EUROPEAN PRODUCT LIABILITY

EUROPEAN PRODUCT LIABILITY

An Analysis of the State of the Art in the Era of New Technologies

Edited by

Piotr MACHNIKOWSKI

INTERSENTIA

Cambridge – Antwerp – Chicago

Intersentia Ltd
8 Wellington Mews | Wellington Street
Cambridge | CB1 1HW | United Kingdom
Tel.: +44 1223 736 170
Email: mail@intersentia.co.uk
www.intersentia.com | www.intersentia.co.uk

Distribution for the UK and Ireland:
NBN International
Airport Business Centre, 10 Thornbury Road
Plymouth, PL6 7 PP | United Kingdom
Tel.: +44 1752 202 301 | Fax: +44 1752 202 331
Email: orders@nbninternational.com

Distribution for Europe and all other countries:
Intersentia Publishing nv
Groenstraat 31
2640 Mortsel | Belgium
Tel.: +32 3 680 15 50 | Fax: +32 3 658 71 21
Email: mail@intersentia.be

Distribution for the USA and Canada:
Independent Publishers Group
Order Department
814 North Franklin Street
Chicago, IL60610 | USA
Tel.: +1 800 888 4741 (toll free) | Fax: +1312 337 5985
Email: orders@ipgbook.com

European Product Liability. An Analysis of the State of the Art in the Era of New Technologies

First published in 2016
Reprinted in 2020

The publication presents results of a research project financed by the Polish National Research Centre (Narodowe Centrum Nauki) on the ground of the decision No. DEC-2013/08/M/HS5/00386.

Artwork on cover: Vers le bleu, Kandinsky Vassily (1866–1944) © Centre Pompidou, MNAM-CCI, Dist. RMN-Grand Palais / Droits réservés

ISBN 978-1-78068-398-0
D/2016/7849/49
NUR 822

GPRC
Guaranteed
Peer Reviewed
Content

British Library Cataloguing in Publication Data. A catalogue record for this book is available from the British Library.

CONTENTS

LIST OF AUTHORS

Marie-Eve Arbour
Full Professor of Civil Law, Université Laval, Québec, Canada

Bjarte Askeland
Professor at Faculty of Law, University of Bergen, Norway

Ewa Bagińska
Professor of Law and head of the Civil Law Department at the School of Law and Administration, University of Gdańsk, Poland

Jean-Sébastien Borghetti
Professor of Private Law, University Panthéon-Assas (Paris II), France

W Jonathan Cardi
Professor of Law and Associate Dean for Research and Development, Wake Forest School of Law, United States

Giovanni Comandé
Scuola Superiore Sant'Anna, Pisa, Italy, and Director of LIDER-Lab and Opinio Juris in Comparatione

Duncan Fairgrieve
Senior Fellow in Comparative Law at the British Institute of International and Comparative Law, London, and *Professeur Associé* at Université de Paris Dauphine PSL, France

Michael Faure
Professor of Comparative and International Environmental Law, Maastricht University, and Professor of Comparative Private Law and Economics, Rotterdam Institute of Law and Economics, Erasmus School of Law, the Netherlands

Israel Gilead
Professor (Emeritus) of Law, Hebrew University of Jerusalem, Professor at the Sha'arey Mada Umishpat Academic Center, and Member of the Israeli Codification Committee

Michael D Green
Williams Professor of Law, Wake Forest University School of Law, United States

Marie-Louise Holle
Assistant Professor at Copenhagen Business School, Denmark

Geraint Howells
Dean and Chair Professor of Commercial Law, City University of Hong Kong

André Janssen
Visiting Professor at the City University Hong Kong, China

Anne Lucienne Maria Keirse
Professor of Private Law at Utrecht University and a judge at the Court of Appeal in Amsterdam, the Netherlands

Bernard A Koch
Full Professor of Civil and Comparative Law and Academic Director of the Medical Law Programme at the University of Innsbruck, Austria

Piotr Machnikowski
Professor of Civil Law and head of the Civil Law and Private International Law Department at the University of Wrocław, Poland

Ulrich Magnus
Professor Emeritus at the University of Hamburg; Judge (retired) at the Court of Appeal of Hamburg; and Affiliate Researcher of the Max Planck Institute Hamburg, Germany

Miquel Martín-Casals
Professor of Civil Law, University of Girona, Spain

Peter Møgelvang-Hansen
Professor of Commercial Law at the Copenhagen Business School, Denmark

Johann Neethling
Senior Professor of Private Law, University of the Free State, Bloemfontein, South Africa and Emeritus Professor, University of South Africa, Pretoria, South Africa

Ken Oliphant
Professor of Tort Law, Faculty of Law, University of Bristol, United Kingdom

Reiner Schulze
Professor of German and European Civil Law, University of Münster, Germany

Josep Solé-Feliu
Senior Lecturer of Civil Law, University of Girona, Spain, and Fellow of the European Centre of Tort and Insurance Law, Austria

Gert Straetmans
Full Professor of European Economic, Consumer and Commercial Law, University of Antwerp, Belgium

Luboš Tichý
Professor of European, International Private and Civil Law and Director of the Centre for Comparative Law, Faculty of Law, Charles University, Prague, Czech Republic

Dimitri Verhoeven
Researcher, Faculty of Law, University of Antwerp, Belgium

Vanessa Wilcox
Senior Legal Researcher, Institute for European Tort Law, Vienna, Austria; Lecturer at the University of Vienna; and Honorary Professor of the Sino-European Tort Law Institute of Yantai University, China

Bénédict Winiger
Full Professor, Faculty of Law, University of Geneva, Switzerland

INTRODUCTION

Piotr Machnikowski

I. LAW AND TECHNOLOGICAL PROGRESS

01 Over the course of its development, the private law has always attempted to respond to the new needs of social entities arising from economic transformations, changes in technology, politics or transformations of systems of values. It has never been an easy task, but it has never been as difficult as it is today.

02 Many modern tort law systems developed their essential framework at the turn of the 19th and 20th centuries. The changes that occurred during the decades that followed aimed at adapting regulations to the changing social and economic environment. They took account of technological progress to a lesser extent because this progress had relatively little impact on the status of the economy and on how society functioned on a daily basis. Technological revolutions that totally transformed society (eg the spread of steam power or electricity) happened, one might say, once a century. In recent years, by contrast, we have observed a sudden increase in the rate of technological development, and we have witnessed a ceaseless technological revolution. We have also seen, and we may anticipate, the increasingly strong impact of new technologies on society in the future – both on the business models of entrepreneurs and the lifestyles of consumers. This is why legislation in the area of liability for damages in the 20th century could afford to take a wait-and-see approach, and respond only to new phenomena that had already occurred and become entrenched in society. This was a measured response, preceded by in-depth thinking and long-term preparations. Nevertheless, there is a lot that indicates that the legislator of the 21st century will not have such comfort.

03 The European law regulating liability for losses caused by defective products is a good example of paths for development of legal regulations in the 20th century. The diversified development of national legislation in this area since the first decades of the 20th century, the increase in legal awareness in the area of losses caused by these products, and the search for new grounds of liability in the 1960s and in the 1970s resulted in efforts to make the substantive law rules pertaining to this liability uniform throughout the European Union. Almost ten years passed between the publication of the first draft and the approval of the directive. It may be safely stated that Directive 85/374 is the legal system's response to the risks that could be identified by observation of the state of technology and the way the economy operated in the 1960s, 1970s and early 1980s. Those were times of constant, but not overly dynamic, technological and organisational progress in the economy.

04 In comparison, the number of contemporary technological innovations has obviously grown and their scope has broadened, while the interval between subsequent ground-breaking achievements of science and technology has shrunk. The same has occurred with the time needed for the implementation of the products of these achievements in manufacturing and the time necessary for distributing new products among entrepreneurs and consumers until the point of market saturation. Moreover, the mass nature of the production of equipment or provision of services based on advanced technologies leads to the reduction of prices, and the growing wealth of societies (which obviously does not pertain to

the whole world and all societies at an equal level) enables them to take advantage of technological innovation to a much greater level than previously. Examples of this phenomenon can easily be found. The spread of the Internet and its impact on the functioning of communication, including in respect of the sale of goods and provision of services, is the most striking. There are, however, further examples. The fastest supercomputer in the world in 1975 cost US$5 million and it performed operations that are now performed by a smartphone worth about US$100. Over the last few decades, the cost of photovoltaic cells has dropped by 85%, and thus their availability for users and profitability of their operation has likewise grown. Improvement of technological capabilities for shale gas extraction in the US within a period of five years (2007–2011) is currently altering the balance of forces in the global market for natural fuels. As a result of a 13-year programme that cost US$2.7 billion, aiming at the exploration of the human genome, we are prepared in terms of expertise and technology for breakthroughs in medicine and health protection and prevention.

05 The above data and information were taken from a broad study on new technologies and their expected impact on life and the economy published in May 2013 by the McKinsey Global Institute.[1] Its authors made an attempt to identify the fastest-developing technologies which feature the greatest potential of impacting human life and work, the operation of industries and the economy, applying a time horizon of 2025. This research does run the risk of certain errors, which is obvious in light of the dynamic and multi-directional development of technology. Despite that fact, the aforementioned study provides a good starting point for an assessment of the extent to which current legislation on product liability will be aligned to the requirements of the economy in 2025, and what kinds of changes will be necessary. There are two major questions that may arise here. Will tort law norms ensure sufficient protection from the risks new technologies will pose to social entities? Will they not decelerate the process of innovation, and will they not disrupt trading of goods and provision of services by performing their function?

II. TECHNOLOGIES THAT MAY AFFECT THE ECONOMY

06 The aforementioned study of the McKinsey Global Institute specifies twelve technologies that are expected to make the greatest impact on the economy by

1 *McKinsey Global Institute*, Disruptive technologies: Advances that will transform life, business, and the global economy <www.mckinsey.com/insights/business_technology/disruptive_technologies>.

2025.[2] These are mainly common application technologies, and thus they are not limited to narrow areas of the economy, but are rather applied across the entire spectrum of economic life (such as the printing press, steam machine, combustion or electric engine were in the past). Such an approach is very useful from the perspective of the legal sciences, because usually whatever has the broadest impact requires a legal response the most.

A. MOBILE INTERNET

07 Nowadays, more than 1 billion people have access to the digital economy by way of mobile electronic devices connecting them to the Internet. This number may even quadruple by 2025. Smartphones and tablets are themselves the objects of trading similarly to applications purchased by their users. Both are designed to find information (including information pertaining to geographical space), execution of contracts, making payments, acquisition, storage and use of products (digital content – books, music, magazines, educational and entertainment content, etc) and ensuring access to digital products and information stored in the computing cloud. These devices have also started to play an important role in health protection for patients as they are fitted out with applications that monitor certain processes occurring in the bodies of their owners, and for physicians by providing information facilitating diagnosis of illnesses. Their significance in the educational service sector continues to grow as they facilitate distance learning. Soon 'intelligent accessories' such as data processing glasses that will shorten the distance between the human brain and the information collected from the external world may partially take over the role of mobile devices.

B. AUTOMATION OF KNOWLEDGE WORK

08 Development of information technologies will enable operations that have been reserved for man to be taken over by computers, including operations that require not only ways of thinking suitable for formalisation, but also complex analyses, subtle judgements and creative ideas. The process with visible effects in the production sector and trade may soon commence in the area of knowledge-based services. The McKinsey Global Institute report estimates that machines may be capable of performing work of this type equivalent to 110–140 million FTEs by 2025. Operation of such equipment may be expected to have an effect not only in simple services (such as information or complaint/claim centres), but also in management, programming, education, medicine and pharmacy, financial services and even legal services.

---

2 Ibid 29 ff.

C. THE INTERNET OF THINGS

09 The aforementioned phenomena are related to ones that will be discussed in the following. Devices are fitted out with tools for communication with the Internet, sensors and components which make it possible to track the environment, transmit and receive information, and make decisions, as well as take actions on the basis of that information. They enable not only remote monitoring (such as of the condition of a patient), but also other tasks including intelligent management of power or communication networks, power consumption and raw materials in an organisation or a household, goods and waste management, and plant farming, among others.

D. CLOUD TECHNOLOGY

10 The significance of this technology does not result from its independent characteristics, but rather from the way, in combination with the aforementioned three, it enables their functioning and development. Storage and processing of data outside the devices that use it, on a shared external server or data warehouse device, totally changes the manner in which mobile devices are used, as in practice it is equivalent to a major enhancement of their data processing capabilities. Simultaneously, the use of a cloud instead of saving data on a local device changes the nature of intangible assets trading – software, digital content and general information are no longer a product, but they rather become the subject of a service.

E. ADVANCED ROBOTICS

11 Advanced robots – mobile devices, adaptive and learning devices may not only overtake the responsibilities of man in the area of physical work, especially requiring precise operations or work performed in dangerous environments (which has already been done by the previous generation of robots), but may also be applied in medicine (both in surgery and prosthetics, and in the construction of exoskeletons) and in the provision of various services.

F. AUTONOMOUS VEHICLES

12 However sensational it may sound, major economic potential has been perceived in the design of an autonomous (driverless) car, presently at the stage of road tests. Based on data from cameras and sensors and their own information (maps), vehicles should be safer, use less fuel and thus emit less pollution, transport more people and goods, and use the throughput of roads more efficiently than vehicles driven by people. They will also liberate hidden work or consumption potential – an average resident of the Western world spends several hundreds of hours per year driving.[3]

G. NEXT-GENERATION GENOMICS AND REGENERATIVE MEDICINE

13 The successful programme aimed at the exploration of human genomes mentioned in the introduction of this text is only the first stage in the expected medical revolution referred to as next-generation genomics. This revolution is made up of DNA sequencing and the technique of modification of organisms by way of genetic re-combination or DNA synthesis. Progress in this area will soon enable fast and affordable (according to forecasts, by means of devices costing up to US$1,000.00 and providing a result within several hours) determination of genetic code. Vast sets of data obtained in this way, combined with the findings of clinical tests and medical statistics, are intended to make it possible to identify these components of a genetic code that determine particular features of an organism, illnesses or the risk of illnesses occurring. A direct 'writing' of DNA and its injection into cells, as well as the development of medication against illnesses that are so far incurable, along with customised therapies, will account for the next stage. Synthetic biology (DNA synthesis and the creation of 'improved' or 'custom-made' organisms) may be a further stage of development, which is much more controversial in ethical terms. Even this area may, however, serve a useful purpose, for example when developing new bio-fuels.

14 Along with the list developed by the McKinsey Global Institute, some attention should be paid to the progress of research in regenerative medicine based on stem cells. In the future, they may allow us not only to repair damaged tissues (which has so far been done in relation to bone marrow),[4] but also to prepare new organs designed for transplant from biological materials.[5]

H. ADVANCED MATERIALS

15 The materials currently being developed in research labs will feature not only greater durability, but capabilities that are yet unknown, such as

---

[3] See also *J Villasenor*, Products Liability and Driverless Cars: Issues and Guiding Principles for Legislation (2014) <www.brookings.edu/research/papers/2014/04/products-liability-driverless-cars-villasenor>.

[4] See eg *I Murnaghan*, Why Perform a Stem Cell Transplant? <www.explorestemcells.co.uk/WhyPerformStemCellTransplant.html>.

[5] See eg <http://stemcells.nih.gov/info/basics/pages/basics6.aspx>.

regenerative or self-cleaning capabilities, resilience, and the capability to transform impacts into electricity. Nanomaterials generated as a result of transforming material at the molecular scale (below 100 nanometres, ie less than a ten-thousandth of a millimetre) become particularly reactive and bio-reactive, and acquire the capability of conducting electricity, heat or resistance. This will enable their use in a broad spectrum of products, including chemicals, medicines (including those for cancer treatments oriented towards cells affected by the disease), prosthetics, cosmetics, electronic devices, displays and batteries, sports equipment, water treatment and desalinating devices, photovoltaic cells construction materials.

I. ENERGY STORAGE

16 The technology of storing electricity has undergone dynamic development. It makes it possible to transform energy into a form that may be stored and re-transformed back into energy whenever needed. This not only enables the production of new types of electricity-driven devices (such as cars), but it might also result in changes in energy distribution systems, including diverging from its continuous generation and transmitting it via a network, switching to the generation and storage of energy in order to make it available at times of increased demand. It may also facilitate the supply of power to areas that do not have the required fuels for the generation of electricity, places that are far away from generation sites and with poorly-developed network infrastructure. This effect will be stronger when combined with the application of renewable energy sources.

J. ADVANCED OIL AND GAS EXPLORATION AND RECOVERY

17 The technologies for obtaining natural gas and so-called 'light oil' from rock formations developed in recent decades are not only highly likely to alter the global market for these fuels, but they will have an impact on the global geopolitical system.

K. RENEWABLE ENERGY SOURCES

18 The decreasing costs and the growing level of financial support (direct, from public funds, and indirect, for example through fees for CO_2 emissions), as well as the growing technical reliability of equipment, are gradually improving the economic efficiency of production of energy from renewable sources, especially that of wind and solar energy, at least in some regions. When combined with new technologies for storing energy, this may result in the dissemination of a new model for electricity generation and distribution that will not be based solely on the operation of large power-generating units and network transmission of energy, but rather on dispersed generation by small power producers for their own needs or in order to transmit energy over relatively small distances.

L. 3D PRINTING

19 The expanding capacities and decreasing prices of devices for contour crafting (3D printers) may lead to a thorough transformation of a major part of the economy, both in terms of the manufacturing sector and the structure of the sales chain. This technology involves manufacturing three-dimensional physical objects made of various materials (plastic, metal, china, glass, paper or live cells) on the basis of a computer model. It has already started to alter medicine, allowing for example the designing and printing of prostheses (work is been done on the technology of bioprinting live organs from a patient's own cells, as mentioned earlier). It will play a major role, however, in consumer applications. The option to self-produce daily-use products (clothing, footwear, kitchenware, decorations and jewellery, toys, smaller furniture and even some food products) or potentially commissioning this service to a specialised entrepreneur (also pertaining to larger facilities, including simple buildings) will reduce demand for some products of serial production and will render all the links in the sales chain of these products redundant. It will also reduce the demand for some production services. A creator's design concept will be made directly available in electronic form to a future user of the given product without any involvement of technologists, production managers, manufacturers of parts and intermediate goods, the manufacturer of a finished product, carriers, wholesalers or retailers. A consumer or a service provider will have the opportunity to choose the design of a product from catalogues made available on the Internet by designers, or they will have the ability to create their own.

III. SOME CONSEQUENCES FOR TORT LAW

A. A CHANGING ROLE OF SUBSTANTIVE PRIVATE LAW

20 The position of traditional tort law as a tool for protection against the risks arising from a third party's business may change in the new reality. There are at least two reasons for this.

21 Firstly, it may be observed in relation to many of the aforementioned technologies that their approval for application and operation involves mainly the public interest or collective interests. They will naturally and principally be governed by public law, which will firstly require a proper level of safety for the surrounding environment. Tort law can, however, supplement public law and incentivise public authorities by imposing tort liability on entities which regulate the safety of products, for failure to perform their task adequately.[6] Such interplay of public duties and private liability may also help to overcome some of the problems mentioned below, such as difficulties in finding causation, unlimited or unspecified spatial scope of operation of the potentially liable party or multiplicity of entities engaged in an unsafe activity.

22 Secondly, all Internet-based and cloud-based computing technologies have an unlimited or even undefined spatial scope of operation, and their functioning involves entities and devices located in various parts of the globe. The same effect is triggered by the globalisation of commerce and the broad availability of goods manufactured in another part of the world in the local market. It increases the significance of conflict-of-laws rules and it also reduces the practical meaning of the national norms of tort law due to the difficulty in enforcement of the obligations it imposes on entities in remote regions around the globe.

B. THE RATE OF TRANSFORMATIONS AND THE CAPABILITY OF THE LEGAL SYSTEM TO RESPOND

23 New technologies – both products and the ways in which they are distributed and applied – have appeared and will appear with increasing frequency. As has been mentioned, the time between development of a new idea and the spread of the product based on the idea has shrunk. The time available to the legislator to prepare legal regulations providing means for the protection of interests of goods purchasers and third parties has also decreased. The requirements of a democratic law-making process do not allow for the rapid acceleration of legislative activity. Thus, there will always be a period in which new goods or new techniques of distribution will be present in the market but still not subject to private legal regulation. This phenomenon will intensify even more in relation to the areas covered by European Union law. The legislative process in the European Union is longer than the national process, there are more factors that influence its course, and the limitations of competences by treaties as well as procedural requirements impede the law from fully addressing current needs. Thus, the amendment of existing European legislation is a more

6 On that see *K Oliphant* (ed), Public Authorities Liability (2016).

difficult and more time-consuming process than the amendment of national legislation.

C. FROM THE MATERIAL PRODUCT MARKET TO A DEMOCRATIC SOCIETY OF SERVICES?

24 The directions of technological development outlined above clearly demonstrate something that could have been observed earlier. The entrepreneur's position in the market and the possibility of earning income will be less and less decided by material resources, capacity of manufacturing material products and the possibility of their broad distribution. Information and the potential to obtain it will play an increasingly significant role. Furthermore, the goods accumulated by consumers no longer only have a material form; more and more frequently they are intellectual goods, or they come in digital form, or they are material objects whose functioning depends on digital contents and access to information from the Internet or the cloud. Dissemination of technologies enabling the generation of energy on a smaller scale from renewable sources and energy storage will enhance the meaning of energy as an object of trading, not only with the involvement of large, specialised suppliers, but also trading between small entrepreneurs and even non-commercial entities.

25 The aforementioned information clearly shows the growing role of services in the economy, which is confirmed by economic research. Combining elements of product sales and service provision into one business relationship is also becoming commonplace. Moreover, one of the features of new technologies is combining tangible and intangible components from numerous entities into one product. 3D printing requires obtaining a design from a creator, material from its supplier, and possibly the printing service from the relevant service provider. Autonomous devices use software and data provided by an individual who is neither their manufacturer nor seller. Moreover, we are experiencing the so-called 'democratisation of technology', which consists of the fact that a large number of small entrepreneurs, due to their flexibility and innovativeness, offer new devices or applications, and thus are leaping ahead of or supplementing the product offerings of major players, and hence playing an increasingly large role in the market.

26 This all means that we should expect growth in the significance of multi-entity and long-term relations based on a network of mutually independent but interrelated agreements. From the perspective of tort law, the effectiveness of regulations attributing liability for injury to product manufacturers needs to be re-considered.

D. SAFETY AND LIABILITY

27 Some of the aforementioned technologies have not yet been examined in terms of safety. This pertains in particular to nanomaterials that may be toxic and hazardous for the environment.[7] Medical procedures based on genomics, organs grown from stem cells, autonomous devices fitted out with programmes enabling value judgements[8], etc should also be evaluated. Ensuring product safety is an issue addressed by public law, but compensation for the losses caused by products that do not ensure the required level of safety is addressed by private law. Thus the question needs to be asked whether the current regulation of liability for losses caused by a dangerous product is fully consistent with the needs of the near future.

28 Limitation of the notion of a product to movables, animals and energy causes serious doubts related to whether the harmonised rules may be applied to goods whose main component is information or digital content, and to those forms of trading which combine the features of transfer of goods and service provision. Moreover, the growing rate of technological development may cause increasing difficulties in the interpretation of the so-called development risk defence. A broad application of this exception may significantly restrict the practical significance of the rules in question. The nature of hazards related to the implementation of technologies whose long-term safety has not been fully investigated in the industry raises doubts as to whether the ten-year period of limitation, calculated from the date of introduction to market of a product, as provided for in the Product Liability Directive, is not too short. Moreover, a number of the aforementioned technologies are related to serious hazards for personal rights other than the life and health of their users and third parties, in particular privacy. Computers and intelligent remote devices are capable of obtaining very detailed information on the interests, preferences, lifestyles and health of their users. Acquisition of information on the genetic code of an individual causes the risk that it may be disclosed to third parties, and it will radically alter the life situation of these people as it will provide others with the potential of anticipating changes in their health (including potential employers or insurers). Therefore, the risk of cases of privacy infringement for purely material reasons continues to grow. Along with the hazards we have noted so far that are inherent in products – risks to life, health and property – there are new ones related to the broader category of non-economic rights and the interests of the user.

---

7 See *G Howells*, Product Liability for Nanotechnology (2009) 32 Journal of Consumer Policy 381.

8 As far as the broad perspective of the development of artificial intelligence is concerned, see *N Bostrom*, Superintelligence: Paths, Dangers, Strategies (2014).

29 There are a few other issues fundamental to liability, especially attributing liability for loss to a specific entity and the role of the causal nexus in this liability (an issue that is outside the regulation of the EU Directive), which need to be considered. The first phenomenon that we have been able to observe for a long time, and which we will continue to see more and more frequently, is uncertainty regarding causality. As the number of entities involved in the production of goods, provision of services or, in broader terms, an event leading to losses, continues to grow, and the process of manufacturing, provision or any other activity becomes increasingly independent on man and based on the operation of a technology, the chances for proving with certainty the cause of a loss and the person whose behaviour lead to this loss continue to decrease. This may be related to the victim's inability to identify which one out of many entities whose conduct could have caused the loss in fact did so (for example in relation to the operation of the Internet, or the movement of an autonomous vehicle). This translates into difficulties in distributing the burden of liability between specific co-liable entities or determining the grounds and the size of recourse liability.[9] This uncertainty may also apply to the cause of the loss itself. With the expansion of human activities and operation of devices using biological or technical processes that are not entirely tested or foreseeable, it becomes increasingly difficult to prove what has actually caused the aggrieved's injury. We already currently encounter such situations (especially in medicine), but the application of new technologies and treatment methods will increase the number of chains of events where a possible causal connection is not comprehensible to the mind of an average person, and often may not be understood even by experts.

30 Another characteristic effect of technological progress is the expansion of the causative range of the impact of individual events. Extended networks and chains of agreements may result in a situation where a relatively small error by one of the participants in trade leads to major losses for other entities – the parties to an agreement and third parties. One good example is the broad consequences of even small errors in data on the basis of which devices conduct their processes.

31 This all leads to the conclusion that the existing European harmonised product liability regime needs to be analysed in detail to determine not only whether it addresses the needs of today, but also whether it will still suffice tomorrow. It is therefore necessary to look at whether the concept of a product, the defect test, development risk defence and the principle of strict liability ensure safety for users of new technologies on the one hand and do not restrict progress on the other. Furthermore, it is advisable to examine whether cases in

---

9 See *I Gilead/MD Green/BA Koch* (eds), Proportional Liability: Analytical and Comparative Perspectives (2013).

which current liability regulation fails to cover the particular risks associated with new technologies are encompassed by other, non-harmonised domestic tort law regimes.

IV. AIM AND SCOPE OF THIS STUDY

32 This book has several aims. The first is to explore the place of liability for defective products within national legal systems, with special focus on the relation between the rules of this liability and other rules of tort law. For EU Member States this concerns the coexistence of European and domestic law, especially where particular aspects of product liability are not regulated in the Directive, but are left to domestic law. Another issue, relevant for all legal systems, is the relation between the special liability regime for defective products and other possible grounds of liability present in domestic law for harm caused by bringing insufficiently safe products to market, both under tort and contract law rules.

33 The second, and potentially more important, aim of the project is to determine whether European law dating from 1985 can ensure sufficient safety for individuals using the goods produced by applying technologies currently under development. If it is determined that European law does not ensure the required level of protection for those making use of new technologies, it will then be necessary to consider whether such protection is provided by other domestic regulations, and whether the Directive should be amended in order to adapt it to new challenges. When discussing this issue, one also has to bear in mind the relationship between the product liability rules and the level of technological development and innovation in an enterprise.

34 The third aim is to check whether development of product liability law in non-EU countries has resulted in more appropriate solutions being created for the future.

35 The book investigates the current condition of EU product liability law, ie Directive 85/374, the structure of relevant domestic implementations in numerous EU Member States, alternative paths for the development of the law applied by countries from outside the EU, and the economic conditions and consequences of product liability regulations. Exploration of domestic legal systems includes the law of European Union Member States from both 'Old Europe' and 'New Europe' (Austria, the Czech Republic, Denmark, England and Wales, France, Germany, Italy, the Netherlands, Poland and Spain) and the European Economic Area (Norway), as well as Switzerland. Thus, European law

in the Roman, German, common law and Nordic traditions are represented. In addition, to compare present European solutions with other models of product liability regulation, the research encompasses two important common law jurisdictions from outside Europe (USA and Canada), as well as two mixed jurisdictions (Israel and South Africa).

PART I

PRODUCT LIABILITY DIRECTIVE

Duncan FAIRGRIEVE, Geraint HOWELLS, Peter MØGELVANG-HANSEN, Gert STRAETMANS, Dimitri VERHOEVEN, Piotr MACHNIKOWSKI, André JANSSEN and Reiner SCHULZE*

* Section I was written by Duncan Fairgrieve; section II by Geraint Howells; section III by Peter Møgelvang-Hansen; sections IV.A, IV.B and IV.C by Gert Straetmans and Dimitri Verhoeven; sections IV.D, IV.E and IV.F by Piotr Machnikowski; section IV.G by André Janssen, Reiner Schulze and Piotr Machnikowski; and section V by Gert Straetmans and Dimitri Verhoeven.

I. INCEPTION OF THE PRODUCT LIABILITY DIRECTIVE

A. HISTORICAL BACKGROUND

01 From a historical perspective, product liability was traditionally seen in many jurisdictions as merely a concrete illustration of the law of obligations to a specific factual matrix, involving the causing of damage by a product. It was only when the mass manufacture of consumer goods started to occur that sufficient impetus was generated towards the identification of an *autonomous* area of law. It was only then that practitioners and scholars commenced specialisation in the sphere of product liability. The US was of course at the vanguard of developments,[1] and a word will thus be said of the evolution in the US, as a background to the European context. Professor David Owen records in his leading US treatise on the topic that the consequence of the spread of industrialisation in the 19th century was that by 1900, products 'cases began to appear with some frequency'.[2] There then followed iconic cases such as *MacPherson v Buick Motor Co*[3] or *Greenman v Yuba Power Products Inc*,[4] which ushered in the modern era of US products liability, accompanied by the various Restatements, with Owen noting that the strict liability rule enshrined in §402A of the Restatement (Second) of Torts resulted in the 'the doctrine of strict products liability in tort, together with a miscellany of secondary principles spread like wildfire around the nation'.[5]

02 The development of product liability in Europe as a distinctive area of the law occurred much later than in the US. It was not until relatively late in the 20th century, after the occurrence of mass product disasters in Europe,[6] and the realisation that traditional responses of the law were inadequate to deal with such situations, that there was a movement towards products liability as

1 As noted *inter alia* by Advocate General Tesauro in Case C-300/95, *Commission v United Kingdom* [1997] ECR I-2649.
2 *D Owen*, Products Liability Law (2005) para 1.2.
3 111 N.E. 1050 (NY 1916).
4 377 P. 2d 897 (Cal. 1963).
5 *D Owen*, Products Liability Law (2005) para 1.3.
6 Such as the thalidomide/Contagen disaster in England, Germany and the Netherlands, and the contaminated colza disaster in Spain.

raising distinct legal issues, for which a tailor-made regime for compensation was potentially required. It should be noted that comparative law played a role in this process in certain European jurisdictions, with Gerhard Wagner describing for instance how in Germany 'product liability was imported from the US, both with regard to the legal problem and its solution'.[7] In a recent study on the historical development of tort/delict in Western Europe since 1850, led by Professors John Bell and David Ibbetson,[8] a volume dedicated to product liability under the responsibility of Simon Whittaker[9] identified a series of common factors which contributed to the development of product liability in Europe.

03 In institutional terms, law reform bodies played an important role in moving forward thinking towards the development of a bespoke regime. This was particularly the case in the UK, where the law reform bodies of the Law Commission and the Scottish Law Commission were charged in November 1971 with considering 'whether the existing law governing compensation for personal injury, damage to property or any other loss caused by defective products is adequate, and to recommend what improvements, if any, in the law are needed to ensure that additional remedies are provided and against whom such remedies should be available'.[10] In December 1972, a Royal Commission on Civil Liability and Compensation for Personal Injury was also established under the chairmanship of Lord Pearson to examine to what extent, and by what means, compensation should be payable in respect of death or personal injury. Such compensation 'through the manufacture, supply or use of goods or services' was expressly included within the terms of reference of the Royal Commission. In their ultimate reports, both the Pearson Royal Commission[11] and the Law Commission[12] recommended the introduction of strict liability for defective products.[13]

04 Over and above the discussions at a national level, it was around this time that developments were also occurring within European organisations, and we will now turn to examine these in more depth.

---

7 See discussion of *G Wagner*, The development of product liability in Germany, in: S Whittaker (ed), The Development of Product Liability (2010) 121.

8 See *J Bell/D Ibbetson*, European Legal Development: the Case of Tort (2012).

9 *S Whittaker* (ed), The Development of Product Liability (2010).

10 As outlined in the resultant report, *Law Commission and Scottish Law Commission*, Liability for Defective Products, Report no 82 (1977) 1.

11 Royal Commission on Civil Liability and Compensation for Personal Injury (Cmnd 7054, 1974).

12 *Law Commission and Scottish Law Commission*, Liability for Defective Products, Report no 82 (1977).

13 Neither of these recommendations were ever put into effect, however, at a national level, for various reasons: see further *S Whittaker*, Liability for Products (2005) 432.

B. EUROPEAN CONVENTION

05 In 1970, the Council of Europe set up a Committee of Experts which was given responsibility for examining harmonisation of the laws of Member States in respect product liability. A draft Convention was prepared, together with an explanatory report. In 1976, the Strasbourg Convention on Products Liability in regard to Personal Injury and Death was duly adopted by the Committee of Ministers of the Council of Europe.[14] The central aspect of the Convention was to introduce or maintain national laws imposing strict liability on producers of defective products, but again only in respect of personal injury and death. One interesting aspect of symmetry with the European Product Liability Directive (further below) was that the basis of liability is premised upon harm *caused by a defect*,[15] defined in the Convention as 'when it does not provide the safety which a person is entitled to expect, having regard to all the circumstances including the presentation of the product'.[16] From other perspectives, there were however significant differences between the instruments,[17] such as the availability of defences. Whittaker has commented on the different context of the two instruments, noting that '[t]he essentially voluntary nature of the Convention meant that those agreeing its content were not under the same pressure to make compromises between the contrasting positions on the appropriate degree of strictness of the product liability which it envisaged nor on the possibility of further defences or exclusions'.[18] The Convention required ratification by individual Member States, and anyway would only enter into force on ratification by three Member States. It was only ever signed by four Member States (Austria, Belgium, France, and Luxembourg) but did not ever enter into force because it was not ratified by any.[19]

C. INCEPTION OF THE PRODUCT LIABILITY DIRECTIVE

06 It was against this backdrop that the European Product Liability Directive emerged. The drafting of the Directive commenced in the mid-1970s, but it enjoyed an unusually long gestation period before finalisation in the 1980s. The first preliminary version of the Directive and accompanying memorandum, albeit in rudimentary form, can be found set out in an Annexe of the Law

---

14 The text of the Convention is available at <http://conventions.coe.int/Treaty/en/Treaties/Html/091.htm>.

15 See further discussion in *S Whittaker* (ed), The Development of Product Liability (2010) 434–435.

16 See art 2(c) of the Convention.

17 See further *S Whittaker* (ed), The Development of Product Liability (2010)435.

18 *S Whittaker*, Liability for Products (2005) 433.

19 For further information, see <http://conventions.coe.int/>.

Commission Working Paper in 1975.[20] Various formal drafts then emerged, with the publication of the first official proposal occurring in 1976.[21] In response to that, two Opinions on the first proposal were given in 1979, one by the European Parliament[22] and another by the Economic and Social Committee.[23] There then followed a second draft Directive, which was submitted by the Commission to the Council of Ministers later in 1979,[24] but reform then slowed as controversy arose between stakeholders as to the appropriate approach. The text was only eventually adopted after lengthy delays on 25 July 1985 as Council Directive 85/374/EEC on the approximation of the laws, regulations and administration provisions of the Member States concerning liability for defective products. As is well known, agreement was only eventually reached due to compromises in controversial areas,[25] namely (i) the exclusion of primary agriculture products and game from the scope of the Directive[26] (an exclusion which was subsequently removed);[27] (ii) the availability of a defence based on the state of scientific and technical knowledge;[28] and (iii) the imposition of a ceiling on liability for death or personal injury caused by identical items with the same defect.[29]

07 The broad effect of the Directive is to require Member States to impose strict liability on producers of defective products, but, unlike the other proposals noted above (and in particular those of the Law Commission and the Scottish Law Commission), the Directive is not confined to cases of death or personal injury. Rather, it extends to damage to property, provided that the property

---

20 See Appendix C of *Law Commission*, Liability for Defective Products: Working Paper No 64 (June 1975) 153–172.

21 Relating to the approximation of the laws, regulations and administrative provisions of the Member States concerning liability for defective products [1976] OJ C241/9 (also EC Bull Supp 11/79).

22 Resolution embodying the opinion of the European Parliament on the proposal from the Commission of the European Communities to the Council for a Directive relating to the approximation of the laws, regulations and administrative provisions of the Member States concerning liability for defective products [1979] OJ C127/61.

23 Opinion on the proposal for a Council Directive relating to the approximation of the laws, regulations and administrative provisions of the Member States concerning liability for defective products [1979] OJ C114/15.

24 Amendment of the proposal for a Council Directive relating to the approximation of the laws, regulations and administrative provisions of the Member States concerning liability for defective products, COM(79)415 final.

25 See some of the issues in discussion in *HC Taschner*, Product Liability: basic problems in a comparative law perspective, in: D Fairgrieve (ed), Product Liability in Comparative Perspective (2005).

26 These were excluded by art 2, with the possibility of inclusion being reserved by art 15(1)(a).

27 See Directive 1999/34/EC of the European Parliament and of the Council of 10 May 1999 [1999] OJ L141/20.

28 The defence is available by virtue of art 7(e), but derogation excluding the defence is permitted by art 15(1)(b).

29 In principle, the Directive does not provide for such a limit, but Member States may adopt one if it is not less than 70 million ECU: see art 16(1).

damaged is of a type ordinarily intended for private use or consumption and is used by the injured person mainly for such use. As shall be seen below, the Directive has been held to be a maximal harmonisation provision.

D. REVIEW AND REFORM OF THE PRODUCT LIABILITY DIRECTIVE

08 Art 21 of the Directive lays down that the Commission must prepare a report to the Council on the application of the Directive on a five-yearly basis. In the early 1990s, an official study was commissioned into the impact of the Directive,[30] but the resultant First Commission report on the implementation of the Directive in 1995[31] was a disappointingly terse document. In this short review, the Commission indicated that it would monitor and evaluate the effect of the exemption in favour of primary agricultural produce and game, and this subsequently resulted in an amendment of the Directive.[32]

09 The Commission's subsequent Green Paper on Liability for Defective Products in 1999[33] examined a further range of issues, including the burden of proof, development risks, financial limits, a ten-year long-stop, supplier's liability, the type of goods covered, the type of damage covered, and access to justice. Responses to the Green Paper were however considered to be inconclusive, and the Commission consequently considered in its Second Report on the Directive in 2000[34] that further investigatory work was required. Two expert groups were formed[35] and two further studies commissioned in order to obtain more data about the practical impact of the Directive across the EU. This renewed research effort resulted in the Lovells report on the application of the Directive of 2003[36] and the Fondazione Rosselli report of 2004 on the development risks defence.[37]

---

30 *McKenna & Co*, Report for the Commission of the European Communities on the Application of Directive 1985/374/EEC on Liability for Defective Products (1994).

31 First report on the application of the Council Directive on the approximation of the laws, regulations and administrative provisions of the Member States concerning liability for defective products (85/374/EEC), 13 December 1995, COM(95)617.

32 Directive 1999/34 of the European Parliament and of the Council of 10 May 1999 amending Council Directive 85/374/EEC on the approximation of the laws, regulations and administrative provisions of the Member States concerning liability for defective products [1999] OJ L141/20.

33 *European Commission*, Liability for Defective Products, COM(99)396.

34 COM(2000)893 final.

35 One comprised of experts designated by national authorities, the other by stakeholders.

36 *Lovells*, Product Liability in the European Union (2003) <http://ec.europa.eu/enterprise/regulation/goods/docs/liability/studies/lovells-study_en.pdf> (Howells was a consultant to that study).

37 *Fondazione Rosselli*, Analysis of the Economic Impact of the Development Risk Clause as provided by Directive 85/374/EEC on Liability for Defective Products (2004).

10 The approach of the Lovells study was to analyse how the Directive was being applied in practice and examine its impact on consumer protection across the EU. The report concluded that there was some experience of the Directive in almost all Member States, but that the Directive had only moderately increased the prospects of product liability claims being brought, and of the success of those claims. However, it was observed in the Lovells study that there was little appetite expressed on the part of respondees for major reform of the Directive. The report thus concluded that it was important to look at the Directive as one part of a broader system involving product safety and consumer protection laws, judicial practices and procedures and cultural and social factors. Significantly it also concluded that it would be hard to compartmentalise strict product liability and make it the exclusive remedy for product-related injuries.

11 The Fondazione Rosselli Report focused upon the specific issue of the development risks defence contained in art 7(e) of the Directive, and the Rosselli study supported the status quo, concluding that the development risks defence was an important feature of the Directive which helped achieve the balance between producers and consumers, and that its removal could stifle innovation. Whilst the study was undertaken in the context of only limited empirical experience of the Directive, as there was a dearth of reported cases in which the defence was applied, the authors nonetheless felt able to conclude that the defence should be maintained as an important contribution to balancing the interests of producers and consumers.

12 It is within this context that the Commission completed its Third Review and published its official position late in 2006.[38] Whilst this document did not consider major changes to be necessary, the Commission did suggest that monitoring should be undertaken of certain central issues, such as the concept of defect, the development risks defence, the burden of proof, the minimum threshold for property damage and a regulatory compliance defence.

13 The Fourth Commission report was published in September 2011 and covers the period of 2006–2010. The Report noted an increase in both the absolute number of cases brought on grounds of product liability and an increase in the *relative* use of the Directive against cases brought on the classic grounds of civil or contractual liability.[39] The review concluded, in common with the third report, that no major changes to the Directive were necessary. The Commission proposed to continue monitoring 'any development likely to affect the balance'

---

38 *European Commission*, Third report on the application of Council Directive on the approximation of laws, regulations and administrative provisions of the Member States concerning liability for defective products, September 2006, COM(2006)496 final.

39 Ibid 4.

between consumer protection and producers' interests.[40] The Commission's Fourth Report accepted that there was little appetite for reform.[41] It was seen as premature to propose a review of the Directive. Within the report, emphasis was again placed on the collection and exchange of information, with specific mention being made of the role of Expert Groups and a database of decisions concerning product liability.[42]

II. PURPOSE AND EFFECT OF THE DIRECTIVE

A. THE PRODUCT LIABILITY DIRECTIVE'S PURPOSE

14 As described above the Product Liability Directive had a long gestation period. Although there was political will for reform in the light of the thalidomide/Contergan tragedy[43] there was also unease at the prospect of importing the perceived product liability crisis from the US.[44] Whilst the US showed how law could be developed to provide compensation in such situations, it also illustrated how the burden could be so high as to make some products uninsurable. However, these problems probably resulted from other features of the US legal system than merely the substantive rules, for example contingency fees, class actions, and punitive damages. Indeed the resulting EU Directive was probably stricter than the Restatement (Second) of Torts and is certainly more demanding that the Restatement of the Law (Third) Torts: Product Liability, and yet Europe has not suffered any litigation crisis.[45]

15 Nevertheless these concerns had caused legislators to be cautious and hesitate. Eventually the EU did adopt a directive in 1985, though there were some compromises to assuage concerns, notably the optional development risks defence and inclusion of an optional cap on damages. The fact that a Directive was adopted was due to the need to satisfy two parallel objectives, which were set out in the first two recitals to the Directive.

Recital 1 provided: 'Whereas approximation of the laws of the Member States concerning the liability of the producer for damage caused by the defectiveness of his products is necessary because the existing divergences may distort competition and affect the movement of goods within the common market and

---

40 Ibid 11.

41 Ibid 11.

42 Product Liability Forum of the British Institute of International and Comparative Law, Product Liability Decisions Database <www.biicl.org/plf/>.

43 *J Stapleton*, Product Liability (1994) 42–46.

44 *G Priest*, The Current Insurance Crisis and Modern Tort Law (1987) 96 Yale Law Journal 1521.

45 See *G Howells/M Mildred*, Is European Products Liability More Protective than the Restatement (Third) of Torts: Product Liability? (1997–8) 65 Tennessee Law Review 985.

entail a differing degree of protection of the consumer against damage caused by a defective product to his health or property'.

Recital 2 provided: 'Whereas liability without fault on the part of the producer is the sole means of adequately solving the problem, peculiar to our age of increasing technicality, of a fair apportionment of the risks inherent in modern technological production'.

The second recital encapsulated the consumer protection agenda, highlighted by the thalidomide tragedy but also becoming apparent as products became more sophisticated and carried with them both increased benefits and risks. These risks were often of a more significant potential scale than existed in a society of less technological advancement.[46] However, the driving force behind the Directive within the Commission was internal market concerns. Dr Taschner[47] always maintained this Directive was primarily based on internal market considerations. How much this position was influenced by the limited legal base available at that time (and indeed to a large extent still today) is unclear, although it must have been a factor. It is questionable whether the existing differences in private law rules impacted on competition and free movement greatly,[48] but what the introduction of a common standard did provide was the confidence for Member States to take the bold move of introducing strict product liability in the knowledge that they were not exposing themselves to a disadvantage compared to other Member States. Arguably those states that did not adopt the development risks defence[49] were potentially exposing themselves, but in truth is was the symbolism of strict liability in light of the US experience that seemed to concern Member States.

B. THE EEC'S COMPETENCE UNDER THE TREATY

16 The Product Liability Directive was promulgated on the basis of art 100 of the Treaty of Rome which provided that:

> 'The Council, acting by means of a unanimous vote on a proposal of the Commission, shall issue directives for the approximation of such legislative and administrative provisions of the Member States as have a direct incidence on the establishment or functioning of the Common Market.
>
> The Assembly and the Economic and Social Committee shall be consulted concerning any directives whose implementation in one or more of the Member States would involve amendment of legislative provisions'.

46 *U Beck*, Risk Society: Towards a New Modernity (1992).

47 *HC Taschner*, Produkthaftung (1986).

48 On the state of Member States law prior to the Directive see, *inter alia*, *G Howells*, Comparative Product Liability (1993) and *J Miller*, Comparative Product Liability (1986).

49 Finland, Luxembourg, Spain (for certain products) and Germany for drugs that was subject to a special regime.

Note that this pre-Single European Act provision required unanimity, and that may have affected some of the negotiations and concessions introduced to ensure adoption. It was before the Treaty was amended to allow internal market measures to be adopted by qualified majority.[50]

17 There was a requirement for 'a direct incidence on the establishment or functioning of the Common Market'; the basis for the Directive was never challenged (probably due to the political concessions), save in the occasional academic piece. Whether private law rules have a strong influence on the common (for which read internal) market is a moot question which is currently hotly disputed in the context of European sales law. Certainly some markets, such as in the United States, seem to operate well without uniform laws. It should also be noted that art 100 calls for approximation, not uniformity. This is significant when we come to look at the actual form harmonisation took.

C. THE METHOD OF HARMONISATION

1) Directive

18 The EU product liability legislation, as is typical of EU private law legislation (especially at that time) took the form of a Directive. Directives are of course 'binding, as to the result to be achieved, upon each Member State to which it is addressed, but shall leave to the national authorities the choice of form and methods'.[51] The intention behind directives was that language and concepts familiar to the national legal system could be used to make it easier to assimilate the Directive's rules into the national system. In practice this has often not been the reality, with quite strict control from the Commission and Court often requiring national law to adhere closely to the Directive's wording.

2) Maximal Character of Directive

19 In fact the Product Liability Directive has become an additional parallel liability regime partly due to art 13 which provides:

> 'This Directive shall not affect any rights which an injured person may have according to the rules of the law of contractual or non-contractual liability or a special liability system existing at the moment when this Directive is notified'.

---

50 Single European Act [1987] OJ L169/1.
51 Art 288 of current Treaty on the Functioning of the European Union.

Thus there was no need to integrate existing national rules. Indeed the French, who tried to do so, eventually abandoned this task. Although, as we shall see, it has had an impact on national rules which sought to provide a general form of strict liability, national rules on fault or sales law remained untouched.

20 Art 13 is one reason why the Product Liability Directive is considered a maximal harmonisation directive. Other factors leading to the same conclusions are the range of measures which were left optional at the national discretion or which refer to national law. Due to these explicit references to national law and continuing discretion, the assumption was that all other rules must be fixed by the Directive as being both the minimum and maximum levels of protection.

3) *Matters Left Optional*

21 Three matters were optional within the original Directive – the inclusion of primary agricultural produce and game, the inclusion of the ceiling on damages and, most controversially, the development risks defence.

a) Primary Agricultural Produce and Game

22 The original definition of 'product' excluded primary agricultural products and game.[52] By derogation Member States were able to include them.[53] This seemed to be a victory for the power of the agricultural lobby, but various justifications were put forward for the exclusion of primary agricultural produce and game. Such products were said to be subject to 'hidden defects' beyond the producer's control and risked deterioration during storage, and also it was said to be difficult to detect at what stage the defect arose. It was also argued that food was already subject to detailed regulation and liability in contract and negligence. These reasons were not very convincing, and indeed the exemption was removed by Directive 1999/34/EC.[54] The impetus behind the removal was to ensure that those infected by mad cow disease would not be excluded from compensation. However, this is just the sort of hidden defect which some had argued justified the original exclusion. Moreover, it is unlikely that the victims of mad cow disease would be able to bring a claim as, given the long latency period of the illness, proving causation would be problematic. Now the exemption has been removed there is no need to go into a detailed discussion of it, but its original inclusion can be still seen as evidence that other matters are not optional and the Directive should be viewed as a maximal harmonisation directive. The possible inclusion of primary agricultural products had to be sanctioned by a specific provision.

---

52 Art 2.
53 Art 15(1)(a).
54 [1999] OJ L141/20.

b) Ceiling on Damages

23 Art 16(1) provides that Member States 'may provide that a producer's total liability for damage resulting for a death or personal injury and caused by identical items with the same defect shall be limited to an amount not less than 70 million ECU'. Some states had the tradition of linking strict liability to ceilings on liability and it was considered by some advantageous to ensure insurance coverage (though insurers could of course build in their own limits in any event). Germany and Portugal have adopted such a limit; Greece also did but has repealed the limit. This is best seen as an option which illustrates that the Directive seeks approximation rather than uniformity, but that the Directive itself regulates the extent of variation allowed.

c) Development Risks Defence

24 The Commission had not originally proposed a development risks defence and continued to oppose the inclusion of such a defence. However, several Member States wanted to have the defence, believing that it might mitigate the extreme impact of strict liability particularly on innovative industries. In the end the defence was included,[55] but Member States were given the option of excluding it.[56] This option was chosen by Luxembourg and Finland, whilst Spain excluded it for certain high-risk products and France for products derived from the human body, and pharmaceuticals in Germany are covered by the Medicines Act 1976, which has a defence which is potentially narrower. The fact that express permission is needed to increase protection by excluding the defence suggests that otherwise this would not be allowed and so the Directive should be classed as a maximal harmonisation Directive.

4) Matters Left to National Law

25 Several matters are left to national law. Thus art 5 prescribes joint and several liability and art 8 no reduction in producer liability even if the damage is also caused by the act or omission of third party, but leaves it to national law to govern matters concerning the rights of contribution and recourse. The rules on damages in art 9 are without prejudice to national provisions relating to non-material damage. The limitation rules in art 10 do not affect Member States' rules on the suspension or interruption of the limitation period.[57] These vestiges of national autonomy indicate that the Directive merely approximates without

---

55 Art 7(e).

56 Art 15(1)(b).

57 However, these rules cannot extend the period beyond the ten-year cut-off period: Case C-358/08, *Aventis Pasteur SA v OB* [2009] ECR I-11305.

creating uniformity, but equally suggests there was a need for such national freedom to be written into the law as otherwise Member States would be bound by the maximal harmonisation character of the Directive.

5) CJEU and Maximal Harmonisation and Art 13

26 There are two important and interlinked questions about the harmonisation character for the Product Liability Directive. The first is whether it is maximal in character, ie not allowing any national laws which are more protective (except to the extent there is express permission to do so on the face of the Directive). The second is the extent to which art 13 allows existing more protective national rules to be maintained.

27 In this section we only consider the first question about the nature of harmonisation, leaving the impact of any form of harmonisation of national laws and the application of art 13 on the relationship between strict liability under the Directive and national laws to the next section.

28 In three decisions the Court confirmed that the Product Liability Directive should be viewed as a maximal harmonisation directive.[58] In reaching this conclusion, the Court was influenced by recital 1 which made out the economic internal market case for harmonisation, which was taken as favouring maximal harmonisation. In addition the lack of a minimum harmonisation clause was relevant, as was the fact that Member States' express powers of derogation were exhaustively specified and narrowly defined. As noted above, the implication is that such derogations were the extent of the Member States' freedom to go beyond the protection laid down in the Directive. It should be noted that these decisions concerned some important issues such as the refusal in *Commission v France* to allow national law to impose similar liability to producer liability on suppliers.[59] In the same case it was also held that whilst there was a freedom to remove the development risks defence, a halfway house imposing more conditions on the use of the defence was not allowed. But this maximal harmonisation rule also extended to relatively minor rules such as the need to

---

[58] See Case C-52/00, *Commission v France* [2002] ECR I-3827, paras 17–20; Case C-154/00, *Commission v Greece* [2002] ECR I-3879, paras 13–16; Case C-183/00, *González Sanchez v Medicina Asturiana SA* [2002] ECR I-3901, paras 26–29.

[59] On this see also later decision of Case C-402/03, *Skov AEG v Bilka Lauprisvarenhus A/S* [2006] 2 CMLR 16. The Court was not influenced by point 2 of the minutes of 1025th meeting of the Council of Ministers of 25 July 1985 which stated: 'With regard to the interpretation of Articles [3] and [13], the Council and the Commission are in agreement that there is nothing to prevent individual Member States from laying down in their national legislation rules regarding liability for intermediaries, since intermediary liability is not covered by the Directive. There is further agreement that under the Directive the Member States may determine rules on the final mutual apportionment of liability among several liable producers (see Article 3) and intermediaries.'

continue the €500 threshold on property damage.[60] The *González Sanchez v Medicina Asturiana* was more concerned with the interpretation of art 13 and the Court's refusal to accept any national rules that could be seen as imposing a general strict product liability regime different to that laid down in the Directive.

29 Finally, however, one needs to recognise that the maximal harmonisation affects of the Directive only extend as far as the scope of the Directive. Thus in *Moteurs Leroy Somer v Dalkia France*[61] national law could continue to apply where the damage was caused to property intended for professionals use, as such damages were outside the scope of the Directive. Equally a national system requiring public healthcare establishments to pay compensation, even when they are not at fault, for damage sustained by a patient as a result of the failure of equipment or products used in the course of treatment was not incompatible with the maximal harmonisation scope as it was a different base of liability and did not affect liability of producers under the Directive.[62]

III. SCOPE OF THE DIRECTIVE'S REGULATION

30 As it is explained elsewhere, the Product Liability Directive entails complete (full/maximum/total) harmonisation with certain exceptions. As emphasised in the preceding chapter[63] the complete harmonisation only applies to matters that are within the scope of the Directive. Whereas this prerequisite is rather obvious, the precise scope of the Directive is not and in some respects the question has given rise to controversial CJEU decisions.

31 This section gives a brief overview of the issues regulated and not regulated by the Directive, including its relation to other liability regimes and the regulatory options of the Member States. The core of the Directive is the requirement that Member States implement a liability scheme according to which 'the producer shall be liable for damage caused by a defect in his product'.[64]

Most of the Directive's basic concepts, for example 'product'[65] and 'producer',[66] contribute to defining its scope and are analysed in detail under section IV. Besides a brief overall overview, the following remarks focus mainly

60 Case C-52/00, *Commission v France* [2002] ECR I-3827 and Case C-154/00, *Commission v Greece* [2002] ECR I-3879.
61 Case C-285/08, *Moteurs Leroy Somer v Dalkia France* [2009] ECR I-4733.
62 Case C-495/10, *Centre hospitalier universitaire de Besançon v Thomas Dutrueux and Caisse primaire d'assurance maladie du Jura* [2011] ECR I-14155.
63 See above no 26 ff.
64 Art 1 of the Directive.
65 Art 2.
66 Art 3.

on some of the questions related to the Directive's concept of damage, to the liable persons and to the legal basis of liability.

A. QUESTIONS RELATED TO 'PRODUCT'

32 The Directive applies to the liability for damage caused by movables, ie tangible goods, and electricity, irrespective of whether the product is distributed as a separate, finished product or as raw material to be processed or as a component part to be incorporated into another movable or immovable.[67]

33 For the applicability of the Directive it does not matter whether the product is distributed by way of sale, hire, leasing or in the course of providing a service.[68]

B. QUESTIONS RELATED TO 'DAMAGE'

34 The Directive regulates the liability for death or personal injury and damage to or destruction of property intended for private use or consumption and mainly used as such by the injured party.[69] For these two heads of damage national law must provide for full and proper compensation, but it is left to national law to determine the precise content thereof without impairing the effectiveness of the Directive. However, insofar as consequences of death or personal injury are concerned, compensation for non-material damage is left to be governed solely by national law.[70]

The CJEU has stated that the three categories mentioned above form three heads of damage that are exhaustive and the only heads of damage possible under the Directive.[71]

35 Financial loss consequential on personal injury or on material damage to or loss of property is within the scope of the Directive insofar as it is recoverable (partly depending on national law). By putting non-material damage on the same footing as the two other headings of damages (personal injury and damage to property) *Veedfald* can be read as if art 9(2) includes *inter alia* pure economic

67 Arts 2 and 3(1) and (2). According to the original directive primary agricultural products and game, were not 'products' but the Member States had the option to exclude this exception (former arts 2 and 15(1)(a)). The special rules on primary agricultural products and game were deleted by Directive 1999/34/EC. See above no 21 ff.

68 Case C-203/99, *Veedfald v Århus Amtskommune* [2001] ECR I-3569, para 12.

69 Art 9. For damage to property there is a deduction/threshold of €500, see below no 148 ff on the different interpretations of the €500 rule.

70 Case C-203/99, *Veedfald v Århus Amtskommune* [2001] ECR I-3569, paras 27 and 28. See for details below no 148 ff.

71 Ibid para 32.

loss.[72] Both the structure of art 9 and recital 9 of the Directive's preamble, however, clearly indicate that pure economic loss which is not a consequence of physical deterioration of property is outside the scope of the Directive.[73]

36 Damage to the defective product itself is explicitly kept outside the scope of the Directive.[74] The interpretation of this exception is influenced by the distinction made in the Directive's definition of 'producer' between the producer of raw material and the manufacturer of a component part of the finished product, and by the express rule in the definition of 'product' that a movable remains a 'product' even if it is incorporated into another movable or into an immovable.[75]

Each of the various persons defined in art 3(1) is a 'producer' and as such 'liable for damage caused by a defect in his product'.[76] The determination of what is the relevant product in this respect thus depends on whom a claim for damages is made against.[77]

When all parts of a finished product are manufactured by the same producer the relevant product is the defective finished product and the Directive does not apply, irrespective of which part of the product was defective and caused the damage to the rest of the product. In addition, when the defectiveness of the finished product is due to a defective component part manufactured by a sub-supplier, the Directive is inapplicable if the consumer makes the claim against the producer of the finished product, as the relevant product in this case is also the finished product. But if the claim in this situation is made against the sub-supplier, the damage is within the scope of the Directive because the defective component part in this case is the relevant product that has caused the damage to other property, ie other parts of the product.

The exception for damage to the defective product itself may have less reasonable effects. When for instance the producer of the finished product is also the manufacturer of the component part that destroyed the finished product the Directive does not apply, whereas it does apply if the producer in question delivers the same type of (defective) component as a spare part in connection with repair work.[78]

---

72 Cf *J-S Borghetti*, in: E Terryn/G Straetmans/V Colaert (eds), Landmark Cases of EU Consumer Law: Essays in honour of Jules Stuyck (2013) 321: 'the drafters' intention most likely was to keep some kinds of damage, such as pure economic loss, outside the Directive. *Veedfald* has brought them into it.'

73 See below no 148 ff, *S Whittaker*, Liability for Products (2005) 506–507 and *B Dahl/M Levy/V Rønne/J Hornsberg*, Produktansvar (1990) Juristen 145, 162 and 173.

74 Art 9(b).

75 Arts 2 and 3(1).

76 Art 1.

77 *B Dahl/M Levy/V Rønne/J Hornsberg*, Produktansvar (1990) Juristen 145, 174 and *V Ulfbeck*, Erstatningsretlige grænseområder (2nd edn 2010) 204–205.

78 *V Ulfbeck*, Erstatningsretlige grænseområder (2nd ed 2010) 205–206.

37 The CJEU has made it clear that damage to property not intended for private use or consumption is outside the scope of the Directive.[79] In *Moteur* the CJEU found no basis in the wording, structure or purpose of the Directive to infer that it rules out that a national liability regime similar to that of the Directive is applied to property intended for professional use and used as such. Commentators have considered this interpretation of the Directive inconsistent with that applied by the Court in cases concerning suppliers' liability under the Directive.[80] However, in the suppliers' liability cases[81] the Court had some concrete basis, although perhaps not a convincing one, in the wording of the Directive.[82]

38 The Directive does not apply to injury or damage arising from nuclear accidents and covered by international conventions ratified by the Member States.[83]

39 The Member States can decide that the producer's total liability for damage resulting from a death or personal injury and caused by identical items with the same defect shall be limited to an amount not be less than €70 million.[84]

C. QUESTIONS RELATED TO PERSONS LIABLE UNDER THE DIRECTIVE

40 The Directive deals with the strict liability of producers as defined by the Directive.[85] According to the CJEU, more surprisingly, it also deals exhaustively with the strict liability of all persons in the chain of distribution of a defect product.[86]

Thus, in the preliminary ruling in *Skov Æg* the CJEU stated that a Danish rule making subsequent suppliers in the chain of distribution vicariously liable for the producer's no fault liability under the Directive 'imposes on the supplier a burden considered by the Community legislature to be unjustified ... it entails a multiplicity of actions, which is precisely what the direct action against the producer ... is intended to avoid'.[87]

---

79 Case C-285/08, *Moteur Leroy Somer v Dalkia France and Ace Europe* [2009] ECR I-4733.

80 See *H Cousy*, in: E Terryn/G. Straetmans/V Colaert (eds), Landmark Cases of EU Consumer Law: Essays in honour of Jules Stuyck (2013) 305 f.

81 Case C-402/03, *Skov Æg v Bilka Lavprisvarehus A/S* [2006] ECR I-199, para 22 and no 11 in the text below.

82 See no 40.

83 Art 14.

84 Art 16.

85 Art 3.

86 Case C-402/03, *Skov Æg v Bilka Lavprisvarehus A/S* [2006] ECR I-199, para 30.

87 Ibid paras 36 and 27–28, referring to Case C-52/00 *Commission v France* [2002] ECR I-3856 and a statement of reasons in a 1976 proposal. The Danish Government based its

According to CJEU's interpretation of the Directive not only 'producers' as defined in art 3 (including suppliers of 'anonymous' products, art 3(3)), are within the scope of the Directive. Based on an inference *a contrario* from art 3(3) the CJEU has established that all other links in the products chain of distribution are also within the scope of the Directive, although in a negative sense.[88] In combination with the interpretation of art 13 to the effect that Member States are not allowed, within the scope of the Directive, to provide other general rules on product liability,[89] this entails that the Member States cannot uphold or introduce rules on the vicarious liability of a supplier for the strict liability of producers under the Directive.[90]

41 The interpretation employed in *Skov Æg* entails that importers, sellers and other suppliers are within the scope of the Directive, also when they are not at the same time 'producers' by virtue of art 3. This means that a service provider may be considered to be a supplier of a product delivered as part of the service provided and as such within the scope of the Directive and thus immune to the strict liability of the Directive. This is for instance the case when a repair mechanic supplies spare parts as part of the repair service.

42 Moreover, a service provider may also be considered to be a 'producer' when employing materials manufactured by itself when performing the service.[91]

43 Service providers using equipment or tools as part of the performance of services are not considered to be links in the chain of distribution of the equipment or tools. They are therefore (if they did not produce the equipment themselves) not within the scope of the Directive and the Member States are free

---

interpretation of the Directive *inter alia* on a statement in the Council minutes (cited above no 26 ff). The CJEU held that the statement had no relevance: 'it must be recalled that, where a statement recorded in Council minutes is not referred to in the wording of a provision of secondary legislation, it cannot be used for the purpose of interpreting that provision' (para 42 of judgment). Given the fact that the wording of the Directive gives no unambiguous answer to the question, one may wonder why the view taken in statements concerning the 1976 proposal on the risk of price increase and a multiplicity of suits should determine the supplier question, whereas the explicit statement made by the decisions makers when the Directive was passed was irrelevant for the interpretation. Apparently the statement in the Council minutes was not present in *Commission v France* from 2002.

88 In the *Skov Æg* ruling the Court concluded that the Directive 'preclud[es] a national rule under which the supplier is answerable, beyond the cases listed exhaustively in Article 3(3) of the Directive, for the no-fault liability which the Directive establishes and imposes on the producer', but also that the Directive does 'not preclud[e] a national rule under which the supplier is answerable without restriction for the producer's fault-based liability.'

89 See no 15.

90 Case C-52/00, *Commission v France* [2002] ECR I-3856 and Case C-402/03, *Skov Æg v Bilka Lavprisvarehus A/S* [2006] ECR I-199.

91 This was the case in Case C-203/99, *Veedfald v Århus Amtskommune* [2001] ECR I-3569. The CJEU did not rule on the question but on the interpretation of 'put into circulation'.

to regulate their liability without the restrictions of the Directive, as long as it does not adversely affect the producer's liability as established by the Directive.[92]

D. QUESTIONS RELATED TO OTHER NATIONAL LIABILITY SCHEMES

44 According to art 13:

> 'This Directive shall not affect any rights which an injured person may have according to the rules of the law of contractual or non-contractual liability or a special liability system existing at the moment when this Directive is notified.'

It is established case law that, on the one hand, Member States cannot maintain a general system of product liability different from that laid down in the Directive,[93] but also that, on the other hand, art 13 'does not preclude the application of other systems of contractual or non-contractual liability based on other grounds, such as fault or a warranty in respect of latent defects.'[94]

The fact that the Directive in general entails complete harmonisation is equivalent to art 13 being interpreted as listing three possible main categories of national liability schemes that may supplement the Directive's scheme, since the rules of the same category as those found in the Directive must be fully harmonised with the exceptions stated in the Directive.

45 The CJEU thus seems to operate with the following categories of national rules concerning damages for physical injury caused by products: (1) contractual rules, (2) fault-based non-contractual rules, (3) general product liability rules (the scheme of the Directive), and (4) special product liability arrangements.

46 The Member States are not allowed to have general rules on product liability other than those stipulated in the Directive (category 3) even if this means a deterioration of the national level of consumer protection. Furthermore, the Member States cannot introduce another 'general system of product liability'.[95]

---

92 Case C-405/10, *Centre hospitalier universitaire de Besançon v Thomas Dutrueux and Caisse primaire d'assurance maladie du Jura* [2011] ECR I-14174. See no 50 below.

93 Case C-402/03, *Skov Æg v Bilka Lavprisvarehus A/S* [2006] ECR I-199, para 39, with reference to Case C-52/00, *Commission v France* [2002] ECR I-3856, para 21; Case C-154/00, *Commission v Greece* [2002] ECR I-3879, para 17; and Case C-183/00, *González Sanchez v Medicina Asturiana SA* [2002] ECR I-3901, para 30.

94 Case C-402/03, *Skov Æg v Bilka Lavprisvarehus A/S* [2006] ECR I-199, para 47, with reference to Case C-52/00, *Commission v France* [2002] ECR I-3856, para 22; Case C-154/00, *Commission v Greece* [2002] ECR I-3879, para 18; and Case C-183/00, *González Sanchez v Medicina Asturiana SA* [2002] ECR I-3901, para 31.

95 Case C-402/03, *Skov Æg v Bilka Lavprisvarehus A/S* [2006] ECR I-199, para 39.

On the other hand, they are free to apply 'other systems of liability based on other grounds such as fault or a warranty in respect of latent defects',[96] ie categories 1 and 2.

Thus, the Directive does not affect the rights of injured persons under national rules of contract law or fault based non-contractual rules, but rules out, within its scope of application, strict product liability rules other than those found in the Directive.

47 It is rather clear that the Directive has not affected sales law in Member States with a tradition of dealing with personal injury and/or damage to property (also) under the general rules sales law, cf art 13. In contrast to what applies to category 4 listed above, the Directive allows the Member States with no such tradition to introduce new rules to the effect that the seller's liability for damage caused by non-conforming goods includes personal injury and damage to property.

Although the Member States are free to make suppliers liable on the basis of contractual rules, this cannot be without restrictions. If, for instance, a Member State upholds or introduces a rule on sellers' liability which for all practical purposes is a 'general product liability rule' it cannot be decisive for its conformity with the Directive that the rule is found in a national sale of goods act and not in an act on product liability.[97] If, on the other hand, the national regulation is expressed in general rules on liability for lack of conformity (as opposed to special rules on personal injury and damage to property) it is most likely to be in accordance with the Directive.[98]

48 The distinction between categories 2 and 3 may be difficult to make in cases where fault (*culpa*) is presumed in relation to products proven to be defective and to have caused damage. According to the line of reasoning that seems to be pertinent to the distinction between categories 1 and 3, the relevant criterion seems to be whether the presumptions and other evidentiary principles applied are unique to product liability cases or just an application of general principles of tort law resulting in product liability cases being ranked in the same category as other types of cases, as for instance damage caused by proven violation of protective public law legislation.[99] The question may also be influenced by the evidentiary strength of the presumption.

49 The Directive allows special product liability arrangements as mentioned under category 4 if they existed at the time of notification of the Directive,

---

96 Ibid para 47.

97 Cf *S Whittaker*, Liability for Products (2005) 443.

98 Cf Betænkning 1502/2008 om visse køberetlige regler om sikkerhedsmangler (Committee Report on certain sales law rules concerning non-conformity regarding lack of security) 81 ff.

99 *V Ulfbeck*, Erstatningsretlige grænseområder (2nd edn 2010) 191.

whereas the introduction of new special arrangements is not allowed. This category covers liability schemes concerning special types of products, and recital 13 of the preamble shows that the primary aim is the sector of pharmaceutical products.

The Member States are entitled to uphold such special arrangements, provided that the arrangement existed at the time of notification of the Directive; in contrast to what applies to the liability schemes mentioned above as categories 1 and 2, the introduction of new special arrangements is not allowed by the Directive.

The issue of what constitutes a 'new' arrangement when a special arrangement that existed at the time of notification is amended was presented to the CJEU by the German Bundesgerichtshof in a recent case, *Novo Nordisk Pharma*.[100] The case did not result in a preliminary ruling on this question because the amendment in question was considered to be outside the scope of the Directive (see no 50 below). Advocate General Szpunar's opinion noted that art 13 does not concern the rules of such arrangements but rather the rights of injured parties. The opinion also emphasised that the exemption should be limited to those rights that existed at the time of the notification of the Directive. It did not concur in the view presented by the German government and the Commission that art 13 allows the Member States to develop the scheme further in order to keep pace with social and economic changes.[101]

50 The restrictions on the Member States following from art 13 only apply to questions that are within the scope of the Directive. However, even if the question is outside the scope of the Directive, the national rules must not adversely affect the effectiveness of the Directive.

In *Centre hospitalier universitaire de Besançon* the service provider's strict liability for damage caused by defective equipment employed by the service provider but produced by another did not violate the Directive, because the service provider was not within its scope.[102] The Court added however that 'it must remain possible for the producer's liability to be put in issue when the conditions laid down by the Directive for such liability to exist are fulfilled. That possibility of putting the producer's liability in issue must be open not only to the injured person but also to the service provider who must thus be entitled to use, to that end, a mechanism such as that of third-party proceedings'.[103]

---

100 Case C-310/13, *Novo Nordisk Pharma GmbH v. S*, Judgment 20 November 2014 [2015] OJ C26/5.

101 Opinion of Advocate General Szpunar in Case C-310/13, *Novo Nordisk Pharma GmbH v. S*, Judgment 20 November 2014 [2015] OJ C26/5, paras 37 and 39.

102 See nos 41–43.

103 Case C-495/10, *Centre hospitalier universitaire de Besançon v Thomas Dutrueux and Caisse primaire d'assurance maladie du Jura* [2011] ECR I-14174, para 30.

Novo Nordisk Pharma[104] concerned national legislation under which the victim has the right to obtain information on the adverse effects of pharmaceutical products. The CJEU stated that although such rules may make it easier for that person to produce the evidence to establish liability on the part of the manufacturer, they do not bring about either a reversal of the burden of proof (in violation of art 4) or a change of the exemptions from liability in art 7. The consumer's right to such information is therefore not within the scope of the Directive.[105]

After having stated that the legislation in question was outside the scope of the Directive, the Court stated that such national legislation must not undermine the effectiveness of the Directive's liability system or the objectives pursued by this system. Legislation on the right to get access to information on the adverse effects of products does not change the nature or the basic elements of the manufacturer liability system established by the Directive.[106]

E. OTHER ISSUES LEFT TO THE MEMBER STATES

51 The Directive makes its optional for the Member States to maintain or provide national legislation that rules out the Directive's development risk exception from the liability of a producer so that the producer is liable even if it proves that the state of scientific and technical knowledge at the time when it put the product into circulation was not such as to enable the existence of a defect to be discovered.[107]

52 The Member States are obliged to provide for joint and several liability for two or more producers liable for the same damage and to uphold the producer's full liability irrespective of a third party also being liable for the damage, but the Directive does not prejudice national rules on the rights of contribution or recourse.[108]

Similarly, the Directive does not affect the national rules regulating suspension or interruption of the three-year limitation period applicable to proceedings for recovery for damages according to the Directive.

---

104 Case C-310/13, *Novo Nordisk Pharma GmbH v S*, Judgment 20 November 2014, [2015] OJ C26/5.

105 Ibid paras 27–29.

106 Ibid paras 31–32.

107 Arts 15(1)(b) and 7(e) Product Liability Directive.

108 Arts 5 and 8(1) Product Liability Directive.

IV. THE CONTENT OF THE PRODUCT LIABILITY DIRECTIVE

A. A PRODUCT

1) *Notion*

53 The Product Liability Directive defines products as 'all movables even if incorporated into another movable or into an immovable'.[109] Art 2 of the Directive also states that the notion of 'product includes electricity'.[110] It follows from its broad definition that the Directive applies to a very wide range of products.[111] In this section the broad scope of the Directive will be analysed in further detail. First, the components of the definition cited above will be analysed successively. Second, the question of goods connected with services will be addressed. Finally, questions relating to specific categories of products will be briefly highlighted.

a) Movable goods

54 The Directive only applies to movable goods. Immovables are excluded, the reason being that liability issues in connection with immovable goods were governed by specific rules in almost all EU Member States.[112] This exclusion has been criticised by legal scholars. They argued that immovables had to be included in the Directive's scope insofar as there is no constructor liability system at Community level.[113] Furthermore, the *ratio legis* of the exclusion was subject of criticism, precisely because of the Product Liability Directive's aim of removing existing divergences of the laws of the EU Member States in this field.[114] However, the Commission was of the opinion that including immovables in the scope of the Directive was not appropriate.[115]

---

109 Art 2 Product Liability Directive.

110 Art 2 *in fine* Product Liability Directive.

111 *C Hodges*, Product liability. European laws and practice (1993) 46; *Y Markovits*, La directive C.E.E. du 25 juillet 1985 sur la responsabilité du fait des produits défectueux (1990) LGDJ 163; *D Wuyts*, The product liability directive – more than two decades of defective products in Europe (2014) 5(1) JETL 3.

112 Explanatory memorandum on the proposal for a Council Directive relating to the approximation of the laws, regulations and administrative provisions of the Member States concerning liability for defective products, Bulletin of the European Communities, Supplement 11/76, 14. See also: *Y Markovits*, La directive C.E.E. du 25 juillet 1985 sur la responsabilité du fait des produits défectueux (1990) LGDJ 165.

113 Green Paper on Liability for Defective Products, COM(1999)396 final, 30.

114 *J-L Fagnart*, La directive du 25 juillet 1985 sur la responsabilité du fait des produits (1987) Cah Dr Eur 3, 22.

115 Report from the Commission on the application of Directive 85/374 on liability for defective products, COM(2000)893 final, 24. Similar arguments were advanced by the Community

55 Movables incorporated into an immovable fall within the scope of the Directive. This extension was inserted into the Directive at the instigation of the European Parliament.[116] Hence, the Directive applies for example to movables which are used in the construction of immovables, such as materials (bricks, windows, etc)[117] used to build a house. In the same vein the Directive's scope also extends to movables incorporated in another movable, for example the components of vehicles or drugs.[118]

b) Tangible Goods

56 The Directive applies to tangible goods only. Even though there is no express exclusion of intangible goods in the Directive, it follows from an *a contrario* interpretation of Art 2 regarding electricity. Electricity is generally perceived as a non-perceptible good. Art 2 explicitly brings electricity into the scope of the Directive. That only makes sense if electricity would otherwise fall outside the scope of the Directive. There would have been no need for an explicit provision if the Directive applied to intangible goods. As a result it must be assumed that the Directive in principle does not apply to intangible goods.[119] It follows that for example services, intellectual property and goodwill are not included in the Directive.[120]

---

legislator for a number of exclusions from the scope of the Directive on consumer rights: 'Contracts related to the transfer of immovable property or of rights in immovable property or to the creation or acquisition of such immovable property or rights, contracts for the construction of new buildings or the substantial conversion of existing buildings as well as contracts for the rental of accommodation for residential purposes *are already subject to a number of specific requirements in national legislation*. Those contracts include for instance sales of immovable property still to be developed and hire-purchase. The provisions of this Directive are not appropriate to those contracts, which should be therefore excluded from its scope. A substantial conversion is a conversion comparable to the construction of a new building, for example where only the façade of an old building is retained. Service contracts in particular those related to the construction of annexes to buildings (for example a garage or a veranda) and those related to repair and renovation of buildings other than substantial conversion, should be included in the scope of this Directive, as well as contracts related to the services of a real estate agent and those related to the rental of accommodation for non-residential purposes' (emphasis added): recital 26, Directive 2011/83/EU of 25 October 2011 on consumer rights, amending Council Directive 93/13/EEC and Directive 1999/44/EC of the European Parliament and of the Council and repealing Council Directive 85/577/EEC and Directive 97/7/EC of the European Parliament and of the Council [2011] OJ L304/64.

116 Resolution embodying the opinion of the European Parliament on the proposal from the Commission of the European Communities to the Council for a Directive relating to the approximation of the laws, regulations and administrative provisions of the Member States concerning liability for defective products, C-127/61, 62.

117 *C Hodges*, Product liability. European laws and practice (1993) 47.

118 Recital 3 to the Directive.

119 *T Vansweevelt/B Weyts*, Handboek buitencontractueel aansprakelijkheidsrecht (2009) 503; *D Wuyts*, The product liability directive – more than two decades of defective products in Europe (2014) 5(1) JETL 5.

120 *D Van de Gehuchte*, Productaansprakelijkheid in België (2000) 35.

57 At this point an interesting parallel may be drawn with the Directive on consumer rights.[121] Art 2(3) defines goods for the purposes of that directive as 'any tangible movable items, with the exception of items sold by way of execution or otherwise by authority of law; water, gas and electricity shall be considered as goods within the meaning of this Directive where they are put up for sale in a limited volume or a set quantity'. It follows that electricity (like water and gas) is a tangible movable item where it is put up for sale in a limited volume or a set quantity. This guidance appeared to be necessary because of the different categorisations of electricity in the laws of the Member States.

58 The aforementioned art 2 of the Product Liability Directive has the advantage of including electricity in the Directive's scope without further specifications about how to categorise electricity. It further illustrates the broad scope of the Directive.

c) Industrially Produced Goods?

59 According to the preamble of the Directive, liability without fault should apply only to movables which have been industrially produced.[122] This view has been confirmed by some legal scholars[123] and Advocate General Colomer in his opinion in the *Henning Veedfald* case.[124]

60 However, other legal scholars have raised some doubts about this requirement,[125] referring to the clear wording of art 2 of the Product Liability Directive. This article makes no distinction between the production methods of goods, nor does the explanatory memorandum to the original proposal of the Directive. Moreover, the explanatory memorandum states that no distinction should be made between industrially manufactured goods and for example handicraft goods.[126] Furthermore, the European Commission seemed to reason along those lines when it answered a parliamentary question on whether craft

---

121 Directive 2011/83/EU of 25 October 2011 on consumer rights, amending Council Directive 93/13/EEC and Directive 1999/44/EC of the European Parliament and of the Council and repealing Council Directive 85/577/EEC and Directive 97/7/EC of the European Parliament and of the Council [2011] OJ L304/64.

122 Recital 3 to the Directive.

123 *M Faure/W Van Buggenhout*, Produktenaansprakelijkheid. De Europese Richtlijn: harmonisatie en consumentenbescherming (deel 1)? (1987–88) 1 RW 1, 6.

124 Opinion of Advocate General Colomer in Case C-203/99, *Veedfald v Århus Amtskommune* [2001] ECR I-3569, recitals 8 and 13.

125 In a similar sense, see: *L Cornelis*, Aansprakelijkheid voor gevaarlijke produkten (1987–88) 34 RW 1139, 1143; *J Peigné*, Quelle responsabilité hospitalière du fait de la greffe d'un organe contaminé (note under CAA Paris 18 October 2006) (2007) 2 RTDSS, 294, 298; *T Vansweevelt/B Weyts*, Handboek buitencontractueel aansprakelijkheidsrecht (2009) 501.

126 Explanatory memorandum on the proposal for a Council Directive relating to the approximation of the laws, regulations and administrative provisions of the Member

and artistic goods fall within the scope of the Directive.[127] All these elements indicate a broad interpretation of the notion of product, regardless of production methods. In the *Henning Veedfald* case, the European Court of Justice applied the Directive to a non-industrially produced good, and did so without even considering the opposing opinion of Advocate General Colomer.[128]

61 As a consequence it seems justified, equally in the light of the Directive's aim of consumer protection, to conclude that the concept of product must be interpreted extensively and that all movable and tangible goods, as well as electricity, are included, irrespective of the method of production of these goods, be it industrial, artisanal or artistic.[129]

d) Goods Used within the Context of Providing a Service?

62 An important question is whether goods used within the context of providing a service fall within the scope of the Directive. In the *Henning Veedfald* case, Advocate General Colomer argued that Directive 85/374/EEC was not intended to apply to services. He had reason to believe that the Product Liability Directive would not cover safety issues relating to equipment used by service providers in the course of their business. According to the Advocate General those safety issues had to be examined in connection with the safety of the service rendered.[130] It followed that goods used within the context of providing a service had to be seen always as accessories of the service placed outside the scope of the Directive.

The European Court of Justice rejected the Advocate General's view. It simply did away with the argument, stating that 'it is sufficient to observe that the case involved the defectiveness of a product – used in the course of providing a service – and not any defect in the service as such.'[131] It follows that even though services as such fall outside the scope of the Directive, the damage caused by a defective product used in the course of providing a service does not benefit automatically from that exclusion.[132] Instead of

States concerning liability for defective products, Bulletin of the European Communities, Supplement 11/76, 14.

127 Question 706/55, G De Vries [1989] OJ C114/42.

128 Case C-203/99, *Veedfald v Århus Amtskommune* [2001] ECR I-3569.

129 *AJO Van Wassenaer van Catwijck*, Produktenaansprakelijkheid in Europees verband (1986) 26; *Y Markovits*, La directive C.E.E. du 25 juillet 1985 sur la responsabilité du fait des produits défectueux (1990) LGDJ 163; *D Van de Gehuchte*, Productaansprakelijkheid in België (2000) 33.

130 Opinion of Advocate General Colomer in Case C-203/99, *Veedfald v Århus Amtskommune* [2001] ECR I-3569, recitals 15–17.

131 Case C-203/99, *Veedfald v Århus Amtskommune* [2001] ECR I-3569, recital 12.

132 *T Vansweevelt/B Weyts*, Handboek buitencontractueel aansprakelijkheidsrecht (2009) 505–506; *D Wuyts*, The product liability directive – more than two decades of defective products in Europe (2014) 5(1) JETL 6.

introducing a so-called *accessorium sequitur principale* rule as advocated by the Advocate General and other intervening parties, the ECJ focuses on whether the damage caused can be linked to either the product or the service. In *Henning Veedfald* the ECJ had no difficulty in concluding that the damage was caused by a defective product. The fluid in which the kidney was prepared for transplantation proved to be defective, whereas the service (the kidney transplant operation) was not.

63 In the same vein, it can be argued that the Product Liability Directive is to be applied for instance when a physiotherapist uses defective oil or when a constructor processes unsafe stones.[133] In practice it is of course not always that easy to assign the damage caused to either one of the products used within the context of providing a service or the service itself. In that regard the guidance offered by the ECJ in *Henning Veedfald* is rather limited. Hence it is not impossible that in the absence of clear cases like in *Henning Veedfald* where the damage caused by the product could be detached from the damage resulting from the service, the ECJ would opt for a kind of *accessorium* reasoning.[134] In contrast, *Centre hospitalier universitaire de Besançon v Dutrueux*[135] rather supports the view that if the user of a product is not the producer of that product he would fall within the notion of service provider and consequently be outside the scope of the Directive.

2) *Some Specific Products*

a) Water and Gas

64 The qualification of water and gas does not raise much concern. It can undeniably be argued that piped water and gas are products within the meaning of the Directive.[136] Indeed, these energy sources can be perceived by our senses and must be considered to be movable and tangible goods.

---

133 *K Schulpen*, De toepassing van de Wet Productaansprakelijkheid op aanneming van werken en diensten (note under Antwerp 24 januari 2007) (2010) 2 T Aann, 173, 176–177; *I Boone/ S Guiliams*, Productaansprakelijkheid en productveiligheid, in: B Tilleman/E Terryn (eds), Beginselen van Belgisch Privaatrecht XIII. Handels- en economisch recht, deel 1 (2011) volume B, 1324, 1327.

134 The ECJ already ventured into similar analyses when distinguishing between free movement of goods and freedom to provide services, especially in the lottery sector. See to that extent: *G Straetmans*, Towards a European public order: comments on Läärä and Zenatti (2000) CMLR 991–1005.

135 Case C-495/10, *Centre hospitalier universitaire de Besançon v Thomas Dutrueux and Caisse primaire d'assurance maladie du Jura* [2011] ECR I-14174.

136 *X Lewis*, The protection of consumers in European community law (1992) YEUL 139, 169–170; *A Geddes*, Product and service liability in the EEC (1992) 12–13; *C Hodges*, Product liability. European laws and practice (1993) 46.

b) Human Body Parts

65 More difficult is the classification of human body parts. It can be generally assumed that parts of the body – such as blood, tissues and sperm – are movable, tangible goods and consequently products within the meaning of the Directive.[137] Having regard in particular to the 'development risk defence',[138] as applied in France, it could be concluded that body material as such falls within the scope of the Directive. The development risk defence is indeed excluded in the French *Code civil* for damage resulting from defective body material.[139] An explicit exclusion would be redundant if body parts did not fall within the substantive scope of the Directive in the first place.

66 And yet, the analysis must be nuanced. Only bodily material which is separated from the human body constitutes a product.[140] A natural person for as long as he is alive cannot be seen as a movable good.[141] Human bodily material is not a product within the meaning of the Product Liability Directive.[142] However, once bodily material has been removed from the human body, it qualifies as a product even after it subsequently again becomes part of (another) human body – for example an organ after a transplant or blood after a transfusion. It simply remains a product, as is illustrated in a number of national blood cases as well as in cases relating to drugs.[143] In none of these cases has it been stated that products which caused damage were no longer products because of their 'absorption' into the human body. In all those cases the real focus was put onto the damage caused by the product, like the ECJ did in *Henning Veedfald*,

---

137 *T Vansweevelt*, Aids en recht (1989) 83–84; *A Van Wassenaer-Van Catwijck*, Produktenaansprakelijkheid in Europees verband (1986) Tjeenk Willink 41; *EH Hondius*, Produktaansprakelijkheid in het ziekenhuis (1990) Tijdschrift voor Gezondheidsrecht 414; *C Hodges*, Product liability. European laws and practice (1993) 51; *CJJM Stolker*, Aansprakelijkheid voor bloedprodukten en bloedtransfusies (1995) 19 NJB 685, 686–687; *P-H Delvaux/L Vandenhouten*, La responsabilité du fait des produits de santé, in: J Cruyplants/J-L Fagnart, Actualités du droit de la santé (1999) 216; *J Herring*, Medical law and ethics (2006) 378; *J Peigné*, Quelle responsabilité hospitalière du fait de la greffe d'un organe contaminé (note under CAA Paris 18 October 2006), (2007) 2 RTDSS 294, 298; *D Marginean-Faure*, note under CAA Lyon 20 December 2007 (2008) 15 AJDA 828, 829; *D Wuyts*, The product liability directive – more than two decades of defective products in Europe (2014) 5(1) JETL 7.

138 Cf *infra* no 145.

139 Article 1386–12, al 1 Civil Code.

140 *CJJM Stolker*, Aansprakelijkheid voor bloedprodukten en bloedtransfusies (1995) 19 NJB 685, 687; *RP Wijne*, Aansprakelijkheid voor zorggerelateerde schade (2013) 331.

141 *J-L Fagnart*, La directive du 25 juillet 1985 sur la responsabilité du fait des produits (1987) Cah Dr Eur 1, 19; *L Cornelis*, Aansprakelijkheid voor gevaarlijke produkten (1987–88) 34 RW 1139, 1143.

142 *HJJ Leenen/JCJ Dute/WR Kastelein*, Handboek gezondheidsrecht (2008) 137.

143 See *inter alia*: Court Amsterdam, 3 February 1999, NJ 1999, 621; *A v National Blood Authority* [2001] 3 All ER 289; and Court of Appeal Brussels, 10 February 2005, T Gez 2007–08, no 4, 284.

regardless of whether the product constituted a separable movable good at the time the damage occurred.

c) Software

67 An important question in the light of recent technical developments is whether software is a product. This question is all the more important now that computer sciences and software are becoming more and more important in the so-called 'information society'.[144] Law doctrine is divided on this subject. Some legal scholars are reluctant to classify software as a product. They argue that it rather constitutes a service[145] or an intangible good.[146] Other scholars add that software is no more than information which then in their view should fall outside the scope of the Directive.[147]

68 In contrast to these views, a parallel is to be drawn with the ECJ's approach mentioned above towards goods used in the context of providing services. Based on the court's straightforward analysis in that respect it could be argued that although the supply of software may be equated with what constitutes a service, that should not be the case for the software itself.[148] It could indeed be seen as the object of the service[149] or a result thereof. In that case it would constitute a product. This broader, more flexible analysis would also be in line with the aim proclaimed in introductory recital 2 of the Product Liability Directive. Therein the Community legislator points out that liability without fault 'is the sole means of adequately solving the problem, peculiar to our age of increasing technicality, of a fair appointment of the risks inherent in modern technological production'.

---

144 *C Stuurman/G Vandenberghe*, Softwarefouten: een 'zaak' van leven of dood? (1988) 24 NJB 1667, 1667.

145 *W Slagter*, Produktenaansprakelijkheid in Nederland (1988) TPR 731, 740.

146 *J-L Fagnart/H Boularbah*, La garantie et la responsabilité en matière de dommages causés par les produits, in: Belgische Vereniging voor Bedrijfsjuristen, Tendensen in het bedrijfsrecht: onderzoek en produktontwikkeling (2000) 132–133; *J Verlinden*, Veiligheid van producten en diensten en productaansprakelijkheid, in: Departement Vorming en Opleiding van de Orde van Advocaten van de balie van Kortrijk (ed), Huur van diensten – Aanneming van werk: vormingsprogramma 2005–2006 (2007) 62; *I Vermeire*, Productenaansprakelijkheidé, in: X, Recht voor de onderneming: risicofactoren in de onderneming (IX.20–1) IX.20–11.

147 *C Stuurman/G Vandenberghe*, Softwarefouten: een 'zaak' van leven of dood? (1988) 24 NJB 1667, 1670; *SSH Wibbens*, Netherlands, in: P Kelly/R Attree, European product liability (1992) 282.

148 *C Stuurman/G Vandenberghe*, Softwarefouten: een 'zaak' van leven of dood? (1988) 24 NJB 1667, 1670; *T Vansweevelt/B Weyts*, Handboek buitencontractueel aansprakelijkheidsrecht (2009) 504; *D Wuyts*, The product liability directive – more than two decades of defective products in Europe (2014) 5(1) JETL 5–6.

149 The service consists of the development of the software whereas the software itself is the product (the result of the service).

69 Further, it seems difficult to uphold, a some legal scholars do, that software is an intangible good. At least when software is for instance 'materialised' in a tangible medium (such as for example a DVD or a USB stick) it must be seen as an tangible good.[150] The European Commission has also approached software stored on a tangible medium as a product.[151] It follows that only in cases where software is supplied in a non-physical manner – for example online –must it be seen as an intangible good falling outside the scope of the Directive.[152] The same however cannot be said of software that is incorporated into a tangible good in such a manner that it can hardly be distinguished from the good, for instance in cases where the software is necessary for the functioning, albeit partially, of the good. In those cases the software becomes an inseverable part of the movable in which it is incorporated. The flight operation software of an aeroplane could serve as an example here. Rather than an intangible good, it must be treated as a product within the meaning of the Directive, given its inextricable link with the product itself.[153]

70 With regard to the argument that software is information which then should not be covered by the Directive, a more nuanced approach is advocated in the following subsection.

d) Information

71 Information can take many forms. One form is 'pure' information such as the piece of paper on which a medical doctor writes a prescription or the recipe book that gives incorrect instructions such that the resulting food is unsafe.[154] What is envisaged here is information that is independent of any specific product as opposed to for instance a product (ie a movable and tangible good) that is accompanied by information. In the latter case the information should be seen as a whole with the product so that the Directive in any case applies.[155]

---

150 *L Dommering-van Rongen*, Produktenaansprakelijkheid en software (1988) 5 Computerr 227, 228; *M Thornton/T Ellis*, United Kingdom, in: P Kelly/R Attree, European product liability (1992) 461.

151 Question 706/88, *De Vries* [1989] OJ C114/42.

152 *D Wuyts*, The product liability directive – more than two decades of defective products in Europe (2014) 5(1) JETL 6. It is interesting to note that the Consumer Rights Directive, cited above, classifies 'digital content (data which are produced and supplied in digital form) which is not supplied on a tangible medium' neither as a tangible good nor as a service. For the purpose of that Directive, this digital content is seen as a *sui generis* category (see recital 19 to the Directive).

153 *K-U Link/T Sambuc*, Federal republic of Germany, in: P Kelly/R Attree, European product liability (1992) 157; *G Howells*, Comparative product liability (1993) 34; *D Van de Gehuchte*, Productaansprakelijkheid in België (2000) 37.

154 *G Howells*, Comparative product liability (1993) 34.

155 *A Geddes*, Product and service liability in the EEC (1992) 10–11; *G Howells*, Comparative product liability (1993) 34.

72 In cases of 'pure' information which is not connected with a specific product, a number of legal scholars reject the application of the Directive because of its reference to movable goods.[156] If information itself is defective or flawed, they submit that in the absence of any defect on the part of the carrier of the information, the Directive does not apply to intangible goods.[157] The argument for this is that while for example a physical book or other printed paper is undeniably a product within the meaning of the Directive, the content that is printed in or on it cannot give rise to a product liability claim.[158]

73 This reasoning can be criticised when viewed from another angle. It could indeed be argued that once the information is 'materialised' on a tangible medium, it becomes a tangible movable good.[159] In consequence the Directive would apply to such 'materialised' information. The fact that in most cases further human intervention is required in order to give rise to an unsafe situation – for example defective information about how to manufacture a product always requires the creation of an unsafe product itself – does not alter this view. An extensive interpretation of the substantive scope of the Product Liability Directive is in line with the interpretation principle developed by the court according to which, in the absence of an express definition in the Directive itself, concepts have to be interpreted in accordance with the purpose and aim pursued by the Directive.[160] The broad interpretation advocated here then clearly contributes to the level of consumer protection the Directive was intended to introduce in the Member States.[161] To automatically exclude 'pure' information

156 *A Geddes*, Product and service liability in the EEC (1992) 10; *C Hodges/M Tyler/H Abbott*, Product safety (1996) 242.

157 *D Van de Gehuchte*, Productaansprakelijkheid in België (2000) 36.

158 *K-U Link/T Sambuc*, Federal republic of Germany, in: P Kelly/R Attree, European product liability (1992) 157.

159 See also: *C Hodges*, Product liability. European laws and practice (1993) 48.

160 Case C-203/99, *Veedfald v Århus Amtskommune* [2001] ECR I-3569, recital 14.

161 See in this respect recitals 1, 4, 5, 6, 8, 9 and 12 to the Directive. Furthermore, art 12 TFEU which is of general application states that 'consumer protection requirements shall be taken into account in defining and implementing other Union policies and activities'. According to art 114(3) TFEU, the Commission in its proposals for the adoption of measures for the approximation of the provisions laid down by law, regulation or administrative action in Member States which have as their object the establishment and functioning of the internal market and which concern health, safety, environmental protection and consumer protection, will take as a base a high level of protection, taking account in particular of any new development based on scientific facts. In the same vein art 38 of the Charter of Fundamental Rights of the European Union ([2000] OJ C364/01) emphasises that Union policies shall ensure a high level of consumer protection. Furthermore, the second sentence of art 35 of the Charter of Fundamental Rights of the European Union requires a high level of human health protection in the definition and implementation of all Union policies and activities. See also art 168(1) TFEU to that effect. Finally also Advocate General Bot emphasised the consumer protection and health protection requirements of the Product Liability Directive: 'Consumer protection is also one of its main objectives, as is shown, inter alia, by an examination of the *travaux préparatoires*, which preceded its adoption and its preamble', see Advocate

from the scope of the Directive would then be at odds with the consumer protection aim of the Directive.

74 The objection that liability without fault would consequently be extended to situations which were hitherto believed to fall outside the Directive is not a convincing argument either. In other domains sensitive to consumer protection, the ECJ has not hesitated to emphasise a high level of consumer protection, even in the absence of an express provision introducing liability without fault. In this respect, the prohibition of misleading commercial practices in the Unfair Commercial Practices Directive[162] is illustrative. In *VHS Tour Services v Team4 Travel* the ECJ had to assess the misleading character of information which was provided by a travel agency in sales brochures offering skiing lessons and snow holidays for groups of schoolchildren. The information concerned the exclusivity that the trader, in this case Team4 Travel, claimed to have on the dates indicated for certain accommodation.

In reality the information relating to exclusivity contained in the brochures distributed by Team4Travel appeared to be objectively incorrect. As a matter of fact, the contractual party (the hotel owner) of Team4 Travel breached the exclusivity contract concluded between them and also offered its hotel accommodation to competitors of Team4 Travel like CHS Tour Services. Even though Team4 Travel contended that it acted with the required professional diligence when drawing up its brochures and that, until the date the brochures were sent out, it had not been aware of the contracts concluded between CHS and the hotels in question, meaning that it was not guilty of any unfair commercial practice, the ECJ concluded 'that, having regard both to the wording and to the structure of Articles 5 and 6(1) of that directive, and to its general scheme, a commercial practice must be regarded as "misleading" within the meaning of the second of those provisions if the criteria set out there are satisfied, and it is not necessary to determine whether the condition of that practice's being contrary to the requirements of professional diligence, laid down in Article 5(2)(a) of that directive, is also met'.[163]

75 According to the ECJ this interpretation was the only one capable of preserving the effectiveness of the specific rules laid down in arts 6–9 of the Unfair Commercial Practices Directive. It follows from the foregoing that the ECJ introduces liability without fault for advertisers who give false information to consumers in their advertising brochures even in situations where they observed the professional diligence required by the Directive when drawing up the brochures. The straightforwardness of the Court of Justice is all the

General Bot, Opinion of 21 October 2014 in Joined Cases C-503 and 504/13, *Boston Scientific Medizintechnik v AOK Sachsen-Anhalt*, not yet published, recital 35.

162 Directive 2005/29/EC.

163 Case C-435/11, *CHS Tour Services v Team4Travel*, recital 45.

more surprising in the presence of a general prohibition on unfair commercial practices that explicitly refers to standards of professional diligence.[164]

76 Returning to the Product Liability Directive, it could be argued in parallel that the acceptance that defective information as such could give rise to liability of the producer of that information would be in line with an effective application of the Product Liability Directive. It would also contribute to an application of the Directive in a way that is favourable to the interests of consumers.

B. DEFECTIVENESS

77 The standard of liability set forth in the Directive is the defectiveness of the product, without negligence or fault of the producer being required. The concept of 'defectiveness' is the touchstone of the strict liability regime of the Product Liability Directive.[165] According to the preamble of the Directive adequate protection of consumers necessitates a liability regime without fault.[166] As cited above, this is, according to the legislator, the sole means of adequately solving the problem particular to our age of increasing technicality, of a fair apportionment of the risks inherent in modern technological production.[167]

According to art 6 of the Product Liability Directive, a product is defective when it does not provide the safety which a person is entitled to expect, taking all the circumstances into account. By way of example, the Directive mentions three specific circumstances: the presentation of the product, the use to which it could reasonably be expected that the product would be put, and the time when the product was put into circulation.[168] Finally, paragraph 2 of art 6 points out that a product may not be considered defective for the sole reason that a better product is subsequently put into circulation.[169]

In the following, the notion of defectiveness and its assessment criteria will be discussed in more detail.

1) Notion

78 As pointed out above, the central concept of the liability regime is the defectiveness of the product. It is important to emphasise that only the safety

164 Article 5(2) of the Directive states: 'A commercial practice shall be unfair if: (a) it is contrary to the requirements of professional diligence …'.

165 *G Howells*, Comparative product liability (1993) 209.

166 Explanatory memorandum on the proposal for a Council Directive relating to the approximation of the laws, regulations and administrative provisions of the Member States concerning liability for defective products, Bulletin of the European Communities, Supplement 11/76, 14.

167 Recital 2 to the Directive.

168 Article 6(1)(a)–(c) Products Liability Directive.

169 Article 6(2) Products Liability Directive.

of the product is captured by the Directive and that it is not concerned with whether the product is unmerchantable or its fitness for purpose.[170] It follows that the defectiveness of a product should not be determined by reference to its fitness for use.[171] The question whether a product is fit or not for the intended purpose belongs to the (national) rules concerning sale of goods.[172] For instance, when a kitchen knife is blunt, meaning that it cannot cut properly, the knife is obviously not fit for its intended purpose, but it is not defective within the meaning of the Directive. In contrast, if the cutting blades of an electric kitchen knife become detached, then that product is defective.[173]

79 It follows from art 6 of the Directive that the defectiveness must be assessed on the basis of what a normal person is entitled to expect. This article is quite clear as it uses only one criterion to establish the defectiveness of a product.[174] As a result, the defectiveness of a product is in principle determined only on the basis of the average consumer expectation test rather than on a risk-utility test.[175] However it should be noted that the wording 'consumer expectation test' is not entirely accurate since the test should be objective and ultimately independent of the interests of both consumers and producers.[176] What is meant in the Directive is therefore not a subjective criterion but an objective and normative criterion of defectiveness of a product.[177]

80 The criterion is in the first place objective because the defectiveness must be assessed on the basis of the legitimate expectations of the public (*in abstracto*) and thus not be based on the subjective expectations of someone.[178] The risks arising from a particular subjective predisposition to cause damage – for example a victim's allergy – should not be borne by the producer unless he has for example failed to indicate these risks and they were sufficiently serious to

---

170 *A Geddes*, Product and service liability in the EEC (1992) 21.

171 Recital 6 to the Directive. See also: *Y Markovits*, La directive C.E.E. du 25 juillet 1985 sur la responsabilité du fait des produits défectueux (1990) LGDJ 194.

172 Explanatory memorandum on the proposal for a Council Directive relating to the approximation of the laws, regulations and administrative provisions of the Member States concerning liability for defective products, Bulletin of the European Communities, Supplement 11/76, 16.

173 *D Van de Gehuchte*, Productaansprakelijkheid in België (2000) 28.

174 *C Van Dam*, European tort law (2006) 377.

175 *F Werro/VV Palmer* (eds), The boundaries of strict liability in European tort law (2004) 438.

176 *C Hodges*, Product liability. European laws and practice (1993) 52; *C Hodges/M Tyler/H Abbott*, Product safety (1996) 243.

177 *D Wuyts*, The product liability directive – more than two decades of defective products in Europe (2014) 5(1) JETL 8.

178 *Y Markovits*, La directive C.E.E. du 25 juillet 1985 sur la responsabilité du fait des produits défectueux, (1990) LGDJ 199; *D Wuyts*, The product liability directive – more than two decades of defective products in Europe (2014) 5(1) JETL 8.

justify a warning.[179] The standard is in fact the safety which the general public is entitled to expect.[180] This shall be judged on the basis of what a normal, prudent person would expect.[181] However, when the product is aimed at a specific group of users and this group is known to the producer, the assessment of the safety of the product has to be geared entirely towards this group.[182] In that case the safety assessment will be done taking into account the objective expectations and perceptions of the members of that specific group.[183]

As it is impossible to determine in advance the standard of safety that the whole range of consumers is entitled to expect for all conceivable products, the defectiveness of a product must be assessed on a case-by-case basis, taking into account all the relevant circumstances, on the basis of objective criteria.[184] Thus the courts have a wide margin of appreciation[185] and can take into account the dynamic aspect of the safety assessment.[186]

81 The criterion is in the second place also normative as it takes the *legitimate* expectations of the general public as the basis for assessment.[187] This means that the courts will establish the level of safety the public is entitled to expect regardless of the actual expectations of the public, regardless of the safety standards applicable in practice and regardless of the standards which the government promulgates.[188] The normative character of the test may therefore work in opposite directions. On the one hand it prevents the public from having

179 Explanatory memorandum on the proposal for a Council Directive relating to the approximation of the laws, regulations and administrative provisions of the Member States concerning liability for defective products, Bulletin of the European Communities, Supplement 11/76, 16.

180 *T Vansweevelt/B Weyts*, Handboek buitencontractueel aansprakelijkheidsrecht (2009) 508.

181 *Y Markovits*, La directive C.E.E. du 25 juillet 1985 sur la responsabilité du fait des produits défectueux (1990) LGDJ 307.

182 *A Geddes*, Product and service liability in the EEC (1992) 22; *WH Van Boom/CJM Van Doorn*, Productaansprakelijkheid en productveiligheid, in: EH Hondius/GJ Rijken, Handboek consumentenrecht. Een overzicht van de rechtspositie van de consument (2006) 264.

183 *T Vansweevelt/B Weyts*, Handboek buitencontractueel aansprakelijkheidsrecht (2009) 509. For instance products aimed at children or medicinal products.

184 Explanatory memorandum on the proposal for a Council Directive relating to the approximation of the laws, regulations and administrative provisions of the Member States concerning liability for defective products, Bulletin of the European Communities, Supplement 11/76, 16; *A Geddes*, Product and service liability in the EEC (1992) 22; *G Howells*, Comparative product liability (1993) 90; *MA Jones*, Medical negligence (2008) 855; *D Wuyts*, The product liability directive – more than two decades of defective products in Europe (2014) 5(1) JETL 9.

185 *RP Wijne*, Aansprakelijkheid voor zorggerelateerde schade (2013) 341. See also: *W Posch*, Reforming European Product Liability Law, in: *U Magnus/J Spier*, European Tort Law (2000) 235.

186 *Y Markovits*, La directive C.E.E. du 25 juillet 1985 sur la responsabilité du fait des produits défectueux (1990) LGDJ 184.

187 *K Van Leeuwen*, Juridische aspecten van produktveiligheid (1990) 10; *D Wuyts*, The product liability directive – more than two decades of defective products in Europe (2014) 5(1) JETL 9.

188 *Y Markovits*, La directive C.E.E. du 25 juillet 1985 sur la responsabilité du fait des produits défectueux (1990) LGDJ 202; *D Van de Gehuchte*, Productaansprakelijkheid in België (2000) 28; *T Vansweevelt/B Weyts*, Handboek buitencontractueel aansprakelijkheidsrecht (2009) 510.

unrealistic expectations but it allows the public on the other hand to expect more in some circumstances than what is laid down in standards.

82 Contrary to the liability regime in the USA, the Directive does not make a distinction between the different types of defect.[189] In the well-known English blood case *A v National Blood Authority*, it has been stated explicitly that the American view cannot be sustained in applying the Directive.[190] And yet it must be submitted that notwithstanding the Court's bold rejection in that case of the layered tripartite approach[191] in the USA, legislative and judicial practice in the Member States is influenced by the American approach.[192] In practice, courts in Member States distinguish between manufacturing defects – to which the consumer expectation test is applied – and design and instruction defects – in which, in addition to the consumer expectation test, other tests such as the risk-utility test and the reasonableness test play a role.[193]

83 In the *Boston Scientific Medizintechnik* case national judges were given further guidance on how to assess the safety which the public at large is entitled to expect.[194] The case concerned pacemakers and cardioverter defibrillators implanted in patients. The quality control system of the producer had established that a component of the pacemaker may experience a gradual degradation and that this defect could lead to premature battery depletion, resulting in loss of telemetry and/or loss of pacing output without warning. As for the cardioverter defibrillators, the quality control system had established a defect in one of its components (a magnetic switch) which could limit the device's therapeutic efficacy. As a consequence, any cardiac dysrhythmia that could be fatal would not be recognised by the defibrillators and no life-saving shock would be given to the patient. In those circumstances the producer recommended treating physicians, respectively, to consider replacing such pacemakers for the patients affected and to deactivate the magnetic switch[195] in the defibrillators concerned.

---

189 See §2 Restatement (Third) of Torts: Product Liability.

190 *A v National Blood Authority* [2001] 3 All ER 289.

191 The safety assessment in the USA is functional to the nature of the defect. More specifically, the consumer expectation test will be used in the presence of a manufacturing defect, whereas the risk-utility test and the reasonableness test are used in the case of a design defect or an instruction defect respectively.

192 *D Wuyts*, The product liability directive – more than two decades of defective products in Europe (2014) 5(1) JETL 12.

193 *S Whittaker*, The EEC Directive on product liability (1985) YEUL 246; *C Van Dam*, European tort law (2006) 377. Compare with *W Posch*, Reforming European Product Liability Law, in: U Magnus/J Spier, European Tort Law (2000) 235.

194 Joined Cases C-503/13 and C-504/13, *Boston Scientific Medizintechnik v AOK Sachsen-Anhalt*, not yet published, recital 38.

195 If that function is deactivated, the patient monitor feature remains unaffected. The fact that temporary suspension of tachyarrhythmia treatment may be performed only with the aid of

84 The preliminary question referred to the ECJ was whether a product in the form of a medical device implanted in the human body is already defective if it is found that products belonging to the same product group or forming part of the same production series have a potential defect without there being any need to establish that the product in question has such defect.

85 The ECJ answered the question in the affirmative, emphasising the preventive function of the Product Liability Directive. It first recalled that the assessment of the defectiveness of a product must be carried out having regard to the reasonable expectations of the public at large. It continued that the safety that the public at large is entitled to expect 'must be assessed by taking into account, *inter alia*, the intended purpose, the objective characteristics and properties of the product in question and the specific requirements of the group of users for whom the product is intended'.[196]

86 Turning again to the defective devices concerned, pacemakers and implantable cardioverter defibrillators, the ECJ then emphasised that 'in the light of their function and the particularly vulnerable situation of patients using such devices, the safety requirements for those devices which such patients are entitled to expect are particularly high'.[197]

87 The potential lack of safety which would give rise to liability on the part of the producer for products such as a pacemaker and an implantable cardioverter defibrillator stems from the *abnormal potential for damage* which those products might cause to the person concerned.[198]

88 Hence, the ECJ had no difficulty in finding that 'where it is found that such products belonging to the same group or forming part of the same production series which have a *potential* defect, it is possible to classify as defective all the

---

a programmer in such a case does not result in a health risk but simply a restriction of the functions which such defibrillator can perform.

196 Joined Cases C-503/13 and C-504/13, *Boston Scientific Medizintechnik v AOK Sachsen-Anhalt*, not yet published, recital 38.

197 Ibid recital 39.

198 See recital 40 of the judgment. Compare with Advocate General Bot, Opinion of 21 October 2014 in Joined Cases C-503 and 504/13, *Boston Scientific Medizintechnik v AOK Sachsen-Anhalt*, not yet published, recital 54: 'In both cases, the fact that devices of the same model are by their manufacturer's own admission, subject to potential failure inhibiting treatment of cardiac rhythm disorders clearly creates an abnormal danger for patients in whom such devices have been implanted. Contrary to the claims made by BS. GmbH at the hearing, I consider that it is irrelevant that the devices are not dangerous per se, and that they are not likely to explode in the patient's chest or to cause an injury. The defect affecting them makes them abnormally dangerous by exposing patients to a risk of heart failure or death'. Requiring the injured person to have died in order to be able to claim reparable loss or injury would be completely contrary to the effectiveness of Directive 85/374/EEC (ibid, recital 68, partim).

products in that group or series, *without there being any need to show that the product in question is defective*' (emphasis added).[199]

89 In doing so, the ECJ followed the Opinion of Advocate General Bot, who also answered the preliminary question in the affirmative, pointing to the fact that the product defect is to be assessed having regard only to safety, which can exist irrespective of any internal fault in the product concerned,[200] the high level of protection the Product Liability Directive seeks to grant consumers,[201] the preventive function of the Directive[202] and the need for the integration of health concerns in European Union policy.[203]

90 Given the particular features of the devices concerned, the judgment of the ECJ must be welcomed. The ECJ rightly emphasises the consumer protection objective of the Product Liability Directive as well as its preventive function in this particular context. Much more so than Advocate General Bot,[204] the ECJ puts the emphasis on the specific nature of the products concerned, which require a consumer-friendly approach. In view of the life-threatening risk presented by a defective device, the patient may reasonably expect the implanted

---

199 Joined Cases C-503/13 and C-504/13, *Boston Scientific Medizintechnik v AOK Sachsen-Anhalt*, not yet published, recital 41.

200 Advocate General Bot, Opinion of 21 October 2014 in Joined Cases C-503 and 504/13, *Boston Scientific Medizintechnik v AOK Sachsen-Anhalt*, not yet published, recital 32.

201 Ibid recital 37: 'The protection which Directive 85/374 seeks to grant consumers would be seriously undermined if, in the event that a number of products of the same model were placed on the market and a safety defect occurred in only some of those products, the probability that the defect was present in other products could not be taken into consideration. In actual fact, all EU legislation on product safety would be called into question if, in that situation, it was necessary to wait for the risk of failure in connection with a lack of safety shown to exist in certain products to materialise in other products through damage occurring'.

202 Ibid recital 38: 'Making proof of a lack of safety subject to the actual occurrence of damage would disregard the preventive function assigned to EU legislation on the safety of products offered on the market and to the specific liability regime established by Directive 85/374, which manifestly pursues a preventive function by imputing liability to the person who, having created the risk most directly by manufacturing a defective product, is in the best position to minimise it and to prevent damage at the lowest cost'.

203 Ibid recital 40.

204 The Advocate General seems to extend his analysis to all medical devices, pointing out that the function of health products for human use lends such products an indisputable specific character, which must be taken into account in assessing the concept of defect. However, this position is further on in the Opinion mitigated by focusing on the specific nature of the products concerned. Compare with: 'Although the notion of legitimate expectation is particularly difficult to define and its perception involves some degree of subjectivity, it may be argued that the expected degree of safety, which depends, among other things, on the nature of the product and its intended use, will be greater for a device implanted in the human body, in respect of which it is difficult to conceive of a situation in which it could be improperly used by the patient, than for a bottle of water or for a cleaning product' (ibid recital 45) and 'it seems clear to me that the legitimate expectations of a patient in whose body a pacemaker or an ICD has been implanted because of a disease suffered by him are not comparable with those of a user of a mobile phone whose battery becomes depleted prematurely' (ibid recital 46, partim).

device to have a failure rate of close to zero. Allowing victims to claim reparable loss or injury in those cases is a fair appointment of the risks inherent in modern technological production between the injured person and the producer.[205] However, extending the ECJ's reasoning to a vast array of products would certainly give rise to questions about the specific nature of the Product Liability Directive and risks of jeopardising the fair apportionment of risks the Directive is intended to foster. The fact that the ECJ, unlike Advocate General Bot, cleverly avoided dwelling on the inclusion of public health standards in the EU policies, as well as making any reference to the Charter of Fundamental Rights of the European Union, seems to indicate its careful analysis tailored to the case at hand. Nevertheless, the judgment must be considered ground-breaking for its assessment of defects in products with similar characteristics.

2) Assessment Criteria

91 When assessing the legitimate safety expectations of the general public, relevant circumstances have to be taken into account. Art 6 of the Directive lists three elements in that respect. It is clear that this guidance of the Community legislator is not exhaustive. Courts are free to take other circumstances into account, including elements of a risk-utility test, the type of the product, the severity of the hazard, etc[206] In the following subsections the analysis will be confined to the three circumstances which are explicitly mentioned in the Directive. We will briefly analyse in turn (i) the presentation of the product, (ii) the reasonable expected use of a product, and (iii) the time when the product was put into circulation.

a) The Presentation of the Product

92 The presentation of a product has a great influence on the safety expectations of the general public.[207] The starting point for each safety assessment is that

---

205 The ECJ also decided that full and proper compensation for persons injured by a defective product relates to all that is necessary to eliminate harmful consequences and to restore the level of safety which a person is entitled to expect. 'As a consequence, in the case of medical devices, such as pacemakers and implantable cardioverter defibrillators, which are defective within the meaning of … Directive 85/374, compensation for damage must cover, inter alia, costs relating to the replacement of the defective product' (recital 50 of the judgment). See also for the concept of compensation for damage, *infra*.

206 See *inter alia*: *S Whittaker*, The EEC Directive on product liability (1985) YEUL 233, 245; *J Knottenbelt*, Richtlijn produktaansprakelijkheid (1988) 43 NJB 1539, 1542; *Y Markovits*, La directive C.E.E. du 25 juillet 1985 sur la responsabilité du fait des produits défectueux, (1990) LGDJ 203; *C Hodges*, Product liability. European laws and practice (1993) 53; *C Hodges/ M Tyler/H Abbott*, Product safety (1996) 243; *F Werro/VV Palmer* (eds), The boundaries of strict liability in European tort law (2004) 439; *C Van Dam*, European tort law (2006) 377; *D Wuyts*, The product liability directive – more than two decades of defective products in Europe (2014) 5(1) JETL 13–14.

207 Article 6(b) Product Liability Directive.

a product must be considered as a whole and assessed in its entirety.[208] In view of this, the presentation of a product must be taken in its broadest meaning, including marketing, advertisements, packaging, instructions, warnings, etc.[209] The presentation of a product thus includes how the product is put into circulation and how it is offered and proposed to the public.[210]

93 In the event of inaccurate, incomplete or missing information, this will certainly be taken into account in the safety assessment.[211] More than this, it is generally accepted that this may render a product defective.[212] Especially in the case of an inherently dangerous product – such as medical products or complicated high tech goods – information about any possible risk is essential to the safety assessment.[213] It follows for example that the producer of the product must provide information on the use of its product, the period within which the product can be used safely and the possible risks connected with the product.[214]

94 An important question in this regard is whether an initially defective product can be transformed into a safe product by giving information. The answer to this question is obviously not always uniform. In some cases the answer may be affirmative, leading courts to conclude, on the basis of the information and warnings provided, that the product meets the legitimate safety expectations. The assumption is thus that the more information is provided to the targeted public, the lower the safety expectations this group may be expected to have.[215]

95 Of course account should be taken of the fact that it is impossible to warn the pubic about all the potential dangers of a product. Thus a producer of

---

208 *T Vansweevelt/B Weyts*, Handboek buitencontractueel aansprakelijkheidsrecht (2009) 511; *D Verhoeven*, Het redelijkerwijze voorzienbaar gebruik van een product en het later ontstaan van gebreken in de wet productenaansprakelijkheid (comment on Court of Appeal Antwerp 28 October 2009) (2011) 8 TBBR 388, 390.

209 *G Howells*, Comparative product liability (1993) 37; *C Hodges*, Product liability. European laws and practice (1993) 53; *D Wuyts*, The product liability directive – more than two decades of defective products in Europe (2014) 5(1) JETL 15.

210 *T Vansweevelt/B Weyts*, Handboek buitencontractueel aansprakelijkheidsrecht (2009) 511.

211 *I Demuynck*, De bescherming van de consument tegen gevaarlijke, gebrekkige en niet-conforme producten, in: Vlaamse Conferentie der Balie van Gent (ed), De consument in het recht: verwend, verwaand of miskend? (2003) 42.

212 *F Werro/VV Palmer* (eds), The boundaries of strict liability in European tort law (2004) 440; *SS Sanbar/MH Firestone/F Buckner et al* (eds), Legal medicine (2004) 410–411; *A Grubb/J Laing/J McHale*, Principles of medical law (2010) 980–981.

213 *D Wuyts*, The product liability directive – more than two decades of defective products in Europe (2014) 5(1) JETL 16.

214 *T Vansweevelt/B Weyts*, Handboek buitencontractueel aansprakelijkheidsrecht (2009) 512.

215 *D Verhoeven*, Het redelijkerwijze voorzienbaar gebruik van een product en het later ontstaan van gebreken in de wet productenaansprakelijkheid (note under Antwerp 28 October 2009) (2011) 8 TBBR 388, 390.

microwave ovens does not have to warn its consumers not to dry a dog in it.[216] According to the Product Safety Directive the producer shall provide consumers with 'the relevant information to enable them to assess the risks inherent in a product throughout the normal or reasonably foreseeable period of its use, where such risks are not immediately obvious without adequate warnings, and to take precautions against those risks'.[217]

96 It follows from the foregoing that a warning or other form of information will not automatically render the unsafe product safe.[218] It may well be that the presentation of a product, despite particular information and warnings, does not correspond to the safety expectations of the general public,[219] especially if the legitimate safety expectations of the general public are higher.[220] It is generally accepted in this regard that a warning is for example insufficient if it is possible to produce a safer product without extra financial burden and this higher safety standard does not affect the benefit of the product.[221] Even the presence of an exhaustive list of warnings and possible dangers does not guarantee that a particular product is safe, as it will be in the end the judge who is entitled to determine the legitimate expectations of the public.[222]

97 In addition, warnings and instructions about the possible use of a product must be taken into account in this assessment. For example if a producer states explicitly or implicitly that a product may be used for a particular purpose or in a particular way, and the consumer uses it for that purpose or in that way and suffers harm, this would weigh very strongly in favour of its defectiveness.[223]

b) The Reasonable Expected Use of a Product

98 The reasonable expected use of a product includes, in addition to consumption, such activities as storage, cleaning, inspection and repair.[224] The producer has to anticipate the reasonable expected conduct of the user. The reasonable expected use of the consumer is not restricted to the normal or

---

216 *S Whittaker*, The EEC Directive on product liability (1985) YEUL 233, 243.
217 Article 5(1) Product Safety Directive.
218 *I Vermeire*, Productenaansprakelijkheid, in: X, Recht voor de onderneming: risicofactoren in de onderneming (IX.20-1) IX.20-17.
219 *D Verhoeven*, Het redelijkerwijze voorzienbaar gebruik van een product en het later ontstaan van gebreken in de wet productenaansprakelijkheid (note under Antwerp 28 October 2009) (2011) 8 TBBR 388, 390.
220 *T Vansweevelt/B Weyts*, Handboek buitencontractueel aansprakelijkheidsrecht (2009) 513.
221 *C Van Dam*, European tort law (2006) 378.
222 *D Wuyts*, The product liability directive – more than two decades of defective products in Europe (2014) 5(1) JETL 18.
223 *S Whittaker*, The EEC Directive on product liability (1985) YEUL 233, 243.
224 *A Geddes*, Product and service liability in the EEC (1992) 22.

anticipated destination of the product.[225] The consumer benefits from a certain margin of reasonable misuse.[226] It means that a certain degree of careless conduct or (too) intensive use of the product must be tolerated.[227]

99 This means that the producer cannot expect that a consumer will always use the product in the normal way or in the way the producer intended the product to be used.[228] The producer has to anticipate this conduct by designing the product in a safer way or, if this is not reasonably feasible, by effectively warning the consumer.[229] In other words, the producer must ensure that its product provides adequate safety even in the event of a reasonably foreseeable misuse of the product.[230] This rather flexible analysis is obviously favourable to the consumer and fosters the goal of consumer protection set forth in the Directive.[231]

100 Some legal scholars advocate that the distinction between reasonable misuse and unreasonable abuse must be assessed on the basis of the 'social acceptance' of that particular use.[232] However, the present authors would rather adhere to what a number of Belgian scholars advance in this respect. They suggest that the appropriate test for distinguishing between reasonable misuse and unreasonable abuse lies in taking into account the gradations of fault. In this, a *culpa levis* is deemed foreseeable, while a serious fault or fraud is not.[233] It must be clear from the foregoing that *de facto* the Directive imposes a duty of consideration on the manufacturer.[234]

---

225 *J-L Fagnart*, La directive du 25 juillet 1985 sur la responsabilité du fait des produits (1987) Cah Dr Eur 3, 33; *D Wuyts*, Productaansprakelijkheid: een Richtlijn voor (n)iets? (2008) 1 TBBR 2, 14.

226 *D Verhoeven*, Het redelijkerwijze voorzienbaar gebruik van een product en het later ontstaan van gebreken in de wet productenaansprakelijkheid (note under Antwerp 28 October 2009) (2011) 8 TBBR 388, 391.

227 *M Faure/W Van Buggenhout*, Produktenaansprakelijkheid. De Europese Richtlijn: harmonisatie en consumentenbescherming (deel 1)? (1987–88) 1 RW 1, 10.

228 *G Howells*, Comparative product liability (1993) 38; *D Wuyts*, The product liability directive – more than two decades of defective products in Europe (2014) 5(1) JETL 20.

229 *C Van Dam*, European tort law (2006) 378.

230 *PM Storm*, Product recall. Het terugroepen van gevaarlijke produkten (1985) 26; *J Verlinden*, Veiligheid van producten en diensten en productaansprakelijkheid, in: Departement Vorming en Opleiding van de Orde van Advocaten van de Balie van Kortrijk (ed), Huur van diensten – Aanneming van werk: vormingsprogramma 2005–2006 (2007) 70; *D Verhoeven*, Het redelijkerwijze voorzienbaar gebruik van een product en het later ontstaan van gebreken in de wet productenaansprakelijkheid (note under Antwerp 28 October 2009) (2011) 8 TBBR 388, 391.

231 *T Vansweevelt/B Weyts*, Handboek buitencontractueel aansprakelijkheidsrecht (2009) 514.

232 *Y Markovits*, La directive C.E.E. du 25 juillet 1985 sur la responsabilité du fait des produits défectueux, (1990) LGDJ 209.

233 *T Vansweevelt/B Weyts*, Handboek buitencontractueel aansprakelijkheidsrecht (2009) 515.

234 *D Wuyts*, The product liability directive – more than two decades of defective products in Europe (2014) 5(1) JETL 20.

101 Finally, it is worthwhile to submit that a producer can warn about certain abuses of a product, but the mere fact that the producer warns against certain behaviour will only lead to an unreasonable abuse of the product in the event of flagrant disregard for warnings or instructions.[235] Ignoring explicit and multiple warnings *can* lead to a serious fault and hence to unreasonable abuse of the product.[236] However, in our opinion, this will not automatically be the case. Together with other legal scholars we are of the opinion that a product that is accompanied by an adequate warning cannot automatically be considered defective if this warning is not respected by the user.[237]

c) The Time when the Product was Put into Circulation

102 Finally the legitimate safety expectations at the time when the product was put into circulation are taken into account and not those that pertained later on.[238] This means that all the elements of the safety assessment must be assessed at the time when the product was put into circulation.[239] Developments in technical and scientific knowledge (see no 145 below) as well as subsequent circumstances that may affect the condition of the product may not be taken into account.[240] Only the development risk defence – pertaining to technical standards, regulatory standards and safety legislation – at the time when the product was put into circulation can be used in the safety assessment.[241]

103 A product cannot be considered defective only as a result of wear and tear of the product.[242] Furthermore, the enactment of stricter safety rules after the product (which met the then-applicable standards) was put into circulation cannot amount to the product being labelled as unsafe just

235 Ibid 21.

236 *T Vansweevelt/B Weyts*, Handboek buitencontractueel aansprakelijkheidsrecht (2009) 516.

237 *AJO Van Wassenaer van Catwijck*, Produktenaansprakelijkheid in Europees verband (1986) 48.

238 *C Van Dam*, European tort law (2006) 378.

239 *J-L Fagnart*, La directive du 25 juillet 1985 sur la responsabilité du fait des produits (1987) Cah Dr Eur 3, 34; *T Vansweevelt/B Weyts*, Handboek buitencontractueel aansprakelijkheidsrecht (2009) 517. See also *I Boone/S Gilliams*, Productaansprakelijkheid en productveiligheid, in: B Tilleman/E Terryn (eds), Beginselen van Belgisch Privaatrecht XIII. Handels- en economisch recht, deel 1, volume B (2011) 1330.

240 *L Cornelis*, Aansprakelijkheid voor gevaarlijke produkten (1987–88) 34 RW 1139, 1146; *H Bocken*, Buitencontractuele aansprakelijkheid voor gebrekkige producten in X., Bijzondere overeenkomsten. XXXIVe postuniversitaite cyclus Willy Delva (2008) 369.

241 *N Reich*, Product safety and product liability (1986) 9 J Cons Pol 133, 139.

242 Explanatory memorandum on the proposal for a Council Directive relating to the approximation of the laws, regulations and administrative provisions of the Member States concerning liability for defective products, Bulletin of the European Communities, Supplement 11/76, 16.

because of these new stricter rules.[243] The car market is illustrative in this respect. The fact that an older car is not equipped with an ABS braking system, which did not exist at the time when the car was put into circulation, does not automatically lead to the conclusion that the car is defective for the mere reason that a better product – namely a new car with an ABS braking system – is put into circulation.[244]

d) The Particular Characteristics and Properties of a Product

104 It was pointed out above, referring to the ECJ's ground-breaking judgment in the *Boston Scientific Medizintechnik* case,[245] that the specific characteristics and properties of a product may have a bearing on the assessment of the product's defectiveness. In particular, the life-threatening risk presented by a defective device may lead to all the products belonging or forming part of that group or series of devices being classified as defective, *without there being any need to show that the individual product in question is defective.*[246]

C. LIABLE PERSON

1) Notion

105 In view of protecting consumers, the Product Liability Directive requires that almost all participants involved in the production process (except mainly for designers) should be made liable and that in some cases this liability should also extend to importers of products, persons who presents themselves as producers or persons who supply a product.[247] Article 1 provides the rule that the producer shall be liable. Article 3 complements this with a definition of the notion of 'producer'. The concept is given an extended definition under the Directive.[248] It follows from the Directive's aim that the term 'producer' must be interpreted broadly so that the victim of a defective product finds a liable person.[249]

---

243 Explanatory memorandum on the proposal for a Council Directive relating to the approximation of the laws, regulations and administrative provisions of the Member States concerning liability for defective products, Bulletin of the European Communities, Supplement 11/76, 16.

244 *T Vansweevelt/B Weyts*, Handboek buitencontractueel aansprakelijkheidsrecht (2009) 517.

245 Joined Cases C-503/13 and C-504/13, *Boston Scientific Medizintechnik v AOK Sachsen-Anhalt*, not yet published, recital 38.

246 See *supra* fn 84–91.

247 Recital 4 to the Directive.

248 *G Howells*, Comparative product liability (1993) 30.

249 *M Thornton/T Ellis*, United Kingdom, in: P Kelly/R Attree, European product liability (1992) 459. See also *Y Markovits*, La directive C.E.E. du 25 juillet 1985 sur la responsabilité du fait des produits défectueux (1990) LGDJ 138.

106 It is from this perspective that the notion of producer will be examined. The ECJ also contributed to a broad reading of the concept. It held that since the European legislator is endowed with the competence to harmonise the laws of the Member States in the field of product liability,[250] it is also competent to determine the persons who have to bear that liability and the conditions under which those can be sued.[251] As a consequence arts 1 and 3 of the Directive are not confined to regulate the liability of the producer of a defective product but also determine whom of the operators who have taken part in the manufacturing and marketing process will have to assume the liability, established by the Directive.[252] It further follows from the case law of the ECJ that the Product Liability Directive sees itself as a complete harmonisation measure[253] of the matters regulated by it so that the determination of the class of persons liable also must be regarded as exhaustively regulated.[254]

a) The Real Producer

107 The producer of the product should be the party primarily responsible for the safety of products.[255] 'Producer' means the manufacturer of a finished product, the producer of any raw material or the manufacturer of a component part.[256] This very broad definition is the most equitable in order to protect the consumer sufficiently.[257]

108 In the event that a composed product is defective the victim may sue both the producer of a component part or of any raw material and the producer of the finished product,[258] provided of course that the component or raw material which

---

250 The general legal base for this competence resides in article 114 TFEU. On this ground Community institutions may 'adopt the measures for the approximation of the provisions laid down by law, regulation or administrative action in Member States which have as their object the establishment and functioning of the internal market'.

251 Case C-52/00, *Commission v France* [2002] ECR I-3827, recital 39.

252 Case C-402/03, *Skov AEG v Bilka Lauprisvarenhus A/S* [2006] ECR I-199, recital 30.

253 See also the contribution of *G Howells* to this work.

254 Case C-402/03, *Skov AEG v Bilka Lauprisvarenhus A/S* [2006] ECR I-199, recitals 32 and 33; Opinion of Advocate General Mengozzi in Case C-405/10, *Centre hospitalier universitaire de Besançon v Thomas Dutrueux and Caisse primaire d'assurance maladie du Jura* [2011] ECR I-14174, recital 37; Case C-405/10, *Centre hospitalier universitaire de Besançon v Thomas Dutrueux and Caisse primaire d'assurance maladie du Jura* [2011] ECR I-14174, recital 26; and *Y Markovits*, La directive C.E.E. du 25 juillet 1985 sur la responsabilité du fait des produits défectueux (1990) LGDJ 153.

255 *G Howells*, Consumer product safety (1998) 12.

256 Art 3(1) Products Liability Directive.

257 Explanatory memorandum on the proposal for a Council Directive relating to the approximation of the laws, regulations and administrative provisions of the Member States concerning liability for defective products, Bulletin of the European Communities, Supplement 11/76, 15.

258 *T Vansweevelt/B Weyts*, Handboek buitencontractueel aansprakelijkheidsrecht (2009) 529.

has been produced by that producer is defective.[259] The producer of the finished product will in principle always be liable,[260] while with regard to the producer of a component part the Directive provides a specific defence under art 7(f).

109 The liability should be channelled to the producer for reasons of prevention and in view of forestalling the spread of damage.[261] The reason for this is that the producer can include the expenditure which he incurs to cover his liability in his production costs when calculating the price and therefore divide it among all consumers of products which are of the same type.[262] The European Economic and Social Committee in its initial opinion on the Directive took the view that the proposed system of liability is based on the principle of passing on – ie in the sale price of goods – the cost of compensation damages so that as a result this cost is borne indirectly by all consumers of a given product.[263] Finally, it seemed to be fair and logical that those who benefit financially from a product (ie the producer) should bear the risk of liability.[264]

b) The Person who Presents Himself as a Producer

110 Furthermore, any person who, by putting his name, trade mark or other distinguishing feature on the product, presents himself as its producer shall be regarded as the producer of that product.[265] This will generally apply to chain-store retailers or mail-order operators who are not involved in the manufacturing of the product but who are selling it under their own name.[266]

---

259 *Y Markovits*, La directive C.E.E. du 25 juillet 1985 sur la responsabilité du fait des produits défectueux (1990) LGDJ 146.

260 *SSH Wibbens*, Netherlands, in: P Kelly/R Attree, European product liability (1992) 285.

261 *DA Fischer*, Products liability – the meaning of defect (1974) 39 Mod L Rev 339, 339–340; *V Pire*, Les limites de la responsabilité du fournisseur au sens de la directive 85/374/CEE relative à la responsabilité du fait des produits défectueux (note under ECJ 10 January 2006 *Skov & Bilka*) (2005) 4 REDC 347, 349; and *T Vansweevelt/B Weyts*, Handboek buitencontractueel aansprakelijkheidsrecht (2009) 527.

262 Explanatory memorandum on the proposal for a Council Directive relating to the approximation of the laws, regulations and administrative provisions of the Member States concerning liability for defective products, Bulletin of the European Communities, Supplement 11/76, 14; *GL Priest*, The current insurance crisis and modern tort law (1987) 96 Yale LJ 1521, 1534; and *A Baker*, Liability without fault and the AIDS plague compel a new approach to cases of transfusion-transmitted disease (1990) 61 U Colo L Rev 81, 97. See also *BA Koch/H Koziol*, Comparative Conclusions, in: BA Koch/H Koziol (eds), Unification of Tort Law: Strict Liability (2002) 403, 413 and 419.

263 Opinion of the Economic and Social Committee on the proposal for a Council Directive relating to the approximation of the laws, regulations and administrative provisions of the Member States concerning liability for defective products [1979] OJ C-114/15, 16–17.

264 *Y Markovits*, La directive C.E.E. du 25 juillet 1985 sur la responsabilité du fait des produits défectueux (1990) LGDJ 137. However, cf *J Stapleton*, Product Liability (1994) 7 ff and 186 ff.

265 Art 3(1) *in fine* Products Liability Directive.

266 *K-U Link/T Sambuc*, Federal republic of Germany, in: P Kelly/R Attree, European product liability (1992) 158; *C Hodges*, Product liability. European laws and practice (1993) 59; *C Hodges/M Tyler/H Abbott*, Product safety (1996) 244.

The *ratio legis* of this is to offer protection to injured parties if they experience difficulties in discovering the identity of the actual producer and ensuring that the person who presents himself as a producer effectively bears the consequences of his conduct.[267]

111 With this extension of the class of liable persons the European legislator targeted companies mainly selling products under their own name that are manufactured by another non-identified company that strictly follows the instructions of the first company.[268] It is more particularly the close economic relationship between the actual producer and his wholesaler, who acts as the producer of the product, that triggered the European legislator to treat the wholesaler as a liable person.[269]

112 Any assessment of whether someone gave the impression that he is the producer of a product must be done *in concreto*, taking into account the view of the ordinary, prudent consumer.[270] The mere fact that someone puts his name on a product is therefore not sufficient to consider him a producer.[271] The decisive factor is the impression made on the average consumer (of the target group of the product) and not the intention of the wholesaler.[272] To avoid liability, the wholesaler must present himself in such a manner that it becomes clear for a normal consumer who is the producer of the product and who is not.[273]

113 It has been mentioned above that the status of apparent producer cannot solely be deduced from the mere application of a name, brand or recognition/

---

267 *Y Markovits*, La directive C.E.E. du 25 juillet 1985 sur la responsabilité du fait des produits défectueux (1990) LGDJ 148 and *T Vansweevelt/B Weyts*, Handboek buitencontractueel aansprakelijkheidsrecht (2009) 530.

268 *Y Markovits*, La directive C.E.E. du 25 juillet 1985 sur la responsabilité du fait des produits défectueux (1990) LGDJ 150.

269 Explanatory memorandum on the proposal for a Council Directive relating to the approximation of the laws, regulations and administrative provisions of the Member States concerning liability for defective products, Bulletin of the European Communities, Supplement 11/76, 15.

270 *G Howells*, Comparative product liability (1993) 31 and *T Vansweevelt/B Weyts*, Handboek buitencontractueel aansprakelijkheidsrecht, (2009) 530.

271 *M Faure/W Van Buggenhout*, Produktenaansprakelijkheid. De Europese Richtlijn: harmonisatie en consumentenbescherming? (deel 1), (1987–88) 1 RW 1, 7 and *D Van de Gehuchte*, Productaansprakelijkheid in België (2000) 41.

272 *S Whittaker*, The EEC Directive on product liability (1985) YEUL 233, 267; *L Cornelis*, Aansprakelijkheid voor gevaarlijke produkten, (1987–88) 34 RW 1139, 1141; *D Van de Gehuchte*, Productaansprakelijkheid in België (2000) 42.

273 *S Whittaker*, The EEC Directive on product liability (1985) YEUL 233, 267 and *D Wuyts*, Productaansprakelijkheid: een Richtlijn voor (n)iets? (2008) 1 TBBR 3, 22.

identification sign for this might be done for purely advertising purposes.[274] The sporting star, for instance, whose name was appended to a product as part of its promotion would not be liable under the Directive as he would not be presenting himself as its producer.[275] In addition, when the law requires a particular person to place his name on the products he sells, that does not make him automatically an apparent producer.[276] Affixing quality labels on the product after inspections have been conducted on it by an independent body does not make this inspection body an apparent producer.[277]

114 Conversely, if the product clearly mentions that it is 'manufactured for' the seller whose mark it bears, this does not automatically relieve the seller of the status of apparent producer.[278] But the opposite is also true since it cannot automatically be derived from the label 'manufactured for' on the product that the seller is presenting himself as a producer.[279] As previously mentioned, the assessment should be made in view of a normal and prudent consumer.

115 The same can be said when the seller's name or brand is affixed to the product which further bears statements like 'Made in Hong Kong' or another country than the seller's home country. In that case the normal consumer can in principle legitimately expect that the seller is presenting himself as a producer, as he cannot be expected to know where the seller is located.[280] However, this will not be the case if the seller clearly indicates that the product was manufactured abroad and a normal consumer knows or should have known that this seller does not possess a company located abroad and consequently could never be the real producer of the product.[281]

---

274 *C Hodges*, Product liability. European laws and practice (1993) 60. Compare with: *M Fallon*, La loi du 25 février 1991 relative à la responsabilité du fait des produits défectueux (1991) JT 465, 470 and *T Vansweevelt*, De Wet van 25 februari 1991 inzake produktenaansprakelijkheid (deel 2) (1992) 3 TBBR 184, 195.

275 *S Whittaker*, The EEC Directive on product liability (1985) YEUL 233, 267. In the same sense, see: *G Howells*, Comparative product liability (1993) 30–31.

276 Explanatory memorandum of the European Convention on Products Liability in regard to Personal Injury and Death, recital 47.

277 *AJO Van Wassenaer van Catwijck*, Produktenaansprakelijkheid in Europees verband (1986) 29; *M Faure/W Van Buggenhout*, Produktenaansprakelijkheid. De Europese Richtlijn: harmonisatie en consumentenbescherming (deel 1)? (1987–88) 1 RW1, 8.

278 *T Vansweevelt*, Art. 3 Wet Productenaansprakelijkheid, in: E Dirix/A Van Oevelen (eds), Bijzondere overeenkomsten: commentaar met overzicht van rechtspraak en rechtsleer (2003) 5.

279 *D Van de Gehuchte*, Productaansprakelijkheid in België (2000) 41–42.

280 *T Vansweevelt/B Weyts*, Handboek buitencontractueel aansprakelijkheidsrecht (2009) 530–531. *Contra*: W Slagter, Produktenaansprakelijkheid in Nederland (1988) TPR 731, 742.

281 *GMF Snijders*, Produktenrecht: drie aspecten in Europees perspectief (1990) 86.

c) The EU Importer

116 Without prejudice to the liability of the producer, any person who imports into the European Union a product for sale, hire, leasing or any form of distribution in the course of his business shall be deemed to be a producer and shall be responsible as a producer.[282] As a result, the victim of a defective product is not required to locate and sue a producer in a non-EU Member State.[283] But despite improvements in the rules of private international law, the victim of a defective product will still find practical difficulties when suing someone in another Member State.[284] Article 3(2) of the Directive contains three conditions that must be fulfilled before the EU importer can be held liable.

117 First, the import must be done with the aim of selling, hiring, leasing or otherwise distributing the product. The import of a product for personal use falls outside the scope of this notion of EU importer,[285] for example a tourist who brings home some souvenirs for his own private use. The decisive criterion is whether the import was done with the intent of transferring the property in the product to another person.[286] In this respect it must also be emphasised that the aim of the Directive to give the injured person in all cases a liable party necessitates a very broad interpretation of the wording of art 3(2). The wording itself is also in turn open, especially the reference to 'any form of distribution'.[287]

It follows that the mere fact of placing a product at one's disposal – even for a very limited period in time – is sufficient to qualify the product as being imported for 'any form of distribution'.[288] For example, a hotel that imports hairdryers for its guests is importing the products for 'a form of distribution'. The same could arguably be said of the airline company that imports an aeroplane, since this is intended to carry passengers.

---

282 Art 3(2) Product Liability Directive.

283 *C Hodges*, Product liability. European laws and practice (1993) 60. See also: Explanatory memorandum on the proposal for a Council Directive relating to the approximation of the laws, regulations and administrative provisions of the Member States concerning liability for defective products, Bulletin of the European Communities, Supplement 11/76, 15; *Y Markovits*, La directive C.E.E. du 25 juillet 1985 sur la responsabilité du fait des produits défectueux (1990) LGDJ 151; and *A Turner*, The EC Product Liability Directive, in: P Kelly/R Attree, European product liability (1992) 5.

284 *G Howells*, Comparative product liability (1993) 31.

285 *T Vansweevelt/B Weyts*, Handboek buitencontractueel aansprakelijkheidsrecht (2009) 532.

286 *D Verhoeven*, De buitencontractuele aansprakelijkheid van de invoerder voor gebrekkige of onveilige producten (2013) 8 TBBR 429, 430.

287 See also: *L Dommering-van Rongen*, Productaansprakelijkheid. Een rechtsvergelijkend overzicht (2000) 90 and *I Demuynck*, De bescherming van de consument tegen gevaarlijke, gebrekkige en niet-conforme producten, in: Vlaamse Conferentie der Balie van Gent (ed), De consument in het recht: verwend, verwaand of miskend? (2003) 35.

288 *D Verhoeven*, De buitencontractuele aansprakelijkheid van de invoerder voor gebrekkige of onveilige producten (2013) 8 TBBR 429, 431.

118 Second, the import of the product should be done 'in the course of his business'. For example, a tourist who brings home some souvenirs for friends is not an EU importer, not even if he is paid for these souvenirs, since he is not acting in the course of his business.[289] This is not to say that a free transfer of products cannot be framed within the commercial and business activities of a person.[290] For example, a company that imports promotional gifts for their customers and business partners clearly qualifies as importer. The assessment of whether the import is done 'in the course of his business' must be done *in concreto*, taking into account *inter alia* the nature of the transfer (free or paid) and the professional activity of the different persons involved in the transaction.[291] It should also be kept in mind that the concept 'in the course of his business' refers to a certain frequency as the term business refers to an activity instead of an isolated act.

119 Third, the product should be imported into the European Union. As a result imports between different Member States are not targeted.[292] This can easily be explained from the angle of free movement of goods. Any extension towards imports between Member States would indeed hinder intra-community trade of products.[293] More importantly, there is no need whatsoever to give the injured party an additional liable person in the case of a mere import between different Member States.[294]

d) The Supplier

120 Finally, where the producer or EU importer of the product cannot be identified, each supplier of the product shall be treated as its producer unless he informs the injured person, within a reasonable time of the identity of the producer or EU importer or of the person who supplied him with the product.[295] In the presence of an anonymous product, the supplier will be the liable person unless he discloses the identity of the producer, EU importer or

289 Ibid 431.

290 *Contra*: *HC Taschner/E Frietsch*, Produkthaftungsgesetz und EG-Produkthaftungsrichtlinie (1990) 350.

291 *T Vansweevelt/B Weyts*, Handboek buitencontractueel aansprakelijkheidsrecht (2009) 532.

292 *AJO van Wassenaer van Catwijck*, Produktenaansprakelijkheid in Europees verband (1986) 29.

293 Articles 34 and 35 TFEU; see also *N Reich*, Product safety and product liability (1986) 9 J Cons Pol 133, 142; *M Faure/W Van Buggenhout*, Produktenaansprakelijkheid. De Europese Richtlijn: harmonisatie en consumentenbescherming (deel 1)? (1987–88) 1 RW 1, 8.

294 *L Dommering-van Rongen*, Productaansprakelijkheid. Een rechtsvergelijkend overzicht (2000) 90.

295 Art 3(3) Product Liability Directive.

his own supplier.[296] If the supplier omits to inform the injured person within a reasonable time, he will be treated as the producer of the product.[297]

121 The notion of 'supplier' is not defined in the Directive. Advocate General Mengozzi deduced from the case law of the Court of Justice that the supplier of a defective product must be regarded as an intermediary involved in the marketing or distribution chain of the product and that this definition should be restrictive in nature.[298] In the same vein, Advocate General Trstenjak submitted that the interpretation of this notion must be functionally similar to the concept of producer, which results in the requirement of a strict link between a producer and a supplier that is so close that the latter is in reality involved in the production process. In her view the concept of producer also encompasses that of a supplier in the presence of such a close link.[299]

122 Decisive in view of classifying a supplier as a functional producer is therefore the producer's *de facto* control over the product after the product has been transferred by him to the supplier. This is the case if the supplier does not operate autonomously in the market but follows the instructions of the producer by whom he is controlled.[300] In the presence of such a close link between the producer and the supplier, the latter must also be seen as the (functional) producer of the product. In other cases, the supplier is just an intermediary involved in the marketing or distribution chain of the product.

123 It has been mentioned above that the supplier will not be liable if he informs the injured person within a reasonable time of the identity of the producer or EU importer or of the person who supplied him with the product. It follows that the supplier *de facto* has the obligation to check the identity of its predecessor and to make an inventory of this information which can be passed on to potential victims.[301] In order to fulfil this requirement it suffices

---

296 Explanatory memorandum on the proposal for a Council Directive relating to the approximation of the laws, regulations and administrative provisions of the Member States concerning liability for defective products, Bulletin of the European Communities, Supplement 11/76, 15.

297 Case C-358/08, *Aventis Pasteur SA v OB* [2009] ECR I-11305, recital 56.

298 Opinion of Advocate General Mengozzi in Case C-405/10, *Centre hospitalier universitaire de Besançon v Thomas Dutrueux and Caisse primaire d'assurance maladie du Jura* [2011] ECR I-14174, recital 29.

299 Opinion of Advocate General Trstenjak in Case C-358/08, *Aventis Pasteur SA v OB* [2009] ECR I-11305, recitals 32 and 34.

300 Ibid recitals 38 and 39.

301 *C Hodges*, Product liability. European laws and practice (1993) 64; *V Pire*, Les limites de la responsabilité du fournisseur au sens de la directive 85/374/CEE relative à la responsabilité du fait des produits défectueux (note under ECJ 10 January 2006 *Skov & Bilka*) (2005) 4 REDC 347, 350; and *S Vandemaele*, De 'gemakkelijke' identificeerbaarheid van de (schijn) producent door de mededeling van de leverancier (note under Mons 13 January 2012) (2013)

to communicate the data of the previous supplier. The current supplier has no obligation to communicate the identity of the real producer.

124 In that respect some legal scholars submit that if the supplier communicates the identity of a previous intermediary – for example a distributor – that is not the manufacturer itself, this previous intermediary will not be liable as he is not a producer. They argue that since art 3(3) of the Directive only refers to the supplier defined as the person who supplies the consumer with a product, he does not have an obligation to inform the injured person of the identity of the producer.[302] However, this reasoning should not be followed. When a supplier reveals the identity of the person who supplied him with the product, the latter should be considered a supplier within the meaning of art 3(3) of the Directive unless he informs the injured person, within a reasonable time, of the identity of the producer, the EU importer or of the person who supplied him with the product. The obligation to inform is explained by the ECJ, which has ruled that the mere statement that the supplier is not the producer of the product without precise information about the identity of for example the producer 'cannot ... suffice for that supplier to be treated as having informed the injured person or therefore for it to be ruled out that it could be treated as a "producer"'.[303] Similarly, the supplier who transmits incorrect, false or useless information will not be freed from his liability.[304]

125 The information also must be revealed within a reasonable time. The Directive does not specify what is to be understood by a reasonable time.[305] Experience shows that the method of formally notifying a supplier of his liability can vary tremendously depending on the Member State, which does not seem to be very satisfactory in view of the aims of the Directive.[306] Nevertheless, although it seems that different EU Member States apply this indication with small variations, the Commission was of the opinion that there is no clear evidence for a need for harmonisation.[307] Anyway, although the Directive says nothing as to how the period within which the supplier must answer is to be

99 DCCR 117, 121: he will be obliged to keep precise records, see further on this *PM Storm*, Een gebrekkig product (1985) 10 TVVS 241, 242.

302 *D Van de Gehuchte*, Productaansprakelijkheid in België (2000) 44–45.

303 Case C-358/08, *Aventis Pasteur SA v OB* [2009] ECR I-11305, recital 57.

304 *T Vansweevelt/B Weyts*, Handboek buitencontractueel aansprakelijkheidsrecht (2009) 534.

305 *A Turner*, The EC Product Liability Directive, in: P Kelly/R Attree, European product liability (1992) 6; *T Vansweevelt/B Weyts*, Handboek buitencontractueel aansprakelijkheidsrecht (2009) 534; and *S Vandemaele*, De 'gemakkelijke' identificeerbaarheid van de (schijn) producent door de mededeling van de leverancier (note under Mons 13 January 2012) (2013) 99 DCCR 117, 124.

306 Green Paper on Liability for Defective Products, COM(1999)396 final, 29 and *C Hodges*, Product liability. European laws and practice (1993) 63.

307 Report from the Commission on the application of Directive 85/374 on liability for defective products, COM(2000)893 final, 23.

calculated, 'it may be generally assumed that this period starts to run from the time when the injured person raises claims under the Directive against the supplier'.[308] This means that the reasonable time requirement begins to run as soon as the supplier knows or must have known that the victim raised a claim under the Directive.

126 Although strict liability for the supplier of products would have been far easier, it was not upheld. The main reason for its rejection was the increasing product costs it would entail, as it would necessitate each supplier to conclude an insurance contract to cover this risk. Furthermore, it would have led to a chain reaction. If strict liability is imposed on a supplier he would address in turn his supplier and go further up the chain to the real producer of the product. The European legislator was also reluctant, stating that the number of cases where a product defect results from the activity of a supplier seems to be relatively limited.[309]

127 Despite all this the question was raised whether the no-fault liability system of the Directive should not be imposed on every professional in the product supply chain, if his activities have affected the safety properties in question of a product placed on the market, such as specific activities involving repackaging, transport or storage.[310] Those professionals should bear the same liability as producers. This proposal is clearly inspired by Directive 2001/95/EC, which includes in its definition of producer each person in the supply chain, insofar as his activities may affect the safety properties of a product placed on the market.

128 However, the European Commission has cut all speculations on this subject short, pointing out that Directive 2001/95/EE aims at prevention, whilst Directive 85/374/EEC fulfils a curative role of compensation. The Commission submits that even though these functions are complementary, it does not mean that in all respects the rules applicable should be exactly the same, which is *inter alia* true for the question whether all the obligations that suppliers have under the Directive on general product safety can be transposed *ipso facto* to the area of product liability.[311] An extension of the strict liability of the Product Liability

[308] Opinion of Advocate General Trstenjak in Case C-358/08, *Aventis Pasteur SA v OB* [2009] ECR I-11305, recital 98.

[309] Explanatory memorandum on the proposal for a Council Directive relating to the approximation of the laws, regulations and administrative provisions of the Member States concerning liability for defective products, Bulletin of the European Communities, Supplement 11/76, 16 and report from the Commission on the application of Directive 85/374 on liability for defective products, COM(2000)893 final, 24.

[310] Green Paper on Liability for Defective Products, COM(1999)396 final, 30.

[311] Report from the Commission on the application of Directive 85/374 on liability for defective products, COM(2000)893 final, 23.

Directive to suppliers whose activities may affect the safety properties of the product is consequently not to be expected. Whether this is the correct approach and whether the arguments advanced for the rejection of the extension are convincing must be discussed further.

e) Other People?

129 It was mentioned above that the Directive seeks to achieve complete harmonisation in the matters regulated by it and that as a result the determination of the class of persons liable under the Directive must be regarded as exhaustive. It follows that all other persons than the (apparent) producer, the EU importer and the supplier cannot be liable under the Directive. This is for example true for the designer of a product, who is not also its manufacturer, or the repairer of a product.[312] They fall outside the scope of the notion of 'producer'.

With regard to the liability of the provider of services, Advocate General Mengozzi pointed out that the person providing a service is distinct from the supplier within the meaning of art 3(3) of the Directive since he does not provide a product but services in the context of which the defective product was used.[313] In this regard, it must be recalled that case law of the ECJ supports the view that the supplier of a product must be regarded as an intermediary involved in the marketing or distribution chain of the product and that it is correct that the service provider 'cannot be considered to be an operator in the production and marketing chain of the product in question'.[314] His liability falls outside the scope of the matters regulated by the Directive. As a consequence national Member States are entitled to stipulate specific liability rules.[315]

130 It was also pointed out above that the ECJ decided in the *Henning Veedfald* case that the Directive was applicable to products used within the context of providing a service.[316] The case was peculiar in that it concerned a service provider who was also the producer of the product used in the context of providing the service. It allowed the ECJ to confine itself to producer's liability, leaving liability aspects relating to service providers unanswered.[317]

---

312 *S Whittaker*, The EEC Directive on product liability (1985) YEUL 233, 269; *K-U Link/ T Sambuc*, Federal republic of Germany, in: P Kelly/R Attree, European product liability (1992) 158; and *C Hodges*, Product liability. European laws and practice (1993) 58.

313 Opinion of Advocate General Mengozzi in Case C-405/10, *Centre hospitalier universitaire de Besançon v Thomas Dutrueux and Caisse primaire d'assurance maladie du Jura* [2011] ECR I-14174, recitals 31 and 32.

314 Case C-405/10, *Centre hospitalier universitaire de Besançon v Thomas Dutrueux and Caisse primaire d'assurance maladie du Jura* [2011] ECR I-14174, recital 28.

315 Ibid recitals 30 and 39.

316 Case C-203/99, *Veedfald v Århus Amtskommune* [2001] ECR I-3569.

317 Case C-405/10, *Centre hospitalier universitaire de Besançon v Thomas Dutrueux and Caisse primaire d'assurance maladie du Jura* [2011] ECR I-14174, recital 37.

2) *Solidary Liability*

131 It follows from the preamble to the Directive that where several persons are liable for the same damage, consumer protection requires that the injured person should be able to claim full compensation for the damage from any one of them.[318] Article 5 of the Directive states that where, as a result of the provisions of this Directive, two or more persons are liable for the same damage, they shall be jointly and severally liable without prejudice to the provisions of national law concerning the rights of contribution or recourse.[319] This joint and several liability is seen as one of the main elements of the Directive.[320]

132 Claims must of course be based on the Product Liability Directive itself and can only be directed to persons liable under the Directive. It gives the injured person the possibility of claiming against the person who, because of his economic position, is best placed to pay compensation for the damage.[321] It also exempts the victim of a defective product from initiating proceedings against all possible producers of the product in order to obtain from each of them the proportion of damages which corresponds to their share in causing the damage.[322]

D. THE STANDARD OF LIABILITY AND DEFENCES

133 In establishing the standard of liability applied in Directive 85/374, of greatest significance is the content of arts 1 and 4, as well as some of the

---

318 Recital 5 to the Directive.

319 This reference to national law was inserted into the Directive at the request of the European Parliament, see further on this: Resolution embodying the opinion of the European Parliament on the proposal from the Commission of the European Communities to the Council for a Directive relating to the approximation of the laws, regulations and administrative provisions of the Member States concerning liability for defective products, [1979] OJ C-127/61, 63.

320 Green Paper on Liability for Defective Products, COM(1999)396 final, 20; Report from the Commission to the Council, the European Parliament and the European Economic and Social Committee on the application of Council Directive on the approximation of laws, regulations and administrative provisions of the Member States concerning liability for defective products (85/374/EEC of 25 July 1985, amended by Directive 1999/34/EC of the European Parliament and of the Council of 10 May 1999), COM(2006)496 final, 4–5.

321 Explanatory memorandum on the proposal for a Council Directive relating to the approximation of the laws, regulations and administrative provisions of the Member States concerning liability for defective products, Bulletin of the European Communities, Supplement 11/76, 16; *Y Markovits*, La directive C.E.E. du 25 juillet 1985 sur la responsabilité du fait des produits défectueux (1990) LGDJ 141; and *A Geddes*, Product liability in the EEC (1992) 29.

322 Explanatory memorandum on the proposal for a Council Directive relating to the approximation of the laws, regulations and administrative provisions of the Member States concerning liability for defective products, Bulletin of the European Communities, Supplement 11/76, 16 and *A Geddes*, Product liability in the EEC (1992) 29.

circumstances enumerated in art 7 excluding liability. These provisions should be interpreted in light of the viewpoint taken by the CJEU that the Directive constitutes an instrument of full harmonisation of domestic laws within the scope encompassed by it.[323]

134 Article 1 states that '[t]he producer shall be liable for damage caused by a defect in his product'. According to art 4, '[t]he injured person shall be required to prove the damage, the defect and the causal relationship between defect and damage'. The second of the aforementioned provisions should be interpreted within the full harmonisation method applied in the Directive as not so much a delimitation of the scope of evidential responsibilities resting on the injured person, but rather as an exhaustive enumeration of the positive conditions which must exist for liability to be borne by the producer. In other words, this provision states that a producer is liable in every event that a causal nexus exists between a defect and injury, and that the burden of proof rests with the injured person.[324] This catalogue of conditions is, however, modified by the list of circumstances excluding liability contained in art 7, which we will return to shortly.

135 This depiction of the conditions for liability is intended primarily to emphasise that the liability of a producer is independent of fault.[325] Thus, the event justifying the assignment of liability for injury to a producer is the mere fact of bringing a dangerous product into circulation, without regard to fault on the part of the producer. The legislator's intention in assigning liability independently of fault was to establish the cornerstone of the liability regime formed by the Directive. This is emphasised in recital 2, which states that 'liability without fault on the part of the producer is the sole means of adequately solving the problem, peculiar to our age of increasing technicality, of a fair apportionment of the risks inherent in modern technological production'. The independence of liability from fault has been the focus of the CJEU's jurisprudence.[326] It is also worth noting a portion of the justification written by the Commission for its proposal, overlooked in the final draft of the Directive,[327] which says that 'an equal and adequate protection of the consumer can be achieved only through the introduction of liability irrespective of fault on the part of the producer of the article which was defective and caused the damage; … any other type of liability imposes on the injured party almost

---

323 See *G Howells* in this chapter.

324 See Case C-183/00, *Maria Victoria González Sánchez v Medicina Asturiana SA* [2002] ECR I-391, para 31.

325 See eg *HC Taschner*, Product liability: basic problems in a comparative law perspective, in: D Fairgrieve (ed), Product Liability in Comparative Perspective (2005) 156 ff.

326 See Case C-300/95, *Commission v United Kingdom* [1997] ECR I-2649; Case C-402/03, *Skov AEG v Bilka Lauprisvarenhus A/S* [2006] ECR I-199, para 19.

327 COM(76)372.

insurmountable difficulties of proof or does not cover the important causes of damage'.

136 This is a crucial issue. Delimiting the liability standard required by the Directive facilitates not only proper transposition of the Directive into domestic legal regimes, but also an accurate determination of the aspect of social life and legal system regulating it which has been encompassed by the harmonising effect of the Directive. This last aspect – determining the scope of the Directive's impact on domestic legal orders – is crucial owing to the maximal nature of harmonisation. Since the Directive does not allow for any other liability regimes (not only ones less beneficial for the protected entity) to be retained in a domestic legal order within the scope encompassed by it, the required effect cannot be achieved without unequivocally determining the scope of the Directive's impact. In the case of Directive 85/374, the situation is complicated by the rule set out in art 13, which establishes the relationship between the liability regime introduced by the Directive and the liability regimes in place in a given domestic legal system. This provision reads: '[t]his Directive shall not affect any rights which an injured person may have according to the rules of the law of contractual or non-contractual liability or a special liability system existing at the moment when this Directive is notified'. Recital 13 goes on to explain that '[w]hereas under the legal systems of the Member States an injured party may have a claim for damages based on grounds of contractual liability or on grounds of non-contractual liability other than that provided for in this Directive; insofar as these provisions also serve to attain the objective of effective protection of consumers, they should remain unaffected by this Directive; whereas, insofar as effective protection of consumers in the sector of pharmaceutical products is already also attained in a Member State under a special liability system, claims based on this system should similarly remain possible'. In practice, determining the permissibility of further application of domestic liability regimes for defective products to the extent that such regimes differ from that set out in the Directive is done by way of a comparison of the scope of application of the two liability regimes and their respective constructions.

137 A competing system regulating liability for injury caused by a defective product can function alongside the system introduced by the Directive either when its application is limited to a specified area of production (eg medicinal products), or when the liability is based on a different principle than the one underlying the regime introduced in the Directive, meaning that of fault or contract liability (eg warranty against hidden product defects).[328]

[328] See Case C-154/00, *Commission v Greece* [2002] ECR I-3879, para 18; Case C-52/00, *Commission v France* [2002] ECR I-3827, para 22; Case C-183/00, *Maria Victoria González Sánchez v Medicina Asturiana SA* [2002] ECR I-391, paras 31–33; Case C-402/03, *Skov AEG v Bilka Lauprisvarenhus A/S* [2006] ECR I-199, para 47.

138 The seemingly clear picture of conditions and of the standard of liability regulated under the Directive becomes slightly muddied when considering the circumstances set out in art 7 freeing a producer from liability. Their introduction is justified in recital 7 by 'a fair apportionment of risk between the injured person and the producer'. However, the reality is that the catalogue of defences available in art 7 is not uniform. Some of them do in fact address the scope of the risk borne by a producer, while others serve to compliment the list of conditions of liability; their placement in art 7 rather than in art 4 results from differences in the apportionment of the burden of proof.

139 Article 7 of the Directive declares that:

> 'The producer shall not be liable as a result of this Directive if he proves:
> (a) that he did not put the product into circulation; or
> (b) that, having regard to the circumstances, it is probable that the defect which caused the damage did not exist at the time when the product was put into circulation by him or that this defect came into being afterwards; or
> (c) that the product was neither manufactured by him for sale or any form of distribution for economic purpose nor manufactured or distributed by him in the course of his business; or
> (d) that the defect is due to compliance of the product with mandatory regulations issued by the public authorities; or
> (e) that the state of scientific and technical knowledge at the time when he put the product into circulation was not such as to enable the existence of the defect to be discovered; or
> (f) in the case of a manufacturer of a component, that the defect is attributable to the design of the product in which the component has been fitted or to the instructions given by the manufacturer of the product'.

140 Before proceeding to a discussion of the individual defences, there are two issues which should first be examined.

141 First, in respect of the 'development risk' defence (art 7(e)) the Directive provides a regulatory option. According to art 15(1) of the Directive, '[e]ach Member State may by way of derogation from Article 7 (e), maintain or, subject to the procedure set out in paragraph 2 of this Article, provide in this legislation that the producer shall be liable even if he proves that the state of scientific and technical knowledge at the time when he put the product into circulation was not such as to enable the existence of a defect to be discovered'.

142 Second, the view of the CJEU is applicable in its entirety to art 7, namely that the Directive implements maximal harmonisation of domestic legal orders within the scope encompassed by it. This means that the Member States are obliged to include in their laws circumstances releasing a producer from

liability consistent with the way in which they are established by the Directive. The regulatory option in art 15 does not constitute an exception – if a domestic regime foresees a development risk defence, it must take the form set out in art 7(e).[329]

143 Taking into consideration the objective of this work, the six facts set out in art 7, which, if the producer proves them, protects him against a judgment for damages, can be divided into two categories. The first consists of facts related to the manner in which the injury visited on the injured person is associated with the producer's activity; what is the causal relationship (the specific course of events) between the activity of the producer and the injury that leads to the producer being liable. This is easier to understand if we invert the provisions of art 7 from their negative orientation (useful for distributing the burden of proof) to an affirmative one. This allows us, applying a slight simplification, to determine that a producer incurs liability for injury caused by a product that he:

(i) manufactured for sale or any form of distribution for economic purposes or manufactured and distributed in the course of his business (art 7(c));
(ii) put into circulation (art 7(a)); and which
(iii) was defective at the time it was put into circulation (art 7(b)).

These facts are all encompassed by a presumption that the producer must rebut in order to free himself of liability. The strength of this presumption varies – in respect of the facts listed in (i) and (ii), the producer must present evidence to the contrary, namely demonstrate that the circumstances did not occur. With regard to the fact presented in (iii), it is not necessary to achieve certainty, but only to demonstrate the likelihood that the defect did not exist at the moment the product was put into circulation. It should be emphasised, however, that in establishing liability the key issue is the existence of the defect at the moment the product is brought to market, not that it was generated by the producer.[330]

144 The meaning of the conditions 'put the product into circulation'[331] and acting 'for economic purpose or in the course of business' was elaborated on by the CJEU in a decision handed down regarding a case in which the defect concerned a fluid involved in preparing kidneys for transplant. The fluid was produced by a hospital owned by a local council in order to be used by another hospital belonging to the same authority; thus it was not manufactured for sale and remained in the sphere of control of public medical facilities offering

329 See Case C-52/00, *Commission v France* [2002] ECR I-3827, para 47.
330 Correctly noted by *J Stapleton*, Product Liability (1994) 192.
331 This ambiguous term also leads to difficulties in interpretation against the background of art 11 of the Directive, concerning the limitation period. See no 176 below.

treatment financed by public money. As to the first condition, the CJEU held that the Directive provides no definition of the expression 'put into circulation' and it must therefore be interpreted in accordance with the purpose and aim of the Directive. The exemption from liability provided for in art 7(a) of the Directive is intended primarily to cover cases in which a person other than the producer has caused the product to leave the process of manufacture. Moreover, uses of the product contrary to the producer's intention, for example where the manufacturing process is not yet complete, and use for private purposes or in similar situations are excluded from the scope of the Directive. However, in that case, the use of the product was characterised by the fact that the person for whom it was intended must bring himself within the producer's sphere of control. The Court held that whether a product used in the provision of a service was made by a third party, by the service provider himself or by an entity linked to the service provider cannot of itself alter the fact that the product was put into circulation. Regarding the second condition, the Court held that 'the fact that products are manufactured for a specific medical service for which the patient does not pay directly but which is financed from public funds maintained out of taxpayers' contributions cannot detract from the economic and business character of that manufacture. The activity in question is not a charitable one which could therefore be covered by the exemption from liability provided for in Article 7(c) of the Directive.'[332]

Furthermore, the facts referred to in art 7(d) and (e) are of a slightly different nature. They do not address the manner in which the defective product was released by the producer, but rather what led to the defect. This casts a somewhat different light on the statement that producer liability is grounded in the assumption that he bears the risk of defects in products that he puts into circulation. The risk is, in fact, limited.

If the source of the defect was adherence to mandatory provisions of law enacted by public authorities, then the producer will not be held responsible for any resulting defect (another legal basis may provide for liability on the part of the public authority that issued the defective regulations). The sense and the objective of this limitation is uncontroversial, as there is no justification for burdening a producer with the negative impact of mistakes by public authorities that he could not oppose. Nonetheless, the practical relevance of this defence is rather limited.

145 The second of the grounds for excluding liability, set out in art 7(e), paints a more complicated picture. A producer bears no liability in spite of putting a defective product into circulation if the state of scientific and technical

---

332 See Case C-203/99, *Veedfald v Århus Amtskommune* [2001] ECR I-3569, paras 14–22. See also *S Whittaker*, Liability for Products: English Law, French Law and European Harmonisation (2005) 516 ff.

knowledge at the time he did so was insufficient to uncover the defect. To put it differently (ignoring the issue of the burden of proof), the producer is only liable for defects that could be uncovered taking into account available knowledge.[333] The CJEU emphasises in its jurisprudence the objective nature of this exclusion – a producer is not released from liability by demonstrating that his subjective knowledge was insufficient to uncover the defect, nor that he made reasonable attempts to acquire such knowledge. Only the 'objective state of scientific and technical knowledge, including the most advanced level of such knowledge, without any restriction as to the industrial sector concerned'[334] counts. In spite of efforts to assign this defence a strictly objective nature, it could still be said that to some degree it make a producer's liability similar to that for negligence,[335] with the difference that rather than a reasonable care, the producer must demonstrate the highest level of diligence and the individual capacity of the producer to ascertain the defectiveness of the product is without significance. In essence, the defence contained in art 7(e) boils down to the producer freeing himself from liability by declaring that, while in possession of all knowledge available at a given moment,[336] the defect in the product could not be avoided. Of course, more important than unsolvable theoretical dilemmas (the concepts of fault and negligence are understood in different manners across different legal systems) is the practical significance of the exception under discussion here. It shifts the risk of injury caused by the introduction into circulation of a technology that has yet to be fully examined in respect of safety from the producer onto the injured person. To put it differently, the risk associated with civilisation failing to achieve a sufficient level of knowledge is assigned to the consumer, and not to the producer, who reaps the benefits of distributing the product. The practical significance of this exclusion of liability may increase as the battle for market dominance transforms into a race to be first in the commercial exploitation of new technologies. However, the provision remains open to interpretation, as the concept of 'the most advanced level of scientific and technical knowledge' is not without ambiguity. Doubts may arise concerning the very concept of 'knowledge', which could, for example, denote any random and not-yet-disproven hypothesis as well as a statement incontrovertibly established as fact. It is also not entirely clear what constitutes an appropriate means of

---

333 Importantly, the defence in art 7(e) refers to a defect in the product, and not only to the risk of its occurrence; see *J Stapleton*, Product Liability (1994) 236 ff.

334 See Case C-300/95, *Commission v United Kingdom* [1997] ECR I-2649, paras 26–29. See also *HC Taschner*, Product liability: basic problems in a comparative law perspective, in: D Fairgrieve (ed), Product Liability in Comparative Perspective (2005) 164. As to the consequences of such an interpretation of art 7(e) see *J Stapleton*, Product Liability (1994) 236 ff.

335 See *J Stapleton*, Product Liability (1994) 236 ff; *S Whittaker*, Liability for Products: English Law, French Law and European Harmonisation (2005) 494 ff and the literature cited therein; also *S Whittaker*, The development of product liability (2010) 35 and authors cited in fn 208.

336 Which itself is difficult to assess, as correctly noted by *S Whittaker*, Liability for Products: English Law, French Law and European Harmonisation (2005) 498 ff.

distribution of knowledge for ascertaining that it is accessible and therefore delineates the standard for evaluating a producer's behaviour.[337]

146 The defence articulated in art 7(f) presents a similar picture to that of the one discussed above. It refers to the producer of a component. While the Directive does not state it directly, it proceeds from both art 1 and recital 4 that the producer of a component can only be held liable when a component of his own production is defective. However, the Directive assumes the existence of a causal link between the activity of that entity and the defect in the component. The presumption of the existence of this link is so strong that it may only be rebutted through demonstrating one of two other sources of the defect – faulty design of the product as a whole or incorrect instructions received from the manufacturer.

147 The characterisation of producer liability envisioned in the Directive is supplemented by the principle expressed in art 12, pursuant to which 'the liability of the producer arising from [the] Directive may not, in relation to the injured person, be limited or excluded by a provision limiting his liability or exempting him from liability.' Domestic provisions implementing the Directive must therefore constitute mandatory law. There should be no doubt that the prohibition set out in art 12 concerns the exclusion or limitation of liability with future effect. It does not, however, extend to contracts (settlements, releases from debt, etc) which the injured person could enter into with the individual responsible for the injury after it has already occurred.

E. INJURED PERSON AND RECOVERABLE DAMAGES

148 The Directive does not directly indicate who may be entitled to damages claims, using the formula 'injured person'.[338] However, wherever it makes mention of the predicted effects of the new provisions, it clearly refers to consumer protection (arts 15(3) and 16(2)). Consumer protection as the objective of the Directive is mentioned multiple times in its recitals.

149 From the perspective of proper legislative technique, it was justified to avoid mention of the term 'consumer' in the content of the Directive. This expression in EU law generally refers to individuals entering into contractual relations with a professional,[339] while the regulation of the Directive does not

---

[337] See *M Mildred*, The development risk defence, in: D Fairgrieve (ed), Product Liability in Comparative Perspective (2005) 184 ff.

[338] See *S Whittaker*, Liability for Products: English Law, French Law and European Harmonisation (2005) 502 ff.

[339] See eg art 2(1) of the Directive 2011/83/EU on consumer rights.

address contracts per se. Protection of the consumer in the economic sense of the word, which is the objective of the regulation, is accomplished by properly regulating injuries giving rise to recoverable damages.

150 Pursuant to art 9 of the Directive,

> 'for the purpose of Article 1, "damage" means:
> (a) damage caused by death or by personal injuries;
> (b) damage to, or destruction of, any item of property other than the defective product itself,[340] with a lower threshold of 500 ECU, provided that the item of property:
> (i) is of a type ordinarily intended for private use or consumption, and
> (ii) was used by the injured person mainly for his own private use or consumption.
> This Article shall be without prejudice to national provisions relating to non-material damage'.

In addition, art 16(1) holds that 'any Member State may provide that a producer's total liability for damage resulting from a death or personal injury and caused by identical items with the same defect shall be limited to an amount which may not be less than 70 million ECU'.[341]

In turn, the relevant recital (9) states that '[w]hereas the protection of the consumer requires compensation for death and personal injury as well as compensation for damage to property; whereas the latter should nevertheless be limited to goods for private use or consumption and be subject to a deduction of a lower threshold of a fixed amount in order to avoid litigation in an excessive number of cases; whereas this Directive should not prejudice compensation for pain and suffering and other non-material damages payable, where appropriate, under the law applicable to the case'.

151 The classification of heads of damage introduced via art 9 is not entirely clear, particularly when attempting to map it to the terminology used in national legal systems.[342] At first glance, one may doubt whether art 9(a) refers to death and personal injury as injuries in and of themselves (which recital 9 would suggest), or rather the material effects of those two violations of the injured person's interests.[343] The latter understanding finds better justification in both

---

340 The exclusion of damage to the very product is based on the assumption that the consumer is sufficiently protected by claims in contractual liability.

341 As to the reasons for such regulation see *HC Taschner*, Product liability: basic problems in a comparative law perspective, in: D Fairgrieve (ed), Product Liability in Comparative Perspective (2005) 161 ff.

342 See eg *J Stapleton*, Product Liability (1994) 275 ff.

343 And also possibly non-material consequences, taken up by *S Whittaker*, Liability for Products: English Law, French Law and European Harmonisation (2005) 508.

the construction of the provision ('damage caused by...') and the separate enumeration of non-material damage, as well as the Directive's protective aim. This leads to the conclusion that the European legislator divides all forms of damage caused by a defective product into two primary categories: material damage and non-material damage. Non-material damage defined under Recital 9 as pain and suffering and other non-material damages remains outside the scope of the Directive's regulation in the sense that the existence and the scope of the obligation to provide compensation is determined exclusively by domestic regulations. The harmonisation introduced by the Directive, however, is intended to encompass material damages, which the Directive in turn divides into material damage to the person (caused by death or personal injury) and material damage to property (caused by destruction or damage to an item of property).

Harmonisation in this case functions by requiring that domestic regulations implementing the Directive must foresee the obligation to provide restitution for damage caused by death and personal injury, and must also provide for a limited obligation in respect of injury to an item of property.

152 The extent of the intervention into domestic laws performed by art 9 of the Directive is not as great as one might assume upon reading the particular provision. Above all, the Directive does not define the concept of damage, leaving it up to national legal systems. The particular types of damage listed in art 9 are also left to be elaborated by domestic law.[344] In addition, the remedies available for repairing damage (types of damages) are a matter of domestic law. Thus it is national law which will determine what, for example, an injured person may demand in the event of personal injury or injury to property that did not belong to the injured person but was used by him under agreement, or whether a remedy is at all available in the event of use with no legal title whatsoever. This leads to the unresolvable contradictions that cropped up in the *Veedfald* case.

153 On the one hand, the Directive clearly fails to define the concept of damage in the manner that it does in the case of a product or a producer, nor does it define the narrower categories of damage resulting from death or from personal injuries and damage to, or destruction of, an item of property. The task of defining them is therefore left to domestic law.[345] On the other hand, the Directive requires that both of those heads of damage be subject to full compensation, which is vital for achieving the Directive's aim.[346] From this it

344 The CJEU draws attention to this in Case C-154/00, *Commission v Greece* [2002] ECR I-3879, para 23.
345 See Case C-203/99, *Veedfald v Århus Amtskommune* [2001] ECR I-3569, paras 25–27.
346 Ibid para 27.

results that 'a Member State cannot ... restrict the types of material damage, resulting from death or personal injury, or from damage to or destruction of an item of property, which are to be made good.'[347] However, it is difficult to establish the criteria which should be applied in determining whether domestic law restricts or does not restrict the types of damage to be made good, since they are not specified in the Directive.[348] Perhaps another approach would be appropriate, under which the legal remedies available to an injured person in the event of injury caused by a defective product should be no less beneficial than those available under other liability regimes regulated exclusively by domestic law. This would, however, constitute an application not of the principle of effectiveness but rather the principle of equivalence. Moreover, it would not remove existing differences between Member States and achieve higher level of convergence of national legal orders, as there still remain large differences in quantum of damages awarded.

154 In addition, the role of the catalogue of types of damage eligible for compensation contained in art 9 of the Directive is not clear, evidence of which can be found in the struggles of the CJEU in *Veedfald*. The Court stated that arts 1 and 9 set out exhaustively the heads of damage that may be possible. 'It follows that the national court is required, under the Directive, to examine under which head the circumstances of the case are to be categorised, namely whether the case concerns damage covered either by point (a) or by point (b) of the first paragraph of Article 9 or non-material damage which may possibly be covered by national law. The national court may, however, not decline to award any damages at all under the Directive on the ground that, where the other conditions of liability are fulfilled, the damage incurred is not such as to fall under any of the foregoing heads.'[349] What results above all from the foregoing is that the exhaustive nature of the enumeration contained in art 9 consists not only in the listing therein of all heads of damage and others not eligible for recovery on the basis of the Directive,[350] but that all of the heads of damage listed therein must be eligible for recovery on the basis of domestic law. In light of the harmonising effect of the Directive, this conclusion is beyond dispute. The Court, however, takes it further and assumes that the enumeration in art 9 is exhaustive in the sense that it encompasses all possible types of damage. Therefore, any damage at all that arises must be qualified as (i) damage resulting from death or from personal injuries or (ii) damage to, or destruction of, an item of property, or

347 Ibid para 28.

348 See the proposals in this respect advanced by *S Whittaker*, Liability for Products: English Law, French Law and European Harmonisation (2005) 504 ff.

349 See Case C-203/99, *Veedfald v Århus Amtskommune* [2001] ECR I-3569, paras 32 and 33.

350 Which leads to particular difficulties in the systems which differentiate economic loss as a separate category of damage; see *S Whittaker*, Liability for Products: English Law, French Law and European Harmonisation (2005) 506.

(iii) non-material damage. This is difficult to accept for two reasons. First, it contradicts the position taken by the Court that the Directive defines neither damage nor its individual forms, but rather leaves the matter to national law. In light of this position, domestic law has little to say about what constitutes personal injury, damage to property or non-material damage considering that if a given set of circumstances is held to be damage it must be qualified under one of those categories. Second, the Court's logic is based on the hidden assumption that the existence of damage has been ascertained in a given matter. Meanwhile, the concept of damage itself is not defined in the Directive, and is also treated differently in national legal systems. A given type of loss may constitute damage in one legal system, while another system might not perceive it as such. This is why, to ensure the proper functioning of EU law (which does not necessarily equate to a drive for coherence and proper functioning of domestic tort law regimes), we should concur with the participants in the *Veedfald* case who argued that the heads of damage listed in art 9 must be defined by EU law so that they are applied uniformly.[351]

155 There are three limitations on the scope of recoverable damages to property introduced by the Directive:

(i) the damaged object is not the defective product itself;
(ii) the object is primarily intended for private consumption, and was used primarily in that manner by the injured person; and
(iii) a lower threshold of liability is in effect.

156 Certain issues require comment. The first of them concerns whether property affected by damage must be a tangible thing, or whether it can also be for examplea computer programme or digital content destroyed as the result of a product defect (eg of electronic equipment). The English version of the Directive uses the phrase 'item of property', which facilitates a broader interpretation. The German and French texts, however, make mention of 'things' (*die Sache, la chose*), which would seem to reflect the intentions of the Directive's authors from the turn of the 1970s and into the 1980s.

157 The scope of harmonisation effected by the Directive is demarcated by the limitation of the scope of damage to property to items intended for personal consumption. As the CJEU has stated, compensation for damage to an item of property intended for professional use and employed for that purpose is not one of the matters regulated by the Directive, such damage not being covered by the

351 Case C-203/99, *Veedfald v Århus Amtskommune* [2001] ECR I-3569, para 24.

term 'damage' for the purposes of art 1. Therefore compensation for damage to such property is not covered by the scope of application of Directive 85/374.[352]

158 Interpretative difficulties also arise out of the application of a monetary threshold on liability. It is not clear whether what is meant is a threshold which, when reached, would allow for pursuing compensation for the entirety of the damage suffered, or whether a sum which is deducted from the compensation owed without regard to the scale of the damage. The English version of the Directive uses the phrase 'lower threshold', which would seem in line with the former interpretation, but recital 9 says 'be subject to a deduction of a lower threshold of a fixed amount', which is difficult to interpret unambiguously (the Polish translation of the Directive is similar here). The French, German and Italian versions, however, lend support to the latter interpretation (*sous déduction d'une franchise de 500 Écus, bei einer Selbstbeteiligung von 500 ECU, previa detrazione di una franchigia di 500 ECU*). The Directive also does not provide a definitive answer to whether the threshold of €500 refers to the value of each individual piece of property damaged or destroyed as a result of a product defect, or to the extent of the damage visited on each of those things (eg in the event of damage to them), or perhaps to the general sum of damage in property caused by a given defect. The wording of the provision lends itself to the interpretation that the threshold of liability concerns the value of each individual damaged piece of property. In turn, the objective of this limitation of liability, which is to prevent the initiation of a large number of court cases for small sums (recital 9), would rather support an interpretation of the provision under discussion referring to the dimension of all damage in property caused by one event arising out of a product defect.

159 These issues cropped up in the CJEU's *Veedfald* decision, as well as in others concerning the improper implementation of the Directive by France and Greece, which did not initially introduce the monetary threshold from art 9(b) into their laws. In these judgments, the CJEU treated the €500 sum as a threshold that, when reached, gave the right to restitution for damage in its entirety, therefore rejecting the reductive mechanism. It also declared that damage of lesser value may be compensated for 'under the ordinary law of contractual or non-contractual liability'. Furthermore, the Court held that the €500 threshold refers not to the value of the damaged property, but rather to the dimensions of the damage incurred by the injured person. It did not determine, however, whether it was about damage to one piece of property or the sum of damage to many items resulting from one event.[353]

---

[352] See Case C-285/08, *Moteurs Leroy Somer v Dalkia France and Ace Europe* [2009] ECR I-4733, paras 24–31.

[353] See Case C-203/99, *Veedfald v Århus Amtskommune* [2001] ECR I-3569, para 26; Case C-154/00, *Commission v Greece* [2002] ECR I-3879, paras 26–35; Case C-52/00, *Commission v France* [2002] ECR I-3827, paras 23–32.

160 Interpretation of the concept of 'personal injury' was at the centre of a recent judgment of the CJEU in *Boston Scientific Medizintechnik GmbH*.[354] Among the questions raised there was that of whether the costs of the operation to remove from the patient's body the defective medicinal product (cardiac pacemaker or defibrillator) and to implant another constitute damage caused by personal injury for the purposes of arts 1 and 9(1)(a) of Directive 85/374.

161 The problem came from the Directive's relatively narrow definition of that form of injury, which, when read literally, would encompass only costs arising out of a previously existing personal injury, but not those associated with prevention of death or personal injury which could potentially result from a product defect. This is also associated with the absence of regulation in the Directive of the duty to recall a defective product from the marketplace.

162 In seeking to resolve this problem, the Court began with the principle of full and proper compensation and declared that in the light of this rule and with regard to the objective of protecting consumer health and safety pursued by the Directive, the notion of 'damage caused by death or personal injuries' must be given a broad interpretation. It thus held that compensation for damage relates to everything that is necessary to eliminate harmful consequences and to restore the level of safety which a person is entitled to expect. At the same time it ruled that, with reference to the prerequisite of the causal relationship contained in art 4 of the Directive, the costs of such an operation also constitute damage to the extent that it is necessary to overcome the defect in the product.

163 It remains to be seen whether this interpretation of the Directive, leading to a blurring of the line between repairing damage and preventing it through repairing the defect in a product, relates solely to personal injury (which would seem appropriate) and only to medical products injected into patients, or whether it will also be applied to other product faults.

F. CAUSATION, MULTIPLE CAUSES AND CONTRIBUTORY NEGLIGENCE

164 Issues of causation are only given piecemeal regulation in Directive 85/374. Article 1 indicates that the producer is liable for damage caused by a defect in his product, while art 4 requires the injured person to prove *inter alia* the causal relationship between defect and damage.

---

354 Joined Cases C-503/13 and C-504/13, *Boston Scientific Medizintechnik v AOK Sachsen-Anhalt*, not yet published, paras 44–55.

165 The only thing in respect of causation that results from these articles is that a causal nexus between the defect in a product and damage is the necessary condition for producer liability. The Directive does not explain what, precisely, the causal link should consist in.[355] Thus it has been left to domestic law to determine whether every link of a *sine qua non* character (the product's defect is a necessary condition in the damage) is sufficient for liability to arise, or whether an additional qualification is necessary, such as directness of the causal link, normality, foreseeability of the damage, lack of remoteness, etc. Therefore, procedural solutions such as the required standard of proof, admissibility of *prima facie* reasoning and solutions to cases of uncertain causation remain matters for national law.[356] The sole limitation for domestic legislators is the principle of effectiveness.

166 This is a significant restriction on the harmonisation pursued by the Directive, especially in light of the declaration contained in recital 1 that approximation of the laws concerning the product liability is necessary because existing divergences may distort competition and affect the movement of goods within the common market and entail a differing degree of protection of the consumer against damage caused by a defective product to his health or property. The legal construction of the causal nexus as a tool for selecting which damage is eligible for recovery and in what scope, is one of the decisive factors in establishing the dimension of the liability borne by producers as well as the scope of protection afforded to the interests of consumers. On the other hand, however, the causal nexus concept is one of the fundamental characteristics of national tort law regimes, and interference in it by the European legislator would negatively impact the internal cohesion of those systems.

167 The Directive does acknowledge that damage may arise out of many causes. If these causes come in the form of the action of two or more of the persons enumerated in art 3, and each of them fulfil the criteria for liability set out in art 4, their liability is joint and several.[357] Article 8 of the Directive addresses cases in which damage is the result of both a product defect and the action or omission of a third party or the injured person himself.

---

[355] See *S Whittaker*, Liability for Products: English Law, French Law and European Harmonisation (2005) 509. CJEU had occasion to address the issue of interpreting the phrase 'damage caused by' in *Veedfald*, yet it declined to do so, which may mean that it left the issue in its entirety to the legislator and national courts.

[356] See examples given by *S Whittaker*, Liability for Products: English Law, French Law and European Harmonisation (2005) 512 ff; *D Wuyts*, The product liability directive – more than two decades of defective products in Europe (2014) 5(1) JETL 25 ff. As for difficulties in proving the causal link see eg *J Stapleton*, Product Liability (1994) 280 ff.

[357] See (b) above.

168 Pursuant to art 8(1) of the Directive, concurrence of causes in the form of a product defect and actions of a third party do not lead to limitation of the producer's liability. This provision remains without prejudice to the provisions of national law concerning the right of contribution or recourse. The Directive therefore regulates only the relationship between the injured person and the producer, and within that scope ensures the injured person has the potential to seek full compensation for damage from the producer. It does not, however, determine whether the injured person may seek damages from those jointly responsible, nor the manner in which the burden of the damages is distributed across the two or more entities held liable.[358] This last aspect serves to slightly weaken the Directive's capacity to achieve its aims, as rules for the assignment of the burden of damages shape an incentive scheme for the producer of potentially defective products.

169 In turn, art 8(2) of the Directive addresses multiple causation in cases where, apart from the product defect, another source of damage is 'the fault of the injured person or any person for whom the injured person is responsible'. In such instances the liability of the producer may be reduced or disallowed. The English version of the Directive is quite misleading here, as it suggests that assessment of whether the fault of the injured party is a joint factor in the damage should be performed 'having regard to all the circumstances',[359] which is rather nonsensical considering that all factual determinations should be made having regard to all the circumstances; furthermore, it may suggest that the entire provision constitutes a regulatory option.[360] The intentions of the legislator are properly expressed in the German ('*Die Haftung des Herstellers kann unter Berücksichtigung aller Umstände gemindert werden oder entfallen*'), French ('*La responsabilité du producteur peut être réduite ou supprimée, compte tenu de toutes les circonstances, lorsque le dommage est causé conjointement...*') and Italian versions ('*La responsabilità del produttore può essere ridotta o soppressa, tenuto conto di tutte le circostanze, quando il danno è provocato congiuntamente...*'). They hold that the circumstances of the case should impact the court's decision to limit or exclude the producer's liability in the event a contribution on the part of the injured party is ascertained.

170 The criteria for qualifying behaviour as a contribution to damage have not been set out in detail in the Directive. It only uses the term 'fault'. It would seem that establishing what constitutes 'fault', the level of care required from the injured person, and whether and to what extent the injured person's individual

358 See *S Whittaker*, Liability for Products: English Law, French Law and European Harmonisation (2005) 509 ff.

359 The same mistake was made in the Polish translation.

360 This last possibility is considered and rejected by *S Whittaker*, Liability for Products: English Law, French Law and European Harmonisation (2005) 510.

characteristics and capacities are relevant in such cases should be done according to criteria set out under domestic law. This is also the case in determining who is a person for whom the injured person is responsible, which should be resolved according to national legislation.[361]

G. TIME RESTRICTIONS ON CLAIMS

1) Introduction

171 In general, the liability of a producer for defective products is not unlimited with regard to time. The Product Liability Directive also follows the approach of placing time restrictions on the producer's liability. The Directive therefore provides a self-standing system that is independent of the general national civil law; the time limitations on claims are therefore contained within the Directive itself. A system of time restriction has been established which has until now received few attention from legal science, for the most part it was discussed merely as a side issue. The system consists, on the one hand, of a prescription period (art 10 Product Liability Directive) and, on the other hand, of a separate extinction period (also referred to as the liability period, cf art 11 Product Liability Directive). Both provisions, as well as the resulting time restriction system, will first be presented and analysed in more detail; thereafter attention will turn to the underlying concept of this volume, namely the transposition of the Product Liability Directive into national law. In conclusion there will be the attempt to find an answer to the question whether the present time restrictions in the Product Liability Directive are adequate or require revision, especially with respect to the challenges posed by new technologies.

2) The Rules on Time Restrictions in the Product Liability Directive

a) The Prescription Period (Art 10)

172 Art 10 Product Liability Directive provides a compulsory prescription period for the EU Member States. This norm obliges the Member States to provide in their legislation that a prescription period of three years shall apply to proceedings for the recovery of damages (see art 10(1) Product Liability Directive). This prescription period begins to run from the day on which the plaintiff becomes aware or should reasonably have become aware of the damage, the defect and the identity of the producer (see art 10(1)(2) Product Liability Directive). The prescription period therefore does not begin with the damage (an

361 See *S Whittaker*, Liability for Products: English Law, French Law and European Harmonisation (2005) 511.

objective point of reference), but rather potentially much later due to the link to subjective criteria. The injured party is therefore not obliged by this rule to resolve the issue as quickly as possible nor with optimal and maximum effect. He merely has to assess the facts known to him, whereby the 'reasonable man' standard is applicable.[362] With regard to policy considerations (which played a considerable role in the drafting of art 10 Product Liability Directive), there is a reference to recital 10 of the Directive:

> 'A uniform period of limitation for the bringing of an action for compensation is in the interests both of the injured person and of the producer'.

This last statement should not be regarded as highly controversial. From the perspective of a producer who distributes his products in many different countries, it would undoubtedly be better if the limitation period for damages claims were the same across the entire European Union. However, the practical significance of this harmonisation should not be overestimated. Since the beginning of the period is associated not with an objectively ascertainable event, but rather with the actual and/or hypothetical knowledge of the injured party as to facts giving rise to liability, and the regulations governing the running of the limitation period remain distinct in different countries, harmonisation does not go very far in improving the situation of entrepreneurs. Taking the side of the injured party, the view that harmonisation of the limitation period is beneficial can be partially justified in the context of art 5 Rome II Regulation; this provision establishes the applicable law as that of the state in which the injured party has his ordinary place of residence, making the harmonisation of limitation periods essentially neutral for the aggrieved, while protection would also be enhanced by including a minimum duration for the limitation period in the Directive. Art 5 Rome II Regulation does, however, allow for an exception in the form of the applicable law of another state, and in these cases the harmonisation of the limitation period would be significant for injured parties as well.

173 Art 10 Product Liability Directive represents a prescription rule, whereby the principle of which is familiar from national legal systems. Accordingly, it is correct that the prescription period in art 10 Product Liability Directive can also be suspended or interrupted. However, art 10(2) Product Liability Directive (in contrast to the remaining provisions of arts 10 and 11 Product Liability Directive) leaves it to national law to give further detail to the suspension and interruption. This does somewhat limit the practical significance of the harmonisation, as Member States can provide stronger or weaker protection

---

362 For more detail see *C Hodges*, Product liability: European laws and practice (1993) no 2-093; *J Schmidt-Salzer/HH Hollmann*, Kommentar EG-Richtlinie Produkthaftung, vol 1 (1986) Art 11 Product Liability Directive no 6.

through expanding or restricting the catalogue of events resulting in suspension of the running of the limitation period, for example by (not) accounting for the time spent by the parties conducting negotiations. Regulations on the renewal of the limitation period can have a similar impact, such as declaring that such an effect can be caused only by the initiation of judicial proceedings for a damages claim, or by various preparatory actions such as a 'private' demand for damages; the effect of a producer's statement acknowledging liability for a defect on the limitation period may also be adjusted, etc. The limits of Member States' freedom in shaping these regulations are only to be found in the objective of the Directive – domestic regulations on limitation periods may not deprive art 10 of the Directive of its practical effect. This line, however, is quite blurred.

b) The Extinction Period (Art 11)

174 Art 11 Product Liability Directive provides that the rights granted under the Product Liability Directive will be extinguished upon expiry of a ten-year period from the date that the producer put into circulation the product that caused the damage. In contrast to the prescription period the judge is to consider this extinction period *ex officio*. Art 11 Product Liability Directive therefore provides an absolute deadline that can neither be suspended nor interrupted. An exception is only possible when the injured person has in the meantime commenced proceedings against the producer. In principle, such an extinction period is necessary as long as the start of the prescription period depends on a subjective criterion. The consequence would otherwise be responsibility for the producer that is not subject to any time restrictions.

175 The introduction of art 11 Product Liability Directive is based for the most part on the negative court experiences of European and American industry in the USA, more specifically the spectacular cases of product liability suits due to harm resulting from products that were already introduced to the market decades before the harm occurred.[363] Such an outcome was to be avoided at European level. The ten-year exclusion period represents a considerable restriction on the previous operation of limitation rules in most national jurisdictions – one has to consider that there are cases in which the defect is latent and remains undiscovered for many years (such as in personal injuries caused by medicinal products).[364] It also seems worth mentioning that in the Commission's original proposal for the Directive the exclusion period could be viewed as a balance against the exclusion of the state-of-the-art defence (a rule that has been subsequently changed in the negotiation process).

---

363 For more detail see *J Schmidt-Salzer/HH Hollmann*, Kommentar EG-Richtlinie Produkthaftung, vol 1 (1986) Art 11 Product Liability Directive no 12.

364 For more detail see *C Hodges*, Product liability: European laws and practice (1993) no 2-095.

176 The interpretation of art 11 Product Liability Directive is rendered difficult above all by the reference to the 'date on which the producer put into circulation the actual product'. The reference to 'the actual product' intends to hinder the argument that the ten-year period runs from the date on which the product with that specification was first put onto the market, for example damage caused to a number of plaintiffs over several years by cars which have all the same braking fault, a separate period according to art 11 of the Directive runs from the date upon which each car was put into circulation by the particular defendant.[365] The 'put into circulation' criterion is not always easy to apply when considering the complexity of various business models. This question has been examined by the CJEU in a case with a rather unique set of facts.[366] A medicinal product was produced in France by Company X, then sold to its subsidiary Company Y with its seat in the United Kingdom and which was engaged in the distribution of products of Company X. Company Y, in turn, sold the product to the UK Ministry of Health, which then distributed it to a hospital, which then released it to a physician's office, where it was applied to a patient. The injured party brought an action against Company Y in the belief that it was the producer. After a certain time, when the actual producer was determined, the plaintiff also brought a claim against Company X. However, by that time the ten-year period had already elapsed when counted from the day of sale of the product by Company X to Company Y, while ten years had (probably) not yet elapsed from the sale of the product by Company Y to the Ministry of Health. The question thus arose of which transaction – one within the group of companies between the producer and distributor, or only an 'external' transaction between the distributor and the hospital – constituted 'putting into circulation' as understood by art 11 of the Directive. The CJEU seemed to accept that the expression 'put into circulation' has a different meaning under art 11 as related to the time limit than under art 7 in excluding producer liability, and thus it can be interpreted differently.[367] In settling the primary issue, the Court stated that a product must be considered as having been put into circulation (within the meaning of art 11 of the Directive) when it leaves the production process operated by the producer and enters a marketing process. Generally, it is not important in that regard that the product is sold directly by the producer to the user or to the consumer or that that sale is carried out as part of a distribution process involving one or more operators. However, when one of the links in the distribution chain is closely connected to the producer (like a wholly-owned subsidiary), it is necessary to establish whether it is a consequence of that link that that entity is in reality involved in

365 Examples taken from *C Hodges*, Product liability: European laws and practice (1993) no 2-095.

366 Which, by the way, shows how debatable the introduction of ten-year term is as far as personal injuries are concerned.

367 See Case C-127/04, *Declan O'Byrne v Sanofi Pasteur MSD Ltd and Sanofi Pasteur SA* [2006] ECR I-1313, paras 23–26.

the manufacturing process of the product concerned. The right test is therefore whether the two entities are carrying out different production activities or one of them acts simply as a distributor or depository for the product manufactured by the other company. If the links between the producer and another entity are so close that the concept of producer within the meaning of arts 7 and 11 of the Directive also includes that another entity, the transfer of the product from one to the other of those entities does not amount to putting it into circulation. In summing up, the Court said that art 11 of the Directive is to be interpreted as meaning that a product is put into circulation when it is taken out of the manufacturing process operated by the producer and enters a marketing process in the form in which it is offered to the public in order to be used or consumed.[368]

177 A particularly interesting point is the legislative purpose that underlies art 11 Product Liability Directive and thus the strict extinction period: this appears to have undergone a change over time and is likely to be of importance for the question of the appropriateness of this rule for new technological challenges. Recital 11 of the Product Liability Directive states the following with regard to the legislative purpose:

> 'Products age in the course of time, higher safety standards are developed and the state of science and technology progresses; … therefore it would not be reasonable to make the producer liable for an unlimited period for the defectiveness of this product; … therefore liability should expire after a reasonable length of time, without prejudice to claim pending at law'.

178 The background is that defects emerging after ten years can often not clearly be attributed to the safety level that the manufacturer had to adhere to at the time the product was put into circulation. A safety defect can in such instance rather also be attributed to the usual wear and tear and use of the product. The extinction of the claim after a ten-year period shall prevent the evidentiary burden for the manufacturer. However, this argument is increasingly rejected and questioned, at least with respect to its catch-all nature.[369] The lack of evidence can arise with regard to manufacturing errors, though not with regard to errors concerning construction and instruction: whether the latter have already been present at the time the product was put into circulation is a matter that can generally be evidenced quite easily.[370] The argument of avoiding

---

368 Ibid paras 27–32.

369 *F Graf von Westphalen*, in: U Foerste/F Graf von Westphalen (eds), Produkthaftungshandbuch (3rd edn 2012) §53 no 14; *G Wagner*, in: Münchener Kommentar (6th edn 2013) §13 Produkthaftungsgesetz no 1; *J Oechsler*, in: J von Staudinger, Kommentar zum Bürgerlichen Gesetzbuch (2013) §13 Produkthaftungsgesetz no 1.

370 *G Wagner*, in: Münchener Kommentar (6th edn 2013) §13 Produkthaftungsgesetz no 1; *J Oeschler*, in: J von Staudinger, Kommentar zum Bürgerlichen Gesetzbuch (2013) §13 Produkthaftungsgesetz no 1.

evidentiary problems for the manufacturer is not valid, at least in these cases and in general.

179 It appears that also the European Commission has since deviated from this original justification and now states an alternative legislative purpose. It argues in the Green Paper 'Liability for Defective Products' that:

> 'Liability limited in time is justified mainly on grounds of fairness: for producers, no-fault liability involves a heavier burden than that laid down in the usual systems of contractual and extra-contractual liability'.[371]

180 The European Commission stated in the (later) Report on the Application of the Product Liability Directive in a similar way that:

> 'This limitation of liability (extinction period) is mainly justified by the fact that strict liability puts a higher burden on producers than liability under the traditional systems of contract or extra-contractual liability'.[372]

181 The European Commission (and many other national legislators that have transposed the Product Liability Directive) thus view the ten-year extinction period as a 'justifiable balance' or 'counterbalance' to the (refutable) strict liability of the manufacturer than is imposed by the Directive.[373] The extinction period should therefore lessen the consequences of strict liability for the manufacturer.[374] This appears to now be the main justification for the existence of art 11 Product Liability Directive.

182 Furthermore, in this context there is an argument at European and national level that only time-limited responsibility ensures that the manufacturer can obtain insurance and to render possible the financing of technological innovations.[375] The latter would only be conceivable with time restrictions as the

---

371 Green Paper on Liability for Defective Products, COM(1999)396 final, 26.

372 Report from the Commission on the Application of Directive 85/374 on Liability for Defective Products, COM(2000)893 final.

373 For Germany see BT-Drucks 11/2447, 25.

374 For information on this aspect see *F Graf von Westphalen*, in: U Foerste/f Graf von Westphalen (eds), Produkthaftungshandbuch (3rd edn 2012) §53 no 14; *J Oeschler*, in: J von Staudinger, Kommentar zum Bürgerlichen Gesetzbuch (2013) §13 Produkthaftungsgesetz no 1.

375 See, for example, Green Paper on Liability for Defective Products, COM(1999)396 final, 26: 'This must be offset by a limitation in time so that technological innovation is not discouraged and insurance cover is available'; Report from the Commission on the Application of Directive 85/374 on Liability for Defective Products, COM(2000)893 final: 'Therefore, the liability period is limited in order not to discourage technological innovation and to allow insurance cover'; *C Hodges*, Product liability: European laws and practice (1993) no 2-098; Münchener Kommentar/*Wagner* (fn 369) §13 Produkthaftungsgesetz no 1; *Staudinger/Oechsler* (fn 369) §13 Produkthaftungsgesetz no 1.

manufacturer would otherwise have to amass considerable financial reserves for the event of possible liability.

c) The Legal Effects of Arts 10 and 11 Product Liability Directive

183 Three spectacular ECJ decisions concerning the Product Liability Directive have conclusively clarified that the Directive displays a fully harmonising effect.[376] This effect therefore extends to arts 10 and 11 Product Liability Directive (with the exception of the aforementioned art 10(2) Product Liability Directive). Accordingly, there may be no deviation either to the disadvantage or to the advantage (eg by more generous time periods) of the injured person. However, the principle of full harmonisation only applies within the scope of the Directive itself:[377] arts 10 and 11 Product Liability Directive can therefore have no effect beyond this. Consequently, they do not regulate additional competing contractual and non-contractual claims and their prescription or exclusion, respectively. They rather expire or are extinguished according to their own national regime. Art 13 Product Liability Directive explicitly provides that the Directive shall not affect any rights which an injured person may have according to the rules of the law of contractual or non-contractual liability or a specific liability system existing at the moment when the Directive was notified. This rule is also described as the 'actual Achilles heel of legal harmonization by the Product Liability Directive' because, in principle, it allows the Member States to maintain and create favoured liability regimes under the heading of contractual or non-contractual liability.[378]

184 New technologies – one thinks, for instance, just of the early years of the internet – often present the law with significant challenges. In the meantime there are further new challenges which the law has to approach: regenerative medicine and nanotechnology are considered as having considerable (economic) potential. Cloud computing is already almost part of day-to-day life and the same can now (or at least in the near future) be said of new computing devices such as digital eyewear, contour crafting and autonomous technologies (eg self-configuring systems, adaptable machines, intelligent transport devices), to name but a few.[379] The present volume attempts to address the specific question of whether the Product Liability Directive in its current form will ensure sufficient

376 See Case C-52/00, *Commission v France* [2002] ECR I-3827, paras 17–20; Case C-154/00, *Commission v Greece* [2002] ECR I-3879, paras 13–16; Case C-183/00, *González Sanchez v Medicina Asturiana SA* [2002] ECR I-3901, paras 26–29. For more detail see *G Howells* in this chapter.

377 See, for example, Case C-285/08, *Moteurs Leroy Somer v Dalkia France* [2009] ECR I-4733.

378 *T Riehm*, 25 Jahre Produkthaftungsrichtlinie: Ein Lehrstück zur Vollharmonsierung (2010) Europäische Zeitschrift für Wirtschaftsrecht 567, 569.

379 See the Introduction to this volume.

safety for individuals using the products produced by applying these and other new technologies.[380] In the event that the Directive (in its present form) manifests itself as being insufficient to overcome these challenges, the next step would be to determine the necessary legal changes. In contrast, the following contribution shall (more modestly) merely examine whether changes to the present rules on time restrictions in the Product Liability Directive (ie arts 10 and 11 Product Liability Directive) are advisable.

A change to the content of art 10 Product Liability Directive, ie the three year prescription period due to the emergence of products produced by means of new technologies, appears to be neither necessary nor appropriate.[381] As the prescription period first begins when the plaintiff became aware, or should reasonably have become aware, of the damage, the defect and the identity of the producer (ie is based on a subjective criterion), it creates a justified balance of interests for new technologies, too. In this respect it is in no apparent need of revision.

185 A more difficult issue concerns the answer to the question of the present correctness of the ten-year extinction period of art 11 Product Liability Directive: it is possible that new technologies create products which are particularly questionable from a safety perspective and which contain latent defects that first become apparent after a long period of time. This could justify a longer extinction period. At present the manufacturer's responsibility would also be excluded for latent defects 'already' after ten years and namely from the date on which the producer put into circulation the actual product.

186 It cannot be denied that the present strict ten-year period (which intends as said before to create a balance to the introduction of the strict liability by the Product Liability Directive) is in general not satisfactory, and this is not just from the perspective of challenges presented by new technologies. The period is certainly too long and only purely theoretical for rapidly deteriorating products such as food stuffs; in contrast it is too short for latent or long-term harm.[382] Nonetheless, in spite of the rule's present weaknesses, one can and must maintain it both in general and specifically with regard to new technologies. The strict ten-year period has not entirely been chosen at random but is rather based on

---

380 Although cloud computing does of course not lead to the manufacture of goods within the context of art 2 Product Liability Directive.

381 Likewise with regard to the result, although it does not specifically consider the challenges posed by new technologies, Green Paper on Liability for Defective Products, COM(1999)396 final, 26: 'With regard to the time limit for instituting proceedings (three years), there is no a priori reason for thinking that the limit should be changed.'

382 *J Schmidt-Salzer/HH Hollmann*, Kommentar EG-Richtlinie Produkthaftung, vol 1 (1986) Art 11 Product Liability Directive no 13; *HC Taschner/E Frietsch*, Produkthaftungsgesetz und EG-Produkthaftungsrichtlinie, Kommentar (2nd edn 1990) Art. 11 Product Liability Directive no 5.

the average life expectancy of durable goods.[383] Despite all justifiable criticism it also guarantees a high degree of legal certainty, especially for manufacturers who use new technologies to manufacture their products and who often had high investment costs. The partially suggested limitation of the manufacturer's responsibility to the 'foreseeable period of the product's use' cannot ensure the necessary legal certainty, especially where the strict liability is concerned.[384] An extension of the strict extinction period under art 11 Product Liability Directive, as has for instance been suggested by the European Parliament (to twenty years for 'hidden defects'),[385] for all products or also just for particular groups of products (eg foodstuffs, pharmaceuticals or products intended for especially long use) would indeed leave legal certainty untouched, but would give rise to considerable financial burdens for the manufacturer. Such an extension of the time period would present the manufacturer with the risk that the long-lasting strict liability would render it very difficult (ie with unfavourable conditions) or impossible to insure his financial risks.[386] The present limitation to ten years appears to be justified and this also applies to the dangers of hidden defects in products that have been created by use of new technologies. One also has to bear in mind that in many legal systems the victim has still the possibility of taking redress against the producer for a longer period under other liability systems.[387] In summary it can be stated that the present time restrictions in arts 10 and 11 Product Liability Directive do not, in principle, require changes in order to overcome the challenges presented by new technologies as they already contain solutions appropriate to the circumstances.

187 The adequacy of the ten-year limitation period may be called into question when considered in the context of the ECtHR judgment of 11 March 2014, *Howald Moor and Others v Switzerland* (52067/10 and 41072/11). The case concerned the fixing of the starting point for the limitation period applicable under Swiss law to victims of asbestos exposure. Given that the latency period for asbestos-related diseases could be several decades, the fixed limitation period of ten years – which began running on the date when the person concerned had been exposed to asbestos dust – would have expired before the victims could

---

383 *HC Taschner/E Frietsch,* Produkthaftungsgesetz und EG-Produkthaftungsrichtlinie, Kommentar (2nd edn 1990) Art 11 Product Liability Directive no 5.

384 *J Schmidt-Salzer/HH Hollmann,* Kommentar EG-Richtlinie Produkthaftung, vol 1 (1986) Art 11 Product Liability Directive no 13; *HC Taschner/E Frietsch,* Produkthaftungsgesetz und EG-Produkthaftungsrichtlinie, Kommentar (2nd edn 1990) Art 11 Product Liability Directive no 5. See also Report from the Commission on the Application of Directive 85/374 on Liability for Defective Products COM(2000)893 final.

385 Opinion of the European Parliament of 5 November 1998 [1998] OJ C359/28.

386 This risk is also referred to in the Green Paper on Liability for Defective Products, COM(1999)396 final, 27.

387 See Report from the Commission on the Application of Directive 85/374 on Liability for Defective Products, COM(2000)893 final.

be aware of their rights. The Court stated that the rules on limitation periods pursue the legitimate aim, *inter alia*, of ensuring legal certainty. As to their proportionality, however, their systematic application to persons suffering from diseases which, like those caused by asbestos, could not be diagnosed until many years after the triggering events, may deprive those persons of the opportunity to assert their claims before the courts. Consequently, the Court found that the application of the limitation period had restricted the victims' access to a court to the point of impairing the very essence of their right.

The primary significance of this judgment lies in the weight it lends to arguments appealing to the protection of the interests of victims, which makes it an important contribution to the discussion on amending art 11 of the Directive. However, it cannot be applied directly in assessing the legality of legislation transposing art 11 of the Directive into national law. This issue must be examined with proper consideration given to art 13 of the Directive, which permits Member States *inter alia* to retain their general liability regimes. The question of national law's compliance with the European Convention on Human Rights would only arise when remedies to injuries to a person caused by a product could not be pursued after the ten years on another basis than that set out in the Directive.

V. OTHER EU LAWS CONCERNING SIMILAR ISSUES

A. GENERAL PRODUCT SAFETY DIRECTIVE 2001/95/EC

1) *In General*

188 Directive 2001/95/EC states that it is important to adopt measures with the aim of improving the functioning of the internal market, comprising an area without internal frontiers in which the free movement of goods, persons, services and capital is assured.[388] One of the objects of this Directive is clearly the need to harmonise the different laws on consumer product safety regulation which Member States were in the course of adopting.[389] Furthermore, the European Union sought to contribute to protecting the health and safety of consumers in order to ensure a high level of consumer protection.[390]

189 A product is defined as 'any product – including in the context of providing a service – which is intended for consumers or likely, under reasonably

388 Recital 2 to the Directive.
389 *C Hodges/ Tyler/H Abbott*, Product safety (1996) 48.
390 Recital 4 to the Directive.

foreseeable conditions, to be used by consumers even if not intended for them, and is supplied or made available whether for consideration or not, in the course of a commercial activity and whether new, used or reconditioned'.[391] It is also stated that this definition shall not apply to second-hand products supplied as antiques or as products to be repaired or reconditioned prior to being used, provided that the supplier clearly informs the person to whom he supplies the product of that fact.[392]

190 It follows from the introductory recitals that the Directive should apply to products irrespective of the selling techniques, including distance and electronic selling.[393] As regards the phrase 'including in the context of providing a service', it can be said that the Directive does not cover services but should apply to products that are supplied or made available to consumers in the context of service provisions for use by them. The safety of the equipment used by service providers themselves to supply a service to consumers does not come within the scope of the Directive since it has to be dealt with in conjunction with the safety of the service provided.[394]

A 'safe product' 'shall mean any product which, under normal or reasonably foreseeable conditions of use including duration … does not present any risk or only the minimum risks compatible with the product's use, considered to be acceptable and consistent with a high level of protection … taking into account the following points in particular: (i) the characteristics of the product …; (ii) the effect on other products …; (iii) the presentation of the product …; (iv) the categories of consumers at risk when using the product, in particular children and the elderly'.[395] Also the feasibility of obtaining higher levels of safety or the availability of other products presenting a lesser degree of risk shall not constitute grounds for considering a product to be 'dangerous'.[396]

191 As the so-called zero risk does not exist, especially not in today's complex technological society,[397] a safe product also bears a certain risk. The decisive element in distinguishing safe from unsafe products is to find out whether a certain (minimum) risk compatible with the product's use is acceptable and

---

391 Art 2(a)(1) Directive 2001/95.
392 Art 2(a)(2) Directive 2001/95.
393 Recital 7 to the Directive.
394 Recital 9 to the Directive.
395 Art 2(b)(1) Directive 2001/95.
396 Art 2(b)(2) Directive 2001/95.
397 *R Dardis/G Davenport/J Kurin/J Marr*, Risk-benefit analysis and the determination of acceptable risk (1983) 17(1) Journal of Consumer Affairs 38, 38; *A Sciascia*, Safe or sorry: how the precautionary principle is changing Europe's consumer safety regulation regime and how the United States' Consumer Product Safety Commission must take notice (2006) 58 Admin L Rev 401.

consistent with a high level of protection.[398] Unsafe products are thus products with an unacceptable risk.[399] Safety must thus be assessed *in abstracto* taking into account the specific factual circumstances of the case, some of which are explicitly mentioned in the Directive.

192 Finally, a producer is defined as '(i) the manufacturer of the product, when he is established in the Union, and any other person presenting himself as the manufacturer … or the person who reconditions the product; (ii) the manufacturer's representative, when the manufacturer is not established in the Union or, if there is no representative established in the Union, the importer of the product; (iii) other professionals in the supply chain, insofar as their activities may affect the safety properties of a product'.[400] A distributor is 'any professional in the supply chain whose activity does not affect the safety properties of a product'.[401]

193 Directive 2001/95/EC contains various obligations for the producers and distributors of products such as the obligation to place only safe products on the market,[402] an information obligation towards consumers[403] and the government[404] and different *post-sale-duties*.[405, 406] Furthermore, the Directive imposes some obligations on the national and European authorities, provides them with different powers in order to ensure the safety of products such as the power to take samples, ban products and even organise an immediate withdrawal.[407] Lastly, it is important to note that the Directive on Product Safety shall be without prejudice to the application of the Directive on Product Liability.[408]

---

398 *T Bourgoignie*, La prevention du risque par le contrôle de la qualité et de la sécurité des produits et des services destinés au consommateur, in: X, Les assurances de l'entreprise. Volume II (1993) 302.

399 *H Dumont*, Sécurité des consommateurs: le droit belge dans un contexte européen (1998) 41 DCCR 291, 306; *A Sciascia*, Safe or sorry: how the precautionary principle is changing Europe's consumer safety regulation regime and how the United States' Consumer Product Safety Commission must take notice (2006) 58 Admin L Rev 689, 701–702; *S Van Camp*, Productveiligheid en product recall (2010) 6 TBH 451, 456.

400 Art 2(e) Directive 2001/95.

401 Art 2(f) Directive 2001/95.

402 Art 3(1) Directive 2001/95.

403 Art 5(1) Directive 2001/95.

404 Art 5(3) Directive 2001/95.

405 Art 5(1) Directive 2001/95.

406 *G Howells*, Consumer product safety (1998) 130–134 and *V Le Gouillou/M Bresson*, Products liability under French law, in: S Woodley (ed), Liability for products in a global economy (2005) 252.

407 Arts 6–13 Directive 2001/95. See also: *G Howells*, Consumer product safety (1998) 135–154.

408 Art 17 Directive 2001/95.

2) Similarities with the Product Liability Directive

194 The Directive on Product Liability in theory only takes a curative approach to product safety.[409] Nevertheless, it undeniably also has a preventive effect through deterrence.[410] The Directive helps to increase the level of protection against defective products for two reasons: it is a 'sword of Damocles' which encourages the producers to do their best to produce without unnecessary risks to health and, once these preventive measures have failed and accidents have happened, it allows the victims to obtain redress from the producers.[411] In this regard legal scholars have pointed out that the threat of product liability may constitute a good incentive to avoid accidents with products, for example by attaching warnings to the product or by carrying out a product recall.[412] As stated above, the Directives on Product Liability and on Product Safety should therefore be regarded as being complementary.[413]

195 It is commonly known that both the Product Liability Directive and the Product Safety Directive promote one and the same policy, which aims to provide the regulatory context that fosters the production and marketing of safe products whilst achieving a high level of consumer protection.[414] Some legal scholars have pointed out that one of the main purposes of the Product Liability Directive is to ensure that all consumers within the European Union have the same high level of protection in relation to damages caused by defective products.[415] As a matter of fact, the Product Liability Directive, like the Product Safety Directive, aims at 'the protection of all those who come into contact with the envisioned products'.[416] The preamble to the Product Safety Directive refers to a high level of consumer protection in this regard.[417]

---

409 *D Van de Gehuchte*, Productaansprakelijkheid in België (2000) 76.

410 *K Van Leeuwen*, Juridische aspecten van produktveiligheid (1990) 23. This preventive function of the Product Liability Directive has been endorsed recently by the ECJ in its *Boston Scientific Medizintechnik* judgment (Joined Cases C-503/13 and C-504/13, *Boston Scientific Medizintechnik v AOK Sachsen-Anhalt*, not yet published).

411 Green Paper on Liability for Defective Products, COM(1999)396 final, 14; Report from the Commission on the application of Directive 85/374 on liability for defective products, COM(2000)893 final, 9.

412 *C Van Dam*, European tort law (2006) 372.

413 *A Geddes*, Product and service liability in the EEC (1992) 2, 36; *C Hodges/M Tyler/H Abbott*, Product safety (1996) 96.

414 *C Hodges/M Tyler/H Abbott*, Product safety (1996) 96; *D Van de Gehuchte*, Productaansprakelijkheid in België (2000) 77.

415 *S Whittaker*, The EEC Directive on product liability (1985) YEUL 233, 235; *AJO Van Wassenaer van Catwijck*, Produktenaansprakelijkheid in Europees verband (1986) 22; *A Geddes*, Product and service liability in the EEC (1992) 8–9.

416 *A Geddes*, Product and service liability in the EEC (1992) 35.

417 Recital 4 to the Directive.

196 In contrast, other legal scholars are less convinced of the similarities between both directives. They submit that the Product Liability Directive is not so much targeted towards protecting consumers but rather seeks to ensure that all possible victims of an accident with a product are protected, regardless of whether they are consumer or not.[418] Only with regard to compensation of property damages are the conditions such as to protect the goods of the private consumer only.[419]

197 However, it does not come as a surprise that in some respect both Directives have marked similarities.[420] Most legal scholars agree that the safety assessment under both Directives will be done in an identical way.[421] The level of safety the general public is entitled to expect is the same or substantially the same as one which only presents such risks as is acceptable and consistent with a high standard of protection, and *vice versa*.[422] Those who disagree submit that a defective product is not necessarily an unsafe product, as the defectiveness requirement involves a consideration of the fair distribution of risks between the producer and the victim while the concept of safety is only about prevention and thus about balancing the risks between the producer and the general public.[423]

198 The latter statement should not be adhered to in our view. As previously stated, the test of defectiveness should be done by considering the legitimate expectations of the general public *in abstracto*. If the assessment were exclusively confined to balancing the risks between producer and victim then it would imply a far more subjective test of defectiveness. As this is not the case, we do agree with the law doctrine that sees the principles of the Product Liability Directive and the Product Safety Directive Product as two sides of the same coin, laying down the same standard of safety in relation to products, with the latter (on product safety) setting out in far greater detail the relevant factors to be taken into account.[424]

---

418 *X Lewis*, The protection of consumers in European community law (1992) YEUL 139, 169.

419 Cf *supra* no 150.

420 *A Geddes*, Product and service liability in the EEC (1992) 36; *C Hodges/M Tyler/H Abbott*, Product safety (1996) 96.

421 *J Calais-Auloy*, Les rapports entre la directive de 1985 sur la responsabilité du fait des produits et celle de 1992 concernant la sécurité des produits (1994) 3 REDC 159, 163; *C Hodges/M Tyler/H Abbott*, Product safety (1996) 96, 121; *G Howells*, The relationship between product liability and product safety – understanding a necessary element in European product liability through a comparison with the U.S. position (1999–2000) 39 Washburn LJ 305, 336.

422 *A Geddes*, Product and service liability in the EEC (1992) 40.

423 *C Van Dam*, European tort law (2006) 372.

424 *A Geddes*, Product and service liability in the EEC (1992) 23, 36; *C Hodges*, Product liability. European laws and practice (1993) 53.

3) *Differences with the Product Liability Directive*

199 It is however also important to note that there are differences between Directive 85/374/EEC – which states that the liability of the producer shall be extinguished upon the expiry of a period of ten years from the date on which the producer put into circulation the actual product – and Directive 2001/95/EC, which requires producers to place only safe products on the market and which fosters the idea that a safe product includes a reference to the foreseeable period of a product's use, which can of course be greater than ten years.[425]

200 A second difference can be found in the scope *rationae materiae* of both Directives. In contrast to the Product Liability Directive, which is only applicable to movable, tangible goods, the Product Safety Directive is not limited to these goods but also applies to immovable products.[426] Furthermore the Product Safety Directive is only applicable to products which are intended for consumers or likely to be used by consumers.[427]

201 These differences have led the European Commission to emphasise that Directive 2001/95/EC and Directive 85/374/EEC have a complementary function: the first instrument ensures that only safe products are put on the market (prevention) and the second establishes the rules under which personal injury and damage to property caused by a defective product are compensated (compensation). Therefore it is justified to deal with the issue of time limits in relation to the producer's liability in a different way than in relation to the general safety of products.[428]

202 This distinction will however often be blurred in practice as many suppliers will be seen as a producer by the (more severe) provisions of the Product Safety Directive, whether or not they are able to identify the previous supplier in the chain or the producer of the product, as is the case in the Product Liability Directive.[429] Distributors, suppliers and other professionals in the supply chain are, however, only caught by the (most important) requirements of the Product Safety Directive to the extent that their activities may affect the safety properties of the marketed product, such as assembly, adaptation, repackaging or labelling of the product.[430]

Nevertheless, as already mentioned above, the Commission is of the opinion that the concept of producer within the Product Liability Directive should not

---

425 Green Paper on Liability for Defective Products, COM(1999)396 final, 27.

426 *D Van de Gehuchte*, Productaansprakelijkheid in België (2000) 77.

427 Art 2(a) Product Safety Directive.

428 Report from the Commission on the application of Directive 85/374 on liability for defective products, COM(2000)893 final, 21.

429 *A Geddes*, Product and service liability in the EEC (1992) 36.

430 Ibid 41.

be extended to suppliers whose activities may affect the safety properties of the product precisely because of the complementary functions of Directive 2001/95/EC and Directive 85/374/EEC.[431] The Commission's reasoning is not totally convincing. Although it must be admitted that the rules applicable should not be exactly the same under both Directives, this is far less convincing for a divergent scope of both Directives. We therefore advocate an identical scope for both Directives on this point. A similar scope would in our view contribute to a coherent and effective liability regime that in accordance with the aim of both directives is designed in a manner that is favourable to consumers. In the absence of an identical scope, the rules bear the risk of becoming unclear, perhaps even unequal, as regards the distribution of responsibilities on all the various people within the production and distribution process. This would be at odds with the clear overlap in scope that already exists between both directives. It is our view that these divergences cannot have been the intention of the European legislator.

B. CONSUMER SALES DIRECTIVE

1) In General

203 The Consumer Sales Directive[432] imposes final seller's liability vis-à-vis consumers for any lack of conformity which exists at the time the goods were delivered. The final seller is liable to the consumer for the lack of conformity regardless of whether he is actually responsible for the non-conformity or ought to know about it. Often, the lack of conformity will result from an act or omission by the producer, a previous seller in the same chain of contracts (for example in case of incorrect handling of the product) or any other intermediary. But even then, it is the final seller who will bear the consequences for the lack of conformity.

204 Whether a good is in conformity with the contract depends not only on the agreement between the final seller and the consumer, and on the seller's descriptions, but also on elements beyond his influence like the purpose for which goods of the same type normally are used or upon the quality the consumer may reasonably expect.[433] According to the Consumer Sales Directive, the final seller is even liable for public statements made by the producer.

431 Report from the Commission on the application of Directive 85/374 on liability for defective products, COM(2000)893 final, 23.

432 Directive 1999/44/EC on certain aspects of the sale of consumer goods and associated guarantees [1999] OJ L172/12.

433 Art 2(2)(d) of the Directive states that consumer goods are presumed to be in conformity with the contract if they 'show the quality and performance which are normal in goods of the same type and which the consumer can reasonably expect, given the nature of the goods and taking into account any public statements on the specific characteristics of the goods made about them by the seller, the producer or his representative, particularly in advertising

205 To that end, the Directive also provides definitions of consumer goods[434] and conformity with the contract[435] that deviate from the concepts of product and defectiveness used in the Product Liability Directive.

206 In the case of a lack of conformity the consumer may require the final seller to repair or replace the goods free of charge, to have an appropriate price reduction or to rescind the contract in accordance with the hierarchy rules of the remedies in art 3 of the Directive.

207 It follows that the Directive applies the traditional contract model on basis of which a contract can generate rights and obligations only for and against the parties to the agreement.[436] Hence, it does not grant consumers a direct claim against members of the distribution chain other than the final seller of the consumer goods, who is held liable to the consumer for the lack of conformity. If the final seller is not responsible for the lack of conformity, he has a right of redress in accordance with art 4 of the Directive.[437] In most EU countries this action can only be brought by a final seller against his supplier. This supplier can in turn pass liability back via the contractual chain and can thus bring an action against his contractual party and so forth. Parties can climb up the chain until liability finally arrives at the party responsible for the non-conformity.[438]

2) Similarities with the Product Liability Directive

208 The Consumer Sales Directive protects consumers against the non-conformity of the goods which exists at the time when the goods were delivered, and also contains rules on consumer guarantees.

---

or on labelling'. See more on this point *M Ebers/A Jansen/O Meyer*, Comparative Report, in: European Perspectives on Producer's Liability (2009 37.

434 Article 1(2)(b) of the Directive states that consumer goods are 'any tangible movable item, with the exception of goods sold by way of execution or otherwise by authority of law, water and gas where they are not put up for sale in a limited volume or set quantity and electricity'. In contrast, as was pointed out above, electricity, water and gas fall within the notion of product used in the Product Liability Directive, even where they are put up for sale in a limited volume or set quantity.

435 See art 2 of the Directive.

436 This is generally referred to as the principle of the relativity of contract or privity of contract.

437 'Where the final seller is liable to the consumer because of a lack of conformity resulting from an act or omission by the producer, a previous seller in the same chain of contracts or any other intermediary, the final seller shall be entitled to pursue remedies against the person or persons liable in the contractual chain. the person or persons liable against whom the final seller may pursue remedies, together with the relevant actions and conditions of exercise, shall be determined by national law' (art 4 of the Directive).

438 However, quite often the contractual chain is broken and liability does not reach the party actually responsible for the non-conformity. See the multiple reasons for this in *M Ebers/ A Jansen/O Meyer*, Comparative Report, in: European Perspectives on Producer's Liability (2009) 39, and more on the academic debate about the right of redress of the final seller at 40–41.

Article 1(2)(d)of the Directive defines the producer as 'the manufacturer of consumer goods, the importer of consumer goods into the territory of the European Community or any person purporting to be a producer by placing his name, trade mark or other distinctive sign on the consumer goods'. It is well known that parts of this definition were inspired by the definition of producer in art 3 of the Directive concerning liability for defective products. In both directives the concept is given a broad scope.[439] The equalisation of persons considered to be producers in both directives is given an identical interpretation in Belgian case law precisely because of the intertwinement of the definitions. By analogy with the case law of the Belgian courts concerning the liability for defective products, the decisive criterion to categorise a person as a producer is whether a normal diligent consumer perceives the trade mark or distinctive sign as an indication that the owner of the trade mark played a role in the manufacturing of the product.[440]

209 Another similarity with product liability cases is that a significant number of non-conformity cases do not arise from the final seller in the distribution chain, but from the producer. For instance, manufacturing defects or public statements made by the producer may lie at the basis of the lack of conformity of the good. However, in contrast with the direct claim consumers are entitled to against producers of defective products, no such direct claim is granted in the Consumer Sales Directive. As was pointed out above, it is the final seller who is liable to the consumer for the lack of conformity of the goods.

210 The European Commission, however, contemplated for a considerable period of time the introduction of a direct claim against the producer, the reasoning being that a system which made the final seller solely liable for non-conformities no longer accords with the situation in modern society, which is based on mass production and distribution.[441] The European Commission was also convinced that consumers would benefit from such a direct claim, especially those consumers who purchase their goods across borders in different Member States.[442] A remainder of this discussion is to be found in recital 23 of the

439 The concept of producer is defined quite broadly in the majority of the EU Member States, see on this point *M Ebers/A Jansen/O Meyer*, Comparative Report, in: European Perspectives on Producer's Liability (2009) 35.

440 Court of Appeal Antwerp, 10 January 2000, Rechtskundig Weekblad 2004–2005, 794; Court Namen 14 November 1997, Revue de Jurisprudence de Liège, Mons et Bruxelles 1998, 644; *D Wuyts*, Productaansprakelijkheid: een Richtlijn voor (n)iets? (2008) 35 TBBR 21–22.

441 See Green Paper on Guarantees for Consumer Goods and After-Sales Services, COM(93)509 final, 86. For a more detailed analysis, see *M Ebers/A Jansen/O Meyer*, Comparative Report, in: European Perspectives on Producer's Liability (2009) 4–6.

442 It would also contribute to increasing consumer confidence in the internal market. See European Commission's Communication on the implementation of the Directive 99/44/EC, COM(2007)210 final [2007] OJ C181/21, 12. See also on this point, *S Rutten/G Straetmans/*

Directive which states that 'it may be necessary to envisage more far-reaching harmonisation, notably by providing for the producer's direct liability for defects for which he is responsible'. A direct claim against the producer for consumers was not introduced in the Consumer Sales Directive, nor was a direct redress claim for the final seller.

3) Differences with the Product Liability Directive

211 Yet, as far as consumers are concerned, the Directive also stipulates in art 8 that the rights resulting from the Directive shall be exercised without prejudice to other rights which the consumer may invoke under the national rules governing contractual or non-contractual liability. Furthermore, unlike the Product Liability Directive, the Consumer Sales Directive is a minimum harmonisation directive, leaving Member States the freedom to adopt or maintain in force more stringent provisions to ensure a higher level of consumer protection, provided that those measures are compatible with the TFEU.[443] Article 4 of the Consumer Sales Directive also leaves considerable leeway to the Member States to regulate the final seller's right of redress.

212 The minimum harmonisation level of the Directive has for instance caused the Belgian legislator to retain the rights of redress existent prior to the implementation of the Consumer Sales Directive. In this regard the case law-based doctrine of qualitative rights[444] developed by the Belgian Court of Cassation is important to note. In answer to a question, raised by legal scholars, as to whether the consumer or retailer (also the second buyer) could claim damages from the producer (also the initial seller) in the case of hidden defects, the Belgian Court of Cassation gave the following fundamental guidelines in its ground-breaking judgment of 5 December 1980.[445]

213 It held that the obligation to deliver the sold goods extended to the so-called accessories (*accessoria*) and everything that is necessary for the durable use of the goods. The right of redress which the first buyer (eg wholesaler) is

---

D Wuyts, Rights of Redress and Direct Producer's Liability in Consumer Sales in Belgium: a Critical Appraisal, in: European Perspectives on Producer's Liability (2009) 207–208 and compare with *M Ebers/A Jansen/O Meyer*, Comparative Report, in: European Perspectives on Producer's Liability (2009) 58–73.

443 See also art 8(2).

444 The doctrine of qualitative rights was taken over from the Dutch legal system. In general terms, qualitative rights may be described as rights that are connected with a certain quality (*in casu* ownership of the goods). See: *E Dirix*, Obligatoire verhoudingen tussen contractanten en derden (1984) 28–29, nos 15–16.

445 Cass. 5 December 1980, Arr. Cass. 1980–1981, 382, Pas. 1981, I, 398; See also *H De Page*, Traité élémentaire de droit civil belge, IV, Les principaux contrats usuels (1975) 139, no 99, and 181, no 146.

entitled to against the producer is such an accessory (*accessorium*) of the goods transferable from the first buyer to the second buyer (eg retailer). Consequently, the second buyer and all subsequent buyers have a direct right against the initial seller further up the chain. Hence, the retailer also has a direct right of redress against the producer without having to bring actions against the first buyer. The doctrine of qualitative rights thus implies that the consumer or retailer has a direct right of redress against all individual sellers upstream in the commercial chain, but only insofar as the sellers upstream in the commercial chain can be held liable for the defect to the party with whom they contracted directly.

214 Thus, the right has a derivative nature which implies that it can only be exercised to the extent of the seller's liability against his buyer. In this regard, it is also important to note that this direct right of redress can be limited by exoneration clauses. The respective downstream buyers/sellers cannot transfer more rights than they actually hold. As a result, the direct action is determined by the various contractual relationships along the contractual chain. It also implies that the producer is allowed to rely on a valid exoneration clause concluded between the wholesaler and the producer, vis-à-vis a consumer or a retailer. In the same vein a producer is entitled to invoke exoneration clauses stipulated in the contract between the wholesaler and the retailer in view of countering a consumer's or retailer's direct claim.[446]

215 It follows that the direct claim in these cases is often short-circuited through exoneration clauses concluded by intermediate parties. The final buyer is indeed subject to all defences that arise from the first sales contract. The producer may also indirectly benefit from exoneration clauses since the scope of the right of redress of the consumer or the retailer is defined by the most rigid exoneration clause. By analogy, the description of the performance in the contract between the consumer and his seller will also affect the consumer's direct right of redress, since any seller further up the distribution chain is entitled to confront the consumer with this description. In the absence of any claim against his seller, the consumer will also be deprived of claims against previous sellers in the contractual chain.

216 The Belgian doctrine of qualitative rights does not as such conflict with the Consumer Sales Directive. However, the improved right of redress which is granted to the final seller[447] on the basis of Belgian law as a consequence of the Consumer Sales Directive gives rise to multiple questions when combined with

---

446 More on this point in *E Dirix*, Obligatoire verhoudingen tussen contractanten en derden (1984) 30; *I Samoy*, Commerciële garanties en het dwingend karakter van de nieuwe regels, in: S Stijns/J Stuyck (eds), Het nieuwe kooprecht (2005) 112, no 19.

447 The consumer does not benefit from this enhanced or improved right of redress.

the qualitative rights doctrine.[448] This is not the place to go into further detail on this.[449] It is simply submitted here that the right of redress introduced by the Consumer Sales Directive for the benefit of the final seller in art 4 has no counterpart in the Product Liability Directive, nor does the hierarchy of rules about the remedies the consumer is entitled to in the case of a lack of conformity of the goods.

217 Finally, although a European direct producers' liability for non-conformity with the contract was heavily debated in academic and European circles, the Directive on Consumer Rights[450] also abstains from introducing a system of direct producers' liability for non-conformity of goods. Although the European Commission admitted that the existence of diverging regimes of direct producers' liability constituted a potential threat for the establishment of the internal market, it concluded that there was 'not enough evidence to determine whether the lack of EU rules on direct producers' liability has a negative effect on consumer confidence in the Internal Market'.[451]

---

448 According to art 1649 *sexies* Belgian Civil Code sets the improved right of redress is termed as follows: 'Where the seller is liable towards the consumer because of a lack of conformity, he [the seller] shall be entitled to pursue remedies against the producer or any other contractual intermediary in the transfer of ownership of the consumer goods based on their contractual liability with regard to the goods, without any clause limiting or excluding liability being opposable to him' (free translation).

449 For a detailed analysis, see *S Rutten/G Straetmans/D Wuyts*, Rights of Redress and Direct Producer's Liability in Consumer Sales in Belgium: a Critical Appraisal, in: European Perspectives on Producer's Liability (2009) 201–203.

450 Directive 2011/83/EU of 25 October 2011 on consumer rights [2011] OJ L304/64. See also *G Straetmans/J Laffineur*, La directive 2011/83 relative aux droits des consommateurs: les modifications de la réglementation concernant les ventes aux consommateurs et les autres droits des consommateurs (2014) European Journal of Consumer Law 475–498.

451 See Proposal for a Directive on Consumer Rights, COM(2008)614 final.

PART II

PRODUCT LIABILITY IN AUSTRIA

Bernhard A Koch

I. SOURCES OF LAW AND THEIR EVOLUTION

A. LIABILITY FOR DEFECTIVE PRODUCTS BEFORE THE ADOPTION OF THE PRODUCT LIABILITY ACT

01 Austrian tort law is traditionally fault-based. Exceptions thereto have been introduced over time, and unlike other European jurisdictions, Austrian courts also grant claims based on a mere analogy to such statutory bases of strict liability, even to the totality of such causes of action, though rather cautiously.[1]

[1] See, eg, *BA Koch/H Koziol*, Austria, in: BA Koch/H Koziol (eds), Unification of Tort Law: Strict Liability (2002) 9 (on the analogous application of strict liability laws: no 25 ff).

However, before the introduction of the *Produkthaftungsgesetz* (PHG),[2] no statutory regime was in force which would have held the producer (or anybody else) liable for the defects of a product irrespective of fault.

02 Fault-based causes of action apart from intentional wrongdoing include in particular neglect of statutory safety regulations or lack of warnings despite awareness of security risks. The latter was recently confirmed in a case concerning an exploding mineral water bottle, where the Austrian Supreme Court *inter alia* granted a fault-based cause of action against the producer for failure to monitor products which after putting them into circulation turn out to be dangerous (possibly triggering recall obligations).[3] The rationale for such duties was found in the so-called *Ingerenzprinzip*,[4] which is well-established in Austrian tort law: whoever creates or controls a source of danger is obliged to invest reasonable efforts into avoiding that such risk materialises.

03 The Austrian Civil Code (*Allgemeines Bürgerliches Gesetzbuch*, ABGB) contains at least one major obstacle, however, that prevents victims of defective products from pursuing tort-based claims against the manufacturer on the basis of a product defect if she did not violate a duty of care herself individually: liability for auxiliaries in Austrian tort law is very limited[5] – outside of contractual or other special relationships, the principal can only be held liable for harmful conduct of her auxiliaries if these were either habitually unfit for the task assigned to them, or if the principal knew that they are dangerous, ie that they are likely to cause harm due to peculiar personal features (§1315 ABGB).[6] Apart from products manufactured by a single individual, this makes it almost impossible in practice to pursue claims in tort law against a producer that employs staff. If there is a contractual bond between the parties, on the other

---

2 Bundesgesetz vom 21. Jänner 1988 über die Haftung für ein fehlerhaftes Produkt, *Bundesgesetzblatt* (Federal Gazette, BGBl) 1988/99. An English translation of the statute as amended (which will be used for citations to the statute in the following) is available on the website of the Austrian Federal Chancellery at <https://www.ris.bka.gv.at/Dokumente/Erv/ERV_1988_99/ERV_1988_99.pdf>. On the history of this legislation, see *infra* no 06 ff.

3 OGH 13.9.2012, 6 Ob 215/11b, *Evidenzblatt der Rechtsmittelentscheidungen* (EvBl) 2013/16 (cmt by *M Spitzer*).

4 Cf art 4:103 PETL: 'A duty to act positively to protect others from damage may exist if law so provides, or if the actor creates or controls a dangerous situation, or when there is a special relationship between parties or when the seriousness of the harm on the one side and the ease of avoiding the damage on the other side point towards such a duty.'

5 See *H Koziol/K Vogel*, Liability for Damage Caused by Others under Austrian law, in: J Spier (ed), Unification of Tort Law: Liability for Damage Caused by Others (2003) 11 (no 3 f).

6 This provision reads: 'Whosoever, for the procurement of his affairs, avails himself either of an unfit person, or knowingly of a dangerous person, is liable for the harm such person causes to another in such capacity.' Translations of the tort law provisions of the ABGB are taken from *B Steininger* (transl), Austria, in: K Oliphant/B Steininger (eds), European Tort Law: Basic Texts (2011) 1.

hand, §1313a ABGB applies,[7] which holds the principal liable for the conduct of her auxiliaries irrespective of such personal qualifications, as long as they had acted within the scope of their assigned duties.

04 This creates a strong incentive to try to find a cause of action in contractual liability, where claimants can not only avail themselves of the aforementioned more favourable provision of vicarious liability, but also benefit from a reversal of the burden of proving fault. Such a contractual relationship was found in the original contract between the manufacturer and her distributor, which was (and still is) held to include protective duties vis-à-vis third parties – those who ultimately use the product. The distribution agreement is therefore a so-called *Vertrag mit Schutzwirkung zugunsten Dritter* (contract with protective effect vis-à-vis third parties),[8] which allows these third parties (ie the product users who become its victims) to avail themselves of the beneficial status of the immediate contracting parties when pursuing liability claims, even though they are not actually parties to that contract.

05 This approach was (and still is) recognised and applied by the Austrian Supreme Court since the mid-1970s.[9] It is commonly referred to as *Produzentenhaftung* (producers' liability) as opposed to *Produkthaftung* (product liability), the latter term at least now being reserved for the statutory strict liability regime introduced by the PHG. However, there were (and still are) limitations which prevent victims from pursuing claims on that (quasi-) contractual basis: First of all, if the manufacturer excludes or limits her liability for defects in her contract with the distributor,[10] such restriction will also curtail the rights of third parties correspondingly, as these cannot have more rights

---

7 This provision reads: 'Whosoever is under an obligation of performance to another is liable towards such person for the fault of his legal representative, and of persons he engages to perform the obligation, as if it were his own fault.'

8 For a fundamental analysis see *F Bydlinski*, Vertragliche Sorgfaltspflichten zugunsten Dritter, JBl 1960, 359, who *inter alia* argued that for example defects of a bicycle which may cause harm to its rider reduce the sales prospects of this product for that very reason, which is why it is in the direct (also economic) interest of the manufacturer not to distribute products which may trigger personal injuries or other damage. See further *G Schmaranzer*, Der Vertrag mit Schutzwirkung zugunsten Dritter (2006).

9 The leading case is OGH 4.2.1976, 1 Ob 190/75, *Entscheidungen des österreichischen Obersten Gerichtshofes in Zivil- und Justizverwaltungssachen* (SZ) 49/14. The most recent Supreme Court case recognising this cause of action was OGH 13.9.2012, 6 Ob 215/11b, SZ 2012/88.

10 However, a contractual exclusion of liability for intentional misconduct is deemed unconscionable and for that reason invalid. It is disputed whether this also applies for the exclusion of liability for grossly negligent behaviour. See OGH RIS-Justiz RS0016582 and RS0038178 (index numbers of case headnotes in the official online database <https://www.ris.bka.gv.at/Jus/>).

than the immediate contracting parties.[11] Furthermore, such liability remains fault-based; even though it is up to the producer to prove that no-one within her sphere was at fault, she might still succeed. Thirdly, innocent bystanders cannot seek compensation for their losses on that basis since they are not perceived to be third parties to the original distribution contract like product buyers or users.

B. THE AUSTRIAN PRODUCT LIABILITY ACT

06 After increasing debates in the late 1970s and early 1980s, Austria adopted a product liability statute in 1988 in order to open up an alternative path towards compensation irrespective of the limitations of the traditional approaches just outlined and – more importantly – irrespective of fault. The Product Liability Act (PHG)[12] was mostly based on the model of Directive 85/374/EEC (PLD).[13] Since Austria was not yet a member of the EEA at the time the Act was adopted, let alone a member of the EU,[14] the statute did not formally implement said Directive, which is why it contained some deviations from its model that were only partly remedied by a subsequent statutory amendment on Austria's entry into the EEA.[15] Further amendments to the PHG became necessary due to Directive 1999/34/EC[16] and on the introduction of the euro.[17]

07 Apart from these deviations that will be addressed throughout the following text where appropriate, the PHG followed the PLD model rather closely and did not add any further aspects of liability to the statutory language. All matters not addressed expressly by the PHG shall be governed by the ABGB instead, as §14 PHG expressly stipulates.[18] Questions of causation and available remedies, for example, are therefore mostly governed by the general principles of Austrian tort law.

---

11 OGH 28.11.1978, 5 Ob 707/78, SZ 51/169. This was rightly criticised *inter alia* by *W Posch*, Produzentenhaftung in Österreich de lege lata et de lege ferenda, in: Verhandlungen des 8. ÖJT Graz 1982 I/3 (1982) 159 ff; *H Koziol*, Grundfragen der Produktehaftung (1980) 20 ff.

12 *Supra* fn 2.

13 The legislator argued that due to strong economic ties with EEC Member States, in particular with Germany, it was quintessential for Austria to follow the lead of the EEC in this respect, even though there was no obligation to do so.

14 Austria joined the EEA as of 1.1.1994 and became a member of the EU one year later.

15 BGBl 1993/95.

16 Directive 1999/34/EC of the European Parliament and of the Council of 10 May 1999 [1999] OJ L141/20, implemented in Austria by BGBl I 1999/185. This Directive eliminated 'the exception of primary agricultural products and game' in art 2 PLD's definition of 'product' and consequently repealed art 15(1)(a) PLD, which had allowed Member States to derogate from the original narrower definition, but now was moot since such derogation was turned into the rule.

17 BGBl I 2001/98.

18 §14 PHG reads: 'Unless otherwise stipulated in this Federal Act, the Civil Code shall be applied to the claims for damages specified hereunder.'

08 As far as the optional elements of the PLD are concerned, the Austrian legislator refrained from taking advantage thereof. The PHG therefore does not foresee caps on liability as possible under art 16(1) PLD. Agricultural products remained outside the scope of the PHG (though with a temporary exception in respect of genetically modified goods)[19] until the PLD itself was reformed accordingly.[20] Finally, Austria also decided to preserve the development risk defence of art 7(e) PLD (implemented by §8 no 2 PHG), even though it could have deviated therefrom according to art 15(1)(b) PLD.[21]

09 There are no further special rules on liability for defective products so, unlike Germany, Austria does not, for example, have a separate statutory regime for medicinal products, which therefore fall under the PHG.

10 In the course of the discussion about a reform of Austrian tort law, it was proposed to include the rules of the PHG into the ABGB.[22] So far, however, it remains a separate statute which refers to the general rules of the ABGB at some points, either expressly (by way of §14 PHG as mentioned)[23] or impliedly.

C. THE NATURE OF PRODUCT LIABILITY UNDER THE PHG

11 There has been some debate in Austria on whether product liability as introduced by the PHG falls within the scope of '*Gefährdungshaftung*',[24] which is the German term for strict liability, but by its name implies that liability attaches to a certain risk or danger. This may be misleading (at least) in this particular instance since products are not necessarily dangerous just because one item of a production series turns out to be defective. In addition, the PHG channels liability onto the manufacturer of a product once she has put it into circulation, so losing control over the product is indeed a prerequisite for liability, which contradicts the classic notion of strict liability in Austria according to which the keeper of the source of harm shall be liable. At best, one could classify the

19 This exception was introduced in 1995 alongside the Austrian Act on Genetic Engineering (*Gentechnikgesetz*, BGBl 1994/510) and remained in force until the next amendment to the PHG implementing Directive 1999/34/EC (fn 16), when it became superfluous.

20 *Supra* fn 16.

21 See *infra* nos 71–72.

22 See the proposal of the Ministry of Justice's working group presented by *BC Steininger*, Austria, in: H Koziol/BC Steininger (eds), European Tort Law 2007 (2008) 134 (with the proposed new §§1332 ff ABGB – which would deviate in many aspects from the existing language of the PHG – cited at 169 ff). The fate of that reform proposal is quite unclear at the moment, however.

23 *Supra* fn 18.

24 *H Koziol/P Apathy/BA Koch*, Österreichisches Haftpflichtrecht III (3rd edn 2014, in the following: HPR III³) no B/17 ff.

PHG as a case of no-fault liability (*verschuldensunabhängige Haftung*), even though this is not entirely true as the conduct of the producer plays at least some role when it comes to defences, in particular the development risk defence or compliance with mandatory regulations.

II. BASIC ELEMENTS OF LIABILITY

12 Despite some deviations in details as already indicated, the PHG follows the general concept of product liability foreseen by the PLD, which therefore applies if the defect of a product causes personal injury or property damage to another, irrespective of whether this victim was a buyer or just a user of the product, or whether she was a mere innocent bystander. Liability is channelled to the producer or – if she is domiciled outside of the EEA – alternatively to the one who imported the product into the common market. Only if neither of the two can be identified is the victim allowed to focus her product liability claims on the supplier, irrespective of any alternative claims she might also have arising out of the sales contract with this secondary defendant. By and large the same defences apply as foreseen by the PLD without the deviations it would have allowed.[25]

A. PRODUCT

1) *The Definition of 'Product' According to the PHG*

13 §4 PHG defines a product as 'any movable *tangible* property',[26] whereas art 2 PLD does not limit movables to tangibles. The reason for this insertion in deviation of the Directive relates to the very broad definition of things in §285 ABGB, which extends to intangibles as well, whereas the corresponding German provision reduces this term to 'corporeal' objects (§90 BGB). It is argued that the understanding of 'movable' in art 2 PLD contains an implicit restriction to the same end.[27]

14 When it comes to defining 'movable', an autonomous European interpretation will ultimately prevail,[28] which is why Austrian specialties such as

25 See *infra* no 70 ff on defences.

26 Emphasis added. §1 para 1 PHG already speaks of 'tangible property' as well. While this and the above citation are taken from the English PHG version cited in fn 2, a better translation would have been 'any movable *corporeal* thing', which comes closer to the actual language of the ABGB ('*bewegliche* körperliche *Sache*').

27 *Koziol/Apathy/Koch*, HPR III³ (fn 24) no B/116.

28 The CJEU will at some point have to clarify whether the definition of 'product' in art 2 PLD is restricted to tangible/corporeal objects, see also *infra* no 98.

the so-called '*Superädifikat*'[29] will be irrelevant. One decisive test will certainly be whether actually physically moving the object to a new location would lower the combined value of object and land.

15 As required by art 2 PLD, §4 PHG foresees that a movable remains to be a 'product' within the meaning of this statute if it is combined with immovable property after it was put into circulation. This has been rightly criticised by Austrian scholars since it leads to unbearable discrepancies:[30]

- If a carpenter produces a wooden bench which collapses, she will be liable under the PHG, but not a construction company that erects a defective bridge – despite dramatically different consequences.
- If the bridge is made of concrete, it is decisive whether it was composed of pre-fabricated concrete parts (in which case the PHG applies) or whether the bridge was cast on site (in which case only the producer of the concrete may be liable, but not the construction company).

16 The problem was aggravated by the *Veedfald* ruling of the ECJ,[31] which made clear that singular, individualised products also fall within the scope of the PLD and not just mass production as originally envisaged.[32]

2) *Special Types of Products*

a) Water and Other Natural Resources

17 §3 PHG and its model, art 3(1) PLD, make it explicitly clear that product liability can also attach to raw material, which raises the question what the term 'manufacturing' means in relation to, for example, agricultural raw materials that are not 'produced' on a farm but collected in nature (such as mushrooms or game hunted in the wild), and more generally whether the mere collection or harvest of natural resources is a 'production' within the meaning of the PLD (and therefore the PHG). This has to be answered in the affirmative, which means that a company that merely bottles spring water without filtering or any

---

29 Such a construction is – at least in theory – not supposed to remain on the land forever. Typically, this would be claimed in the contract between the land owner and the developer, whereas in practice the construction may be as massive as a shopping centre. See *BA Koch/K Nemeth*, Property Law, in: M Schauer/C Grabenwarter (eds), Introduction to the Law of Austria (2015) §7.01[B].

30 See *Koziol/Apathy/Koch*, HPR III^3 (fn 24) no B/114 f, B/128 f with further references.

31 ECJ 10.5.2001, Case C-203/99, *Veedfald v Århus Amtskommune*, ECLI:EU:C:2001:258 [2001] ECR I-3569.

32 Cf recitals 2 and 3 of the PLD Preamble. But see already the explanatory memorandum to the original draft of the PLD (Bulletin of the European Communities, Supplement 11/76, 14), which states that '[n]o distinction should be made between industrial and craft products'.

other modification is still a 'producer' within the meaning of the PLD and PHG since the water would not have been put into circulation without such human intervention, even though it did not bring the bottled content into existence, which a narrow understanding of 'manufacturing' would imply.[33]

b) Energy

18 In contrast to art 2 PLD, §4 PHG includes 'energy' under the definition of 'product', not just 'electricity'. The Austrian legislator did not see a conflict with the Directive, though, as it proceeded from the assumption that the qualification of other energy resources (or at least of their carriers) such as coal or oil would undoubtedly be 'movable tangible property', whereas the existing dispute on this point with respect to electricity had to be resolved with an explicit mention in the Directive.[34] The question as to *when* electricity is put into circulation – at the moment when it is fed into the mains connection of the customer or already when it enters the mains network – is still disputed.[35]

c) Body Parts

19 Body parts or blood are 'things' within the meaning of §285 ABGB[36] once they are separated from the body they originate from. However it is illegal to make commercial use of one's own body parts,[37] let alone professionally. Still, third parties can dispose and make use of them and subsequently put them into circulation, eg in the form of blood or plasma units. However, while the entrepreneur who does so may be liable under the PHG,[38] she will not be able to seek recourse from the donor if the blood was already infected.[39]

---

33 The same of course applies correspondingly if the water is distributed via a pipeline system. *Koziol/Apathy/Koch*, HPR III^3 (fn 24) no B/119; *S Strahwald*, Produkthaftung für vergiftetes Trinkwasser, VR 2003, 178 (179, 181).

34 Explanatory Memorandum to the PHG Draft (<www.parlament.gv.at/PAKT/VHG/XVII/I/I_00272/imfname_264133.pdf>) 9.

35 In favour of the former *W Posch*, in: M Schwimann (ed), Praxiskommentar zum ABGB VII (3rd edn 2005) §6 PHG Rz 4; *contra H Fitz/A Grau*, in: H Fitz/A Grau/P Reindl (eds), Produkthaftung (2nd ed 2004, in the following: *Fitz/Grau* in PHG^2) §6 Rz 28; *R Welser*, Blitzschlag und Produkthaftung, ecolex 1990, 465. It may well be that the Austrian Supreme Court will follow its German counterpart in this respect, which has recently ruled in favour of the first option: *Bundesgerichtshof* (BGH) 25.2.2014, VI ZR 144/13, Neue Juristische Wochenschrift (NJW) 2014, 2106. On the defectiveness of electricity, see *A Grau*, Produktfehler (2002) 105 f.

36 *Supra* no 13.

37 §4 para 2 Organ Transplant Act (*Organtransplantationsgesetz*, OTPG, BGBl I 2012/108); §8 para 4 Blood Safety Act 1999 (*Blutsicherheitsgesetz*, BGBl I 1999/44).

38 *Koziol/Apathy/Koch*, HPR III^3 (fn 24) no B/141.

39 *M Preslmayr*, Handbuch der Produkthaftung (2nd ed 2002) 58 f; *W Posch*, in: M Schwimann (fn 35) §4 PHG Rz 7.

d) Intellectual Products in General[40]

20 Since the definition of 'product' in the PHG is reduced to corporeal things, the question arises whether intellectual products can be defective solely because of flaws relating to their (intellectual and as such intangible) content. It is obvious that a carrier of information per se can trigger product liability: someone who is injured by toxic chemicals used for producing a book cover, for example, will most certainly have a claim in product liability against the manufacturer of the book, as will the user of a DVD that is unevenly shaped and for that reason ruins the drive in which it is played.

21 However, when it comes to the contents of the book or the DVD, opinions in Austria are split. Still, this question should be answered in the affirmative for several reasons. To begin with, the typical buyer acquires the carrier because of the information it contains, and not because the colour of the book cover looks nice on her bookshelves. The use one makes of this product is to consume and digest the information, not to exercise one's fingers by flipping the pages. Considering the – undisputed – fact that the producer is liable for errors in an instruction manual attached to a product, it would be insupportable to treat this case differently if the buyer acquired the same product without the manual and bought the latter separately.[41]

22 A natural limit to liability for intellectual products because of flaws in the information they carry is the range of compensable losses under the PLD as implemented by the PHG. Since the product will only trigger liability under this regime if it causes personal injury or certain property damage, but not in cases of pure economic loss, the only publications relevant in practice will be instruction manuals, guidebooks, maps, and the like.

23 One of the prime difficulties in confirming product liability for information as distributed on some carrier media is drawing the borderline to liability for services, of course. However, this problem is a natural consequence of legislating in one specific area without providing for the border areas as well, as was done by the European legislator when imposing the PLD without ensuring that there is a

---

40 See generally *BA Koch*, Product Liability for Information in Europe? in J Potgieter/ J Knobel/R Jansen (eds), Essays in Honour of / Huldigingsbundel vir Johann Neethling (2015) 245.

41 This is equally obvious in the more and more typical case when only a fragmentary printed introduction (if any) is included in the packaging of a product which contains a hyperlink to further information provided online: the manufacturer cannot escape liability for false information by physically detaching the information from the actual product for which such information is designed.

compatible regime of liability for services as well.[42] The problem was aggravated once it was clear that individualised products also fall within the scope of the Directive.[43] The question therefore arises whether an expert opinion by a legal scholar on an individual case, neatly printed and bound, also counts as a product within the meaning of the PLD and therefore the PHG, despite the fact that it was produced for an individual client and not for some anonymous readership. The only (but necessary) way to distinguish this from a publication aimed at a larger audience is by pointing to the fact that the *Veedfald* ruling cannot be applied to this expert opinion since it could have taken any other form as well (such as an oral presentation),[44] whereas the perfusion fluid concocted for the kidney transplantation was the only form in which this product could exist.[45]

e) Software and Digital Content in Particular

24 As long as intellectual products are tangible carriers of information, the definition of §4 PHG (and art 2 PLD) poses no problem. However, if the information is provided in digital form only, eg via download, the question arises whether this is still 'movable tangible property'.

25 If product liability attaches to tangible carriers of information, however, it would be inconsistent not to extend it to mere digital downloads of the same content as well – in modern society, it should not make a difference whether one buys a printed book or an e-book.[46] One should also bear in mind in this context that the definition of things in the ABGB is more than 200 years old, written at a time when electronic data was not yet an item of interest.[47] What matters to the product liability theory is the fact that the product leaves the sphere of the manufacturer, perhaps makes a stopover at some intermediary

---

42 As is well known, a subsequent Proposal for a Council Directive on the Liability of Suppliers of Services, COM(1990)482, was ultimately withdrawn by COM(1994)260, with no follow-up project in sight.

43 *Supra* no 16.

44 On the unsatisfactory result that product liability for intellectual products only attaches to tangible media, whereas the presentation of their content in any other way, such as by a public reading or in a TV show, will not suffice, see *Koziol/Apathy/Koch*, HPR III^3 (fn 24) no B/135.

45 Cf recital 19 of the recently proposed Directive on certain aspects concerning contracts for the supply of digital content COM(2015)634 final, which could also be helpful in this context: 'This Directive ... should not apply to services, which are performed personally by the supplier and where the digital means are only used for access or delivery purposes, such as a translation offered by a person or other professional advice services where only the output of the service is delivered to the consumer by digital means.'

46 Cf *G Wagner*, in: Münchener Kommentar zum BGB (6th 2013, in the following: *MünchKomm*) §2 ProdHaftG no 12 ff, who rightly argues that there is no adequate reason to reduce the PLD to the risks of the 'old economy' and to completely exclude the predominant economic good of modern-day commerce – information.

47 Cf *P Bydlinski*, Der Sachbegriff im elektronischen Zeitalter: zeitlos oder anpassungsbedürftig?, Archiv für die civilistische Praxis (AcP) 198 (1998) 288, 305 ff.

distributor, and that it ultimately arrives within the sphere of a consumer or user where it causes harm. The actual physical route it took from one point to another is irrelevant.[48] If in modern society we no longer buy music on CDs, but download it as MP3 files online, neither the producer's perspective nor the buyer's interest have changed, even though there may no longer be a tangible object passed from the one (ultimately) to the other.

26 Still, opinions are split in Austria over whether digital content falls within the scope of the PHG's definition of a product or not. This is equally true for software.[49] At least in the past, some distinguished between operating systems and user software (with the former commonly acquired together with the hardware),[50] but even if one believed in such a distinction in the past, it is certainly moot now, where operating systems are no longer necessarily sold bundled with the hardware. Operating systems were treated differently because they are essential for using the hardware and perceived to be a vital part of it, making the 'tangible' item usable. However, again this should not be decisive. If one accepted that the producer shall be liable for a defect in the software (or even just the operating system) pre-installed in the hardware, with the latter being the final product and the former being equivalent to a component thereof, it would be inconsistent to treat the producer of the same software differently if she subsequently sold a newer version of that operating system which replaces the one originally shipped. There is no difference in design, manufacturing and marketing of that software, so it should not make a difference in product liability either.

---

48 If something happens en route, it may be considered as a defence according to art 7(b) PLD, but what is crucial then is not *what* happened en route, but *that* it happened after leaving the sphere of the producer.

49 The Austrian Supreme Court answered this in the affirmative at least with respect to software on tangible media (OGH 5 Ob 504, 505/96, SZ 70/202). In favour *Holzinger*, Produkthaftpflicht und Software, EDV und Recht (EDVuR) 1988, Issue 4, 10; *Ch Horwath*, Software – ein Produkt? ecolex 2000, 784; *Koziol/Apathy/Koch*, HPR III^3 (fn 24) no B/136 ff. Support in favour can also be found in a response by *Lord Cockfield* on behalf of the Commission to a question posed by the European Parliament [1989] OJ C114/42, after pointing to the definition of a product in art 2 PLD: 'Consequently, the Directive applies to software in the same way, moreover, that it applies to handicraft and artistic products.'
Contra eg *M Andréewitch*, Zur Anwendbarkeit des Produkthaftungsgesetzes für Softwarefehler, EDVuR 1990, 50; *Eccher/Riss*, in: H Koziol/P Bydlinski/R Bollenberger (eds), Kurzkommentar zum ABGB (4th edn 2014, in the following: KBB^4) §§292 no 1 (but also with respect to electricity, which is even expressly listed as a product in §4 PHG). Some insist that software must be saved on some tangible medium in order to fall within the definition of a product, eg *Preslmayr*, Handbuch (fn 39) 55; *R Welser/C Rabl*, Produkthaftungsgesetz (2nd ed 2004, in the following: PHG^2) §4 no 11. *Fitz/Grau* in PHG^2 (fn 35) §4 no 33, are undecided and argue that public perception should be decisive, which in the case of software would presumably speak in favour of a product, at least by now.

50 See the references cited by *A Eustacchio*, Produkthaftung (2002) 34.

f) Waste

27 Waste is commonly understood to fall within the product definition of the PHG, but only if produced[51] for some economically relevant purpose, not if it was just made ready for final disposal, which is why mere by-products such as wood shavings are only products if collected for recycling or for use in a heating system. Waste therefore needs to be put (back) into circulation, not taken out of circulation for good in order to qualify as a product under the PHG.[52]

B. DEFECT

1) Overview

28 §5 PHG follows art 6 PLD rather closely when defining the defect of the product that must have triggered the harm at stake. It reads:

> '(1) A product shall be deemed defective if it does not provide the safety which, taking all circumstances into account, may be reasonably expected, in particular with respect to:
> 1. the presentation of the product,
> 2. the use to which it can reasonably be expected that the product would be put,
> 3. the time when the product was put into circulation.
>
> (2) A product shall not be considered defective for the sole reason that an improved product was subsequently put into circulation.'

29 This seems to impose a three-step analysis to assess the defectiveness of a product. First, the product must have shown a lack of safety, although only with respect to the interests protected by the PHG. Next, this safety deficit must have deviated from the actual expectations in this respect; and finally, these expectations must have been 'reasonable' under the circumstances. This test has to focus on the time when the product was put into circulation, so any subsequent changes in the perception of safety and risks must not be considered,[53] even though they may not only have an impact on products of the same line which are put into circulation after such change, but also on the producer's duty to monitor her (already circulated) products, which – if breached – may trigger fault-based liability.[54]

---

51 The requirement of some transformation, ie production, applies here as well, of course, so throwing away an item without further ado does not thereby transform it into a product.

52 *Koziol/Apathy/Koch*, HPR III^3 (fn 24) no B/145.

53 See also *infra* no 73 ff on the development risk defence.

54 See *supra* no 02.

2) *Dangerousness vs Safety*

30 The dangerousness of a product does not necessarily mean that it is defective – a kitchen knife is a likely cause of personal injury, but that does not render it defective within the meaning of the PLD in light of reasonable expectations with respect to this particular product. The likelihood of causing harm of a kind covered by the PHG (and the PLD) is nevertheless an indicator for the safety of the product, which means that its safeness is not a fixed measure, but flexible, so that the first step in the analysis is necessarily coupled with the next one, ie the expectations of safety.

3) *Whose Expectations Count?*

31 The crucial question for the latter is, of course, whose expectations count.[55] Needless to say, the buyers of a product as well as its typical users are relevant. As to the latter, Austrian courts use the notion of the '*Idealtypus des durchschnittlichen Produktbenützers*' (ideal type of average product user),[56] which is obviously a rather empty phrase, and it does not get more helpful if this is determined according to the '*am wenigsten informierten und damit gefährdetsten Benutzergruppe*' (least informed user groups which for that reason are most at risk).[57] However, identifying whose expectations are relevant cannot stop there, even though it must not (or at least not always) extend to the general public at large. Instead, it depends upon the type of product and the range of people who might be exposed to its risks,[58] which has to be determined objectively, so the personal expectations of the actual victim cannot be decisive as such.[59]

32 In light of these difficulties in narrowing down the target group whose expectations count, it has been argued that it is not the expectations of any group of people that is relevant, but rather the expectations of the law.[60] However, while shifting the focus in this way may help to come to a conclusion, the necessary steps to assess what the law expects are not that different from the analysis described before, as – again – the use of the product will *inter alia* be decisive,

---

55 *Koziol/Apathy/Koch*, HPR III³ (fn 24) no B/155 ff.

56 Starting with OGH 11.11.1992, 1 Ob 644/92, SZ 65/149.

57 eg OGH 30.3.2001, 7 Ob 49/01h, SZ 74/62.

58 *Koziol/Apathy/Koch*, HPR III³ (fn 24) no B/158 ff.

59 Some Supreme Court decisions asked for expert opinions on what these legitimate expectations were under the circumstances, without clarifying what kind of expertise may be relevant for such analysis. However, the OGH explicitly ruled out that public opinion research might help in this context: OGH 11.11.1992, 1 Ob 644/92, SZ 65/149. See also OGH 12.10.1995, 6 Ob 626/95, ecolex 1996, 166; 16.7.1998, 6 Ob 157/98a, Recht der Wirtschaft (RdW) 1998, 735.

60 *Grau*, Produktfehler (fn 35) 132 f.

which in turn has to be examined in light of those who actually use it or are at least expected to do so.

4) Which Expectations are 'Reasonable under the Circumstances'?

33 Once the expectations in respect of product safety have been identified (whether those imposed by law or actual expectations of a certain group of people), they have to be checked to determine whether they were 'reasonable under the circumstances', which obviously again needs to be assessed objectively. All safety features prescribed by law[61] and those developed in the respective industry[62] undoubtedly have to be fulfilled, but 'reasonable expectations' will clearly go beyond that minimum standard. Again, the perspective of expected users and those who will typically get into the product's proximity will provide important guidelines. Exclusively personal or remote aspects, however, such as rare allergies or phobias, will not meet the reasonableness test, unless the producer ought to have foreseen that members of such specific groups may come into contact with the product, in which case at least certain warnings must be attached to the product.

34 The 'reasonableness' of safety expectations must not be equated with whatever is technically possible to increase the product safety. It is common knowledge that certain safety features will not be added to a product in order to preserve its marketability for a larger audience, since any improvement in this respect will trigger costs that will inevitably have to be passed on to consumers. Buyers of a car necessarily have to make an informed choice regarding how much they want to invest in the safety of their vehicle beyond what is required by law, and each add-on will typically cost extra. Reasonableness is therefore not only determined by technical feasibility, but also by economic affordability (for both the producer and the targeted buyers).[63]

35 As expressed in §5 para 1 PHG, aspects which determine reasonableness include – apart from the time when it was put into circulation – the presentation of the product and the expected use thereof. The former not only includes marketing aspects and information provided when the product is circulated, but also choices made in the design phase – the appearance of the product itself may also contribute to raising certain safety expectations. When it comes to the expected use of the product, Austrian courts are rather generous and also hold

61 See also *infra* nos 71–72 on the possibility to escape liability if compliance with mandatory regulations is proven.

62 In Austria, the so-called Ö-Normen will have to be considered in this respect, which are voluntary national standards drawn up by the Austrian Standards Institute <https://www.austrian-standards.at>. See, eg, OGH 28.4.2011, 1 Ob 62/11s, RdW 2011, 468.

63 *Koziol/Apathy/Koch*, HPR III^3 (fn 24) no B/169.

that misuse of a product still has to be expected as long as it is not completely foolish under the circumstances. Apart from typical aberrations of the intended use (such as chewing on a pencil) any conduct in respect of the product will be relevant that is not just theoretically possible, but commonly imaginable in light of the features of the product and its average user. It was held, for example, that keeping a bottle of soda over more than twenty hours in the trunk of a car at high outside temperatures without cooling may still be socially acceptable use,[64] as would ignoring one of several safety measures when parking a tractor if compliance with all of the measures would have made the use of the tractor more cumbersome.[65]

5) *Types of Defects*

36 As in other jurisdictions, Austrian courts distinguish between:

- design defects;
- manufacturing defects; and
- marketing defects.

37 There is no apparent Austrian peculiarity with respect to the interpretation of these categories, so the first one relates to the development of the product, the second one to its actual production (ie the implementation of the design), and the third one to the distribution stage (including – but not limited to – failure to warn).

38 There is some debate in Austria about whether products are deemed defective if they are simply ineffective, ie do not fulfil certain expectations of their users without reducing their physical well-being or the condition of their property.[66] Examples include pharmaceuticals or safety devices such as smoke detectors or lightning protection devices. If a medicine not only has no harmful side effects, but indeed no effect at all, the health of the patient does not deteriorate because of the drug as such. However, since she expects her health to improve because of this medication, she abstains from taking alternatives, which ultimately will nevertheless negatively affect her overall condition. The same is true for smoke detectors – the fact that they fail to go off did not start the fire, but counter-action will most likely be taken too late, so the ineffectiveness of this gadget will at least contribute indirectly to the overall damage. This is why the majority opinion in Austria confirms that product liability should also attach to ineffective (and for that very reason defective) products.[67]

64 OGH 8.4.1997, 4 Ob 87/97s, SZ 70/61.
65 OGH 28.2.2012 8 Ob 21/11p, RdW 2012, 334.
66 See *Koziol/Apathy/Koch*, HPR III³ (fn 24) no B/199 ff.
67 OGH 21.6.2007, 6 Ob 162/05z, SZ 2007/98 (wood preserver). See also *Grau*, Produktfehler (fn 35) 98, who rightly argues that the perspective of the producer in such cases speaks even

C. PUTTING A PRODUCT INTO CIRCULATION[68]

39 Many aspects of product liability depend upon the question whether, when and by whom a product was put into circulation, starting with attributing the product to the defendant (§§1, 7 para 1 PHG), further when identifying a product defect (§§5 para 1 no 3, 5 para 2, and 7 para 2 PHG), the development risk defence (§8 para 2 PHG), recourse options (§12 para 3 PHG) as well as the start of the extinction period of §13 PHG.

40 Oddly enough, the PLD fails to offer any guidance in this respect. While the Austrian legislator tried to fill this gap by providing a statutory definition, it is highly doubtful whether this is of any help at all. §6 PHG provides:

> 'A product shall be deemed put into circulation as soon as the entrepreneur – irrespective of the title – has transferred it to another person into the latter's power of disposition or for the latter's use. Dispatching the product to the customer shall be deemed sufficient.'

41 According to the PHG drafters, the core aspect of this magic moment is that the producer voluntarily gives up and thereby loses 'even a theoretical possibility to control the risk inherent in the product' when putting it into circulation.[69] However, the drafters contradict themselves in this respect when arguing that this term not only includes the sale of a product, but also extends to service contracts and leases. The lessor of a product, however, does not lose 'even a theoretical possibility' to control the product that she merely leased to another.

42 The *Veedfald* decision of the ECJ[70] made clear that 'circulation' does not necessarily entail that the product leaves the sphere of the producer. It therefore seems to be decisive instead that the producer is aware of and agrees to the fact that third parties will from now on be exposed to her product, which already takes place, for example, in a showroom on the producer's own premises where products are put on display for potential customers.[71] General opinion in Austria holds that a product is even put into circulation if used internally by the producer

more in favour of product liability: Whereas it is hard to foresee defects of a product in the classic sense, the intended effects of the product and the consequences of their failure are very much predictable for the producer.

68 See, generally, *Koziol/Apathy/Koch*, HPR III^3 (fn 24) no B/208 ff.

69 *'Wesentlicher Kern des Begriffs ist es, daß das Produkt mit dem Willen desjenigen, dessen Haftung in Frage steht, aus seinem Verfügungsbereich herausgetreten ist und er dadurch jede auch nur theoretische Möglichkeit verloren hat, die potentiell in dem Produkt steckende Gefahr zu beherrschen.'* Explanatory Memorandum to the PHG Draft (fn 34) 10.

70 *Supra* fn 31.

71 Cf OGH 9.7.2002 2 Ob 253/01x, *Juristische Blätter* (JBl) 2003, 249: prototype self-defence spray passed on to the husband of a potential future distributor of the product.

as long as it is at least possible that third parties may be harmed, since it must not make a difference for the victim whether the person using the defective product produced it herself or acquired it from another.[72] If, for example, a construction company produces its own scaffolding which collapses on a building site and thereby injures a passer-by, the latter's claims against the producer should not be barred by the fact that the product was used internally (but in a context where third parties may be harmed).[73]

III. THE PERSON LIABLE FOR DAMAGE

A. PRODUCER

43 Presumably the most important deviation from the PLD in Austrian law is the fact that the PHG uses a different approach to identify the defendant:[74] instead of focusing on the 'producer' (with the importer or supplier being 'responsible as' or 'treated as' a producer) as proposed by the Directive, the PHG speaks of two different 'entrepreneurs' – the one who produced it and put it into circulation (the 'producer'), the other who imported it into the EEA (the 'importer'). The supplier is yet another 'entrepreneur'. This was justified by pointing at art 7(c) PLD, according to which the producer can escape liability by proving 'that the product was neither manufactured by him for sale or any form of distribution for economic purpose nor manufactured or distributed by him in the course of his business'. In the eyes of the PHG drafters, this meant that the person liable under the PLD has to be an 'entrepreneur', which of course is not entirely correct, certainly not if one defines this term by applying §1 para 1 no 1 of the Austrian Consumer Protection Statute (*Konsumentenschutz-gesetz*, KSchG),[75] as was done originally despite convincing criticism.[76]

44 Other than that, the concept of 'producer' is in line with the PLD, so §3 PHG in that respect corresponds to art 3(1) PLD, extending the definition

72 Needless to say, both production and use must still have been part of the commercial activity of the producer.

73 *Koziol/Apathy/Koch*, HPR III³ (fn 24) no B/213 with further references.

74 According to the drafters of the 1993 amending statute (fn 15), which would have offered the occasion to remedy said deviation from the Directive, 'representatives of the EC Commission' had confirmed that the peculiar approach adopted by the Austrian statute was in compliance with the PLD (Explanatory Memorandum, <www.parlament.gv.at/PAKT/VHG/XVIII/I/I_00648/imfname_261744.pdf> 3). Needless to say, no source was actually cited thereto.

75 Federal Act Establishing Provisions for the Protection of Consumers, BGBl 1979/140 as amended (English language version available at <https://www.ris.bka.gv.at/Dokumente/Erv/ERV_1979_140/ERV_1979_140.pdf>). §1 para 1 no 1 KSchG defines 'entrepreneur' as 'a person who makes the transaction in the course of carrying on his business', with 'business' being defined by §1 para 2 KSchG as 'any organisation, which is intended to be permanent, for the purposes of independent commercial activity, even though it may be a non-profit enterprise'.

76 *M Spitzer*, Der Unternehmer im PHG, JBl 2003, 414.

beyond the immediate manufacturer of the final product to the producer of raw materials or components as well as to own branders.[77]

45 Those who merely provide make-ready services (ie finishing of an otherwise already complete product) fall outside the scope of said definition, whereas assemblers who create something new by putting together individual parts prefabricated by others stay within it. Drawing the line between the two is not always easy, though – the Austrian courts focus on the expertise of the provider, the expectations of their customers, and public perception of the product(s).[78] The less individual creativity is needed to complete the product, the more likely this last step will be mere make-ready service. For example, if pre-packaged individual parts of a piece of furniture are put together by the seller according to the instructions attached to the parts, this final act will merely make the furniture ready for sale rather than creating something new. On the other hand, if a new table is put together by combining a table-top produced by one company with a frame manufactured by another, a new product may have been assembled out of these two components, unless joining these parts could have been achieved by anybody without further expertise.[79]

46 Public entities can be held liable for *acta iure gestionis* if they thereby produce something and put it into circulation.[80]

B. IMPORTER

47 When Austria joined the EEA, the original wording of the PHG also had to be adjusted[81] in respect of the definition of the importer, who according to the original version was someone who imported goods into Austria. The new wording of §1 para 1 no 2 PHG now speaks of 'the entrepreneur by whom it was imported into and put into circulation in *the European Economic Area*' (emphasis added), in line with art 3(2) PLD and Annex III, adaptation (a)(i), to

---

77 §3 PHG reads: 'The term "producer" (§1 para 1 subpara 1) shall mean the person who has manufactured the finished product, a raw material or component part, as well as anybody who presents himself as producer by affixing to the product his name, trade mark or other distinguishing feature.'

78 *Koziol/Apathy/Koch*, HPR III³ (fn 24) no B/42 ff.

79 Cf OGH 23.11.2006, 8 Ob 136/06t, EvBl 2007/53 (cmt by *M Leitner*): a bistro table was sold to a company which used it on its trade fair stand. The table consisted of two parts – a glass top and a frame, each produced by different manufacturers. The seller of the table had put together this combination (without attaching its name, brand or label to it). Employees of the buyer were hurt when the glass top burst without external influence. The OGH could not deliver a final ruling, but at least considered that this was mere make-ready service since apparently neither special expertise nor creativity were decisive in bringing about said bistro table.

80 *Fitz/Grau* in PHG² (fn 35) §1 Rz 51. The *Veedfald* ruling (fn 31) has clarified this further.

81 *Supra* fn 15.

the EEA Agreement.[82] The wording of adaptation (a)(ii) of said Annex III was in essence copied into a new §17 PHG.[83] There are two major problems with these amendments, however:

- The Austrian legislator had acted prematurely – the EEA Agreement was adjusted by another Protocol[84] only one month after the promulgation of the amendments to the PHG in the Federal Gazette. This Protocol had become necessary because Switzerland after all had not joined the EEA like all the other EFTA states, which is why the definition of the term 'EFTA state' for purposes of the EEA Agreement was retrospectively changed to address all EFTA states *with the exception of Switzerland*. This subsequent modification of the EEA Agreement was never reflected in the wording of the PHG, though, and since Switzerland is still an EFTA state and has ratified the Lugano Convention in the meantime as required by §17 PHG as it stands, an importer into Switzerland is a possible defendant under the PHG even though this is in conflict with the PLD regime as amended by the EEA Agreement and the Protocol thereto.
- Another question arises with respect of Liechtenstein: does §1 para 1 no 2 PHG take precedence over §17 PHG? According to the former provision, importers into Liechtenstein can be sued under the PHG since they bring goods 'into ... the European Economic Area' (of which Liechtenstein is a member), whereas the latter rule postulates that the importer is the one that introduces products from an EFTA state (like Liechtenstein) 'into the European Economic Community' until said EFTA state has ratified the Lugano Convention, which Liechtenstein never has and most likely will not do in the foreseeable future. §17 PHG starts with the word 'moreover', which seems to indicate that it speaks of *further* importers *in addition to* those already included under §1 para 1 no 2 PHG. The model for §17 PHG – adaptation (a)(ii) of Annex III to the EEA Agreement – is not equally outspoken, though. Furthermore, the rationale for expanding product

82 [1994] OJ L1/321.

83 §17 PHG reads: 'Moreover, the term "importer" within the meaning of §1 para 1 subpara 2 shall mean the entrepreneur who imported the product for distribution from an EFTA state into the European Economic Community or from the European Economic Community into an EFTA state, or from an EFTA state into another EFTA state and put it into circulation. From the date when the Lugano Convention ... enters into force for an EC Member State or an EFTA state, this shall cease to be valid for states that have ratified the Convention, insofar as on the basis of these ratifications a national judgment, obtained to the benefit of the injured person, is enforceable against the producer or importer as defined by §1 para 1 subpara 2.' The legislator forgot to repeal the heading of the previous version of §17 PHG (which had been about increasing the lower threshold of property damage), so it now still carries the rather unsuitable heading 'Extra Charges', which of course has nothing to do with the current content of this provision.

84 Protocol Adjusting the Agreement on the European Economic Area of 17 March 1993 [1994] OJ L 1/572.

liability to importers in a country different from the victim's domicile is undoubtedly that the Brussels/Lugano regime[85] set out the procedural basis for pursuing and (more importantly) enforcing such claims, a possibility which would be entirely absent if said regime did not apply.[86] From a teleological point of view, therefore, importers into Liechtenstein should *not* fall under §1 para 1 no 2 PHG (despite its wording), so victims should (at least also) be able to raise claims against the first entity that imported goods from Liechtenstein into a jurisdiction where the Brussels/Lugano regime applies, ie into one of the EU Member States, Norway or Iceland.

C. SUPPLIER

48 In line with art 3(3) PLD, §1 para 2 PHG identifies the supplier as a 'backup' defendant if the producer or importer cannot be identified.[87] Again, though, the focus is exclusively on 'entrepreneurs' who supply the defective product,[88] which may lead to some deviations from the PLD model in Austrian practice.[89]

49 The supplier can escape liability if she names the producer or – where applicable – the importer of the defective product, but it equally suffices to nominate her own supplier (or anyone in the chain of distribution leading to her) who surprisingly need not have been an entrepreneur. In the latter case the victim consequently loses her claims under the PHG altogether since the supplier goes free and the person she nominated for that purpose is not covered by product liability at all.[90]

50 As is commonly accepted, providing only the name is not enough to free the supplier from liability under §1 para 2 PHG. Instead, sufficient contact details must be provided that enable the victim to successfully address her claims to the person nominated.[91] In contrast to other EU Member States, Austria abstained

85 The Brussels Convention was meanwhile replaced by the (now even recast) Brussels I Regulation, of course.

86 See also the explanations for §17 PHG given by the drafters of this rule at p 3 f of the explanatory memorandum cited *supra* fn 74, which clearly indicate that the new wording of §1 para 1 no 2 and §17 PHG combined shall only apply to importers against whom claims can be enforced under the Brussels/Lugano regime, which is still not true for Liechtenstein.

87 §1 para 2 PHG reads: 'Where the producer or – in the event of imported products – the importer (para 1 subpara 2 above) cannot be identified, any entrepreneur who has put the product into circulation shall be liable under para 1 above, unless he supplies the injured party within a reasonable period with the name of the producer or – in the case of imported products – of the importer or the party who has supplied the product.'

88 Cf *supra* no 43.

89 *Koziol/Apathy/Koch*, HPR III³ (fn 24) no B/70.

90 *Koziol/Apathy/Koch*, HPR III³ (fn 24) no B/75.

91 eg OGH 30.7.1992, 7 Ob 581/92.

from defining an exact time period within which the supplier has to provide said information. The drafters of the PHG thought that typically 'one or two weeks' would suffice.[92]

D. MULTIPLE TORTFEASORS

51 Multiple tortfeasors are generally jointly and severally liable in Austria,[93] unless their exact shares in causing the loss can be attributed individually.[94] The former is repeated for the special case of product liability by §10 PHG (implementing art 5 PLD), though without the latter exception. Joint and several liability for product defects therefore also applies if the loss is divisible and each part can be attributed to a specific liable person (eg if the defect of one specific component of the final product is the proven cause of an identifiable part of the victim's damage such as personal injury to a specific body part, whereas another component injures the victim elsewhere).[95]

E. RECOURSE

52 If one of multiple tortfeasors indemnifies the victim, she can seek recourse from the other tortfeasors for the part of the damages paid that exceed her own share,[96] which in case of doubt is ultimately determined per capita, even though

---

92 Explanatory Memorandum to the PHG Draft (fn 34) 9. In court practice, 16 days were still accepted (OGH 21.2.1995, 4 Ob 503/95, SZ 68/33), whereas more than five weeks was deemed too long (OGH 23.9.1999, 2 Ob 240/99d, SZ 72/141).

93 See generally *BA Koch/P Schwarzenegger*, Multiple Tortfeasors under Austrian Law, in: WVH Rogers (ed), Unification of Tort Law: Multiple Tortfeasors (2004) 9.

94 This is determined by §§1301 f ABGB, which read:
'§1301 ABGB. Multiple persons may become liable for unlawfully inflicted damage by contributing thereto jointly, in a direct or indirect manner, by instigating, threatening, ordering, helping, concealing or the like; or, by omitting to comply with a special duty to prevent the harm.
§1302 ABGB. In such a case, if the damage was caused negligently and the contributions to it can be determined, each participant is liable only for the part of the damage caused through his negligence. If, however, the damage was caused intentionally; or, if the contributions of each to the damage cannot be ascertained, all are liable for one, and one for all; the person having compensated the damage will, however, have a right of recourse against the others.'

95 This is expressly confirmed by the Explanatory Memorandum to the PHG Draft (fn 34) 13, but considered to be a rare case ('*seltenen Fällen*').

96 §12 para 1 PHG provides (without covering the entire range of options): 'If a person liable for compensation has paid damages and the defect of the product was caused neither by him nor by one of his agents, he shall be entitled to claim reimbursement from the producer of the defective finished product, raw material or component part. If several parties are liable for reimbursement, they shall be jointly and severally liable.'

§12 para 2 PHG requires the bases of liability attributable to the tortfeasors to be assessed first, and not just their shares in causing the harm.[97]

53 §12 para 3 PHG extends the concept of subsidiary liability of the supplier to the recourse action: if the person that indemnified the victim fails to identify an addressee of recourse claims under para 1 or 2 of said section, 'any entrepreneur who put the product into circulation prior to the party entitled to claim reimbursement shall be liable for reimbursement, unless he indicates within a reasonable period the producer or the party having supplied the product'. Again, the latter need not be an entrepreneur.[98]

54 These recourse claims are not deemed to be tort claims, which is why the short prescription period in §1489 ABGB does not apply,[99] but rather the standard thirty-year period in §1478 ABGB.[100]

IV. THE AGGRIEVED PERSON AND DAMAGE

A. THE AGGRIEVED PERSON

55 There are no limitations on to who may file claims under the PHG apart from the restrictions on the recoverability of property damage incurred by entrepreneurs.[101] The victim may therefore have bought the product herself, used it with or without the permission of its owner, or she might have been a third party who just happened to be in the wrong place at the wrong time when the product defect caused her harm.

B. THE NOTION OF DAMAGE

1) *Damage in General*

56 The PHG by and large[102] incorporates the provisions of the PLD when it comes to the definition of damage: only personal injury and property damage

97 §12 para 2 PHG reads: 'If several liable parties have contributed to the defect, the extent of the claim for reimbursement of the party that has compensated the damage against the other parties shall depend on the circumstances, in particular on the extent to which one or the other party is responsible for the damage or to which the damage was caused by bringing about a product defect.'

98 Cf *supra* no 49.

99 See *infra* nos 91–92 (with the relevant wording of §1489 ABGB in fn 159).

100 *Koziol/Apathy/Koch*, HPR III^3 (fn 24) no B/87.

101 See *infra* no 57.

102 See the qualifications and deviations in the following.

is covered, whereas pure economic loss is excluded (though not expressly).[103] As permitted by art 9 PLD, the 'national provisions relating to non-material damage' are not affected by the PHG, so that the provisions of the ABGB referred to by §14 PHG[104] also apply in product liability cases.[105]

2) *Business Property*

57 Deviating from art 9(b) PLD, the PHG originally failed to limit the recoverability of property damage to items 'intended for private use or consumption' and actually mainly used for such purpose by the victim. When the Austrian legislator tried to amend this when joining the EEA,[106] it committed the same mistake that was made when defining the defendant:[107] instead of referring to the damaged object's *use* as the language of art 9 PLD foresees, §2 no 1 PHG now requires that the property damage 'was not suffered by an entrepreneur who has used the object predominantly in his enterprise'. This leads to a conflict with the PLD regime in cases where, for example, an object normally used professionally is exceptionally in private use. If a defective product damages a professional kitchen appliance which an enthusiastic hobby chef has acquired for her home, such harm must be compensated by the producer under the PHG since the appliance 'was not suffered by an entrepreneur', whereas the PLD would exclude such harm because this gadget is not 'of a type ordinarily intended for private use'.[108]

3) *Damage to the Product Itself*

58 One of the most disputed questions of product liability (presumably not only) in Austria is whether product liability also applies in cases where the final

---

103 As to the latter, see eg OGH 24.11.1998, 1 Ob 184/98k, EvBl 1999/76; 29.4.1999, 2 Ob 162/97f, *Baurechtliche Blätter* (bbl) 1999/228 f.

104 *Supra* fn 18.

105 §1325 ABGB requires that 'damages for pain and suffering' have to paid for bodily injury. While jurisprudence awards damages for bereavement since about a decade, this is only true for fatal injuries inflicted by at least gross negligence or intent, which is why this is not available in product (or any other strict) liability cases: *Koziol/Apathy/Koch*, HPR III^3 (fn 24) no B/225.

106 *Supra* fn 15. As the Explanatory Memorandum to the amending act explains (fn 74, 4), this would not have been necessary as confirmed by the Commission: extending the scope of liability to objects not used or consumed privately, but in a business, would not have been in conflict with the PLD since these items were not within its scope anyhow. However, the Austrian legislator still tried to implement art 9(b) PLD fully 'since it was suggested by representatives of the industry' ('*zumal dies auch von Vertretern der Wirtschaft vorgeschlagen wird*' – an explanation which did not really come as a major surprise).

107 *Supra* no 43.

108 *Koziol/Apathy/Koch*, HPR III^3 (fn 24) no B/102 ff.

product itself is damaged due to a defect of one of its components (so-called '*Weiterfresserschäden*').[109]

59 It is clear that the producer of the final product cannot be held liable for such damage since §1 para 1 PHG (in line with art 9(b) PLD) makes clear that property damage is only covered 'if any tangible property *other than the product* is damaged' (emphasis added). This is a problem the victim has to solve on the basis of contract law with her supplier.[110]

60 The follow-up question remains, however, whether the manufacturer of the defective component can be held liable under the PHG for damage to the rest of the product, which should be answered in the affirmative,[111] even though the Austrian Supreme Court has ruled otherwise.[112] The component producer puts her parts into circulation by passing them on to the manufacturer of the final product. It would be an unbearable discrepancy if she were liable for spare parts delivered to a DIY store (which she undoubtedly would be), but not if items from the same production line (!) instead went to someone who built these parts into another (final) product.[113] This is not only true for single pieces of mass production that have some exceptional defect, but even more so in cases of construction defects, of course. One also has to bear in mind that art 2 PLD insists that a product remains one 'even if incorporated into another movable'.

4) Loss of Chance

61 The loss of a chance is not recognised as a distinct head of damage in Austrian law.[114]

---

109 There is no literal translation of this term, the closest being 'eat-through damage' (like acid 'eating through' some material). The term '*Weiterfresser*' implies that damage spreads within the product.

110 *Koziol/Apathy/Koch*, HPR III^3 (fn 24) no B/96.

111 Opponents argue that a component producer should not be liable for more than the manufacturer of the final product. This misses the point, however – the latter did not put the defective component as such into circulation, but the finished composed product which had the defective part inside. It is not the final product that causes damage to something else; rather, it carries the risk of damage to itself inside. See *Koziol/Apathy/Koch*, HPR III^3 (fn 24) no B/98 with further references.

112 OGH 3.2.1994, 8 Ob 536/93, SZ 67/22 (bursting cooling water hose in a car). Due to a more fundamental misapplication of the PHG by the OGH in this case (confusing the role of the importer), the 'ruling' is rather an *obiter dictum* with respect to the problem of '*Weiterfresserschäden*', see *Koziol/Apathy/Koch*, HPR III^3 (fn 24) no B/96 fn 230).

113 In the car example of fn 112, the producer of the hose is clearly liable if it had been sold to the car owner directly or added to her car by a garage during repair.

114 See also no 68 (at fn 126).

5) *Nuclear Damage*

62 The exception for nuclear damage contained in the original version of §15 para 2 PHG did not accurately reflect the contents of art 14 PLD: damage arising from nuclear accidents was excluded from the statute's scope altogether, even if these were not 'covered by international conventions ratified by the Member States' as the PLD had required. This was corrected by the 1993 amending statute.[115]

C. CAPS AND LIMITATIONS

63 Austria has abstained from introducing caps on liability as is possible under art 16(1) PLD.[116]

64 As far as property damage is concerned, Austria was forced to adopt the lower threshold of €500[117] foreseen by art 9(b) PLD like all other Member States,[118] which is unanimously frowned upon by academics[119] since such a lower limit was previously unknown to Austrian tort law and is seen just as critically as it was (unsuccessfully) litigated by France.[120]

V. CAUSALITY

A. CAUSATION IN GENERAL

65 The standard rules on causation apply to product liability as well. While art 4 PLD requires the victim *inter alia* to prove 'the causal relationship between

115 *Supra* fn 15.

116 See already *supra* no 08.

117 In the original version of the PHG, this threshold was lower: instead of 500 ECU, it had been set at ATS 5,000 (approximately €364), as the Directive's limit was deemed to be too high (see the Explanatory Memorandum to the PHG Draft, fn 34, 9). This was adjusted when Austria joined the EEA (fn 15).

118 One of the prime flaws of art 9 PLD is the fact that it fails to properly define the effect of the €500 lower threshold (apart from introducing it in the first place). Some jurisdictions, such as the Netherlands or the United Kingdom, perceive this to be a minimum damage rule, so that the full loss is compensated once it exceeds this amount. Others (including Austria) instead treat this as a deductible, so that the first €500 cannot be recovered at all. Cf the Third Report on the Application of the PLD, COM(2006)496 final, 11.

119 See eg *Koziol/Apathy/Koch*, HPR III^{3} (fn 24) no B/232 f.

120 ECJ 25.4.2002, Case C-52/00, *Commission v France*, ECLI:EU:C:2002:252 [2002] ECR I-3827; see also the follow-up decision of ECJ 14.3.2006, Case C-177/04, *Commission v France*, ECLI:EU:C:2006:173 [2006] ECR I-2461.

defect and damage', the Austrian legislator did not see any need to copy such wording into the PLD since it was deemed self-evident.[121]

66 This means that also in product liability, one has to differentiate between factual and legal causation, the former building upon the *conditio sine qua non*, the latter being referred to as the '*Adäquanzzusammenhang*' (adequacy of causation). Exceptions to the *conditio sine qua non* are recognised particularly in cases of uncertain causation due for example to alternative causes.[122]

B. ALTERNATIVE CAUSATION

67 If several external causes could alternatively have caused the harm in question, established practice holds all potential tortfeasors jointly and severally liable for the loss. This is based upon an analogy to §1301 f ABGB,[123] which apply via §14 PHG.[124]

68 If one of these alternative causes lies within the victim's own sphere, however, which was as prone to trigger the damage she suffered, and if there is a strong and convincing reason to attribute the loss to those responsible for the other potential causes, Austrian courts apply proportional liability as suggested by Bydlinski.[125] The loss of a chance theory is, however, commonly rejected,[126] not only because its results can often be achieved via Bydlinski's approach anyhow.

C. COMPARATIVE NEGLIGENCE

69 If one of several actual causes of the harm are attributable to the victim herself, either because of her own conduct, a source of harm within her own sphere, or some other risk that cannot be attributed to another, liability of the tortfeasor is reduced or even excluded altogether (depending upon the

121 See the Explanatory Memorandum to the PHG Draft (fn 34) 11: An express provision on the burden of proving harm, defect and causation was 'superfluous already in the Directive' ('*schon in der Richtlinie überflüssig*') as this corresponded to the national (tort) laws in force at the time anyhow.

122 See eg *H Koziol*, Causation under Austrian Law, in: J Spier (ed), Unification of Tort Law: Causation (2000) 11. Cf *id*, Basic Questions of Tort Law from a Germanic Perspective (2012) no 7/8.

123 These provisions are cited *supra* fn 94.

124 *Supra* fn 18.

125 See *BA Koch*, Causal Uncertainty and Proportional Liability in Austria, in: I Gilead/M Green/BA Koch (eds), Proportional Liability: Analytical and Comparative Perspectives (2013) 77 (in particular 83 ff).

126 See eg *H Koziol*, Basic Questions (fn 122) no 5/93 ff.

corresponding degree of impact) according to §1304 ABGB.[127] §11 PHG explicitly refers to said provision despite the fact that §14 PHG points to the ABGB in general anyhow.[128] There is one major difference in the way §1304 ABGB is applied in product liability as opposed to general tort law, though: while the wording of §1304 ABGB equally speaks of 'fault' by the victim, other causes within her own sphere also commonly lead to a reduction or exclusion of the defendant's liability, so for example if such cause would trigger strict liability if a third person had been harmed rather than the victim herself.[129] However, such other risks will not be considered in product liability, as the repetition of the term 'fault' in §11 PHG in line with art 8(2) PLD intended to express. It is therefore indeed just adverse conduct attributable to the victim (either by herself or by some auxiliary) that may have an impact on the extent of the producer's liability.[130]

VI. DEFENCES AND EXCLUSIONS

A. DEFENCES

70 §8 PHG lists a series of defences, which are meant to implement art 7(d)–(f) PLD:

> 'Liability shall not be excluded through lack of guilt but only by proving that:
> 1. the defect can be attributed to a legal provision or official instruction with which the product had to comply,
> 2. according to the state of technology at the time when the product was put into circulation by the person against whom an action is brought, its properties could not be recognised as a defect, or
> 3. if the person against whom an action is brought has produced merely a raw material or a component part – the defect was caused by the design of the product in which the raw material or component part was fitted, or by the instructions given by the producer of the product.'

---

127 This provision reads: 'If, in a case of damage, there is also fault on the part of the person harmed; he has to bear the loss proportionately with the injurer; and, if the proportion cannot be determined, in equal shares.' §1304 ABGB is used analogously in combination with §§1301 f ABGB in support of *Bydlinski's* proportional liability solution described *supra* no 67.

128 §11 PHG reads: 'If the injured person or a party for whose conduct he is responsible is at fault, §1304 of the Austrian Civil Code (ABGB) shall be applied mutatis mutandis.'

129 A typical example is a traffic accident case, where the victim is the keeper of a vehicle (falling under the strict liability rules of the Train and Motor Vehicle Liability Act) that was one of the causes of her own harm. See the extensive analysis of *Koziol*, Basic Questions (fn 122) no 6/204 ff, pointing *inter alia* to the fact that the term 'fault' is unsuitable in this context because the victim cannot act wrongfully vis-à-vis herself (no 6/215). Instead, one should rather speak of carelessness vis-à-vis one's own interests.

130 *Koziol/Apathy/Koch*, HPR III^3 (fn 24) no B/247.

1) *Compliance with Mandatory Regulations*

71 In line with art 7(d) PLD, §8 no 1 PHG excludes product liability if the defect resulted from the fact that the product had to comply with 'a legal provision or official instruction'.[131] The language of this provision already shall underline that there must have been a causal link between the norm and the defect – if the product were defective but the rule had been disobeyed, the defence would not apply. While norms of general application as well as individual orders and decrees are covered, compliance with mere industry standards or usage will not suffice.[132]

72 While it is clear that rules applicable at the place where the product is put into circulation are covered by this defence, those in force at the production site or in the export jurisdiction will have to be disregarded. Otherwise the producer could escape product liability by producing in or exporting from a jurisdiction where favourable rules (within the meaning of §8 no 1 PHG) apply.[133]

2) *Development Risk*

73 §5 para 1 no 3 PHG makes clear that the existence of a product defect must be determined in light of the circumstances at the time the product was put into circulation by the defendant, which means that a scientific discovery *after* the product left the manufacturer's sphere, but *before* the supplier passed it on to the victim will be relevant for the latter's (subsidiary) liability under §1 para 2 PHG. §8 no 2 PHG adds that it also must have been detectable at these points in time. Austria thereby implemented the development risk defence of art 7(e) PLD despite the fact that it was optional according to art 15(1)(b) PLD. As in the Directive's model, this defence does not focus on the defect as such or whether it could have been avoided, but on the possibility of discovering it.

74 The 'state of technology at the time when the product was put into circulation' is considered to be the highest imaginable standard of conduct, determined by the totality of any expertise available in science and technology.[134]

---

131 The latter is a slightly imprecise translation; the German original speaks of an order by an authority, so it must have been an act of the executive branch 'instructing' the manufacturer, importer or supplier. Whether this still falls within the scope of 'mandatory regulations issued by the public authorities' as expressed by art 7(d) PLD is disputed and will ultimately have to be clarified by the CJEU, but other language versions of the Directive seem to be in support of the Austrian solution by avoiding a technical term such as 'regulation' (cf the French, Spanish and Italian version: *'règles impératives émanant des pouvoirs publics', 'normas imperativas dictadas por los poderes públicos', 'regole imperative emanate dai poteri pubblici'*).

132 But see their relevance for defining the justified safety expectations *supra* fn 62.

133 See *Koziol/Apathy/Koch*, HPR III^3 (fn 24) no B/236.

134 The Explanatory Memorandum to the PHG Draft (fn 34) 12 speaks of the *'Inbegriff der Sachkunde ..., die im wissenschaftlichen und technischen Bereich allgemein zur Verfügung*

A single scientifically sound opinion published and accessible (which in times of the Internet is almost universally true) may suffice to increase the standard. Knowledge and expertise in the trade merely define the minimum, it is irrelevant whether the liable person had actually known or even could have become aware of the advance of science, as long as it has advanced.[135]

3) *Defect Originating from Another Co-Producer*

75 §8 no 3 PHG implements art 7(f) PLD and thereby makes clear that the producer of raw material or some component of the final product can escape liability vis-à-vis the victim if the former can prove that the origin of the defect was not in her sphere. In the case of raw materials, this necessarily means that the defect will not have existed at the time these were put into circulation (ie passed on to the producer of the final product), so that the supplier of raw materials will already succeed under §7 para 2 PHG.[136]

76 The first possible defence provided by §8 no 3 PHG relates to 'the design of the product in which the raw material or component part was fitted'. The defendant escapes liability if some other manufacturing step was already completed by another, and adding her own component did not contribute to the overall defectiveness of the product, which was already triggered by the previous construction (or the design of the product in general).[137] The second variant of the defence provided by §8 no 3 PHG to one of several contributors to a final product in its core resembles §8 no 1 PHG – compliance with orders, but this time instructions not by the authorities, but by another producer which are merely binding *inter partes*. This may be unsatisfactory for victims who have no insight into the production process and are unaware of such internal instructions (although they at least in theory could know the statutory norms

---

steht. Der Inbegriff der Sachkunde ist die Summe von Wissenschaft und Technik, die allgemein anerkannt ist und allgemein zur Verfügung steht.'

135 See eg OGH 30.6.2010, 9 Ob 60/09b, SZ 2010/77: it is irrelevant whether the actual producer had access to the latest state of science and technology or if he had taken all reasonable efforts to meet this standard. The decisive point is solely whether the defectiveness of the product could have been detected in the abstract.

136 See *infra* no 86 (at fn 154) and no 87. §8 no 3 PHG may still be helpful if the product is passed on from one contributing producer to another and the defendant receives an already defective unfinished product, adds her own (flawless) component and then passes it on to the next (or final) producer.

137 The first defence must not be interpreted narrowly, as *Grau*, Produktfehler (fn 35) 80, rightly argues, so any defectiveness of the product existing already at the time the defendant contributed to the manufacturing process must be relevant, not just 'the design of the product in which the raw material or component part was fitted'. In light of the reluctance of the CJEU (to say the least) to interpret exceptions or defences generously, it is doubtful, though, whether this opinion will stand the test of that court.

falling under §8 no 1 PHG). However, this is part of the policy underlying the Directive and therefore an unavoidable outcome.[138]

B. CONTRACTUAL EXCLUSION OF LIABILITY

77 As §9 PHG makes clear, product liability under this statute 'may be neither excluded nor limited beforehand'. Unlike art 12 PLD, this does not seem to be limited to the liability vis-à-vis the victim, but even extends to recourse actions. Common opinion holds, however, that the Directive's solution should be preferred and §9 PHG therefore interpreted narrowly.[139]

78 Apart from explicit waivers of liability also indirect variations of limiting or excluding liability are forbidden, such as *ex ante* definitions of what might constitute a defect or a waiver of certain instructions.[140]

VII. REMEDIES

79 Since neither the PLD nor the PHG define which remedies are available if product liability is given, the general rules of tort law apply via §14 PHG.

80 The language of the ABGB gives priority to restoration in kind,[141] which has little practical relevance, however. In practice, tort law claimants will typically ask for monetary compensation instead.

A. PERSONAL INJURY

81 If the victim was physically injured by a defective product, §1325 ABGB prescribes that the liable person 'must bear the costs of healing and compensate him for lost earnings, and, if the person harmed loses his earning capacity, also for the loss of future earnings, and moreover has to pay, on demand, damages for pain and suffering'.[142] Furthermore, if the injuries lead to some disfigurement of

---

138 *Koziol/Apathy/Koch*, HPR III^3 (fn 24) no B/243.

139 *Fitz/Grau*, PHG^2 (fn 35) §9 no 3.

140 See *Koziol/Apathy/Koch*, HPR III^3 (fn 24) no B/255 for details.

141 See the first sentence of §1323 ABGB quoted *infra* fn 145.

142 Compensable pecuniary loss not only includes the cost of treatment, but also, for example, rehabilitation, necessary adjustments of the victim's residence and other special needs, nursing costs, and even extends to costs of close relatives visiting the victim in the hospital or gratuities for the nursing staff. If home care is provided by family members, the costs of a professional nurse (including ancillary wage costs) will be awarded. Similarly, if the victim is no longer able to take care of the household, the costs of a household helper shall be covered

the victim, a separate amount may be awarded for the monetary consequences thereof (eg reduced prospects of finding a job).[143]

B. DEATH

82 The survivors of a deceased immediate victim can ask for the reimbursement of the funeral expenses (as long as these were reasonably spent) or the like, but also – more importantly – claim maintenance to the extent the deceased would have been obliged to pay.[144]

C. PROPERTY DAMAGE

83 The general rules also apply to property damage.[145] Since lost profits are only available in the event of gross negligence or intent, they are not recoverable in product liability, which attaches irrespective of fault.[146]

D. NON-COMPENSATORY DAMAGES

84 Non-compensatory forms of damages such as punitive damages are not recognised under Austrian law and are therefore unavailable. There is no exception in cases of product liability.

---

even if none is hired because a relative steps in. On details, see eg *K Danzl* in KBB[4] (fn 49) §1325 no 1 ff.

143 Originally, §1326 ABGB thought of reduced chances to find a spouse, which is why it still speaks primarily of female victims.

144 §1327 ABGB reads: 'If bodily injury results in death, not only must all expenses be compensated, but also what is lost thereby by the surviving dependants for whose maintenance the deceased was obliged to provide by law.' On damages for bereavement, which are only available if the harmful conduct was at least grossly negligent, see *supra* fn 105.

145 §§1323 f ABGB provide:
'§1323. In order to compensate for damage caused, everything must be re-turned to its previous state, or, if this is inappropriate, the estimated value must be reimbursed. If compensation relates only to the damage suffered, it is termed actual indemnification; insofar as it also includes lost profit and reparation of the offence suffered, it is termed full satisfaction.
§1324. If damage was caused through malicious intent or conspicuous negligence, the person harmed is entitled to claim full satisfaction; otherwise, he can only claim actual indemnification. Pursuant to this, when the law uses the general expression "compensation", it falls to be assessed which type of compensation is to be provided.'

146 *Koziol/Apathy/Koch*, HPR III[3] (fn 24) no B/228. For the same reason, the value of the damaged object according to the particular preferences as foreseen by §1331 ABGB cannot be recovered in product liability since this requires 'an act forbidden by criminal law, … wantonness and spitefulness'.

VIII. PROCEDURAL AND EVIDENTIAL ISSUES

A. BURDEN AND STANDARD OF PROOF[147]

1) *Burden of Proof*

85 It may come as no surprise that as a general rule, claimants in Austria have to prove that all the constituent elements of their claims are present in their case.[148] In the product liability scenario, the victim therefore has to prove that she incurred some damage which is recoverable under the PHG and which was caused by the defect of a product attributable to the defendant.[149] There is no need to specify what exactly was defective about or within the product, however. The claimant has to prove that the actual harmful product originated from the sphere of the defendant – which may be easier when suing the manufacturer, but gets trickier the closer one gets on the chain of distribution. In case of action against the importer, the product must have been part of the lot in fact imported by her, and if the supplier is the defendant under §1 para 2 PHG, the product must have been acquired from her and not from some alternative distributor, which may get difficult if it is a consumer good sold by many alternative providers on the market, even though the claimant may also benefit from the recognition of *prima facie* evidence in product liability cases.[150]

86 §7 PHG specifically assigns the burden of proof in three scenarios:[151]

- The victim need not establish that it was the defendant who put the defective product into circulation – this is presumed according to §7 para 1 PHG (in line with art 7(a) PLD) unless the defendant succeeds in proving the opposite.
- While the requirement that the defendant must have acted as an entrepreneur is questionable,[152] it is at least not for the victim to prove, but instead the defendant has to defeat such a presumption (§7 para 1 PHG). This is only true, however, if the defendant is either the producer or importer as defined by §1 para 1 PHG, whereas if the claimant seeks compensation from the supplier

147 *Koziol/Apathy/Koch*, HPR III³ (fn 24) no B/217 ff.

148 *H Koziol*, Österreichisches Haftpflichtrecht I (3rd edn 1997) no 16/6.

149 See also the Explanatory Memorandum to the PHG Draft (fn 34) 11.

150 *Fitz/Grau* in PHG² (fn 35) §7 no 5.

151 §7 PHG reads: '(1) If a producer or importer claims not to have put the object into circulation or not to have acted as an entrepreneur, the burden of proof shall rest with him. (2) If a person against whom an action is brought claims that the defect which caused the damage did not exist at the time of its being put into circulation, he shall show that, having regard to the circumstances, his claim is plausible.'

152 *Supra* no 43 ff.

(§1 para 2 PHG), the former has to prove that the latter was an entrepreneur in line with the general rule.[153]

- Furthermore, the defendant has to prove that the product was not (yet) defective at the time it was put into circulation.[154] However, the threshold is set in her favour: it suffices if the denial of defectiveness is merely probable under the circumstances.[155]

2) *Standard of Proof*

87 According to §272 *Zivilprozessordnung* (Austrian Code of Civil Procedure, ZPO), the relevant standard of proof is a 'high' degree of probability.[156] A mere preponderance of the evidence is generally considered unsuitable for Austrian civil procedure.[157] An exception to this is, however, the above-mentioned §7 para 2 PHG:[158] in order to prove that the product was not defective at the time it was put into circulation, the defendant only needs to prove that this was more likely than not under the circumstances ('*unter Berücksichtigung der Umstände wahrscheinlich*').

B. EXTINCTION OF CLAIMS (ART 11 PLD)

88 Rather than implementing art 11 PLD properly, the ten-year period was originally introduced by the 1988 PHG as an (objective) prescription period, thereby cutting the thirty-year long-term period of §1489 ABGB which otherwise applies to tort claims to one third.[159] Instead of extinguishing the

153 The supplier was not mentioned in §7 para 1 PHG on purpose, as the Explanatory Memorandum to the PHG Draft (fn 34) 11 expressly confirms.

154 §7 para 2 PHG. Unlike para 1, this also applies to the supplier.

155 This is in line with art 7(b) PLD. The PHG translation used in this text (fn 2) speaks of 'plausible' rather than 'probable'; the latter term is preferable in light of the English language version of the PLD.

156 *WH Rechberger*, in: HW Fasching/A Konecny (eds), Kommentar zu den Zivilprozessgesetzen, vol 3 (2nd edn 2004), vor §266 no 11. See also *Koziol* (fn 148) no 16/11.

157 *Rechberger* (fn 156) vor §266 no 11.

158 This provision reads: 'If a person against whom an action is brought claims that the defect which caused the damage did not exist at the time of its being put into circulation, he shall show that, having regard to the circumstances, his claim is plausible.'

159 §1489 ABGB reads: 'Compensation claims prescribe within three years starting with the time when the person harmed becomes aware of the damage and the identity of the wrongdoer, irrespective of the question whether damage was caused by the breach of a contractual duty or independently of any contract. If the person harmed has not become aware of the damage or the identity of the injurer or if the damage arose from one or more criminal offences, which can only be committed intentionally and are punishable with imprisonment of more than one year, the claim only expires after 30 years.' The thirty-year period starts to run from the harmful event (although this is increasingly disputed, cf *Koziol*, Basic Questions (fn 122), no 9/21 ff), whereas the three-year period cannot commence before the victim can pursue her claim (see *infra* no 91).

product liability claim altogether a decade after the defective product had been put into circulation, the claim was therefore merely converted into an *obligatio naturalis*,[160] and the standard rules on the consequences of an interruption of the limitation period applied as well. This deviation from art 11 PLD was corrected, however, when the PHG was amended on Austria's entry into the EEA.[161]

89 Unlike prescription, the passing of the ten-year extinction period must be recognised and applied by the judge *ex officio*, whereas prescription needs to be claimed and proven.[162]

C. PRESCRIPTION

90 When it comes to art 10 PLD, the Austrian legislator saw no need to specifically mention its three-year (subjective) prescription period in the PHG, since this was already (and still is) the standard short (subjective) limitation period in tort law under §1489 ABGB.[163]

91 However, the wording of §1489 ABGB[164] does not entirely match the requirements of art 10(1) PLD as the former only foresees knowledge of the damage and the identity of the wrongdoer as the trigger of the short prescription period, whereas art 10(1) PLD in addition requires awareness of the defect. Austrian court practice nevertheless applies §1489 ABGB in a way that complies with the Directive: the claimant has to know or at least should have known the major facts linking her harm with the sphere of the defendant before the three-year period can start to run,[165] so at least potential knowledge of the defect is necessary in product liability cases even though it is not expressly foreseen by statutory language.

IX. ALTERNATIVE REGULATIONS AND REMEDIES

92 As has already been explained in the introduction, the quasi-contractual concept of 'producers' liability' is still a valid cause of action that many victims of defective products may choose to pursue as an alternative route to compensation.[166]

---

160 A *Naturalobligation* cannot be enforced, but once paid cannot be recovered.
161 *Supra* fn 15.
162 *Welser/Rabl*, PHG^2 (fn 49) §13 no 8.
163 See the wording of the first sentence of this provision *supra* fn 159.
164 *Supra* fn 159.
165 See, eg, *W Dehn* in: KBB^4 (fn 49) §1489 no 5.
166 See *supra* no 04 f including the citations in fn 9.

93 Buyers of defective products may instead sue their seller for breach of contract, which not only allows them to seek redress for damage to the product itself,[167] but also claim compensation on under contractual liability. However, if the problem exclusively originated from within the producer's sphere,[168] the defendant may not be liable since the manufacturer is typically not deemed to be an auxiliary of a supplier unless the goods are specifically ordered for a client, which is why the defendant may successfully prove that she is not to blame for the claimant's loss.

94 Furthermore, but less likely, delictual bases of liability may come into play, for example based on violations of mandatory product specifications or breach of monitoring and/or recall obligations.[169]

95 Since most of Austria's population is covered by a social insurance regime,[170] the immediate consequences of bodily injury will be remedied by health insurance, which applies irrespective of the cause, thereby shifting the product liability question to the recourse stage, but only if the social insurance carrier decides to pursue such action against the producer.

X. ASSESSMENT OF DOMESTIC LAW

96 The Product Liability Act was received very well in practice – the number of Supreme Court decisions on this PLD-based regime by far exceeds the number of such cases in other EU jurisdictions. This was also recognised by the Commission's second report on the application of the PLD, where Austria was singled out as a model pupil.[171] To date, the Austrian Supreme Court alone has decided more than one hundred cases where the PHG was at least considered as a cause of action.

97 This does not mean, however, that the predecessor of product liability, the above-mentioned producers' liability on the basis of a quasi-contractual theory, is no longer relevant – it has been confirmed ever since, not only by the Austrian legislator when introducing the PHG, but also by the courts, that

167 Cf *supra* no 58 ff.

168 This is not the case, though, if the defect could and should have been detected by the seller before passing it on to her client.

169 See *supra* no 02 (at fn 3).

170 In fact, 99.9% of the Austrian population are covered by at least some social health insurance scheme, see *Hauptverband der österreichischen Sozialversicherungsträger* (ed), Die österreichische Sozialversicherung in Zahlen (33rd edn 2014) 13.

171 'In Austria nearly all product liability cases are solved on the sole basis of the system provided by the Directive': COM(2000)893 final, 6.

this cause of action remains valid alongside the delictual basis provided by the PHG. In the aforementioned mineral water bottle case of 2014, for example, the OGH confirmed both (alternative) causes of action against the mineral water producer.[172]

98 As to future challenges of product liability, whether and how these will be mastered on the basis of the existing regime will depend upon the suitability of its rules from a European perspective. One key question that is currently unresolved and awaiting clarification from the CJEU is whether digital content can contribute to the defectiveness of a product, and whether such a product must indeed be distributed on some tangible medium as the language of §4 PHG might imply, or whether a merely digital format would suffice. This will have an impact on products such as driverless cars or any other novel gadget with significant control and steering exercised by software, particularly if this software is updated after the original product was put into circulation. More generally, the reduction of the term 'movable' to tangible or corporeal objects by the Austrian statue yet has to stand the test of the CJEU.

99 When it comes to 3D printing, the manufacturer of the printer can easily be held liable under the existing system, even though the output of the 3D printer will not be attributable to its producer – if a user prints gun components, the victims of a shooting in which such a gun is used will not have claims against the printer manufacturer, just as victims of a stabbing cannot sue the knife producer under product liability. More challenging will be the question whether the user herself becomes a producer within the meaning of the Directive whenever she prints a (very tangible) product, even though this is often by using an STL file downloaded from the Internet. As long as the further qualifications are fulfilled (in particular if the product was manufactured for further distribution in the course of the printer's business), it is hard to see why she should not be deemed a producer within the meaning of the PLD.

100 If one had to add to a to-do-list for the European legislator, another important question is how to draw the line between services and other performances, which has been particularly tricky ever since it turned out that the PLD regime not only applied to mass production, but also to singular tailor-made items for a specific customer. Perhaps this latter decision has to be reconsidered, with individualised production, as well as personal counselling and other services, submitted to a different, more suitable liability regime.[173]

---

172 OGH 13.9.2012, 6 Ob 215/11b, EvBl 2013/16 (cmt by *M Spitzer*, cited already *supra* fn 3).

173 Cf *supra* fn 45.

PRODUCT LIABILITY IN THE CZECH REPUBLIC

Luboš Tichý

I. SOURCES OF LAW AND THEIR DEVELOPMENT

01 Czech law did not provide for product liability prior to the adoption of an act implementing Directive 85/374/EEC. It was possible to claim product liability within the general liability regime governed by the Civil Code of 1964 (Act No 40/1964 Sb), under which everybody was liable for damage that occurred as a result of a breach of one's legal duty (see §420(1) Civil Code). I am not aware of any such claims nor of the existence of any relevant case law. Such claims would therefore be raised only exceptionally, if at all.

02 The Directive was firstly implemented by Act No 59/1998 Sb on Product Liability, which came into force on 1 June 1998 – six years prior to the accession of the Czech Republic to the EU in 2004. Act No 59/1998 Sb was amended by Act No 209/2000 Sb, with a date of effect of 1 September 2000, to reflect further amendments of the Directive itself.

03 Both the formal and material characteristics of Act No 59/1998 Sb strongly resembled the Directive. It was divided into 12 sections and elements of liability governed by Act No 59/1998 Sb constituted an autonomous regulation, which resembled a regulation contained in the Civil Code, yet remained separate and distinctive.

04 A major change was brought about by the adoption of the new Civil Code (Act No 89/2012 Coll) that repealed Act No 59/1998 Sb and provided for product liability in provisions governing non-contractual liability. Thus product liability was made equal to other material elements of delictual liability such as liability for damage caused by movables or immovables. The Civil Code contains only five sections, whereas basic elements of liability are provided for in general provisions. It follows the Directive only loosely and its implementation is partially inaccurate. It provides only for derogations from a general liability regime for product defects. This is a major difference from the previous regulation, which also stipulated basic elements of liability.

05 Czech law does not provide for any other liability regimes for damage caused by new technologies.

II. BASIC ELEMENTS OF LIABILITY

06 The concept of 'a product' is not sufficiently defined. Švestka[1] refers to the wording of the then effective law and subsequently defines a product as a manufactured or otherwise produced movable irrespective of the manufacturing method that is used to bring it to market. Products are also component parts of a thing, appurtenances to a movable item or even an immovable. Electricity is also a product.

07 The legal definitions of the term are equally remarkable. §3 of Act No 59/1998 Sb defined a product as 'any movable that was manufactured, mined or otherwise produced or gained irrespective of the degree to which it was manufactured or brought to market.' Appurtenances to movables, immovables and electricity are products too. The Civil Code considers a product to be a new thing (see §2939(1): 'damaged caused by a movable thing that is to be brought to market as a product for the purpose of sale, lease or other utilization').

08 Clearly, the Civil Code contains inaccuracies. The definition does not explicitly mention electricity and even classes objects (things) built into movables or immovables as products.

09 Perhaps the only contribution of legal theory to this issue can be found in the textbook *Evropské parvo*, which explicitly states that electricity, gas, heat and other forms of energy must also be considered products. The category of product also involves human organs, blood and even garbage.[2]

---

1 *J Švestka*, in: M Knappová/J Švestka et al, Občanské právo hmotné (2002) 577.
2 *L Tichý*, in: Tichý et al., Evropské právo (5th ed 2014) 499.

10 Unfortunately, neither legal theory nor case law deals with recent technological developments. Textbooks merely refer to directives or laws. While §4 of Act No 59/1998 Sb adopted art 6 of the Directive, the Civil Code does not provide for any definition of 'defect'. §2941 stipulates that a defective product is a product whose use is not as safe as may be reasonably expected with regard to all circumstances, notably with regard to the manner in which the product was brought to market or advertised, or the supposed purpose for which the product is to be used, as well as with regard to the period in which the bringing to market occurred.

11 This issue of marketing of a product is completely omitted. Neither Act No 59/1998 Sb nor the Civil Code define 'putting into circulation' but use 'bringing to market' instead. There is no analysis of bringing to market whatsoever.

12 Czech law does not provide for any differentiation between various categories of products.

III. THE PERSON LIABLE FOR DAMAGE

13 Act No 59/1998 Sb defines a liable person as a person that manufactured, produced, mined, cultivated or otherwise extracted the product or its part. The person who provided his/her own name, brand or trademark (§2939(1) of the 2012 Civil Code) is then jointly and severally liable with the producer, as is the person who imported the product to place it on the market within his/her own business activity (§2939(2)of the Civil Code).

14 It follows that neither the producer nor provider of the name, brand or trademark must have any specific characteristics or qualifications. It may be anyone. It does not have to an entrepreneur. It may be an entity from the public sector or even a public body. It is only the importer who undertakes this conduct as/during his/her own business activity.

15 Recourse against producers is directly proportionate to their participation as stipulated by §7a of Act No 59/1998 Sb. This solution is also contained in general provision of §2916 the 2012 Civil Code governing recourse among the liable persons.

IV. THE AGGRIEVED PERSON AND DAMAGE

16 A claim may be raised by the aggrieved person in accordance with the general liability regime. Neither the 2012 Civil Code nor Act No 59/1998 Sb provide for any autonomous regulation.

17 According to §1 of Act No 59/1998 Sb the damage must have explicitly been done to 'a thing that is different from the defective product'. The Civil Code does not expressly provide for that. It is unclear whether or not this provision was omitted from the current legislation on purpose in order to enable compensation for damage caused by product defects.

18 The extent of damage and its type are governed by the general regime. Thus it is permissible to claim compensation for subsequent damage connected to the defects of the product, compensation for pure economic damage, compensation for loss of chance or compensation for immaterial damage. Compensation for objects used for or designed for a purpose that is predominantly something other than business-related is restricted in Act No 59/1998 Sb (see §1). These restrictions were also adopted by the 2012 Civil Code (§2943).

19 The only restriction applies to compensation for damage of a thing. The damage can be claimed only if the damage exceeded the amount of €500 on the day the damage occurred.

V. CAUSALITY

20 The issue of causality/direct link is not governed by product liability. In fact, there is no definition of this category in Czech law at all. Neither legal theory nor case law deals with this issue in these circumstances. Thus it is necessary to apply general principles as developed in case law and legal theory, which, unfortunately, are part of the most under-developed area of Czech tort law. Prevailing opinion does not distinguish between legal and factual causality. The current approach is based on the *conditio sine qua non* rule and on a doctrine of adequacy. Proportionate liability is permissible and is governed in cases of fault liability. According to prevailing opinion it is necessary to identify the decisive cause by reconstructing the usual course of events and usual experience.[3]

VI. DEFENCES AND EXCLUSIONS

21 Czech Republic did not use the opportunity to exclude the development risk defence. One may be released from liability if it is proved that 'the stage of scientific and technological knowledge did not enable one to identify origin of the product at the time when it was brought to market' (see §2942(2)(e)of the 2012 Civil Code) that was repeated word-for-word from the previous law.

3 *J Švestka* (fn 1) 459.

22 Compliance with legal regulations that are binding for producers is a factor in exclusion of the liability. In fact, this amounts to complete liberation from liability (§2942(2)(d) of the 2012 Civil Code). Any preliminary limitations of a right to compensation regime of damages are null and void (§2942(4) of the 2012 Civil Code).

VII. REMEDIES

23 Compensation for damage is governed by the general damage contained in the 2012 Civil Code. Pecuniary damage is compensated by restitution of the initial state and eventually by monetary compensation provided that such restoration is not possible or the injured expressly requests it (§2951(1) of the 2012 Civil Code).

24 Punitive, exemplary or nominal damages are impermissible. It is permissible to request removal of the product from the market or an *actio negatoria* preventing a product being put on the market.

VIII. PROCEDURAL AND EVIDENTIAL ISSUES

25 The objective standard of proof is the judge's conviction about the veracity of the evidence.[4] Any other standard of assessment thereof, including its binding relevance for the court and the extent to which it is prescribed by law, is impermissible.

26 While Act No 59/1998 Sb contained a special regulation of statutory bar, it is currently the general regime of the 2012 Civil Code that applies (§609). The limitation period is three years and claims for damage compensation lapse ten years after the day the damage occurred. A two-year limitation period starts to run from the occasion on which it was possible to raise the claim for the very first time, ie the moment the injured party became aware of the damage, the defect and the identity of the producer, or at least the moment the party could have and should have become aware (see §§619 and 620(2) of the 2012 Civil Code). The limitation period is suspended where the entitled person is prevented from raising the claim and in cases of *vis maior* (§§650 and 651 of the 2012 Civil Code). In cases where the limitation period continues after the disappearance of the obstacle, the limitation period may not expire earlier than six months from the day on which the said obstacle disappeared.

4 Judgment of the Supreme Court, SJ 93/2001.

27 The claimant is required to cover all damages to property and court fees of 4% of the compensation sought. The injured party does not have to be represented by a lawyer. Mass actions have not been governed so far.

IX. ALTERNATIVE REGULATIONS AND REMEDIES

28 The injured party may seek to initiate administrative proceedings with the producer in cases where, for instance, the producer breached technical standards requirements (Act No 22/1997 Coll.) or distributes or places to a greater extent on the market products that do not meet the expectations of consumers and that may be potentially harmful to them (see Act No 634/1992 Coll, on Protection of Consumers). This also applies to goods which cannot be classified as products for the purpose of product liability law. There is no duty to recall defective products from the market. According to §253 of the Penal Code (Act No 40/2009 Coll), causing harm to a consumer may result in criminal responsibility.

X. ASSESSMENT OF DOMESTIC LAW

29 Product liability law is rarely applied in practice; it is difficult to find the reasons for this. The Directive has been implemented in national law. The Czech Republic did not implement arts 4, 8(1) or 9(b). The definition of product is very general and therefore seems to be sufficient to cover new technologies.

PRODUCT LIABILITY IN DENMARK

Marie-Louise Holle and Peter Møgelvang-Hansen

I. SOURCES OF LAW AND THEIR EVOLUTION

A. DANISH LAW BEFORE THE PRODUCT LIABILITY DIRECTIVE

01 The original Danish rules on product liability constituted a rather simple system. The liability of producers and suppliers for physical damage caused by dangerous/defective products was based on fault/negligence (*culpa*) following the ordinary principles of Danish judge-made tort law. A special feature was a court-developed principle of professional suppliers' vicarious liability for product liability incurred by a previous link in the chain of production or distribution.[1] The main justification for this principle is generally sought in the fact that the supplier is usually in a better position than the injured party to influence and to seek recourse against the producer and other previous links in the chain of distribution.

02 The principles mentioned above are based on (non-statutory) tort law and have no counterpart in sales law. Personal injury and damage caused to property (other than the defective product itself) are outside the scope of the seller's liability for breach of contract. This is not stipulated explicitly in any of the provisions of the Sale of Goods Act (from 1906) but has been and still is the way the Act is interpreted based on the *travaux préparatoires* of the Act.[2] An exception to this, concerning damage to the buyer's property, is found in international non-consumer sales, see CISG arts 5 ff.

B. IMPLEMENTATION OF THE PRODUCT LIABILITY DIRECTIVE

03 In order to maintain the pre-existing rules as far as possible and going no further than required by the Directive, the Danish rules implementing the Directive were added 'on top' of the existing non-statutory rules. Thus, the 1989 Danish Product Liability Act (PLA)[3] introduced the Directive's strict (no-fault) defect liability for the 'producer' (with a development risk defence) and codified the pre-existing principle of professional suppliers' vicarious liability for product liability incurred by a previous link in the chain of production and distribution. Apart from codifying the rule on vicarious liability and adopting the rules of the Directive, the PLA does not lay down rules on questions not dealt with by the Directive, leaving such questions (on for instance causation, the concept and assessment of damages, etc) to be determined in accordance with the general rules and principles of Danish tort law. The Act does not include any maximum of the amount of the indemnity or compensation. As is the case with the Directive, the PLA is limited to personal injury and damage to consumers' property.

---

1 The leading Supreme Court case is *Ugeskrift for Retsvæsen* 1939 p. 16; see *B Dahl*, Produktansvarsstudier (1984) 33.

2 According to a well-established legal tradition common to the Nordic countries, the *travaux préparatoires* constitute an important aid to interpreting legislation, see eg Case C-478/99, *Commission v Sweden* [2002] ECR I-4147, concerning the implementation of the Unfair Contract Terms Directive 93/13/EEC.

3 Act no 371/1989.

04 The PLA of 1989 originally stipulated that suppliers were vicariously liable for the producers' strict liability. In its preliminary ruling in *Skov Æg*[4] the CJEU ruled that the supplier's vicarious liability for the producer's no-fault liability was in conflict with the Directive. The vicarious liability rule of the PLA was amended accordingly to the effect that suppliers are now vicariously liable only for the producer's (and other previous commercial links') fault-based liability, see section 10a of the PLA.[5] In addition a new rule, PLA section 10 presuming supplier's fault in cases of injury caused by defective products, was enacted in order to maintain as much as possible of the suppliers' previous (pre-*Skov Æg*) liability.

C. PRESENT SOURCES OF PRODUCT LIABILITY LAW

05 As a result of the implementation process and the corrections made necessary by *Skov Æg*, the question concerning liability for personal injury and damage to consumers' property is now regulated by two sets of rules: the original non-statutory ones developed by the courts, and the rules dictated by the Directive. Thus, both the court-developed principles (CDPL) and the rules of the PLA apply to personal injury and damage to consumers' property whereas only the court-developed principles apply to damage to non-consumer property.

06 Under Danish law personal injury and damage caused to property (other than the defective product itself) are outside the scope of a seller's liability for breach of contract. No explicit rule to this effect is found in the Sale of Goods Act but the Act has been and still is understood in this way by the courts.[6] In the wake of *Skov Æg* the Danish Minister of Justice appointed a committee to consider an amendment of the Danish Sale of Goods Act in order to improve the protection of consumers without placing disproportionate burdens on the sellers. In its report the committee recommended an amendment of the Sale of Goods Act to the effect that the seller's liability for damage caused by non-conforming goods would include personal injury and damage to property.[7] The report has not resulted in a bill (so far).

07 Special rules on product liability are found in the Act on Access to Complaint and Compensation within the Health Service, see below no 27 ff.

---

4 Case C-402/03, *Skov Æg v Bilka Lavprisvarehus* [2006] ECR I-199.

5 As amended by Act no 541/2006.

6 *J Lookofsky/V Ulfbeck*, Køb. Dansk indenlandsk købsret (4th ed 2015) 205–206.

7 Report no 1502/2008 on certain rules lack of conformity due to security defects (*Betænkning 1502/2008 om visse køberetlige regler om sikkerhedsmangler*).

II. BASIC ELEMENTS OF LIABILITY

A. ACCORDING TO THE PRODUCT LIABILITY ACT

08 The Act consists of 18 sections. With regard to scope, terminology and level of detail, the rules in PLA are very close to the rules of the Directive. The only noticeable deviations from the Directive are a few rules on suppliers' liability and recourse against producers, sections 10, 10a and 11.[8]

09 Section 1 lays down the scope of the PLA by stating that it deals with the liability of a producer and a supplier for damage caused by a defective product produced or supplied.

10 Whereas the requirement of a causal link between the defect and the damage is not defined in the Act, the other basic operative/constitutive terms (damage, product, producer and defect) are defined in the subsequent sections of the Act, in Chapter 2.[9] The Act applies only to personal injury and damage to consumer property (other than damage to the product itself).[10]

11 Legal causation is also a condition for liability under the CDPL and this condition is understood and applied in the same way under both sets of liability rules.[11] The same is true as far as the assessment of damages is concerned (except the rule of deduction of a self-risk in case of damage to property).[12] Section 9[13] deals with the injured person's contributory negligence which may lead to reduction of a claim for damages.[14] This rule is also the same as the one applicable according to the CDPL.[15] There is no rule limiting the total amount of damage resulting from personal injury caused by identical items having the same effect.[16]

12 Section 7 contains exemptions from liability in various special cases (the burden of proof being with the manufacturer).[17] Limitation rules are found in PLA section 14.[18]

---

8 See below no 30 ff.

9 Sections 2–5.

10 Section 2 implementing art 9 of the Directive.

11 *A Schønbeck*, Produktansvar – overblik og kontraktuel håndtering (2015) 25 and *Dahl/Møgelvang-Hansen*, Karnov online, Kommentarer til produktansvarsloven, note 82. See below no 40 ff.

12 *Dahl/Møgelvang-Hansen* (fn 11) note 15.

13 Implementing art 8(2) of the Directive.

14 See below no 40 ff for details.

15 *Dahl/Møgelvang-Hansen* (fn 11) note 110.

16 Art 16(1) Directive.

17 *Schønbeck* (fn 11) 45 ff.

18 Implementing art 10 of the Directive.

B. COURT-DEVELOPED PRODUCT LIABILITY

13 As a rule the CDPL does not entail that special liability rules are applied but merely the application of the general non-statutory tort law principles which are flexible enough to allow the courts (as is the case in many other special areas of tort law) to apply the general rules in a way that takes into account the special circumstances characterising the type of case at hand, for instance the need for a more or less strict evaluation of the basic requirement of fault. This means that generally (as far as the CDPL is concerned) the importance of the classification of a case as a product liability case should not be exaggerated as the same liability rules to a large extent may also be applied in a similar manner in a case with many of the characteristics of the typical product liability case although it is not a product liability case in a strict doctrinal sense.[19]

14 One important exception to the general tort rules is the principle of suppliers' vicarious liability which is now a firm rule applied in product liability cases (and certain other types of cases, eg employer's liability), whereas in other areas of tort law vicarious liability is only applied on an *ad hoc* basis taking into account all the circumstances of the individual case.[20]

15 The basis of liability under the CDPL is fault/negligence (*culpa*).[21] This is in accordance with the general rules of Danish tort law and the plaintiff must show this. However, in court practice it is often sufficient for the plaintiff to demonstrate that the product is dangerous/defective, because based on the nature of the defect the courts assume that the producer has acted in a negligent manner, thereby inferring liability on the part of the producer.[22] An example of this, bordering on strict liability, is the Western High Court case from 1986 concerning dental damage caused by a pebble in wholegrain rye bread.[23]

16 The CDPL supplement the PLA not only in cases that are outside the scope of the PLA and the Directive, but also in cases that are within the scope of the Act and the Directive, because neither the PLA nor the Directive affect the general fault-based tort rules.[24] This means *inter alia* that the self-risk/

---

19 See *Bryde Andersen/Lookofsky*, Lærebog i Obligationsret I (4th ed 2015) 468 ff and *V Ulfbeck*, Erstatningsretlige grænseområder (2nd ed 2010) 190 f.

20 Furthermore the classification of a case as a product liability case is important in that it defines one aspect of the scope of the Sale of Goods Act. See above nos 01–02 and below no 17 ff. See also *M-L Holle*, Hæftelsesansvar for selvstændigt virkende tredjemænd (2013) 79 ff.

21 *Bryde Andersen/Lookofsky* (fn 19) 490 ff.

22 *Schønbeck* (fn 11) 44; *Bryde Andersen/Lookofsky* (fn 19) 493 f.

23 *Ugeskrift for Retsvæsen* 1986 p 205 V.

24 Art 13 of the Directive and PLA section 13.

threshold rule (required by the Directive as far as damage to consumer property is concerned)[25] has no effect in cases where the producer etc acted negligently.

C. WHICH PRODUCTS?

17 The term 'product' is defined in PLA section 3, which follows the definition in art 2 of the Directive. A product means any movable, whether this has been manufactured, is a natural product or whether it has been used as a component part of another movable or attached to real property as a fixture. As for the concept 'movable', Danish authors do not seem to be sure whether 'movable' should be defined according to national law (which in the case of Danish law would be the definition following from the Credit Agreement Act, section 4(1)(15)) or whether it is an autonomous notion of EU law. However, Danish authors believe that either way the concepts are identical or at least not conflicting.[26]

18 While immovable property as such is clearly excluded from the PLA, prefabricated buildings ready for delivery are not. Standard houses are also not included, but the various things making up for example a house, such as bricks and tiles, are considered products within the meaning of the PLA.[27] Property attached to immovable property also falls within the scope of the PLA. Components taken away from immovable property are also included, such as gravel and plants.[28] Generally, products do not cease to be products in the meaning of the Act if they are mixed and become a new product. For instance, wheat flour remains a 'product' even though it is integrated into another product, bread.[29]

19 Furthermore, energy sources such as electricity, gas and water are 'products' in the sense of the PLA.

20 Services do not fall within the sphere of application of PLA.[30] However, if the performance of the service includes the delivery of material things, for example spare parts during repair, the latter are considered to be products within the scope of the Act.

21 Immaterial performances are outside the scope of the PLA. It has been discussed to what extent an immaterial performance, for example information, appearing on for instance nautical charts or a software media, are 'products'

25 Art 9 of the Directive and PLA section 8.
26 *Dahl/Møgelvang-Hansen* (fn 11) note 27.
27 *Schønbeck* (fn 11) 33.
28 *Dahl/Møgelvang-Hansen* (fn 11) note 27.
29 See for instance *Ugeskrift for Retsvæsen* 1986 p 205 V and above no 13 ff.
30 *Schønbeck* (fn 11) 34.

within the scope of PLA. In a case from 2007, the Maritime and Commercial Court had initially ruled that the publisher (a public agency) of a nautical chart was liable according to PLA for the damage to a boat owner's boat that ran aground. The chart indicated an incorrect water depth due to information that had disappeared during the conversion of the old maps to digital form some years earlier. On appeal the Supreme Court decided the case in favour of the publisher without deciding upon the question whether the chart was a 'product'.[31] Parts of the legal doctrine argue in favour of the interpretation that publications are not 'products' insofar as the information content of the publication (eg a naval chart) is concerned[32] and that the same goes for software with the possible qualification that software 'information' may be considered an integrated part of a 'product' (eg a chip) if the 'information' is directed to hardware, whereas information directed to the user of the device, etc is not.[33]

22 The 'product' concept according to the CDPL is much broader but without clear boundaries. Thus, not only do all material objects produced, sold and consumed fall within the scope of the CDPL, but so do services.[34] As mentioned above no 13 ff, the practical importance of a precise delimitation of the CDPL is often rather modest. In some instances, however, the classification may have important legal effects, see for instance the 2008 Supreme Court decision where a fire in a power plant was caused by a negligently installed safety membrane.[35] The construction company that performed the installation pleaded without success that consequential loss caused by the fire was within the scope of a contract term limiting liability. The Supreme Court held that the contract term in question applied to contractual liability loss only. As the case did not concern the contractor's contractual liability for the non-conforming installation, but rather product liability, the loss was not within the scope of the liability limitation term.[36]

D. THE CONCEPT OF DEFECT

23 The basic requirement according to the CDPL was originally that the product is 'dangerous', ie had properties that entail an unacceptable risk of damage to its surroundings during the usual consumption process, stressing

---

31 *Ugeskrift for Retsvæsen* 2007 p. 2128.

32 *Ulfbeck* (fn 19) 273 f; *Bryde Andersen/Lookofsky* (fn 19) 454 and 499 f. Cf *Dahl/Møgelvang-Hansen* (fn 11) note 27; *B Gomard*, Obligationsret Del 2 (4th ed 2011) 285.

33 See *B Gano*, Publikationer og softwares produktkarakter i henhold til produktansvarsdirektivet – Er visse immaterielle produkter omfattet af art. 2? (2009) 3 Justitia 46.

34 See *B Dahl et al*, in: Juristen 1990, 147.

35 *Ugeskrift for Retsvæsen* 2008 p. 982.

36 See for details *P Møgelvang-Hansen*, in: G Cordero-Moss (ed), Boilerplate Clauses, International Commercial Contracts and the Applicable Law (2011) 251 ff.

that the damage-causing potential is not due to the consumer's own inadequate handling of the product. In addition, the CDPL requires fault/negligence. The concept of 'dangerousness' is quite similar to the concept of 'defect' in PLA section 5, ie that the product is not as safe as may reasonably be expected.[37]

24 A 'defective' product may often also constitute breach of contract, but the test is not the same as a lack of conformity test under the Sale of Goods Act.[38] 'Defect' can be understood both in a positive and a negative sense. In a positive sense it means that the product lacks properties that it may reasonably be expected to have; in a negative sense, it means that the product has properties it cannot reasonably be expected to have. The risk of damage depends not only on the product itself but also on how it used. When the interplay between product and use results in damage, the fundamental question becomes whether the damage is due to the use or a defect.[39] The marketing of the product is also evaluated in this objective and general analysis. Three types of defects are envisaged in doctrine and case law: errors of construction or design (general problems with the product series), of fabrication (problems with a single product unit), and of instruction (the instructions accompanying or not accompanying the product are either wrong or insufficient).

25 A Supreme Court case from 2015 about damage to non-consumer property was decided on the basis of the CDPL: a grill bar burned down in a fire caused by a deep-fat fryer which had been re-assembled after its weekly cleaning in a different way than explicitly indicated by the operating instructions. There was a considerable risk of fire if the deep-fat fryer was not assembled in the right way. As it was uncomplicated to design the deep-fat fryer in such way that it could not be switched on unless it was assembled correctly, the Supreme Court ruled that the deep-fat fryer was defective due to a design error and that this triggered producer liability on the basis of negligence, and also the supplier's vicarious liability. The information given in the operating instructions could not lead to another result, and the rules on the injured party's contributory negligence could not justify a reduction of the liability.[40]

26 All activities and all information fit to influence consumers' expectations may entail that the product is defective.[41] The marketing may in itself cause a defect; this also goes for the instructions accompanying the product. See for instance the 1994 Supreme Court case where the majority of the Supreme Court (three of five justices) ruled that the producer of a kitchen stove ought to have

---

37 *Bryde Andersen/Lookofsky* (fn 19) 475 and 501.
38 *Ulfbeck* (fn 19) 199 ff; *Schønbeck* (fn 11) 37.
39 *Dahl/Møgelvang-Hansen* (fn 11) note 60 ff; *Schønbeck* (fn 11) 37 f.
40 *Ugeskrift for Retsvæsen* 2015 p 2455.
41 *Dahl/Møgelvang-Hansen* (fn 11) note 64.

taken into consideration that some consumers might place the stove on a socle and that the consumers ought to have been warned against the risk that the stove might slip from the socle and cause serious personal injury. The case was decided on the basis of the CDPL.[42]

E. THE ACT ON ACCESS TO COMPLAINT AND COMPENSATION WITHIN THE HEALTH SERVICE[43]

27 The Act contains special rules offering patients compensation to a wider extent than do the PLA and the CDPL in that the schemes also cover the development risk, the burden of proof of causation is less onerous, and the patient's conduct may lead to a reduction of the compensation only in the case of gross negligence.

28 Part 4 of the Act provides a special scheme concerning pharmaceutical injury, ie physical injury suffered by patients as a result of properties in pharmaceuticals used in connection with examination, treatment and the like. The scheme applies to pharmaceuticals approved for marketing in Denmark and dispensed through a pharmacy, physician, hospital, etc. It covers injury that occurs as a result of adverse drug reactions if the nature or extent of these reactions exceeds what the injured person should reasonably accept. The provision comprises both known and unknown adverse drugs reactions as well as concretely foreseeable and unforeseeable adverse drug reactions. Damages are paid if there is a preponderance of evidence that the injury was caused by the use of pharmaceuticals. The compensation may be reduced only if the patient contributed to the injury intentionally or by gross negligence. The compensation is paid by the state. The state is subrogated to the patient's claim against pharmaceutical producers and suppliers in pursuance of the PLA.

29 Furthermore, Part 3 of the Act on Access to Complaint and Compensation within the Health Service has established a patients' insurance scheme covering (*inter alia*) injury caused with a preponderance of evidence by the malfunction or failure of technical apparatus, instruments or other equipment used for or in connection with examination, treatment or the like. Compensation for the patient can be reduced only if the patient contributed to the injury wilfully or through gross negligence. Insofar as there is a liability to pay compensation pursuant to the provisions of the PLA, compensation paid under the patients' insurance scheme forms basis for a recourse claim.

---

42 *Ugeskrift for Retsvæsen* 1994 p 53.

43 Consolidated Act no 1113/2011 as amended most recently by Act no 742/2015.

III. THE PERSONS LIABLE FOR DAMAGE

30 All business links in the chain of distribution are liable for injury and damage caused by their own negligence/fault. In some cases the defect per se may give sufficient basis for assuming negligence, see above no 13 ff.

31 According to the CDPL, all business links in the chain of distribution are vicariously liable for the producer's and other previous links' product liability with a right of full recourse against all liable previous links according to general tort law. See below no 40 ff.

32 Also as far as the PLA liability is concerned, business suppliers[44] are vicariously liable for the producer's (and other previous links') fault-based liability, but not the producer's strict liability, see section 10a of the PLA.[45] A vicariously liable supplier has the right of full recourse against the previous suppliers in the line of distribution and the producer, PLA section 11(3). This rule is mandatory to the benefit of a vicariously liable supplier, PLA section 12.

33 Furthermore, suppliers are liable for their own fault/negligence according to PLA section 10, which lays down a presumption of negligence.

34 Public entities may be producers or suppliers and may as such be liable under the PLA and the CDPL.[46]

IV. THE AGGRIEVED PERSON AND DAMAGE

35 Product liability concerns physical damage to person or property, including consequential economic loss in accordance with the general tort law rules. Pure economic loss is outside the scope of the PLA. Whereas pure economic loss may often trigger liability in accordance with the general, non-statutory tort law, such damage is not considered to be within the scope of the CDPL.[47]

36 The person injured, or in the case of death the dependants, may claim damages in accordance with the general tort rules, according to which the injured person is entitled to compensation also for non-economic loss, ie pain and suffering and permanent injury.

---

44 According to PLA section 4(3) a supplier is an entity that puts a product in circulation without being a producer in the meaning of PLA (and the Directive).

45 See above nos 03–04 on *Skov Æg* and amendment Act no 541/2006.

46 Cf Case C-203/99, *Veedfald* [2001] ECR I-3569 and *Ugeskrift for Retsvæsen* 2007 p 2128 (see above no 17 ff).

47 The practical impact of this is rather limited, see above no 13 ff.

37 According to PLA section 8 an amount of DKK 4,000 (ECU 500) is to be deducted from the amount of compensation for damage to consumer property.[48] However, if the injured person is able to prove that the damage was caused by negligence, the CDPL may be invoked to the effect that the consumer is entitled to full compensation for any damage to items of property.

38 Damage to the product itself is neither within the scope of PLA nor the scope of the CDPL; see nos 01–02 and 05–07.

39 The Act does not include any maximum concerning the amount of the indemnity or compensation.

V. CAUSALITY

40 General tort law rules on factual and legal causation also govern product liability, meaning the causal relationship between the defective product and the damage.[49] The rules on causation are developed by the courts. To a large extent the decision depends on the specific context. The question is closely connected with procedural questions and the burden of proof. As elsewhere in tort law, the burden of proof for causation generally is with the plaintiff.[50]

41 However, in product liability cases courts often assume causation once the plaintiff has proven a violation of safety rules or clear negligence.[51] Other factors may also influence the burden of proof of causation, see below no 55 ff.

42 Proof of causation may be either direct in the sense that circumstances are sufficient to establish a causal relation by supplying eye-witnesses or registrations/recordings by technical appliances, or indirect in the sense that a causal relation between the manufacturer's conduct and the damage can be deducted from the circumstances at hand, for example by way of excluding alternative explanations. For illustration, in a 19

48 PLA section 8 and art 9(b) of the Directive.

49 *Bryde Andersen/Lookofsky* (fn 19) 484 ff and 505; *B Von Eyben/H Isager*, Lærebog i erstatningsret (8th ed 2015) 303 ff.

50 *J Rostock-Jensen/A Kvist-Kristensen*, Produktansvar – Produktansvarsloven (2004) 81 ff; *Schønbeck* (fn 11) 42.

51 *Ulfbeck* (fn 19) 191; *Schønbeck* (fn 11) 44; *Bryde Andersen/Lookofsky* (fn 19) 484.

39 case, the Supreme Court majority held that there was a causal relation between defect molasses and dead cows; the only piece of evidence was the fact that the dead cows were fed with the molasses and that three calves that were still alive were not.[52]

43 The special compensation schemes codified in the Danish Act on the Access to Complaint and Compensation within the Health Service[53] obey other rules. Causation is particularly difficult to prove in this area, as the determination of the origin of the injury may often be difficult to determine, and because plaintiffs (who are already patients or victims of accidents) often suffer several damages.[54] According to the Act a preponderance of evidence showing that the injury was caused by the use of pharmaceuticals, etc is sufficient proof of causation.

44 The preponderance of evidence rule is in contrast to what is considered to be the general rule in tort law. However, it is not easy to state as a general rule how much more than a preponderance of evidence is required in other areas of product liability law, because in case law the question depends to a large extent on the particulars of the individual case.[55]

45 PLA section 11(1) provides that two or more liable entities are jointly and severally liable vis-à-vis the injured party. This is in accordance with the solution under the general rules of tort law, and it also applies under the CDPL.[56]

46 In the absence of an agreement between two or more liable entities who are the actual producers or present themselves as such,[57] liability is apportioned according to the cause of the defect, the individual producer's opportunity and possibility of controlling the product, existing liability insurance policies, etc, see PLA section 11(2).[58] The same principle applies in cases outside the scope of PLA.[59] Vicariously liable suppliers have full recourse against earlier links, see PLA section 11(3) and above no 30 ff.

47 Contributory negligence from the injured party is governed by PLA section 9(1). Negligence on the part of the injured party may result in a reduction of damages. Under the general tort law rules, when the court holds that the injured party contributed to the injury with negligence of a certain importance,

---

52 *Ugeskrift for Retsvæsen* 1939 p 16; *Bryde Andersen/Lookofsky* (fn 19) 484 ff.
53 See above no 27 ff.
54 *Von Eyben/Isager* (fn 49) 416 f.
55 *Von Eyben/Isager* (fn 49) 303 ff.
56 *Schønbeck* (fn 11) 53; *Von Eyben/Isager* (fn 49) 457 ff.
57 ie producer as defined in art 3(1) of the Directive implemented in PLA section 4(1).
58 *Rostock-Jensen/Kvist-Kristensen* (fn 50) 188 f.
59 Section 25 of the Consolidated Liability Act no 266/2014.

damages are reduced by either a third, a half or two-thirds, depending on the degree of negligence. The principle codified in PLA section 9(1) reflects a general principle and also applies as such under the CDPL.[60] Acceptance of risk is dealt with in the same manner as negligence.[61] The rule on imputed contributory negligence[62] also applies both under the PLA and the CDPL, meaning that if the damage was caused partly by a defect in the product and partly by a person for whom the injured party was vicariously liable, damages may be reduced or even not awarded at all.[63] This is in accordance with the general rules on imputed contributory negligence.[64]

VI. DEFENCES AND EXCLUSIONS

48 The wording of section 7 of the PLA is very close to art 7 of the Directive. Thus according to PLA section 7(1), the producer is not liable if:

'1. the producer did not place the product on the market,
2. the producer did not make or gather the product and did not place the product on the market as part of commercial activities,
3. if the defect is caused by the product having to conform to mandatory statutory requirements, or
4. if the scientific or technical knowledge, available at the time when the product was placed on the market, did not allow the defect to be discovered.'

49 Furthermore, PLA section 7(2) provides that a producer is not liable if it must be presumed that the defect causing the injury or damage did not exist at the time when the producer placed the product on the market. In addition, under this provision, a producer of a component part is not liable if it is proven that the defect is caused by the design of a product of which the component part forms part or by the directions of the producer of the final product.

50 Liability according to the CDPL is based on fault/negligence. This entails *inter alia* that the development risk defence also applies outside the scope of the PLA. It also means that in cases within the scope of the PLA the CDPL rules may result in liability in cases where strict liability according to the PLA is excluded by PLA section 7. A producer who is not liable under the PLA because of the development risk exception may thus be liable under the CDPL for fault/

---

60 *Rostock-Jensen/Kvist-Kristensen* (fn 50) 175 ff; *Schønbeck* (fn 11) 52.

61 *Rostock-Jensen/Kvist-Kristensen* (fn 50) 175.

62 Art 8(2) of the Directive.

63 *M-L Holle*, in: *Ugeskrift for Retsvæsen* 2015 B p 147 ff; *Rostock-Jensen/Kvist-Kristensen* (fn 50) 176 f; *Von Eyben/Isager* (fn 49) 444.

64 *Rostock-Jensen/Kvist-Kristensen* (fn 50) 176.

negligence if the producer did not warn the consumers, etc or did not recall, etc the product when it became possible to discover the defect.

51 The PLA is mandatory not only to the benefit of the injured party but also to the benefit of a supplier who has paid damages to the injured party according to PLA section 10a, ie on the basis of the supplier's vicarious liability for fault-based liability of a previous link.[65] This means that a contract term excluding or limiting liability claims between commercial parties is not binding on suppliers seeking recourse against a previous link in the chain of distribution. The mandatory rule applies only within the scope of the PLA, ie in cases of personal injury and damage to consumer property.[66]

VII. REMEDIES

52 Product liability triggers monetary compensation. Punitive damages are not available.

53 Defective/unsafe products also often do not conform with the contract, meaning that the injured party in its capacity as a party to the contract can pursue contractual remedies according to, for example, the Sale of Goods Act. See above nos 01–02.

54 The marketing of defective/unsafe products may also trigger prohibitory and mandatory injunctions according to the product safety legislation and the Marketing Practices Act, see below no 60 ff.

VIII. PROCEDURAL AND EVIDENTIAL ISSUES

55 According to PLA section 6(2), the injured party must prove the damage, the defect and the causal relationship between the defect and the damage. There are no codified rules or strict case law principles stating what degree of certainty is required. The doctrinal view seems to be that the requirements are the same under the PLA and the CDPL.[67] The courts take into account the possibilities of and impediments to proving the extent of the damage and the amount of the loss.[68] Other specific circumstances of the case, such as the nature of the defect

---

65 Cf sections 12 and 11.3 of the Act.

66 *Møgelvang-Hansen* (fn 36) 233–253.

67 *Dahl/Møgelvang-Hansen* (fn 11) note 79; *Ulfbeck* (fn 19) 195.

68 *Dahl/Møgelvang-Hansen* (fn 11) note 80; *B Gomard/M Kistrup*, Civilprocessen (7th ed 2013) 649 ff.

and circumstances pertaining to the defendant, may also be taken into account. In general, the burden of proof is less onerous once negligence is proven.[69] See also above no 40 ff.

56 The main rule, according to PLA section 14(1), is that the general rules of the Limitation Act[70] also apply to product liability claims, meaning that the limitation period is three years. This goes both for claims under the PLA and for claims under the CDPL. The three-year period runs from the day the plaintiff knew or ought to have known about the damage, the defect and the manufacturer's name and address, see PLA section 14(1).

57 PLA section 14(2) implements art 11 of the Directive by stating that the producer's liability according to the PLA (and also as a consequence thereof a supplier's vicarious liability) becomes time-barred after ten years from the time the product was put into circulation.[71] In addition, the liability of the supplier under the PLA and the liability of all links in the supply chain under the CDPL become time-barred after thirty years (personal injury) or ten years (damage to property) from the time the actual product was put into circulation.[72] The limitation periods are renewed if the claim is acknowledged or legal proceedings are initiated.

58 Cases on product liability are tried by the courts in the ordinary civil procedure. A small claims court procedure was introduced in 2008 as part of comprehensive reform of the court system.[73] The procedure applies to claims not exceeding DKK 50,000 (approximately €6,660). Furthermore, cases concerning claims for damage to consumer property may be brought before the Consumer Complaints Board or one of the approved private complaints boards under the Consumer Complaints Act scheme.[74]

59 Group actions are a new civil procedural device that were introduced in 2008[75] in order to enable the courts to deal with disputes concerning a large number of uniform claims in a more effective way than under the traditional rules and to improve access to the courts in cases concerning small claims from a large number of individuals. The basic conditions for bringing a group action are that the group action is deemed to be the best method of dealing with the claims,

---

69 *Bryde Andersen/Lookofsky* (fn 19) 474.

70 Consolidated Act no 1063/2013.

71 *Schønbeck* (fn 11) 56 ff; *Dahl/Møgelvang-Hansen* (fn 11) note 145 ff.

72 *B von Eyben*, Forældelse efter forældelsesloven af 2007 (2012) 615 f and *Bryde Andersen/Lookofsky* (fn 19) 497 f and 513 f.

73 Sections 400–410 of Consolidated Administration of Justice Act no 1308/2014.

74 Act no 504/2015.

75 Sections 254a–254k of the Administration of Justice Act.

that the group members can be identified and notified about the proceedings in an appropriate manner, and that a group representative can be appointed. The main rule is that a group action only includes group members who positively ask to participate. So far, only a few group actions have been brought.

IX. ALTERNATIVE REGULATIONS AND REMEDIES

60 In private law, the contracting parties are free to agree on which requirements a product has to fulfil. In the absence of an agreement to the contrary, it will constitute lack of conformity of the goods, ie breach of contract, if the product sold cannot be used in the usual manner or fulfil its usual or specified purpose without a significant risk of injury to person or damage to property, unless the buyer was made aware of the risk.[76]

61 Personal injury and damage caused to property (other than damage to the defective product itself) is not within the scope of the seller's liability for breach of contract, see above nos 01–02.

62 Public law regulation concerning a wide range of products provides that products must be safe, so that they are not capable of causing injury to persons or damage to property when handled or consumed in a normal way. General safety rules are found in the Product Safety Act,[77] which implements the Product Safety Directive.[78] The scope of the Act is the same as the Directive's, ie consumer products. The Act constitutes the basic safety regulation for all consumer products and supplements the product safety rules in specific sectors. Only safe products may be put on the market.[79] The producer is the one who is mainly responsible for the product. Distributors who resell the product without influencing the safety of the product must endeavour to resell only safe products, and have to look after the products they deal with. Both the producer and the distributor have the duty to monitor the product put on the market and to intervene if it later turns out that the product is not safe.[80] A product is safe when it is used in conformity with its purpose and handled in the expected way without danger to health or safety.[81] A product is considered safe when it complies with the legal requirements, the harmonised European or Danish standards and the actual technical standards.[82] The public authorities of control

---

[76] Sections 75a and 76 of the Sale of Goods Act.
[77] Act no 1262/2009.
[78] Directive 2001/95/EC.
[79] Section 5 Product Safety Act.
[80] Sections 10 and 11 Product Safety Act.
[81] Section 4, 1 Product Safety Act.
[82] Section 6 Product Safety Act.

that safeguard product safety may order the issuance of public warnings and the withdrawal or destruction of products.[83] In the event of an order of withdrawal or destruction, the seller of the product may not invoke the two-year limitation rule on remedies under the Sale of Goods Act.[84] The Product Safety Act is administered by the Safety Technology Authority (*Sikkerhedsstyrelsen*) which is the coordinating authority concerning product safety, including responsibilities under the EU rapid alert system (Rapex). The regulatory functions for other various product lines under the Product Safety Act are assumed by different specialised regulatory bodies. Services are not subject to general safety legislation. The level of security for services is regulated by requirements on professional skill and authorisation for persons who have undertaken to perform services.

63 The marketing of unsafe products or services is also a violation of the general clause on 'good marketing practices' in section 1 of the Marketing Practices Act[85] and may as such trigger intervention from the Consumer Ombudsman and/or private intervention from for example a consumer organisation with sufficient legal interest in suing for an injunction. In practice such cases are referred to the Safety Technology Authority to be dealt with under the Product Safety Act.

X. ASSESSMENT OF DOMESTIC LAW

64 Product liability rules are not applied very frequently. This goes for both the PLA and the CDPL. The most likely reason for this is that products on the Danish market are generally relatively safe, because product safety tends to be more a question of preventing than curing. Thus, there are detailed obligations that producers and suppliers must comply with before products can be put onto the market. In addition, the relevant authorities generally seem to be rather active enforcing rules on safety, both before and after products are put into circulation.

65 Another reason for the small number of cases may be that victims of defective products consider the cost of a lawsuit and the level of damages awarded, and therefore judge that a lawsuit is not worthwhile. However, there are no studies or statistics supporting this hypothesis. As for personal injury of

---

83 Section 20 Product Safety Act.
84 Sections 54 and 83 of the Sale of Goods Act.
85 Consolidated Act no 1216/2013. See *P Bo Madsen*, Markedsret 2 (6th ed 2015) 164.

a more severe and/or lasting kind, social welfare and health systems cover losses and expenses to a large extent, as does private insurance.[86]

66 Should a plaintiff decide to make a claim in court, that person is in a rather favourable position where evidence is concerned, because the product liability is strict and the burden of proof may be less onerous than in other tort cases.

67 The relative strictness of liability and product safety rules may be considered to come at a high price for producers who have to be careful when developing and constructing new products. This also goes for the instructions and marketing information relating to products. On the other hand, these control and safety measures can be seen as the price for a relatively high level of safety.

68 Recent developments in technology mean that it may be harder to determine whether a given element (material/immaterial) put on the market falls within the scope of 'product', since scientific and technical progress are challenging the concept of a 'product' – and probably continue to do more so in the future. At least in theory, the non-statutory CDPL might be sufficiently flexible to develop further such that they also become applicable in such cases, irrespective of the restrictions resulting from the current concept of a 'product'.[87] A development in this direction should probably not be limited to national law.

86 *Von Eyben/Isager* (fn 49) 52 ff and 59 ff.

87 See above no 13 ff.

PRODUCT LIABILITY IN ENGLAND AND WALES

Ken OLIPHANT and Vanessa WILCOX

I. SOURCES OF LAW AND THEIR EVOLUTION

A. PRE-DIRECTIVE 85/374/EEC RIGHTS AND REMEDIES

01 Prior to the implementation of Directive 85/374/EEC a victim of a product defect could bring himself within one or more of several legal categories, all of which continue to exist today. In particular, an action lay in tort and contract, and criminal consequences could also follow.

1) An Action in Tort

02 It was in the spring of 1932 that the (then) House of Lords handed down judgment in what would arguably become the most famous case in the common law: *Donoghue v Stevenson.*[1] Their Lordships ruled there that the manufacturer of any article, apart entirely from contract, owes a duty to its 'neighbour' – on the facts, the ultimate consumer of a bottle of ginger beer – to take reasonable care to ensure that the article is carefully produced. The case created the modern concept of negligence, the most common basis of litigation in *tort*. Tort's appeal lay in its extension to persons other than the actual ultimate purchaser, the drink in *Donoghue v Stevenson* having been paid for by the claimant's friend. Its major disadvantage, however, was and remains the need to prove negligence. *Daniels and Daniels v R White & Sons Ltd and Tarbard*[2] – a case that arose subsequently – is illustrative of the difficulties that inhered in framing one's action in tort. The facts, personal injury arising from a defective bottle of lemonade, relate closely to those in *Donoghue v Stevenson,* but the claim against the manufacturer in tort failed in *Daniels and Daniels* since the manufacturer was found to have adopted a 'fool-proof method of cleaning, washing and filling bottles'[3] and effectively supervised the process so that the presence in the bottle of 38 grains of carbolic acid could not have been attributed to its negligence.

2) An Action in Contract

03 A right of action founded on *breach of contract* co-existed alongside that in tort. However, the former action was and is of course limited to instances where there is a direct contractual relationship between the parties (cf the position under the Contracts (Rights of Third Parties) Act 1999, discussed in no 75). Thus, despite the fact that '[b]oth husband and wife drank almost simultaneously'[4] in *Daniels and Daniels* above, while Mr Daniels succeeded against the retailer,

---

1 [1932] AC 562. Cf *Winterbottom v Wright* (1842) 10 M&W 109.
2 [1938] 4 All ER 258.
3 [1938] 4 All ER 258, 262 per Lewis J.
4 [1938] 4 All ER 258, 260 per Lewis J.

the absence of privity was fatal to Mrs Daniels' action.[5] Mr Daniels' claim was based on implied conditions as to quality or fitness of goods sold in the course of a business under sec 14 of the Sale of Goods Act 1893 (now sec 14 of the Sale of Goods Act 1979 and in the case of an agreement between a trader and a consumer, as on the facts in *Daniels and Daniels*, secs 9 and 10 of the Consumer Rights Act 2015, which entered into force on 1 October 2015). In addition, an action lies, *inter alia*, for breach of sec 13 of the Sale of Goods Act 1979 (implied term in sales by description; now sec 11 of the Consumer Rights Act 2015 in the case of consumers) which states that goods are to be sold as described. Equivalent terms also exist in respect of hire-purchase agreements[6] and other contracts.[7] The legislature has also stepped in to ensure that the above implied terms, among others, cannot be excluded or restricted by reference to any contract term as against a person dealing as a consumer.[8] Despite the mentioned drawback of privity, an action in contract benefits from the fact that, in contrast to tort, fault generally need not be proved. Moreover, all reasonably foreseeable damage, whether to persons, property or pocket, is compensable.

B. IMPLEMENTING DIRECTIVE 85/374/EEC

04 The inadequacies inherent in the existing causes of action led to huge debates in the USA and the changes effected there fed into discussions in the UK, as well as influencing the European legal landscape. Around the time when the Council of Europe was setting out the terms of what would become the European Convention on Products Liability,[9] which sought to introduce a strict product liability regime into Europe, Britain was still coming to terms with the thalidomide disaster. A Royal Commission on Civil Liability and Compensation for Personal Injury, under the leadership of Lord Pearson, sat to consider the law relating to compensation for personal injury caused, *inter alia*, 'through the manufacture, supply or use of goods or services'.[10] This was followed by consultations and subsequent recommendations by the English and Scottish Law Commissions whose terms of reference, insofar as protected interests were

5 Cf *Priest v Last* [1903] 2 KB 148 where the claimant recovered expenses incurred in the treatment of his wife for the injury occasioned to her by the use of a hot-water bottle he had purchased.

6 Supply of Goods (Implied Terms) Act 1973, sec 9 f. The Consumer Rights Act 2015 also covers hire-purchase agreements between traders and consumers: sec 3(2)(c).

7 Supply of Goods and Services Act 1982, secs 3 f and 9 f. The Consumer Rights Act 2015 also covers contracts between traders and consumers for the hire and transfer of goods (sec 3(2)(b) and (d)) and contracts for the supply of digital content (Chapter 3) and services (Chapter 4).

8 Formerly regulated under the Unfair Contract Terms Act 1977; now contained in sec 31 of the Consumer Rights Act 2015 in the case of consumer contracts. See also Consumer Rights Act 2015, secs 47 and 57, and Part 2.

9 CETS No 091. Strasbourg, 27.01.1977.

10 (1978) Cmnd 7054, vol 1, Ch 22 (para 1193).

concerned, were much broader than those of the Pearson Commission.[11] As the above investigations coincided with the European Commission's preliminary draft directive for defective products, which was eventually adopted as Directive 85/374/EEC, the English and Scottish Law Commissions' work came to naught. Instead, Directive 85/374/EEC was implemented by way of Part I of the Consumer Protection Act 1987 (CPA). Part I of the Act entered into force on 1 March 1988. Directive 85/374/EEC was subsequently amended by Directive 1999/34/EC and the changes required by it were given effect to in the Consumer Protection Act 1987 (Product Liability) (Modification) Order 2000 (see no 06 below).[12] Section 1(1) of the CPA expressly provides that the Act shall be construed to comply with the Directive. Although criticised,[13] at least one judge has ruled that 'insofar as the wording of the CPA ... differs from the equivalent Articles in the Directive, it should not be construed differently from the Directive; and consequently the practical course [is] to go straight to the fount, the Directive itself.'[14]

05 Directive 85/374/EEC allowed Member States options in three areas: first, they could, by way of derogation, provide in their legislation that a 'product' under art 2 also meant primary agricultural products and game: art 15(1)(a); second, they could derogate from the development risk defence under art 7(e) which allows a producer to escape liability where the state of scientific and technical knowledge at the time when he put the product into circulation was not such as to enable the existence of the defect to be discovered: art 15(1)(b); and finally, they could limit a producer's total liability for damage resulting from a death or personal injury to an amount which may not be less than 70 million ECU: art 16(1). How the UK exercised these options is set out below.

06 First, like the Directive, the UK adopted a vague *definition of 'product'* under sec 1(2) of the CPA: 'product' means any goods or electricity and includes a product which is comprised in another product, whether by virtue of being a component part or raw material or otherwise. Moreover, 'product' extended to things subjected to 'an industrial or other process': sec 1(2)(c). The UK did not derogate from art 2 of the Directive so that only *processed* primary agricultural products and game were caught. As former sec 2(4) stated, the CPA did not apply 'to a person in respect of any defect in any game or agricultural produce if the only supply of the game or produce by that person to another was at a time when it had not undergone an industrial process.' Liability for processed food did not attach to the primary producer, therefore, but to the processor and, where applicable, the producer of the final product, ie 'the fruit pulp producer and fruit

11 Liability for Defective Products (1977) Cmnd 6831.
12 Statutory Instrument 2000 No 2771.
13 *A Arnull*, Product Liability and the Effect of Directives (2001) 26 European Law Review 213, 214.
14 *A v The National Blood Authority* [2001] 3 All ER 289, at [2] per Burton J.

pie maker but not the fruit grower'.[15] As mentioned in no 04 above, Directive 1999/34/EC (in its art 1(2)) eventually amended Directive 85/374/EEC to extend the scope of the provisions of the latter Directive to *primary agricultural products and game*, whether processed or otherwise, as a result of concerns over BSE (bovine spongiform encephalopathy). This change was implemented by the Consumer Protection Act 1987 (Product Liability) (Modification) Order 2000, which entered into force on 4 December 2000. Article 2(3) of the Order provides for the omission of sec 2(4) from the CPA.

07 Second, the UK chose not to exclude the *development risk defence*, which is laid down in sec 4(1)(e) of the CPA. The provision, which was subject to an unsuccessful challenge by the European Commission, reads that it shall be a defence for the producer 'that the state of scientific and technical knowledge at the relevant time was not such that a producer of products of the same description as the product in question might be expected to have discovered the defect if it had existed in his products while they were under his control'. The Commission had argued unsuccessfully that, unlike the relevant article of the Directive, which calls for an objective assessment, sec 4(1)(e) of the CPA depends on the subjective knowledge of a producer taking reasonable care.[16] The defence is given fuller treatment in no 64 below.

08 Third, the UK declined to impose a *ceiling on liability*. In response to the Commission's Green Paper on Liability for Defective Products,[17] the UK said that it continued in its belief that setting such a limit could lead to injustices in cases with multiple claims on the one hand and lengthy delays in the payment of compensation awards where there is a possibility of further claims in respect of the same products on the other.[18]

C. SCOPE OF THE CONSUMER PROTECTION ACT 1987

09 The UK legislature adopted a mixed bag approach insofar as transposing the 1985 Directive was concerned: (i) some aspects of the Directive are given effect in the CPA; (ii) the CPA also delegates issues encompassed in the 1985 Directive to certain enactments; (iii) as it does issues not encompassed in the Directive but nevertheless related to product liability; and finally (iv) some issues are left to general principles of national law. In particular:

---

15 *J Stapleton*, Product Liability (1994) 304.

16 Case C-300/95 *Commission v United Kingdom* [1997] ECR I-2649.

17 COM(1999)396 final.

18 United Kingdom response to the Commission's Green Paper on Liability for Defective Products, 15 January 2014, Ares(2014)74687, 4 <http://ec.europa.eu/DocsRoom/documents/1496/attachments/1/translations/en/renditions/pdf>.

(i) The core sections of the 1987 insofar as defective products are concerned are secs 1–7. Section 1 sets out the purpose and construction of Part I of the 1987 Act (including the definition of 'product'). This corresponds with art 2 of the Directive; sec 2 defines who may be liable (corresponding with arts 1 and 3), and it lays down the rule of liability in the case of multiple tortfeasors (implementing art 5) and expressly states that a claim under the Directive operates without prejudice to other rights and remedies (enacting art 13). The meaning of 'defect' is dealt with under sec 3 (cf art 6), available civil defences are enumerated in sec 4 (cf art 7) and damage is defined in sec 5 (cf art 9). The prohibition on exclusions from liability under sec 7 corresponds with art 12.

(ii) Section 6 deals with the application of certain enactments and in particular sec 6(8) – on nuclear installations – finds its equivalent in art 14 of the Directive. The short- and long-stop limitation periods set out in arts 10 and 11 of the Directive respectively are not given effect in the 1987 Act itself, but rather the Directive precipitated an amendment to the Limitation Act 1980 which since then has regulated actions in respect of defective products under the thereby inserted sec 11A.[19] Articles 5 and 8 of the Directive refer to the preservation of national law concerning the right of contribution or recourse (which is regulated by the Civil Liability (Contribution) Act 1978). In line with art 8(2) of the Directive, on contributory negligence, sec 6(4) CPA refers to the Law Reform (Contributory Negligence) Act 1945. Under art 9 of the Directive, damage includes damage caused by death, an issue dealt with under the Fatal Accidents Act 1976.

(iii) As mentioned, the CPA also deals with the application of certain enactments not expressly covered by the Directive, including the Congenital Disability (Civil Liability) Act 1976. Suffice to say at this stage that the effect of the section is to flesh out the liability element of those provisions in respect of claims arising in the context of defective products.

(iv) General principles of national law are left to govern certain issues such as causation, the quantum of damages, procedure (including the burden of proof (cf art 4)) and the calculation of interest payable.

D. IMPACT OF THE CONSUMER PROTECTION ACT 1987 ON EXISTING RIGHTS AND REMEDIES

10 In practice, relatively few claims are brought under the 1987 Act (see no 86 ff), which can be relied upon in addition to existing rights and remedies (as envisaged by sec 2(6) CPA).[20]

---

[19] See sec 6(6) and sch 1 CPA.

[20] Section 2 lays down the liability for defective products. Section 2(6) reads: 'This section shall be without prejudice to any liability arising otherwise than by virtue of this Part.' See

E. SPECIAL LIABILITY REGIMES FOR NEW TECHNOLOGIES

11 The difficulty with addressing the topic of special liability regimes for new technologies is that what is 'new' is of course relative. Moreover, 'old' special liability regimes exist but are capable of applying to emerging technologies in the industries in question. This is the case, for example, with respect to sec 1 of the Employer's Liability (Defective Equipment) Act 1969 which imposes strict liability on an employer for personal injury to an employee as a result of a defect in equipment provided by his employer where the defect is attributable wholly or partly to the fault of a third party (whether identified or not). The Act only applies where the damage arose in the course of the employee's employment. The provision cannot be excluded or limited but applies without prejudice to the law relating to contributory negligence and any remedy by way of contribution or in contract or otherwise which is available to the employer in respect of the injury: sec 1. If the damage is caused by a 3D printer, for example, or some other 'newly' developed equipment, there is no doubt that the provision would nonetheless apply.

12 Two other, more specific liability regimes may also be mentioned. First, the Vaccine Damage Payments Act 1979 provides, *inter alia*, for the payment of a statutory sum by a person who is severely disabled as a result of vaccination against any of the diseases to which the Act applies.[21] New vaccines are periodically developed and approved and this may involve the use of new technologies. However, it appears that these would still be regulated under the 1979 Act.

13 Second, the Human Fertilisation and Embryology Act 1990 (as amended)[22] regulates aspects of reproductive and regenerative medicine. In particular, sec 44 amends the Congenital Disabilities (Civil Liability) Act 1976 so that the latter provides, in its sec 1A, for a civil action for disabled children who were born 'as the result of the placing in [their mother] of an embryo or of sperm and eggs or her artificial insemination'. In 2015, Parliament approved new Regulations under the 1990 Act that allow the practice of a novel form of reproductive medicine, mitochondrial donation (resulting in what are popularly known as 'three-person babies').[23] Liability continues to be regulated under the Act of 1976. Though use of the new technique is the provision of a service as opposed to the supply of a product, the service is one which may well rely on medical products.

M Lunney/K Oliphant, Tort Law: Text and Materials (2013) 595 for possible reasons as to why consumers are slow in bringing actions under the CPA.

21 That is, diphtheria, tetanus, whooping cough, poliomyelitis, measles, rubella, tuberculosis, smallpox, and any other disease which is specified by the Secretary of State for the purposes of this Act by order made by statutory instrument: sec 1(2).

22 See also Human Fertilisation and Embryology Act 2008, sch 6 clause 14 f.

23 Human Fertilisation and Embryology (Mitochondrial Donation) Regulations 2015.

14 Moving on to possible reforms: in February 2015 the Department for Transport (DfT) published a document, 'The Pathway to Driverless Cars: A Detailed Review of Regulations for Automated Vehicle Technologies',[24] which included a summary of responses to a consultation on the subject. The brief section on liability issues is reproduced here:[25]

> 'The major theme throughout many of the questions posed to stakeholders was liability. Respondents were concerned about how liability would be apportioned in the event of a collision and who would take responsibility for this if the vehicle was in control at the time.
>
> While many felt the existing liability regime would be sufficient for testing to go ahead, almost equal numbers foresaw problems and the need for changes to be made.
>
> There was general agreement that vehicle manufacturers should continue to be held strictly liable for mechanical and system failures as is already the case for emergency braking and cruise control systems. It was suggested that vehicle manufactures should also accept liability for the software in their vehicles.
>
> Many respondents focused on the difficulty of establishing whether the driver or the automated system was in control of the vehicle at the time of a collision or other event. The use of independent event data recorders and camera systems were recommended to address this.
>
> It was suggested that thought should be given to the wider liabilities, for example road maintenance and information providers.'

15 The report also highlighted potential difficulties for claimants seeking to rely on existing rights and remedies:[26]

> 'Due to the complexity of the technologies involved, a claimant may need to call on expert evidence. For example, an expert may be needed to prove to a court that a collision could only have happened through a malfunction of the technology and not by any other action of the claimant.
>
> Equally, establishing exactly what may have been considered to be "state of the art" at the time of the vehicle's development could again require detailed technical expertise.
>
> The complexity of the technologies involved, the cost of obtaining expert witnesses and the potential for evidence of any manufacturing defect to be destroyed in a subsequent collision could mean that the chances of bringing successful product liability claims against automated vehicle manufacturers are limited.'

---

24 <https://www.gov.uk/government/uploads/system/uploads/attachment_data/file/401565/pathway-driverless-cars-main.pdf>.

25 Para 16.4 ff.

26 Para 7.48 ff (para numbers omitted).

16 The DfT concluded that there was 'need to consider how liability would be decided if that vehicle is subsequently involved in a collision'[27] and that some actions were required in relation to regulations on electric personal vehicles and 'remote control' vehicles.[28] The target for making these amendments to domestic legislation is summer 2017.[29] The need for a review of the allocation of civil liability between driver and manufacturer and to amend the appropriate legislation was echoed in the DfT's Summary Report and Action Plan.[30] In July 2015 the DfT issued a Code of Practice for the testing of automated vehicle technologies, which reads: 'Failure to follow the Code may be relevant to liability in any legal proceedings. Similarly, compliance with the Code does not guarantee immunity from liability in such circumstances.'[31]

17 In other areas, there is much discussion and consensus that current product liability laws will need to be reviewed to ensure they are suitable for emerging technologies.[32]

II. BASIC ELEMENTS OF LIABILITY

A. OVERVIEW

18 A claimant seeking to rely upon the CPA will need to establish (as to the burden of proof, see no 71), subject to defences (see no 60 ff), that a defect (see no 27 ff) in a product or component thereof (see no 19 ff) caused (see no 55 ff) him damage (see no 47 ff). The regime under the CPA is strict (see no 41) with primary liability being channelled to the producer (see no 43 f). Provision is made for instances where the latter cannot be identified (no 45). The statutory scheme limits the categories of recoverable damages (see no 68 ff).

---

27 Para 18.6.

28 Para 18.8.

29 Para 18.9.

30 Para 18 <https://www.gov.uk/government/uploads/system/uploads/attachment_data/file/401562/pathway-driverless-cars-summary.pdf>.

31 Para 1.5 <https://www.gov.uk/government/uploads/system/uploads/attachment_data/file/446316/pathway-driverless-cars.pdf>. See also the work of the Automated Driving Insurer Group.

32 See, for example, the discussion of nanotechnology liability in *Royal Society and Royal Academy of Engineering*, Nanoscience and Nanotechnologies: Opportunities and Uncertainties (2004), available here: <www.nanotec.org.uk/finalReport.htm>; and *Better Regulation Task Force*, Scientific Research: Innovation with Controls (2003). In a more specific context, see also *BB Chatterjee*, Rethinking *Alcock* in the New Media Age, Journal of European Tort Law (forthcoming), which focuses on psychiatric damage to secondary victims resulting from the communication of images through new technologies and media platforms.

B. PRODUCT

19 As mentioned above (no 6), a 'product' is defined as goods or electricity and includes components and raw materials: sec 1(2)(c) CPA. The term 'goods' encompasses substances, growing crops and things comprised in land by virtue of being attached to it and any ship, aircraft or vehicle: sec 45(1). Section 2(4) on the restriction of the Act's application to processed game and agricultural produce has been omitted so that the Act now applies to game and agricultural produce, processed or otherwise, in compliance with Directive 1999/34/EC. The use of the term 'goods' points in the direction of tangible assets. Thus, it would seem that intellectual property and digital content, of themselves, are not envisaged as falling within it. Similarly, 'where software is supplied non-physically – for example, over the internet – it seems hard to escape the conclusion that no "product" is involved and hence there can be no liability [for the software producer].'[33] The physical media upon which digital content is recorded do, however, fall within the scope of the CPA. Moreover, it is thought that if 'a malfunction or glitch in the software as written causes a machine to malfunction and injure the claimant there will be liability [for the software producer] under the 1987 Act.'[34] The basis of this conclusion is an analogy drawn with a case before the Court of Appeal in which it was stated *obiter* that a disk including the software encoded on it would be 'goods' for the purposes of the Sale of Goods Act 1979 and the Supply of Goods and Services Act 1982.[35]

20 The Directive does not extend to pure information, service or advice.[36] However, 'any instructions for, or warnings with respect to, doing or refraining from doing anything with or in relation to the product' are relevant in determining whether a product as a whole is defective: sec 3(2)(a) (see no 28). Where such instructions are printed, it is the producer of the product and not the person undertaking the printing that is *prima facie* liable for errors which result in damage (assuming the latter did not introduce errors that were not in the material sent for printing).

21 Water and gas are expressly mentioned as goods under the Act and hence fall within its definition of 'product'.[37]

---

33 Clerk & Lindsell on Torts (21st edn 2014) para 11-51. See no 14 above (on software in driverless cars), however.

34 Ibid para 11-51.

35 *St Albans City and DC v International Computers Ltd* [1996] 4 All ER 481, 493 per Sir Iain Glidewell.

36 Clerk & Lindsell on Torts (fn 33) para 11–49 f. Cf *St Albans City Council v ICL Ltd* [1996] 4 All ER 481, 493 where Sir Iain Glidewell thought a book containing dangerous misinformation was a defective good under sec 14 of the Sale of Goods Act 1979.

37 Section 46(1).

22 In the case of *A v The National Blood Authority*, it was conceded that blood was a product within the meaning of the 1985 Directive.[38] Other bodily fluids (eg sperm) have been held to constitute 'property' within the meaning of sec 32(9)(c) of the Human Tissue Act 2004[39] and some have concluded that they are products.[40] Nevertheless, there are those who argue against such a conclusion.[41] The same applies for body parts.

23 As stated in sec 45(1) CPA, things attached to land may constitute 'products'. However, sec 46(3) reads: 'the performance of any contract by the erection of any building or structure on any land or by the carrying out of any other building works shall be treated for the purposes of this Act as a supply of goods insofar as, but only insofar as, it involves the provision of any goods to any person by means of their incorporation into the building, structure or works.' In short, buildings and land fall outside the scope of the Act; construction materials (eg bricks and mortar) fall within it.[42] A further limitation is to be found in sec 46(4), which states that 'references in this Act to supplying goods shall not include references to supplying goods comprised in land where the supply is effected by the creation or disposal of an interest in the land.' Relief may, however, be available in the case of defectively constructed property under the Defective Premises Act 1972. In response to the Commission's Green Paper on Liability for Defective Products, the UK stated that 'construction activities are largely a service activity. We believe that liability for defective working practices (as opposed to the supply of defective products) is best considered under any separate initiative which the Commission may propose for defective services.'[43]

24 Where a component is incorporated into a movable, an action may be brought against the producer of the defective component or that of the final product. Where a defective component is incorporated into an immovable, the claim is against the producer of the component.[44]

25 Crafts and customised items are included within the meaning of 'product' but a maker of such products may bring himself within the defence under sec 4(1)(c), for example, where the product was not supplied in the course of a business with a view to profit.[45]

---

38 [2001] 3 All ER 289, at [17] per Burton J.

39 *Yearworth v North Bristol NHS Trust* [2010] QBD 1.

40 For example, Clerk & Lindsell on Torts (fn 33) para 11-49; *G Howells*, The Law of Product Liability (2nd edn 2007) para 4.52.

41 *Stapleton* (fn 15) 310.

42 *Howells* (fn 40) para 4.41 f.

43 United Kingdom response to the Commission's Green Paper on Liability for Defective Products (fn 18) 6.

44 *Howells* (fn 40) para 4.71.

45 'Business' includes a trade or profession and the activities of a professional or trade association or of a local authority or other public authority: sec 45(1) CPA.

26 The proportion of the value of materials and services, and the categorisation of the contract as a contract of sale or one of service, are quite irrelevant. The courts will look to substance rather than form. An aspect of 'service' comes with every product. Indeed, most suppliers, importers and own branders are doing no more than proving a service but the CPA nonetheless provides for their liability. The only question is whether there is a 'product' within the meaning of the CPA whose defect caused damage.

C. DEFECT

27 It is for the claimant to 'establish on the balance of probabilities that there was a defect in the product'.[46] An inference that a particular product was defective may, however, be drawn under the appropriate facts.[47]

28 Section 3(1) CPA provides that: 'there is a defect in a product for the purposes of this Part *if the safety of the product is not such as persons generally are entitled to expect*'.[48] A 'legitimate expectations test' is thus central to the question of defectiveness under the CPA. A number of considerations are to be taken into account in determining whether a product is defective, as listed in sec 3(2). In particular: '(a) the manner in which, and purposes for which, the product has been marketed, its get-up, the use of any mark in relation to the product and any instructions for, or warnings with respect to, doing or refraining from doing anything with or in relation to the product; (b) what might reasonably be expected to be done with or in relation to the product; and (c) the time when the product was supplied by its producer to another …'.

29 While art 6 of the Directive, in defining 'defect', refers to 'taking all circumstances into account'[49] in conducting the legitimate expectations test, one judge has interpreted this to mean taking 'all *relevant* circumstances' into account,[50] with the consequence that some questions – namely, the avoidability of the harmful characteristic in relation to precautionary measures, the impracticality, cost or difficulty of taking such measures, and the benefit to society or utility of the product – would be considered irrelevant.[51] Some have argued that an exclusionary approach to risk/utility considerations goes

---

46 *Foster v Biosil* (2001) 59 BMLR 178 per Booth QC.

47 *Ide v ATB Sales Ltd* [2008] EWCA Civ 424, [2009] RTR 85.

48 Emphasis added. 'Safety', in relation to a product, includes safety with respect to products comprised in that product and safety in the context of risks of damage to property, as well as in the context of risks of death or personal injury: sec 3(1) CPA.

49 See also sec 3(2) CPA 1987 which states that 'all the circumstances shall be taken into account' in determining whether there was a defect in a product.

50 *A v The National Blood Authority* [2001] 3 All ER 289, at [57] per Burton J.

51 *A v The National Blood Authority* [2001] 3 All ER 289, at [68] per Burton J.

too far[52] and is indeed inconsistent with other authorities. In *B (A Child) v McDonald's Restaurants Ltd*,[53] for example, utility was a factor which led the court to conclude that the products – hot drinks – were not defective. Similarly, avoidability was also a relevant consideration in finding the product in question defective in *Abouzaid v Mothercare (UK) Ltd*.[54]

30 In determining the issue of defectiveness, a distinction is drawn between standard and non-standard products. The former are products which perform as the producer intends and the latter are specific specimens which are deficient or inferior in terms of safety to other products of the same or a similar series.[55] It is the harmful characteristic in the non-standard product that causes the injury or damage.[56] Non-standard products are not to be considered as automatically defective but it may be easier to prove defectiveness if the product in question differs from the standard product.[57]

31 Note also that the mere fact that a product is inherently dangerous – eg poison – does not necessarily mean that it is defective, 'provided that the injury resulted from that known danger.'[58] In such a case, 'there may not need to be any further consideration ... of whether it was safe and the level of safety to be legitimately expected.'[59]

32 The distinction between standard and non-standard products is thought to 'serve broadly the same purpose as that which is sometimes made between design defects and manufacturing defects'.[60] However, the CPA itself does not draw such a distinction and in at least one case a judge has ruled that 'there are no such boxes or categories in the Directive, unlike the Third Restatement.'[61] Though criticised, there is a ruling to the effect that design standards are not the relevant benchmark since members of the public as a whole are unlikely to know what safety standard the product they are buying has been designed to.[62] In particular, Howells, a leading academic commentator, writes that the approach taken in the case in question was weak insofar as the consumer expectation test focused on 'the "actual" expectations of consumers rather than the legal

---

52 *Lunney/Oliphant* (fn 20) 586 f.
53 [2002] EWHC 490.
54 Times, 20 February 2001.
55 The equivalent of 'rogue products' or 'lemons' in the US or '*Ausreisser*' or 'off the road' products in Germany.
56 *A v The National Blood Authority* [2001] 3 All ER 289, at [36] per Burton J.
57 *A v The National Blood Authority* [2001] 3 All ER 289, at [38] per Burton J.
58 *A v The National Blood Authority* [2001] 3 All ER 289, at [35] per Burton J.
59 *A v The National Blood Authority* [2001] 3 All ER 289, at [35] per Burton J.
60 See *Lunney/Oliphant* (fn 20) 588.
61 *A v The National Blood Authority* [2001] 3 All ER 289, at [39] per Burton J.
62 *Pollard v Tesco Stores Ltd* [2006] EWCA CIV 393, at [17] per Laws LJ.

test that requires consideration of what the persons generally are "entitled" to expect.'[63]

33 As to defects to digital content and misleading information, see no 19 above. As regards electricity (which by virtue of sec 1(2) is a product under the CPA), it is thought that surges in current may constitute a 'defect'.[64]

34 As the standard is that expected by members of the public as a whole at any given time, it may well be that what such members consider safe today will not be so considered tomorrow and *vice versa*.

D. MARKETING OF PRODUCT

35 The CPA does not use the Directive's phrase 'put into circulation'[65] but instead employs the term 'supply'. This has been held to mean when a product enters a marketing process in the form in which it is offered to the public in order to be used or consumed.[66]

36 The manner in which the product was marketed is closely intertwined with the question of defectiveness.

37 If a defect 'did not exist in the product at the relevant time', this could serve as a valid defence under sec 4(1)(d) CPA (see no 63). Generally, the relevant time is the time the product, other than electricity,[67] is supplied to another: sec 4(2). If the defect arose before, liability may attach. As is implicit in sec 3(2)(b), foreseeable misuse or mishandling is a relevant consideration and this may well extend to improper storage or handling. But where a product is supplied with appropriate instructions for its use, the producer should not generally be expected to cater for users who throw them away or lose them.[68]

E. PRODUCER'S OBLIGATIONS

38 Though Part I of the CPA does not itself use the language of 'duty', it may be said that producers owe a strict duty to consumers and others to ensure that

63 *Howells* (fn 40) para 4.151.

64 Clerk & Lindsell on Torts (fn 33) para 11-49, fn 221.

65 See arts 6 and 7 of the Directive.

66 See Case 127/04, *O'Byrne v Sanofi Pasteur MSD Ltd* [2006] 1 WLR 1606, 1620 f as referred to in *O'Byrne v Aventis Pasteur MSD Ltd* [2010] 1 WLR 1412, 1420 f per Lord Rodger.

67 In relation to electricity, it means the time at which it was generated, being a time before it was transmitted or distributed: sec 4(2) CPA.

68 *Worsley v Tambrands Ltd* [2000] PIQR P95.

their products are not defective. The duty is implicit in the definition of 'defect' contained in sec 3 of the Act and shaped by the defences set out in sec 4.[69] More concrete statements as to the obligations of a producer are provided by safety regulations issued by the Secretary of State under Part II of the 1987 Act, especially the General Product Safety Regulations 2005 (see nos 79 ff and 83 ff), though these are not decisive in determining liability issues under Part I.

F. SPECIAL PRODUCTS

39 Products which could result in congenital disabilities are given specific treatment under the CPA. Section 1 of the Congenital Disabilities (Civil Liability) Act 1976 provides that a person responsible for an occurrence affecting the parent of a child, which causes the child to be born disabled, will be liable to the child if he would have been liable in tort to the affected parent. The child's claim is thus derivative and distinct from that of the parent. The Act does not apply where either or both of the parents knew the risk of their child being born disabled.[70]

40 Section 6(3) of the CPA deals with how the 1976 Act is to be given effect in relation to product liability. It provides, so far as is material, that a child born disabled has the right to pursue the tortfeasor under the CPA where it was a defective product that caused the ante-natal injury.[71] Unlike under sec 1(6) of the Congenital Disabilities (Civil Liability) Act 1976, which permits a parent to exclude or limit the tortfeasor's liability towards the child, any purported exclusion or limitation of liability is void as a result of secs 6(3)(c) and 7 CPA. See also no 67.

G. STANDARD OF LIABILITY

41 The CPA may be considered to establish a strict liability regime (ie one which requires no proof of fault on the defendant's part). Claims under the CPA are therefore not claims in negligence. Nevertheless, the liability 'is to be treated as liability in tort'.[72] The wrong is complete where the elements specified in the statute are established. Liability under the CPA is not absolute, in the sense of not admitting defences (no 60 ff).

---

69 *S Deakin/A Johnston/B Markesinis*, Markesinis and Deakin's Tort Law (7th edn 2012) 615.

70 Section 1(4) (subject to exception).

71 For an example of such a claim, see *Multiple Claimants v Sanofi-Synthelabo Ltd* [2007] EWHC 1860.

72 Section 6(7) CPA.

42 Interpretation of the statutory requirements may be influenced by views as to the strictness of the liability introduced. Thus, because liability under the Directive is defect- as opposed to fault-based, Burton J in *A v The National Blood Authority* concluded that this tacitly countermanded the express wording of art 6, requiring consideration of *all circumstances* in assessing defectiveness, as this would open the door to a risk/utility analysis typical of negligence.[73] As noted above (no 29), the reasoning has been criticised and Burton J may be thought to have gone too far in precluding any balancing at all of risk with utility.[74]

III. THE PERSON LIABLE FOR THE DAMAGE

43 Section 2(2) and (3) CPA deals with the persons who may be liable. While primary liability attaches to the producer of the product, any person who puts his name, trade mark or other distinguishing mark on the product, the first commercial importer of the product into the EU for the purpose of supply or a supplier may also be liable. Public authorities are not excluded from the purview of the Act.[75]

44 A 'producer' is defined under sec 1(2)(a) as the person who manufactured a product. This covers both a product component and a finished product. In the case of a substance which has not been manufactured but has been won or abstracted, it is the person who won or abstracted it. Where a product does not fit within those categories but essential characteristics are attributable to an industrial or other process, it is the person who carried out that process.

45 Under sec 2(3), a supplier is only liable if the person who suffered the damage requests him to identify the producer, own brander or importer and he fails to do so within a reasonable period of time. What constitutes a 'reasonable period of time' is left to the courts to determine. By virtue of sec 1(3) a person who supplies any product in which products are comprised is not treated by reason only of his supply of that product as supplying any of the products so comprised. The effect of this provision is that a supplier need only identify a producer of the entire product and not the producer of a specific defective part. There is a defence for those who supply products otherwise than in the course of business and who do so otherwise than with a view to profit: sec 4(1)(c), see no 62.

46 As arts 5 and 8 of the Directive state, the Directive applies without prejudice to the provisions of national law concerning the right of contribution

---

73 *A v The National Blood Authority* [2001] 3 All ER 289, at [57]–[63].

74 See *Lunney/Oliphant* (fn 20) 586 f.

75 Section 9 CPA (referring specifically to the Crown). See also *A v The National Blood Authority* [2001] 3 All ER 289, at [42] per Burton J. Nor are non-profit making organisations.

or recourse. Under the CPA, where two or more persons are liable for the same damage, their liability is joint and several: sec 2(5). By sec 1(1) of the Civil Liability (Contribution) Act 1978, 'any person liable in respect of any damage suffered by another person may recover contribution from any other person liable in respect of the same damage (whether jointly with him or otherwise).' The amount of the contribution recoverable from any person is as may be found by the court to be just and equitable having regard to the extent of that person's responsibility for the damage in question: sec 2(1) of the same Act.

IV. THE AGGRIEVED PERSON AND DAMAGE

47 There is little guidance on who can bring an action under the Act. Presumably, any person who suffers personal injury or any loss of or damage to any property (including land)[76] as a result of a product defect, or the personal representatives of a person who dies, can do so. Section 5(5) CPA does, however, specifically mention that only a 'person with an interest in ... property' can pursue an action for loss of or damage to property caused by a defective product.

48 In parallel with art 9 of the 1985 Directive, the concept of actionable damage is limited in a number of respect under the 1987 Act. First, while damage consequential upon personal injury and the other losses discussed above is actionable, pure economic loss is not because it does not fit into the categories of damage giving rise to liability specified in sec 5 CPA. This is in line with the general exclusionary rule applied in negligence actions but exceptions exist even there. The CPA admits no such exceptions. Pure economic loss is, of course, readily recoverable in contract.

49 Second, 'damage to the product itself or ... the loss of or any damage to the whole or any part of any product which has been supplied with the product in question comprised in it'[77] is also excluded. Again, this maps onto the normal approach taken in negligence,[78] though exceptions are sometimes suggested – for example, in the case of component parts of 'complex structures'.[79] The Act does not seem to allow any exception of that nature.

50 Third, loss of or damage to property does not extend to property which, at the time it is lost or damaged, was not ordinarily intended for private use, occupation or consumption *and* was not intended by the person suffering the

---

76 Section 5(1).
77 Section 5(2).
78 *D & F Estates Ltd v Church Commissioners* [1989] AC 177.
79 Ibid, per Lord Bridge.

loss or damage mainly for his own private use, occupation or consumption: sec 5(3).[80] Domestic tort actions do not segregate business from non-business use of goods or other property although some torts specifically refer to harm to business interests (eg malicious falsehood), and others (eg the economic torts) are more likely to arise in a commercial context. In contract, the terms are agreed upon by the parties and there is no categorical bar to their agreeing to exclude liability for particular forms of damage. However, there are legislative controls on what can and cannot be agreed in consumer contracts, including the exclusion of liability.[81]

51 Finally, a threshold of £275 applies insofar as loss of or damage to property is concerned: sec 5(4). This reflects the policy expressed in the recital to the Directive: 'to avoid litigation in an excessive number of cases'. As the CPA applies without prejudice to any liability arising otherwise (sec 2(6) CPA), an action in negligence may still be maintained for any loss or damage excluded as a result of the application of the threshold. However, the onus of adducing evidence on fault falls on the claimant. The UK Government has revealed that it does not intend to modify the threshold, which it considers to be reasonably modest and does not unduly disadvantage consumers. It points out that, in most cases, the damage would in any case be covered by the consumer's home insurance policy.[82] Though a *de minimis* threshold applies generally to the compensation of damage under domestic law,[83] the adoption of a pecuniary threshold is unusual.

52 Under domestic tort law, the type (but not the extent) of the damage must normally have been reasonably foreseeable.[84] This rule of remoteness appears also to apply to claims under the CPA. In contract, a very substantial degree of probability is required.[85]

53 The issue of loss of a chance was specifically raised in *A v The National Blood Authority*.[86] The defendants argued that they were not liable for all the consequences of the claimants' blood infection but only for that damage which resulted from the failure to introduce surrogate testing and/or to implement routine screening earlier. However, Burton J refused to reduce the claimants'

---

80 See sec 5(5) ff.

81 See especially Consumer Rights Act 2015, Part 2 (Unfair Terms).

82 United Kingdom response to the Commission's Green Paper on Liability for Defective Products (fn 18) 4.

83 *K Oliphant*, Basic Questions on Tort Law from the Perspective of England and the Commonwealth, in: H Koziol, Basic Questions on Tort Law from a Comparative Perspective (2015) no 5/119. But note that some torts (eg trespass in its various forms) are actionable without proof of any damage at all.

84 *Overseas Tankship (UK) Ltd v Morts Dock and Engineering Co Ltd* [1961] AC 388.

85 *Koufos v C Czarnikow Ltd, The Heron II* [1969] 1 AC 350.

86 [2001] 3 All ER 289, at [176] ff per Burton.

damages by reference to any loss of chance argument. The judge found it unnecessary to address the contention of counsel for the claimants that the CPA does not allow claims for loss of a chance because they are claims for pure economic loss, which is not damage for which liability can arise under sec 5(1) CPA, or counsel's further submission, referring to *Hotson v East Berkshire Health Authority*,[87] that the issue in personal injury cases is simply one of causation, and thus results in either total success or total failure.[88]

54 As indicated in no 08, the UK legislature did not exercise the option of capping the defendant's potential liability.

V. CAUSALITY

55 Section 2(1) CPA imposes liability 'where any damage is *caused* wholly or partly by a defect in a product' (emphasis added). It is 'unnecessary to ascertain the cause of the defect'.[89] It is, however, for the claimant to prove on a balance of probabilities that a defect had caused the damage sustained.

56 The theory of proportional liability under the CPA is yet to be ruled upon by the English courts.[90] But in answering the question in the Commission's Green Paper on Liability for Defective Products whether 'market share liability' would be feasible for cases in which there are several producers of the same product and it is not possible to identify the producer of the product in question, the UK argued that such a concept was superfluous since, if the producer cannot be identified, the liability falls on the supplier. It also warned that the introduction of market share liability 'would have far reaching consequences for producers and might discourage record keeping for traceability purposes.'[91] The cognate issue of loss of a chance has already been broached in no 53 and, as it is best regarded as relating to the definition of damage rather than causation, is not pursued further here.

57 All relevant circumstances can be taken into consideration in determining the cause of the damage. Domestic rules on causation apply. English law proceeds on the basis of both factual and legal causation. Factual causation is

---

87 [1987] AC 750.

88 As to why this is the case, see McGregor on Damages (19th edn 2014) Chapter 10.

89 *Ide v ATB Sales Ltd* [2008] EWCA Civ 424, at [19] per Thomas LJ.

90 On proportional liability in English law see *K Oliphant*, Causal Uncertainty and Proportional Liability in England and Wales, in: I Gilead/MD Green/BA Koch (eds), Proportional Liability: Analytical and Comparative Perspectives (2013).

91 United Kingdom response to the Commission's Green Paper on Liability for Defective Products (fn 18) 3.

generally approached under the 'but for' test, though there are exceptions. Where there are two or more acts or events which would each be sufficient to bring about the claimant's injury but the claimant is unable to prove which act or event in fact caused the loss (ie *multiple concurrent or alternative causes*), a broader view of causation may be taken on grounds of fairness and reasonableness. In such cases, it is sufficient to show that the defendant's conduct 'materially contributed' to the claimant's injury[92] or to the risk of the same.[93] In the case of *overtaken causes* – that is, where a claimant is injured by a defendant's negligence but prior to trial suffers similar loss as a result of an independent supervening event – the initial injury may still be considered the cause of the damage and damages will be awarded against the initial defendant where the supervening event was tortious; otherwise the supervening event is treated as a risk within the claimant's sphere and curtails the defendant's liability.[94] Where the successive event is hypothetical rather than actual, a reduction of damages will ensue.[95]

58 As regards legal causation, a *voluntary intervening act of a third party* breaks the chain of causation unless the defendant was under an exceptional duty to protect against third-party interference.[96] No hard and fast rules can be laid down as to lawful or negligent intervening acts of a third party.[97] As regards an *involuntary intervening act of a third party*, the starting point is to ask whether the intervention was reasonably foreseeable. If it was, liability is likely to stick. In the case of *intervening events*, the position is that '[w]here the event is dependent upon the defendant's act in the sense that it would not have occurred had the defendant not acted as he did, the defendant will be liable for all the damage.'[98]

59 Where the aggrieved party contributes to the damage in question, recourse may be had to the Law Reform (Contributory Negligence) Act 1945: see sec 6(4) CPA. Similar rules of thumb as are stated above in respect of intervening acts of a third party apply to *intervening acts by the claimant*. A claimant cannot be found to have been 100% contributorily negligent.[99] In exceptional circumstances, however, the (full) defence of *volenti non fit iniuria* may apply.[100]

---

92 *Bonnington Castings Ltd v Wardlaw* [1956] AC 613.
93 *McGhee v National Coal Board* [1973] 1 WLR 1; *Fairchild v Glenhaven Funeral Services Ltd* [2003] 1 AC 32.
94 *Baker v Willoughby* [1970] AC 467; *Jobling v Associated Dairies* [1982] AC 794.
95 *Heil v Rankin* [2001] QB 272. See McGregor (fn 88) para 6-040.
96 See *Lamb v Camden LBC* [1981] 2 All ER 408.
97 McGregor (fn 88) paras 6-040 and 6-046.
98 Ibid para 6-072.
99 *Pitts v Hunt* [1990] All ER 344.
100 See, in a different context, *Morris v Murray* [1991] 2 QB 6.

VI. DEFENCES AND EXCLUSIONS

60 Section 4 CPA implements the defences specified in art 7 of the Directive. Under sec 4(1)(a) it is a defence if the 'defect is attributable to compliance with any requirement imposed by or under any enactment' or with any EU obligation. In practice, most legislation tends to set minimum standards whereas the defence only applies in respect of mandatory obligations.[101] Insofar as domestic legislation goes, the provision applies to 'enactments'; consequently, voluntary standards set by bodies governing particular industries do not count.[102]

61 By sec 4(1)(b), it is a defence if 'the person proceeded against did not at any time supply the product to another'. The rule seeks to protect producers in such circumstances as 'where accidents occur before distribution or where products are stolen and supplied through irregular channels.'[103]

62 Section 4(1)(c) applies where the defendant's supply of products was neither in the course of a business nor with a view to profit (see also no 45). In *Henning Veedfald v Århus Amtskommune*, the European Court of Justice (ECJ) made it clear that the equivalent provision in the Directive (art 7(c)) does not exclude a defective product which is manufactured and used in the course of providing a specific medical service, financed entirely from public funds, for which the injured patient is not required to pay any contribution. The fact that a product is manufactured for a specific medical service that is financed from public funds maintained out of taxpayers' contributions cannot detract from the economic and business character of that manufacture.[104]

63 We have already considered the exculpatory ground under sec 4(1)(d) (see no 37). The defence seeks to exclude liability where 'the defect did not exist in the product at the relevant time'[105] and is quite broad in its application. *Piper v JRI (Manufacturing) Ltd* concerned an allegedly defective prosthesis that was implanted into the claimant's right hip.[106] It was held there that it was sufficient to show that the manufacturing and inspection process was such that any imperfections would have been identified before the final inspection process. On the facts, the court inferred that the defect would have been detected had it been present prior to delivery at the hospital, a decision upheld on appeal. The efficacy of this defence is further illustrated by the recent case of *Love v Halfords*

101 *Howells* (fn 40) para 4.252.
102 Ibid para 4.252.
103 Ibid para 4.256.
104 Case C-203/99, [2001] ECR I-3569, at [19] ff.
105 See no 37 on the meaning of the relevant time.
106 [2006] EWCA Civ 1344.

Ltd.[107] The claimant there alleged that his bicycle's steerer tube was defective and thus caused him to lose control and fall, sustaining very serious injuries. In connection with the sec 4(1)(d), the evidential burden fell upon the defendant to show that there was no defect in the steerer tube at the point of sale but was discharged on the facts: as a matter of reasonable inference from the scientific evidence, there was nothing defective about the steerer tube, its design, assembly or the steel from which it was made.[108] Rather, the evidence was that 'some accident in the nature of a collision, or aggressive jumping or similar riding on the bike involving the placing of excessive bending force on the tube took place and there was a botched attempt to repair it which made it worse.'[109]

64 Sec 4(1)(e) enacts the development risk defence. A person is not liable if 'the state of scientific and technical knowledge at the relevant time was not such that a producer of products of the same description as the product in question might be expected to have discovered the defect if it had existed in his products while they were under his control'. The inclusion of the above defence is said to be justified by a number of considerations, 'such as encouragement of technological innovation, keeping down insurance costs, preserving a competitive advantage and (no doubt) to protect the pharmaceutical industry.'[110] Whether sec 4(1)(e) accords to its corresponding provision in the Directive was the question in *Commission v United Kingdom.* Advocate General Tesauro elucidated in his Opinion in the case, and the ECJ agreed, that the defence refers solely to 'scientific and technical knowledge', not safety standards in use in the industry, at the time the product was put into circulation.[111] The Court further ruled that the defence does not contemplate the state of knowledge of which the producer in question was actually or subjectively in or could have been apprised. Rather, the test is objective: the state of scientific and technical knowledge, including *the most advanced level of such knowledge* at the time the product was put into circulation, of which the producer is presumed to have been informed. Only serious or scientific opinions are relevant. The Court went on to add that the relevant scientific and technical knowledge must have been accessible at the time when the product was put into circulation. To illustrate the requirement of accessibility, the Advocate General gave the example of research carried out by an academic in Manchuria published in a local scientific journal in Chinese as knowledge which would not be accessible because the information does not circulate outside the boundaries of the region. In *A v The National Blood Authority*, Burton J thought that 'the right approach is to look at "accessibility" and to regard as Manchuria perhaps an unpublished document or unpublished research not available to

107 [2014] EWHC 1057, [2014] RTR 470.
108 [2014] EWHC 1057, at [50] per Sir Colin Mackay.
109 [2014] EWHC 1057, at [49] per Sir Colin Mackay.
110 Clerk & Lindsell on Torts (fn 33) para 11-71.
111 Case C-300/95 [1997] ECR I-2649, at [26] ff.

the general public, retained within the laboratory or research department of a particular company.'[112] In that case, the claimants had argued that, once the defect in blood is known, it is a known risk and a known risk does not qualify under the defence even if it is unavoidable. Burton J agreed but added that if the risk is one within the legitimate expectations of the public at large it might bear on the separate issue of whether the product was defective.[113] On the facts, the defence was found not to be applicable and the defendant's liability stuck.

65 Finally, it is a defence under sec 4(1)(f) if the defect constituted a defect in a subsequent product in which the original product was comprised and the defect was wholly attributable to the design of the subsequent product or to compliance by the producer of the product in question with instructions given by the producer of the subsequent product.

66 It is for the defendant to prove his case when relying upon the above defences, hence the reference to 'for him to show' in sec 4(1) of the CPA. This can also be inferred from the recital of Directive 85/374/EEC, which reads: 'a fair apportionment of risk between the injured person and the producer implies that the producer should be able to free himself from liability *if he furnishes proof* as the existence of certain exonerating circumstances'.[114]

67 Section 7 CPA prohibits the exclusion or restriction of liability.[115] Any term or notice purporting to have such effect would thus be invalid.

VII. REMEDIES

68 Damages are available for damage to the interests specified in no 47 ff above. English courts do not allow the reduction of the claimant's award by reference to the defendant's economic position or on other equitable grounds. It is very unlikely that punitive or exemplary damages could be awarded under the CPA, given the 1985 Directive's foundation on the need to approximate national laws.[116] Such a conclusion is also consistent with the lack of express

112 [2001] 3 All ER 289, at [49].

113 For criticisms of this aspect of the decision see *Lunney/Oliphant* (fn 20) 594 f.

114 Emphasis added. See also *Love v Halfords Ltd* [2014] EWHC 1057, at [25] f per Sir Colin Mackay.

115 'The liability of a person by virtue of this Part to a person who has suffered damage caused wholly or partly by a defect in a product, or to a dependant or relative of such a person, shall not be limited or excluded by any contract term, by any notice or by any other provision.'

116 On the availability of such damages in England and in Continental Europe generally, see *H Koziol/V Wilcox*, Punitive Damages: Common Law and Civil Law Perspectives (2009). See also Clerk & Lindsell on Torts (fn 33) para 11-84.

mention of the availability of such damages in the CPA and the non-availability of exemplary (and indeed aggravated) damages in the tort of negligence.[117]

69 An action lies under the Fatal Accidents Act 1976 in the case of death. Bereavement damages are available to a fixed category of eligible persons (including the spouse of the deceased).[118] A fixed statutory sum, currently set at £12,980, is paid.[119] Any damage for which a person is liable under sec 2 of the CPA is deemed to have been caused, for the purposes of the 1976 Act, by that person's wrongful act, neglect or default: sec 6(1)(a) CPA. See no 71.

70 It is not possible to seek an injunction in respect of a defective product under the CPA. The UK Government has said that it 'do[es] not see a case for extending the right of a consumer to seek an injunction if injured by a defective product. We feel this goes beyond the aims of the Directive. And furthermore, such a change would fundamentally alter the present safety regime for products. It is not clear what benefit this would have for consumers or businesses.'[120] The UK Government also has no plans to introduce a special compensation scheme for the victims of defective products in cases where the development risks defence applies and has noted that it would 'be difficult to assess the likely demand on such a fund.'[121]

VIII. PROCEDURAL AND EVIDENTIAL ISSUES

71 Although not expressly stated under the CPA, a claimant is required to prove certain aspects of his case (including the existence of a defect, causation and damage: see nos 27 ff, 55 ff and 47 ff respectively) as is a defendant as regards the available defences (see no 60 ff). As in all civil proceedings, the standard of proof is the balance of probabilities (see nos 27 and 55). In applying this standard, the court may be prepared to work on the basis of inferences, as mentioned under nos 27 and 63 above.

72 Schedule 1 CPA amended the Limitation Act 1980 in its application in relation to the bringing of actions under Part I CPA. In the case of defective products, the relevant period is three years from the date on which the cause of action accrued and the date of knowledge of the injured person or, in the

117 *Kralj v McGrath* [1986] 1 All ER 54 (aggravated damages); *Kuddus v Chief Constable of Leicestershire* [2001] UKHL 29 [2002] 2 AC 122, at [122] per Lord Scott (exemplary damages).
118 Section 1A(2). See proposed changes under the Negligence and Damages Bill 2015–16.
119 Section 1A(3).
120 United Kingdom response to the Commission's Green Paper on Liability for Defective Products (fn 18) 7.
121 Ibid 4.

case of loss of or damage to property, the date of knowledge of the plaintiff or (if earlier) of any person in whom his cause of action was previously vested, whichever is the later.[122] In the case of death the period is three years from the date of death or the date of the personal representative's knowledge, whichever is the later.[123] There is a long-stop period of ten years from the relevant time (as to which see no 37).[124] In response to the question in the Commission's Green Paper of whether the latter period would benefit from modification, the UK Government stated that sympathy lay with those who advocate increasing the period of liability as some injuries (such as BSE) have long incubation periods and may appear later than ten years after the product was supplied; however, it felt that doubling the period, for example, would add significantly to business costs and would bear particularly heavily on smaller enterprises. It was also concerned about the practicability of deciding to which sectors to apply longer time limits. Finally, it added that such an added layer of complexity would not be in the interests of business or consumers.[125]

IX. ALTERNATIVE REGULATIONS AND REMEDIES

A. CONSEQUENCES OF PURSUING DOMESTIC REMEDIES

73 As mentioned in no 10, an action in contract and tort may be brought alongside or instead of one under the CPA, provided only that the claimant does not recover damages several times over. A claimant will be advised as to which course to pursue in light of the precise circumstances of his case.

74 Strict liability is the default rule in contract unless the contract imposes a fault standard (so that a contractual duty of care arises). The alternative action in tort will generally be in respect of negligence, which as its name suggests requires fault. It is noteworthy that English courts have generally refused to rely on the doctrine of *res ipsa loquitur* in domestic product liability cases to infer negligence from the very nature of an accident or injury (cf no 27).[126] However, in *Grant v Australian Knitting Mills Ltd*, a case in which a claimant who contracted dermatitis alleged that this was the result of wearing a woollen garment in which

122 Limitation Act 1980, sec 11A(4). 'Personal injuries' includes any disease and any impairment of a person's physical or mental condition, and 'injury' and cognate expressions shall be construed accordingly: sec 38(1) Limitation Act 1980.

123 Limitation Act 1980, sec 11A(5).

124 Limitation Act 1980, sec 11A(3).

125 United Kingdom response to the Commission's Green Paper on Liability for Defective Products (fn 18) 5.

126 *Mason v Williams & Williams Ltd* [1955] 1 WLR 549, 551 f per Finnemore J. *See also Evans v Triplex Safety Glass Co Ltd* [1936] 1 All ER 283.

excess sulphites were found, the Privy Council ruled that: 'If excess sulphites were left in the garment, that could only be because some one was at fault ... Negligence is found *as a matter of inference* from the existence of the defects taken in connection with all the known circumstances: even if the manufacturers could by apt evidence have rebutted that inference they have not done so.'[127] In effect, therefore, the same outcome is reached as if *res ipsa loquitur* had been applied. A more concrete advantage in pursuing one's claim in negligence (or in contract) is that such actions are not limited to products but rather they can extend, *inter alia*, to services – for example, damage arising from hire-purchase agreements or from those who conduct repair or installation work (see also the liability for misstatements in no 76).[128] This is not the case under the CPA (see no 20 above). Also, unlike the CPA which is effectively limited to protecting consumers, most actions in contract and tort extend to business claimants.

75 The difficulty arising from the doctrine of privity of contract is somewhat alleviated by the Contracts (Rights of Third Parties) Act 1999, which entitles third parties to enforce a term of a contract if the contract expressly provides that they may or if the term purports to confer a benefit on them. This is no help to a bystander, however (cf an action in tort). Moreover, where goods are sold via a distribution chain, liability is *prima facie* limited to the immediate contracting party and does not automatically extend to the manufacturer. While the seller will invariably have a contract with the supplier and he with his supplier until the contractual chain reaches back to the manufacturer, suing along a contractual chain is not altogether efficient. Moreover, a difficulty arises where one party in the chain has ceased to trade for whatever reason or is uninsured, out of the jurisdiction or can benefit from an exclusion clause.[129] Admittedly, certain warranties are implied into contracts for sale in the course of business (see no 03) including correspondence with quality or fitness and sample supplied.[130] Yet this is not the case where (for example) a fault was specifically drawn to the buyer's attention before the contract was made and/or would have been apparent on a reasonable examination in the case of a sale by sample.[131] Nonetheless, the

---

127 [1936] AC 85, 101 per Lord Wright (emphasis added).

128 Markesinis and Deakin's Tort Law (fn 69) 610.

129 Ibid 608.

130 See sec 14 f of the Sale of Goods Act 1979; sec 10 f of the Supply of Goods (Implied Terms) Act 1973; secs 4 f and 9 f of the Supply of Goods and Services Act 1985. In the case of consumers see, among others, secs 9 f and 13 of the Consumer Rights Act 2015.

131 On implied terms about quality or fitness see, for example, sec 14(2C)(a) of the Sale of Goods Act 1979; sec 10(2C)(a) of the Supply of Goods (Implied Terms) Act 1973 and secs 4(3)(c) and 9(3)(c) of the Supply of Goods and Services Act 1985. In the case of sale by sample see secs 14(2C)(c) and 15(2)(c) of the Sale of Goods Act 1979; secs 10(2C)(c) and 11(1)(c) of the Supply of Goods (Implied Terms) Act 1973 and secs 4(3)(c), 5(2)(c), 9(3)(c) and 10(2)(c) of the Supply of Goods and Services Act 1982. In the case of consumers see, among others, sec 9(4)(a) of the Consumer Rights Act 2015 on satisfactory quality and secs 9(4)(a) and 13(2) on sale by sample.

effect of implied terms is that a purchaser is protected in contract even if the goods were not 'unsafe' and thus caused no damage but were merely shoddy. Purchasers also benefit from a statutory presumption that goods which do not conform to the contract of sale within a period of six months from the date of delivery are taken not to have conformed to it on that day.[132]

76 Should one choose to seek redress in the form of an action for breach of contract or tort, one 'lets in all the consequences of that form of action.'[133] The aim of contractual damages is to put the non-breaching party in the position he would have occupied had the contract been fulfilled, while that in tort is the restoration of the *status quo ante* (more exactly: putting the victim in the position he would have been in had the tort not occurred). An advantageous consequence in both cases is the availability of damages for pure economic loss (cf CPA, no 48). In tort, however, such losses are mostly restricted to cases where one can establish a relationship of proximity through an assumption of responsibility by the defendant to the claimant. A 'defective' or negligently made statement may fall within the so-called *Hedley Byrne* exception, thus entitling a successful claimant to such damages.[134] Damage to the product itself is also recoverable in contract and (perhaps) in tort. Exemplary and aggravated damages can be pursued under (some) torts. A greater number of defences also exist, for example exclusion of liability in tort and duress and frustration in contract.

77 One who frames his action in contract can seek to rely upon general contractual remedies such as rescission and specific performance. Moreover, certain statutory remedies serve to benefit consumers: by sec 24 of the Consumer Protection Act 2015, for example, a right to require the seller to repair or replace the problematic goods or to require him to reduce the purchase price is implied.

78 In addition, restitutionary remedies may be sought as a basis for redress in contract and tort, though this option is not often available and is seldom pursued. An injunction can also be sought in contract but not in tort claims based on negligence.

---

132 See Consumer Rights Act 2015, sec 19(14). The provision does not apply if it is established that the goods did so conform to the contract on that day or its application is incompatible with the nature of the goods or with how they fail to conform to the contract.

133 *Addis v Gramophone Co Ltd* [1909] AC 488, 496 per Lord Atkinson.

134 *Hedley Byrne & Co Ltd v Heller & Partners Ltd* [1964] AC 465. See also liability under the Misrepresentation Act 1967.

B. DUTY TO RECALL

79 The CPA does not itself provide for a producer's liability for damage caused by its failure to recall a dangerous product, but in appropriate circumstances a duty to recall and a corresponding liability for breach of that duty can arise at common law.[135] In practice, the content of that duty is likely to be shaped by the regulations relating to recall notices (considered below).

80 Regulation 15 of the General Product Safety Regulations 2005 deals specifically with recall notices. Subregulation 1 reads: 'where an enforcement authority has reasonable grounds for believing that a product is a dangerous product and that it has already been supplied or made available to consumers, the authority may serve a notice ("a recall notice") requiring the person on whom it is served to use his reasonable endeavours to organise the return of the product from consumers to that person or to such other person as is specified in the notice.' Regulation 2 defines an 'enforcement authority' as 'the Secretary of State, any other Minister of the Crown in charge of a government department, any such department and any authority or council mentioned in regulation 10'.[136] A 'product' is rather wordily described in reg 2. In short, any product intended or likely to be used by consumers, whether or not this was paid for, is covered. The provision extends to both new and second-hand products but is restricted to items supplied in the course of a commercial activity.[137] A 'dangerous product' is defined as a product other than a safe product, and a 'safe product' means 'a product which, under normal or reasonably foreseeable conditions of use including duration and, where applicable, putting into service, installation and maintenance requirements, does not present any risk or only the minimum risks compatible with the product's use, considered to be acceptable and consistent with a high level of protection for the safety and health of persons': reg 2. In determining the foregoing, the following shall be taken into account: '(a) the characteristics of the product, including its composition, packaging, instructions for assembly and, where applicable, instructions for installation and maintenance, (b) the effect of the product on other products, where it is reasonably foreseeable that it will be used with other products, (c) the

135 *Rivtow Marine Ltd v Washington Iron Works* [1974] SCR 1189 (Canadian Supreme Court).

136 Ie a county council, district council, London Borough Council, the Common Council of the City of London in its capacity as a local authority: reg 10(4).

137 The precise definition is: 'a product which is intended for consumers or likely, under reasonably foreseeable conditions, to be used by consumers even if not intended for them and which is supplied or made available, whether for consideration or not, in the course of a commercial activity and whether it is new, used or reconditioned and includes a product that is supplied or made available to consumers for their own use in the context of providing a service. "Product" does not include equipment used by service providers themselves to supply a service to consumers, in particular equipment on which consumers ride or travel which is operated by a service provider'.

presentation of the product, the labelling, any warnings and instructions for its use and disposal and any other indication or information regarding the product, and (d) the categories of consumers at risk when using the product, in particular children and the elderly. The feasibility of obtaining higher levels of safety or the availability of other products presenting a lesser degree of risk shall not constitute grounds for considering a product to be a dangerous product'.

81 A recall notice may only be issued in specific instances, namely where: '(a) other action which an enforcement authority may require under [the General Product Safety Regulations 2005] would not suffice to prevent the risks concerned to the health and safety of persons, (b) the action being undertaken by the producer or the distributor concerned in fulfilment of his obligations under these Regulations is unsatisfactory or insufficient to prevent the risks concerned to the health and safety of persons, and (c) the authority has given not less than seven days notice to the person on whom the recall notice is to be served of its intention to serve such a notice and where that person has before the expiry of that period by notice required the authority to seek the advice of such person as the Chartered Institute of Arbitrators determines on the questions of – (i) whether the product is a dangerous product, (ii) whether the issue of a recall notice is proportionate to the seriousness of the risk, and the authority has taken account of such advice': reg 15(4). The details of what the recall notice may require are stated in reg 15(2). Where an enforcement authority has been unable to identify any person on whom to serve a recall notice, or the person on whom such a notice has been served has failed to comply with it, then the authority may itself take such action as could have been required by a recall notice: reg 15(9). In the latter case, the authority may recover from the person on whom the notice was served summarily as a civil debt, any costs or expenses reasonably incurred by it: reg 15(10).[138] Of course, a person who has suffered personal injury or property damage as a result of using the dangerous product may pursue a civil action against the producer, etc, of the product under the CPA, among other avenues. However, reg 42 states that the Regulations shall not be construed as conferring any right of action in civil proceedings in respect of any loss or damage suffered in consequence of a contravention of these Regulations. As noted above, the Regulations may yet be relevant in construing the content of the common law duty to recall. Further, the authority may be liable to pay compensation to a person on whom an improper notice was served in respect of any loss or damage suffered by reason of the notice: reg 16. Criminal liability may ensue for the contravention of various provisions under the Regulations: reg 20 (see no 83 f).

---

138 Magistrates' Courts Act 1980, sec 58.

C. SOCIAL SECURITY

82 A person injured by a defective product would of course be entitled to rely on his social security rights. In particular, he may seek free medical consultation before a practitioner that is contracted by the National Health Service (NHS) and he may also seek free NHS hospital treatment. The NHS has a (capped) right of recourse against the tortfeasor under sec 150 of the Health and Social Care (Communities Health Standards) Act 2003, a task undertaken by the Department for Work and Pensions' Compensation Recovery Unit (CRU). An injured person could also be entitled to other social security benefits, for example disability benefits. The value of such benefits may be liable to recoupment by the CRU on behalf of the Secretary of State under the Social Security (Recovery of Benefits) Act 1997.

D. CRIMINAL OFFENCES

83 A whole host of potential criminal offences can arise in connection with defective products. In the case of death or personal injury, these include manslaughter and causing actual bodily harm (ABH). Companies may be liable under the Corporate Manslaughter and Corporate Homicide Act 2007. There is no individual liability under that Act; therefore, the penalty is limited to a fine, albeit of unlimited amount. A director or employee could also be liable for the common law offence of manslaughter, but this is unlikely in the product liability context. The General Product Safety Regulations 2005 also establish a number of criminal offences. In addition to the criminal liability for breach of the regulations on recall notices discussed above (see no 79 ff), it may be noted that a person who contravenes reg 5 (placement of an unsafe product on the market), *inter alia*, is guilty of an offence and may be punished by fine, imprisonment or both: reg 20(1). A defence of due diligence (ie that the person took all reasonable steps and exercised all due diligence to avoid committing the offence) exists under reg 29.

84 The Health and Safety at Work Act 1974 supplements the General Product Safety Regulations 2005 which do not apply in the case of products used in the workplace. Section 6 of the 1974 Act imposes a duty on any person who designs, manufactures, imports or supplies any article for use at work or any article of fairground equipment, *inter alia*, to ensure, so far as is reasonably practicable, that the article is safe and without risks to health. In addition to civil liability under sec 47, breach of the above duty is also an offence under sec 33 and is punishable by fine, imprisonment or both.

E. ADMINISTRATIVE LAW

85 Relevant government authorities are also equipped with administrative powers under the General Product Safety Regulations 2005 including the power to suspend sale (reg 11), organise appropriate checks on the safety properties of a product (reg 21) and to enter and search business premises connected with the production of a product (reg 22).

X. ASSESSMENT OF DOMESTIC LAW

86 It took 12 years after its entry into force for a claim resulting in a reported judgment to be brought under the CPA. This notwithstanding, an increasing number of persons seek to rely upon the Act; this is more a trickle than it is a flood, though. Moreover, such actions have been pursued with various degrees of success.

87 Several reasons have been posited as to why the scale of product-related litigation under the Act has not taken off as expected, including the Act's limited scope. There might be advantages of suing in tort (eg where a product was not put into circulation) or for defects in quality in contract (since the seller is more likely to be local). There is also evidence in the UK that consumers have always been less active in respect of damage by defective products. An empirical examination of pre- and post-implementation data could confirm the generally held view that claims consciousness is localised to specific wrongs. Expenses involved (eg for discovery of documents and experts) as well as to the influence of the legal profession, as gatekeepers of the courts, are other explanations. Regard must be had, in the former case, to the restriction of contingency fees to or their predominance in select areas, for example personal injury at work or on the road. The availability of non-legal avenues is a further factor. It is also very likely that a large proportion of claims settle informally out of court.[139]

88 As to the question of whether the Directive has been correctly implemented in national law, the litigation by the Commission (see no 64) illustrates that the latter had some reservations. However, the ECJ did not consider the UK implementing legislation to be manifestly contrary to the Directive, at least insofar as the defence under art 7(e) of the Product Liability Directive was concerned, but it did give guidance as to how it considered it should be interpreted. Indeed, at least one commentator has said that the CPA 'probably

---

139 See *Lunney/Oliphant* (fn 20) 595 for further details.

represents the truest implementation' of the 1985 Directive among the major EU Member States.[140]

89 In the authors' view, the definition of a 'product' does seem apt to cover the new technologies specifically discussed in the introduction to this book. That is not to say, however, that claimants would not face difficulties in proving certain aspects of their claim.

140 *W van Gerven/J Lever/P Larouche*, Cases, Material and Text on National, Supranational and International Tort Law (2000) 668.

PRODUCT LIABILITY IN FRANCE

Jean-Sébastien BORGHETTI

I. SOURCES OF LAW AND THEIR EVOLUTION

A. PRODUCT LIABILITY IN FRANCE BEFORE 1985

01 There was no specific regulation of product liability in France before the implementation of Directive 85/374/EC. The courts had managed to impose strict liability on producers and suppliers of defective products, however, using existing provisions of the Civil Code (CC).

02 When consumer goods started to cause a significant number of accidents, most victims relied on contract law, and more specifically on *garantie des vices cachés*, in order to obtain compensation from manufacturers and/or sellers. *Garantie des vices cachés* (latent defects guarantee; art 1641 ff CC) is of Roman origin and had equivalents in most continental civil codes drafted during the 19th century. The French version provides that when the buyer of a defective product discovers the defect, he has the choice between rescinding the sale or paying a discounted price. As in Roman law, this action was initially intended to remedy the insufficient quality of the thing sold, rather than its insufficient safety.[1] However, the CC provides that when the defect causes injuries or damage distinct from a diminution in value of the thing sold, the buyer can receive damages, but only if the seller knew of the defect (art 1645 CC). This could have posed a formidable obstacle to the compensation of victims, had it not been removed by the *Cour de cassation*, France's supreme judicial court. In the 1960s, the *Cour de cassation* decided that if the seller is a dealer by profession, there is an irrebuttable presumption that he knew of the existence of the defect of the product he sold.[2] Should the defect in the thing sold cause death, injuries or damage to the buyer, the seller is thus bound to compensate him, even if it was materially impossible for the seller to discover the defect.

03 In the 1960s, *garantie des vices cachés* thus became a major weapon in the hands of victims of defective products. They could base a claim on *garantie des vices cachés*, provided they had bought the damaging product. The claim could be directed against the direct seller, but also against any person higher up the chain of sales, including the manufacturer, thanks to *action directe*, an exception

1 *P Malaurie/L Aynès/P-Y Gautier*, Les contrats spéciaux (7th ed 2014) no 379.

2 Cass. com., 1 July 1969, *Bull. civ.* IV, n° 243, *Gaz. Pal.* 1970, 1, tables, v° vente, n° 43; Cass. com., 20 January 1970, *JCP.* 1972, II, 17280, note M Boitard and A Rabut; Cass. com., 27 April 1971, *D.* 1971, somm. 144; Cass. com., 15 November 1971, *D.* 1972, jur. 211, JCP G 1971, IV, 293; Cass. 1re civ., 21 November 1972, *JCP* G 1974, II, 17890, note J Ghestin, *RTD civ.* 1975, 126, obs. G Cornu; Cass. com., 27 November 1973, *Bull. civ.* IV, no 344 and 345, *JCP* G 1974, II, 17887, note Ph Malinvaud, *RTD civ.* 1975, 126, obs. G Cornu.

to privity of contract.[3] Provided they had bought the defective product, victims therefore did not lack people they could sue.

04 Of course, in order to obtain compensation, victims had to prove that their damage had been caused by a defect in the product, and that this defect already existed at the time the product left the defendant. Besides, the CC provided that the buyer had to bring the action only a short time after the defect had been discovered (art 1648 CC).[4] But when these requirements were met, *garantie des vices cachés* allowed for the compensation of any type of damage, be it death, personal injury, damage to property or pure economic loss.

05 If the victim of a defective product did not happen to also be the buyer of this product, he could not avail himself of contract law remedies and *garantie des vices cachés*. He therefore had to rely on delictual liability. In most cases, the only action available to him was that grounded in article 1382 CC, which sets a general liability for fault rule.[5] Theoretically, it meant that in order to receive compensation the victim had to demonstrate that the manufacturer or the seller of the product had been at fault. There again, however, the courts had succeeded in alleviating the burden on the claimant.

06 As early as the 1930s, the *Cour de cassation* had decided in some cases that the mere fact of selling a defective product could constitute negligence towards third parties on the part of a professional seller.[6] This judicial trend got stronger in the 1960s, ie precisely at the time when French lawyers became

---

3 When there exists a 'chain of contracts along which the property of a thing has been transferred' (*chaîne contractuelle translative de propriété*), ie when the property of a thing has been transferred several times in a row, usually through sales contracts, the latest owner of the thing can raise a claim in contract against any of the previous owners of that thing, even though he himself has not entered a contract with that owner. For example, if A sells a product to B who sells it to C who sells it to D, and if the product proves to be defective, D can raise a claim in contract against either C or B or A, as long as he demonstrates that the product was defective when it left the defendant's hands.

4 The length of this 'short period' was not set by the CC and had to be determined by judges according to the facts of the case. It usually did not exceed 12 months. Since a 2005 statute entered into force, an action grounded on *guarantie des vices cachés* must be brought within two years after the defect was discovered or should have been discovered by the buyer.

5 Art 1382 CC states that 'every act whatever of man that causes damage to another, obliges him by whose fault it occurred to repair it.' (The English version of the CC is borrowed from the English translation of the Code Civil edited by A Levasseur, D Grunning and R Trahan, and available on the official French legal website <legifrance.gouv.fr>). A reform of the French common law of contract was adopted in February 2016 and will come into force on 1 October 2016. It affects neither the rules on delictual liability nor the ones pertaining to specific contracts such as the contract of sale. It will however entail a re-numbering of the provisions on delictual liability. Art 1382 CC will thus become art 1240 as of 1 October 2016.

6 See Cass. civ., 22 July 1931, *Gaz. Pal.* 1931, 2, 683; Cass. req., 8 March 1937, *S.* 1937, 1, 241, rapp. Pilon, *D.* 1938, 1, 76, note R Savatier; Cass. req., 7 October 1940, *DH* 1940, jur. 180, *Gaz. Pal.* 1940, 2, 64.

aware of the growing number of accidents caused by consumer goods. It became a general rule that the putting into circulation or the sale of a defective good by a professional, whether a manufacturer or a mere seller, constituted an act of negligence, on which an action based on article 1382 CC could be grounded.[7] This was all the more favourable to claimants, as French law does not usually distinguish between different types of damage and article 1382 allows for the compensation of death, personal injuries, damage to property or even pure economic loss.

07 By so doing, the *Cour de cassation* nearly harmonised the situation of victims regardless of their contractual status. Whether or not they had bought the defective product themselves, victims only had to demonstrate the defectiveness of the product in order to obtain compensation from either the professional seller or the manufacturer of the product.[8] Although the divide between liability in contract and liability in tort theoretically remained essential, the situation of victims was scarcely affected by their contractual status.[9]

08 Another striking feature of French product liability law before 1985 was that it put manufacturers and professional sellers or dealers on an equal footing. In most European countries, no-fault product liability, when it existed, rested solely on manufacturers. Sellers incurred no liability in tort for a defect in the product they had sold if they had committed no negligence. On the contrary, from the outset, French law made the professional seller liable in damages for a defect in his product, even if he had not been aware of it and even when he was sued in tort and not in contract. Of course, when a professional seller was sued in relation to a defect in the product he had sold, he could bring a reverse action against the manufacturer of this product. It was the manufacturer who had to bear the final cost of compensation, at least if the defect in the product dated

---

7 Cass. com., 20 March 1961, *Bull. civ.* III, no 148; Cass. 1re civ., 11 December 1961, *Bull. civ.* I, no 595; Cass. 2e civ., 16 March 1966, *Bull. civ.* II, no 350; Cass. 3e civ., 18 April 1972, *Bull. civ.* III, no 233; Cass. 1re civ., 18 July 1972, *Bull. civ.* I, no 189; *D.* 1973, somm. 39; Cass. 3e civ., 5 December 1972, *D.* 1973, jur. 401, note J Mazeaud; Cass. com., 26 June 1978, *Bull. civ.* IV, no 177; Cass. 1re civ., 27 June 1978, *Bull. civ.* I, no 243, *D.* 1978, inf. rap. 409, obs. C Larroumet.

8 Quite paradoxically, victims who were not buyers of the product were in an even better position than the ones who had bought the product, since the latter had to bring their claim within the 'short period' (in practice around one year) mentioned by art 1648 CC, whereas the former were submitted to the prescription period applicable to non-contractual liability law claims, which was thirty years until 1985 and was then reduced to ten years. A new reform of prescription law took place in 2008, however.

9 *J Ghestin*, 'L'application des règles spécifiques de la vente à la responsabilité des fabricants et distributeurs de produits en droit français', in: C Gavalda (ed), La responsabilité des fabricants et distributeurs (1975) 3–67, no 5; *P Malinvaud*, 'La responsabilité civile du fabricant en droit français', in: La responsabilité du fabricant dans les États membres du Marché Commun (1974) 131–159, *in fine*; *H Mazeaud*, La responsabilité civile du vendeur-fabricant, *RTD civ.* 1955, 611–621, *in fine*.

back to the production stage.[10] Nevertheless, from the victim's point of view, the manufacturer and the professional seller were equally liable for the consequences of the product's defect, regardless of any negligence on their part. This important feature of French law partly explains France's reaction to the 1985 Directive.

B. PRODUCT LIABILITY IN FRANCE BETWEEN 1985 AND THE IMPLEMENTATION OF THE DIRECTIVE

09 The adoption of the Directive did not go unnoticed in France. Nevertheless, it took nearly 13 years before the statute implementing it was approved. The main reason for this delay was the controversial nature of the development risk defence.

10 Before 1985, the notion of development risk was almost totally unknown to French lawyers.[11] The Directive and the option created by article 15(1)(b) made them realise that the handling of unknown risks at the time the product is put into circulation was a crucial feature in any product liability regime. The importance of the development risk defence was further enhanced by the breakout of the notorious *affaire du sang contaminé* in the middle of the 1980s. This tainted blood scandal has had great repercussions on French politics and even French law.[12] Although the media and the general public focused on the criminal aspect of the scandal, it also had an impact on product liability law.

11 When civil courts were faced with claims in damages from tainted blood victims, they had to deal with the question as to whether the blood purveyors had been or could have been aware of the presence of HIV in the contaminated blood samples. And when some purveyors were found to have been legitimately ignorant of the existing risks, courts had to decide what the legal consequences of such ignorance had to be. The *Cour de cassation* finally decided that the undiscoverable character of the virus constituted no defence for the blood purveyors, who therefore had to answer for the deaths, injuries and damage caused by the contaminated blood they had distributed.[13]

12 Although the liability of blood purveyors was a liability in contract, most French scholars assumed it to be a general rule of French product liability

---

10 *J-S Borghetti*, La responsabilité du fait des produits. Étude de droit comparé (2004) no 234.

11 *O Berg*, La notion de risque de développement en matière de responsabilité du fait des produits défectueux, *JCP* G 1996, I, 3945, p. 271.

12 For a comprehensive presentation – in English – of this scandal and its impact on French liability law, see *S Whittaker*, Liability for Products: English Law, French Law, and European Harmonization (2005) 149–151, 315–319, 394–401.

13 Cass. 1re civ., 12 avril 1995, *JCP* G 1995, II, 22467, note P Jourdain, ibid I, 3893, no 20, obs. G Viney.

law, whether contractual or delictual, that the existence of a development risk constituted no defence for the producers and dealers. A close examination of case law shows that this opinion rested on no firm ground, since it is not possible to find a single case in which the *Cour de cassation* found a manufacturer or a dealer liable in tort in a development risk context.[14] However, it became a widespread belief among French lawyers that the development risk defence was totally alien to French law.[15] As a consequence, many scholars considered that the defence provided for by the Directive was unacceptable, since it meant a step back for consumer protection. On the other hand, French industry favoured the development risk defence, for obvious reasons.

13 This debate between proponents and opponents of the development risk defence reached Parliament. Between 1988 and 1998, various attempts were made to implement the 1985 Directive into French law, but the defence was a point of permanent contention between consumer-friendly and industry-friendly MPs.[16] Although development risks were never a real issue for the general public, the various French governments proved incapable of taking a firm stance on the question. This explains why it took France 13 years and one condemnation by the European Court of Justice[17] to transpose the Directive. In the meantime, however, the Directive exerted a strong influence on French product liability law, owing to judicial activism.

14 Between 1989 and 1998, the *Cour de cassation* developed a new product liability regime, directly inspired by the 1985 Directive.[18] The Court decided that manufacturers and professional sellers must deliver products free from any 'safety defect' (*défaut de sécurité*).[19] The concept of a 'safety defect' was defined

14 *Borghetti* (fn 10) no 412 ff.

15 See *P Jourdain*, Commentaire de la loi n° 98–389 du 19 mai 1998 sur la responsabilité du fait des produits défectueux, *JCP* E 1998, 1204–1215, no 37; *S Lambert*, La loi du 19 mai 1998 relative à la responsabilité du fait des produits défectueux (2000), 128; *C Larroumet*, La responsabilité du fait des produits défectueux après la loi du 19 mai 1998, *D.* 1998, chron. 311–316, no 23; *G Viney*, L'introduction en droit français de la directive communautaire du 25 juillet 1985, *D.* 1998, 291–299, no 18. For a more balanced point of view, see *M Charmant*, Rapport au nom de la Commission des lois, Assemblée nationale, n° 2136, 20 June 1991, 26.

16 *H, L and J Mazeaud/F Chabas*, Leçons de droit civil. Obligations. Théorie générale, t II, vol I, 9th edition by F. Chabas (1998) no 558-1.

17 ECJ, 13 January 1993, Case C-293/91, *Commission v France.*

18 *Borghetti* (fn 10) no 218 ff.

19 Cass. 1re civ., 20 March 1989, *D.* 1989, jur. 381, note P Malaurie, *RTD civ.* 1989, 756, obs. P Jourdain; Cass. 1re civ., 22 January 1991, *Bull. civ.* I, no 30, *RTD civ.* 1991, 539, obs. P Jourdain; Cass. 1re civ., 11 June 1991, *Bull. civ.* I, no 201, *D.* 1993, somm. 241, obs. O Tournafond, *JCP* G 1992, I, 3572, no 158, obs. G Viney, *RTD civ.* 1992, 114, obs. P Jourdain; Cass. 1re civ., 27 January 1993, *Bull. civ.*, I, no 44, *D.* 1994, somm. 238, obs. O Tournafond, *RTD civ.* 1993, 592, obs. P Jourdain; Cass. 1re civ., 17 January 1995, *D.* 1995, jur. 350, note P Jourdain, *JCP* G 1995, I, 3853, no 9, obs. G Viney; Cass. 1re civ., 15 October 1996, *Bull. civ.* I, no 354, *D.* 1997, somm. 287, obs. P Jourdain and 348, obs. Ph Brun, *JCP* G 1997, I, 4025 no 13,

in exactly the same way as in the 1985 Directive. A product was thus defective if it did not provide the safety which a person is entitled to expect.[20] Should the security defect in a product cause death, injuries or damage, the manufacturer or professional seller of the product was to be held liable in damages. This liability was of contractual nature but was distinct from the liability incurred on the basis of *guarantie des vices cachés*. This was very interesting from the victims' point of view, as it meant that plaintiffs did not have to bring their action within the short period characteristic of the latter. It was the ordinary limitation period for actions in contract which applied, ie thirty years at that time.[21] Another striking feature of this new regime was that, despite its contractual nature, it benefited any victim, whatever his contractual status.[22] A bystander could thus get damages on the basis of this liability regime.

C. THE IMPLEMENTATION OF THE DIRECTIVE

15 France at last implemented the 1985 Directive through a law of 19 May 1998.[23] The new product liability provisions have been inserted into the CC and now form a new section of it.[24]

16 When the Directive was finally implemented in French law, the Government and Parliament chose to depart on several points from the black letter of the Directive in order to improve the level of consumer protection.[25] This should come as no surprise, given France's obsession with consumer protection. But this was not accepted by European authorities, and France was penalised by the ECJ in 2002.[26] Some changes were made to the new CC

---

obs. G Viney; Cass. 1re civ., 3 March 1998, *Bull. civ.* I, no 95, *D.* 1999, jur. 36, note G Pignarre and Ph Brun, *JCP* G 1998, II, 10049, concl. P Sargos, *JCP* G1998, I, 144, no 18, obs. G Viney, *RTD civ.* 1998, 683, obs. P Jourdain; Cass. 1re civ., 28 April 1998, *Bull. civ.* I, no 104, *JCP* G 1998, II, 10088, concl. P Sargos, *JCP* G 1998, I, 185, no 19, obs. G Viney, *RTD civ.* 1998, 684, obs. P Jourdain.

20 Cass. 1re civ., 3 March 1998 (fn 19).

21 Prescription law was reformed in 2008 and the normal prescription period is now five years (art 2224), but it is extended to ten years in case of bodily injuries (art 2226); see *infra* no 72.

22 Cass. 1re civ., 17 January 1995 (fn 19); Cass. 1re civ., 28 April 1998 (fn 19); Cass. 1re civ., 13 February 2001, *Bull. civ.* I, no 35, *D.* 2001, somm. 2234, obs. Ph Delebecque, *JCP* G 2002, II, 10099, note C Lisanti-Kalczynski, *RTD civ.* 2001, 367, obs. P Jourdain.

23 *Loi* n° 98-389 of 19 May 1998.

24 Art 1386-1 to 1386-18 CC. As of 1 October 2016, they will become arts 1245 – 1245-17 CC (see fn 5).

25 *Borghetti* (fn 10) n° 532.

26 ECJ, 25 April 2002, Case C-52/00, *Commission v France*, *D.* 2002, act. 1670, note C Rondey, somm. 2935, obs. J-P Pizzio, doctr. 2458, note J Calais-Auloy, jur. 2462, note C Larroumet, *JCP* G 2002, I, 177, note G Viney, *RTD civ.* 2002, 523, obs. P Jourdain, 868, obs. J Raynard. The ECJ ruled that France had failed to fulfil its obligations under the Directive by including damage of less than €500 in art 1386-2 CC, by providing in the first paragraph of art 1386-7

provisions through a law of 9 December 2004, in order to comply with the 2002 ECJ decision. These changes, however, were deemed insufficient by the European Commission and France was condemned anew by the ECJ in 2006.[27] A new modification of the CC was then voted in as an emergency measure, which should prevent any further condemnation.[28] If one excludes the issue of recoverable damage,[29] the scope of the CC provisions on product liability is now exactly the same as the Directive's. They only regulate those issues addressed in the Directive.

17 A major question, following the Directive's official implementation in 1998, has been the impact of this implementation on the judge-made product liability regime developed by the *Cour de cassation* in the 1990s. Since this regime was more or less a translation of the 1985 Directive, it should have disappeared when the Directive was officially implemented into the CC. However, there were some significant differences between this regime and the Directive's regime, now to be found in the CC. The main one was that the CC regime channels liability to the producer, whereas the judge-made regime theoretically put the producer and the professional seller on an equal footing. It was therefore much more consumer-friendly, and the question was whether this regime could be kept alive.

18 According to the ECJ's *González Sánchez* decision,[30] Member States are not allowed to maintain a product liability regime that has a general scope and the same basis as that put in place by the Directive, but that is distinct from the Directive's regime.[31] The French judge-made product liability regime thus seemed to be condemned by this interpretation of the Directive, since it rests on the product's defectiveness. However, some argued that the *Cour de cassation* could easily amend its previous case law in order to comply with the ECJ's interpretation of the Directive without giving up sellers' liability.[32] This position gained further support from the 2006 *Skov* decision,[33] in which the ECJ ruled that the 1985 Directive does not preclude a national rule under which the

---

that the supplier of a defective product was to be liable in all cases and on the same basis as the producer, and by providing in the second paragraph of art 1386-12 that the producer had to prove that he had taken appropriate steps to avert the consequences of a defective product in order to be able to rely on the grounds of exemption from liability provided for in art 7(d) and (e) of the Directive.

27 ECJ, 14 March 2006, Case C-177/04, *Commission v France*.

28 *Loi* n° 2006-409 of 5 April 2006, which amended art 1386-7 CC.

29 See *infra* no 53.

30 ECJ, 25 April 2002, Case C-183/00, *Maria Victoria González Sánchez v Medicina Asturiana SA*.

31 Point 33.

32 *Borghetti* (fn 10) no 601 ff.

33 ECJ, 10 January 2006, Case C-402/03, *Skov Æg v Bilka Lavprisvarehus A/S and Bilka Lavprisvarehus A/S v Jette Mikkelsen, Michael Due Nielsen*.

supplier is answerable without restriction for the producer's fault-based liability. As a matter of fact, it might have been possible for the *Cour de cassation* to fall back on the position it adopted in the 1960s and to decide that the putting into circulation or the sale of a defective product constitutes per se a fault on the part of the professional manufacturer or seller.

19 The *Cour de cassation*, however, clearly declined to take this path, and rather chose to abide by the Directive's spirit. In a 2007 decision, it ruled that a professional supplier that was not a manufacturer could not be made liable towards the victim of a product's defect on the basis of the judge-made product liability regime.[34] This, in effect, means that this regime cannot be relied on to reach solutions different from those provided for by the Directive. The harmonised European regime therefore now reigns supreme. The judge-made regime remains nominally applicable only to those products put into circulation between the expiration date of the implementation delay that had been set for the Directive (30 July 1988), and the entry into force of the CC provisions (21 May 1998). As the Directive's regime should apply to these products, but they cannot formally be subjected to the CC provisions, the *Cour de cassation* rules that they should be subjected to judge-made product liability 'interpreted in the light of the Directive'. The differences that existed between the judge-made regime and the Directive's are thus erased, and it is the Directive's rules that are directly applied under the guise of the judge-made regime. The only exception concerns the development risk defence: the *Cour de cassation* ruled that, since this defence was only optional, it should not apply to products put into circulation before the coming into force of the CC provisions, which marked the legislator's intention to introduce this defence, without retroactivity, into French law.[35]

20 It must also be noted that the *Cour de cassation*, departing from the solution it followed in the 1960s, refuses to regard the mere selling or putting into circulation of a defective product as a fault[36] – thus preventing the circumvention of the Directive's regime through the use of classical liability for fault rules. According to the *Cour de cassation*, liability for fault can only be relied on if a fault has been characterised that is 'distinct from the defect'.[37]

---

34 Cass. 1re civ. 15 May 2007, *Bull. civ.* I, no 186, JCP G 2007, I, 185, no 8, obs. Ph Stoffel-Munck, *RDC* 2007, 1147, obs. J-S Borghetti, *RTD civ.* 2007, 580, obs. P Jourdain.

35 Cass. 1re civ. 15 May 2007, *Bull. civ.* I, no 185, *RDC* 2007, 1147, obs. J-S Borghetti; Cass. 1re civ., 9 July 2009, *CCC* 2009, 261, obs. L Leveneur.

36 See *supra* no 06.

37 See Cass. com. 26 May 2010, *Bull. civ.* IV, no 99, *JCP* G 2010, 1015, obs. Ph Stoffel-Munck; *RDC* 2010, 1266, obs. S Carval, *RTD civ.* 2010, 790, obs. P Jourdain; Cass 1re civ, 10 December 2014, no 13-14.314.

21 The regime resulting from the Directive's implementation is thus the only product liability regime applicable under French law. Depending on the circumstances, other liability regimes might apply to damage caused by a defective product,[38] but they do not qualify as product liability regimes, in the sense of regimes based on the product's defectiveness and that would apply either to all products and to certain specific categories.

II. BASIC ELEMENTS OF LIABILITY

22 French law closely follows the Directive as far as the elements giving rise to liability are concerned. No other elements than damage, the product's defect and a causal link between the two are required. Article 1386-9 CC[39] further provides that the plaintiff must prove all three elements.

23 The defences are also the same as the ones mentioned by the Directive. The only difference between the French implementation provisions and the Directive concerns the development risk defence when elements of the human body or by-products derived therefrom are at stake.[40]

A. PRODUCTS

24 Article 1386-3 CC[41] closely follows the Directive and provides: 'A product is any movable thing, even though incorporated into an immovable, including the products of the soil, of stock-farming, and of hunting and fishing. Electricity is deemed a product.' There is hardly any case law on the issue of what is a product under the special product liability regime, however.

25 As far as 'intellectual products' are concerned, there has been some debate among French scholars on whether they are covered by the Directive and the new CC provisions. The prevailing view, supported by this report's author, is that they should not, as this was not the intention of the Directive's drafters and the European product liability regime is obviously designed for physical products, but is rather ill-suited for intellectual products.[42] There has been no judicial decision on this issue so far to either confirm or deny this view.

---

38 Such as liability for fault, or liability for the deed of things.
39 As of 1 October 2016: art 1245-8 CC.
40 See *infra* no 26.
41 As of 1 October 2016: art 1245-2 CC.
42 *Borghetti* (fn 10) no 494-495.

26 Another issue is that of elements of the human body. That these can be products in the sense of the French implementation provisions is made clear by article 1386–12 CC,[43] which provides that 'a producer may not invoke the exonerating circumstance provided for in Article 1386–11, 4° [development risk defence],[44] when the damage was caused by an element of the human body or by products derived therefrom.' This article restricts the application of the development risk defence and is the result of the compromise struck between proponents and opponents of the defence, when the Directive was finally implemented into French law: the defence was retained, according to the wishes of business circles, but it was not made applicable to blood products, in order not to undo the solutions which had been reached by the courts after the tainted blood scandal;[45] besides, the legislator chose to extend the exclusion of the defence to all 'elements of the human body or product derived therefrom', for reasons that are not totally clear.[46]

27 Following article 2 of the Directive, article 1386–3 CC provides that items of movable property attached to immovable property should be treated as products. This apparently has not raised difficulties so far, but it is obvious that the producer of the item of movable property that has been incorporated into the immovable can be made liable on the basis of product liability rules only if damage can be attributed to the first item's distinct features or (lack of) quality.

28 There is no reason why a thing created by an entrepreneur based on an individualised order from a client should not be held as a product, regardless of whether the entrepreneur himself or the client provided the necessary materials. A problem might of course arise if the product proves to be defective due to the client's specific instructions. In such a case, none of the defences provided for in the Directive or in the CC section on product liability would apply, and the entrepreneur, regarded as the producer, would be liable vis-à-vis the victim, even if the latter were the client himself. The entrepreneur, however, might have recourse against the client based on the contract existing between them.

B. DEFECT

29 The definition of 'defect' given at article 1386–4 mirrors exactly the definition given by article 6 of the Directive. Authors in France, like elsewhere,

---

43 As of 1 October 2016: art 1245–11 CC.

44 As of 1 October 2016: art 1245–10, 4° CC.

45 See *supra* nos 10–11.

46 That the development risk defence should not apply to products derived from human blood is understandable, as human blood is not always used pure, but is often transformed before being transfused. It is the extension of the defence to parts of the human body other than blood, and products derived therefrom, that lacks a clear rationale.

have been critical of the vagueness of this definition. They generally agree, however, that the legitimate expectations criterion must be assessed objectively (ie from the standpoint of the general public) and that a product does not offer the safety which a person is entitled to expect when it is abnormally dangerous.[47]

30 There is little case law so far on the issue of defectiveness. The few decisions that have been handed down are rather in line with the scholarly approach, but they also indicate that French courts are quite willing to assess defectiveness by looking at the result of the product's use, and without necessarily identifying the distinct material characteristics that make it defective.[48]

31 Pharmaceutical products are currently giving rise to a significant amount of litigation. Several authors have argued that a specific test should apply to such products, namely the risk/benefit balance. This criterion has been endorsed in some appellate courts' decisions,[49] but the *Cour de cassation* recently decided on two occasions that a vaccine's defectiveness could not be ruled out on the sole ground that the risk/benefit balance of the vaccine was positive.[50] Unfortunately, the Court did not say what other criterion could or should apply. A possible interpretation of these decisions could be that the risk/benefit balance may possibly apply when assessing the existence of a design defect, but that a positive balance is not enough to rule out the existence of a manufacturing defect.

32 This is only a hypothesis, however, if only because the distinction between manufacturing, design and presentation defects is absent from the CC and has never been made explicitly by the courts. It has been suggested that courts do apply the distinction, albeit unknowingly, insofar as they characterise these different kinds of defect differently.[51] Furthermore, the above-mentioned decisions, along with other ones, suggest that courts are actually increasingly acknowledging that defects can fall into different categories that may call for the application of different rules, at least on the issue of evidence.[52] But judges have yet not created a clear and coherent classification of defects.

---

47 See eg *Borghetti* (fn 10) no 451; *G Viney/P Jourdain*, Les conditions de la responsabilité (3rd edn 2006) no 774; *Ph Brun*, Responsabilité civile extracontractuelle (3rd edn 2014) no 739.

48 TGI Aix-en-Provence, 2 October 2001, *D.* 2001, inf. rap. 3092; Cass. 1re civ., 26 September 2012, *D.* 2012, 2304, obs. I Gallmeister, ibid 2853, note J-S Borghetti, ibid 2013, 40, obs. Ph Brun; Cass. 1re civ., 10 July 2013, *D.* 2013, 2306 avis Mellottée, ibid 2312, note Ph Brun, ibid 2315, note J-S Borghetti.

49 See eg CA Versailles, 17 March 2006, no 04/08435; CA Versailles, 16 March 2007, no 05/09525; CA Versailles, 29 March 2007, no 06/00496; CA Versailles, 5 November 2007, no 06/06435; CA Paris, 19 June 2009, no 06/13741.

50 Cass. 1re civ., 26 September 2012 (fn 48); Cass. 1re civ., 10 July 2013 (fn 48).

51 *Borghetti* (fn 10) no 350–352.

52 *Borghetti* (fn 10) no 350–352.

33 One clear point, however, is that a defect in the sense of article 1386-4 CC can be either inherent in the product, or 'external', ie result not from its intrinsic characteristics but from the way it was presented, or from the instructions and warnings that came, or did not come, along with it.

34 There are hardly any published cases on specific types of products, other than pharmaceuticals, the characteristics of which could raise specific difficulties as far as the appraisal of defectiveness is concerned. Some cases can however be mentioned in which electricity was alleged to be defective, due to unexpected variations in voltage. Appellate courts in one or two cases at least have accepted this.[53] The author finds this solution quite debatable, and rather approves of the position taken in another case, where the appellate court ruled that variations in voltage do not constitute an internal defect of electricity, which could give rise to the application of product liability rules, but rather a breach of the contract concluded between the plaintiff and his electricity provider.[54]

35 There is no case law concerning products performing their function owing to their digital content (programmes) or intellectual content (eg the content of a book). As explained previously, the dominant scholarly view is that programmes or information as such should not be regarded as a product in the sense of the CC provisions; however, there is no doubt that the digital content of a product, such as a programme, can make a product defective, for example if it causes this product to malfunction. Whether the mere fact that the intellectual content of a product (such as a book) is false can make this product defective is much more doubtful. The author of this report believes that this should not be the case, but there have been no cases on this issue so far.

C. PUTTING INTO CIRCULATION

36 The Directive gives no definition of 'putting into circulation', even though it is a central aspect of the regime it creates. The French legislator purported to fill this gap, and article 1386-5 CC[55] provides: 'A product is put into circulation when the producer has voluntarily released it. A product is put into circulation only once.' Since the time when this provision was adopted, however, the ECJ has given some indications on how 'putting into circulation' in the sense of the Directive should be interpreted. In the *Declan O'Byrne* case, it ruled that 'a product is put into circulation when it is taken out of the manufacturing process

[53] CA Rennes, 4 June 2010, no 09/04002; CA Caen, 23 October 2012, no 09/02445.
[54] CA Montpellier, 3 July 2013, no 11/09032.
[55] As of 1 October 2016: art 1245-4 CC.

operated by the producer and enters a marketing process in the form in which it is offered to the public in order to be used or consumed'.[56]

37 The definition of putting into circulation given at article 1386–5 does not fit exactly with the one given by the ECJ. Since the latter should prevail, it is suggested that the 'voluntary release' of the product, mentioned in the CC, could be interpreted as creating a rebuttable presumption that the product entered the marketing process, ie was put into circulation according to the ECJ's view. There have been no published cases on this issue so far, however.

D. PRODUCERS' DUTIES AND THE NATURE OF PRODUCT LIABILITY

38 When the French legislator implemented the Directive in 1998, it mentioned an additional obligation for the producer, which is not found in the Directive. Article 1386–12 al 2 CC then provided that 'the producer cannot invoke the grounds of exemption from liability under subparagraphs 4 and 5 of Article 1386–11 [ie the development risk defence and compliance with mandatory regulations] if, in the event of a defect manifesting itself within a period of ten years after the product was put into circulation, he has failed to take appropriate measures to avert the harmful consequences thereof'. A duty for the producer to follow up on the product after it is put into circulation was thus created. But the ECJ condemned this departure from the Directive[57] and the second paragraph of article 1386–12 had to be suppressed by the French legislator.[58]

39 As a result, the French CC now mentions no specific duties for producers. There is no doubt, however, that producers must demonstrate reasonable care in designing, manufacturing and distributing their products, as well as in monitoring them after their putting into circulation. In the case of a breach of these duties of care, a producer can be made liable on the basis of the general liability for fault principle (article 1382 CC), independently from the special product liability rules. The possibility of applying liability for fault, in addition to the product liability provisions, is explicitly mentioned at article 1386–18 al 2 CC[59] and has been confirmed by the ECJ.[60]

---

56 ECJ, 9 February 2006, Case C-127/04, *Declan O'Byrne contre Sanofi Pasteur MSD Ltd et Sanofi Pasteur SA*.

57 ECJ, 25 April 2002, Case C-52/00 (fn 26).

58 *Loi* n° 2004–1343 of 9 December 2004.

59 'The producer remains liable for the consequences of his fault or for the fault of persons for whom he is answerable.' This article will become art 1245–17, al 2 CC as of 1 October 2016.

60 See ECJ, 25 April 2002, Case C-183/00 (fn 30).

40 This possibility confirms the general view, substantiated by the Directive itself, that the special product liability regime is a strict liability regime (*responsabilité sans faute*). This has been contested, however, mainly on the ground that proving the product's defect often amounts to proving someone's fault (though not necessarily the producer's).[61] Yet, from a formal point of view, there is no denying that product liability must be classified as strict liability, inasmuch as a proof that there was a fault is not formally required in order to make the producer, or any other defendant, liable. This classification has little importance anyway, except in the case of recourse or regress actions, where the basis of the defendant's liability has an influence on the final share of liability which the latter must bear.[62]

III. THE PERSON LIABLE FOR DAMAGE

A. LIABLE PERSONS

41 When the Directive was implemented in 1998, the French legislator chose to widen the circle of liable persons, as compared to the Directive's provisions. Article 1386-7 CC then provided that a professional supplier was liable for damage caused by the product's defect, exactly like the producer, but he of course had recourse against the producer. In its previously cited 2002 decision,[63] the ECJ ruled that this was a violation of the Directive, and the CC provisions have been amended so as to reflect more closely the Directive's.[64]

42 Articles 1386-6 and 1386-7 CC,[65] which purport to implement article 3 of the Directive, are actually not formulated exactly as the latter. Article 1386-6 al 1 and 2 provides: 'Is a producer, when he acts in a professional capacity, the manufacturer of a finished product, the producer of a raw material and the manufacturer of a component part. / … Any person acting in a professional capacity is considered a producer when: 1° He presents himself as the producer

61 See eg *W Lorenz*, Europäische Rechtsangleichung auf dem Gebiet der Produzentenhaftung: Zur Richtlinie des Rates der Europäischen Gemeinschaften vom 25 Juli. 1985, ZGH 1987, 1-39, 31; *J Stapleton*, Products Liability in the United Kingdom: The Myths of Reform (1999) Tex Int'l LJ 34, 45-70, 9; *S Whittaker*, The EEC Directive on Product Liability, in: *Yearbook of European Law* (1986) 233-286, 256.

62 See *infra* no 46.

63 ECJ, 25 April 2002, Case C-52/00 (fn 26).

64 Art 1386-7 CC was initially modified through *loi* n° 2004-1343 of 9 December 2004, but the ECJ ruled that the new version was not yet in line with the Directive (ECJ, 124 March 2006, Case C-177/04, *Commission v France*). A new legislative modification was thus made necessary, through *loi* n° 2006-406 of 5 April 2006, which led to the current version of art 1386-7 CC being adopted.

65 As of 1 October 2016: arts 1245-5 and 1245-6 CC.

by affixing his name, trade mark or other distinguishing sign on the product; 2° He imports a product into the European Community to sell it, lease it, with or without a promise of sale, or to carry out any other form of distribution.' Article 1386-7 adds: 'If the producer cannot be identified, the seller, the lessor, with the exception of a lending lessor or a lessor similar to a lending lessor, or any other professional supplier is liable for the defect in the safety of the product in the same conditions as a producer, unless he names his own supplier or the producer within three months from the date he received notice of the demand from the victim.'

43 There seem to be only two possibly significant differences between the French provisions and the Directive's. First of all, article 1386-7 CC provides that the lending lessor and lessors similar to the lending lessor do not bear the liability that rests on the supplier when the producer cannot be identified. It is doubtful, however, whether a lending lessor would qualify as a supplier under the Directive, meaning that French law probably does not depart from the Directive on this point. The second difference is that, whereas article 3(3) of the Directive provides that the supplier is liable for the product's defect if the producer cannot be identified and does not inform the injured person of the identity of the producer within a reasonable time, article 1386-7 sets a three-month delay in lieu of this reference to a reasonable time. Other countries have also done so,[66] however, and this has not been criticised by the European Commission. Here again, therefore, the departure from the Directive does not appear significant.

44 Even though there is a sharp divide in France between private and public law, there is no reason why public entities, such as hospitals, should not be liable under the special product liability provisions, provided they fall into one of the categories of potentially liable persons. There has actually been no published case so far in which a public entity has been regarded as a producer or a supplier in the sense of the Directive, but French administrative courts have imposed strict liability on public hospitals for damage caused by defects in the products they use.[67] Besides, a specific legislative provision on the liability of public and private hospitals implicitly confirms that they can be made liable on the basis of the CC product liability provisions.[68]

---

66 See eg Germany, Italy, Spain and Portugal, on which *Borghetti* (fn 10) no 553.

67 CE, 9 July 2003, no 220437, concl. T Olson, AJDA 2003, 1946, note M Deguergue, Lebon 338; CE, 12 March 2012, no 327449, D. 2013, 40, obs. Ph Brun and O Gout; CE, 25 July 2013, D. 2013, 2438, note M Bacache, ibid 2014, 47, obs. O Gout.

68 Art L2241-1 *Code de la santé publique* (public health code).

B. MULTIPLE TORTFEASORS

45 The traditional rule under French law is that multiple tortfeasors are jointly and severally liable to the plaintiff.[69] This rule also applies to product liability. Article 5 of the Directive expressly provides so when several persons are liable on the basis of the Directive's provisions. Surprisingly, this text has only been partially transposed into French law. Article 1386–8 CC[70] provides: 'In the case of a damage caused by the defect in a product incorporated into another, the producer of the component part and the one who has affected the incorporation are solidarily liable.' This article does not cover all situations in which several persons may be liable under product liability rules.[71] Yet, even in cases not mentioned by article 1386–8 CC, joint and several liability must apply, both because the Directive so provides and because this is the ordinary rule under French law. When there are several tortfeasors, but not all of them are liable under the product liability provisions, joint and several liability also applies to all of them, since this is the normal rule.

46 The Directive sets no rules of recourse among joint tortfeasors, even when all of them are liable on the basis of product liability provisions. Quite to the contrary, both article 5 and article 8 of the Directive expressly state that the latter applies without prejudice to the provisions of national law concerning the rights of contribution or recourse. In a case where the producer of a product had brought recourse against the producer of a component part, a defect in which had caused the product to be defective and to cause damage, the *Cour de cassation* ruled that the normal French rule on recourse actions must apply. Under this rule, when there are several tortfeasors and all of them are liable on a no-fault basis, liability must be split equally among them. In that case, this meant that the producer of the product and the producer of the component part each had to bear one half of the final weight of liability.[72]

47 It can be doubted whether this result reflects the logic behind the Directive. The position taken by the ECJ in the *Skov* case suggests that, even though the Directive does not officially purport to regulate recourse or regulate claims, it requires that, among the various operators who have taken part in the

---

69 French law actually makes a distinction between *responsabilité solidaire* and *responsabilité in solidum*. Depending on the circumstances, the one or the other will apply. The difference between the two is extremely slight, however, and both substantially amount to joint and several liability.

70 As of 1 October 2016: art 1245–7 CC.

71 For example, art 1386–8 CC does not cover the case in which both the producer and the person who, by putting his name, trade mark or other distinguishing feature on the product, presented himself as its producer (art 3(1) of the Directive); see, on such a case, Cass. 1re civ., 4 June 2014, *RDC* 2014, 613, obs. J-S Borghetti.

72 Cass. 1re civ., Civ. 1re, 26 November 2014, *D.* 2015, 405, note J-S Borghetti.

manufacture and marketing processes of the product, the cost of a defect be channelled to the party which was in the best position to control the risk, and thus to avoid the defect.[73] In the case of a product being defective due to a defect in a component part, this would mean that it is the producer of that part who should bear the full final cost of damage.

IV. THE AGGRIEVED PERSON AND DAMAGE

A. POSSIBLE PLAINTIFFS

48 Any person suffering damage caused by a product's defect can claim compensation on the basis of product liability law. Since French courts are quite lax on the issue of causation, this means that 'indirect victims' ('*victimes par ricochet*') can be compensated, if they suffer pecuniary or non-pecuniary damage as result of a relative being physically injured due to a product's defect.

B. DAMAGE

49 Damage under French law is defined neither by the Civil Code nor by case law, but it is understood in a very broad way by courts and can basically be defined as the violation of any interest whatsoever, provided that interest is not unlawful. All types of damage are thus normally compensable. A major difference between the Directive and 'ordinary' French law is that the former only provides for the compensation of certain types of damage. This raises at least two questions.

50 The first is whether French law may extend the range of damages that can be compensated in application of the specific product liability provisions. The French legislator thought so and took a more liberal approach to damage to property than the Directive. Whereas article 9 of the former provides that damage to property other than the defective product itself can be compensated only when the item of property is of a type ordinarily intended for private use or consumption, and was used by the injured person mainly for his private use or consumption, article 1386–2 al 2 CC[74] states that any damage caused to an item of property other than the defective product itself can be compensated, ie regardless of the type of this product and of the use to which it was put.

51 In the *Leroy Somer* case, the ECJ ruled that types of damage not covered by the Directive lie outside its scope of application, and that national laws are thus

[73] ECJ, 10 January 2006, Case C-402/03 (fn 33) pt 30.
[74] As of 1 October 2016: art 1245–1 CC.

free to organise their compensation as they wish.[75] As a result, article 1386-2 CC is not contrary to the Directive, insofar as it extends the scope of compensable damage.

52 The second issue, as far as damage is concerned, has to do with the fact that the Directive does not mention all possible types of damage. As a matter of fact, it only considers damage caused by death of personal injuries (art 9(1)(a)), damage caused to an item of property (art 9(1)(b)) and immaterial damage (art 9(2)). The question is thus: can types of damage not mentioned by the Directive be compensated under it? Such types of damage include, for example, loss of chance[76] or the cost of preventive measures.[77]

53 This question is easily answered, however, in the context of French law. Given that (i) national laws can extend product liability provisions to cover types of damage that are not normally compensable under the Directive, and (ii) French law normally compensates all types of damage, it seems quite clear that the CC's special product liability provisions can be relied on to compensate any kind of damage, as is otherwise the case under French law, with the only exception being those types of damage for which compensation is explicitly excluded by the Directive, ie damage to the defective product itself and damage to another item property that is worth less than €500. As a result, damage to business property, consequential economic loss[78] and pure economic loss, loss of chance, and non-economic loss should all be compensable under the French product liability regime. In a defective pacemaker case, the *Cour de cassation* accepted that the plaintiff living with the defective product in his chest was entitled to receive damages compensating non-pecuniary damage resulting from the exposure to the risk that the pacemaker should fail.[79]

54 When implementing the Directive, French law set no maximum limit on product liability, as such limits are rather alien to the French legal tradition. The only limit is the lower €500 'threshold' set by article 9 of the Directive. As is well known, though, there is an ambiguity on this point. While the English version of the Directive speaks of 'threshold', the French version speaks of a '*franchise*',

---

75 ECJ, 4 June 2009, Case C-285/08, *Moteurs Leroy Somer v Dalkia France and Ace Europe*.

76 For a case involving (possibly) such damage, see ECJ, 10 May 2001, Case C-203/99, *Henning Veedfald v Århus Amtskommune*.

77 On this issue, see ECJ, 5 March 2015, Cases C-503/13 and C-504/13, *Boston Scientific Medizintechnik GmbH v AOK Sachsen-Anhalt – Die Gesundheitskasse and Betriebskrankenkasse RWE*.

78 The only exception should be consequential economic loss resulting from damage caused to the defective product itself.

79 Cass. 1re civ. 19 December 2006, *D.* 2007, 2897, obs. Ph Brun, *JCP* G 2007, II, 10052, note S Hocquet-Berg, *RTD civ.* 2007, 352, obs. P Jourdain.

ie a franchise or deductible. However, article 1386-2 CC suggests that the €500 limit should be interpreted as a threshold, and not as a franchise.[80]

V. CAUSALITY

A. APPRAISING AND PROVING CAUSATION

55 There are no specific rules concerning causation in respect of product liability. This should come as no surprise, as the Directive does not contain any, and French liability law does not have any detailed rules on causation. The CC provisions on product liability, like other provisions on liability, only speak of causation, without any more detail, and the *Cour de cassation* has consistently declined to give a precise definition of this concept. The only requirement is that causation be certain and direct, which leaves much leeway to judges in practice.[81]

56 In the field of pharmaceuticals liability, French courts have demonstrated their willingness to ease proof of causation by plaintiffs, albeit without giving any precise definition of causation, nor of its components. In cases involving vaccines against hepatitis B, which some plaintiffs have alleged can cause demyelinating diseases like multiple sclerosis, the *Cour de cassation* ruled that, despite the state of scientific uncertainty concerning the aetiology of demyelinating diseases and the absence of epidemiologic evidence as to the link between hepatitis B vaccination and such diseases, lower judges are allowed to presume causation on the facts of the case.[82] In cases brought against DES producers, the *Cour de cassation* ruled that, if the plaintiff has demonstrated that she was exposed to DES in her mother's womb and that her pathology was caused by this exposure, she may claim full compensation of her damage from any of the producers that commercialised the product in France at the time.[83] In theory, the defendant producer can escape this liability by proving that its was not his product that caused damage, but rather that from another producer; in practice, however, such proof is impossible, and the *Cour de cassation* has thus in effect reversed the burden of proof not of causation, but of the producer's identity.

---

80 The text provides for the compensation of 'damage which is greater than' €500 (in French: '*dommage supérieur à*', and not '*sous déduction d'une franchise de*').

81 *Brun* (fn 47) no 244.

82 Cass. 1re civ., 22 May 2008, *Bull. civ.* I, no 148 and 149, *D.* 2008, 2894, obs. P Jourdain, *JCP* G 2008, II, 10131, note L Grynbaum, ibid I, 186, no 3, obs. Ph Stoffel-Munck, *RTD civ.* 2008, 492, obs. P Jourdain, *RDC* 2008, 1186, obs. J-S Borghetti. On this issue, see *J-S Borghetti*, Litigation on Hepatitis B vaccination and demyelinating diseases in France: breaking through scientific uncertainty?, in: M Martín-Casals/DM Papayannis (eds), Uncertain Causation in Tort Law (2015).

83 Cass. 1re civ., 24 September 2009, *Bull. civ.* I, no 186, *RTD civ.* 2010, 111, obs. P Jourdain, *RDC* 2010, 90, obs. J-S Borghetti.

57 It must also be noted that, in cases involving pharmaceuticals, there is very often confusion between causation that unites the use of the product and damage, on the one hand, and causation that unites the product's defect and damage, on the other hand. The Directive and its implementing provisions only mention the latter, but it is the former that is most often decisive in such cases, and on which debates usually concentrate.

B. MULTIPLE CAUSES

58 If the product's defect is only one of several causes of the damage suffered by the plaintiff, the ordinary rules of French law on the issue of multiple causation apply. The producer is liable in full towards the plaintiffs – as article 8(1) of the Directive (implemented as article 1386–14 CC)[84] requires – regardless of the potentially tortious nature of the other causes of damage. However, if another of these causes is also a source of liability for someone else, then both tortfeasors will be jointly and severally liable to the plaintiff; and the producer, if he has fully compensated the victim, will have recourse against the other tortfeasor. The magnitude of this recourse will depend on the nature of this other tortfeasor's liability. If the latter is also strictly liable to the plaintiff, then liability should be split equally between him and the producer; but if his liability to the plaintiff is based on fault, then he will have to bear the full final cost of compensation.

C. THE AGGRIEVED PARTY'S CONTRIBUTION TO HIS OWN DAMAGE

59 If the aggrieved party has contributed to his own damage, this will have an impact on his right to be compensated only if this contribution amounts to a fault. This is the solution set by the Directive, which has been transposed at article 1386–13 CC.[85] If the aggrieved contributed to his own damage but without being at fault, this shall have no effect on his right to compensation. A fairly common situation is that the aggrieved suffered from a particular frailty or was especially exposed to a certain type of damage due to some physiological characteristics of his.[86]

---

84 As of 1 October 2016: art 1245–13 CC.

85 'The liability of the producer may be reduced or suppressed if, taking into account all the circumstances, the damage was caused both by a defect in the product and by the fault of the victim or of a person for whom the victim is responsible.' This article will become art 1245–12 CC as of 1 October 2016.

86 This is actually a complex question, as the plaintiff's particular frailty could sometimes impact the way in which defectiveness is assessed. There are however hardly any cases addressing openly this issue in France.

VI. DEFENCES AND EXCLUSIONS

A. THE DEVELOPMENT RISK DEFENCE

60 Concerning defences, article 1386–11 CC closely follows article 7 of the Directive. As explained above, the French legislator chose to introduce the development risk defence, except 'when the damage was caused by an element of the human body or by products derived therefrom' (article 1386–12 CC). There is hardly any case law on the development risk defence, however.[87]

61 As French law does not formally recognise the difference between manufacturing, design and warning defects, there is apparently no reason why the development risk defence should apply to design and warning defects, and not to manufacturing ones. This way of restricting the ambit of the defence might appeal to French judges, though, insofar as they are usually eager to foster victim compensation. But the near absence of cases applying the defence so far prevents any realistic prediction on this issue.

B. COMPLIANCE WITH STANDARDS

62 It has long been an established rule in French law that compliance with standards (as opposed to mandatory regulations; cf article 7 of the Directive), whether they be administrative or voluntary, does not per se preclude the finding of a fault. Article 1386–10 CC[88] confirms this solution in the case of a defect: 'A producer may be liable for a defect although the product was manufactured in accordance with the rules of the trade or the existing standards or although it had been the object of an administrative authorization.' Though not expressed in the Directive, this rule is certainly in accordance with it. To regard compliance with standards as a defence would indeed violate article 7 of the Directive, which gives a limitative list of applicable defences. The *Cour de cassation* has had no difficulty in applying the rule, at any rate.[89]

C. CONTRACTUAL EXCLUSION OF LIABILITY

63 The Directive forbids any contractual limitation or exclusion of the liability it establishes (article 12). This rule has naturally been transposed into the Civil

---

[87] One case can be cited, in which an appellate court allowed the defence and ruled that the producer of a pharmaceutical was not liable for not having warned against a risk that was not certain: CA Paris, 23 September 2004, no 02/16712, *D.* 2005, 1012.

[88] As of 1 October 2016: art 1245–9 CC.

[89] Cass. 1re civ., 25 June 2009, no 08–12632, 08–14197 and 08–20706.

Code (as article 1386–15)[90] and appears all the more natural as the same rule generally applies in French law where liability in tort is concerned. Article 1386–12 al 2 CC sets an exception, though, and provides that exclusion or limitation clauses are valid 'as to damages caused to things not used by the victim mainly for his own private use or consumption', if stipulated between professionals. The reason for this exception is fairly easy to understand, since the latter covers precisely those types of damage which are not compensable under the Directive, but which the French legislator chose to include into the scope of the product liability regime.[91]

VII. REMEDIES

64 Neither the Directive nor the CC provisions indicate whether the aggrieved party can only claim damages under the special product liability provisions, or if he can also require compensation in kind. It could thus be considered that both options are normally possible. In French law, the judge is normally free to choose the type of compensation he regards as most appropriate, and he can therefore grant damages to a plaintiff who asked for compensation in kind, or vice versa.

65 In practice, however, compensation in kind is extremely rare in French liability law, and is mostly found in cases of infringements of personality rights. Thus, even if one accepts that compensation in kind is possible under the Directive (even though its drafters probably only had damages in mind when they dealt with compensation), it is hard to imagine cases where such compensation would actually be more pertinent than damages, and would be awarded by judges.

66 Damages must exactly compensate damage suffered by the plaintiff, without his becoming richer or poorer than he would have been had the damage not occurred.[92] Under this so-called 'full-compensation' principle, non-compensatory forms of damages are not allowed in French law, whether they are exemplary, punitive or nominal. It is often said, though, that judges have a tendency to exaggerate the amount of damage suffered by the plaintiff when they regard the defendant's behaviour as particularly culpable, so as to raise the amount of damages and to punish the tortfeasor, but the number of cases of such covert punitive damages is thought to remain rather small, and product liability is probably not the field where they are most likely to be found.[93]

---

[90] As of 1 October 2016: art 1245–14 CC.

[91] See *supra* nos 50–51.

[92] See eg Cass. 2e civ., 8 July 2004, *Bull. civ.* II, no 393: '*Les dommages-intérêts alloués à une victime doivent réparer le préjudice subi sans qu'il résulte pour elle ni perte ni profit*'.

[93] On this issue, see *J-S Borghetti*, Punitive Damages in France, in: H Koziol/V Wilcox (eds), Punitive Damages: Common Law and Civil Law Perspectives (2009) 55–73, nos 25–30.

67 Neither the Directive nor the CC provisions on product liability provide for the possibility of claiming injunctions, eg the withdrawal of a product from circulation. Such withdrawal can be ordered by public authorities under the Product Safety Directive,[94] but there is no specific procedure whereby an 'ordinary' person can require a court to order such a withdrawal. Could such an injunction nevertheless be granted in application of 'ordinary' liability rules?

68 Although the case law is neither very abundant nor very explicit on this issue, many French authors are of the opinion that injunctions are a generally available remedy in tort law. As a result, someone may be required to stop a tortious conduct, or to suppress a tortious state of things under his control, if this conduct or state of things threatens to cause damage to the plaintiff.[95] Even if this truly reflects the state of French law, however, it remains to be seen whether someone could require a producer to withdraw from the market all products from a given category, on the basis of their being defective, even though the plaintiff himself is not at risk of being adversely affected by all of them. This seems doubtful. A plaintiff could probably not obtain the withdrawal of products that are not likely to cause damage to him personally. And if one item of a defective product does threaten to cause damage to the plaintiff, there might be more efficient ways to avoid damage than to withdraw the product: more often than not, the easiest thing will be for the plaintiff to stop using the product. It is therefore doubtful that a French judge will ever order the withdrawal of a product at the request of an individual.

VIII. PROCEDURAL AND EVIDENTIAL ISSUES

A. BURDEN OF PROOF

69 According to the general rule, it is for the plaintiff to demonstrate, if need be, the existence of the elements that are necessary for his claim to succeed.[96] This traditional allocation of the burden of proof is confirmed, in the field of product liability, by article 1386-9 CC (implementing article 4 of the Directive): 'The plaintiff must prove the damage, the defect, and the causal link between the defect and the damage.'

70 In civil matters, French law does not have standards of proof. Proof of facts (as opposed to contracts) can be achieved by any means, and lower judges are sovereign in deciding whether the elements put forward to them by the parties

94 Directive 2001/95/EC of the European Parliament and of the Council of 3 December 2001 on general product safety; see especially arts 5 and 8.

95 On this issue, see *C Bloch*, La Cessation de l'illicite (2008).

96 See art 9 of the Code of Civil Procedure.

are sufficiently convincing or not. This means that the *Cour de cassation* is not allowed to review lower judges' decisions when it comes to the appreciation of evidence. Besides, article 1353 CC[97] explicitly provides that proof of facts can be made by presumption, ie that judges are allowed to deduce the existence of a fact that has not be proven directly from the existence of other facts, the existence of which is certain. In practice, this leaves much leeway to judges, and it is their personal conviction that is decisive.

71 As explained earlier, French courts have tried to make proof of causation easier for some plaintiffs in pharmaceutical cases.[98] Most striking is the insistence by the *Cour de cassation*, in hepatitis B vaccine cases, that lower judges should assess causation on the facts of the case, and resort if need be to presumptions, even when they are faced with a state of scientific uncertainty.[99] In two fairly recent cases, the *Cour de cassation* even suggested that lower judges should consider whether the elements that allow a presumption of causation do not also allow a presumption that the vaccine doses used by the plaintiff were defective.[100] This solution shows how plaintiff-friendly French judges can be, but it is probably not in accordance with the Directive, since it results in the requirement of the product's defect being in effect squeezed out. The ECJ will soon have an occasion to clarify this point, as the *Cour de cassation* recently referred three questions to it that have to do precisely with the use of presumptions in order to prove causation and defectiveness under the Directive's regime.[101]

B. PRESCRIPTION

72 The normal prescription period in French law is five years. According to article 2224 CC: 'Personal actions or movable rights of action prescribe in five years from the day the holder of a right knew or should have known the facts enabling him to exercise his right.' In the case of bodily injuries, a longer prescription period applies, regardless of the nature of the claim (ie whether it be in contract and in tort). Article 2226 al 2 provides: 'An action in civil liability arising from an event that resulted in bodily injury, brought by the direct or indirect victim of the harm, prescribes in ten years from the date of

97 As of 1 October 2016: art 1382 CC.
98 See *supra* no 56.
99 Cass. 1re civ., 22 May 2008 (fn 82).
100 Cass. 1re civ., 26 September 2012 (fn 48); Cass. 1re civ., 10 July 2013 (fn 48).
101 Cass. 1re civ., 12 November 2015, *D.* 2015, 2602, note J-S Borghetti, see case C-621/15, Request for a preliminary ruling from the Cour de cassation (France) lodged on 23 November 2015 – *W and Others v Sanofi Pasteur MSD SNC, Caisse primaire d'assurance maladie des Hauts-de-Seine, Caisse Carpimko.*

the consolidation of the initial or of the aggravated injury'. Ordinary claims are further subjected to a twenty-year 'long-stop' period,[102] but this limit does not apply to claims for the compensation of damage arising from a bodily injury.

73 In contrast, but in accordance with the Directive, article 1386–17 provides that claims based on the special product liability rules have a prescription period of 'three years from the date the plaintiff knew or ought to have known of the damage, the defect, and the identity of the producer.' A ten-year long-stop period also applies. According to article 1386–16, '[e]xcept in the case of fault of the producer, his liability under the [product liability rules] is extinguished after ten years following the putting into circulation of the actual product that caused the damage, unless the victim has in the meantime instituted proceedings.' Prescription rules applicable to product liability claims are thus much less favourable to plaintiffs than the ordinary rules set by the CC, especially when plaintiffs suffered bodily injuries. The starting point of the 'normal' prescription period is defined more or less in the same way under both categories of rules, but the length of the former is much shorter than that of the latter. This, in practice, can make the possibility of bringing a claim on another basis than product liability quite attractive.[103]

74 Ordinary rules of French law concerning the suspension and interruption of prescription should apply to the three-year delay provided for at article 1386–17 CC. But they obviously do not apply to the ten-year long-stop period, since this would run counter to the *ratio legis* of this rule.

75 Prescription being a defence, it is the defendant who must prove that the three-year delay has expired. It is not self-evident, however, whether it is the defendant who must prove when the delay started to run (ie the time when the plaintiff knew or ought to have known of the damage, the defect, and the identity of the producer), or the plaintiff who must prove that he did not immediately know of the defect and the identity of the producer when the damage happened. There is no clear case law on this issue,[104] but the best solution is certainly the second one.[105]

76 Things are easier when it comes to the ten-year long-stop period. It is certainly the defendant who must prove that the delay has expired, and he is

102 Art 2232 al 1 CC: 'The deferral of the starting point, the suspension or the interruption of the prescription cannot have the effect of extending the period of the extinctive prescription beyond twenty years from the day of the birth of the right.'

103 See *infra* nos 79–85.

104 See however Cass. 1re civ., 10 July 2013 (fn 48), which seems to adopt the second branch of the option.

105 See *R Zimmermann*, Comparative Foundations of European Law of Set-Off and Prescription (2006) 107–108.

obviously the one who is in the best position to establish when the damaging product was put into circulation, ie when the delay started to run.

C. GENERAL PROCEDURAL RULES

77 It is reasonably easy to bring a liability claim before the courts under French law. Judicial aid is quite developed, and courts' and attorney's fees are, as a rule, not too expensive. Class actions used to not be possible under French law. They were first introduced in the field of consumer law in 2014, but could then only be brought for the compensation of pecuniary damage suffered by consumers.[106] A law of January 2016 has created a new hypothesis of class action, whereby victims of damage caused by producers or suppliers of 'health products' (*produits de santé*)[107] can claim compensation for any harm they have personally suffered.[108] The new rules, which are quite complex,[109] will come into force on 1 July 2016. It remains to be seen whether they will often be relied on. The example of class actions in the field of consumer law suggests that this may not be the case.

IX. ALTERNATIVE REGULATIONS AND REMEDIES

78 Product liability rules are obviously part of a larger set of rules and remedies available to victims of defective products. Depending on the circumstances, these victims may be in a position to rely on other liability rules, or on other mechanisms, such as social security or criminal law rules.

A. OTHER LIABILITY RULES

79 Other liability regimes than product liability may apply in the event of damage caused by a defective product. Article 13 of the Directive expressly provides that 'the Directive shall not affect any rights which an injured person may have according to the rules of the law of contractual or non-contractual liability or a special liability system existing at the moment when the Directive is notified'. It has been implemented as article 1386–18 CC. The ambit of this rule is more restrictive than might appear at first sight, though. As a matter of fact, French law has no special liability system in the sense of article 13. Besides, the ECJ has given a restrictive interpretation of this provision, by ruling that it 'does

106 Art L423–1 *Code de la consommation* (Consumer code).
107 As defined by art L5311–1 *Code de la santé publique* (public health code).
108 *Loi* n° 2016–41 du 26 janvier 2016 de modernisation de notre système de santé.
109 They will form arts L1143–1 – L1143–22 *Code de la santé publique* (public health code).

not preclude the application of other systems of contractual or non-contractual liability *based on other grounds, such as fault or a warranty in respect of latent defects*'.[110]

80 In effect, this means that, under French law, a person who suffered damage caused by the defect in a product can bring a claim in damages against the producer or any other operator who took part in the manufacture and marketing processes of the product only on the basis of delictual liability for fault,[111] or of the contractual latent defects warranty.

81 Delictual liability for fault, based on article 1382 CC, requires proof of fault, damage and causation between these two first elements. Given the so-called *non-cumul rule*, however, it can only be relied on by plaintiffs who do not have a claim in contract against the defendant.[112] Besides, French law has a rather lax conception of privity in contract, with the result that many plaintiffs do have a claim in contract, even though they do not have a direct contractual relationship with the defendant.

82 As a matter of principle, any person who acquired ownership of a product has a claim in contract against any previous seller of the product.[113] This means that if the plaintiff was the owner of the defective product, he will normally only have a claim in contract against the producer or any seller down the sales chain (next to his claim based on the Directive's product liability regime). This contractual claim will normally be based on the latent defects warranty (article 1641 ff CC). To rely on this warranty, the owner must prove that the product had a hidden defect at the time the defendant sold the product. A security defect will normally qualify as a defect under the latent defects warranty, provided it is internal; but a warning defect will usually not be regarded as a defect in the sense of the warranty. The latter appears more favourable than the product liability regime as far as the prescription period is concerned, though. The period is only two years, but it starts to run as of the discovery of the product's vice.[114]

83 The restrictions set by the Directive concerning the other liability regimes that victims of defective products may rely on only concern those actions

---

110 ECJ, 25 April 2002, Case C-183/00 (fn 30) pt 31.

111 The possibility to bring a claim on this basis, when damage was caused by a defective product, is expressly mentioned at art 1386-18 CC.

112 Under this rule, liability between two parties can only be in contract, and not in tort, whenever damage is connected to the execution of a valid contract between the parties.

113 See *supra* fn 3.

114 Art 1648 CC: 'An action resulting from redhibitory defects must be brought by the buyer within two years from the discovery of the vice.' The current version of this text dates back to 2005. Previously, the buyer had to bring his claim within a 'short delay' after the discovery of the defect: see *supra* no 04.

directed against 'operators taking part in the manufacture and marketing processes of the product'.[115] Under certain circumstances, aggrieved persons may be in a position to bring claims against persons who have not taken part in these processes. The Directive has no impact on these claims. In particular, the victim of a defective product, if he is not its owner, may have a claim against the latter based on the 'liability for the deed of things' regime. Under this regime, derived from article 1384 al 1 CC,[116] the 'keeper' of a thing (normally its owner) is strictly liable for any damage caused by the abnormal behaviour of this thing. When the defect in a product causes the latter to malfunction, an action based on article 1384 al 1 CC against the owner of the product will thus normally be available to any victim who is not himself the owner.[117]

84 French administrative courts have developed another strict liability regime, which may be relied on by some victims of defective products. Under this regime, a public hospital is liable, even when it is not at fault, for damage caused to users as a result of the failure of products or equipment used in connection with their treatment.[118] The ECJ explicitly ruled that this regime does not fall within the scope of the Directive, and that its application is thus unhampered by the latter.[119]

85 These various liability regimes may of course apply outside the scope of the Directive, provided their conditions of application are met. Delictual liability for fault may be of special interest when damage has been caused in the course of a service being provided, since French law has no specific liability regime applicable to defective services. When there is a contractual relationship between the service provider and the plaintiff, however, liability must necessarily be in contract.[120] Contractual liability under French law is normally strict, which means that, if a breach of contract is established, the debtor can only avoid the payment of damages to the creditor by proving that this breach was a consequence of *force majeure*. Yet, in practice, contractual liability, when the contract was for the procurement of a service, looks very much like liability for fault, since the claimant will more often than not have to demonstrate that the debtor did not act like a reasonable professional in order to prove that the service was not performed as it should have been.

---

115 ECJ, 21 December 2011, Case C-495/10, *Centre hospitalier universitaire de Besançon v Thomas Dutrueux and Caisse primaire d'assurance maladie du Jura*, para 25.

116 'We are responsible not only for the damage caused by our own act, but also for that which is caused by the acts of persons for whom we are responsible, or by things that are in our custody.' This article will become art 1242, al 1 CC as of 1 October 2016.

117 Of course, the owner of the thing shall be able to bring a recourse claim against the producer, if the conditions of liability under the Directive's regime are met.

118 CE, 9 July 2003 (fn 67).

119 ECJ, 21 December 2011, Case C-495/10 (fn 115).

120 See fn 112.

B. OTHER AREAS OF LAW

86 Victims of defective products may also find some relief through other legal mechanisms than the rules of civil (or administrative) liability. Social security is obviously one of them, and normally benefits any person suffering a bodily injury, as well as a physical or psychiatric disease, regardless of its cause. Social security has recourse against the tortfeasor when it has compensated damage that is the consequence of a tort or of a breach of contract, but it is likely that such recourse is not often carried out when damage is the result of a defective product, if only because social security might not even be aware that damage was actually caused by such a product, or might not be able to prove it.

87 Private direct insurance is also a possible remedy, but it is little developed in France, at least as far as bodily injuries are concerned, except as a complement to social security.

88 In certain cases, the putting into circulation, or keeping in circulation, of a defective product may also constitute a criminal offence. Depending on the circumstances, offences like poisoning (*empoisonnement*),[121] voluntary endangering of somebody else's life (*mise en danger volontaire de la vie d'autrui*),[122] involuntary homicide (*homicide involontaire*),[123] or lack of assistance to someone in peril (*non-assistance à personne en danger*)[124] may apply. There are not many published cases, however.

89 If damage caused by a defective product coincides with a criminal offence, French law allows the victim to initiate criminal proceedings. In the case of such proceedings – regardless of who initiated them – any person who directly suffered damage due to the alleged criminal offence can chose to claim compensation from the defendant either before a civil court or before the criminal court dealing with the case.[125] If compensation is awarded, though, it will always be on the basis of civil liability rules, which criminal courts are allowed to apply. If the criminal court finds the defendant guilty of a criminal offence, there will always be a ground for civil liability, since criminal liability necessary rests on fault, and, under French law, a criminal fault is always also a civil fault. When the criminal court finds that there has been no criminal offence, it may nevertheless grant compensation to the claimant if the conditions of application of a civil liability regime, such as product liability, are met.

---

121 Art 221-5 *Code pénal* (Criminal Code).
122 Art 121-3 *Code pénal*.
123 Art 221-6 *Code pénal*.
124 Art 223-6 *Code pénal*.
125 Arts 2, 3 and 4 *Code de procédure pénale* (Code of Criminal Procedure).

90 Strictly speaking, criminal law does not offer any remedy to the victim of a defective product, since its function is to punish offenders, and not compensate damage.[126] It may nevertheless contribute to the success of the compensation claim. As a matter of fact, if such a claim is linked to criminal proceedings, the plaintiff will be allowed to rely on the findings of the criminal inquiry carried out under a judge's authority. The linking of civil and criminal proceedings may therefore considerably ease the evidentiary burden that rests on the plaintiff.

X. ASSESSMENT OF DOMESTIC LAW

91 The 'putting into circulation' of the special product liability regime in French law has been rather difficult. The limited protection this regime offers to victims of defective products, as compared to pre-existing rules of French law, greatly contributed to the delayed implementation of the Directive, and also incited the French legislator to depart from it; this, in turn, resulted in France's initial implementation being censored on several points by the ECJ. Things now to seem to be in order, however, and plaintiffs, who initially tended to shun the new CC provisions on product liability, are now relying more and more on them. According to court statistics, a few hundred claims based on these provisions are brought before first instance courts each year,[127] and tens of them have already reached the *Cour de cassation*. Thus, product liability now appears to be an established part of liability law.

92 Product-related litigation is not massive, though, and nothing indicates that the new product liability regime has had significant negative consequences on economic operators. There was much concern, before and at the time of the Directive's implementation, that it would result in a massive rise in insurance premiums,[128] but these fears do not appear to have materialised. In retrospect, this is not really surprising, as the new product liability regime did not fundamentally change the conditions of producers' liability. Its main effect may actually have been to make the possibility of rendering producers liable for damage caused by defects in their products more conspicuous. It may thus have created an incitation to sue, but without radically altering the technical conditions required for a successful claim.

126 Unless one considers that the producer being criminally convicted constitutes a kind of moral compensation for the victim.

127 See Annuaire statistique de la justice. Édition 2011–2012, 61, for the latest statistics available.

128 See eg *J Schmidt-Salzer*, Die EG-Richtlinie Produkthaftung, Betriebs-Berater 1986, 1103, no 52–55; *A Benoit-Moury*, L'enjeu d'une directive européenne récente sur la responsabilité du fait des produits défectueux, Annales de droit de Liège 1987, 337, 343.

93 Published product liability cases also illustrate the limits of the new regime. One of them concerns pharmaceuticals. A significant share of product liability litigation in France, especially before the *Cour de cassation*, deals with such products. It is becoming more and more obvious, though, that the Directive's regime, designed to deal with 'ordinary' products, is not perfectly suited to pharmaceuticals. Whether it be on the issue of causation or on the one of defectiveness, these products raise specific questions or difficulties, which probably call for tailored rules. The Directive, unfortunately, neither contains such rules, nor allows Member States to develop them, at least officially (in practice, national courts may have no choice but to bend the Directive's rules in order to adapt to these products).[129]

94 It is more difficult to say whether the special product liability regime will prove to be adapted to new technological products, such as those discussed in the introduction. There is hardly any case law concerning such products so far, but this absence may have various causes. The inappropriateness of product liability rules may be one, yet it is more likely that litigation simply has not had the time to develop.

[129] See ECJ, 20 November 2014, Case C-310/13, *Novo Nordisk Pharma GmbH v. S.*

PRODUCT LIABILITY IN GERMANY

Ulrich Magnus

I. SOURCES OF LAW AND THEIR EVOLUTION

A. SHORT HISTORY OF PRODUCT LIABILITY LAW IN GERMANY

01 The legal history of a special product liability law in Germany started with the famous *Hühnerpest* case of 1968.[1] In this case a chicken farmer, the claimant, had mandated a veterinarian to vaccinate his chickens against fowl pest. The veterinarian vaccinated the animals with a serum that the defendant pharmaceutical business had produced and which for unknown reasons contained active viruses. The consequence of the vaccination was an outbreak of fowl pest. Over 4,000 chickens died. The claimant sued the defendant for compensation of his loss. Under traditional contract and tort law the claimant would have lost his case because he had no contract with the defendant and could not prove that the latter's negligence had caused the damage as is necessary under §823 (1) *Bürgerliches Gesetzbuch* (BGB), the central norm of German tort law. The Federal Supreme Court (*Bundesgerichtshof*, BGH) decided that in such cases of product liability the burden of proof must be reversed. The victim of a product defect need no longer prove that the manufacturer was at fault; the latter now has

1 BGHZ 51, 91; for an English translation see *BS Markesinis/H Unberath*, The German Law of Torts (4th edn 2002) 555 ff.

to prove that he was not. The central argument was that for the victim it is often difficult and sometimes impossible to prove detailed circumstances of production which exclusively occur in the sphere of the manufacturer who organises and controls these circumstances. The manufacturer is closer to them (*näherdaran*) and should therefore bear the burden to prove the absence of fault. Because in the *Hühnerpest* case the defendant could not prove that the product defect was not his fault and could not have happened in his factory, the claimant succeeded.

02 Since the *Hühnerpest* case many decisions have confirmed and refined this special burden of proof rule for product liability cases; since then product liability became a specifically regulated part of general tort law which already existed before the enactment of the Product Liability Act of 1989 (which implemented the EU Directive of 1985). This product liability under general tort law still continues to exist side by side with the Product Liability Act.

03 Also before the *Hühnerpest* case a person who was injured by a defect of a product could be entitled to damages. A claim could be based on several causes of action; however, the prospects of being successful were limited. In contract law the prospects are theoretically promising: fault is presumed[2] and a debtor is – contrary to tort law – liable for its auxiliaries without the possibility of exoneration.[3] Yet these favourable rules only very rarely apply. Often, the division of production and marketing in industry and trade means that the injured person did not conclude a direct contract with the manufacturer. All instruments which in German law can extend the scope of the contractual protection even to persons only indirectly related to the contract (for instance, contracts either directly in favour of third parties or with protective effects towards them, further the so-called *Drittschadensliquidation* which allows the contract partner to claim the loss a third person had, or an implied special guaranty contract, etc) do not cover the situation of the user of a defective product or a bystander being injured. The Federal Supreme Court thoroughly examined but expressly rejected all these contractual help constructions in the *Hühnerpest* decision[4] and clarified that they do not apply to 'normal' product liability cases.

04 Traditional German tort law bases liability on fault which the claimant must prove (§823 (1) BGB). In product liability cases this is, without the mentioned reversal of burden of proof, often extremely difficult for injured persons. Moreover, a defendant business can exonerate itself from liability where an employee has caused the damage. The employing enterprise is exempted from vicarious liability if it can prove that it had selected and controlled the employee with sufficient care (§831 BGB). Although the courts established a

2 See today §280 (1) sentence 2 BGB.
3 §278 BGB.
4 BGHZ 51, 91.

specific duty of organisation which the business itself must observe and although the exoneration possibility was not accepted for leading employees, this rarely helped claimants in product liability cases.

05 Another cause of action in product liability cases is sometimes provided by §823 (2) BGB in connection with specific statutory law. The interpretation of §823 (2) BGB leads to a slight mitigation concerning the burden of proof in product liability cases. Under this provision a wrongdoer is liable if he or she has – at least negligently[5] – violated a statutory provision which specifically intends to protect such persons as the injured as well as precisely the interests which were infringed. If a breach of such a so-called *Schutzgesetz* (protective norm) is established – which the victim must prove – the courts assume a presumption of fault which the wrongdoer must rebut.[6] There exist some protective norms with respect to the production of certain goods, for instance for the production of feed,[7] of pesticides[8] or of drinking water.[9] Generally, §§3 and 6 *Produktsicherheitsgesetz* (Product Safety Act) require that products are sufficiently safe when they are marketed. The Product Safety Act does not itself provide for a separate liability; but it has been held by courts[10] and suggested by legal writers[11] that the Act's provisions are also protective norms. Yet, because the number of protective norms is limited and because the victim is still obliged to prove that the damage he/she suffered was caused by a defect of the product, the advantage the reversed burden of proof rule under §823 (2) BGB has is moderate.

06 In essence, before the implementation of the EU Directive on Product Liability, German law had solved product liability cases primarily on the basis of tort law and, with respect to fault, had introduced a reversal of the burden of proof that victims of torts generally have to bear.

B. THE IMPLEMENTATION OF THE PRODUCT LIABILITY DIRECTIVE

07 In 1989 the German legislator enacted the *Gesetz über die Haftung für fehlerhafte Produkte* (*Produkthaftungsgesetz*, ProdHaftG), which implemented

5 If the protective norm requires intent (as most relevant provisions of the Criminal Code) this degree of fault is also necessary to trigger liability under §823 (2) BGB. Where the protective norm requires no fault, under §823 (2) BGB at least negligence must be present (§823 (2) sentence 2 BGB).

6 See BGH VersR 1968, 593; BGH VersR 1985, 452; BGHZ 116, 104 (114).

7 §§3 and 17 Futtermittelgesetz (Feed Act); see BGH NJW 1987, 1694 (1695).

8 §20 (2) Pflanzenschutzgesetz (Pesticides Act); see BGH NJW 1981, 1606.

9 §§3 and 8 Trinkwasserverordnung (Drinking Water Regulation); see BGH NJW 1983, 2935.

10 See LG Bonn BeckRS 2011, 09538.

11 MünchKommBGB/Wagner (6th edn 2013) §823; *Palandt/Grüneberg* (74th edn 2015) §823 n 68; *Wagner*, VersR 2014, 905 (913).

the EU Directive 85/374/EEC of 1985 concerning liability for defective products with a delay of one and a half years. The ProdHaftG follows the Directive closely. On the other hand, German law considerably influenced the Directive.[12] The Directive's implementation as a separate Act outside the Civil Code was regarded as the easier way to adapt it to German law and to adjust it to future changes. The existing special statutes and the regulation of tort law in the BGB remained entirely unaffected by the new Act.

08 When implementing the Directive, the German legislator originally made use of all the possible options in the Directive in a victim-unfriendly way:

- 'Primary agricultural products and game', which the Directive originally did not cover but the coverage of which it allowed (art 15(1)(a)), were excluded from the ProdHaftG of 1989. Only after the Directive had been respectively amended[13] were these products also included into the scope of the ProdHaftG.[14]
- The Directive excludes manufacturer's liability for so-called development risks that a seemingly safe product is afterwards revealed to be dangerous (art 7(e)) but allows the Member States to derogate from this exclusion and to hold producers liable even if they prove that at the time of marketing the product appeared to be safe (art 15(1)(b)). The German ProdHaftG used this option and excluded and still excludes liability for development risks.[15]
- The Directive entitles the Member States, but does not oblige them, to limit a producer's maximum liability for damages for death and personal injury if caused by identical items with the same defect to the amount of 70 million ECU (art 16). Germany introduced the limit with the qualification that the maximum amount shall apply not only in the case of a mass defect of identical goods but also in the case of damage by a single defective product (with many injured persons).[16] It is doubted whether this regulation complies with art 16(1), which does not mention the case of damage by a single defective product.[17]
- The Directive leaves unaffected national rules on the recoverability of 'non-material damage' (art 9). The original version of the German ProdHaftG

---

12 See the general concept to regulate the problem in tort law (contrary to the French solution), the wide definition of producer which includes part suppliers, importers etc, and further features. As to the legislative history of the Directive see *HC Taschner/E Frietsch*, Produkthaftungsgesetz und EG-Produkthaftungsrichtlinie. Kommentar (2nd edn 1990) Einführung n 163 ff (Taschner was the EU official who was responsible for the Product Liability Directive).

13 Directive 1999/34/EEC.

14 Amending Act of 2 November 2000 (BGBl 2000 I 1478).

15 See §1 (2) no 5 ProdHaftG.

16 See §10 (1) ProdHaftG; the maximum amount is now €85 million.

17 See *Staudinger/Oechsler* §10 ProdHaftG n 6.

excluded any compensation for non-material damage. However, in 2002 the German law of damages was revised (separately from the famous reform of the German law of obligations) and compensation for non-pecuniary loss was introduced in the ProdHaftG[18] and in all other strict liability statutes which so far had excluded it.

09 Thus, though originally always taking the user-unfriendly option, in later steps German legislation improved the legal situation of victims of product liability cases by including agricultural products and by admitting compensation for immaterial harm.

C. SCOPE OF THE GERMAN PRODUCT LIABILITY ACT

10 As already mentioned the German Product Liability Act follows closely the Directive, often verbatim. The Act therefore regulates all the issues encompassed by the Directive but also a few additional matters: (i) according to §5 ProdHaftG several producers are jointly liable, while the redress between them depends on the circumstances;[19] and (ii) §§7–9 ProdHaftG provide special rules on the amount and form of damages in the case of death and bodily injury; however, these rules mainly repeat the corresponding provisions of the Civil Code (§§842–845 BGB).

11 On the other hand does the Product Liability Act not regulate general issues of tort law such as causation, the general concept of recoverable damage or the responsibility for auxiliaries. These issues are left to the tort and damages law and the general law of obligations of the Civil Code.

D. THE IMPACT OF THE GERMAN PRODUCT LIABILITY ACT

12 The German Product Liability Act had no impact on German statutory law as no existing provision was abrogated or modified. All existing provisions remained in force.

13 In addition, in legal practice the new Act had almost no effect at least for the first twelve years. This was for the following reasons. As mentioned, originally the Product Liability Act excluded compensation for immaterial loss. Therefore, persons with bodily injuries always had to rely on the rules of general tort law

18 §8 sentence 2 ProdHaftG.

19 Furthermore, a reference to the BGB provisions on redress between joint debtors is made (§5 sentence 2 ProdHaftG).

– with its fault requirement – if they claimed compensation. With respect to property losses, the Act (like the Directive) covers only damage to privately used 'items of property' and further provides for a €500 threshold for such losses. There are hardly incentives for claimants to base their cause of action for these 'private losses' on the Directive since in many cases the property damage will remain below the threshold or so close to the threshold that there is a 'rational disinterest' not to litigate in such cases. Then, again, only the general tort regime can provide compensation.

14 The situation changed to some extent when in 2002, twelve years after the entry into force of the Product Liability Act, the legislator allowed compensation for immaterial damage under the Act. Since then the Act has been more often used in practice than before because the Act does not require the proof of fault as condition for liability.[20]

E. FURTHER LIABILITY REGIMES ON NEW TECHNOLOGIES

15 Although German law provides special liability statutes for certain technologies such as the *Gesetz zur Regelung der Gentechnik* (Act on the Regulation of Gene Technique, GenTG) or the *Atomgesetz* (Nuclear Power Act, AtomG) thus far there do not exist liability regulations on those new technologies discussed here. For instance, the *Stammzellgesetz* (StemCell Act, StZG) allows the import and use of embryonic stem cells only under narrow conditions.[21] However, the Act, though containing provisions on criminal sanctions, does not provide for any civil liability. Similarly restrictive is the *Embryonenschutzgesetz* (Embryos Protection Act, EschG). This Act also provides for criminal sanctions if reproduction techniques are used which the Act prohibits. But the Act does not contain provisions on civil liability. Likewise, for nanotechnology there are a number of EU Regulations which regulate the administrative admission or registration of nano-particles in certain goods, for instance in cosmetics, food for human consumption[22] or biocides.[23]

16 Therefore, presently the traditional rules of general tort law are applicable to these new technologies such as reproductive medicine, nanotechnology, cloud computing, 3D printing, autonomous technologies, etc.

---

20 For recent decisions see, eg, BGH NJW 2014, 2106; BGH VersR 2013, 1451; BGH NJW 2013, 1302; BGHZ 181, 253; BGH NJW 2009, 1669; BGH NJW 2009, 1080.

21 See §4 StZG.

22 EU Regulation no 1223/2009.

23 EU Regulation no 528/2012.

II. BASIC ELEMENTS OF LIABILITY

A. OVERVIEW

17 German product liability law is still split into the traditional fault-based rules under the Civil Code and the quasi-strict liability under the Product Liability Act. The latter does not apply to property damage that affects goods ('*Sachen*', 'items') for non-private use. In these cases only the general tort rules can provide compensation. The aforementioned reversal of burden of proof under general tort law of product liability is however applicable irrespective of whether professionally or privately used property has been damaged or destroyed.

18 Under the traditional tort regime, liability is incurred if one of the absolutely protected rights (in principle life, body, health, freedom and property)[24] has been unlawfully and culpably infringed and damage has been caused as a result. As mentioned, where a defect of a product has been proved by the victim as the cause of the damage the producer must prove the non-existence of fault.

19 Under the Product Liability Act fault is not required. It is sufficient and must be proved by the victim that the product had a defect which caused the damage. But the producer has the possibility of exonerating himself from liability if he proves certain exempting reasons.[25]

B. THE CONCEPT OF PRODUCT

20 There are slight but not unimportant differences between the definition of 'product' under general tort law and under the Product Liability Act. Under the Act[26] – like under the Directive[27] – products are exclusively movables. Product liability under general tort law also covers immovables, which can be defective products but do not fall within the scope of the Product Liability Act.[28]

21 Immaterial things are generally not products under the Product Liability Act because they are not corporeal movables;[29] general product liability law, on

[24] The term 'property' includes immaterial property rights; the courts have recognised some further absolute rights, in particular the general personality right and the right of an established and operating business.

[25] §1 (2) and (3) ProdHaftG which fully correspond to art 7 Product Liability Directive.

[26] §2 ProdHaftG.

[27] Art 2 Product Liability Directive.

[28] See MünchKommBGB/Wagner §2 ProdHaftG n 1; *Staudinger/Oechsler* §2 ProdHaftG n 1, 17; *Taschner/Frietsch* §2 ProdHaftG n 7 f.

[29] See *Palandt/Sprau* §2 ProdHaftG n 1; *Staudinger/Oechsler* §2 ProdHaftG n 1.

the other hand, does not exclude them. However, it is the prevailing view that for the purposes of the Product Liability Act software is regarded as a product at least where it is stored on a carrier CD or a similar corporeal medium. If the software is the cause of the damage, liability under the Act as well as under general tort law is incurred if the other requirements of responsibility are fulfilled.[30] On the other hand, is it disputed whether software that is used online counts as product in the sense of the Product Liability Act. The preferable view is in favour of this solution,[31] while the contrary view rejects it.[32] A slightly reduced corporality requirement is already indicated by the express mention of electricity in §2 Product Liability Act and art 2 Directive. It is further accepted that fluids like water, oil, etc are also movables. Moreover, the use of the software generally leads to visibility and thus a certain degree of corporality on a screen (like words or pictures in a book, which also represent the intellectual content of the work and can as such be defective).

22 In all other respects the definition of 'product' is identical for general and special product liability law.

23 Movables as such have the same meaning in general tort law and under the Product Liability Act. Since the size of the movable does not play any role, nano-particles also fall under the term and can constitute products or parts of products.[33] Where a movable is inseparably attached to an immovable – for instance defective joists in building a house – the movable material remains a separate product in the sense of the product liability law, although under German domestic property law the movable becomes part of the immovable property.[34] In the example the producer of the joists is therefore liable for their defects, whereas the business which uses the joists for building the house is not liable under the Product Liability Act because it produces an immovable. Under general tort law the assembling business may nonetheless be liable either for using the wrong joists or for negligently overlooking their defects.

30 In this sense, *Cahn*, NJW 1996, 2899 (2904); *Erman/Schiemann* §2 ProdHaftG n 2; *Foerste/von Westphalen*, Produkthaftungshandbuch (3rd edn 2012) §47 n 42 f; MünchKommBGB/Wagner §2 ProdHaftG n 15; *Palandt/Sprau* §2 ProdHaftG n 1; *Staudinger/Oechsler* §2 ProdHaftG n 64; *Taschner/Frietsch* §2 ProdHaftG n 22 f; however contra older contributions: Bundesfinanzhof (Federal Tax Court, BFH) CR 1987, 576; *Honsell*, JuS 1995, 211 (212).

31 See *Cahn*, NJW 1996, 2899 (2904); *Foerste/von Westphalen* Produkthaftungshandbuch (3rd edn 2012) §47 n 42 f; Hoeren PHI 1989, 138 (139 f); MünchKommBGB/Wagner §2 ProdHaftG n 15; *Palandt/Sprau* §2 ProdHaftG n 1.

32 *Erman/Schiemann* §2 ProdHaftG n 2; *Staudinger/Oechsler* §2 ProdHaftG n 67; *Taschner/Frietsch* §2 ProdHaftG n 22 f.

33 MünchKommBGB/Wagner §2 ProdHaftG n 3.

34 See §94 BGB; further MünchKommBGB/Wagner §2 ProdHaftG n 7; *Staudinger/Oechsler* §2 ProdHaftG n 21 ff.

24 Animals of agricultural or private breeds constitute products both under general tort law as well as under the Product Liability Act.[35] Since the size of the animals does not matter, micro-organisms are also covered.[36] If these micro-organisms are genetically modified, the GenTG and its liability provision[37] are also applicable. Wild animals, even if caught and sold, are probably not products because there is no producer. On the contrary, tamed wild animals (circus elephants, etc) should be regarded as products.

25 Electricity is expressly mentioned in §2 ProdHaftG as a product and is also regarded as a product under general tort law.[38] The same is true for other energy sources as oil and gas, and also for water.[39]

26 Parts of the human body (organs, blood, urine, sperm, hair) become products after they are separated and being processed in whatever way (deep-frozen, etc).[40] The donor is however not regarded as the producer; he or she gives something away but does not produce it.[41] Prostheses and artificial body parts (eg defibrillators, or breast, ear and other implants) are also products that fall under general and special product liability law.[42] This remains true even after such parts are implanted.[43] Human corpses or their parts, as far as their use is permitted, are movables and can become products.[44]

---

35 *Foerste/von Westphalen*, Produkthaftungshandbuch §47 n 22; MünchKommBGB/Wagner §2 ProdHaftG n 4; *Staudinger/Oechsler* §2 ProdHaftG n 71.

36 *Foerste/von Westphalen*, Produkthaftungshandbuch §47 n 23; MünchKommBGB/Wagner §2 ProdHaftG n 4; *Staudinger/Oechsler* §2 ProdHaftG n 72.

37 §32 GenTG; where the liability under the GenTG and the ProdHaftG concur, §37 (2) GenTG provides that the liability for development risks is not excluded.

38 See BGH NJW 2014, 2106 (damage through too high electric tension).

39 *Foerste/von Westphalen*, Produkthaftungshandbuch §47 n 5; MünchKommBGB/Wagner §2 ProdHaftG n 3; *Staudinger/Oechsler* §2 ProdHaftG n 48; *Taschner/Frietsch* §2 ProdHaftG n 19.

40 ECJ, Case C-203/99, *Veedfald v Aarhus Amtskommune* [2001] ECR I-3569 (transfer of kidney through hospital); OLG Hamburg NJW 1990, 2322 (bloodcans); *Foerste/von Westphalen*, Produkthaftungshandbuch §47 n 5; MünchKommBGB/Wagner §2 ProdHaftG n 17; *Palandt/Sprau* §2 ProdHaftG n 1; *Staudinger/Oechsler* §2 ProdHaftG n 34; *Taschner/Frietsch* §2 ProdHaftG n 27.

41 In this sense *Deutsch*, VersR 1992, 521 (525); also *Foerste/von Westphalen*, Produkthaftungshandbuch §47 n 18; MünchKommBGB/Wagner §2 ProdHaftG n 17; *Staudinger/Oechsler* §2 ProdHaftG n 38; *Taschner/Frietsch* §2 ProdHaftG n 27; indirectly probably also ECJ, Case C-203/99, *Veedfald v Aarhus Amtskommune* [2001] ECR I-3569 (failed transfer of donor's kidney through hospital).

42 ECJ, 5 March 2015, Case C-503/13 and C-504/13, *Boston Scientific Medizintechnik GmbH v AOK Sachsen-Anhalt et al* (implanted defribillator) and BGH VersR 2013, 1451 (the reference decision in that case), see further *Foerste/von Westphalen*, Produkthaftungshandbuch §47 n 20; MünchKommBGB/Wagner §2 ProdHaftG n 17; *Staudinger/Oechsler* §2 ProdHaftG n 39; *Taschner/Frietsch* §2 ProdHaftG n 28.

43 See ECJ, 5 March 2015, Case C-503/13 and C-504/13, *Boston Scientific Medizintechnik GmbH v AOK Sachsen-Anhalt et al* (implanted defribillator).

44 *Foerste/von Westphalen*, Produkthaftungshandbuch §47 n 21; MünchKommBGB/Wagner §2 ProdHaftG n 17; *Staudinger/Oechsler* §2 ProdHaftG n 40.

27 The Product Liability Act excludes the liability for medical pharmaceuticals. The liability for their defects is separately regulated by the *Arzneimittelgesetz* (Medical Pharmaceuticals Act, AMG).[45] Article 13 Product Liability Directive allowed the continued existence of this special regime.

28 Where a manufacturer produces the product according to the specifications prescribed by the victim, and the product is therefore defective, this is still a product. However, in accordance with §6 (1) ProdHaftG on contributory negligence, the victim is not entitled to compensation.[46]

C. THE CONCEPT OF DEFECT

29 In respect of the definition of 'defect', §3 ProdHaftG repeats almost verbatim the wording of art 6 Product Liability Directive. In accordance with this definition, a product is defective if it does not provide the safety that in all the circumstances can be justly expected.

30 Under general tort law no statutory definition of 'defect' exists. However, it had become usual to distinguish four types of defects:[47]

- design defects (*Konstruktionsfehler*): the construction of the product is defective;
- fabrication defects (*Fabrikationsfehler*): a defect occurs in the production process;
- instruction defects (*Instruktionsfehler*): the instruction for the use of the product is defective; and
- development risks (*Entwicklungsfehler*): the product develops dangers which were unknown and could not be discovered at the time of marketing the product.

31 These types of defects follow the different stages of the production process. Under general tort law on all levels the producer must observe the standard of diligence that complies with the acknowledged state of technology and science. If a defect is proved to be the cause of the victim's damage, the fault of the producer is presumed with respect to the first three categories of defects; but the presumption can be rebutted. The courts declined however to also accept the presumption of fault for development risks. Therefore, in such cases liability has been denied, at least with regard to the first victims whose injuries lead to

45 See §15 ProdHaftG.

46 So far no case law on this issue seems to exist.

47 See as representative: *Palandt/Sprau* §823 n 173 ff; slightly differently MünchKommBGB/Wagner §823 n 642 in whose list development risks is replaced by defects concerning the later observance of the product (*Produktbeobachtungsfehler*).

the discovery of the development risk. Yet, particularly but not exclusively with respect to this defect category, the courts developed a duty of producers to observe the later development of the product (*Produktbeobachtungspflicht*)[48] and to warn or take other preventive measures if dangers have become apparent (*Gefahrabwendungspflicht*).[49] For each type of defect specific duties of care have been developed which *in abstracto* can be summarised as requiring at each level care that the normal user or the public not be unreasonably endangered by the product. The producer must avoid those dangers which can be avoided with acceptable means provided that the goods are used in their intended or likely function. There is even a duty of care to warn, give advice or take other measures if the product has no effect but the user justifiably relies on promised effects.[50] According to a disputed view, the producer's duties extend over the whole lifespan of the product and even cover the phase of its disposal, meaning that waste can also be 'defective'.[51]

32 Thus, in general tort law the term 'defect' is closely linked to the duty of care that the producer owes with respect to the specific product and with respect to the specific phase in the life of the product. It is not necessary that the good as such needs to be defective per se. It is sufficient that the producer neglected the duty to provide reasonable safety. The level of care is influenced by a number of elements: the intensity of danger the product and an eventual defect creates, in particular whether the life, body and health of persons are endangered; the legitimate safety expectations of the envisaged user and of users where the product invites, or easily allows, certain abuse; the extent to which the danger can be avoided by reasonable means; the recognised standard which science and technology in the production of the respective goods generally require; and the phase in the product's lifecycle.[52]

33 With regard to defects of specific goods there is apparently no difference between general tort law and the Product Liability Act. It has been held – under the Product Liability Act but the result would be identical under general tort law – that the delivery of electric energy can be defective if, for instance, the supplier changes the tension thereby damaging electric devices of users.[53] Even a mere suspicion of a defect can already constitute a defect, at least under certain circumstances. Thus, an implanted defibrillator has been regarded as defective

---

48 See thereto BGHZ 80, 199; BGH NJW 1990, 906; *Palandt/Sprau* §823 n 175; *Wagner*, VersR 2014, 905.

49 BGH NJW 1990, 2560; BGH VersR 2009, 272; *Palandt/Sprau* §823 n 176.

50 BGHZ 80, 186; BGHZ 80, 199; BGH NJW 1985, 194.

51 See *Gesmann-Nuissl/Wenzel*, NJW 2004, 117 (118); MünchKommBGB/Wagner §823 n 644.

52 See, eg, BGHZ 106, 273; BGHZ 181, 253; BGH NJW 2009, 1669; MünchKommBGB/Wagner §823 n 645 ff; NK-BGB/Katzenmeier §823 n 307.

53 BGH NJW 2014, 2106.

if some defibrillators of the same brand were already found defective in other patients, although the defibrillator in the concrete case did not cause problems in that respect.[54] The CJEU argued that for medical devices such as pacemakers and implanted defibrillators 'it is clear that, in the light of their function and the particularly vulnerable situation of patients using such devices, the safety requirements for those devices which such patients are entitled to expect are particularly high.'[55] Therefore, 'where it is found that such products belonging to the same group or forming part of the same production series have a potential defect, it is possible to classify as defective all products in that group or series, without there being any need to show that the product in question is defective.'[56] Where goods are in use and their defects cause damage after some time, it is still the duty of the producer to observe how the product reacts in practice, and not only to stop further production and marketing of that product but also to warn users or to withdraw the product from the market. The producer of motorbikes which became extremely dangerous when certain attachments (of another producer) were installed was therefore liable for warning users and for damages.[57] It did not matter in that case that the motorbike was a second-hand bike that was bought from another user. Because the producer had specifically prepared the bike for such attachments and because of the extreme risk (the driver had a fatal accident), the BGH held that the producer was obliged to observe how the widely used attachments changed the stability of the motorbike at high speed (and was liable in damages for neglect of the duty).[58]

34 It has already been mentioned that computer programmes and books can also be defective, for instance, if they contain wrong information.[59]

35 It is hardly doubtful that an existing standard of care can be increased for the future by a kind of prospective overruling. The BGH has accepted this method with respect to general duties of care (*Verkehrssicherungspflichten*).[60] In the relevant case a 13-year-old boy had climbed on an unfenced carriage of the defendant railway company and suffered severe burns when he came

54 CJEU, 5 March 2015, Case C-503/13 and C-504/13, *Boston Scientific Medizintechnik GmbH v AOK Sachsen-Anhalt et al*; see the reference by the BGH VersR 2013, 1451.

55 CJEU, 5 March 2015, Case C-503/13 and C-504/13, *Boston Scientific Medizintechnik GmbH v AOK Sachsen-Anhalt et al*, para 39.

56 CJEU, 5 March 2015, Case C-503/13 and C-504/13, *Boston Scientific Medizintechnik GmbH v AOK Sachsen-Anhalt et al*, para 41.

57 BGH NJW 1987, 1009.

58 BGH NJW 1987, 1009.

59 See BGH NJW 1970, 1963 (wrong information in a medical work leads to wrong treatment of patient who almost dies = publisher not liable because author was responsible); see also BGH NJW 1973, 843 (a case of contractual liability where a book on notarial duties for mayors contained wrong information on how to draft a valid emergency testament – the claim was justified in principle but prescribed).

60 BGH NJW 1995, 2631.

close to the power line above the carriage. The Court held that the warnings (a lightning sign) were not sufficient but that the company was not at fault since the lower courts had increased the duty to warn only after the accident. The same reasoning can be expected for the level of product liability duties.

D. MARKETING OF A PRODUCT

36 Both in general product liability law and under the Product Liability Act, the producer becomes liable for defects of the product only if he has put the latter into circulation.[61, 62] With respect to the Product Liability Directive, the CJEU decided as a result that a product is put into circulation if its production process has been finished and it is used for its intended or possible purpose.[63] This is often but not exclusively the case when the product has left the sphere of the producer.[64] In a rather special case a hospital had produced a medical fluid for use in another hospital where the fluid caused damage to a kidney that the plaintiff's brother had donated for transplant to the plaintiff. Both hospitals were owned by the defendant. The fluid was defective and made the kidney unfit for the transplant. The CJEU held that the use of the fluid in the defendant's own hospital still meant it had been put into circulation in the sense of art 7(a) Directive.[65]

37 This interpretation has also to be followed for §1 (2) no 1 German Product Liability Act, which implements art 7(a) Directive. For the traditional product liability law of the BGB it was always the position that the producer must have put the product to public use ('*in Verkehrgebrachthaben*').[66] This means the marketing of the product, its delivery to third persons or its otherwise deliberate putting into circulation for the public.[67] Thus, where an employee suffers damage during the process of production the employer may be liable under general

---

61 MünchKommBGB/Wagner §1 ProdHaftG n 25 criticises the decision as mixing product liability and liability for services; he argues that the CJEU would establish an unjustified strict liability for services. However, in its decision the CJEU clearly distinguishes between the production of the defective fluid – for which the defendant is liable without fault – and the use of the fluid during the medical services which led to the damage. The Court exclusively addresses the product liability; in the – correct – view of the Court it is the defect of the product that makes liable, not the medical service which was rendered. Critical to the decision also *Staudinger/Oechsler* §1 ProdHaftG n 50 where the author however seems to assume that the kidney was the product.

62 See *Palandt/Sprau* §823 n 181.

63 See CJEU, Case C-203/99, *Veedfald v Aarhus Amtskommune* [2001] ECR I-3569; CJEU, Case C-127/04, *O'Byrne v Sanofi Pasteur MSD Ltd et al* [2006] ECR I-1313.

64 See CJEU, Case C-127/04,*O'Byrne v Sanofi Pasteur MSD Ltd et al* [2006] ECR I-1313.

65 CJEU, Case C-203/99, *Veedfald v Aarhus Amtskommune* [2001] ECR I-3569.

66 See BGHZ 104, 323; BGHZ 114, 284; LG Berlin BeckRS 2008, 09725; *Palandt/Sprau* §823 n 181.

67 See already BGHZ 51, 91 ('delivery' ('*Auslieferung*') of the vaccine thus putting it into circulation); also the special case of LG Berlin BeckRS 2008, 09725.

contract and tort law but not under tortious product liability law.[68] The same is true where a person is injured who has stolen the unfinished product from the producer or has used it before its completion without the producer's consent.[69] However, it is disputed how cases must be solved where the producer still works on the product that is already outside its plant. In a case where the producer (and defendant) had installed the electronic system in the power station of the claimant, due to a software defect the station exploded while employees of the defendant were still working on the optimisation of the system, the court held that the system was already put into circulation as soon as the defendant had allowed the claimant to start using the system.[70] However, the court denied the defendant's liability because the software was changed after its installation and the claimant could prove neither that the defect existed already at the time when the product was put into circulation nor that the defendant was liable for the later modification of the software programme. As a result, the burden of proof was not reversed.[71]

38 If the product as such is not defective, however, its use may create dangers against which the producer must provide reasonable instructions and warnings.[72] If there are not sufficient warnings – even against an abuse which the product readily invites[73] – the producer is liable both under general product liability law and under the ProdHaftG.

39 Where a product becomes defective on its way to public circulation, for instance due to improper storage during transport from the production place to the place of distribution, this may still be a case of product liability if the product later causes damage to users, provided that the producer transported the product to the place of distribution or did not properly instruct an independent carrier.

E. THE PRODUCER'S DUTIES

40 The statutory law does not define the duties of care of the producer in greater detail. It was the courts which developed such duties and extended them further and further. The whole system of product liability can also be described as a system of duties of care which are specific to the time before and after the product is put into circulation.[74] The producer is obliged to design and

68 *Staudinger/Oechsler* §1 ProdHaftG n 51.
69 See LG Berlin BeckRS 2008, 09725; *Palandt/Sprau* §1 ProdHaftG n 14.
70 LG Berlin BeckRS 2008, 09725.
71 LG Berlin BeckRS 2008, 09725.
72 See for instance BGHZ 64, 46 (49); BGHZ 116, 60 (65); BGHZ 139, 79 (83); BGHZ 181, 253 (para 23).
73 eg BGHZ 105, 346 (351); BGH NJW 1999, 2815.
74 See *Bamberger/Roth/Spindler* §823 n 492; *Staudinger/OechslerEinl* zum ProdHaftG n 31.

manufacture the goods with reasonable care, as well as to prepare the necessary instructions and warnings for users. If safer products have been developed by others, the producer must adapt its own production to the improved standard. With respect to particularly dangerous goods, the producer is obliged to document that the goods were not defective when put into circulation.[75] The BGH therefore held that glass bottles must be specifically checked before they are re-used and the check must be documented; if not, it is presumed a bottle that explodes and injures a person was defective when leaving the factory.[76]

41 After having put the goods into circulation the producer is obliged to react if the goods systematically cause damage. To a certain extent the courts have established a duty to actively observe the fate of the goods.[77] If a specific dangerousness of the goods develops over time, the producer must warn users[78] or even withdraw the goods from the market.[79] In principle this duty is unlimited in time,[80] although the intensity of the duty decreases the longer the product is on the market and appears to do no harm.

F. SPECIAL REGULATIONS FOR CERTAIN KINDS OF PRODUCTS

42 German law provides for special rules for medical pharmaceuticals in the *Arzneimittelgesetz* (Medicinal Products Act, AMG). The Act establishes a system of strict liability for damage caused by a medical pharmaceutical that has dangerous effects which exceed the measure that is acceptable in view of the present state of medical science or where the damage was caused by instructions that do not conform to this state of knowledge.[81] This liability replaces the liability under the Product Liability Act (§15 ProdHaftG which implemented

75 See, eg, BGHZ 129, 353 (361 f).

76 BGHZ 129, 353 (361 f).

77 BGHZ 80, 186; BGHZ 80, 199; BGHZ 116, 60; BGH NJW 1990, 906.

78 See, eg, BGHZ 179, 157.

79 BGHZ 179, 157; OLG Düsseldorf NJW-RR 1997, 1344; also under criminal law BGHSt 37, 106.

80 *Bamberger/Roth/Spindler* §823 n 512; *Staudinger/Hager* §823 n F 21; but contrary LG Frankfurt.

81 §84 (1) AMG: '*Wird infolge der Anwendung eines zum Gebrauch bei Menschen bestimmten Arzneimittels, das im Geltungsbereich dieses Gesetzes an den Verbraucher abgegeben wurde und der Pflicht zur Zulassung unterliegt oder durch Rechtsverordnung von der Zulassung befreit worden ist, ein Mensch getötet oder der Körper oder die Gesundheit eines Menschen nicht unerheblich verletzt, so ist der pharmazeutische Unternehmer, der das Arzneimittel im Geltungsbereich dieses Gesetzes in den Verkehr gebracht hat, verpflichtet dem Verletzten den daraus entstandenen Schaden zu ersetzen. Die Ersatzpflicht besteht nur, wenn*

1. *das Arzneimittel bei bestimmungsgemäßem Gebrauch schädliche Wirkungen hat, die über ein nach den Erkenntnissen der medizinischen Wissenschaft vertretbares Maß hinausgehen oder*

art 13 Product Liability Directive; the latter was addressed to reserve priority to the existing AMG).

G. THE MODEL OF PRODUCT LIABILITY

43 German product liability law still has two different routes: product liability law under the BGB, which is characterised as liability based on presumed fault, and liability under the Product Liability Act, which the prevailing view qualifies as a system of strict liability,[82] but with a number of specific grounds for exemption. The strict liability under the AMG belongs to this second route. Whereas the courts treat most elements of general and special product liability as broadly identical,[83] the basis and scope of liability is nonetheless different. In contrast to fault-based general product liability law, the strict Product Liability Act covers only some of the possible product liability cases and sets limits for compensation.

III. THE PERSON LIABLE FOR DAMAGE

A. THE PRODUCER

44 General and special product liability law do not use exactly the same definition of the person who is liable as producer. Differences exist insofar as under general product liability law leading employees can also become liable, like the producer,[84] whereas the Product Liability Act does not provide for this possibility.[85] On the contrary, importers and distributors are generally not producers under general product liability law, but they are under the Product Liability Act.[86]

45 In principle the producer is the person or entity under whose responsibility the final product that was put into circulation was in fact directly manufactured.

2. *der Schaden infolge einer nicht an den Erkenntnissen der medizinischen Wissenschaft entsprechenden Kennzeichnung, Fachinformation oder Gebrauchsinformation eingetreten ist.'*

82 See *Foerste/von Westphalen*, Produkthaftungshandbuch§24 n 298; Hk-BGB/Staudinger §823 n 162; *Jauernig/Teichmann* §823 n 140; NK-BGB/Katzenmeier §823 n 284; *Palandt/Sprau* Einführung vor §1 ProdHaftG n 5; differently – as a mixture of liability for illegal conduct and risk: *Staudinger/Oechsler*, Einl zum ProdHaftG n 27 f; mixture of fault and strict liability with the first dominating: MünchKommBGB/Wagner Einleitung ProdHaftG n 19.

83 See with respect to the notion of defect: BGHZ 181, 253 (para 12); also MünchKommBGB/Wagner Einleitung ProdHaftG n 16.

84 See BGH NJW 1975, 1827.

85 See *Staudinger/Oechsler* §4 ProdHaftG n 5.

86 See §4 ProdHaftG; *Palandt/Sprau* §823 n 181.

This producer remains responsible even if he markets the product via a distributor whom he has entitled to put their own name on the product so that the distributor appears as the producer.[87] The latter then becomes a quasi-producer.[88] Furthermore, if a business improves a product that another business has produced, the improving business also becomes a producer and will be liable if it is the improvement that is defective and causes damage.[89]

46 Suppliers of components of the final product are also producers, however only of their parts, while an assembler is responsible for the construction and fabrication of the complete end-product. Any business that is involved in the production of a final product is in principle allowed to trust that the other contributing businesses will perform their part in a reliable and defect-free way.[90] Nonetheless, the assembler must reasonably examine the fitness of the components for the final product.[91]

47 Importers of defective goods are regarded as their producers by §4 ProdHaftG (in accordance with art 3(2) Product Liability Directive). Under general product liability law they are not deemed to be producers but still have certain special duties, namely to observe the goods and to react by issuing warnings, etc if dangers become apparent. Thus, the German exclusive importer of Japanese motorbikes was held liable for not warning users that certain attachments of other producers made the bikes extremely unsafe.[92]

48 §4 (3) ProdHaftG (implementing art 3(3) Directive) further provides that the supplier of a product is to be treated as its producer if he does not inform the injured person of the identity of the producer within a month after being asked.[93] This rule does not apply in general product liability law.

49 In the case of agricultural products, their mere harvesting still does not count as production. The person harvesting them is not their producer, but does become so if he processes the harvested product in any way before putting it into circulation.[94]

50 Generally the business as such or the single entrepreneur is liable as producer. Employees are not personally liable under general product liability law

---

87 BGH NJW 1987, 372.

88 See for general product liability law: OLG Karlsuhe NJW-RR 1994, 798; OLG Stuttgart ZMR 2010, 307; *Palandt/Sprau* §823 n 181; §4 (1) sentence 2 ProdHaftG.

89 See BGH NJW 1992, 1678.

90 MünchKommBGB/Wagner §823 n 627.

91 BGH BB 1977, 1117; BGH VersR 1978, 550.

92 BGH NJW 1987, 1009.

93 Art 3(3) Product Liability Directive requires information within a 'reasonable time'.

94 OLG Hamm DB 1973, 325; *Palandt/Sprau* §823 n 181.

or under the Product Liability Act. As already mentioned, an exception applies under general product liability law if the employee has a leading position in the business and is responsible for instance for the construction of the product.[95] However, a cook employed by a restaurant who has prepared a wedding meal is not personally liable under the general product liability law; liability still rests on the owner of the restaurant.[96]

51 To fulfil the role of producer it is irrelevant whether a business puts its products into circulation for commercial or non-commercial purposes. However, thus far it is necessary that a business, not a private person, has produced the product. The size of the business – whether an international company with thousands of employees, small family enterprise or one-man business – does not matter.[97] In a case in which a person invites guests to a private party and prepares an infected meal courts will probably not apply product liability principles. In the leading *Hühnerpest* case the Federal Supreme Court made it always a requirement that a business (*ein Betrieb*) must have manufactured the product.[98]

52 Public entities which are acting in the private sector (for instance hospitals) are subject to general and special product liability law in the same way as private entities. For the interpretation of the Product Liability Act this already follows from related case law of the CJEU.[99] But it is also true for general product liability law.[100]

B. JOINT AND SEVERAL LIABILITY

53 Where several producers are liable, for instance the assembler of the wrongly constructed final product and the supplier of a defective component, they are jointly and severally liable.[101] The injured person can recover compensation from each of them in full, though on the whole only once.[102]

95 See BGH NJW 1975, 1827; but also BGH NJW 1987, 372 where the Court denied the liability of the head of the defendant's laboratory for insufficient instructions on a dangerous product because the head was not responsible in the business for the instructions.

96 BGHZ 116, 104.

97 BGHZ 116, 104.

98 BGHZ 51, 91.

99 ECJ, Case C-203/99, *Veedfald v Aarhus Amtskommune* [2001] ECR I-3569 (production of special serum by hospital of the community for transfer of kidney in another hospital of same community).

100 BGH NJW 1991, 1948 and OLG Hamburg NJW 1990, 2322 (with HIV infected blood cans produced in public hospital); see also BGH NJW 1982, 699 (production of insterile infusion though open whether in public or private hospital).

101 For general product liability law see §840 (1) BGB and BGH NJW-RR 1990, 406; for the Product Liability Act see §5 sentence 1 ProdHaftG.

102 See §421 BGB.

C. RECOURSE

54 If debtors are jointly and severally liable, they are obliged in relation to each other to bear such shares as agreements (for instance, a quality assurance agreement) or the circumstances determine.[103] As for the circumstances, the extent each debtor caused the damage is particularly relevant;[104] secondly, the degree of fault matters.[105] The same principles are applied as for contributory negligence.[106]

IV. THE AGGRIEVED PERSON AND DAMAGE

A. WHO CAN CLAIM?

55 Only the injured person him- or herself as well as the owner of damaged property is entitled to damages. In the case of death the dependants of the deceased (who were entitled in law to maintenance) can claim the lost maintenance;[107] the heirs can claim the burial costs.[108] The heirs can further claim compensation for those losses which the deceased could have claimed him- or herself had he or she survived, for instance damages for pain and suffering (*Schmerzensgeld*) for significant pain before death or costs for medical treatment during that phase.[109] German law does not provide for damages to close relatives for bereavement. If, however, a close relative suffers their own medically diagnosed injury because of the death or severe injury of their relative, he or she has his/her own claim against the tortfeasor.[110]

56 It does not matter under either general or special product liability law whether the injured or deceased person was the intended or an accidental user of the product or a mere bystander.[111] They are all entitled to compensation if

[103] §426 (1) sentence 1 BGB for the general product liability law and §5 sentence 2 ProdHaftG for the Product Liability Act. §426 (1) sentence 1 BGB provides as a further default rule that joint tortfeasors have to bear equal shares in relation to each other. This default rule is lacking in §5 ProdHaftG.

[104] See *Palandt/Grüneberg* §426 n 14 for the general law and §5 sentence 2 ProdHaftG specifically for the Product Liability Act.

[105] See *Palandt/Grüneberg* §426 n 14; §5 sentence 2 ProdHaftG refers insofar to the general provision of §426 BGB.

[106] BGH NJW 1955, 1314; BGH NJW 1972, 1802; MünchKommBGB/Wagner §5 ProdHaftG n 10; *Staudinger/Oechsler* §5 ProdHaftG n 16.

[107] §844 (2) BGB, §7 (2) ProdHaftG.

[108] §844 (1) BGB, §7 (1) sentence 2 ProdHaftG.

[109] See explicitly §7 (1) sentence 1 ProdHaftG which expresses a rule also applicable in general tort law (including general product liability law).

[110] See most recently BGH BeckRS 2015, 02887.

[111] *Palandt/Sprau* §823 n 170 and §1 ProdHaftG n 10.

the product was defective, caused the damage and the producer cannot rebut the presumption of fault or prove a ground for exemption.

B. DAMAGE

1) *Concept of Damage*

57 German law did not develop a specific concept of damage for product liability but uses the general concept of damage as enshrined in §§249 ff BGB. It requires a diminution of a legally protected position of the aggrieved person. In tort law the legally protected positions are: life, body, health, sexual self-determination, freedom, personality, and all kinds of property (movable, immovable, immaterial).[112] Pure economic loss is recoverable in tort only under specific, rather restrictive conditions.[113] General product liability law follows this concept in full, whereas under the Product Liability Act compensation can be granted only for a restricted number of legally protected positions, namely life, body, health and damage to specific property.[114]

2) *Recoverable Damage*

58 As just indicated, German law grants damages in a different way in different kinds of product liability cases: general product liability law is more generous than the Product Liability Act. However, the difference exclusively concerns property damage. With respect to injury to life, body and health there is no difference.

59 In accordance with the Product Liability Directive,[115] §1 (1) sentence 2 Product Liability Act only covers damage to the claimant's privately used movables. Movables that are used for business purposes do not fall under the Product Liability Act. The *Hühnerpest* case and many of the major product liability cases would therefore not have been covered by this special Act.

60 Moreover, the text of the provision (*'eine andere Sache als das fehlerhafte Produkt beschädigt'*) excludes – again in accordance with the Directive – damage to the defective product itself. The main underlying reason is that these kinds of damage shall be governed by contract law. It appears to be the

---

112 See also the list of protected rights in §823 (1) BGB.

113 Either a protective statutory provision, for instance, of criminal law, must have been violated (§823 (2) BGB) or the tortfeasor must have acted with intent and in violation of good morals (§826 BGB).

114 See §1 (1) ProdHaftG.

115 Art 9(b) Directive.

prevailing, though heavily disputed view, that the quoted formulation does not allow damages to be claimed if only a component of the product is defective and causes damage to the whole product.[116] This is however different where the component is *the* product that is merely inserted into the claimant's movable or immovable.[117] Whereas the Product Liability Act, according to the prevailing view, excludes any compensation for damage to the product itself, under general product liability law the German courts grant such damages under special conditions: the cause of the damage to the product itself must be a separate, functionally independent – and defective – part of the product which can easily be removed and replaced; and the damage must not be identical with the reduced value of the product because of the defective part (no '*Stoffgleichheit*' between the defect and the damage).[118] Compensation for the reduced value is to be dealt with exclusively by contract law. If the aforementioned conditions are met (so-called '*Weiterfresserschäden*') the damage to the product itself is recoverable. In the leading case, the BGH therefore accepted a damages claim where a huge machine the defendant had delivered burned down because a small switch swimming in a fluid and designed to protect against overheating was defective and did not work.[119] This and later decisions are still criticised,[120] but the Court upheld its view even after the Product Liability Act introduced the opposite solution.

61 If a protected right has been violated any consequential damage (cost of healing or for repair, loss of income, lost profit, increased needs, etc) is also recoverable – both under general and under special product liability law.[121] But the compensation of these economic losses always depends on the fact that a protected right must first have been infringed. Pure economic loss without such an infringement is not recoverable under tortious product liability law. The exceptions where such loss can be recovered in tort[122] do regularly not occur in product liability situations.

62 German law does not recognise the loss of a chance as such. The courts do not assess a certain percentage of probability and compensate for its loss. Nonetheless, in the case of a child's lost future income, for instance, the courts

---

116 Against any compensation for damage to the product itself: *Erman/Schiemann* §1 ProdHaftG n 3; MünchKommBGB/Wagner §1 ProdHaftG n 8 ff; *Taschner/Frietsch* §1 ProdHaftG n 39; for compensation at least in certain cases NK-BGB/Katzenmeier §1 ProdHaftG n 12; *Staudinger/Oechsler* §1 ProdHaftG n 20; open: *Palandt/Sprau* §1 ProdHaftG n 6.

117 See OLG Stuttgart NZM 2010, 626 (installation of defective devices in building).

118 See BGHZ 67, 359; BGHZ 86, 256; BGH NJW 1992, 1678; BGHZ 117, 183.

119 BGHZ 67, 359 ('*Schwimmerschalter*').

120 See, for instance, *Kötz/Wagner* n 151 f.

121 See also MünchKommBGB/Wagner §1 ProdHaftG n 2.

122 See *supra* fn 113.

meticulously assess the prospects of the future life of the injured person, its probable length, the person's probable career and probable income, etc.[123]

63 In the case of bodily harm it is undisputed that the injured person can claim compensation for pain and suffering – both under general[124] and under special product liability law.[125]

C. LIMITS OF LIABILITY

64 Only the Product Liability Act provides for certain monetary limits on compensation. General product liability law does not contain any similar restrictions. For cases of death and bodily injury the Act provides that the producer can be held liable up to a maximum amount of €85 million.[126] This cap applies in cases where a single product is defective and causes damage, as well as in cases of a product series of identical items. In the case of a single defective product, the maximum sum will be reached only if a product leads to the death or injury of many persons, for instance if a product defect causes an aeroplane to crash, affecting with hundreds of people on board and on the ground. However, it is doubtful whether the Product Liability Directive allows a maximum amount for this situation since the relevant provision of the Directive (art 16) refers merely to 'damage resulting from death or personal injury and caused by identical items with the same defect.' A literal interpretation would not allow the implementation of a cap for single products.[127] Moreover, the CJEU interprets the Directive as a fully harmonising instrument from which the Member States are not allowed to deviate.[128] Yet it remains to be seen how the CJEU will interpret art 16 of the Product Liability Directive in a concrete case.

65 The Product Liability Act – this time clearly in accordance with the Directive – also contains a monetary limit for property damage.[129] If property

---

123 See, eg, BGH NJW 2011, 1145; for the prospects of an adult see BGH NJW 2011, 1148; further *Palandt/Grüneberg* §253 n 17.

124 See insofar §253 (2) BGB.

125 See §8 sentence 2 ProdHaftG. This possibility was introduced only in 2002. The Product Liability Directive (art 9) leaves it to national law whether or not non-pecuniary damage shall be recoverable.

126 §10 (1) ProdHaftG.

127 In this sense *Erman/Schiemann* §10 ProdHaftG n 1; *Taschner/Frietsch* Art. 16 Richtlinie n 4; *Staudinger/Oechsler* §10 ProdHaftG n 6; doubting: MünchKommBGB/Wagner §10 ProdHaftG n 3; *Palandt/Sprau* §10 ProdHaftG n 2.

128 CJEU, Case C-52/00, *Commission v France* [2002] ECR I-3227, para 24; CJEU, Case C-154/00, *Commission v Greece* [2002] ECR I-3901, para 20; CJEU, Case C-402/03, *Skov v Bilka; Mikkelsen v Bilka* [2006] ECR I-223, para 23.

129 §11 ProdHaftG which in this respect implemented art 9(b) Product Liability Directive.

damage does not exceed the sum of €500 it is not recoverable under the Act, and if it exceeds the threshold only the amount in excess can be recovered.[130]

66 Under general product liability law, neither the maximum amount of €85 million nor the threshold of €500 is applicable. As a consequence the aggrieved person can claim the full amount of damages under general product liability law if the producer cannot prove the absence of fault. The cap and the threshold of the Product Liability Act do not bar recourse to general product liability law.

V. CAUSALITY

A. CONCEPT OF CAUSATION AND TRIGGERING EVENT

67 Product liability law uses the general concept of causation without any specific modification. In German law causation is proven if, first, the *conditio sine qua non* formula is fulfilled, and secondly the damage is the adequate consequence of the condition which the tortfeasor set. Other policy considerations must often be applied, in particular whether the damage falls within the protective scope and purpose of the norm involved.

68 German law recognises neither proportional liability nor market share liability as a concept of causation or damages.[131] If several tortfeasors are liable they are jointly liable towards the victim irrespective of whether or not they acted in concert and how important the contribution of each tortfeasor in relation to the others was.[132]

69 The triggering event for product liability under both general and special product liability law is the damage which the product must have caused. It must be possible to trace this damage back to a defect in the product that has been put to use by persons other than the producer and its auxiliaries. The 'defect' can be either a design, fabrication or instruction defect. As already mentioned, neither under general product liability law nor under the Product Liability Act is liability incurred for development risks, and only under the general product liability law can neglect of the duty to actively observe the product result in liability.

B. MULTIPLE CAUSES OF DAMAGE

70 Where causes external to the producer and to the aggrieved person contributed to the damage, this generally does not influence the producer's

---

130 See MünchKommBGB/Wagner §11 ProdHaftG n 3; *Palandt/Sprau* §11 ProdHaftG n 1.

131 See particularly for product liability law *Staudinger/Oechsler* §4 ProdHaftG n 50 ff.

132 See NK-BGB/Katzenmeier §830 n 1 ff; *Palandt/Sprau* §830 n 1.

liability unless these causes were the exclusive cause of the damage. §5 (2) ProdHaftG explicitly provides – in accordance with art 8(1) Directive – that it does not affect the liability of the producer if both a defect of the product and the act of a third person caused the damage. Thus, if for instance terrorists poison oranges harvested, processed and stored by a farmer, the latter remains liable as the producer if he still delivers the fruits after becoming aware of the poisoning. If, on the contrary, the farmer can prove that he had no knowledge when marketing the oranges and that he could not reasonably avoid the poisoning, then, under general product liability law, there is an absence of fault and the farmer is not liable if a person is poisoned by one of the oranges (as soon as the farmer learns of the poisoning he is however obliged to take reasonable measures to warn, etc).[133] Under the Product Liability Act none of the causes for exemption (§1 (2) ProdHaftG) covers this case. Therefore it is likely, though thus far undecided, that the farmer would be liable under the Act.[134]

C. MULTIPLE CAUSES AND CONTRIBUTORY NEGLIGENCE

71 In cases where several tortfeasors are liable and the aggrieved person contributed to their own damage, the courts distinguish whether the tortfeasors acted in concert or independently. Since in the first case each tortfeasor is identified with the contributions of the others, the causal weight and gravity of fault of all these contributions must be balanced against the contributory negligence of the victim.[135] The calculation is more difficult if the tortfeasors acted independently. Then, the victim is regarded as a further tortfeasor and his or her contribution set in relation to each of the other tortfeasors.[136] The joint liability of all tortfeasors merely goes as far as their individual contribution in relation to that of the victim.[137]

---

133 To such cases see *Bamberger/Roth/Spindler* §823 n 520.

134 In this sense MünchKommBGB/Wagner §1 ProdHaftG n 33; *Staudinger/Oechsler* §1 ProdHaftG n 68.

135 BGH NJW 1959, 1772.

136 See for instance BGH NJW 2006, 897; BGH NJW 2011, 292.

137 If, for example the entire damage is €12,000 caused by three tortfeasors A, B, C and by the victim V to equal shares V is on the whole entitled to €9,000. However, in relation to each tortfeasor V can only claim half of the damage because the own contributory negligence equals a share of each tortfeasor. This leads to €4,500 against each tortfeasor (the half of €9,000). For this sum each tortfeasor is jointly liable. Since V is finally entitled to €9,000, each tortfeasor alone and separately is further liable for €1,500; see BGHZ 30, 203; OLG Celle OLGZ 1974, 203; to this method of calculation see further MünchKommBGB/Oetker §254 n 119 ff; *Palandt/Grüneberg* §254 n 69 ff.

VI. DEFENCES AND EXCLUSIONS

A. REGULATION OF DEFENCES

72 While the Product Liability Act – in accordance with the Product Liability Directive –contains a list of specific exemption causes, the courts did not develop a similar list under general product liability law. Because the latter requires fault, such a list of exemption causes is unnecessary.

73 The exemption causes listed in §1 (2) ProdHaftG correspond almost word-for-word with those of art 7(a)–(e) Product Liability Directive and must be interpreted in conformity with them. Since the exemption causes constitute exceptions from the general rule of – strict – liability, they have to be interpreted restrictively.[138]

German law has made use of the option of the Directive[139] and allows the development risk defence (§1(2) no 5 ProdHaftG). The provision relieves the producer of liability if 'the defect according to the state of scientific and technical knowledge at the time when [the producer] put the product into circulation could not be discovered'. This provision is accompanied by §3 (2) ProdHaftG which provides that 'a product is not defective solely because later a better product has been put into circulation.'[140] Technical innovations thus do not make earlier products defective. However, if it is later discovered that certain materials that have been used in the production are inherently dangerous, the product qualifies as defective; however, the producer is not liable for this development risk if he can prove that at the time of leaving the product to others (not involved in the process of production) the defect could not be discovered.

74 The state of scientific and technical knowledge is an objective standard.[141] It requires that the producer uses the newest available and recognised scientific and technical information on the risks posed by materials, constructions or safety measures.[142] However, there must be clear and specific indications of dangers; the general possibility that some risk may develop is insufficient. Therefore, the BGH has held that the mere possibility or non-specific suspicion that resistance to apple scab may develop due to a treatment with a pharmaceutical, which the defendant producer had delivered to the claimant farmers, did not suffice.[143] The state of scientific and technical knowledge means that the knowledge must be more or less certain and accepted by the respective community of scientists and

138 See ECJ, Case C-203/99, *Veedfald v Aarhus Amtskommune* [2001] ECR I-3569, para 15.
139 See art 7(e) and 15(1)(b) Product Liability Directive.
140 This provision implemented art 6(2) Product Liability Directive.
141 See BGHZ 181, 253.
142 BGHZ 181, 253.
143 BGHZ 80, 186; also BGHZ 80, 199.

technicians.[144] This standard with which producers must comply may be higher than the usages observed in certain industry branches.[145] On the other hand, it is necessary that a real alternative already exists that has been successfully tested and shown to be better than the present product, and that it can be produced with reasonable means and efforts.[146]

75 If the state of scientific and technical knowledge does not enable a risk to be fully excluding using technically possible and economically reasonable, means and the product is nevertheless allowed to be put into circulation, the producer must at least warn that there are risks that are not generally known.[147]

76 Under general product liability law the same considerations as under §1 (2) no 5 ProdHaftG apply with respect to fault. In the case of development risks which could not be discovered, the producer is not at fault if he observed the state of scientific and technical knowledge at the time of putting the product into circulation.

B. SCOPE OF THE DEVELOPMENT RISK DEFENCE

77 The development risk defence is primarily available in the case of defects of construction which were not discoverable at the time the product was put into circulation.[148] However, the BGH extended this defence to instruction defects.[149] Where the instruction was defective because it did not warn against dangers which were not known at the time the product and the instruction were put into circulation, the development risk defence exonerates the producer as well. The Court argued that it is the purpose of the defence to exempt the producer from liability for development risks. This purpose covers both construction and instruction defects.[150]

78 On the other hand, the development risk defence of §1 (2) no 5 ProdHaftG does not apply to fabrication defects.[151] The BGH held that this provision and the underlying provision of the Directive did not intend to allow the development risk defence for fabrication defects even if the latter were unavoidable (so-called '*Ausreißer*' (outliers)).[152] The Directive and the Act aimed to abolish this *Ausreißer* defence. The strict liability for *Ausreißer* exists only under the Product

144 See BGHZ 80, 186; also BGHZ 80, 199; BGHZ 181, 253.
145 BGHZ 181, 253 (para 16).
146 BGHZ 181, 253.
147 BGHZ 181, 253.
148 BGHZ 181, 253.
149 BGHZ 181, 253 (para 27 ff).
150 BGHZ 181, 253 (para 27).
151 BGHZ 129, 353.
152 BGHZ 129, 353.

Liability Act. Under general product liability law the producer is liable if the victim can prove that the product was defective and caused the damage and if the producer cannot rebut the presumption of fault.[153] It is often difficult for the victim to prove that a defect existed and was the cause of the damage. Sometimes the courts help by using the instrument of the *prima facie* evidence.[154] In the case of an exploding soda bottle the producer was obliged to document that each bottle left the business without defect. If this could not be proven the producer was held liable.[155]

C. COMPLIANCE WITH PUBLIC LAW STANDARDS AS DEFENCE?

79 According to §1 (2) no 4 ProdHaftG,[156] a further exonerating cause is if the defect is due to the product having to comply with mandatory regulations and thus a legal provision specifically forces the producer to manufacture defective products.[157] There are hardly any such mandatory provisions. The public law on product safety regularly leaves room for the producer to construe and produce its products[158] and is therefore not mandatory in the required sense; and more precise administrative regulations are not norms that fall under §1 (2) no 4 ProdHaftG.[159] Compliance with such norms does not exonerate the producer from its otherwise existing liability for product defects.[160] This rule applies under both the Act and general product liability law.

D. CONTRACTUAL EXCLUSION OF LIABILITY

80 Liability under the Product Liability Act cannot be excluded or limited in advance (§14 ProdHaftG). Agreements to the contrary are invalid. Agreements and settlements after the product has caused damage are however permitted.[161]

---

153 BGHZ 104, 323.

154 See BGHZ 104, 323.

155 BGHZ 104, 323.

156 The provision implemented art 7(d) Product Liability Directive.

157 See MünchKommBGB/Wagner §1 ProdHaftG n 42 ff; *Staudinger/Oechsler* §1 ProdHaftG n 100 ff.

158 See §4 (2) *Produktsicherheitsgesetz* (Product Safety Act, PSG). The provision merely establishes a presumption that a product that conforms to specific regulations meets the safety requirements of the PSG.

159 See MünchKommBGB/Wagner §1 ProdHaftG n 42 ff; *Staudinger/Oechsler* §1 ProdHaftG n 100 ff.

160 BGH NJW 1994, 3349 (liability of producer of a breath surveillance device despite compliance of the product with DIN norms); BGHZ 139, 43 (sale of imported fireworks to children, although legally permitted, does not relieve seller from further duties of care).

161 See MünchKommBGB/Wagner §14 ProdHaftG n 3; *Palandt/Sprau* §14 ProdHaftG n 1; *Staudinger/Oechsler* §14 ProdHaftG n 11.

81 Liability under general product liability law is in principle open to party autonomy. However, in pure tort situations, it will normally not be possible to agree on a reduction of liability in advance unless the parties already had prior contact. Moreover, any contractual exclusion or reduction of liability is subject to certain limitations: the liability for intent cannot be excluded in advance (§276 (3) BGB); where the exclusion is provided for in standard contract terms it is not possible to exclude or limit liability for gross negligence or in the case of personal injury for negligence (§309 no 7 BGB). Such clauses are invalid.

VII. REMEDIES

A. POSSIBLE CLAIMS

82 If the aggrieved party is entitled to damages he or she may claim restoration in kind or the sum of money which is necessary for such restoration (§249 (1) and (2) sentence 1 BGB). Generally, a sum of money will be claimed. The same is true for the compensation for pain and suffering (§253 BGB) although in theory even in those cases restoration in kind could be claimed.

B. NON-COMPENSATORY DAMAGES AVAILABLE?

83 The general aim of the German law of damages is the compensation of the loss the aggrieved party suffered.[162] Non-compensatory, in particular punitive, damages are viewed with caution and suspicion.[163] Indeed, in principle, punitive damages are rejected.[164] Only in certain situations does the Federal Supreme Court accept a special preventive function of damages which allows higher damages than the actual loss to be awarded. The most prominent case, and indeed the only one, concerns the violation of the general personality right. Here, the BGH stresses the principle of prevention, primarily in order to prevent the reckless exploitation and marketing of a personality without the latter's consent.[165]

84 The German law of damages also does not provide for nominal damages. However, German law recognises of the possibility of a declaratory judgment (§256 *Zivilprozessordnung* (Code of Civil Procedure, ZPO)). A claimant can request such a judgment where he or she can demonstrate a sufficient interest

162 See §249 (1) BGB; NK-BGB/Magnus Vor §§249–255 n 8; *Palandt/Grüneberg* Vorbem §249 n 2.
163 See BGHZ 118, 312.
164 BGHZ 118, 312.
165 See BGHZ 128, 1; BGH NJW 1996, 984.

that a legal relationship be established or denied. A legal relationship is for instance the existence of a claim of one person against another.[166] Since the claim for a declaratory judgment is a subsidiary remedy, it is available in tort or product liability cases only if a direct damages claim is not yet possible, for instance because the the damage is still ongoing.[167]

C. INJUNCTIONS

85 It is possible, but relatively rare,[168] for a claimant to be entitled to claim the withdrawal of a product from circulation. The basis for such a claim would be §1004 in connection with §823 BGB. It requires that the product endangers one of the claimant's protected rights and that this danger cannot otherwise be avoided.[169] In any event the claimant can only request the recall of the product to which he or she is exposed. Under German law individuals cannot initiate proceedings in the public interest. Thus a single claimant cannot sue for the product's general withdrawal from the market. This is a task of the public authorities which supervise the safety of product.

86 In a leading case, a hospital had bought medical beds that then caught fire when their electrical components became wet. The hospital claimed the costs for repair of the beds. The producer argued that its warning was already sufficient. The BGH confirmed this latter view.[170] A recall or a warning to no longer use the beds was sufficient. The typical contractual remedies of replacement or repair are generally not available in tort law.[171] A superficial view may suspect a contradiction with the aforementioned *Boston Scientific Medizintechnik* case. There, the CJEU held that claimants can recover the costs of the removal of a potentially defective defibrillator or pacemaker, as well as the costs of the implantation of a new and safe device.[172] However, since these costs do not concern the repair of the defective product but merely its removal and the implantation of a new one, they rightly do not fall under the exclusive regime of contract law and are recoverable in general and special product liability law.

---

166 BGH NJW-RR 1992, 252.
167 BGH NJW-RR 2008, 1520.
168 A respective case is for instance BGHZ 179, 157.
169 See BGHZ 179, 157 (para 11); also BGHSt 37, 106 (119 ff); further MünchKommBGB/Wagner §823 n 681.
170 BGHZ 179, 157.
171 BGHZ 179, 157 (para 19).
172 ECLI:EU:C:2015:148, Case C-503/13 and C-504/13, *Boston Scientific Medizintechnik GmbH v AOK Sachsen-Anhalt – die Gesundheitskasse et al.*

VIII. PROCEDURAL AND EVIDENTIAL ISSUES

A. BURDEN OF PROOF

87 The allocation of the burden of proof in product liability cases is rather complex[173] and differs in certain respects in general and special product liability law. Under general product liability law the claimant must prove the product's defectiveness, the damage and the causation between these two elements, namely that the defect caused the damage. Concerning the defect, the claimant must also prove that the defect has its origin in the producer's sphere and existed when the product was put into circulation.[174] This includes the exclusion of other possible causes.[175] The instrument of *prima facie* evidence can facilitate the proof if the type and kind of the damage speaks to a defect of the product, for instance if concrete slabs immediately collapse when installed in a building.[176] The defect is then presumed and the producer must rebut this presumption. The same facilitation of proof can apply in cases where a defective product is particularly dangerous for life, body or health and the producer did not document that each product was flawless when it was put into circulation. This was held to be so in cases of exploding glass bottles which led to severe eye injuries.[177] To prove causation in relation to defects in instructions, it is presumed that the victim would have behaved in accordance with correct instructions and warnings if the damage would then have been prevented.[178]

88 Contrary to the general burden of proof in tort law, the claimant need not prove the producer's fault. In this respect, the burden of proof is reversed from the victim to the producer. This reversal of the burden of proof applies with respect to defects in the construction[179] and fabrication of the product.[180] The reversal does not however apply to defective instructions.[181]

89 Under the Product Liability Act too, the claimant must also prove the defect, the damage and the causation between the two. In this respect no differences exist between the two regimes. However, the producer bears the burden of proof for facts which may relieve him of his liability (§1 (4) ProdHaftG).

---

173 Also MünchKommBGB/Wagner §823 n 684.
174 BGHZ 51, 91 (105); BGHZ 80, 186 (196); BGH NJW 1973, 1602.
175 See, eg, OLG Köln NJW-RR 2012, 922.
176 BGH VersR 1958, 107.
177 See BGHZ 104, 323; BGH NJW 1993, 528.
178 BGHZ 116, 60 (73).
179 BGHZ 67, 359; BGH VersR 1971, 80; BGHZ 80, 186.
180 See BGHZ 51, 91; BGHZ 80, 186.
181 BGHZ 80, 186.

90 The evidentiary standard is always the full conviction of the judge so that 'reasonable doubts are silenced'.[182]

B. LIMITATION PERIOD

91 The usual limitation period under both general and special product liability law is three years.[183] Under the Product Liability Act this period starts from the day on which the claimant became or reasonably should have become aware of the damage, the defect and the identity of the producer.[184] Negligent lack of awareness of the necessary facts suffices to start the limitation period running.[185] Moreover, any claims are extinguished ten years after the product has been put into circulation, independently of the claimant's lack of knowledge.[186]

92 The limitation rules for general product liability and tort law differ on a number of points: the three-year period starts to run only at the end of the year in which the claimant became aware of the relevant facts giving rise to the claim and of the identity of the tortfeasor. Further only *grossly* negligent lack of awareness sets the limitation period in motion.[187] There is also an objective limitation period, which is independent of the knowledge of the claimant, of ten years from the date the claim came into existence or of thirty years from the date of the tortious conduct, whichever is the earlier.[188] In the case of injuries to life, body or health, this objective limitation period is always thirty years.[189]

93 The running of the limitation period is suspended as long as the parties are in negotiations over the claim.[190] This time does not count for the calculation of the limitation period.[191] The limitation period is interrupted and starts anew if the debtor acknowledges the debt, for instance by part payment, payment of

---

182 BGH NJW-RR 1994, 567 (568: '*Es genügt vielmehr ein für das praktische Leben brauchbarer Grad von Gewißheit, der den Zweifeln Schweigen gebietet, ohne sie völlig auszuschließen*'); also BGHZ 53, 245 (256).

183 §195 BGB; §12 (1) ProdHaftG.

184 §12 (1) ProdHaftGwhich implements art 10(1) Product Liability Directive.

185 See MünchKommBGB/Wagner §12 ProdHaftG n 2; *Palandt/Sprau* §12 ProdHaftG n 2/3.

186 §13 ProdHaftG (implementation of art 11 Product Liability Directive).

187 §199 (1) BGB.

188 §199 (3) BGB.

189 §199 (2) BGB.

190 §203 BGB; §12 (2) ProdHaftG. Art 10(2) Product Liability Directive leaves maters of suspension and interruption to the law of the Member States.

191 §209 BGB which is also applicable to cases falling under the ProdHaftG; see §12 (3) ProdHaftG.

interest, provision of a security or in another way, or if an official act of execution is undertaken or applied for.[192]

C. OTHER RELEVANT PROCEDURAL RULES

94 German law does not provide for special procedural rules for product liability cases. Where the damage is small, victims will often not pursue their claims because the outcome is not worth the effort. Small claims (up to €5,000) need no representation by a lawyer. For a claim for the amount of €500 the present court fees are €105,[193] which the losing party has to pay.[194] There may be a 'rational disinterest' not to invest €105 for the chance to get €500 or to lose and to be obliged to pay the costs of the court and of the other party.

95 German law also does not provide for the general possibility of class actions. In product liability cases no such possibility exists.

IX. ALTERNATIVE REGULATIONS AND REMEDIES

A. CONCURRENT CLAIMS

96 There are few other bases for claims, besides general and special product liability law, that provide for damages when a person suffers loss because of a defective product.

97 Where a contract exists between the victim and the producer, a damages claim can simultaneously be based on contract law. In contract law, if an obligation has been infringed, the debtor's fault is generally presumed (§280 (1) sentence 2 BGB). Further, the liability for auxiliaries is stricter in contract law than in tort law; pure economic loss can also be recovered in contract law, as well as non-pecuniary damage for personal harm. On the other hand, liability – except for intent – can be contractually excluded.

98 A further concurring basis of claim is §32 (1) *Gentechnikgesetz* (Act on Genetic Engineering, GenTG). The provision prescribes strict liability if genetically modified organisms cause damage to persons or property. The Act contains a special presumption of causation: if the organism caused damage it is presumed that the genetic modification was the cause, unless it is probable that

---

192 §212 (1) no 1 and 2 BGB.

193 See §34 *Gerichtskostengesetz* (Act on Court Fees, GKG).

194 §91 (1) ZPO.

other reasons led to the damage (§34 GenTG). The Act further provides that the person responsible for the genetic modification must also provide compensation for development risks (§37 (2) GenTG). The related provision of the ProdHaftG (§1 (2) no 5) is explicitly excluded.

99 A separate regime that supersedes the Product Liability Act, though not general product liability law, is the Law on Medicinal Products (*Arzneimittelgesetz*, AMG). Its §84 implements strict liability of the producer for damage caused by a medicinal product. Article 13 Product Liability Directive explicitly left such special regimes intact and the CJEU recently held that the German AMG may be even further developed as long as amendments do not concern matters regulated in the Product Liability Directive and do not undermine the effectiveness of the Directive, which aims at full harmonisation.[195]

100 The victim can choose freely between the different bases for a claim. Generally it is not necessary to make a choice. The victim or his/her lawyer will regularly base this claim on all possible bases.

B. DEFECTIVE SERVICES

101 If services are defective, general contract and tort law applies. German law does not provide for a special regime for such cases, comparable to the product liability regime. In general, this means that a person who suffers damage because of a service must prove that there is recoverable damage wrongfully caused by the defendant. In addition, the defendant's fault is required. As mentioned, in contract law, the fault is presumed if the violation of a contractual duty is established. In tort law, fault must generally be proved.

102 However, there are special rules for certain services. For instance, new provisions have recently been enacted on medical treatment in contract, which mainly codify the pre-existing case law (§§630a–h BGB). Of particular interest is §630h BGB. It codifies a number of presumptions which apply to medical treatment not only in contract but essentially also in tort:[196] (i) negligent malpractice is presumed if a fully manageable risk of treatment materialises; (ii) the doctor must prove the patient's informed consent; (iii) non-documented treatment measures are presumed to have not taken place; (iv) if a not (fully) qualified doctor carries out measures, it is presumed that injuries were caused by the lack of qualification; and (v) in the case of gross malpractice, causation

195 ECLI:EU:C:2014:2385, Case C-310/13, *Novo NordiskPharma GmbH v S.*

196 See *Palandt/Sprau* §823 n 144.

of an injury is presumed provided that the malpractice is of a kind that can generally cause such injuries.

C. DUTY TO RECALL DEFECTIVE PRODUCTS

103 As already indicated, the producer has the duty to actively observe how the products 'behave' on the market. If they have inherent dangers, the producer must warn users and, if the dangers are severe for life and limb, must recall the products (see *supra* no 83 ff).[197] This latter duty can rarely be invoked by an individual user and if so only with respect to the product he or she uses. But the violation of the duty to warn and, if necessary for the protection of important rights of others, to withdraw the product from the market can result in damages claims if the danger materialised or in claims for the costs of the removal and even a new installation of a safe product.[198]

D. OTHER REMEDIES OF AGGRIEVED PARTIES

104 Persons who have suffered bodily injuries will often first approach their social or private health insurance, which in turn may seek redress from a liable tortfeasor. With respect to property damage, (private) insurance coverage is less common. However, if it does exist then the insurance company also has a redress claim against a liable tortfeasor.

105 In administrative law persons may and often will inform the authority that is competent for the supervision of the safety of products of product defects or suspected defects. There is rarely a direct possibility for individual claimants to enforce the withdrawal of products from the market by way of a suit before the administrative courts.

106 Somewhat relatedly, a person injured by a defective product may inform the police and thus initiate a criminal prosecution. There is furthermore a special criminal proceeding ('*Privatklage*')[199] that private persons can institute for specific crimes (including bodily injury and property damage) that may lead to a criminal verdict. Another possibility is the right to join the criminal proceeding as a private accessory prosecutor ('*Nebenkläger*')[200] or to pursue the civil claim arising out of the crime in the criminal court.[201]

197 BGHZ 179, 157.

198 See ECLI:EU:C:2015:148, C-503/13 and C-504/13, *Boston Scientific Medizintechnik GmbH v AOK Sachsen-Anhalt – die Gesundheitskasse et al.*

199 §§374 ff *Strafprozessordnung* (Code of Criminal Procedure, StPO).

200 §§395 ff StPO.

201 §§405 ff StPO.

X. ASSESSMENT OF DOMESTIC LAW

A. APPLICATION OF PRODUCT LIABILITY LAW IN PRACTICE

107 Product liability law is rather often applied in practice. The many decisions of the Supreme Court cited above provide evidence of this fact. Until 2002 it was mainly the general product liability rules developed by the courts under the BGB that were applied, whereas the Product Liability Act played no great role because until that time the Act denied compensation for pain and suffering. This shortcoming was removed in 2002 and since then the Act has played a much greater role in practice.

B. DIFFICULTIES IN THE PRACTICAL APPLICATION

108 In particular, the various duties of producers and the precise range of these duties, as well as the different rules on the burden of proof, again and again necessitate judicial decisions, often even of the highest civil court. It is evidently often difficult to fix these duties, their scope and the respective burden of proof in the concrete case. And it is likewise difficult to assess whether this state of affairs is owing to the inherent complexity of the subject or to the structure of German product liability law. I am inclined to consider both to be responsible. A clear system of strict product liability would probably provide greater foreseeability, but also less flexibility.

C. NEGATIVE EFFECTS OF THE REGULATION

109 From the viewpoint of aggrieved product users, the whole system might appear too restrictive in compensating damage caused by defective products. For both the general and the special product regulation regimes, it will often be very difficult for injured persons to prove that the defect caused the damage. The courts only sometimes help via the instrument of *prima facie* evidence. Furthermore, liability under the Product Liability Act has its shortcomings. In particular, the deductible of €500 for property damage under the Product Liability Act (and the Product Liability Directive) might appear rather high and act as a deterrent. Equally, the restriction of the Act to privately used property might be regarded as unconvincing. With respect to development risks, German law could abolish this excuse under the Act.

110 From the viewpoint of producers, it might appear particularly unfair to be made liable for defects of fabrication that could not be discovered.

111 Seen from a neutral viewpoint, the compromise between the liability of the producer and the entitlement of the product user seems acceptable. Where the producer does not achieve a high standard of product safety, it is just to oblige him to compensate damage that is the consequence of this shortcoming. The safety standard, though high, should, however, not be out of reach or economically unbearable.

D. CORRECT IMPLEMENTATION OF THE DIRECTIVE

112 The German Product Liability Act has by and large correctly implemented the Product Liability Directive. Even the special German Act on Medicinal Products has thus far not infringed the Directive.[202] An open, though thus far theoretical, question is whether art 16(1) Directive has been correctly implemented in §10 (1) ProdHaftG, which provides that the maximum amount also applies to situations where a defect in a single product caused damage exceeding €85 million.

E. PRESENT PRODUCT LIABILITY LAW APT FOR NEW TECHNOLOGIES?

113 New technologies, in particular nanotechnology and autonomous technologies ('intelligent agents'), seem to raise primarily factual questions in relation to proving defects, causation between the defect and the damage, and the person who should be held responsible for the technology.[203] It is arguable that the more refined and complex the technology becomes, the more straightforward proof and identification of the person responsible needs to be made. The German GenTG and AMG, with their facilitated burden of proof of causation, are examples of this development. The present Product Liability Act and the Directive also demonstrate the same trend in their extended definition of producer, taking into account the development of international division of labour in trade and industry. In the case of nanotechnology, it could be suggested that a rebuttable presumption of a defect applies if a nanotechnology causes damage and no other causes are apparent; a similar presumption is imaginable for damage caused by intelligent agents. If the identification of the person responsible is difficult, a similar extension as for the definition

202 See ECLI:EU:C:2014:2385, Case C-310/13, *Novo NordiskPharma GmbH v S.*
203 See also *Müller-Hengstenberg/Kirn*, MMR 2014, 307 (309 ff).

of producer appears acceptable. Since new technologies not only create risks and dangers but also provide advantages, the liability regime should not be too strict in order not to stifle technical evolution. On the other hand, the regime must provide for reasonable compensation rules so that it is not only the victims who pay the costs of the technological evolution. Thus, a cautious though continuous adaptation of the existing rules is necessary to take into account this evolution.

PRODUCT LIABILITY IN ITALY

Giovanni Comandé*

* I am grateful to Miss Francesca Episcopo for her important research and assistance in this project; any remaining error is my responsibility.

I. SOURCES OF LAW AND THEIR EVOLUTION

A. REGULATIONS FOR PRODUCT LIABILITY THAT EXISTED PRIOR TO THE IMPLEMENTATION OF DIRECTIVE 85/374/EEC

01 When Directive 85/374/EEC was adopted many legal systems had already implemented a specific regime for product liability. In the Italian system, in the absence of specific legislation, scholars and courts have attempted to overcome the gap by resorting to contractual or tort liability and in particular that of the seller for damages resulting from defects (art 1494 of the Civil Code (CC)).[1] These rules soon proved insufficient to ensure full and effective protection: liability for defects can only be enforced against the assignor within the short period of limitation and forfeiture referred to in art 1495 CC,[2] and can be countered by the seller proving the absence of fault. In fact, the seller can easily claim to have in good faith ignored the defects of packaged goods sold by the manufacturer, meaning that the manufacturer is therefore the only person required to ensure the quality and safety of products put on the market.[3]

02 The application of liability for defects in the sale contract excluded the possibility of a direct action against both the manufacturer and the first seller. It also prevented a claim by a third party who had not been involved in the negotiation of the contract.[4]

---

1 Art 1494 CC: '*In ogni casi il venditore è tenuto verso il compratore al risarcimento del danno, se non prova di aver ignorato senza colpa i vizi della cosa. Il venditore deve altresì risarcire al compratore i danni derivanti dai vizi della cosa.*'

2 Art 1495 CC: '*Il compratore decade dal diritto alla garanzia, se non denunzia al venditore i vizi entro otto giorni dalla scoperta, salvo il diverso termine stabilito dalle parti o dalla legge. La denunzia non è necessaria se il venditore ha riconosciuto l'esistenza del vizio o l'ha occultato. L'azione si prescrive, in ogni caso, in un anno dalla consegna; ma il compratore, che sia convenuto per l'esecuzione del contratto, può sempre far valere la garanzia, purché il vizio della cosa sia stato denunziato entro otto giorni dalla scoperta e prima del decorso dell'anno dalla consegna.*'

3 Contractual liability was insufficient even after the introduction of the legislation on the sales of consumer goods, since its application depends on the defectiveness of the product under the 'guarantee of conformity' perspective, and it is limited, as far as actions are concerned, to the contractual relation between the consumer and the seller.

4 *G Alpa/M Bessone*, Responsabilità del produttore (4th edn 2005) 923 ff.

03 Some authors have tried to solve the problem by configuring the liability of the manufacturer as a case of pre-contractual liability, based on the obligation to protect towards any individual intended to come into contact with the product once it has entered the production chain.[5]

04 In a second step, scholars and judges tried to expand the effectiveness of the compensation for damages caused by a defective product, assigning liability for the harm caused directly to the producer (or, in general, to those involved in the production chain other than the final seller). In the absence of specific legislation that is able to provide the level of protection required in the case of damage caused by a defective product, courts and scholars have tried to shape the rules of civil liability in order to better protect consumers' needs. These attempts have expanded the operation of art 2043 CC or relied on provisions that do not require proof of fault or are based on the presumption of fault (such as arts 2049, 2050 and 2051 CC).

05 Several theories have been developed in the search for the most advantageous solution from the point of view of substantive law and the easing of the burden of proof for the victim in court.[6]

06 One theory has traced product liability to the breach of the general principle of *neminem laedere* encompassed in art 2043 CC.[7] According to this theory, fault of the producer (manufacturer or importer) could be proved by presumptions that the producer is inherently connected to the defectiveness of the product,[8] or that the producer failed to comply with a duty of care particularly broad and rigorous so as to require to foresee all possible reckless conduct by users (especially in the case of products intended to be used by minors).[9]

07 Alternatively, scholars and judges have tried to frame product liability cases under art 2049 CC[10] so as to attribute to manufacturers directly and objectively

---

5 For this specific reading of the broader theory of 'social contact', see *E Ghidini*, La responsabilità del produttore per beni di consumo (1970) 774 ff. In opposite terms: *M Cinelli*, Sul problema della responsabilità dell'imprenditore verso i terzi (esame critico di una tesi sul preteso fondamento precontrattuale) (1971) 2 Rivista di diritto civile (Riv. dir. civ.) 457 ff; *G Alpa*, Prassi negoziale d'impresa e teoria del contratto sociale nell'elaborazione di un rapporto tra produttore e consumatore (1957) 623 ff.

6 On this topic: *G Ponzanelli*, Dal biscotto alla 'mountainbike': la responsabilità da prodotto difettoso (1994) 1 Foro italiano (Foro it.) 252 ff.

7 Art 2043 CC: '*Qualunque fatto doloso o colposo, che cagiona ad altri un fatto ingiusto, obbliga colui che ha commesso il fatto a risarcire il danno.*'

8 The leading case is *Saiwa*, Cass. civ., 25 May 1964, no 1270 (1965) 1 Foro it. 2098 ff.

9 Cass. civ., 10 October 1957, no 4004 (1958) 1 Foro it. 46 ff; App. Genova, 5 June 1964 (1964) 1 Foro it. 373 ff.

10 Art 2049 CC: '*Responsabilità dei padroni e dei committenti: I padroni e i committenti sono responsabili per i danni arrecati dal fatto illecito dei loro domestici e commessi nell'esercizio delle incombenze a cui sono adibiti.*'

any defect negligently caused by their employees (identifiable or not) in the course of the production.[11]

08 The same rationale (aiming at channelling to the manufacturer damages resulting from a 'defect' of the organisation and of the productive activity in general) can be found in the theory, based on the concept of 'business risk'.[12] This links manufacturers' liability to the dangerousness of the activity pursuant to art 2050 CC[13] As a result, manufacturers would pay damages if they could not prove that they took all reasonable steps to prevent the harm. In particular, art 2050 CC was applied to damages resulting from the use of drugs. In these instances, the manufacturer, the importer and the supplier of the drug that was considered defective have been found jointly and severally liable[14] as subjects 'running an inherently dangerous activity.'

09 Finally, for cases of harm arising at the retailer level, the special liability for damage caused by things (chattel) under one's own control has been applied pursuant to art 2051. The keeper – namely the manufacturer – was held liable for any damage that was not caused by an act of God.[15]

B. IMPLEMENTATION OF THE DIRECTIVE

10 The Directive was originally implemented by Presidential Decree 224/88, and then repealed by Legislative Decree 206/2005, establishing the Italian Consumer Code (Cons Code), which has transposed, with some changes, the rules on product liability in arts 114–127. This legislation has fully implemented the EU Directive and identified the rules applicable to personal injuries or economic damage caused by the use and consumption of defective products.

---

11 This approach was applied in App. Roma, 24 February 1976 (1978) 1, 2 Giurisprudenza italiana (Giur. it.) 430 ff, and defended in: *S Rodotà*, Il problema della responsabilità civile (1964) 164; *M Bessone*, Prodotti dannosi e responsabilità d'impresa (1971) 1 Rivista trimestrale di diritto processuale civile (Riv. trim. dir. proc. civ.) 102; *G Alpa*, Responsabilità d'impresa e tutela del consumatore (1975) 394; *C Castronovo*, Problema e sistema del danno da prodotto (1979) 774.

12 *P. Trimarchi*, Istituzioni di diritto privato (2009) 126.

13 Art 2050 CC: '*Chiunque cagiona danno ad altri nello svolgimento di un'attività pericolosa, per sua natura o per la natura dei mezzi adoperati, è tenuto al risarcimento, se non prova di avere adottato tutte le misure idonee a evitare il danno.*' See Cass. civ., 15 July 1987, no 6241 and Trib. Milano, 19 November 1987 (1988) 1 Foro it. 144.

14 For the relevant case law on the matter, see below (fn 19).

15 App. Roma, 8 October 1986 (1987) 1 Foro it. 1589; Trib. Monza, 10 November 1982 (1983) 6 Responsabilità civile e previdenza (Resp. civ. e prev.) 789; Trib. Roma, 23 April 1984 (1985) 1 Foro it. 588. On the contrary, Cass. civ., 1 April 1987 (1987) 1 Foro it. 1590, considered that no custody duties could be invoked, since the explosion happened when the bottle was already been given to the buyer.

11 With regard to the regulatory options proposed by the Directive in arts 15 and 16, the Italian legislator chose respectively:

- not to admit the liability of the manufacturer in case of development risk (which was then included in the causes excluding liability in art 118 Cons Code);
- to include the so-called natural agricultural products within the definition of 'product' (but only as a result of the Law no 25 of 2 February 2001, implementing the Directive 34/1999, which repealed the third paragraph of art 2 Presidential Decree 224/88); and
- not to specify a cap that limits the producer's total liability for damages resulting from death or personal injury pursuant to art 9 of the Directive.

12 The legislation implementing the Directive transposes the provisions contained in it, regulating all aspects it has identified. Like the Directive, the implementing legislation does not define some concepts it makes reference to, such as those of causation and damages. Consequently, these notions are considered to have the same meaning that have in the general rules; reference must be made to the interpretation that they have been given over time by scholars and case law.[16]

13 The general rule of tort liability, art 2043 CC, while not defining what constitutes 'damage', assigned to it two meanings: that of 'wrongful damage' and that of 'compensable damage'.

14 The first concerns the harmful event, which is considered relevant for compensation only if caused by wrongful conduct (*contra ius*) – that is, conduct which is detrimental to legally protected interest – and *non jure* – that is, conduct performed with no valid justification for infringing the right (eg self-defence, state of necessity, or exercise of the right in a non-abusive way). In the law implementing the Directive, elements of liability are specifically set out. Hence, it

16 For a further description of the principles of the Italian liability system, see: *FD Busnelli*, Italy: Answers to the Hypotheticals under Italian Law, in: J Spier (ed) The Limits of Expanding Liability: Eight Fundamental Cases in a Comparative Perspective, (1998); *FD Busnelli/G Comandè*, Wrongfulness in the Italian Legal System. Some Remarks on the Borderline between Contract and Tort Liability, in: H Koziol (ed), Unification of Tort Law: Wrongfulness (1998) 69 ff; *FD Busnelli/G Comandè*, Italy, in: J Spier (ed), Unification of Tort Law: Causation (2000) 79 ff; *FD Busnelli/G Comandè*, Italy, in: U Magnus (ed), Unification of Tort Law: Damages (2001) 117 ff; *FD Busnelli/G Comandè*, Italy, in: *BA Koch/H Koziol* (eds), Unification of Tort Law: Strict Liability (2002) 207 ff; *FD Busnelli/E Bargelli/G Comandè*, Italy, in: J Spier (ed), Unification of Tort Law: Liability for Damage Caused by Others (2003) 159 ff; *FD Busnelli/E Bargelli/G Comandè*, Italy, in: U Magnus/MM Casals (eds), Unification of Tort Law: Contributory Negligence (2004) 119 ff; *FD Busnelli/E Bargelli/G Comandè*, Italy, in: WVH Rogers (ed), Unification of Tort Law: Multiple Tortfeasors (2004) 117 ff; *FD Busnelli/G Comandè/M Gagliardi*, Italy, in: P Wimer (ed), Unification of Tort Law: Fault (2005) 115 ff.

is not left to the judge to determine the wrongfulness of the damage, but rather it is established in advance by the legislation: damage caused by defective products is inherently wrongful and does not require any further assessment.

15 The second issue identified by art 2043 CC concerns the harmful consequences of the injury that can be either economic or not economic ones. Pecuniary losses encompass the negative effects on the victim's assets of the infringement of the victim's legally protected interests (not necessarily a patrimonial one), negative effects that can be measured objectively in economic terms. According to art 1223 CC, this type of damage is either a loss that has actually occurred (*damnum emergens*) and/or a loss of earnings (lost profits/*lucrum cessans*).

16 Non-pecuniary damages are the detrimental effects of the injury to values related to the individual that do not have economic significance. This kind of damage is only compensable, pursuant to art 2059 CC, in cases predetermined by law. Yet this principle has been interpreted on the basis of a constitutionally informed reading of art 2059 CC.[17] Accordingly, today compensation for non-pecuniary losses also ensues from the harm to constitutional and inviolable right (even if the case is not predetermined by law as requested by art 2059 CC) if the harm meets the threshold criteria of 'severity of the injury' and 'seriousness of harm'.

17 Turning to the second concept recalled but not defined by the regulations on defective products, we realise that the causal link selects recoverable damages based on the causal (factual and legal) traceability of the wrongful harm to the tort. At first the research aims at identifying the actual entity responsible for the harm caused, considered as a normal consequence of the wrongful conduct according to a logical-probabilistic reconstruction of the actual case based on the criterion of 'more likely than not', in relation to individual cases of liability and their means of attribution. The intervention of human or natural causes that interrupt the causal link or concur to determine the harm (arts 2055 CC

---

17 Cass. civ., 11 November 2008, nos 26972, 26973, 26974, 2675, in: (2009) 1–2 Resp. civ. prev. 38 ff, commented by *PG Monateri*, Il pregiudizio esistenziale come voce di danno non patrimoniale; *C Scognamiglio*, Il sistema del danno non patrimoniale dopo le Sezioni Unite; (2009) 2 Nuova giurisprudenza civile commentata (Nuova giur. civ. comm.) 102 ff, commented by *E Bargelli*, Danno non patrimoniale: la messa a punto delle Sezioni Unite; (2009) 1 Foro it. 120 ff, commented by *G Ponzanelli*, Sezioni Unite: il nuovo statuto del danno non patrimoniale; (2009) 3 Corriere giuridico (Corriere giur.) 410 ff, commented by *A Di Majo*, Danno esistenziale o di tipo esistenziale: quale l'esito?; (2009) 1 Danno e responsabilità (Danno e resp.) 19 ff, commented by *C Castronovo*, Danno esistenziale: il lungo addio; (2009) Riv. dir. civ. 97 ff, commented by *FD Busnelli*, Le Sezioni Unite e il danno non patrimoniale. An updated and exhaustive analysis on the topic of non pecuniary damages was made by *AAVV*, Il danno non patrimoniale. Guida commentata alle decisioni delle S.U. 11 novembre 2008, nn. 269072/3/4/5, Milano, 2009.

and 1227 CC section 2 paragraph 1, referred to by art 2056 CC) is relevant for excluding or limiting liability.

18 In a second step, consequences attributable to the person or persons identified as 'liable' must be selected as compensable: the tortfeasor is liable to compensate pecuniary damages and, where required by law (art 2059 CC as 'constitutionally interpreted'), non-pecuniary ones arising from the injury. In general, one can say that all damages must be compensated (but only those) that are a result of the non-performance/tort according to the criterion of the so-called 'causal regularity'. Both damages 'direct and immediate' and 'indirect and mediated' that fall within the range of the normal consequences of the harming event fulfil the criterion of causal regularity (art 1223 CC, referring to pecuniary damages, expressly provides for the recoverability of both the emerging damage and lost profits).

19 Damage that the creditor/victim could have avoided through ordinary diligence are not recoverable, according to a principle of fairness and self-responsibility.[18]

20 The rules governing liability that were used, sometimes forcibly, to allow compensation before adoption of the Product Liability Directive, remain fully valid and applicable. In particular, liability 'presumed' under the reported interpretation of art 2043 CC, and that for dangerous activities pursuant to art 2050 CC, seem to be still preferred to the special EU-derived rules: their preferential use has long been one of the main reasons for the failure of the Directive.[19] Note that these regimes, being general rules of tort law, do not conflict with the reading of the ECJ in 2002.

---

18 Art 1227 CC: '*Concorso del fatto colposo del creditore. Se il fatto colposo del creditore ha concorso a cagionare il danno, il risarcimento è diminuito secondo la gravità della colpa e l'entità delle conseguenze che ne sono derivate.*' On the selection of the recoverable damages: *FD Busnelli/G Comandè*, Italy, in: J Spier (ed), Causation (fn 16) 79 ff; *FD Busnelli/G Comandè*, Italy, in: U Magnus (ed), Damages (fn 16) 117 ff. On the matter of the contributory negligence of the victim in the causation and the gravity of the damage, see *AP Benedetti*, La colpa del danneggiato nell'illecito civile: un'analisi storico-comparativa (2012) 5 Nuova giur. civ. comm. 358 ff; *V Bachelet*, Concorso omissivo colposo del danneggiato: il quasi inestricabile intreccio tra la causalità e la colpa e l'irruzione sul campo della solidarietà (2012) 5 Nuova giur. civ. comm. 436 ff; *U Violante*, Principio causalistico e declino del principio di autoresponsabilità (2010) 8–9 Danno e resp. 794 ff; *FD Busnelli/G Comandè*, Italy, in: U Magnus/MM Casals (eds), Contributory Negligence (fn 16) 119 ff.

19 This is especially the case of damages caused by defective medicine and drugs derived from human blood, whose costs were ascribed jointly to the Italian Health Minister (Ministero della Salute) ex art 2043 CC and to the producer ex art 2050 CC: *ex multis*, Trib. Potenza, 16 May 2013 no 63; Trib. Roma, 14 May 2013 no 1038; Cass. civ., 11 July 2006 no 576–581; Cass. civ., 14 July 2011, no 1543; Trib. Napoli, 29 April 2013, no 5466; Cass. civ. 30 May 2014 no 12277; Cass. civ., 21 October 2005, no 20359; Cass. civ., 31 May 2005, no 11609 alla <www.diritto24.ilsole24ore.com/lex24>.

21 There are no specific forms of regulation for new technologies referred to in the introductory chapter.

II. BASIC ELEMENTS OF LIABILITY

A. OVERVIEW

22 The manufacturer/importer of the product within the European Community (art 115 Cons Code)[20] is responsible pursuant to art 114 Cons Code, for the harm (art 123) caused by the defect (art 117) of a product (art 115) existing at the time of its entry into circulation (arts 118, 119), unless the manufacturer/importer can prove the existence of the causes excluding liability under art 118. The supplier of the defective product is liable for damages if the manufacturer is not identified, or if the supplier does not fulfil its duty to disclose the identity and domicile of the manufacturer (art 116).

23 The injured party must prove only damage, defect and the causal link between the two (art 120). The kind of liability thus identified was qualified, not without debate, as strict liability,[21] since it is not based on fault but on causal attribution of damage in the presence of a defect in the product.[22] Such a liability is not 'absolute' because it is related to the existence of a defect and an injury causally linked to it, and since there are a series of exhaustive conditions designed to free the manufacturer from liability (art 118).

---

20 Unless specified reference to articles is always to rules in the consumer code.

21 *G Ponzanelli*, Art. 1. Responsabilità del produttore, in: R Pardolesi/G Ponzanelli (eds), La responsabilità per danno da prodotti difettosi, (1989) Nuove leggi civ. comm. 596 ff; *G Alpa/M Bessone/V Zeno-Zencovich*, I fatti illeciti, in: P Rescigno, Trattato di diritto privato, Obbligazioni e contratti (1995) 14, 391; *CM Verardi*, L'esclusione della responsabilità, in: G Alpa (ed), Responsabilità per danno da prodotti (1990) 84; *M Franzoni*, L'illecito, in: M Franzoni (ed), Trattato della responsabilità civile (2004) 450. On the contrary, *L Bigliazzi Geri/U Breccia/FD Busnelli/U Natoli*, Diritto civile (1989) 770, who considered liability for defective products as a intermediate form of liability, combining elements from both the fault model and the strict one: '*dal combinato disposto degli art. 1 e 5, 1°comma, emerge dunque una peculiare ipotesi di responsabilità che, in virtù della sua graduazione intermedia tra il modello della responsabilità (puramente) oggettiva ed il modello della responsabilità (puramente) soggettiva può essere avvicinata – in una prospettiva di coerente inquadramento sistematico delle varie previsioni normative speciali di responsabilità civile – alle ipotesi di responsabilità semi-oggettiva delineate, sia pure con formule diverse, degli artt. 2050, 2051, 2052 cod. civ.*'

22 On this topic, *G Alpa*, Il diritto dei consumatori: un laboratorio per i giuristi, in: Liber Amicorum per Francesco D. Busnelli. Il diritto civile tra regole e principi, vol 2 (2008) 173, 180–181; *P Bortone*, La responsabilità per danno da prodotti difettosi, in: P Bortone/L Buffoni, La responsabilità per prodotto difettoso e la garanzia di conformità nel codice del consumo (2007) 29. For the distinction between '*per colpa*' (fault), '*oggettiva*' (no fault) and '*assoluta*' (strict), see *G Ponzanelli*, La responsabilità civile: profili di diritto comparato (1992) passim.

24 More recently, it seems that case law tends to qualify product liability in terms of 'presumed liability', ie based on the traditional canon of culpability, but declined to do so in order to allow the victim to resort to presumptions – provided they are based on facts (and not on other presumptions), and are direct and consistent – to prove the fault of the tortfeasor.[23] This interpretation would result in generally making the procedural position of the injured party more difficult, especially if compared to the interpretation that finds the basis for product liability in the mere causal relationship between defect and damage under the Directive's regime.

25 The responsibility of suppliers/contractors would seem to be strict because they bear the risk of not identifying the manufacturer.[24]

B. THE NOTION OF PRODUCT

26 The concept of 'product' is defined by the first two paragraphs of art 115, which reads: 'Product, for purposes of this title, is all movables even if incorporated into another movable or immovable. Electricity as well is considered product'.[25]

27 In its original formulation, art 2 Presidential Decree 224/88 excluded liability for defects in relation to 'non-industrial' products, namely 'agricultural products of the soil and of farming, fishing or hunting.' The exclusion of agricultural products of the soil, livestock, hunting or fishing did not apply if they had undergone some transformation, understood as a process to change the characteristics of the product or add additional substances to its natural composition. Such processing had the same legal effect of industrial packaging or any other process that would create an expectation as to the safety of the product, or that would make it difficult for a consumer to monitor it. After the first transformation, thus understood, the processing enterprise was responsible for all hazards that arose from the product even if not directly related to the transformation.[26]

28 In the wake of considerable technological development which invested the agricultural market, leading, in some respects, to a kind of equivalence with the

---

23 Cass. civ., 29 May 2013, no 13458 (2014) 1 Corr. giur. 31 ff, with commentary of *L De Benedetto*, Legittimazione ad agire, oneri probatori del danneggiato, conferme e richiami della Suprema Corte in materia di responsabilità da prodotto difettoso (2014) 5 Danno e resp. 489 ff, commented by *C Baldassarre*, Responsabilità del produttore: danno risarcibile, onere della prova e logica giuridica.

24 Cass. civ., 1 June 2010, no 13432 (2010) 8–9 Resp. civ. e prev. 630 ff.

25 *O Triano*, Art. 2. Prodotto, in: P Pardolesi/G Ponzanelli (eds) (fn 21) 497, 516.

26 On this topic, *PG Monateri*, La responsabilità civile (1998) 707.

industrial sector, and associated concerns about the damages caused by certain animal viruses and the use of GMOs, Directive 34/1999/EC and Legislative Decree 25/2001 led to the repeal of the third paragraph of art 2 Presidential Decree 224/88. Thus, even natural agricultural products were included in the concept of product relevant for the application of the special product liability rules.[27]

29 To date, the law does not allow the concept of product to encompass the following: real estate, intangible property and services. As for real estate, the exclusion is justified by the fact that they cannot be subject to circulation relevant to the free exchange of goods within the common market. Hence, they remain outside the scope of the Directive.[28]

30 Services are excluded because they are not so much the outcome of an activity, but rather the *quid proprium* of the same activity.[29] One could perhaps come to a different conclusion through the coordination with the broader notion of 'product' and (above all) of 'producer' pursuant to art 3 al 1 lit d and e. However, it seems preferable to opt for the reconstruction of the relationship between the two articles as marked by the criterion of specialty. Yet even in the varied services sector there can be situations where the various types of liability overlap. This is the case where the provision of a service causes harm because of a defective product used in the provision of the service,[30] or in cases of plain defective product liability, as happens with damage caused by information systems.[31]

31 The exclusion of intangible goods from the notion of product determines the non-applicability of product liability rules to the case of 'digital content and intellectual property'.

32 Movable property incorporated into a building and second-hand goods – also including products made from recycled materials[32] – fall within the concept of 'product' defined by art 115. Similar results are achieved for software,[33] drugs and products of human origin prepared and used for medical purposes.[34]

---

27 *G Ponzanelli*, Estensione della responsabilità oggettiva anche all'agricoltore, all'allevatore, al pescatore e al cacciatore (2001) 8–9 Danno e resp. 792.

28 *A Lupoli*, La responsabilità per danno da prodotti difettosi, in: F Bocchini (ed) Diritto dei consumatori e nuove tecnologie (2003) 52.

29 *PG Monateri*, La responsabilità da prodotti, in: M Bessone (ed), Trattato di diritto privato (2002) 253.

30 On the product as a result of the service: *Triano* (fn 26) 514.

31 On this point, *C Rossello/F Toriello*, Responsabilità del produttore, in: G Alpa/P Zatti, Commentario breve al Codice Civile – Leggi complementari (2003) 2035.

32 *Monateri* (fn 29) 234.

33 Ibid 235; *Lupoli* (fn 28) 69; *G Stella*, La responsabilità del produttore per danno da prodotto difettoso nel nuovo codice del consumo (2006) 10 Resp. civ. prev. 1589, 1062.

34 *Franzoni* (fn 21) 580; Case C-203/99, *Henning Veedfald v Århus Amtskommune* [2001] ECR I-3569, with commentary of *LK Dosi*, Trapianto di rene e responsabilità per danno da

33 As for the inclusion of software within the concept of 'product', the European Commission itself has intervened, endorsing the opinion of those who argue that software, when put into circulation, acquires a material state that allows it to contribute to the functioning of a certain machine.[35]

34 In spite of the clear direction at the European level, some Italian scholars distinguish between individual software (individual programmes created specifically for a client), which is brought within the concept of provision of services, and software produced in series and built-in hard disk or in hardware components, which are considered fully subject to the relevant product liability rules.[36]

35 Blood used for transfusion purposes,[37] liquids manufactured by the laboratories of a hospital in preparing a human organ for transplantation,[38] and a haemophiliac vaccine that caused serious injury to the person who received it have all been considered products as well.[39]

36 It is worth pointing out that liability of the producer and the distributor of drugs containing human gamma globulins for inoculation in the body, which, being infected, had caused the spread of blood-borne diseases (such as hepatitis B or HIV) has often been framed under art 2050 CC.[40] Scholars and court decisions have stated that liability under art 2050 CC need not only involve an

---

prodotti difettosi: un'interpretazione ardita della Corte di Lussemburgo (2002) 1 Nuova giur. civ. comm. 181.

35 Question for written answer to the Commission [1989] OJ C-114/42. On this matter see *JP Triaille*, L'applicazione della direttiva comunitaria sulla responsabilità del produttore nel campo del software (1990) 2 Dir. inf. 725 ff.

36 *Monateri* (fn 29). For an opposite approach: *G Alpa*, Responsabilità extracontrattuale ed elaboratore elettronico (1986) 2 Dir. inf. e informatica 385.

37 *Monateri* (fn 29) 236. The opposite thesis is based on the assumption that the transfusion is based on gratuitous donations (art 2, L 219/2005, no 219, and can therefore be considered not relevant for the purpose of the discipline under analysis (art 118: the manufacturer can defence himself by proving that he have not manufactured the product 'for sale or for any other form of distribution for consideration'): *U Izzo*, Sangue infetto e responsabilità civile: responsabilità, rischio e prevenzione (2000) 3 Danno e resp. 229 ff; *id*, La precauzione nella responsabilità civile. Analisi di un concetto sul tema del danno da contagio per via trasfusionale (2004) 282 ff; *S Guizzi*, I danni da 'contagio' da sangue infetto (e da impiego di 'emoderivati') e quelli da 'fumo attivo': due ipotesi a confronto, in: G Vettori (ed), Il danno risarcibile (2004) 1275 ff; *A Fusaro*, Attività pericolose e dintorni. Nuove applicazioni dell'art. 2050 CC (2013) 6 Riv. dir. civ. 1337 ff. For a deeper analysis of the liability derived by medical product and drugs: *U Izzo*, La precauzione nella responsabilità civile. Analisi di un concetto sul tema del danno da contagio per via trasfusionale (2004); *A Querci*, Sicurezza e danno da prodotti medicali (2011); *P Recano*, La responsabilità civile da attività pericolose (2001).

38 Case C-203/99, *Henning Veedfald v Århus Amtskommune* [2001] ECR I-3569.

39 Case C-127/04, *Declan O'Byrne v Sanofi Pasteur MSD Ltd and Sanofi Pasteur SA* [2006] ECR I-1313.

40 Cass. civ., 27 July 1991, no 8395 (1992) 1 Foro it. 1992, 164; App. Trieste, 16 June 1987 (1989) 2 Resp. civ. 344; Trib. Torino, 5 March 1993, (1993) D. econ. ass. 561; Trib. Parma,

activity that is considered dangerous in itself, but also where 'the danger has materialized and transfused in the objects of the same activity', particularly when the products 'by imperfect construction, in design or packaging, maintain an inherent potential dangerousness, linked to the performance of the activity for which they constitute the outcome'.[41] In the specific case of products derived from blood, it was commonly acknowledged that the circulation (marketing) of products falls under the activity considered relevant for liability under art 2050 CC, as the products retain in themselves, and spread, that same potential dangerousness that characterised the activity producing them.[42]

37 The fact that the source of the harm is often not reconnected to the danger of the good, but to a defect, it seems to legitimate (preferably, according to some)[43] recourse to product liability law. Later we will be able to analyse the reasons why case law has continued to apply the rules on dangerous activities to other damages caused by defective products (such as those resulting from the explosion of gas cylinders) even after the transposition of Directive 85/374/EEC.[44]

38 As for the reference to electricity, a fundamental distinction was made. It falls under the specific discipline of product liability rules when the damage derives from electricity in and of itself (eg because it does not provide the required voltage);[45] otherwise, if harm is a result of the operations of delivery art 2050 CC will be applied to compensate for damages.[46] However, when harm is a result of a defect in the method of supply, that is, of the machinery, equipment and tools that provide or operate on electricity, it is possible to assume liability of various subjects (such as the manufacturer of the equipment or the utility company supplying the service).[47]

C. THE CONCEPT OF DEFECTIVENESS

39 The notion of 'defect' is different from that of 'defect' in the thing sold pursuant to art 1490 CC.[48] It is defined by art 117, as the product that 'does not

30 September 1998 (1999) 4 Danno e resp. 455, commented by *G Facci*, La trasfusione di sangue ed il rapporto di causalità.

41 Cass. 30 August 2004, no 17369 (2005) 1 Foro it. 245.

42 Cass. 15 July 1987, no 6241 (fn 13).

43 *Franzoni* (fn 21) 500.

44 On this topic see *A Maietta*, Scoppio di bombola a gas: esercizio di attività pericolosa o danni da prodotto difettoso? (2009) 6 Danno e resp. 656.

45 *U Carnevali*, Responsabilità del produttore, in: II Aggiornamento. Enciclopedia giuridica (1998) 940.

46 *Franzoni* (fn 21) 581; *Carnevali* (fn 45) 940.

47 *Bortone* (fn 22) 30.

48 Art 1490 CC: '*Il venditore è tenuto a garantire che la cosa venduta sia immune da vizi che la rendano inidonea all'uso a cui è destinata o ne diminuiscano in modo apprezzabile il valore.*

provide the safety which one is entitled to expect taking into account all the circumstances, including: the way in which the product was put into circulation, its presentation, its evident features, instructions and warnings; the use to which the product can be reasonably allocated and behaviours that, in relation to it, can reasonably be expected; the time in which the product has been put into circulation … A product is defective if it does not provide the safety normally offered by other samples from the same series'.

40 Statutory provisions establish a link between defects and lack of security:[49] a product that is 'not harmless' is not necessarily defective, but rather the product is defective if it 'does not meet the security requirements generally required by users in the circumstances listed in art 117 and does not meet the standards imposed from industry regulations' (see art 118).[50]

41 When deciding on whether the product is defective, judges refer to the standard of 'normal conditions of use of the product itself', and to the 'reasonable expectation of consumer safety'.[51] In this way, damage can be considered to be the result of a product defect only when the product was used in a way it was designed to be used and which the manufacturer could reasonably expect. Abnormal use – ie the abuse, unauthorised use, or particular health conditions of the injured party able to make a product dangerous which is inherently harmless – does not allow the specific European liability regime to be applied to the manufacturer.[52]

42 It should be noted that this criterion of reasonableness and predictability, as it aims to achieve a proper allocation of risks arising from the use of a product,[53] must be understood as referring not to an abstract user, but to the actual characteristics of the potential recipients of the given product.[54]

Il patto con cui si esclude o limita la garanzia non ha effetto, se il venditore ha in mala fede taciuto al compratore i vizi della cosa.'

49 'The notion of defective product, for the purpose of the application of the product liability as defined by 7 d.P.R. 24 May 1988, no 224, identifies with that of unsafe product', Trib. Vercelli, 7 April 2003 (2003) 10 Danno e resp. 1001, commented by *G Ponzanelli*, Responsabilità oggettiva del produttore e difetto di informazione.

50 Cass. civ., 29 May 2013, no 13458 (fn 23).

51 Trib. Monza, 20 July 1993 (1994) 1 Foro it. 251; App. Roma, 30 July 1992 (1996) 3–4 Resp. civ. e prev. 672, commented by *A De Bernardinis* La responsabilità extracontrattuale per danno da prodotti difettosi.

52 Cass. civ., 29 September 1995, no 10274 (1996) 1 Foro it. 954 with commentary of *F Caringella*, La ragionevolezza dell'uso della res quale condizione della responsabilità del produttore: il caso di prodotti destinati ai minori; Cass. civ., 13 December 2010, no 25116 (2011) 10 Danno e resp. 975.

53 In this sense: *D Campilongo*, La responsabilità civile, in: P Cendon, Trattato di responsabilità civile (1998) 518 and *C Cossu*, Sicurezza del prodotto e uso prevedibile (1996) 1 Danno e resp. 91.

54 Cass. civ., 21 October 1957, no 4004 (fn 9) 46; Cass. civ., 29 September 1995, no 10274 (fn 52); Trib. Roma, 12 May 2004 (2005) 1 Resp. civ. prev. 217, commented by *S Della Bella*, La responsabilità del produttore di tute sportive.

43 The standard of 'no defectiveness' analysed here is therefore the result of both reference to specific regulatory legal rationales, as well as to consistent case law aimed at finding, case by case, the level of 'security' that the consumer could reasonably have expected from the product. Both standards do not seem to be at risk of being modified via 'prospective overruling'.

44 The second paragraph of art 117, in conjunction with art 118 al 1 lit e, excludes from the definition of 'defect' the specific kind of overexposure to risk determined by the level of technological development at the time of the putting into circulation of the product.[55]

45 The notion of defect is then attributed to the lack in the product of the expected quality and safety, a deficiency described as a 'trilogy of defects':[56]

- design defects[57] (for which the defect is inherent in the very way in which the product was designed pursuant to art 117 al 1 lit b);
- manufacturing defects[58] (for which a single product has a lower security level than the other items of the same series pursuant to art 117 al 3);
- and deficiency in the information provided (or the lack or absence of information accompanying the product itself pursuant to art 117 al 1 lit a.[59]

46 With regard to this latter category, considering the relational perspective of the concept of defect, it is possible to identify an inverse proportionality between increasing product safety and quantity/quality of information provided by

---

55 Art 117, 2: 'A product cannot be considered defective for the sole reason that a better product is at any time been put on the market'; art 118: 'liability is excluded … if the state of scientific and technological knowledge at the time when the producer put into circulation the product, yet did not made it possible to consider the product as defective'.

56 *Carnevali* (fn 45) 30.

57 Applied in Trib. Milano, 13 April 1995 (1996) 3 Danno e resp. 381, with commentary of *G Ponzanelli*, Crollo di un letto a castello: responsabilità del produttore-progettista e del montatore.

58 Applied, *ex multis*, in: Trib. La Spezia, 27 October 2005 (2006) Corr. merito 169, with commentary of *L Cabella Pisu*, Il costo di una caduta dagli stivali; (2006) 4 Resp. civ. 465, commented by *M Gorgoni*, La responsabilità ex d.P.R. 224/88 tra rigurgiti giurisprudenziali e manovre normative; (2006) 2 Danno e Resp. 173, commented by *G Ponzanelli*, Stacco del tacco e difetto da prodotto; Trib. Milano, 31 January 2003 in (2003) 3–4 Resp. civ. prev. 1151, commented by *S Della Bella*, Cedimento di scala estensibile e responsabilità del produttore-progettista, and (2003) 6 Danno e resp. 634, with commentary of *AL Bitetto*, Oltre la siepe, la scala del giardiniere e la responsabilità del prodotto difettoso: la nozione di danneggiato nella disciplina sulla responsabilità del produttore; Trib. Roma, 14 November 2003 (2004) 1 Foro it. 1632; Cass. civ., 14 June 2005, no 12750 (2006) 3 Danno e resp. 259, commented by *L Bitetto*, Responsabilità da prodotto difettoso: strict liability or negligence rule?

59 Cf: Cass. civ., 6 August 2013, no 18654 (2014) 5 Danno e resp. 498, with commentary of *C Baldassarre*, Responsabilità del produttore: danno risarcibile, onere della prova e logica giuridica; Trib. Vercelli, 7 April 2003 (fn 49).

the manufacturer. Correct and full information could also exclude the danger of certain characteristics in the product, as in the case of contraindications of drugs.[60]

D. MARKETING OF A PRODUCT

47 The marketing of a product is defined by art 119 as 'delivery to the purchaser, user or a person connected to these, also for demonstration or sampling it', 'delivery to the carrier or shipper for sending to the purchaser or user' and the 'circulation as a result of forced selling', unless the debtor has not communicated the existence of the defect to the bailiff or the creditor. In essence, putting into circulation consists in the entry of the product into the market,[61] corresponding to a moment when the product leaves the legal sphere of control of the manufacturer and becomes potentially harmful to any future consumers and bystanders.[62] The ECJ has followed this reading of the concept of 'putting into circulation', considering that such a prerequisite of liability has to be present even when the product has been used for the provision of a service.[63]

48 Sending the product for demolition or disposal (as opposed to what happens for recycling), referral to a specialised institution for quality control, or storage in special warehouses or deposits do not constitute acts of putting into circulation.

49 The release into circulation of a product that is known at the time to be defective constitutes a fundamental condition for product liability rules (art 117 lit a and c). Specific causes of exclusion of liability relate to it. They are all connected, according to the Court of Justice, to cases where 'the putting into circulation is a result of the activity of someone other than the manufacturer, has occurred against the will of the producer, or the product is used for private purposes'. Among the specific causes of exclusion are: failure of putting the product into circulation, the (at least likely) non-existence of the defect at the time of putting it into circulation, the non-professional nature of the activity or

---

60 *G Ghidini*, Art 5 – Prodotto difettoso, in: G Alpa (fn 21) 49.

61 *C Cossu*, La messa in circolazione del prodotto, in: G Alpa/M Bin/P Cendon, La responsabilità del produttore, in: F Galgano (ed), Trattato di diritto commerciale e diritto pubblico dell'economia, vol 13 (1989) 153.

62 This also happened in the case law before the introduction of the European discipline: cf App. Genova 5 June 1964 (fn 9).

63 'Article 7(a) of the Directive is to be interpreted as meaning that a defective product is put into circulation when it is used during the provision of a specific medical service, consisting in preparing a human organ for transplantation, and the damage caused to the organ results from that preparatory treatment': Case C-203/99, *Henning Veedfald v Århus Amtskommune* [2001] ECR I-3569, para 18.

the fact that the manufacturing or distribution was done for free (art 118). In addition, entry into circulation is the starting point for calculating the limitation period for actions for damages under art 126 Cons Code.

50 Entry into circulation can determine some of the factors that cause the defectiveness itself,[64] such as the absence or deficiency of the instructions[65] or bad packaging of the product itself (considered a 'manufacturing defect').[66]

51 It is worth mentioning that if it cannot be shown that the product was put into circulation, it is still possible to pursue a general action for liability under art 2043 CC.

E. DUTIES OF THE PRODUCER

52 The Cons Code implementing Directive 85/374/EEC does not specifically define the obligations and standards of care the violation of which gives to liability for damages to be paid by the manufacturer. However, other legal provisions establish the safety standards of the product the violation of which can make the product defective within the meaning of art 114 ff Cons Code.

53 In order to identify the manufacturer's duties of care, systematic coordination with product safety rules, which are also transposed in the Consumer Code, and in particular in arts 104[67] and 105, is particularly important.[68]

54 Under product safety regulation, any product in normal and reasonably foreseeable use, including duration, is safe if it does not present any risk or minimum risks compatible with the product's use or considered acceptable by observing a high level of protection of the health and safety of individuals. Accordingly, in addition to administrative controls aimed at testing the safety of the product, the legislator sets out specific obligations on the manufacturer and the distributor of the product to provide information, to warn of risks, avoid marketing unsafe products, and to adapt or withdraw from market any product not complying with safety standards.

---

64 Trib. Massa Carrara, 20 March 2000 (2002) 1 Arch. civ. 343.

65 Cass. civ., 6 August 2013, no 18654 (fn 59). It has been commonly recognised, both in doctrine and case law, that the producer's duty of disclosure has to be shaped according to the concrete use the product has been designed for (or that which it is reasonably predictable that it could be used for): eg Trib. Roma, 12 May 2004 (fn 54).

66 Trib. Rimini 31 December 2008 (2009) 4 Danno e resp. 432.

67 See art 104 Cons Code ('Obligations of the producer and distributor').

68 See art 105 Cons Code ('Safety presumptions and appraisals').

F. PARTICULAR SORTS OF PRODUCTS

55 The statute implementing Directive 85/374/EEC does not specify different treatment of the notion of defect and of consumer expectations with reference to certain types of products, but the vagueness of the law allows for differences in special regulated areas

56 A particularly high level of safety is required, for example, for medical devices: Law 46/97 implementing Directive 93/42/EEC concerning medical devices, as amended by Legislative Decree 37/2010, identifies the 'essential requirements', ie those safety and performance features that every device, each in accordance with their risk category, must have in order to be marketed and used in the health sector.[69]

57 Similar rigorous rules apply to the production and distribution of drugs, activities unanimously recognised as 'dangerous': no medicinal product may be sold in Italy without an authorisation from the AIFA (Italian Agency for Pharmaceuticals) or the EU in accordance with Regulation (EC) No 726/2004 – for which it is necessary to submit an application containing all the data that demonstrate its safety and effectiveness, according to the precautionary principle pursuant to which 'no health and safety data, no market'.[70] In addition, continuous monitoring (pharmacovigilance) must accompany the sale and use of pharmaceutical products in order to promptly detect and curb any possible harmful side effects that were not revealed in the clinical trial.

G. MODEL OF LIABILITY

58 Product liability was originally considered a form of strict liability (because it is independent of the finding of fault), but not absolute (because it identifies certain causes of exclusion of liability).[71] The most recent rulings on the subject, departing in some respects from the Directive, rather speak in terms of 'presumed liability'.[72] A result of this different qualification of liability is a significant increase of the burden of proof identified in art 120, especially with reference to the use of presumptions.

---

69 See 1st attachment to the D.Lgs 46/97.

70 See art 8 Dl 219/2006.

71 Cass. 14 June 2005, no 12750 (fn 58).

72 Cass. 29 May 2013, no 13458 (fn 24).

III. THE PERSON LIABLE FOR DAMAGE

A. LIABLE ENTITIES

59 The notion of producer was originally identified by art 3 Presidential Decree 224/88. It indicated that the manufacturer of the finished product, the manufacturer of the component parts and the producer of the raw material, as well as those who had affixed their trademark[73] or other distinguishing mark on the product, could be held liable. The importer of a product from a non-EU country into the European Community was treated as the producer for the purposes of liability along with the person who identified himself as such.[74]

60 The content of art 3 Presidential Decree 224/88 has not been faithfully repeated in the Consumer Code while, for the application of the rules on defective products, reference is made to the general definition provided in art 3 lit d, according to which the producer is 'the manufacturer of the good or the service provider, or his intermediary, as well as the importer of the goods or services in the territory of the European Union or any other person or entity presenting itself as the producer identifying the good or service with its name, trademark or other distinctive sign', without prejudice to what is established by art 103 al 1 lit d, and art 115 al 2bis.

61 Art 115 al 2 lit a defines the producer as 'the manufacturer of the finished product or a component thereof, the producer of the raw material, as well as, for the agricultural products of the soil and for those of the farming, fishing and hunting, respectively the 'farmer, the breeder, the fisherman and the hunter.' Hence, if the term 'producer' that is applicable for the purposes of liability under art 114 ff of the Consumer Code must be obtained from a systematic reading of art 3 lit d and art 115 al 2, it does not seem possible to admit the inclusion of the 'service provider' (which seems to be suggested by art 3), because that concept is precluded by the very notion of product obtainable from the first two paragraphs of art 115.

62 As for the specific role of the supplier or the person enabling goods to pass from producers to consumers,[75] the legislation does not make their position entirely equal to that of the manufacturer, since it attributes to it a subsidiary

---

[73] The producer is commonly identified by the trademark on the product; in this way, see Trib. Monza, 20 July 1993 (fn 51); Cass. civ., 21 November 1995, no 12023 (1996) 3 Danno e resp. 363 ff, commented by *G. Ponzanelli*, Batteria anonima e responsabilità del 'vero' produttore.

[74] Trib. Viterbo, 17 October 2001 (2001) Rass. giur. umbra 206, commented by *L Mezzasoma*, L'importatore all'interno della C.E. di prodotti difettosi fabbricati in altro stato comunitario, 207; Cass. civ., 14 June 2005, no 12750 (fn 58).

[75] *Monateri* (fn 29) 241.

nature[76] intended to encourage retailers to cooperate to make sure that the manufacturer or the link in the distribution chain can always be identified.[77] If the manufacturer is not identifiable, the target of the action, pursuant to art 116, will be 'the supplier having distributed the product in the exercise of commercial activity.'

63 The supplier may be called to trial: (i) directly, if the victim does not know the identity of the manufacturer (and, in this case, the supplier may be freed from liability by communicating within three months the identity and address of the manufacturer) or, once requested, if the supplier does not fulfil its obligation to notify the victim within three months of the identity and address of the manufacturer (in the event of late communication the supplier remains subject to the liability rules);[78] or (ii) as a third party pursuant to art 106 Code of Civil Procedure, if the victim has sued, as manufacturer, a party that contests to be the manufacturer.

64 The onus, and the relative risk of failure, is on the supplier to effectively identify the manufacturer, because only this allows the supplier to be excluded from the trial (to be regarded as the termination of the dispute), with compensation of court costs from the manufacturer if the supplier is not found liable for the introduction of the proceedings against the supplier.[79] However, if the manufacturer, the preceding supplier or importer no longer exist, as a result of the death of the natural person or liquidation of the company, the supplier is still freed from liability if it identifies the producer, ie fulfils the exonerating requirements of the Community legislation.[80]

65 Suppliers' liability is solely governed by Directive 85/374/EEC, and Member States are not allowed to extend it.[81]

66 Likewise, the importer of a product into the EU is subject to product liability only when the manufacturer is located outside the EU.[82] By virtue of the principles behind the regulation, namely the protection of consumers with respect to the defects inherent in processed products put into circulation

---

76 *V Carfì*, Art. 116, in: V Cuffaro (ed), Codice del Consumo (2008) 425.

77 *A Stoppa*, Responsabilità del produttore (1998) 17 Digesto delle discipline privatistiche 128.

78 *Ponzanelli* (fn 73) 363, and *Lupoli* (fn 28) 51.

79 Cass. civ., 1 June 2010, no 13432 (fn 24). To the case of the non-identified producer is compared that of the producer who has been correctly identify but remains unreachable; in this sense, *Lupoli* (fn 28) 51.

80 *Lupoli* (fn 28) 51.

81 Case C-402/03, *Skov Æg v Bilka Lavprisvarehus A/S and Bilka Lavprisvarehus A/S v Jette Mikkelsen and Michael Due Nielsen* [2006] ECR I-199.

82 Cass. civ., 20 May 2009, no 11710 (2009) 1 Foro it. 2662.

by professional traders, the fact that the importer sold the goods without the necessary qualifying title will not be relevant to exclude it from liability.[83]

67 For the attribution of liability, the commercial nature of the transaction is crucial, as well as the professional character of the activity (art 118: 'liability is excluded … if the manufacturer did not manufacture the product for sale or for any other form of distribution for consideration, nor manufactured or distributed it in the exercise of her professional activity'; art 116 refers to the 'supplier that has distributed the product in the course of a commercial activity').

68 Some commentators have denied that the fact that the product was put into circulation for free should always be understood as exempting liability in accordance with art 118 lit c: the overall interpretation of the rule would seem to exclude its application in cases where the entry into circulation has taken place free of charge, but still in the exercise of the professional activity, for example with promotional, advertising or demonstration aims.[84]

69 The key issue is rather that the tortfeasor is a professional entity (public or private), that has produced or distributed the product in connection with an activity characterised by organisation, economic efficiency and professionalism, so that failing these characteristics the application of product liability rules should be excluded. In the case of products purchased on eBay directly between consumers, for example, the only person who could be held liable for damages resulting from the defect of the product is the producer of the product (as long as it is possible to show a causal link to the actions of the latter): the consumer-seller, in the absence of any commercial qualification, cannot be treated either as a 'producer', nor as 'supplier', with subsidiary liability pursuant to art 116, thus remaining completely immune from the application of the EU Directive (however, the consumer-seller may still be equally liable under art 2043 CC).

B. LIABILITY OF MULTIPLE ENTITIES

70 Pursuant to art 121, 'if several persons are liable for the same damage, all are jointly liable to pay compensation'.[85]

---

83 Cass. civ., 14 June 2005, no 12750 (fn 58).

84 *Cossu* (fn 61) 177.

85 For a further analysis of this matter, see: *D Poletti*, Art. 9. Pluralità di responsabili, in: R Pardolesi/G Ponzanelli (eds) (fn 21) 597 ff; *E Bellisario*, Art. 121, Pluralità di responsabili (fn 21) 764; *V Carfì*, Art. 121, in: V Cuffaro (ed), Codice del consumo (fn 76) 442 ff. As for case law, cf: Trib. Firenze, 5 April 2000 (2001) 1 Arch. civ. 208, which considered liable for the damages caused by a defective bike both the seller (ex art 1494 CC) and the producer (under the product liability discipline); the same kind of joint liability was also recognised in Trib. Milano, 13 April 1995 (fn 57).

71 In order to extend consumer protection, the special regulation on product liability overcomes the principle of 'channelling' liability to the manufacturer of the final product that had been developed in previous years. It involves the direct liability of all those who have contributed to the creation of the defective product, so as to involve for compensation all the liable 'producers'.[86] Victims appear to be strongly protected, as they can act against any individual who participates in the design, manufacture and distribution of the product.[87]

72 'He who has paid damages has recourse against the others to the extent determined by the magnitude of the risk attributable to each, by the seriousness of their faults and the amount of the consequences that ensued. When in doubt, the allocation is done in equal parts'. The mechanism of recourse, modelled on the general rules of art 2055 CC (with the addition of the reference to the risk), is marked by the identification of their respective 'liability' in the determination of the defect and associated damages. While accepting a qualification in terms of strict liability, it admits the importance of ascertaining fault for the purposes of the internal allocation of liability between the various defendants.

IV. THE AGGRIEVED PERSON AND DAMAGE

A. POSSIBLE CLAIMANTS

73 On the basis of product liability law, all subjects that somehow found themselves exposed, even on an occasional basis, to the risk deriving from a defective product have legal standing. The protection afforded refers to 'user' in a broad sense, not limited to the 'consumer' or 'non-professional user':[88] potential injured parties will certainly include the end-user of the production, bystanders, or third parties not related to the process of commercialisation of the product.

74 In general, one can say that the injured party is entitled to sue if the kind of damage suffered is considered compensable under art 123 (always in the case of damage resulting from death or personal injury; as a 'consumer' in the case of damage to goods other than the product itself); in case of death, the heirs of the victim will be entitled to claim compensation for damages. Accordingly, the issue of what compensable damages are is directly connected to the general issue of recoverability of damages in case of death.

---

86 *Bortone* (fn 17) 87.

87 In the same way, before the introduction of the product liability regime: Cass. civ., 9 June 1986, no 3816 (1987) 1, 1 Giur. it. 1252; Cass. civ., 13 May 1980, no 1696 (1980) 1, 1 Giur. it. 1460; App. Milano, 10 October 1978 (1978) 2 Resp. civ. prev. 875; Trib. Roma, 27 June 1987 (1988) I Nuova giur. civ. com. 1475; Trib. Forlì, 7 May 1976 (1978) 1, 2 Giur. it. 442.

88 Cass. civ., 29 May 2013, no 13458 (fn 23).

75 The entry into force of Law 281/98 introduced another form of protection for consumers: on the basis of arts 139 and 140 Cons Code, consumer groups may take legal action for the protection of health and to ensure the safety and quality of products and services. They can both encourage inhibitory protection to correct deficiencies in information regarding a product, and pursue a producer's obligation to withdraw an unsafe product from the market.

76 The systemic coordination with other provisions of the Consumer Code allows collective action to protect the rights of consumers. Art 140 bis Cons Code establishes: 'Class action has the goal of finding liability and condemning to compensation and refunds in favour of users consumers. The action protects: a) the contractual rights of a plurality of consumers and users who are, in respect of a single undertaking, in a homogeneous situation, including the rights related to contracts entered into pursuant to articles 1341 and 1342 of the Civil Code articles; b) the uniform rights that final consumers of a particular product or service have towards the respective manufacturer, even without a direct contractual relationship'.

B. COMPENSABLE DAMAGE

77 The concept of damage is not identified by the special legislation, as the definition from general civil liability is used. Qualitative and quantitative limits on compensable damages are identified in art 123 Cons Code (see the following paragraphs).

78 Compensable damages, under art 123, are limited to two categories: those caused by death or personal injury and those involving the destruction or deterioration of property other than the defective product. For the first category, compensation must include all items of pecuniary and non-pecuniary losses.[89]

79 If damage consists of the destruction or deterioration of property other than the defective product, it is only possible to get compensation if the product is for private consumption and thus primarily used by the injured person, and only when the damage exceeds the sum of €387.34. *A contrario*, compensation is excluded for damage to property intended for professional use.[90]

---

89 In this way: Trib. Roma, 4 December 2003 (2004) 5 Danno e resp. 527, commented by *G Ponzanelli*, Causa probabile del danno e responsabilità del produttore; Trib. Vercelli, 7 April 2003 (fn 49) 1001; Cass. 31 May 2003, nos 8822–8828. For the opposite conclusion: Trib. La Spezia, 27 October 2005 (fn 58); Trib. Roma, 20 June 2002 (2002) 1 Foro it. 2882, with commentary of *L La Battaglia*, Uno nessuno centomila: il destino costituzionale del danno da perdita del congiunto.

90 Cass. civ., 22 August 2013, no 19414 (2014) 5 Danno e resp. 498.

80 Damage to defective products themselves are not compensable under the rules implementing the Directive, but they may eventually be requested both pursuant to art 2043 and by way of the remedies provided by the law on the sale of consumer goods (art 128 ff Cons Code).[91]

81 The expression 'thing other than' the defective product must be understood in the most logical and coherent way, so that the resulting damage to the thing as a whole caused by the defect of a component thereof cannot be compensated under art 123 lit b,[92] where action is brought against the manufacturer of the final product. If the action is directed against the manufacturer of the individual components of a good composed of various elements (and not characterised by an intrinsic inseparability of the components),[93] then this manufacturer will also be liable to compensate the damage to the remaining parts of the product.[94]

82 In the case of personal injuries and death, all kind of damages that may be connected to the defect must be compensated.[95]

83 There are no caps on the limitation of liability, because the Italian legislator chose not to opt for the option of art 16 of Directive.[96] No further limits are provided from a subjective point of view or from the point of view of the kind of products used or events that have occurred.

V. CAUSALITY

A. RULES ON CAUSATION

84 The rules that govern factual and legal causation in product liability are those of general liability (see above), and in particular those applicable to strict liability.[97] Such liability is linked to the simple causal link between the defect

91 *Bortone* (fn 17) 106.
92 Trib. Roma, ord. 18 October 2006.
93 App. Nimes, 25 April 1960, in: G Alpa/M Bessone (fn 4) 172.
94 *Verardi* (fn 21) 249.
95 In the first place, many decision excluded the recoverability of non-pecuniary damages, since the non fault base structure of this form of liability was considered incompatible with such awards; in this sense: Trib. Roma, 17 March 1998 (1998) 1 Foro it. 3659 commented by *A Palmieri*, Dalla mountainbike alla bottiglia d'acqua minerale: un nuovo capitolo per un'opera incompiuta; Trib. Milano, 31 January 2003 and Trib. La Spezia, 27 October 2005 (both fn 58). Such a trend was then definitely overcome with the more recent case law on non pecuniary damages following the leading cases (fn 17).
96 Art 16 Directive 85/374/EEC: 'Any Member State may provide that a producer's total liability for damage resulting from a death or personal injury and caused by identical items with the same defect shall be limited to an amount which may not be less than 70 million ECU.'
97 *Verardi* (fn 21) 249.

and the damage that occurred, while the manufacturer is relieved from liability by establishing one of the exhaustive criteria provided for by the Directive. These exclusions of liability are linked to the fact that 'the harmful event is not attributable to the manufacturer'. Therefore they are conditions negating the allocation *prima facie* of strict liability to the producer.[98]

85 The elements taken into account for the causality tests are those established by arts 114, 115 and 116: the production of the good, its putting into circulation and the defective nature of the good – in other words, those elements necessary to define the concept of defect, as a prerequisite of liability.

86 Currently, with a few exceptions,[99] the Italian civil liability system does not recognise the operation of proportional liability. The allocation of liability according to an 'all or nothing' rule is preferred instead. According to scholars who view this option favourably, in most cases, product liability brings together the three categories of damage where proportionate liability could generate a fair and efficient allocation of costs for damages between the different stakeholders: uncertainty about the *conditio sine qua non* for damages; uncertainty about the extent of the various causal contributions; and uncertainty about the risk to which the tortfeasor has exposed others.[100]

B. MULTIPLE CAUSES OF DAMAGE

87 The implementing statute does not refer to cases where circumstances or third parties have contributed to cause the harm (if the causes of exclusion of liability in art 118 Cons Code do not apply). On the contrary, the Directive, at art 8, explicitly states that the responsibility of the producer shall not be reduced when the damage is caused both by a defect in the product and by intervention of a third party.

88 Despite that aspect of the Directive not being specifically transposed, and by virtue of the direct enforceability of the provision mentioned above, the Consumer Code must be interpreted in the sense that the direct allocation of

---

98 *Bortone* (fn 17) 73; on this topic, see *Castronovo* (fn 11) 507.

99 For a deeper analysis of the precautionary principle, see *G Comandè*, L'assicurazione e la responsabilità civile come strumenti e veicoli del principio di precauzione, in: G Comandè (ed), Gli strumenti di precauzione: nuovi rischi, assicurazione e responsabilità (2006) 23 ff; *L Nocco*, Causalità: dalla probabilità logica (nuovamente) alla probabilità statistica: la Cassazione civile fa retromarcia (2006) 12 Danno e resp. 1238; *ME Arbour*, A proposito della nebulosa. Principio di precauzione-responsabilità civile, in: Liber Amicorum per Francesco D. Busnelli. Il diritto civile tra regole e principi, vol 2 (2008) 513.

100 *G Comandè/L Nocco*, Proportional Liability as an Application of the Precautionary Principle. Comparative Analysis of the Italian Experience (2013) 1 Op. J. 1.

liability to the producer makes it possible to exclude liability only where the intervention of a third party has led to an interruption in the causal relationship between defect and damage.

89 The victim may possibly rely simultaneously on different titles of liability against the third party (eg the retailer of the good, the person who assembled the defective product), by virtue of the provisions of art 127 Cons Code. This has no impact on both *an* and *quantum* of compensation payable by the producer of the defective product.

C. CONTRIBUTION OF THE VICTIM

90 Art 127 provides that, in cases where the wrongful conduct of the victim has contributed to the harm, damages should be assessed according to the provisions of art 1227 CC, taking into account the seriousness of victim's own fault, the extent of the consequences that ensued from it,[101] and excluding damage that the victim could have avoided through ordinary diligence.[102]

91 In addition, compensation is not due if the injured party was aware of the defect in the product and the danger resulting therefrom and yet was voluntarily exposed to it (art 127 al 2 Cons Code).

92 Finally, art 127 al 3 states that the individual who has the product in her possession who negligently contributes to determining the harm to property other than the product is treated as the victim in calculating the respective liabilities.

93 In identifying the standard of care required, it is necessary to refer to the category of consumers for whom the product was intended, and the use that it could reasonably be anticipated that they would make of it.[103] In order to exclude or decrease producer responsibility, it is necessary that the fault of the victim is more serious and, in some ways, more important than the seriousness of the risk caused by the defect,[104] as can be inferred from the function of the applicable rules and from the definition of defect and causation associated with it.

---

101 *G Visitini*, Trattato breve della responsabilità civile. Illeciti. Inadempimento. Danno risarcibile (3rd edn 2005) 555. For a case law application of art 127, see Cass. civ., 15 October 1999, no 11629 (200) 1 Foro it. 1917.

102 The criterion of the contributory negligence was used to exclude or reduce the producer liability also before the introduction of Directive 85/374/EEC: cf Trib. Roma, 22 December 1972 (1974) 1, 2 Giur. it. 749.

103 For the case law which applied this principle before the introduction of the defective product liability, see fn 6.

104 *F Di Giovanni*, Colpa del danneggiato, in: G Alpa (fn 21).

VI. DEFENCES AND EXCLUSIONS

94 The manufacturer has several defences under art 118. He can show:

(i) that he did not put the product into circulation;
(ii) that the defect did not exist when he put the product into circulation (evidence that is 'sufficiently probable');
(iii) that he did not manufacture the product for sale or for any other form of distribution for consideration;
(iv) that he did not distribute the product as part of his professional activities;
(v) that the defect was due to the product's compliance with a mandatory provision or a binding measure;
(vi) that the state of scientific and technical knowledge at the time the producer put the product into circulation did not yet make it possible to discover that the product was defective; or
(vii) that the defect was attributable to the design of the product or to another component (this only applies to the supplier/manufacturer of a component or raw material).

95 The first defence (i) concerns the situation where the distribution of the good has taken place against the will of the entrepreneur (typically with the theft of goods from a third party), so that the marketing of unsafe products could not be attributed directly to the producer.

96 The next point (ii) refers to the occurrence of a defect after marketing. In order to be considered a cause for exclusion of liability, it is necessary that the defect does not result from a 'normal' use of the good, but rather from the onset of independent causal factors (such as the 'abnormal or unreasonable' use by the consumer), and that it is not of the case that the defect was originally present in the product but did still not clearly manifest itself before the product was put on the market.[105]

97 The circumstance taken into account at (iii) concerns the non-professional nature of the activity, in compliance with the spirit of the legislation intended to deal with situations of danger associated with the mass production of commercial goods.

98 Point (iv) instead is coherent with the principle of non-contradiction. Compliance with 'mandatory rules' refers both to laws and regulations and to

---

[105] *Bortone* (fn 17) 53. This specific clause has been considered as an obstacle to the application of the defective product discipline in case of damages in case of off label treatment: *A Querci*, Responsabilità per danno da farmaci: quali rimedi a tutela della salute? (2012) 4 Danno e resp. 656 ff.

binding administrative measures, which constitute structural standards of production that manufacturers cannot disregard in the course of business.

99 The subsequent cause for exclusion of liability (v) is generally known as the 'development risk defence'. It consists in showing that, when put into circulation, the product could not be considered defective according to the relevant technical and scientific knowledge of that time. This provision, particularly relevant for pharmaceuticals, is read by case law as requiring complying with the maximum level of science and technology offered at the time of marketing, and allows the producer to be exempted only from those damages that could no longer be avoided or limited upon the discovery of the risk factor.

100 Finally, (vi) covers the case where the defect is due solely to the design methods of the product and the related instructions for the production of the individual parts: in such cases, the producer of the raw material or component cannot be held to be responsible for an error not attributable to them.

101 As for the development risk, we must specify that the manufacturer is obliged to only put safe products on the market and to only keep products with these characteristics on the market. If the manufacturer does not do so, the burden of adapting to product to meet the requirements of safety or of withdrawing the unsafe products from the market falls on the manufacturer at its own expense. The legislator intervenes therefore in a preventive manner, allocating to producers the burden of acquiring all the information aimed at preventing risks, by adopting a dynamic definition of safety related to the entire life of the product. Accordingly, a product may not be defective and yet still be unsafe because a risk that was unknown before its circulation may later emerge. In this situation, the manufacturer is not liable under art 118, but will be subject to the penalties provided for by the legislation on product safety.

102 As anticipated, the development risk defence is accepted. It consists of the evidence that the defect is down to a general ignorance of the specific risk factors because of the state of technical and scientific knowledge at the time of production or circulation of the product. It applies to both the design defect and to the defect in information.

103 The fact that a specific injury was caused by a defect attributable to the state of scientific and technical evolution means that the manufacturer will not be liable on the basis of product liability law. However, this does not exclude liability under arts 2043 or 2050 CC.

104 Compliance with mandatory rules or a binding order excludes liability, while the adherence to certain standards of production, as well as a successful homologation, are absolutely irrelevant from the perspective of excluding liability.

105 Pursuant to art 124, 'every agreement excluding or limiting beforehand, in relation to the injured, liability under this title' is void. Unlike the provisions of art 1229 CC, the admissibility of clauses limiting liability is excluded even in the event of liability for slight negligence.[106]

VII. REMEDIES

106 The injured party may, pursuant to art 123, claim compensation for damages caused by the defective product. Since implementing legislation does not preclude the possibility of repairing the harm by restoration in kind, it is possible to use this remedy along with economic compensation, according to the general rules of civil liability. Thus, according to art 2058 CC, the injured party may claim restoration in kind, where it is totally or partially possible, and if it is not too burdensome for the debtor.

107 Punitive damages are not permitted because this kind of damages is incompatible with public order.[107]

108 The implementing legislation does not provide for other instruments in addition to compensation. Yet injunctions and ordering the withdrawal of the product from the market are possible through a systematic coordination of the various applicable regulations. Art 140 of the Consumer Code provides that '[t]he subjects named at art. 139 (consumer associations) have standing in cases provided for therein to act to protect the collective interests of consumers and users by requiring the court: to inhibit the acts and conduct prejudicial to the interests of consumers and users; to adopt appropriate measures to correct or eliminate the harmful effects of ascertained violations; to order the publication of the order on one or more newspapers with national or local circulation in cases where the publicity of the measure can help to correct or eliminate the effects of the ascertained violations'.

---

106 *V Carfì*, Art. 124, in: V Cuffaro (fn 76) 451.

107 Explicitly in this sense: Cass. civ., 19 January 2007 (2007) 1 Nuova giur. civ. comm. 981, commented by *G Ponzanelli*, I danni punitivi bussano alla porta: la Cassazione non apre; Cass. civ. 8 February 2012, no 1781 (2012) 5, 1 Foro it. 1449.

VIII. PROCEDURAL AND EVIDENTIAL ISSUES

A. PROOF

109 Art 120 provides that the claimant must prove the defect (as defined by art 117), the harm (as defined in art 123) and the causal relationship between the two. First then, in line with the provisions of art 2697 CC regarding the allocation of the burden of proof, the claimants must prove the existence of the facts constituting their right. They are also required to prove the identity of the producer when acting directly against him.

110 The proof of the constituent elements of the right to compensation can be given through presumptions, provided that they are clear, precise and coherent, based on facts and not on further presumptions.[108]

111 The wording of art 1 Presidential Decree 224/88, in making the producer's special liability for defective products conditional on a causal link between the harm and the defect in the product, creates a prerequisite for such liability. It delimits the scope of its applicability. Therefore, of the constituent elements of this right, the victim claiming damages must prove the causal connection not between product and damage, but between the 'defect and damage' suffered during the normal use of the product (art 8 Presidential Decree 224/88, now art 120 Cons Code).[109] As clearly stated by the Supreme Court:

> '[T]he simple proof of a causal link between the product and damage is not sufficient to transfer the burden on the manufacturer to show that the product was not defective. The test of the defectiveness of the product can be based on mere presumptions, provided that the presumptions: (a) are based on facts, not on assumptions or assessments; (b) have the requirement of seriousness (i.e. the existence of the unknown fact must be inferred with reasonable certainty, even probabilistic, the so called probabilistic inference); (c) have the requirement of accuracy (i.e. the presumption did not present multiple probabilistic inferences); (d) have the requirement of consistency (i.e. there is no evidence dissonant with respect to the presumption); (e) do not result in a double presumption, not being able to appreciate a presumption as a known fact, to derive from it another presumption'.[110]

112 The victim must prove that the use of the product led abnormal results compared to what could reasonably be expected, such as to indicate the existence of a defect or the lack of reasonably expected safety, and must also prove that he did not use the product in an abnormal way.

---

108 *Carnevali* (fn 46) 947.

109 *Stella* (fn 33) 1606. On the burden of proving that the damage occurred during the ordinary use of the product: Trib. Benevento, 24 February 2006 (2006) 12 Resp. civ. prev. 1254.

110 Cass. civ., 29 May 2013, no 13458 (fn 23).

113 It is not enough that the victim alleges causality, shifting the burden of proof to the producer.[111] This trend of making it more difficult to fulfil the burden of proof for the victim is in line with the case law, which recognises the liability of the producer as strict, but based 'on presumed fault'.[112] The claimant is exempted from proving the cause or origin of the defect. Therefore, it is the manufacturer who must prove that the defect was caused by a factor external to her actions, without preventing the manufacturer from making use of the presumption provided for by art 118 lit b.[113] This allocation of the burden of proof is less burdensome for the producer than the concurrent and different presumption of the existence of a defect normally burdening the producer.

114 Such a lifting of the burden of proof is not allowed with respect to other causes of exemption specified by law.[114]

115 The manufacturer must prove the facts negating the claim for compensation: the non-existence of the defect, the non-existence of damage, the lack of a causal link between the two, the contributory negligence of the injured party, the abnormality in use of the product, or the presence of causes excluding liability named in art 118. The supplier must indicate the identity and address of the manufacturer, and prove that the latter was the manufacturer.

116 As for the means of proof, in addition to rebuttable presumptions, the parties concerned may resort to untypical evidence (forms of evidence not listed in the Code of Civil Procedure), if the court allows it, as well as making use of typical evidence, for example a witness or an expert (the costs of which, if it appears likely that the damage was caused by a defective product, will be initially covered by the manufacturer), formal interrogation, swearing, etc.

117 It is worth mentioning that the framework outlined above on the victim's burden of proof is the result of recent case law, increasing the burden in sharp contrast to the attitude prevalent in previous years. This is especially the case in relation to showing defect and causation. The use of presumptions was widely accepted without restriction, to the point that some scholars even talked about the 'futility of the category of defect',[115] while others stressed that, given the

---

111 Cass. civ., 15 March 2007, no 6007 (2007) 12 Danno e resp. 1216 states that the causal nexus between the defect and the damages plays the role of a 'pre-requisite' for the application of the defective product liability, and that it has to be proven by the victim accordingly to the general rule of the burden of proof (art 2697 CC).

112 *A Palmieri*, Difetto e condizioni di impiego del prodotto: ritorno alla responsabilità per colpa? (2007) 1 Foro it. 2415.

113 *Bortone* (fn 17) 65 ff.

114 Cass. civ., 8 October 2007, no 20985 in (2008) Resp. civ. 354.

115 *C Castronovo*, voce 'Danno (danno da prodotti, dir. it. e stran.)', in: 10 Aggiornamento. Enciclopedia giuridica (1995) 10.

interplay of the various presumptions, the victim simply had to identify the possible sources of damage providing some indication of the causal link with the defect.[116]

B. LIMITATION PERIODS

118 The right to compensation shall be extinguished within three years (and not five, as in the general rules of non-contractual liability) from the day on which the injured person had or should have had knowledge of the damage, the defect[117] or the identity of the person liable. In the case of damage that gets worse over time, reference for the purpose of limitation is made to the time when the damage assumed sufficient seriousness to justify a claim being brought.

119 In the case of the right to compensation for damages caused by a crime, the limitation period under art 2947 al 3 CC applies.[118]

120 The general rules for the interruption or suspension of the limitation period apply. Entitlement to compensation is time-barred ten years from the day the product was into circulation (unless there is a trial), or from the request to be admitted as a creditor in a bankruptcy proceeding, or from the explicit recognition of the right by the liable party.

121 The manufacturer must demonstrate the time the product was put into circulation, in line with the general principles of evidence.[119]

IX. ALTERNATIVE REGULATIONS AND REMEDIES

A. CIVIL LAW LIABILITY

122 Consistent with the provisions of art 13 of the Directive requiring that the system of protection provided therein should not affect the protection guaranteed by each national system both in contract and tort, art 127 al 1 of the Consumer Code provides that 'the provisions of this Title shall not affect nor limit any rights which the injured person enjoys from other laws.' Accordingly, the remedies offered by the special legislation on product liability would not

---

116 *Monateri* (fn 26) 733.

117 For the purpose of the limitation of the claim, it must be taken in consideration the time when the victim knew, or could reasonably know the defectiveness of the product, meant not as a specific defect or it's cause, but rather as a 'generic lack of safety'.

118 Cass. pen., 23 July 2008, no 30818 in DeJure, last visited 9 March 2016.

119 *M Franzoni*, Il danno risarcibile, in: M Franzoni (fn 21) 114.

replace national solutions that are more favourable to the consumer, but would constitute the minimum content of that protection.[120] In particular, other forms of liability that may be invoked, if all necessary requirements to establish them are shown, are:

- non-contractual liability (art 2043 CC);[121]
- liability for dangerous activities under art 2050 CC (see cases regarding damages for bursting of gas cylinders and contagion by infected blood products); and
- strict liability regimes in general.

123 In addition, the victim, if relevant requirements are present, can always bring the concurring action of her choice against the manufacturer, including contractual liability for defects in the good (art 1494 CC) and for the guarantee of conformity referred to in art 129 ff Cons Code.

124 A different reconstruction of the relationships between the various applicable rules, aimed at obtaining maximum harmonisation, was envisaged by European Court of Justice in its pronunciations of 25 May 2002.[122] According to the Court, art 13 of the Directive allows other forms of liability to coexist with the legislation implementing the Directive only if the former includes different elements or special rules, except in relation to recovery of damages not compensated under art 11 Presidential Decree 224/88.

125 Such an interpretation would preclude the use of any other form of strict liability, such as that in art 2050 CC, when the conditions for the application of product liability law are met.[123]

---

120 In this sense: *Monateri* (fn 26) 705.

121 Trib. Brescia, 31 March 2003 (2004) 6 Danno e resp. 666, commented by *R Breda*, Danno da emoderivato infetto e responsabilità della casa produttrice, where the producer of drugs derived from infected human blood was condemned under art 2043 CC since it had not used the safest technology available despite the fact that the risk of transmitting the disease was commonly known.

122 Case C-52/00, *Commission v France* [2002] ECR I-3822; Case C-183/00, *María Victoria González Sánchez v Medicina Asturiana SA* [2002] ECR I-3901, both in (2002) 4 Foro it. 294, with commentary of *A Palmieri/R Pardolesi*, Difetti del prodotto e del diritto privato europeo; (2002) 7 Danno e resp. 725, commented by *G Ponzanelli*, Armonizzazione del diritto v. Protezione del consumatore: il caso della responsabilità del produttore. In the same direction, Case C-285/08, *Moteurs Leroy Somer v Dalkia France and Ace Europe* [2009] ECR I-4733, and in (2010) 5 Resp. civ. 1006, with commentary of *A Venchiarutti*, Applicazione estensiva della direttiva sulla responsabilità dei danni da prodotti difettosi: un nuovo equilibro tra competenze comunitarie e interne?

123 Meaning that, in cases such as those of infected drugs derived by human blood, the victim could act under the guarantee from the hidden defect or under the general clause ex art 2043 CC, but she could not benefit from a strict liability regime, such as that of Directive 85/374/EEC: *Fusaro* (fn 37) 1357.

126 This approach has been strongly criticised by scholars because it restricts consumer protection, in marked contrast to the pro-consumer approach implemented over the last decades.[124]

B. ADMINISTRATIVE LAW MEASURES

127 Administrative remedies are available in the event of a confirmed danger posed by a product. They are identified in the first title of the Consumer Code implementing the Directive on product safety.[125] Pursuant to art 107 Cons Code, the regulatory bodies indicated under art 106 may: ban the marketing of a hazardous product and take the necessary measures to ensure compliance with the ban; order or organise the immediate withdrawal of the product from sale; alert consumers to the risks it presents; order or coordinate its recall from consumers; and destroy it under suitable conditions.

128 Moreover, again with reference to unsafe products, it is provided that, unless the facts constitute a more serious crime, the producer and the distributor who placed the unsafe product on the market in violation of the prohibition under art 107 may be punished by imprisonment, a fine and the payment of an administrative sanction according to art 108.

129 There is no duty on producers to be insured in order to avoid problems of insolvency or bankruptcy which might result in the victim's inability (especially for the most seriously injured) to obtain compensation.

X. ASSESSMENT OF DOMESTIC LAW

A. IMPLEMENTATION AND APPLICATION OF THE LAW

130 As mentioned, the number of cases on product liability is not particularly high. Moreover, cases often refer to general rules of tort liability under arts 2043 and 2050 CC especially for medicinal products. It is not simple to assess why this is so, in the absence of empirical data. Yet it seems fair to assume that the reversals of the burden of proof built into art 2050 CC and developed by case law under art 2043 CC remain still highly attractive for plaintiffs as compared to the mechanism of the Directive.

---

124 See: *Palmieri/Pardolesi* (fn 122) and *Ponzanelli* (fn 122); *ME Arbour*, Corte di Giustizia e protezione delle tradizioni giuridiche nell'interpretazione della direttiva CEE/374/85 (2003) 4 Danno e resp. 375.

125 Art 107 Cons Code ('Checks').

131 Such a pattern does not seem to conflict with the principle of maximum harmonisation established by the ECJ in the 2002 trilogy on the Product Liability Directive as arts 2043 and 2050 CC are rules of liability of general applicability as provided for by art 13 of the Directive. In addition, actual cases that apply the Civil Code give the impression that the ways in which showing (ie reversing the burden of proving) fault has been made easier have an impact on the requirements of establishing the causal link between the damaging fact (the product defect) and damages that occurred.

132 Over the years, some difficulties and contrasting interpretations have been found with reference to the notion of product (see above nos 29–41).

133 Most probably the rather rare application of the Directive in Italy is not linked to specific negative effects arising from it, but rather to the perception of the traditional rules, as developed in case law, as a familiar and easier pattern for the plaintiff to follow. In addition these traditional rules reduce the impact of several defences provided for by art 118 Cons Code. For instance, the fact of not having 'manufactured the product for sale or for any other form of distribution' would not be per se an impediment to compensation under arts 2043 or 2050 CC. Moreover, the development risk defence might not have such a strict reading under the relevant Civil Code provisions since it would be analysed in the process of establishing fault.

134 The implementing national law correctly reflects the content of the Directive. Still, like the Directive, it does not define many of the notions (eg harmful event, damages) to which it refers, instead resorting to the meaning generally developed by national law. This simple fact opens the law up to divergences in the results reached in various Member States.

B. APPLICATION OF PRODUCT LIABILITY LAW TO NEW TECHNOLOGIES

135 In principle, the scope of the Directive and of the Italian implementation is broad enough to encompass 'new' products as described in the introduction. After all, movable property incorporated into immovable goods (such as a building) or used goods fall within the concept of product as defined by art 115 Cons Code. Case law has already reached the same conclusion for software, drugs and products of human origin, subjecting them to the regime of the Directive. The European Commission itself has endorsed the opinion that software, when put into circulation, acquires a material state that allows it to contribute to the functioning of a certain machine (see above no 33). Following this line of

reasoning, the Directive can easily cover products incorporating greater levels of information and communications technology.

136 Still, several issues might require further analysis, for instance: (i) the actual scope of the development risk defence; (ii) the possible interplay between product safety regulations and the Product Liability Directive; and (iii) a potential reading of such rules in light of the precautionary principle due to the uncertainties related to new technologies employed in production.

137 The development risk defence has been read as a state of art defence. Yet the advent of new technologies in putting innovative products (or old products manufactured in innovative ways) into circulation calls for a more careful reading of that defence and a discussion of the level and diffusion of scientific knowledge required to trigger the defence.

138 As for the possible interplay between product safety regulations and the Product Liability Directive, further comparative analysis would be useful to explore the role of product liability rules in closing the gaps between the advances in knowledge about a technology and the way it is regulated. In other words, product safety regulations and product liability law have so far mostly been mutually indifferent. Extensive use of new and insufficiently tested technologies might mean that product liability has to play the role of an inter-temporal *ex post* regulator. Whether or not this is a predictable or a desirable outcome is a different matter.

139 If 'new' technologies and products present the same characteristics as traditional ones, the Directive is well equipped to cover them. However, in case of technologies that present significant risks such as to trigger the precautionary principle as defined by the European Commission,[126] it is easy to conjecture that the scope of the Directive will need to be refined to address such high levels of scientific uncertainties involved in innovative production activities.

---

126 Communication from the Commission of 2 February 2000 on the precautionary principle, COM(2000)1 final: 'when a phenomenon, product or process may have a dangerous effect, identified by a scientific and objective evaluation, if this evaluation does not allow the risk to be determined with sufficient certainty.'

PRODUCT LIABILITY IN THE NETHERLANDS

Anne Lucienne Maria KEIRSE

I. SOURCES OF LAW AND THEIR EVOLUTION

A. REGULATING PRODUCT LIABILITY PRIOR TO THE IMPLEMENTATION OF DIRECTIVE 85/374/EEC

01 Prior to the implementation of Directive 85/374/EEC, there was no specific legal regime for product liability in Dutch legislation. In the original proposal for a new *Burgerlijk Wetboek* (Dutch Civil Code, BW), dating back to 1961, a statute provision regarding product liability was included (art 6.3.13).[1] However, this provision was removed from the proposal in 1976, when the legislator decided that the introduction of the European regulation, which was already proposed at that time, should be awaited.[2] Due to this lack of statutory rules, tailored rules on product liability had been developed in case law on the basis of the tort law clause, art 6:162 BW (at that time art 1401 BW).[3]

B. IMPLEMENTATION OF DIRECTIVE 85/374/EEC IN DUTCH LAW

1) *Type of Legal Act*

02 Directive 85/374/EEC has been implemented in Dutch law by the introduction of a separate section of the civil code; at that time arts 1407a–1407j BW (old). These provisions were replaced by arts 6:185–193 in the new BW, which entered into force in 1992. In addition, some statutory provisions were amended as a result of the implementation of the Directive. An example is art 6:173 BW (at that time art 6.3.2.5), which regulates liability for dangerous equipment. Paragraph 2 was added to this provision, excluding liability on the basis of art 6:173 BW for damage that falls within the ambit of art 6:185 ff BW, unless the criteria of subsections (a) and (b) are met (see more on this in section IX.A.4).[4]

2) *Regulatory Options*

03 Directive 85/374/EEC granted the Member States the option to derogate from the Directive in specific situations. Firstly, Member States were allowed to codify that the definition of 'product' also includes primary agricultural products and game (art 15(1)(a)). Secondly, Member States could eliminate the state-of-the-art defence, thus leaving out the exclusion that the producer is not to be held liable if he proved that the state of scientific and technical knowledge at the time when the product was put into circulation was not such as to enable the existence of the defect to be discovered (art 15(1)(b)), thereby broadening the scope of the product liability. Finally, a maximum amount could be imposed on the producer's total liability for damage resulting in a death or personal injury

---

1 *AJO van Wassenaer van Catwijck*, Productenaansprakelijkheid in Europees verband (1991) 3–4.

2 *H Duintjer Tebbens/M Zilinsky*, Productaansprakelijkheid (2009) 19 ff.

3 *ALM Keirse*, Richtlijn 1985/374/EG inzake de aansprakelijkheid voor producten met gebreken, in: AS Hartkamp/CH Sieburgh/LAD Keus et al (eds), De invloed van het Europese recht op het Nederlandse privaatrecht. 2: bijzonder deel (2014); HR, 25.03.1966, NJ 1966, 279 (*Moffenkit*); HR, 02.02.1973, NJ 1973, 315 (*Lekkende babykruik*); HR, 30.06.1989, NJ 1990, 652 (*Halcion*).

4 *Kamerstukken II* 17 541, no 11, 10; *Kamerstukken II MvA*, 19 636, no 6, 13.

(art 16(1)). When the Directive was amended in 1999, the first regulatory option was deleted.

04 The Dutch legislator did not make use of the above-mentioned regulatory options. Consequently, a producer is absolved of liability for his defective product when it concerns a so-called development risk, if he can prove that the state of scientific and technical knowledge, at the time when he put the product into circulation, was not such as to enable the existence of the defect to be discovered. In addition, no limit to the producer's total liability is currently in force. Finally, before the amendment of the Directive, primary agricultural products and game were not governed by the Dutch product liability regime. Now they are, as of 4 December 2000.

C. SCOPE OF THE LAW IMPLEMENTING DIRECTIVE 85/374/EEC

05 The scope of the Dutch product liability regime is almost identical to the scope of the Directive; even the wording resembles that of the European provisions. Therefore, the Dutch law regulates all issues encompassed by the Directive. One minor difference is that art 14 of the Directive, which states that the Directive shall not apply to injury or damage arising from nuclear accidents and covered by international conventions, does not have an equivalent in Dutch law. Such an equivalent was not necessary, as the international conventions to which the Netherlands is a party would supersede the Dutch product liability regime.[5]

06 The Directive also leaves some issues to national laws, such as the concept of damage, the rules on causality and the issue of recourse (pursuant to art 9 and art 5 in conjunction with art 8 of the Directive). These issues have not been regulated by the regime of art 6:185 ff BW, but have been left to general principles of tort law. Thus, the law implementing the Directive does not regulate issues which are not encompassed by the Directive.

D. IMPACT OF THE NEW LAW ON EXISTING REGIMES

07 The question then arises as to what impact the Directive has had on existing liability regimes. The maximum nature of the Directive implies that it fully and exhaustively regulates strict liability of the producer for damage caused by defective

5 *Kamerstukken II* Mvt 1985/86, 19 636, no 3, 4; *van Wassenaer van Catwijck* (fn 1) 19.

products.[6] Since the Dutch legislator had not enacted any separate legislation or specific rule for product liability prior to the implementation of the Directive, there was no need to abrogate such an earlier provision. Nevertheless under Dutch law the principle of maximum harmonisation has been complied with by channelling liability towards the producer in cases where several grounds of liability of different actors for defective products exist. Consequently the product liability regime has its effect on both tortious liability of the possessor of dangerous equipment for damage caused by this equipment and contractual liability of the seller for selling a defective, and therefore non-conforming, product to a consumer. To be more concrete, a second limb was added to the provision concerning the liability of possessors of dangerous equipment (art 6:173 BW), stipulating that liability of the possessor shall not ensue if it the possession has a safety defect as stipulated in art 6:186 BW. Liability of the possessor will then resurface, the second limb further stipulates, if it can be established that the damage does not exceed €500 or that the producer did not put the product into circulation. Similarly, the provision regarding the seller's liability in a consumer sale was amended. Generally a seller of a product that does not meet the standards that were reasonably to be expected on the basis of the contract shall be liable for damage caused by that product. But in the case of a consumer sale the second limb of art 7:24 BW stipulates that where the failure in performance comes about because of a defect which causes a safety risk as meant in art 6:185 ff BW, the seller will not be liable for damage as referred to in art 6:190 BW, unless the seller was aware or ought to have been aware of the defect, he guaranteed the absence of the defect, or the damage would not be recoverable under the product liability regime either.

08 From another perspective, the maximum nature of the Directive does not imply that the product liability regime is exclusive. Art 13 of the Directive, which stipulates that the Directive shall not affect any rights which an injured person may have according to the rules of the law of contractual or non-contractual liability or a special liability system existing at the moment when this Directive was notified, has been implemented in art 6:193 BW. This provision reads as follows: 'The right to damages of the injured person against the producer pursuant to this section (art 6:185–6:193), is without prejudice to all other rights or actions'. Thus, this article acknowledges the injured person's possibility of bringing a case before the court based upon another liability regime than art 6:185 ff BW, such as art 6:162 BW (tort). After all, general liability regimes have remained in force and can under certain circumstance substantiate claims for damages against producers. It is acknowledged in case law and generally accepted amongst academics that art 6:162 BW legitimately offers an opening

6 *Keirse* (fn 3) 57. See Case C-52/00, *Commission v France* [2002] ECR I-3827; Case C-154/00, *Commission v Greece* [2002] ECR I-3879; Case C-183/00, *Gonzáles Sánchez v Medicina Asturiana* [2002] ECR I-30901; Case C-402/03 *Skov v Bilka Lavprisvarehus* [2006] ECR I-199.

where the strict product liability regime offers none, for instance for products brought into circulation before 1990, to avoid the limitation period of strict product liability, or in the case of damage to non-privately used property.[7]

E. SPECIAL LIABILITY REGIMES WITH REGARD TO NEW TECHNOLOGIES

09 Over the last couple of years, the influence of new technologies, such as nanotechnology, cloud computing, 3D printing and autonomous technologies on our daily life has increased enormously. With regard to these new risks, there is no separate liability regime in Dutch law. These new technologies have only been discussed in literature within the context of arts 6:185 or 6:162 BW. In this context, the question has been addressed whether the existing regimes encompass these new technologies adequately (see more on this section X).[8]

II. BASIC ELEMENTS OF LIABILITY

A. OVERVIEW

10 The conditions for liability are set out in art 6:185(1) BW, which states that a producer shall be liable for damage caused by a defect in his product. Consequently, five concepts attain independent meaning: (i) product, (ii) producer, (iii) defect (see more on the definition of defect in section II.C), (iv) damage (see more on the definition of damage in section IV.B), and (v) causal link (see more on causality in section V). If the aforementioned conditions are met, the producer can nevertheless free himself from liability if he can appeal to one of the defence grounds stipulated in art 6:185(1)(a)–(f) (see section VI.A ff).

---

7 See *CJM van Doorn/SB Pape*, Productaansprakelijkheid en productveiligheid, in: EH Hondius/GJ Rijken (eds), Handboek Consumentenrecht (2011) 282; *Keirse* (fn 3) 57; *E Bauw*, Onrechtmatige daad: aansprakelijkheid voor zaken (2015) 87. However, some wonder whether this development of circumventing the strict product liability regime is entirely acceptable given the maximum harmonisation envisaged by the Directive. See *MY Schaub*, De invloed van de Wet OHP op dwaling (2011) 10 Nederlands Tijdschrift voor Burgerlijk Recht 565–575.

8 See on nanotechnology: *ER de Jong*, Tussen fabel en feit, over aansprakelijkheidsrechtelijke normstelling aan de hand van nanotechnologie (2011) 42 Nederlands Juristenblad (NJ) 2836–2843; *P Stroetenga*, Nanotechnologie en Productaansprakelijkheid. Aansprakelijkheid voor nanoproducten (2009). See on autonomous technologies, in particular autonomous cars: *KAPC van Wees*, Aansprakelijkheidsaspecten van elektronische rijtaakondersteunende systemen in het wegverkeer (2004) 5 Verkeersrecht Artikelen (VRA), 133 ff; *AI Schreuder*, Aansprakelijkheid voor 'zelfdenkende' apparatuur (2014) 5/6 Aansprakelijkheid, Verzekering & Schade (AV&S); *CNJ de Vey Mestdagh/J Lubbers*, 'Nee hoor, u wilt helemaal niet naar Den Haag…': Over de techniek, het recht en de toekomst van de zelfrijdende auto (2015) 4 Ars Aequi.

B. PRODUCT

11 Art 6:185 BW introduces liability for damage caused by a defective *product*. Art 6:187(1) BW reads: 'a "product" means all movable things, even those incorporated in another movable or immovable thing, as well as electricity'. Pursuant to Dutch law, a 'thing' must be understood as a tangible object that can be subject to human control (art 3:2 BW). Accordingly, all intangible objects, such as services, advice and information fall outside the scope of the Directive.

12 Electricity is explicitly mentioned in the definition of a 'product'. The reason for this is that electricity is not a tangible object which can be subject to human control. Therefore, it cannot be defined as a thing according to Dutch law.[9] Consequently, electricity would have fallen outside the scope of this liability regime had it not been explicitly mentioned. The situation is different for water and gas. Unlike electricity, they can be perceived and controlled by humans and are therefore defined as tangible things. Accordingly, they fall within the ambit of the product liability regime of the BW.[10]

13 Pursuant to the statutory text of art 6:187(1) BW, immovable things fall outside the scope of the product liability regime. However, a movable thing that has been incorporated in an immovable (or another movable) thing must be considered a 'product'. This means that liability does not cease to exist when the product is attached to another thing, even though it may no longer be regarded as an independent object pursuant to art 3:4 BW.[11] In this respect, it is not required that the product can be easily distinguished; even things that disappear almost entirely during the production process (such as glue or preservatives) fall under the notion of 'product'.[12]

14 It should be mentioned that the concept of 'product' should not be narrowly interpreted. In this sense, the product liability regime is not restricted to products made by specific production methods. Even objects that are not industrially manufactured can fall under the notion of 'product'; a striking example is human body parts. Although living human beings are not considered to be things pursuant to art 3(2) BW and can therefore not fall under the product liability regime of 6:185 BW as such, it is assumed that this is different when it concerns body parts, such as organs, blood or other bodily fluids, that are

---

9 *Kamerstukken II* MvA 1987–1988, 19 636, no 6, 25.

10 *Kamerstukken II* Mvt 1985/86, 19 636, no 3, 10.

11 Ibid.

12 *J Spier/T Hartlief/ALM Keirse et al*, Verbintenissen uit de wet en schadevergoeding (7th edn 2015) no 135.

separated from the human body. These body parts can be considered products.[13] With regard to blood separated from the human body, the District Court Amsterdam already held in the *Scholten/Sanquin Bloedvoorziening* case that it is a product in the sense of art 6:185 BW.[14]

15 Another point of discussion concerns the question whether intellectual property and digital content can be defined as a 'product' in the sense of art 6:187(1) BW. It has been argued that a distinction should be made between intellectual property or information with and without a material carrier. Information or intellectual property without such a carrier (for instance when it concerns digital content) falls outside the ambit of the regime, as it does not concern a movable thing.[15] As regards intellectual property or digital content that is carried on through a movable thing, this may fall within the ambit of the product liability regime.[16] An example is software;[17] the European Commission, in answering a preliminary question, has stated that software is also a product if it is stored on a tangible object.[18]

16 In principle, if the object meets the requirements as laid down in art 6:187 BW, it can be qualified as a 'product'. However, it may be relevant – to a certain extent – whether the object or good in question is created on the basis of an individualised order from a client. In this respect, it depends on the degree to which the customer was involved in the production process. If the client has decided on the design of the object or good, and has given instructions to the entrepreneur, it may be qualified as a service rather than as a product. An example of such a service would be the construction agreement (art 7:750 ff BW).[19]

---

13 *CJJM Stolker* (ed), Onrechtmatige Daad. Art. 6:187, note 5.1 (online resource). See also: *van Wassenaer van Catwijck* (fn 1) 38 ff; *L Dommering-van Rongen*, Productenaansprakelijkheid. Een nieuwe privaatrechtelijke regeling vergeleken met de productenaansprakelijkheid in de Verenigde Staten (1991), 86 ff; *CJJM Stolker*, Aansprakelijkheid voor bloedproducten en bloedtransfusies (1995) NJB 685 ff; *D Wuyts*, The Product Liability Directive – More than two Decades of Defective Products in Europe (2014) 5(1) Journal of European Tort Law, 7.

14 District Court Amsterdam, 03.02.1999, NJ 1999, 621 (*Scholten v Sanquin Bloedvoorziening*). The claimant in this case argued that he was infected with HIV via a blood transfusion. The district court held that the blood product was defective, but it applied the defendant's development risk-defence.

15 *Dommering-van Rongen* (fn 13) 94, 95.

16 Ibid 93; *CJJM Stolker* (ed), Onrechtmatige Daad. Art. 6:187, aant. 5.1 (online resource); see also Van Boom and Van Doorn, who argue that although the information is not a product, the carrier is: *WH van Boom/CJM van Doorn*, Productaansprakelijkheid en productveiligheid, in: EH Hondius/GJ Rijken, Handboek Consumentenrecht: een overzicht van de rechtspositie van de consument (2006) 264.

17 *RJJ Westerdijk*, Productenaansprakelijkheid voor software (1995); *Wuyts* (fn 13) 5–6.

18 Written Question No 706/88 by Mr Gijs de Vries to the Commission: Product Liability for Computer Programs [1989] OJ C114/42.

19 Under such an agreement, one of the parties engages himself towards the other party to make and deliver a tangible construction on another basis than an employment agreement, in exchange for a price to be paid in money.

C. DEFECT

17 Pursuant to art 6:186(1) BW, a product is defective when it does not provide the safety that a person is entitled to expect, taking into account all the circumstances of the case at hand. As to the level of safety that a person is entitled to expect, it is not the subjective safety standard of the individual that is relevant, but rather the objective standard of the general public.[20] The statutory provision mentions three elements which can be taken into consideration.

18 Firstly, the presentation of the product can give rise to liability. The product must be assessed as a whole, including aspects as advertising, packaging and manual, to the extent that they may be relevant for a safe use of the product. A product will be considered defective if the producer has refrained from providing necessary instructions or has neglected to warn adequately of the potential dangers.[21] However, it must be noted that a proper warning does not prevent a defect from being qualified as such, if the defectiveness could have been prevented in some other way.[22] Furthermore, a seal of quality does not automatically imply that a product is without defects.[23]

19 Secondly, the reasonably expected use of the product may be relevant. The producer cannot automatically be held liable for a defect which arises due to the extensive misuse by the user. He is in principle only liable if the product has been used in a reasonable way and the product nevertheless shows signs of having a defect. However, this does not mean that the producer is freed from any kind of liability if the user has neglected to take the necessary precautionary measures when using the product in question. The producer should always be aware of the fact that some users will not be as cautious as they should be. Therefore, when designing a product, the producer should not focus on the individuals who always take the necessary precautions, but instead have in mind the general public, some of whom will be imprudent and will neglect taking safety measures.[24]

20 Thirdly, the time the product was put into circulation must be considered to establish defectiveness. It is important in this regard that the defectiveness must be examined according to the safety norms existing at the moment the product was marketed. Otherwise the product can be deemed to be defective for

---

20 *Bauw* (fn 7) no 74; Court of Appeal The Hague, 18.09.2012, JA 2012/212; HR, 06.09.2013, RvdW 2013/1253.

21 *Kamerstukken II* Mvt 1985/86, 19 636, no 3, 9; See also: HR, 30.06.1989, NJ 1990/652 (*CJHB*) (*Halcion*).

22 *Dommering-van Rongen* (fn 13) 96.

23 *CJJM Stolker* (ed), Onrechtmatige Daad. Art. 6:187, note 5.1 (online resource).

24 HR, 02.02.1973, NJ 1973/315 (HB) (*Lekkende Kruik I*).

the sole reason that new safety norms have entered into force.[25] This situation is closely related to the situation in which a better product is marketed. According to art 6:186(2), a product is not deemed to be defective for the sole reason that a better product has been put on the market afterwards. In this regard, the notion of 'better' must be understood as 'safer'.

21 The time the product was put into circulation also plays a role in the context of used objects. It has been argued that one cannot expect the same level of safety from a used product as from a product that has been purchased recently. Such a situation is also closely related to art 186(1)(b), since an used object might show signs of wear arising from normal usage of the product. However, if a product shows signs of excessive wear, despite normal usage, liability of the producer might be invoked.[26]

22 As regards energy, defectiveness might arise in the event of variation of the mains voltage, for instance if it suddenly spikes or drops.[27] Besides such variation, it has been somewhat unclear what constitutes defectiveness. It is not very likely that a power cut would constitute defectiveness.[28] After all, power cuts are regularly caused by external causes, such as cable breaks, lightning or problems at the substation.

23 An ineffective product can be defective and can, therefore, fall under the product liability regime. Even an increased risk of failure can constitute defectiveness. Where it is found that products belonging to the same group or forming part of the same production series (such as pacemakers or implantable cardioverter defibrillators) have a potential defect, such a product may be classified as defective without there being any need to establish that that product has such a defect. This follows from the *Boston Scientific Medizintechnik GmbH* case, which has recently been decided by the CJEU, and is discussed in the chapter on the Product Liability Directive in this book.[29]

24 Although no distinction between manufacturing, design or presentation defects can be found in national law, such a distinction has been used in legal doctrine. However, it has been pointed out that it does not have any normative meaning, and must solely be treated as a means to categorise or establish the defectiveness.[30]

---

25 *Kamerstukken II* Mvt 1985/86, 19 636, no 3, 9–10.

26 *Dommering-van Rongen* (fn 13) 182.

27 *Wuyts* (fn 13) 4.

28 *Spier/Hartlief/Keirse et al* (fn 12) no 135.

29 Joined Cases C-503/13 and C-504/13, *Boston Scientific Medizintechnik GmbH v AOK Sachsen-Anhalt – Die gesundheidskasse en Beriebskrankenkasse RWE*, ECLI:EU:C:2015:148, paras 14–17, 19–23.

30 *Dommering-van Rongen* (fn 13) 144.

25 The established standard of defectiveness is constructed by statutory provisions and case law (both from the CJEU and from the Dutch courts) and may be influenced – to some extent – by scholarly literature. The question arises as to what extent this established standard might be changed in the future by means of prospective overruling. The Dutch civil law system adheres to a type of persuasive precedent, which provides enough flexibility for the courts to deviate from or overrule previous decisions.[31] On the one hand, the established rule is that there is no system of precedent and that therefore the judges are not bound by previous judicial decisions, but on the other hand judgments, especially those of the Dutch *Hoge Raad*, are very authoritative and persuasive. Consequently, court rulings are, as a general rule, relevant retrospectively, but the technique of prospective overruling is nevertheless used in practice. Especially when open-ended norms are to be applied or when formerly established case law is being reversed, retrospective effect may not always be acceptable, and instead deciding *ex nunc* or by way of prospective overruling may be the better alternative.[32]

D. MARKETING OF A PRODUCT

26 Pursuant to art 6:185(1)(a) BW, a producer is liable for a defective product if it has been 'put into circulation'. If the producer did not market the product, eg if the product was put into circulation due to theft or if it concerns a fake product, the producer cannot be held liable. What exactly constitutes the phrase 'bringing the product on the market' has been somewhat vague, since it has not been defined, neither by the European legislator nor by the national legislator.[33] The interpretations differ in scholarly doctrine; it has been stated that it refers to the time of transfer or the title of delivery,[34] to the moment the product leaves the factory,[35] or the moment the product has reached the end-user/consumer.[36] However, the definition of 'passing something on in the chain of distribution' has been used by the court.[37] In this respect, it is not necessary that the product

31 *E Hondius*, Precedent and the Law (Report for the Netherlands Comparative Law Association) (2007) 11(3) Electronic Journal of Comparative Law 10.

32 *CH van Rhee/W van der Woude*, Effects in time of judgments in the Netherlands: prospective overruling and related techniques, in: E Steiner (ed), Comparing the Prospective Effect of Judicial Rulings Across Jurisdictions (2015) 65–80.

33 *I Giesen/M Loos*, Liability for defective products and services: The Netherlands (2002) 4 Electronic Journal of Comparative Law 79.

34 *GMF Snijders*, Productveiligheid en aansprakelijkheid (1987) 165 ff.

35 *DWF Verkade/MPh van Sint Truiden/JFC Maassen*, Product in gebreke: producten-aansprakelijkheid naar Nederlands en EEG-recht (1990) 86.

36 *Van Wassenaer van Catwijck* (fn 1) 71.

37 Court of Appeal Leeuwarden, 18.03.1998, NJ 1998, 867 (*Tetra Werke/Kuiper*) para 4; *Giesen/Loos* (fn 33) 79; such an interpretation has also been advocated by the legislature at the time of the implementation of the Directive, see: *Kamerstukken II MvA*, 19 636, no 6, 15.

has reached the consumer.[38] This definition is also in line with case law of the CJEU.[39]

27 No specific rules exist regarding defects which arise due to the means of putting a product into circulation, instead of the characteristics of a given product. Defects that might arise due to improper storage or forwarding might give rise to liability, depending on the moment the product has been put on the market. If this has been before the moment of storage, the producer cannot be held liable. If it concerns faulty instructions at the time the product was marketed, liability can be incurred. As has been mentioned before, such a situation might fall under the notion of a defective presentation of the product.

E. OBLIGATIONS, DILIGENCE OR DUTY OF CARE OF THE PRODUCER

28 The product liability regime of art 6:185 ff BW does not define in greater detail the obligations, diligence or duty of care on the part of the producer. However, such duties have been established in scholarly literature and in case law, notably as in the *Koolhaas/Rockwool* case. In this case the *Hoge Raad* established a general duty of care for producers to instate safety measures so as to prevent the supply of defective products as well as to keep end-users/consumers informed about potential applications of the product. This case concerned the production of stone wool, which was used for the production of a certain type of potting soil. This potting soil was bought by growers of yuccas. At a certain point, the producer of the stone wool changed the composition of the product without notifying the end-users (the producer of the potting soil was however informed). Due to the changed composition of the product, the end-users suffered damage since the renewed product turned out not to be suitable for growing yuccas. The growers decided to bring the case before the court and to ask for compensation for their losses. The *Hoge Raad* established that the producer has to act as a 'careful producer' and has to take all the necessary measures to prevent the product from causing damage. In addition, the producer has a duty to investigate the potentially negative effects of a new or renewed product. If the product has been renewed or changed, the producer has a duty to warn or inform the end-users or consumers about this change. Accordingly, this also applies to producers of the raw material or component; it

---

38 *Spier/Hartlief/Keirse et al* (fn 12) no 137.

39 Case C-203/99, *Veedfald v Arhus Amtskommune* [2001] ECR I-3569; Case C-127/06, *O'Byrne v Sanofi Pasteur* [2006] ECR I-1313; See also: *CJM van Doorn/SB Pape*, Kroniek Productaansprakelijkheid en productveiligheid 2005–2008 (2009) 2 Tijdschrift voor Consumentenrecht en Handelspraktijken 50–51.

is not enough for the producer of such a product to only inform the producer of the end-product.[40]

In academic doctrine, a more general duty to warn has been elaborated on. In this respect, the producer should always notify the consumer if the potential risk posed by the product cannot be prevented by some other means. The question then arises as to what kind of risks the producer should warn about. First of all, the producer should warn about potential risks that can materialise in the normal usage of the product, for instance side effects of medication. Secondly, a warning is necessary for risks that may materialise due to inattention, carelessness and/or a lack of time on the side of the user. Thirdly, the producer has to inform the consumers about risks which can materialise due to incorrect, but nevertheless foreseeable, usage of the product.[41]

F. SPECIAL PRODUCTS

29 In certain circumstances, it might be necessary to undertake a so-called risk/utility test in order to establish whether a product is defective. This is often the case for medical products, such as medicines. As these medicines might have side effects, the question often arises as to whether these side effects are still acceptable. In this respect, the utility of the medicine must be weighed against the risks of usage. If the side effects prove to be a threat to the patient's health, the product must be considered to be defective. On the other hand, if the side effects are not substantial enough as compared to the advantages of the medicine, the product might not deemed to be defective, provided that the producer has warned about these potential side effects.[42]

G. CLASSIFICATION OF PRODUCT LIABILITY

30 Dutch law makes a distinction between fault-based liability for wrongful acts (art 6:162 BW) and so-called qualitative liability, a form of strict liability. This form of strict liability can be characterised as liability *qualitate qua* for which the fault of the liable person themselves is not required.[43] It can be divided into two categories: strict liability for wrongful acts of other individuals

---

40 HR, 22.10.1999, NJ 2000, 159 (*Koolhaas/Rockwool*); see also: *KJO Jansen*, Informatieplichten. Over kennis en verantwoordlijkheid in contractenrecht en buitencontractueel aansprakelijkheidsrecht (2011) 481–483.

41 *SB Pape*, De betekenis van het *Jetblast*-arrest voor de waarschuwing in het productaansprakelijkheidsrecht (2006) 56 Nederlands Tijdschrift voor Burgerlijk Recht 374–382.

42 *Spier/Hartlief/Keirse et al* (fn 12) no 138; *AML Broekhuijsen-Molenaar/CJJM Stolker*, Geneesmiddelen en aansprakelijkheid (1986), 30.

43 *Spier/Hartlief/Keirse et al* (fn 12) no 139.

and strict liability for defective objects and substances. Art 6:185 ff BW can be – in line with the Directive[44] – classified as the second category. It reflects the characteristic of strict liability, since fault in the sense of culpability is not required. The question whether the product is defective is important, and not whether the producer has acted negligently.[45]

31 As has been stipulated before, injured parties can still bring a product liability claim before the courts based on other liability regimes, such as art 6:162 BW. This tort law standard is one of fault-based liability. Over recent years, however, the *Hoge Raad* has moulded the standard for liability of the producer under general tort law according to the standard of product liability under the regime of art 6:185 ff BW. In the *Halcion* case of 1989, the *Hoge Raad* decided that a product is defective under art 6:162 BW, if 'it does not offer the safety a consumer or user is entitled to expect, given the circumstances of the case'.[46] In later cases, the *Hoge Raad* ruled that it is wrongful if a product is put into circulation that, when used in a normal fashion and for the intended purpose, causes damage.[47] In *Dupont v Hermans*, the *Hoge Raad* referred explicitly to *Halcion*.[48] Since this standard resembles the standard of art 6:185 ff BW, the standard under tort law is more or less similar to the specific product liability standard. In that sense, the relationship between European product liability law and domestic tort law has been considered to have become very close.[49]

III. THE PERSON LIABLE FOR DAMAGE

A. PRODUCER: DEFINITION

32 Within the product liability regime, a 'producer' is defined in a broad manner. It includes the manufacturer of a finished product, the producer of any raw material or the manufacturer of a component part and any person who, by putting his name, trade mark or other distinguishing feature on the product, presents himself as its producer.

---

44 See Preamble of Directive 85/374/EEC, in which it is stated that the Directive embraces liability without fault. The reason for this is consumer protection, prevention and a fair distribution of risks. See also: *I Giesen*, Bewijs en aansprakelijkheid. Een rechtsvergelijkend onderzoek naar de bewijslast, de bewijsvoeringslast, het bewijsrisico en de bewijsrisico-omkering in het aansprakelijkheidsrecht (2001) 194.

45 *Kamerstukken II MvA*, 19 636, no 6, 5; *Giesen* (fn 44) 200–201.

46 HR, 30.06.1989, NJ 1990, 652 (*Halcion*).

47 HR, 06.12.1996, NJ 1997, 219 (*DuPont/Hermans*); HR, 22.10.1999, NJ 2000, 159 (*Koolhaas/Rockwool*).

48 HR, 06.12.1996, NJ 1997, 219 (*DuPont/Hermans*).

49 *I Giesen*, Product liability in the Netherlands, in: S Whittaker, The Development of Product Liability (2010) 154, 155, 166, 167.

33 It can be difficult to determine whether a certain producer is the manufacturer of a component part or of a finished product, since it may be unclear when the manufacturing process has ended and the distribution process has started. Decisive is then whether the product already has the actual form in which it is going to be sold or that assemblage or composition is still needed.[50] With regard to the manufacturer of a component part, he remains liable, even if the material has ceased to be an independent thing (this is in line with art 6:185(1) BW).

34 As has been stipulated before, any person who presents himself as being the producer can also be held liable. The rationale for this rule is that the putting of the name, trade mark or other distinguishing feature on a product shows evidence of a strong economic relationship between the actual producer and the person acting as the producer.[51] Contrary to this, the person who lends his name to a product for advertising reasons is not considered to be the producer of the product.[52]

B. OTHER ENTITIES BEARING LIABILITY

35 Besides the producer, any person who imports a product into the European Economic Area for the purpose of it being sold, hired, leased or in any other way distributed in the course of his business, can be held liable, according to art 6:187(e) BW. Because of the phrase 'in the course of his business', this provision only applies to entrepreneurs. However, it has been somewhat unclear as to whether import for own use also falls within the scope of art 6:187(e) BW.[53]

36 The supplier can also be held liable for a defective product if the producer of the product cannot be identified. However, he can free himself from this liability if he informs the injured person, within reasonable time, of the identity of the producer or the person who supplied him with the product. The same rule applies when it concerns a product that has been imported into the European Economic Area.

37 When a product is sold by a business to a consumer (B2C sale) and the product turns out to be defective in the sense of art 6:185 BW, and if this leads to damage in the sense of art 6:190 BW, the consumer cannot hold the seller liable, pursuant to art 7:24(2) BW. However, this rule is not absolute; the consumer

---

50 *CJJM Stolker* (ed), Onrechtmatige Daad. Art 6:187(2), note 17 (online resource).

51 Ibid.

52 *Kamerstukken II* Mvt 1985/86, 19 636, no 3, 10.

53 See for two differing opinions: *Dommering-van Rongen* (fn 13) 130; *Verkade/van Sint Truiden/Maassen* (fn 35) 112.

can bring a claim against the seller in the event that (i) the seller was aware or ought to have been aware of the defect, (ii) the seller had promised the product would be free of the defect, or (iii) it concerns damage to any object other than the product itself for which there is no right to compensation under art 6:185 ff BW. Art 7:24 BW seeks to direct the liability to the producer, as the protection of the consumer-buyer should not be at the expense of the retailer.[54] It must be emphasised that art 7:24 BW only applies to B2C sales. If it concerns any other type of sales (B2B, C2C), the seller can be held liable under contract law.

38 Pursuant to the defence codified in art 6:185(1)(c) BW, a producer can free himself from liability if he can prove that the product was not manufactured or distributed for economic purposes.[55] Thus, the commercial or non-commercial character of a given transaction putting a product on the market does have some kind of significance. Additionally, the producer can free himself from liability if he can prove that the product was not manufactured or distributed by him in the course of his professional practice or business. This means that a distinction is made between entrepreneurs (ie professionals and businesses) and consumers.

39 As mentioned in the parliamentary materials, the Dutch legislator has stated that public entities (ie entities operated by the state or local government) can also fall under the notion of 'business' as mentioned in art 6:185(1)(c) BW.[56] Thus, it can be presumed that public entities can also fall under the notion of 'producer' in the sense of the product liability regime.

C. MULTIPLE ENTITIES

40 Pursuant to art 6:187 BW, multiple entities can be held liable for the same defective product. In such a situation, each of them is joint and several liable according to art 6:189 BW.

If both the manufacturer of the product and the manufacturer of a component or raw material which is fitted into the product are liable, art 6:185(1)(f) BW channels the liability to the first, provided that the component's manufacturer

---

54 *KJO Jansen*, Samenloop en kanalisering van aansprakelijkheid. Over de exclusieve aansprakelijkheid van bepaalde personen, mede in het licht van de toezichthouders-problematiek, in: ISJ Houben (ed), Samenloop (2007) 172.

55 See also: Case C-203/99, *Veedfald v Arhus Amtskommune* [2001] ECR I-3569, in which was decided that a hospital was liable for the producing of a product that was used during a procedure. The fact that this procedure was paid from public financial means and was completely free of charge for the patient did not stand in the way of declaring to be made for economic purposes.

56 *Kamerstukken II* Mvt 1985/86, 19 636, no 3, 8.

can prove that the defect is due to the design of the product itself or to the instructions given by the manufacturer of the product.[57]

If the seller of a defective product is liable under contract law and the producer of the defective product is liable under art 6:185 ff BW, the liability is channelled to the seller if the value of the damage is less than €500 (art 6:190(1)(b) BW in conjunction with art 7:24(2)(c) BW).[58]

41 Art 5 of the Directive leaves the regulation of contribution or recourse up to the Member States. The general provisions regarding the apportionment of recourse in case of joint and several liability, arts 6:10 and 6:102 BW, are therefore applicable. According to art 6:10 BW, every debtor must contribute in relation to the part of the joint obligation for which he is accountable in his internal relationship with the other solidary debtors. This rule has been elaborated on in art 6:102(1) BW, which states that, in order to establish what part a debtor is accountable for, art 6:101 BW is applicable. Pursuant to this provision, it is decisive to what extent the circumstances that have contributed to the damage can be attributed to them individually (see no 66 for more on art 6:101 BW).

IV. THE AGGRIEVED PERSON AND DAMAGE

A. THE AGGRIEVED PERSON

42 The scope of the product liability regime is limited to three types of damage; only those who have suffered damage in the sense of 6:190 BW can bring a claim under art 6:185 ff BW. The liability regulated by the Directive and Title 6.3.3. BW is thus limited to liability for death or personal injury, and damage to or destruction of property intended for private use or consumption and used as such by the injured party. This means that claims are generally pursued by consumers.

43 In the event of damage caused by death or personal injury (art 6:190 BW), the product liability regime does not impose any limitations on the potential group of aggrieved persons. However, this group is limited by provisions of tort law. Although those limitations are not laid down specifically for product liability cases, they do apply to such situations.

44 With respect to damage caused by death, art 6:108 BW determines the different categories of persons who might pursue a claim. Firstly, the spouses and minor children can be deemed to be aggrieved persons, provided that

57 *Jansen* (fn 54) 173.
58 Ibid.

they suffer damage due to the loss of the deceased's prospective income (sub (a)). Secondly, other blood and legal relatives can pursue a claim, provided that they were supported financially by the deceased at the time of death (sub (b)). Thirdly, a person who lived together with the deceased in a family relationship and who was financially supported by the deceased can pursue claims, provided that it is likely that the financial support would have continued and that he or she cannot provide for his/her own maintenance (sub (c)). Finally, a person who lived together with the deceased and ran their common household can claim compensation for losses (sub (d)).

45 With regard to damage caused by personal injury, the person who has suffered the injury can pursue a claim based on art 6:185 ff BW, according to art 6:106 BW. The same applies in the event of damage to another object which is privately used; in that sense, the rightful owner can pursue a claim. Additionally, if a third party – not being an insurer – has incurred costs on behalf of the injured person, that party must also be compensated (art 6:107(1) BW). However, this rule only applies if the injured person, had he incurred the costs, would also be entitled to compensation.

46 If a person suffers damage, insurance companies often immediately compensate this. If such a company does not compensate the total amount of damages suffered, the aggrieved party may decide to bring a claim for the remaining losses. In such a case, the aggrieved person can only claim the amount of money that is not compensated for by the insurer. The insurer for his part can, by means of subrogation, claim before the courts the amount of money that has been paid. However, this situation does not apply to product liability law. Pursuant to art 6:197 BW, the rights arising from art 6:185 BW are not accessible for subrogation. Therefore, an insurer cannot bring a claim based upon the product liability regime, not even if he has set this out in an agreement or by means of exercising the rights in someone else's name.

47 A person who has suffered damage due to a faulty product but whose damage is not listed in art 6:190 BW can nevertheless pursue claims under tort law (art 6:162 BW) or under contract law (art 6:74 BW) (see more on this section IX.A.2). The same applies to insurers.

B. DAMAGE

48 Article 6:190 BW states that a producer is liable for damage caused by death or by personal injuries and for damages caused by the defective product to another asset of a type which is ordinarily intended for private use or consumption. In the light of recent case law, it seems that the CJEU leaves the interpretation and scope of this concept of damage to national law.[59]

49 The interpretation and scope of the notion 'damage caused by death' (art 6:190(1)(a) BW) is elaborated on by the general law of damage, more specifically by art 6:108 BW. Pursuant to this statutory provision, it includes loss of financial support (art 6:108(1)(a)–(c) BW), costs for someone to attend to the common household (art 6:108(1)(d) BW), and the costs of the funeral and the disposal of the dead (art 6:108(2) BW). In the recent *Boston Scientific Medizintechnik GmbH* case, the CJEU has broadened the definition of damage caused by death or personal injury. In this case, no deaths or personal injuries were suffered, but the physicians intervened in order to prevent such damage. The referring court asked whether damage related to the replacement of a surgical pacemaker or an implanted cardioverter defibrillator constituted 'damage caused by death or by personal injuries' for which the producer is liable.[60] According to the court, 'as a consequence, in the case of medical devices, such as pacemakers and implantable cardioverter defibrillators, which are defective ..., compensation for damage must cover, inter alia, the costs relating to the replacement of the defective product'.[61] Therefore, the Court found that the costs relating to the preventive measures fell within the notion of 'damage' of the Directive.

50 With regard to damage to another thing, this will only be compensated if this thing was intended to be used in the private sphere and if it was actually used in such context. Consequently, damage to a thing used in the professional sphere does not fall within the protective ambit of art 6:185 ff BW. Damage to another thing includes not only 'direct' damage, such as the costs of repair, but also the costs incurred due to the absence of the object.[62]

51 When it comes to damage to the product itself, no compensation is granted to the user or consumer under the product liability regime. If the product has been obtained on the basis of a contract, the consumer can make a contractual claim based upon art 7:17 BW (non-conformity) in conjunction with art 7:24 BW (consumer sale) against the seller of the product.

---

59 However, the CJEU decided that the national laws must provide for 'full and proper compensation for persons injured by a defective product'. It also stipulated that '[a]pplication of national rules may not impair the effectiveness of the Directive and the national court must interpret its national law in the light of the wording and the purpose of the Directive'. See: Case C-203/99, *Veedfald v Arhus Amtskommune* [2001] ECR I-3569, para 27.

60 Joined Cases C-503/13 and C-504/13, *Boston Scientific Medizintechnik GmbH v AOK Sachsen-Anhalt – Die gesundheidskasse en Beriebskrankenkasse RWE*, ECLI:EU:C:2015:148, para 44.

61 Ibid para 50.

62 *Dommering-van Rongen* (fn 13) 260.

52 Since art 6:190 BW only mentions damage caused by death, personal injury or damage to another thing, the question arises as to whether pure economic loss can fall within the ambit of the concept of damage. In the literature, it is presumed that pure economic loss is not governed by art 6:185 ff BW, and that for such a loss a claim must be made based on art 6:162 BW.[63] With regard to economic loss as a consequence of damage to a thing, it has been presumed that this can be compensated on the basis of art 6:185 in conjunction with art 6:190 BW, provided that the loss is incurred in the private sphere.[64]

53 Art 9 of the Directive states that it applies without prejudice to national provisions relating to non-material damage. As also emphasised by the CJEU, it is left to the Member States to regulate whether and in what situation non-material damage is eligible for compensation.[65] Accordingly, if the product is defective in the sense of art 6:185 BW and this leads to non-material damage that falls within the ambit of art 6:190 BW, it can be compensated, provided that Title 6.1.10 of the BW gives this possibility. With regard to non-material damage, two requirements have to be met. Firstly, it must be established whether it falls under the notion of 'damage' in the sense of art 6:190 BW. Secondly, it must be determined whether it is eligible for compensation pursuant to art 6:106 BW, the rule of general liability law on compensation for non-material damage. This statutory provision determines that the injured person has a right to compensation for non-material damage if the person suffering the loss is physically injured, if his honour or reputation has been harmed, or if his person has been otherwise afflicted.

The Court of Appeal of 's-Hertogenbosch ruled on the question whether non-material damage falls under the notion of 'damage' in the sense of art 6:190 BW in 2009. The case was about a couple whose car broke down on one of the motorways in France during a holiday. Shortly after the couple stopped their car at the side of the road and got out of the vehicle, the car caught fire and burned down completely. The couple brought the case before the court and argued that they suffered mental damage due to the incident. They claimed compensation on the basis of art 6:185 BW in conjunction with art 6:187(3) BW.[66] The Court of Appeal decided that a claim for compensation for non-material damage caused by a defective product cannot be successful if the mental damage is not the result of physical injury, since the applicability of art 6:190 BW is restricted to death or physical injury. Therefore, solely non-material damage does not fall within that scope.[67] Although not discussed in

63 *Bauw* (fn 7) 86; *Pape* (fn 41) 374–382.
64 *Spier/Hartlief/Keirse et al* (fn 12) no 144.
65 Case C-203/99, *Veedfald v Arhus Amtskommune* [2001] ECR I-3569.
66 Court of Appeal 's-Hertogenbosch, 01.09.2009, JA 2010, 7, paras 4.1.3–4.2.1.
67 Ibid para 4.3.3.

this case, it would also not have met the test of art 6:106 BW, since it requires more than just non-material damage (his person must be afflicted). One may wonder whether the Court of Appeal has interpreted the notion 'damage caused by death or personal injuries' too narrowly.[68]

Conversely, non-material damage as a result of physical damage does fall within the ambit of art 6:190 BW, and can be eligible for compensation pursuant to the statutory text of art 6:106 BW. Two cases where immaterial damages were claimed successfully can be mentioned. In the case *Claimant/Vlissinge Transportbeton* the claimant had sustained severe burns to the legs as a result of coming into direct contact with liquid concrete. The Middelburg District Court held that the producer who supplied the defective product was liable, and awarded €5,000 in immaterial damages.[69] In the case *Claimant/Evuco Vuurwerk* the claimant lost her eye due to defective fireworks and was awarded €25,000 in immaterial damages by the Court of Appeal in Leeuwarden.[70]

54 It should also be mentioned that nuclear damage is not governed by the product liability regime. Art 14 of the Directive states that it shall not apply to such damage, provided that it will be covered by international conventions ratified by the Member States.

C. MONETARY LIMITS

55 In accordance with Art 9 of the Directive, art 6:190(1)(b) BW provides for a minimum threshold for liability regarding damage to a thing privately used: €500. There has been discussion on whether an injured person can be compensated wholly if the monetary amount of the damage exceeds the limit of €500, or whether compensation is only possible for the amount left after the €500 is deducted. The Dutch legislator opted for the first situation. This can be derived from the initial proposal for art 6:190 BW, which stated that damage to an object should only be compensated if the monetary amount were more than fl. 1263.85. However, the proposal was amended at this point, as the legislator wanted a more neutral wording in case the CJEU were to interpret art 9 of the Directive differently.[71] However, the interpretation of the new statutory text remained the same.

---

68 See also the annotation of I van der Zalm under Court of Appeal 's-Hertogenbosch, 01.09.2009, JA 2010, 7.

69 District Court Middelburg, 13.07.2005, ECLI:NL:RBMID:2005:AZ5281 (*Claimant/Vlissingse Transportbeton*).

70 Court of Appeal Leeuwarden, 08.02.2011, ECLI:NL:GHLEE:2011:BQ0194 (*Claimant/Evuco Vuurwerk*).

71 *CJJM Stolker* (ed), Onrechtmatige Daad. Art 6:190, note 11 (online resource). See also: *GMF Snijders*, Productenrecht: Drie aspecten in Europees perspectief (1990) 83, 84.

56 Art 16 of the Directive provides the possibility for Member States to limit the liability to a maximum amount of €70 million. The Netherlands did not make use of this option. Thus, there are no maximum limits on monetary compensation within the Dutch product liability regime.

57 Under general Dutch liability law, the judge can moderate the compensatory pursuant to art 6:109 BW. According to this statutory provision, compensation can be reduced if a full award of damages would lead to unacceptable results in view of the circumstances of the given situation, including the nature of the liability, the legal relationship between the parties, and their financial resources. Furthermore, the compensation cannot be reduced to a lower amount than the amount for which the debtor is covered by insurance or was compelled to do so. However, it is very much debated whether this provision is also applicable to product liability cases. Thus far, there is no reason to assume that this is the case.[72] Anyway, in practice the provision of art 6:109 BW is rarely applied; full compensation is the main rule.

V. CAUSALITY

A. GENERAL RULES

58 Causation is mentioned several times in the product liability regime of art 6:185 ff BW. Firstly, art 6:185(1) BW states that damage must be *caused* by a defect. Secondly, art 6:188 BW, which deals with the burden of proof, requires the injured person to prove the *causal* relationship between defect and damage. Thirdly, art 6:185(3) BW deals with the situation that there are multiple *causes* of damage.

59 However, the product liability regime does not offer any rules on causality. Therefore, there has been a discussion as to whether the general rules of national law on causality are automatically applicable to product liability cases falling under the product liability regime. Since the Directive does not give a definition of causation, it is likely that the scope and definition of the causation requirement will be interpreted in line with national law (art 6:98 BW).[73] The same may apply to the application of proportional liability or the loss of a chance doctrine, both of which are accepted under Dutch law. Since it is likely that

72 *Spier/Hartlief/Keirse et al* (fn 12) no 148.

73 Ibid no 148. See also Dommering-Van Rongen, who discusses the question whether 'causality' must be interpreted according to national or European law. She states that it might be difficult to emanate from a European interpretation of causation, as this concept has been embedded in national tort law; *Dommering-van Rongen* (fn 13) 153; *Wuyts* (fn 13) 25.

causality issues are left to national laws, it can be argued that Dutch courts can also apply proportional liability in product liability cases. It is important to note that no such case has been brought before the courts so far.

60 In general Dutch liability law, causation is a requirement to establish liability. The requirement of causation consists of two stages: causation in fact and legal causation. The first stage, which concerns the factual establishment of a causal link between the defect, the tortious act or breach of contract and the damage suffered, is embodied in the wording of arts 6:185, 6:162, 6:74 BW, and others. Factual causation concerns the *conditio sine qua non*; this factual causal connection exists between a particular tortious act and an injury when the injury would not have arisen but for the act. The second stage is addressed in art 6:98 BW, which reads: 'Only damage that is related in such a way to the event giving rise to the liability of the debtor that it, in regard of the nature of liability and the damage, it can be attributed to him as a consequence of the event is eligible for compensation.'

61 In some situations, it might however be difficult to prove either the factual or the legal causality. This uncertain causality poses difficulties for the plaintiff, as the burden of proof lies on him. Traditionally, Dutch law adhered to a so-called 'all-or-nothing' approach. If the plaintiff was unable to prove the causation, the defendant's liability could not be established. Over the years, the *Hoge Raad* adopted a more 'proportional' approach to prevent less unfair outcomes.[74] This eventually led to the development of two closely related doctrines: proportional liability and loss of a chance.

62 The doctrine of proportional liability covers situations where the *conditio sine qua non* connection cannot be established, as it might be unclear whether the tortious conduct was the factual cause of the damage, or whether it was caused by an act or event that the aggrieved contributed to himself.[75] The doctrine of proportional liability was acknowledged in the landmark case of

---

74 *ALM Keirse*, Going Dutch: How to Address Cases of Causal Uncertainty, in: I Gilead/MD Green/BA Koch, Proportional Liability: Analytical and Comparative Perspectives (Volume 33 2013), 1, 2.

75 Note that the problem of causal uncertainty only occurs in the situation that it is unclear whether the damage was due to the tortious act of the defendant or to an act/event that could be contributed to the claimant himself. It does not apply to the situation in which it is unclear whether the damage has been caused by the tortious act of the defendant or by external factors. In the latter situation, art 6:99 BW (alternative causality) applies. This article reads: 'Where the damage is caused by two or more events, for each of which another person is liable, and its ascertained that the damage originates from at least one of these events, then each of these liable persons is joint and several liable for that damage, unless a liable person proves that this specific damage is not caused by the event for which he himself is liable'. See also: HR, 09.10.1992, NJ 1994, 535 (*Des Dochters*).

Nefalit/Karamus in 2006.[76] The case was about Karamus, an employee of Nefalit. When working for Nefalit, Karamus had been exposed to asbestos. After a couple of years, Karamus had developed lung cancer, which he claimed to be caused by the exposure to asbestos. Therefore, he claimed damages from his employer, based on art 7:658 BW (liability of the employer). However, it was not possible to determine whether the lung cancer had actually been caused by the asbestos exposure or by the fact that Karamus had been smoking for several years. An expert had established that the probability that the asbestos exposure was the actual cause was 55%. The *Hoge Raad* declared that in the case of uncertain factual causality, an expert must be appointed to establish the likelihood that the claimant's damage was the cause of the defendant's tortious act or neglect. If this likelihood is very small or very high, the judge can either reject or sustain the claim. If the likelihood is neither very small nor very high, the application of the all-or-nothing approach would be unreasonable. Therefore, the *Hoge Raad* provided a new solution. It held that:

> 'Taking into account the principles which underlie articles 6:99 and 6:101 BW, it has to be accepted that when an employee suffers damage which, considering the aforementioned probabilities, can be caused both by attributable negligence on the part of the employer in his duty to exercise reasonable care ... as well as through a circumstance which can be attributed to the employee himself or, as mentioned before, through a combination of these, where it cannot be established with sufficient certainty to which extent the damage suffered by the employee has been caused by all of these circumstances or one of them, the judge can order the employer to compensate the entire damage of the employee, but reducing the employer's duty to compensate proportionally, based on a well-reasoned estimate, to the extent to which circumstances which can be attributed to the employee have also contributed to the damage.'[77]

In follow-up case law, the proportional liability was confirmed and it was established that it could be applied to other legal areas as well.[78] However, the applicability must always be determined on a case-by-case basis.[79] The purpose of the rule of proportional liability requires the purpose of the standard that has been violated, the nature of the violation and the nature of the damage to be taken into account. As is explicitly mentioned by the *Hoge Raad* (more than once), the rule of proportional liability should be applied restrictively. After all,

---

76 *Nefalit/Karamus* was however not the first case in which proportional liability was applied. This was *Schaier/De Schelde*, see also: District Court Middelburg, 01.02.1999, NJ kort 1999/35 (*Schaider/De Schelde*).

77 HR, 13.03.2006, NJ 2001, 250 (*Nefalit/Karamus*).

78 HR, 24.12.2010, RvdW 2011/35 (*Fortis/Bourgonje*); HR, 14.12.2012, RvdW 2013, 37 (*Nationale Nederlanden/Mother and son*); HR, 21.12.2012, NJ 2013/237 (*Tax advice*).

79 *Keirse* (fn 74) 53.

the rule implies that persons might be held liable even though their tortious behaviour did not cause any damage.

63 The theory of loss of a chance concerns the situation in which the factual causation (the *conditio sine qua non* connection) is established, but in which it is unclear *if* there is damage that is eligible for compensation and, if so, what the size of the damage is.[80] As with proportional liability, an 'all-or-nothing' approach can – in some situations – be unreasonable. Loss of a chance was first recognised by the District Court Amsterdam in the *Wever/De Kraker* case. In this case, medical specialist De Kraker had made a diagnostic error; he had not detected a cerebral haemorrhage of the baby daughter of the Wever family at the first consultation. Instead, this haemorrhage had only been detected at the second consultation round, a day later. The cerebral haemorrhage led to the baby girl becoming permanently disabled. The parents claimed that the baby could not have made a full recovery due to this medical malpractice. The defendant claimed that the damage would have occurred regardless of whether the haemorrhage had been detected a day sooner. This view was supported by an expert. The District Court (whose view was underlined by the Court of Appeals) held that the baby girl was denied the possibility of a better end result due to the medical error. Since the chance of a better recovery was 25%, the Court held the defendant liable for 25% of the damage.[81]

The *Hoge Raad* first acknowledged the theory of loss of a change in the *Baijings/H* case. The case dealt with a client (Baijings), who was involved in a labour law conflict with his former employer. Baijings lost the case at the first instance, but decided to appeal against the district court's decision. However, his attorney neglected to file the appeal in due time. Consequently, Baijings lost his chance for a better result. Therefore, he decided to bring a claim against his attorney. The *Hoge Raad* confirmed that the theory of loss of a chance could be applied, on the basis of which damages were awarded in proportion to the probability of obtaining a benefit and/or avoiding a loss.[82]

In follow-up case law the theory of loss of a chance was affirmed.[83] More recently the *Hoge Raad* has made clear that the rule of proportional liability must be distinguished from the rule of loss of a chance.[84] As mentioned above, the latter rule requires a causal link between the fault and the loss of a chance. Once it becomes clear that a causal link exists, the defendant is liable for the

---

80 *CJM Klaassen*, Monografieën BW, Schadevergoeding algemeen, deel 2 (2007) 57; See also: HR, 21.12.2012, RvdW 2013, 85 (*Tax advice*).

81 District Court Amsterdam, 15.12.1993, and Court of Appeals Amsterdam, 04.01.1996, NJ 1997, 213 (*Wever/De Kraker*).

82 HR, 24.10.1997, NJ 1998, 257 (*Baijings/H*).

83 HR, 19.1.2007, NJ 2007, 63 (*Kranendonk/Holding*); HR, 16.02.2007, NJ 2007/256 (*Tuin Beheer*).

84 HR, 21.12.2012, NJ 2013/237 (*Tax advice*).

chance that no damage would have arisen had he taken due care. The principle of restrictive application, applicable to proportional liability, does not extend to the rule of loss of a chance.

64 When applying the causality test as mentioned at no 59, several elements should be taken into consideration as contributing to the damage. Among these elements are: whether the product can cause damage equal to the damage the injured person has suffered (general causality); whether the defective product can indeed have caused the damage suffered by the injured person (specific causality); the failure to provide adequate information; the production of the product; putting it into circulation; and the foreseeability of the damage.[85]

B. MULTIPLE CAUSES OF DAMAGE

1) Third Party Contributed to the Damage

65 The damage suffered by the injured person can come from multiple sources – not only from the defective product, but also from the acts or omissions of a third party or from other circumstances external to the producer and the aggrieved party. In such a case, the liability of the producer will not be limited pursuant to art 6:185(3) BW. This is however different when the damage is also caused by a third party for whom the injured party is liable. In such a case, the liability of the producer may be reduced or disallowed (art 6:185(2) BW).

2) Aggrieved Party Contributed to the Damage

66 If the damage suffered by the injured person is also caused by the aggrieved himself, the liability of the producer may be reduced or disallowed (art 6:185(2) BW). Whether this occurs depends on the circumstances of the case.[86] In the event of such a reduction or disallowance, the degree to which this will be done will be determined according to art 6:101 BW, the general Dutch clause concerning contributory negligence. Art 6:101 BW reads:

> 'Where circumstances which can be imputed to the victim have contributed to the damage, the obligation to repair is diminished by apportioning the damage between the victim and the person who has the obligation to repair, in proportion to the degree in which the circumstances which can be imputed to each of them, have contributed to the damage. The apportionment may vary or the obligation to repair can either be completely extinguished or not apportioned at all, if equity so

85 *Dommering-van Rongen* (fn 13) 154 ff.
86 *Spier/Hartlief/Keirse et al* (fn 12) no 141.

requires due to the different degree of gravity of the faults committed or any other circumstances of the case.'

Art 6:101 BW thus contains a double apportionment criterion that offers sufficient scope to weigh the circumstances that pertain to a particular situation. The basic rule is the extent to which each of the parties contributed to the damage. However, in the interest of equity, apportionment may also be governed by other factors. The equity correction of art 6:101 BW allows a different apportionment if the relative causal contributions appear to offer an unsatisfactory result. The relative gravity of the faults is offered as the first criterion that can be used for that purpose, but the text also indicates other criteria, such as degree of culpability, the nature of the tortfeasor's liability, the type and gravity of the damage incurred. The age and the social, physical and psychological circumstances of both parties can also be taken into account. So can economic conditions or the presence of insurance. In short, the circumstances of an individual case, considered in relation to each other and in their overall context, determine the equity correction. This can result in any form of apportionment, ranging from a completely upheld to a completely extinguished duty to compensate. In general, if the tortfeasor or debtor acts intentionally, the duty to compensate the damage may be completely upheld, even if there is some contributory negligence. On the other hand, intentional behaviour on the part of the injured person may completely extinguish the duty to compensate.

VI. DEFENCES AND EXCLUSIONS

A. REGULATION AND INTERPRETATION OF DEFENCES

67 The producer of a defective product can free himself from liability if he can prove that one or more of the defences laid down in art 6:185(1) BW is applicable. The defences which are listed include: (i) the producer did not put the product into circulation; (ii) the defect did not exist at the time the product was put on the market or the defect came into being afterwards; (iii) the product was neither manufactured or distributed for economic purposes, nor in the course of professional practice or business; (iv) the defect was due to compliance with mandatory regulations issued by public authorities; (v) the defect could not have been discovered due to the state of the scientific and technical knowledge at that time; or (vi) the defect was due to the design of the product of which the defective part forms a component, or the defect was caused by the instructions of the producer of the end-product (this defence is only applicable to the manufacturers of components).

68 If the producer wants to free himself from liability upon the ground laid down in art 6:185(1)(a) BW, he must prove that he did not put the faulty product on the market. As has been stipulated in no 29 above, it has been somewhat unclear what the phrase 'bringing the product on the market' entails. Although the different interpretations vary among scholars, there has been a consensus that it must be defined as 'passing something on in the chain of distribution'.[87] In this respect, it is not necessary that the product has reached the consumer.[88]

69 Art 6:185(1)(b) BW grants the producer the possibility to prove that either the defect did not exist at the time the product was put into circulation, or that another event or act of a third party for whom he is not liable caused the defect. The legislator included such a dichotomy as it might be very difficult for the producer to prove that the defect did not exist at the time of putting the product into circulation. Instead, it might be easier to prove that the defect was caused by another third party or event afterwards.[89] It should also be mentioned that the legislator intended, with the wording 'it is probable' in art 6:185(1)(b) BW, to incorporate a less stringent burden of proof.[90]

70 If the producer wants to successfully make a claim based upon 6:185(1)(c) BW, he must meet both criteria mentioned: the product must neither be manufactured or distributed for economic purposes, nor be manufactured or distributed in the course of professional activities or business.

71 Pursuant to art 6:185(1)(e) BW, the producer can also free himself from liability if the defect could not have been discovered due to the state of the scientific and technical knowledge at time, the so-called development risk defence. This defence is often applied to design defects, but its applicability to manufacturing or presentation defects should not be excluded.[91]

There has been a consensus that the development risk defence must be interpreted restrictively.[92] The CJEU clarified the scope and meaning of the concept of 'scientific and technical knowledge' in *Commission v United*

---

87 Court of Appeal Leeuwarden, 18.03.1998, NJ 1998, 867 (*Tetra Werke/Kuiper*); *Giesen/Loos* (fn 33) 79.

88 *Spier/Hartlief/Keirse et al* (fn 12) no 137.

89 *CJJM Stolker* (ed), Onrechtmatige Daad. Art. 6:185, note 5.1 (online resource).

90 *Kamerstukken II* Mvt 1985/86, 19 636, no 3, 8.

91 *Dommering-van Rongen* (fn 13) 237.

92 Within legal doctrine, it is still not clear as to how restrictive the development-risk defence must be interpreted. Stolker has argued that it must had been impossible to discover the defect. In this sense, it does not matter whether the information was easily accessible, but whether it could have been obtained by further research. See also: *CJJM Stolker*, Vijf argumenten tegen het ontwikkelingsrisicoverweer (1989) NJB 647; Verkade, Sint Truiden and Maassen were less stringent, as they argued that the producer was obliged to peruse all relevant national and international publications, provided that those were accessible. See also: *Snijders* (fn 34) 165 ff; *Verkade/van Sint Truiden/Maassen* (fn 35) 77.

Kingdom, by stating that it 'is not specifically directed at the practices and safety standards in use in the industrial sector in which the producer is operating, but, unreservedly, at the state of scientific and technical knowledge, including the most advanced level of such knowledge, at the time when the product in question was put into circulation'.[93] Furthermore, the CJEU has clarified that the state of knowledge which the producer in question had is not relevant, but that the 'objective state of scientific and technical knowledge of which the producer is presumed to have been informed' must be taken into account. This scientific and technical knowledge must also have been accessible to the producer.[94]

72 The last defence of art 6:185(1) BW offers the manufacturer of a component or raw material the possibility to free himself from liability if he can prove that the defect was due to the design of the product of which that part forms a component, or that the defect was caused by the instructions of the end-product's producer. A claim based upon the first part of this defence must be dismissed if the manufacturer of the component or raw material is involved in producing the end-product, or if he was aware of the defects of the product. The same applies if a manufacturer of a component or raw material was aware that the instructions were incorrect.[95]

B. COMPLIANCE WITH PUBLIC, GENERAL ADMINISTRATIVE OR VOLUNTARY STANDARDS

73 Compliance with mandatory regulations issued by public authorities might also constitute a valid defence, according to art 6:185(1)(d) BW. However, this defence does not apply to *every* public or administrative standard; only those that cover the design and/or composition of the product fall within the ambit of the provision. Therefore, in order to free himself from liability, the producer must prove that the design and/or composition of the defective product in question was prescribed mandatorily by the public authorities, and that the damage is due to the defectiveness of this design or composition. However, it is very unlikely that such a situation would occur, as such mandatory regulations are almost non-existent in Dutch legislation.[96]

The *Halcion* case shows how strict the defence of art 6:185(1)(d) BW is. In this case, the *Hoge Raad* determined that the registration of a medicine in the national database of human medicines, which was in line with mandatory

---

93 Case C-300/95, *Commission v United Kingdom* [1997] ECR I-2649, para 26.
94 Ibid paras 27–28.
95 *Dommering-van Rongen* (fn 13) 86.
96 *Kamerstukken II* 1988/1989, 19 636, no 13, 8.

regulations issued by the Dutch government, did not free the producer from liability.[97]

74 Additionally, not all types of regulations issued by public authorities fall within the scope of the defence clause; compliance with non-mandatory standards issued by a public authority does not free the producer from liability. The regulations must be mandatory in the sense that the producer was either obliged to comply with the standards or was prohibited from producing the product. In this sense, compliance with minimum standards is also not sufficient to free the producer from liability.[98] The same applies to regulations for which deviation is in certain exceptional cases allowed. Since there is sufficient margin of discretion in such a situation, the regulations cannot be deemed mandatory.[99]

75 Compliance with standards issued by a private authority does not constitute a defence under art 6:185(1)(d) BW, as those are not public standards and are not mandatory. However, this might be different in the event that the government has obliged producers to comply with the standards issued by a private authority, provided that the obligation is not based upon a private contract.

76 If all the criteria of art 6:185(1)(d) BW are met, the producer can in principle successfully free himself from liability on the basis of art 6:185 BW. In such a situation, the aggrieved party can decide to bring a claim against the public authorities for issuing defective standards.[100] However, there might be circumstances in which it is not reasonable for the producer to hide behind a faulty mandatory standard issued by a public authority. This might be the case if the producer was aware of the defectiveness of the standard.[101]

C. CONTRIBUTORY NEGLIGENCE

77 According to art 6:185(2) BW, the liability of the producer is reduced or extinguished, having regard to all the circumstances, if the damage has been caused both by a defect in the product and by the fault of the injured person or of a person for whom the injured person is liable. Although the wording of this provision differs from the wording in the general clause on contributory negligence, to be found in art 6:101 BW, the same principles and criteria apply.[102]

---

97 HR, 30.06.1989, NJ 1990, 652 (*Halcion*) para 4.4.1.

98 *CJJM Stolker* (ed), Onrechtmatige Daad. Art. 6:185, note 7.1 (online resource).

99 District Court Amsterdam, 03.02.1999, NJ 1999, 621 (*Scholten v Sanquin Bloedvoorziening*) paras 8–9.

100 *Kamerstukken II* 1988/1989, 19 636, no 13, 8.

101 *Dommering-van Rongen* (fn 13) 69.

102 *ALM Keirse*, Schadebeperkingsplicht; over eigen schuld aan de omvang van de schade (2003) 61.

This means that the obligation to compensate harm is to be reduced if the harm was also caused by circumstances which are attributable to the aggrieved person. In such a case the harm will be apportioned to the aggrieved person and to the liable person in proportion to the degree in which each of them contributed to them. However another apportionment shall be made, or the obligation to compensate the harm shall be extinguished completely or maintained in full if this is required by fairness in view of the relative gravity of the faults or other circumstances, such as the degree of culpability, in the underlying situation. If, for example, the plaintiff has continued using the defective product despite becoming aware of the defect, a reduction of the claim for damages may follow.

D. CONTRACTUAL EXCLUSION AND EXPANSION OF LIABILITY

78 The liability of the producer based upon the product liability regime of art 6:185 ff BW cannot be limited or excluded by contract, according to art 6:192(1) BW. Whether the exclusion or limitation clause has been laid down in the general terms and conditions or in some other way does not make a difference.[103] Thus, the product liability regime is of a mandatory nature. In the event that the producer did incorporate an exclusion or limitation clause in his contract, such a clause will be void pursuant to art 6:192(1) in conjunction with art 3:40 BW. The latter article regulates that a clause will be null and void if it violates a statutory provision of mandatory law.

79 The product liability regime does not, however, prohibit the expansion of the producer's liability by means of contract. Therefore, it is likely that this has also been left to domestic law. Since the contractual expansion of liability is possible under Dutch contract law, it is not ruled out that it is also possible under special product liability law.

VII. REMEDIES

A. TYPES OF CLAIMS

80 The product liability regime of art 6:185 ff BW does not determine the types of claims that the injured person can pursue. However, Dutch liability law does. First of all, pursuant to art 6:103 BW, a provision of general liability law, damage is compensated monetarily. The court may, nevertheless, grant another kind of compensation (such as restoration in kind) if the injured party so requests.

103 *Keirse* (fn 3) 55.

If the liable person, after such a judgment, does not supply another type of compensation within a reasonable period of time, the injured person regains the right to demand monetary compensation.

B. NON-COMPENSATORY FORMS OF DAMAGES

81 In the Netherlands, punitive, exemplary, or other non-compensatory forms of damage are not recoverable, regardless of whether the case falls under general liability law or the product liability regime.[104]

An exception exists for restitutionary damages. A general provision regarding this type of damages is laid down in art 6:104 BW of section 6.1.10 BW. It reads: 'If someone who is liable towards another on the basis of a tortious act or a failure in the performance of an obligation has gained a profit because of the tortious act or failure, the court may, upon the request of the injured person, assess the damage in line with the amount of the profit or a part of it.' The rationale for this provision is that it is unreasonable for someone to profit from committing a tortious act or from failing to perform an obligation, which might have resulted in the fact – although it is very difficult to prove – that someone else has suffered damage.[105]

C. INJUNCTIONS

82 The Directive (including the Dutch law implementing the Directive) does not include the right of individuals or consumer groups to claim injunctions, ie withdrawal of a product from circulation, if the health and/or safety of consumers is harmed by a defective product.[106] However, it is possible for consumers to claim an injunction based on general liability law (more specifically art 3:296 BW), by stating that the producer is acting unlawfully by refraining from withdrawing the product from circulation (see section IX.B for more on the duty to recall). Art 3:296 BW reads: 'Where a person is legally obliged towards another person to give, to do or not to do something, the court shall order him, upon a request or claim of the entitled person, to carry out this specific performance, unless something else results from law, the nature of the obligation or a juridical act'. This statutory provision is also applicable in product liability cases.

---

104 *Giesen* (fn 49) 184; *Dommering-van Rongen* (fn 13) 200.

105 *MvA II*, Parliamentary History, Introduction of Book 6, 1269.

106 Green Paper on Liability for Defective Products, COM(1999)396 of 28 July 1999, 33; Council Directive 2009/22/EC of 23 April 2009 on injunctions for the protection of consumers' interest [2009] OJ L110/30 does not cover Directive 85/374/EEC.

VIII. PROCEDURAL AND EVIDENTIAL ISSUES

A. BURDEN OF PROOF

83 The burden of proof has been laid down in art 6:188 BW, which states that the injured person will have to prove the damage, the defect and the causal relationship between the defect and the damage. This is different if the producer claims that one of the defences mentioned in art 6:185(1) BW is applicable; in that case, the burden of proof of facts justifying the defence lies on him.

In the initial proposal for the implementation of the Directive, the Dutch legislator did not implement art 4 of the Directive. The reason for this was that a similar burden of proof was already laid down in art 177 (old), now art 150 of the Code of Civil Procedure (*Wetboek van Burgerlijke Rechtsvordering*, Rv), which reads: 'the party that invokes legal consequences of asserted facts and rights, bears the burden of proof for those facts and rights, unless a different distribution of the burden of proof arises from a special provision or from the requirements of reasonableness and fairness'. Art 6:188 BW was nevertheless adopted by amendment. However, this statutory provision does not establish what standard of proof is required for a claimant to succeed and it does not determine the manner in which this proof has to be established. Therefore, national courts need to rely on their domestic law.[107]

84 With regard to the national standards of proof, there are no such evidentiary standards that the court uses to acknowledge a fact as proven. Often, it will depend on the case as to which standard applies. Nevertheless, it is presumed that the burden of proof must not be rendered too strict. Otherwise, it would be very difficult to achieve adequate protection for the consumers. A recent case that was brought before the District Court of Oost-Brabant underlines this. In this case, a woman was injured when a ladder she was using suddenly folded. The woman claimed before the court that the ladder was defective and that this was the cause of her injuries. The Court held that if a ladder, when being used in a normal manner, suddenly folds and causes damage, a defect is presumed. It is then up to the producer of the ladder to rebut this presumption.[108] A similar example is the *Leebeek* case, in which the aggrieved party claimed to have suffered lacerations when trying to open a bottle of Pepsi and the neck of the bottle broke. The *Hoge Raad* ruled that, if it is established that the injured person tried to open the bottle in a normal manner, it must be presumed that the bottle is defective. It is then up to the producer to rebut this presumption.[109]

---

107 *Wuyts* (fn 13) 24.

108 District Court Oost-Brabant, 20.03.2013, JA 2013/82.

109 HR, 24.12.1993, NJ 1994, 214 (*Leebeek/Vrumona*) para 3.6.

Although the *Hoge Raad* applied a less stringent standard in the aforementioned case, it must be emphasised that the standard should not be interpreted *too* leniently, as this might lead to the unwanted situation that the producer is held liable for damage that is not the result of the product in question.[110]

85 Regarding the manner in which the proof has to be established, this also depends on the circumstances of the case. In some situations, it might be very difficult for the injured person to prove his claim, due to the technical complexity of certain products, the high costs of expert evidence, or because of limited access to certain information (for instance laboratory data). In such cases, it has been presumed that art 6:188 BW does not prevent the judge from applying national rules on the reversal or alleviation of the burden of proof.[111] In this sense, the judge has the discretion to apply several methods: reversal of the burden of proof as regards the causality; the *res ipsa loquitur* rule (negligence is inferred from the very nature of an accident or injury) as regards the defect and the causality (see also the aforementioned *Leebeek* case); and the reversal of the burden of proof based upon reasonableness and fairness (also stipulated in art 150 Rv).

B. LIMITATION PERIOD

1) Limitation Period under Product Liability Regime

86 The limitation period for product liability claims is laid down in art 6:191 BW. This provision consists of two limitation periods: a relative, short time limit that is determined using a subjective test, and an absolute, long time limit based on an objective test.

87 The relative period is laid down in 6:191(1) BW, which states that the time limit for the injured person to commence a legal claim for the recovery of damages against the producer is three years. This period will start on the day the injured person becomes aware, or should reasonably become aware, of the damage, the defect and the identity of the producer. With regard to the damage,

---

110 *Spier/Hartlief/Keirse et al* (fn 12) no 143.

111 Ibid no 143; *Giesen* (fn 44) 195; See also Case C-310/13, *Novo Nordisk Pharma GmbH*, ECLI:EU:C:2014:2385, paras 25, 27, 29, 30. In this case, the CJEU held that the Directive does not regulate the consumer's right to obtain information on the adverse effects of a product and that this has been left to national law. Although national laws may regulate such a right to information in specific situations, it is not allowed that national legislation brings about a general reversal of the burden of proof or that it undermines the effectiveness of the Directive in some other way.

it is not required that the exact amount of damage has been established yet; the fact that damage has been suffered is sufficient.[112] Where there are multiple producers liable for the damage suffered, the limitation period commences for each of them at the time the aggrieved becomes aware of their identity. Consequently, the limitation period with regard to a claim against one producer can lapse at a different moment in time from the limitation period for a claim against another producer.[113]

88 The absolute limitation period is laid down in art 6:191(2) BW. Pursuant to this provision, the injured person's right to claim damages from the producer shall be extinguished ten years from the date on which the producer put the product that caused the damage into circulation. Thus, if an injured person does not become aware, and there are no reasons to assume that he *should* have become aware, of the damage, the defect and the identity of the producer within ten years of the product being put into circulation, the injured person loses his right to claim damages. However, the right shall not be extinguished after ten years if the injured person has instituted proceedings against the producer before the end of that term.

2) Interruption and Suspension of the Limitation Period

89 Art 10(2) of the Directive determines that the suspension and interruption of the limitation period under the product liability regime is left to national law. As the product liability regime of art 6:185 ff BW does not provide for rules regarding interruption and suspension, reference has to be made to general liability law.

A distinction should first be made between the interruption of the limitation period of art 6:191(1) BW and the extinction period of art 6:191(2) BW. With regard to the latter period, general rules on interruption and suspension are not applicable. Accordingly, the extinction period cannot be interrupted, except if the injured person has already instituted proceedings within ten years of the product being put into circulation.[114]

With regard to the limitation period mentioned in art 6:191(1) BW, general rules on interruption do apply. Consequently, the limitation period can be interrupted by three types of actions. First of all, interruption can take place by means of starting a legal action (art 3:316(1) BW). However, when such a filed legal claim is rejected by the court, the limitation period is only interrupted if, within six months after the legal proceedings have ended, a new legal claim

112 *Kamerstukken II* 1987/88, 19 363, no 6, 28.

113 Ibid.

114 *Kamerstukken II* 1987/88, 19 363, no 6, 29; *WH van Boom/CJM van Doorn,* Productaansprakelijkheid en productveiligheid, in: EH Hondius/GJ Rijken, Handboek Consumentenrecht: een overzicht van de rechtspositie van de consument (2006) 270.

is filed which is after all permitted by the court. It should also be mentioned that if a legal action is withdrawn, the limitation period is not interrupted (art 3:316(2) BW). If such a filed legal claim is rejected, the limitation period can still be interrupted if the court of arbitration or the court has declared itself incompetent to rule on the issue, and if this ruling becomes final.[115] In addition, the limitation period cannot only be interrupted by bringing a legal claim before a court, but also by an act to obtain a binding third-party ruling, provided that the opposing party is informed within a short time and that it results in binding ruling. When no such binding ruling is obtained, the period will not be interrupted (art 3:316(3) BW).

Secondly, the period is also interrupted by a letter of formal notice in which performance is demanded, or by any other written announcement in which a right to performance is claimed, provided that it is followed within six months by a legal action (art 3:317 BW).

Thirdly, acknowledgment of the right which a right of action serves to protect shall interrupt the prescription of the right of action as against the person who acknowledges the right (art 3:318 BW).

90 After the limitation period has been interrupted in any other way than by the commencement of a legal action that has been awarded by the court, a new limitation period will start to run as of the day following the day of interruption (art 3:319(1) BW). If a binding third-party ruling, as laid down in art 3:316(3) BW, is the reason for the interruption, the new limitation period will start to run as of the day following the one on which the binding ruling has been given. The duration of the new limitation period will be the same as the original, which will be three years if the claim is based on art 6:185 BW.[116] The same applies to interruption on the basis of art 3:316(4) BW, pursuant to art 3:319(3) BW.

91 It is not possible, either under the product liability regime or under general liability law, to suspend the limitation period.[117]

3) Limitation Period under General Liability Law

92 The limitation period under the product liability regime differs from the one under the general liability regime, which is laid down in art 3:310 BW.

---

115 Art 3:316(4) BW in conjunction with art 1052(5) *Wetboek van Burgerlijke Rechtsvordering* (Code of Civil Procedure), and arts 1022(1), 1067 or 1074(d) *Wetboek van Burgerlijke Rechtsvordering.*

116 This may be longer in case a claim is brought on the basis of tort law or contract law (see next section), provided that the maximum term will not exceed five years. It is also important to stipulate that a legal claim cannot be prescribed before the end of the original term.

117 With the introduction of the New *Burgerlijk Wetboek*, the possibility to suspend the limitation period has been omitted.

However, similarly to art 6:191 BW, art 3:310 BW also makes a distinction between a relative, short limitation period and an absolute, long limitation period. The relative period is five years and starts on the date that the victim becomes aware of both the damage and the identity of the tortfeasor. The absolute period of limitation is in principle twenty years after the occurrence of the liability-creating event, except for harm suffered due to exposure to harmful substances as defined in art 6:175 BW (which is also understood to cover asbestos and nicotine). In that case, the right to claim damages shall expire thirty years from the date on which the liability-creating event occurred.[118]

93 Contrary to these general rules, a different rule applies with regard to injuries or death (art 3:310(5) BW). In such a case, a right of action to claim damages on account of an injury or death becomes prescribed five years from the day following the one on which the injured person becomes aware of both the damage and the identity of the person who is liable for it. Where the injured person was a minor on the day on which he became aware of both the damage and the identity of the person liable for it, the right of action shall only prescribe five years from the day following the one on which he reaches the age of legal majority. This provision includes only a relative, short limitation period, as the absolute limitation period for personal harm incurred as a result of death or injury was lifted on 1 February 2004.

94 To sum up, the limitation periods under general liability law are considerably longer than the ones under the product liability regime. The relative, short limitation periods differ by two years (three years under product liability law and five years under general liability law), whereas the absolute limitation periods differ even more (ten years under product liability regime compared to twenty years in general, thirty years in relation to harmful substances, and unlimited period in the case of injuries or death). Therefore, if an injured person's claim has been prescribed or extinguished based upon art 6:185 BW in conjunction with art 6:191 BW, he can often still bring a claim based upon art 6:162 BW in conjunction with arts 3:310 and 6:193 BW.

C. OTHER PROCEDURAL RULES

95 Other important procedural rules might also affect the injured person's real possibility of pursuing claims. These might include: formal requirements to bring a claim, court and attorney's fees, and the possibility and ease of pursuing class action claims.

---

118 Art 3:310(2) and (3) BW. See for an asbestos case: HR, 25.11.2005, NJ 2009, 103. See for a nicotine case: District Court Amsterdam, 17.12.2003, NJ 2008, 311 (*Römer/BAT*).

96 In the case of product liability cases, the civil procedure commences by having a bailiff serving a writ of summons to the other party. This writ of summons must meet the criteria laid down in art 111(2) Rv, which include: information on the competent court, the trial date, information regarding court fees, and the claim and grounds upon which the claim is based. If the elements listed in art 111(2)(a)–(l) are not incorporated in the writ of summons, the writ will be declared void.[119]

97 In order to bring a claim before the court, both the plaintiff and the defendant are required to pay court fees.[120] This is different when it concerns a claim for less than €25,000; in that case, only the plaintiff has to pay court fees.[121] For 2015, the fees at the district courts ranged between €78 and €3,864, depending on the type of claim and the income of parties.[122]

98 For claims for €25,000 or more, the assistance of an attorney is mandatory.[123] Parties must, in this respect, pay their own attorney's fees. However, legal aid is available for persons of limited means on the basis of the Acts on Legal Aid. Dutch lawyers are typically paid on an hourly basis, and they are in principle prohibited from making their fees dependent on the outcome of the case. However, an exception is now made for personal injury lawyers for a five-year trial period. As of January 2014, an experimental pilot project started, allowing lawyers to work on a no-win-no-fee basis in personal injury cases. They are permitted, by way of an experiment, to take on an injury or loss of dependency case on the basis of the no-win-no-fee principle, subject to the proviso that there is a realistic expectation of a discussion on the question of liability. However, the fee that can be charged in the end is capped and still depends on the number of hours spent on the case. The lawyer can in principle collect no more than 25% of the damages and much less in the case that requires a minimal amount of effort.[124]

99 Dutch law has two possibilities to pursue collective redress: art 3:305a BW and the Dutch Act on Collective Settlements for Mass Damages (*Wet collectieve afhandeling massaschade*, WCAM). The representative action mechanism of art 3:305a BW determines that only a foundation or association with full legal capacity that represents the interests of the aggrieved may bring a claim

119 Art 120(1) Ro.

120 Art 3(1) *Wet griffierechten burgerlijke zaken* (The Court Fees (Civil Cases) Act).

121 Art 4(1)(b) *Wet griffierechten burgerlijke zaken* (The Court Fees (Civil Cases) Act).

122 See annex to the *Wet griffierechten burgerlijke zaken* (The Court Fees (Civil Cases) Act).

123 *A contrario*, art 79(1) Ro in conjunction with art 93(1) Ro.

124 Regulation amending the Regulation on Best Practice (*Verordening tot wijziging van de Verordening op de praktijkuitoefening*) of 25.07.2013, as established by the Dutch Bar Association, Staatscourant 2013, 20779.

before the court. However, such a claim cannot be filed to obtain compensatory damages.[125] In 2005, the WCAM was introduced (implemented in art 7:907 ff BW), which has made it easier to deal with cases of mass tort. Although the regulation does not provide for the possibility of claiming compensatory damages, it does offer the defendant and the representatives of the aggrieved persons to agree on a collective settlement. This settlement can be declared binding on the whole group of aggrieved persons by the court.[126] Individuals can then bring individual claims before the court to claim compensatory damages based upon the collective settlement.

At the time of writing, there is a proposal for a bill on redress of mass damages in a collective action, which would also make it possible to claim compensatory damages.[127]

IX. ALTERNATIVE REGULATIONS AND REMEDIES

A. OTHER BASES AND RULES OF LIABILITY FOR DEFECTIVE PRODUCTS

1) General

100 As has been stipulated in no 7, the special product liability regime did not replace prior regimes; an injured person may at any time revert to other, more general liability regimes. The aggrieved is probably inclined to do so if the claim does not fall within the – more restricted – scope of art 6:185 BW. In such a case, the aggrieved can revert to several other regimes: art 6:162 BW (tort law), arts 6:74 and 7:17 BW (contract law), art 6:173 BW (liability for dangerous equipment), art 6:174 BW (liability for dangerous constructed immovable things), or art 6:179 BW (liability for animals).

2) Liability for Defective Products under Tort Law

101 If the aggrieved person decides to bring a claim based upon another liability regime, he may opt for art 6:162 BW (the general clause on tort law). The scope of this article is broader than the one of art 6:185 BW, since the restrictions of the latter provision do not apply. In this sense, applicability is not restricted to products that have been put into circulation after 1 November 1990, nor to only those products mentioned in art 6:187(1) BW, nor to only those types of

125 Art 3:305a(3) BW.

126 Art 7:907 BW in conjunction with arts 1013–1018 Ro.

127 See English consultation version of the draft bill on Redress of Mass Damages in a Collective Action: www.internetconsultatie.nl/motiedijksma (accessed 16.3.2015). See also *JM Emaus/ ALM Keirse*, The Netherlands, in: E Karner/BC Steininger (eds), ETL 2014 (2015) nos 3–6.

damages as mentioned in art 6:190 BW. Furthermore, the limitation period for claims based upon art 6:162 BW is considerably longer than for those based upon art 6:185 BW (see also section 8.2). This means that if a claim under art 6:185 BW has been prescribed or has been extinguished, the injured person can still bring a claim under art 6:162 BW, provided that it is within the limitation period as laid down in art 3:310 BW.

102 In order to ensure that the claim under art 6:162 BW succeeds, it should be established not only that there is an unlawful act, but also that this act is attributable to the procuder. By determining whether the putting into circulation of a product that has caused damage is unlawful, the *Hoge Raad* uses a standard which is similar to the one under art 6:185 ff BW. In the *Koolhaas/Rockwool* case, the *Hoge Raad* ruled that it is wrongful to put a product into circulation that, when used in a normal fashion and for the intended purpose, causes damage.[128] In this respect, the criterion used to determine the defectiveness of a product under art 6:185 ff BW is also used to determine the unlawfulness under art 6:162 BW.[129]

Besides the unlawfulness of the act, art 6:162(3) BW also requires that the unlawful act is attributable to the tortfeasor. This is the case if the unlawful act results from the tortfeasor's fault or from a cause for which the tortfeasor is accountable by virtue of law or generally accepted principles. It is due to the nature of the act that the putting into circulation of a faulty product can be attributed to the person who put the product into circulation, unless he can free himself by claiming that exculpatory circumstances apply.[130] In theory, the producer can exculpate himself by proving that he complied with his duty of care, but it is hard to imagine situations in which the producer might be able to escape liability and in practice there are no examples of such situations. As a rule the act of putting a defective product on the market will be attributable to the producer because generally accepted standards justify such attribution. This follows from the case law of the *Hoge Raad* and especially from the *Koolhaas/Rockwool* case. In this case the *Hoge Raad* established a general duty of care for producers to instate safety measures so as to prevent the supply of defective products as well as to keep end-users/consumer informed about potential applications of the product.[131] This further equates liability under art 6:162 BW with liability under art 6:185 BW.

---

128 HR, 22.10.1999, NJ 2000, 159 (*Koolhaas/Rockwool*); See also: HR, 06.12.1996, NJ 1997, 219 (*DuPont/Hermans*).

129 *Spier/Hartlief/Keirse et al* (fn 12) no 149.

130 See also: HR, 06.12.1996, NJ 1997, 219 (*DuPont/Hermans*); *Spier/Hartlief/Keirse et al* (fn 12) no 149.

131 HR, 22.10.1999, NJ 2000, 159 (*Koolhaas/Rockwool*).

3) *Liability for Defective Products under Contract Law*

103 The injured person can also decide to bring a claim under contract law. In that sense, he can hold the seller of the defective product liable for the damage – both economic loss and consequential loss – which he has incurred (art 6:74 BW). This is different in the case of a B2C sale. In that respect, the seller cannot be held liable pursuant to art 7:24(2) BW, unless the seller was aware or ought to have been aware of the defect; the seller had promised the product would be free of the defect; or if it concerns damage to any object other than the product itself, for which no right to compensation exists under art 6:185 ff BW.

4) *Liability for Dangerous Products, Dangerous Constructed Immovable Things and Animals*

104 The possessor of a defective product can also be held liable. Based upon art 6:173 BW, the possessor of a movable thing that is known to pose a great danger to people and property if it does not meet the standards which in the given circumstances may be set for such a thing is liable if this potential danger materialises, unless the possessor would not have acted with fault had he known of the danger at the time it occurred. However, no such liability exists in relation to a safety defect as defined by art 6:185 ff BW, unless: (i) the defect did not exist at the time that the thing was put into circulation or the defect arose afterwards; or (ii) the damage has a value of less than €500. In those cases, the possessor can be held liable.

105 Liability also exists for dangerous constructed immovable things. Art 6:174 BW states that the possessor of a constructed immovable thing that poses a danger to people or property because it does not meet the standards which in the given circumstances may be set for such things is liable if this potential danger materialises. However, the possessor cannot be held liable if he would not have acted negligently had he known of the danger at the time it occurred.

106 Pursuant to art 6:179 BW, a possessor of an animal can be held liable for the damage caused by that animal. As the legislation regarding things is also applicable to animals, application of both art 6:179 BW and art 6:185 BW is possible.[132] In this sense, both the possessor and the producer (ie breeder) can be held liable. However, such a concurrence is very rare.[133]

---

132 Art 3:2a BW.

133 The example given in the literature is that of an inbred pitbull terrier, which attacks someone and causes personal injuries. In such a case, the aggrieved person can sue the possessor of the pitbull, as well as the breeder. See also: *Keirse* (fn 3) 59.

107 If a thing, ie a constructed immovable thing or an animal (as mentioned in arts 6:173, 6:174 and 6:179 BW), is used in the course of business, it is not the possessor but rather the person who conducts this business who will be held liable. This follows from art 6:181 BW.

5) Liability for Defective Services

108 If a service is not a 'product' as understood by the product liability regime, the aggrieved person can turn to other liability regimes. With regard to liability for defective services, a claim can in principle either be brought under tort law, or, if a contractual basis exists, under contract law.[134] General rules on the supply of services (*overeenkomst van opdracht*) are laid down in Book 7 addressing specific contracts. Title 7 of Book 7 consist of a general part on the supply of services applicable to services that are supplied independently, ie otherwise than on the basis of a contract of employment (arts 7:400–413 BW), a part on mandate (section 2, 7:414–424 BW), a part on agency contracts (section 3, 7:425–427) and a part on medical services (section 5, 7:446–468). Contracts for works, such as construction and processing services, are dealt with in Title 12 of Book 7 and storage services are subject to the provisions of Title 9.

Under both tort and contract law, one criterion applies to determine whether a service provider is liable for a defective service: a producer must have breached a standard of care. This standard is whether the service provider in question exercised, in the conduct of his work, the standard of care expected of a good provider of services, which implies that he has to operate as a reasonably able provider of services, acting in a reasonable way, would have done.[135]

B. DUTY TO RECALL

109 The aim of the duty to recall is to prevent a consumer suffering damage due to a product that is already established to be defective and that the producer has neglected to withdraw from circulation. Under the special product liability regime, no such duty to recall exists. Liability is only incurred under the special product liability regime for *putting* a defective product into circulation, not for *neglecting to withdraw* it.[136]

---

134 In practice, claims are however more often based upon contract law (whenever there is such a contract), than on tort law. The reason for this is that the burden of proof is slightly more lenient under contract law, than under tort law. See also: *Giesen/Loos* (fn 33) 89.

135 *Giesen/Loos* (fn 33) 88; See also the general rule of art 7:401 BW, which states that a service provider must always observe the 'care of a good provider'.

136 At the time of the introduction of the product liability regime in Dutch law, the Dutch legislator had considered to regulate recall into the product liability regime. However, it was argued that the Regulation on Product Safety already deals sufficiently with product recalls. See also: *Kamerstukken II* MvA 1987–1988, 19 636, no 6, 12–13; *van Wassenaer van Catwijck* (fn 1) 12 ff.

110 Furthermore, no statutory duty to recall exists in Dutch law.[137] Nevertheless, not withdrawing a defective product can – in some situations – be regarded as unlawful under tort law (art 6:162 BW). In this respect, it can either be contrary to a statutory duty, or it can violate a standard of due care (*maatschappelijke zorgvuldigheid*).

With regard to the first category, not recalling a defective product can be contrary to the *Warenwet* (Commodities Act), which implemented Directive 2001/95/EC on product safety. On the basis of this legislation, the producer is prohibited from putting an unlawful or unsafe product on the market. If the producer refrains from recalling a product which is deemed to be unlawful or unsafe, the Minister of Health, Welfare and Sport can decide to recall the product in question. In such a case, the producer is obliged to comply.[138]

Secondly, not recalling a defective product might be wrongful as it might violate a standard of due care (*maatschappelijke zorgvuldigheid*). If a producer is aware – or should reasonably be aware – that a product is defective, it can be contrary to his standard of due care if he waits to act until the moment the product causes damage or if he does not act at all.[139] To determine whether the producer's lack of action is contrary to the standard of due care and to establish what kind of recall measures he ought to have taken, the so-called *Kelderluik* factors have to be taken into account.[140] The landmark *Kelderluik* (Cellar Hatch) case was about an employee of the Coca-Cola Company, who, while making a delivery at an Amsterdam pub and placing the bottles in the cellar, left the cellar hatch open. Although the employee placed some crates with bottles next to the door as a precautionary measure, one of the customers of the pub did not pay attention and fell through the open cellar hatch. The customer claimed compensation for the injuries he incurred. The central question of this case was whether the Coca-Cola employee had taken adequate precautionary measures. The *Hoge Raad* formulated four factors that could be taken into account: (i) the degree of probability that the required attention and care could be disregarded; (ii) the degree of likelihood that this might lead to accidents; (iii) the gravity of the consequences of such accidents (ie the nature of the damage); and (iv) the

137 Although the *Warenwet* (Commodities Act) prohibits the trading of unlawful or unsafe products, it does not impose a duty to recall for the producer. It only obliges the producers to comply with a command of the Minister of Health, Welfare and Sport regarding product recall. See also art 21(1) *Warenwet*. The *Warenwetbesluit algemene productveiligheid* (Commodities Decree on general product safety) compels the producer to stay informed of his product's potential risks, and to prepare precautionary measures that can be used in order to avoid safety or health risks. Among these are also the possibility of taking recall measures (art 2(1)(b)(2) *Warenwetbesluit algemene productveiligheid*). However, this statutory provision does not include an actual obligation to take those measures; it only obliges the producer to be able to take those measures.

138 Art 18, 21 *Warenwet* (Commodities Act).

139 *CF Kroes*, Product recall. Enkele vermogensrechtelijke gezichtspunten (2005) 3 VrA 52.

140 Ibid 46.

burden of taking adequate precautions.[141] When applying these criteria to product recall cases, the following elements must be taken into account to determine whether a producer has breached his standard of care: (i) the degree of likelihood that the defective product would cause damages; (ii) the degree of probability that the consumer would disregard the required attention and care when using the product; (iii) the severity of the damage (ie death, personal injury or damage to a thing); and (iv) whether it was possible and not too burdensome to take precautionary measures (such as issuing a warning or recalling the product).[142]

C. REMEDIES UNDER OTHER AREAS OF LAW

111 Injured parties can also turn to their insurers to receive compensation for their losses due to a defective product. Medical expenses are often covered by health insurance. Such insurance also compensates sickness due to unlawful behaviour. Damage to a thing can be covered by an *inboedelverzekering* (insurance aimed at insuring against the risk of a loss of property from one's house). With regard to non-material damage, such damage is not covered by insurance.[143]

112 There are also remedies available under Dutch administrative law. As mentioned above (no 110), it is stipulated in the *Warenwet* (Commodities Act) that it is prohibited to put an unlawful or unsafe product into circulation.[144] If an unlawful or unsafe product is nevertheless marketed, the Minister of Health, Welfare and Sport has the competence to warn the consumers and/or users about the product, and, if necessary, to recall the product.[145]

If a producer violates arts 18 and/or 21 of the *Warenwet*, this is deemed to be an economic offence under the *Wet op de Economische Delicten* (Economic Offences Act).[146] Such a breach will be punished by imprisonment for a maximum of six months, or a fine of up to €20,250.[147] The putting into circulation of a defective product might also breach more general provisions of criminal law, such art 174 *Wetboek van Strafrecht* (Dutch Criminal Code). This provision states that it is punishable to sell or distribute products which the seller/distributor is aware pose threat to health or life, without notifying the buyer/user. If a producer violates this provision, he risks imprisonment of up to

---

141 HR, 05.12.1964 (*Kelderluik*) NJ 1966, 136; English translation of the *Kelderluik* factors: *G van Maanen/D Townend/A Teffera*, The Dutch 'Cellar Hatch' Judgment as a Landmark Case for Tort Law in Europe: A Brief Comparison with English, French and German Law with a Law and Economics Falvour (2008) 5 European Review of Private Law 873.

142 *CF Kroes* (fn 139) 46, 47.

143 *Giesen* (fn 44) 188, 189.

144 Art 18 *Warenwet* (Commodities Act).

145 Arts 18, 21 *Warenwet* (Commodities Act).

146 Art 1(4) *Wet op de Economische Delicten* (Economic Offences Act).

147 Art 23(4) *Wetboek van Strafrecht* (Dutch Criminal Code).

fifteen years, or a fine of up to €81,000.[148] If the violation of this provision results in the death of the buyer/user, the producer can be sentenced to thirty years' imprisonment.[149]

X. ASSESSMENT OF DOMESTIC LAW

A. APPLICATION OF SPECIAL PRODUCT LIABILITY IN PRACTICE

113 Although it was thought that the introduction of the special product liability law in Dutch law would lead to an enormous increase in the number of product liability cases, the actual number of such cases has not risen that significantly over the last couple of years.[150] There might be various reasons for this. First of all, it has been noted that most of the cases are settled out of court.[151] It might be the case that the rules on product liability are quite clear and facilitate negotiations and settlements, thus preventing product liability cases from going to court. In addition, the fear of losing goodwill may also incline producers to give in more easily. Secondly, a defective product can also be part of a service or subscription (for instance, subscriptions for mobile networks in which the mobile phone is included). If the product is defective and causes damage, the liable party is often the provider of the service/subscription rather than the producer of the product. Thirdly, due to the high standard of social security within the Netherlands, injured persons are not forced to bring a claim under tort law in order to ensure their livelihood.[152] As has been stipulated before, most damages are already covered by insurance schemes, such as the *inboedelverzekering* or by healthcare. The part that is not covered (costs relating to immaterial damages, such as mental damage) is very difficult to claim before a court (see also no 55). With regard to damages that are reimbursed by the insurance companies, it is important to note that social security schemes do not have the possibility of starting proceedings against a producer of a defective product to claim these reimbursements (see also no 47, in which it is explained that, pursuant to art 6:197 BW, the rights arising from art 6:195 BW can not be subrogated).[153]

[148] Art 174(1) *Wetboek van Strafrecht.*

[149] Art 174(2) *Wetboek van Strafrecht.*

[150] *MG Faure*, Productaansprakelijkheid in Europa: kritische rechtseconomische reflecties (2004) 1 Aansprakelijkheid, Verzekering & Schade; *I Giesen/E de Kezel*, Product Liability: the Development in the Netherlands, in: HJ Kullmann et al, Produzentenhaftung (2015) 3.

[151] Insurance companies have claimed that this would be about 90% of all product liability cases. See also: *Faure* (fn 150) 11; *Giesen/de Kezel* (fn 150) 20.

[152] *Faure* (fn 150) 10–11.

[153] Report from the Commission on the Application of Directive 85/374 on Liability for Defective Products, COM(2000)893 final, 11.

B. DIFFICULTIES IN PRACTICAL APPLICATION

114 One of the most important difficulties in the practical application of special product law is the strict limitation of the regime. Since the criteria are more stringent under art 6:185 ff BW than they were in regimes prior to implementation of the Directive, special product liability law cannot always be applied. This can be the case in various situations: firstly, if the defective product in question was put into circulation before 1 November 1990; secondly, when it concerns a type of damage or product not mentioned in special product liability law; and thirdly, when the claim has been prescribed or extinguished due to the limitation periods, which are significantly shorter than those under general liability law.

C. EFFECTS EVOKED BY SPECIAL PRODUCT LIABILITY LAW

115 One of the most significant effects of special product liability law is the fact that it has also influenced the negligence standard under tort law as regards product liability cases. Since the *Hoge Raad* merged both standards into a similar one, the product liability standard under tort law has become more strict.[154]

116 One of the main negative effects of special product liability law for the aggrieved is the channelling of liability from the seller to the producer in B2C sales (art 7:24(2) BW; see also no 36). Provided that the exceptions to this statutory provision are not met, the aggrieved party cannot seek compensation from the party who is closest to him. Instead, he has to reach out to the producer, who may not be as accessible as the seller is. In that sense, there might be more reluctance on the part of the aggrieved to bring a claim.[155]

D. ASSESSMENT OF IMPLEMENTATION OF THE DIRECTIVE

117 The Directive has been implemented correctly, as the wording of the special product liability provisions are almost identical to those of the Directive and since all the articles have been implemented in Dutch law. However, it has been argued that the implementation was not effective in the light of the maximum harmonisation principle. Harmonisation has not been fully achieved,

---

[154] *Giesen/Loos* (fn 33) 98.

[155] See for critique on this provision: *HJ Rossel*, De invloed van de regeling inzake produktenaansprakelijkheid op de aansprakelijkheid ex art. 6:173 ex art. 7:24 (1992) 6057–6058 WPNR 535–577.

as the implementation of the Directive has not succeeded in reducing the role of other liability regimes when it comes to product liability.[156]

E. NEW TECHNOLOGY: A PRODUCT IN THE SENSE OF THE PRODUCT LIABILITY REGIME?

118 As explained in section II.B, a product is defined as a movable thing, even if it is incorporated in another movable or immovable thing, including electricity (art 6:187(1) BW). 'Thing' is understood to mean a tangible object that can be subject to human control (art 3:2 BW). The question is whether new technologies, such as autonomous technologies, cloud computing, 3D printing or nanotechnology, fall within the definition of 'product' in the sense of art 6:185 BW.

119 Autonomous technologies, of which self-driving cars are the most famous, have been discussed in the context of product liability most frequently.[157] With regard to such technologies, these are not devices that are directly controlled by humans, but which operate – to a certain extent – fully autonomously.[158] Taking the example of a self-driving car, it becomes clear that it is a combination of a car and software. It consists not only of typical car parts, but also of sensors, computers and automatic control components.[159] The car as such can be understood as a 'product' in the sense of art 6:185 BW, since it is a tangible object. But the software used in the car can also be defined as a 'product', since it is carried on a material carrier.

120 Another example of a new technology is cloud computing. This is defined by the EU as 'the storing, processing and use of data on remotely located computers accessed over the internet'.[160] Thus, without much effort or capital investments, users are able to have access to several computing resources, such as networks, servers, storage, applications, and services, almost everywhere.[161] This whole process of storing, processing and use of data can be defined as a service, rather than a product.[162] Therefore, it might fall outside the scope of art 6:185 ff BW.

121 3D printing is the process by which a model of a 3D object, created in a computer aided design programme, is constructed by a 3D printer out of a

156 *Giesen/Loos* (fn 33) 103.
157 *Van Wees* (fn 8) 133 ff; *Schreuder* (fn 8); *de Vey Mestdagh/Lubbers* (fn 8).
158 *De Vey Mestdagh/Lubbers* (fn 8).
159 Ibid.
160 Unleashing the Potential of Cloud Computing in Europe, COM(2012)529 final of 27.09.2012.
161 Ibid.
162 See also Daniels and Kits, who discuss cloud computing as a service rather than a product; *K Daniels/P Kits*, Contracteren in de cloud: ken uw risico's (2015) 1 Contracteren 2–16.

polymer into a real object.[163] Although most of production using 3D printing is still done by professionals, a growing number of consumers have purchased a 'home' 3D printer.[164] With regard to professional 3D printing, two situations may occur: (i) a consumer buys an object that is made with the 3D printer; or (ii) a consumer commissions someone else to print a certain object designed by the consumer himself. With regard to the first situation, the object that is bought might fall within the notion of 'product', as it is a tangible which can be controlled by humans. With regard to the second situation, this likely falls outside the concept of 'product', as it should be characterised as a service.

122 Another example is nanotechnology. This technology refers to structures and devices at the scale of one billionth of a metre (one nanometre).[165] The applications of nanotechnology are numerous and are still in development. Thus, the potential applications and potential risks might be – to some extent – still unclear to us.[166] In general, nanotechnology can be used to produce or manufacture products (such as with the use of a nano-laser), or it can form part of a product. In that capacity it may not only 'improve' the product in question, but can also pose dangers to health and property.[167] If such a product is a tangible thing, it can be deemed a 'product' in the sense of art 6:185 BW. Interestingly, the literature only discusses whether the notion of 'damage' in the sense of art 6:190 BW is sufficiently broad to also include damage caused by nanotechnology, or whether the development risk defence might be a problem. These authors seem to imply that nanotechnology is a product in the sense of art 6:185 BW.[168]

---

163 *AP Engelfriet*, 3D printen: revolutie of de nieuwe Napster? (2011) Tijdschrift voor Internetrecht 141–144.

164 See on the potential product liability problems that can arise regarding consumer 3D printing: *N Freeman Engstrom*, 3-D Printing and Product Liability: Identifying the Obstacles (2013) 162 University of Pennsylvania Law Review Online 35–41; *ND Berkowitz*, Strict Liability for Individuals? The Impact of 3-D Printing on Product Liability Law (2015) Washington University in Saint Louis, available at: <http://ssrn.com/abstract=2548317>.

165 *G Howells*, Product Liability for Nanotechnology (2009) 32 J Consum Policy 381–391.

166 *M van Zijverden/AJAM Sips*, Nanotechnologie in perspectief. Risico's voor mens en milieu (RIVM report 2008).

167 See for the different applications (the so-called 'four generations' nanotechnology) and the potential risks: *M van Zijverden/AJAM Sips*, Nanotechnologie in perspectief. Risico's voor mens en milieu (RIVM report 2008).

168 In addition, the new risks involved with nanotechnology pose the question whether potential damages would fall within the scope of the notion 'damage' of special product liability law. Also, it is questioned whether the development risk-defence would not stand in the way of a claim under art 6:185 ff. See more on this: *Howells* (fn 165) 381–391; *EM Vogelezang-Stoute/JR Popma/MVC Aalders/JM Gaarthuis*, Regulering van onzekere risico's van nano-materialen. Mogelijkheden en knelpunten in de regelgeving op het gebied van milieu, consumentenbescherming en arbeidsomstandigheden (STEM publication 2010); *ER de Jong* (fn 8) 2836–2843.

PRODUCT LIABILITY IN NORWAY

Bjarte Askeland

I. SOURCES OF LAW AND THEIR EVOLUTION

01 The Norwegian Act on Product Liability was enacted in 1988. The history of product liability within Norwegian law started, however, in the decades before. Several theorists had discussed the problem in Norwegian and Scandinavian literature.[1] The doctrine accepted that damage that resulted from the dangerous properties of a thing should fall under the doctrine of strict liability for dangerous objects. The doctrine is based on Supreme Court practice and the content is that an owner may be liable for damage caused by a risk that is deemed to be 'typical, continuous and extraordinary' stemming from an activity or the use of a thing or property. The doctrine was developed in the decades before 1900.[2] Liability for dangerous things might also be regarded as liability based on the Act on the Sale of Movable Goods 1907. In the literature there was a debate

1 See *T Sandvik*, Ansvar for skadevoldende egenskaper (1964) 49 Norsk forsikringsforenings publikasjoner 3–5 with further references.

2 On the development of and content of the doctrine of strict liability, see *N Nygaard*, Skade og ansvar (2007) 253–282.

on this question, partly generated by the fact that the preparatory works of the Sales Act was unclear on the relevant point. The view that §43 third section of the Sales Act provided a legal basis for liability for dangerous things prevailed and was supported by a majority of commentators.[3] There was, however, some disagreement regarding the extent of liability and rules of adequacy in this respect.[4]

02 Typically for Norwegian tort law, the fact that one legal basis is available does not preclude other legal bases from being applied. The liability was in the last part of the 20th century perceived to be based on two legal instruments: firstly the aforementioned provision in the Sales Act, and secondly the uncodified rule on strict liability for dangerous objects or activity.[5]

03 In 1975 a committee was appointed with a mandate to investigate the liability of producers and distributors of dangerous objects produced and/or sold. The government was informed of and referred to the international investigations on the same matters. Otherwise, the initiative was, however, independent of the international discussions on the subject.[6]

The committee submitted a *Norsk offentlig utredning* (Norwegian Public Investigation/Report, NOU 1980: 29) in 1980. In the mandate it was made clear that the committee was obliged to pay attention to international developments in the relevant field. The committee proposed an Act on Product Liability. The proposal was taken further by the Ministry of Justice in 1988. By this time the EU Directive on Product Liability had been submitted. The Ministry proposed an Act that was based on the NOU 1980: 29, yet it was basically adapted in line with the EU Directive.[7] The Act was enacted on 23 December 1988.[8]

04 The current product liability regulation consists of two parts. The main part of the Product Liability Act (PLA) aims at ordinary products, such as things, machines and other movables defined according to the EU Directive. A special part of the Act (Chapter 3) concerns, however, drugs or other kinds of medical products.[9] The ordinary rules in the Act apply also to drugs, but in the special part there are also some special regulations, all in favour of the potential

---

3 See *Sandvik* (fn 1) 17.

4 The debate on this point is summarised by Sandvik, see *Sandvik* (fn 1) 17–19. Sandvik himself held the view that the liability was merely limited by ordinary rules of adequate causation, see *Sandvik* (fn 1) 23.

5 See the historical overview in *S Rognlien*, Produktansvaret, lov, konvensjoner og lovvalg (1992) 17.

6 See NOU 1980: 29, 11.

7 See *Rognlien* (fn 4) 21.

8 *Lov om produktansvar* 23 December 1988 no 104.

9 See Chapter 3 PLA.

claimant.[10] The liability for damage stemming from drugs is completely strict, whereas the general liability clause in §2–1 may be characterised as almost strict. The requirement of in §2–1 PLA that there must be a defect is thus covered by a provision prescribing strict liability for the producers and vendors of drugs, see §3–3 (1) PLA. There is also a requirement of compulsory liability insurance for producers and vendors, see §3–4 PLA.

05 There have not been any new amendments of the Act to take into account new technologies. Whenever questions of liability arise from damage caused by products using new technologies, they have to be solved by the provisions in the PLA as interpreted in the light of general tort law principles. Only some of the rules of product liability have been enacted, whereas others must be inferred from the general rules and principles of tort law. Hence, only the legal basis of liability is described in a manner that provides any guidance for the judge, see no 06 ff.

II. BASIC ELEMENTS OF LIABILITY

06 The requirement for liability is that a product has a defect (*sikkerhetsmangel*) in the eyes of the law, that there is damage, and that there is a causal link between the defect and the damage. The formulation of the requirement of there being defect establishes a normative standard with guidelines presented in §2–1 (1) second sentence. This provision reads that the consideration of whether there is a safety defect must take into account all the circumstances connected to the product, the presentation and the marketing of the product, and the expected use of the product. The producer may, however free himself from liability if he can prove that the cause of the defect was that the product was satisfying mandatory provisions of safety imposed by the authorities, see §2–2 (c) PLA.

07 The concept of 'product' is defined as 'all kinds of goods or movables', see §1–2 (1) PLA. It is additionally specified that the concept comprises both natural products and industrial products, part of a product and a whole product. It is clearly stated in the Act that a movable attached to immovable property falls under the Act, see §1–2 (1) PLA. In the early doctrine it was discussed whether or not computers and discs may be products, something which has been answered in the affirmative.[11] There is, however, an established delimitation of the concept of product that rests on the idea that the Act only comprises material products. Hence software and other kinds of intellectual property fall outside the scope of the Act. In connection with this, it has been discussed whether or not ready-

10 On the special features of regulation of drugs within product liability law, see *O André Oftebro/KW Kielland*, Produktansvarsloven med kommentarer (2015) 15–21.

11 See *Rognlien* (fn 4).

made *kasetter* (this must probably be translated as 'cassettes') – for practical purposes discs or other kinds of physical objects with programmes and/or content on them, and corresponding properties – fall within the definition of a product. It is suggested that a guideline for determining this is whether the item can be looked at mainly as a *konsulent tjeneste*, meaning an immaterial service of programming. If so, the service falls outside the scope of the Act. If, however, the immaterial service also comprises a material object, it is suggested that the object may generate liability on the basis of the PLA. In the preparatory works of the Act the Ministry of Justice stated that electricity in itself is not a product, an interpretation that seems a bit problematic in view of the Directive.[12] This shortcoming was, however, amended at a later stage: In connection with Norway's bilateral agreement with the EU of 1992, it was clearly stated in the wording of §1–2 (1) second sentence that electricity is covered by the concept of product under the Act.[13] As for water, gas and petroleum, these are objects that are clearly included in the scope of the Act, according to the preparatory works.[14] As for blood and body parts, these items are not specifically mentioned in the preparatory works or case law within the field. It is however in theoretical works assumed that blood may fall within the concept of product.[15] This does not contradict the wording of the Act, which broadly mentions drugs or substances employed to prevent, heal or ease illness; see §3–2 PLA, which refers to the definitions in *Legemiddelloven* §2.[16] Interpreting the Act so that it covers blood is still a faithful interpretation of the Act.

08 Items or objects created using specific individual designs are regarded as products. As long as the product is material in nature, the fact that the individual design or construction represents the major part of the value of the object does not preclude the object from being a product in the eyes of the law. The proportion between the value created by the design and the value of the material itself is of no importance.

09 The concept of defect is expressed by a new invention within Norwegian tort law, namely the concept of a *sikkerhetsmangel* – see the wording in §2–1 (1) PLA. The Norwegian words may be directly translated as a 'lack of security'. This expression intends to capture the situation where an object represents a greater danger than what could normally be expected. In the preparatory works for the Act, it was stated by the Ministry of Justice that the concept of *sikkerhetsmangel* is meant to be equivalent to the concept of 'defect' within the Directive.[17]

12 See NOU 1980: 29, 180.
13 Cf Ot. prp. no 72 (1991–92) 28–30.
14 See Ot. prp. no 48 (1987–88) 47.
15 *Rognlien* (fn 4) 279.
16 See *Lov om legemidler med videre* 20 June 1964 no 5 §2.
17 See Ot. prp. no 48 (1987–88) 33.

10 The basis of liability is formulated in a manner that makes manufacturing, design or presentation defects relevant to the standard. This follows from the second sentence in the provision in §2-1 (1) PLA. In the assessment of whether a defect is present, one should consider all aspects of the product, its presentation, marketing and foreseeable application. This does not actually make a distinction between the three kinds of defect (manufacturing, design or presentation), but rather clarifies that all three aspects are relevant to the question of liability.

11 The standard may in principle and theoretically be changed by prospective overruling. It falls within the tradition of the Supreme Court to point out the direction for the future, typically as *obiter dicta*. In recent decades the courts have, however, been modest regarding *obiter dicta* that may have a prospective overruling effect. It is therefore not very likely that such decisions will occur.

12 When it comes to the digital or intellectual content of products, the preparatory works have set out clear constraints. It has been held that the Product Liability Act only covers material products; hence, mere intellectual products and software products fall outside the scope of the Act.[18] It has been consistently held that a map containing incorrect information should not be considered a product that renders a producer liable; such cases should be governed by the normal *culpa* rule.[19] A book analysing the Act makes a clear division between merely intellectual presentations or products and products of a material nature.[20]

13 The committee held that a product may not render liability based on the Act in the time period before the product is '*satt i omsetning*', an expression which means 'put into the commercial sphere', see §1-1 PLA. This criterion sought to exclude liability based on events taking place after the product has been finished, but before it has been put into circulation.[21] The initial goal of the drafters of the law was to use an expression that fitted the Directive.[22] It is decisive that the product has left the production process and entered the sphere of marketing and sales, so that it is offered to consumers.[23] The intention of the drafters was to make the producer or seller responsible for any event arising from the time period before the product was left to the consumer. Hence the Act was meant to set a time limit for the responsibility at the point in time when the product was no longer under the producer or seller's physical control. The original wording

18 See *Rognlien* (fn 4) 147–148; also *Oftebro/Kielland* (fn 10) 40.
19 See *Oftebro/Kielland* (fn 10) 40.
20 *Rognlien* (fn 4) 147–148. This work was written by the leader of the committee that drafted the Act, Stein Rognlien.
21 See Ot. prp. no 48 (1987–88) 63.
22 See Ot. prp. no 72 (1991–92), 64.
23 *Oftebro/Kielland* (fn 10) 31 with reference to the ECJ case C-86/09.

of the Act at this point was, however, changed because it did not fit the wording of the Directive.[24] It is assumed by academics that where the producer sends a product to a retailer, but still has control over the transport and hence being able to stop it, the product has not yet been put into circulation in the eyes of the law.[25] Accordingly the development on this point may still be interpreted such that defects stemming from improper storage or forwarding may give rise to product liability.

14 The expression '*satt i omsetning*' ('put into circulation') is paired with the requirement that only products put into circulation in connection with professional activity may lead to liability on the basis of the Act. In the preparatory works it is mentioned that this avoids production merely for the producer's own use falling within the scope of liability. The requirement must be coordinated with the criterion '*gitt til forbruk*' in §1–2 (2), which may be translated as 'made available to consumer'. In §1–2 (2) PLA this is defined as the point in time when the consumer has 'taken over' or 'started using' the product.

15 As for instructions, they may in principle be regarded as a defect of the product, provided that they mislead the customer such that a risk is created.[26] Commentators on the Product Liability Act seem, however, to emphasise that one cannot expect very much from the producer regarding instructions.[27]

16 The law does not define in detail the standard expected from the producer. The legislator seems to lean very much on the standard of what may normally be expected by the probable group of customers. The producer will therefore have to take the measures necessary to make the products safe, without any specific guidance from the Product Liability Act. There is, however, a realm of administrative regulation governing manufacturing, which for practical purposes may be relevant to the question of whether a defect has occurred. If for example food products have not been prepared properly according to standards described in administrative regulations, this violation of an administrative rule may in itself be relevant to the question of whether or not there is a defect. Under Norwegian law there is a long tradition of applying administrative regulations when examining how tortfeasor has behaved.[28] In general, failing to comply with administrative regulations will count against the alleged tortfeasor; however, it will not be decisive in itself.

---

24 See Ot. prp. no 72 (1991–92) 34, cf *Oftebro/Kielland* (fn 10) 31.

25 See *Oftebro/Kielland* (fn 10) 31.

26 The consequences of faulty or misleading instructions are elaborated in *Rognlien* (fn 4) 193–194.

27 *Rognlien* (fn 4) 193–194.

28 See on this subject *B Askeland,* Tort and regulatory law in Norway, in: W van Boom/M Lukas/C Kissling (eds), Tort and regulatory law (2007) 205–218.

17 As explained above, there is a special liability and insurance regime for medical products. The liability is completely strict and there is compulsory insurance. The whole regime on drug products is very strict and the expectations of consumers are correspondingly high. It should be mentioned that the regulation of drugs is severe. Many drugs allowed in other EU countries are not allowed or sold in Norway. Other than this, there are no special regulations for special products; hence the general rules otherwise apply.

18 Scholars have classified product liability as a certain kind of strict (no fault) liability for which elements of the *culpa* standard are integrated into the requirement of liability. The liability clause in §2-1 PLA has thus been compared to a subcategory within the case law that falls under the uncodified rule of strict liability, the so-called '*objektivt ansvar for uforsvarlig ordning*', which may be translated as 'strict liability for negligent arrangements'.[29] Hence the basis of liability is a sort of hybrid between culpa and strict liability. The main feature of this category is that even though the legal basis is strict, weight is given to the fact that the alleged tortfeasor could have acted differently in order to avoid the accident. This is liability for 'avoidable' damage, in contrast to strict liability, which concerns 'unavoidable' damage.[30] Even though the basis of liability is theoretically categorised as explained above there have not been any cases where the product liability clause in §2-1 PLA has been interpreted in the light of the cases of strict liability mentioned above. This is probably because there are merely theoretical similarities between the categories, such as that the bases for liability in both may be said to be located in the 'grey area' between *culpa* and strict liability. Still, there may be profound differences in the actual structure and argumentation in the cases of 'strict liability for negligent arrangement' mentioned above and the basis of product liability. After all, product liability has at its core the sale of goods, whereas the mentioned special kind of strict liability applies to many other areas of life. Another point that should also be mentioned is that, according to the legal method within Norwegian law, it is not conventional to interpret a statutory provision in the light of other parallel, uncodified rules of liability based on case law. The product liability clause in §2-1 PLA seems to live its life of its own, where the key requirement seems to be what level of security the probable users generally expect.

19 In this respect the consumer cannot claim damage that is caused by a risk that was known beforehand. This interpretation of the provision came to the fore in a case about an allergic dentist, Rt. 2004, 122. A dentist used a mixture

---

29 See *N Nygaard*, Skade og ansvar (6th edn 2007) 254–257. Cases of this category are for example Rt. 1991, 1303 and Rt. 2000, 388.

30 A resembling legal basis of liability is established under Swedish law, named '*bristfälliga anordningar*', see on the subject *H Andersson*, Ansvarsproblem (2013) 111–134.

made for preserving teeth. The mixture contained chemical substances, Syntac, Tetric and Fermit, which the dentist was allergic to. He wore gloves in order to avoid allergic reactions, but nevertheless developed a rash and other allergic reactions. He had to terminate his work and business as a dentist. He claimed compensation for his loss of income from the importer of the mixture he had used. The Supreme Court found that the importer was not responsible for the damage because the risk was known to the dentist. The court found support for this view in the preparatory works of the Product Liability Act. There were statements saying that the user of the product must bear the risk when the risk is known beforehand and is a necessary feature of the function of the product.[31] Hence the Supreme Court found that the risk in question must be looked upon as an unavoidable occupational hazard for which the Product Liability Act provided for grounds for liability. In a case against a tobacco producer where a smoker claimed compensation for loss stemming from cancer caused by smoking, the Supreme Court stated that the risk of smoking was known to the public and hence that there could be no liability on the basis of §2–1 PLA.[32]

III. THE PERSON LIABLE FOR DAMAGE

20 The liable persons are described in §1–3 PLA, which nominates six categories of possible liable persons: (i) the producer or manufacturer of the product; (ii) 'anyone' who offers a product for sale by placing their name, trade mark or other sign of identification or recognition on the product; (iii) a seller of the product, provided that the producer cannot be identified without difficulties and the seller does not provide information on the name of the producer or a previous seller within a reasonable time; (iv) sellers of unrefined products of nature; (v) importers of products from a foreign country; and (vi) sellers of imported products, if the seller does not provide information on the name of the importer within a reasonable time.

21 The PLA and the liability clause apply only to producers who put their product into circulation in connection with their professional business. This may be inferred from the special wording in §1–1, '*i tilknytning til yrkesmessig sammenheng*', which means that the sale must be connected to business activity. The reason for this delimitation was specified in the preparatory works: the aim was to avoid producers becoming liable for products made for their own use, meaning that the liability regime of the PLA should not cover so-called 'hobby products'.[33]

---

31 See NOU 1992: 29, 83 and Ot. prp. no 48 (1987–88) 127.

32 See the case referred in Rt. 2003, 1546.

33 See NOU 1980: 29, 99 and Ot. prp. no 48 (1991–92), 7.

22 These rules also apply to public entities. Hospitals owned by the state may accordingly be liable. Public entities providing different kinds of control or supervision of products in the market may, however, not be liable on the basis of the PLA, even if the public entity ought to have discovered a defect.[34] An entity controlling lifts may thus not be liable for overlooking a defect in a lift being controlled by the entity.

23 If more than one person fulfils the requirements for liability, the general rule on solidary liability applies, see the Norwegian Compensatory Damages Act (*Skadeserstatningsloven* 13 June 1969 no 26, skl.), §5–3.[35] This rule has the same effect as arts 9:101 and 9:102 of the Principles of European Tort Law. Each of the liable parties is obliged to pay all of the damages when rightfully claimed, see skl. §5–3 first section. The responsible parties may on the other hand bring a recourse action against each other, see skl. §5–3 second section. This recourse action against the other tortfeasor(s) and the contribution allocated to each of them are governed by the proportionate quality or quantity of their contribution to the damage. If there are no specific arguments against dividing the loss equally between each of the tortfeasors, the loss will be divided equally.[36]

IV. THE AGGRIEVED PERSON AND DAMAGE

24 §2–3 of the Product Liability Act delimits the sphere of potential claimants by requiring that the damage must have struck a person (§2–3 (1) (a)) – as a personal injury – or a thing that normally for the main part is used in the capacity of being a consumer or a thing that *in fact* has been used for the main part in the capacity of a consumer. The question of whether the law applies to a thing must be taken on the basis of the use of the thing at the time the damage occurred. However, the formulation '*hovedsaklig*' – 'for the main part' – makes it possible to put weight on the normal private use of the thing, even if it was being used otherwise at the time the damage occurred.[37] As an additional limitation the Act expresses that the damage to the thing itself is not covered by liability under the Act. Likewise damage to another thing that the product is incorporated in is excluded, provided that the incorporation of the damaging thing is done before the product is put into circulation. The delimitations mean that damage to things used for business purposes are not protected by the Act.

34 See *Oftebro/Kielland* (fn 10) 45.
35 This follows from regular tort law principles, see also *Rognlien* (fn 4) 163.
36 See *B Askeland*, Tapsfordeling og regress ved erstatningsoppgjør (2006) 206–209.
37 *Oftebro/Kielland* (fn 10) 77.

25 The concept of damage is based on the general concept of damage within tort law. It is, however, suggested that pure economic loss arising from the damaging event is not comprised.[38] This is consistent with the tradition regarding strict liability. This tradition has, however, come under pressure. Theorists now claim that there is no reason to treat pure economic loss differently from other types of loss.[39] There is also good support for such a view in case law.[40] This change in the prevailing view may also affect the view on product liability, meaning that it will be possible to have a claim despite the fact that no physical or material damage has occurred. There have, however, so far not been any cases addressing this kind of problem.

26 Damage that is eligible for redress is first and foremost personal injuries and pecuniary loss stemming from damage to things for a consumer's personal use. Damage to the product itself, damage to business property and pure economic loss are not eligible due to the exclusion clauses in the Act noted for above. Loss of chance has a very insecure position within Norwegian doctrine.[41] Hence it is highly uncertain whether it would be feasible to win a case based on harm of that nature. The area of product liability does not in itself particularly invite claims for this kind of harm.

There is a lower limit of liability, a sort of *de minimis* rule expressed in §2-3 (3) PLA. This rule is formulated as a rule on reduction of the damage by NOK 4,000 (approximately €400). The aim of the provision is to avoid small claims. The reduction is automatic, hence for every award of compensation there will be a subtraction of NOK 4,000. There is no upper limit or cap on the possible award. However, the general reduction clause in skl. §5-2 applies. This means that if the award is considered to be unreasonably high in view of the tortfeasor's financial capacity, the gravity of his conduct and other circumstances, the award may be reduced to a proportion that is realistic for the tortfeasor to pay. The possibility of claiming reduction is weaker whenever the tortfeasor has third-party liability insurance. All these guidelines are directly set out in the text of skl. §5-2.

V. CAUSALITY

27 The general rules of factual and legal causation are applicable in respect of product liability.[42] Thus the general rules apply to the question of whether there

---

38 *Rognlien* (fn 4) 233.
39 See *B Thorson*, Erstatningsrettslig vern for rent formuestap (2011) 61.
40 See Rt. 2006, 690.
41 See *M Strandberg*, Skadelidte hypotetiske inntekt (2005) 105–113.
42 *Rognlien* (fn 4) 204–209.

is adequate causation between the defect and the damage. There are no special principles or rules of causality regarding product liability. Neither proportionate liability nor loss of a chance have any tradition within Norwegian tort law, hence none of these legal instruments comes into play.

28 The structure of the Norwegian liability rules on product liability focuses the causal questions on the connection between the defective product and the damage. Of course there are also elements of causation on other points in the rules to be applied, but the causation problems of whether A or B have produced a product or whether A or B has put it into circulation have not come to the fore. An important case on product liability and causation was Rt. 1992, 64. The case concerned a woman who suffered from severe heart disease while using contraceptive pills. The crucial point of the case was whether the use of the pills was a sufficient cause when taking into consideration other causes and conditions involved, for example the woman's smoking habits. The question of evidence was also at stake: it had to be proved that it was sufficiently probable that the use of the contraceptive pill had had a negative impact on the woman's health conditions. This question of evidence was governed by the general rule on evidence under civil law: the fact that the pill was a cause must be proven to be more likely than not. The Supreme Court found that it was more likely than not that the defective contraceptive pill had had an impact, *and* that this impact was necessary and not entirely immaterial for the occurrence of the heart disease. Hence the requirements of causation and evidence in this respect were met. As a result, the manufacturer of the pill was held responsible on the basis of strict liability. The facts of the case took place before the Product Liability Act was enacted (1988). Hence the decision was based on the uncodified rules of strict liability that were the only option before the statutory provision came into force. The result would, however, have been exactly the same had the PLA been applied. As mentioned above, medical products are governed by a special part of the PLA. For medical products the rules are entirely of strict liability, hence the regulation is more advantageous for the victim than elsewhere and for other products.

29 In the event that a third party external to the producer and the aggrieved party contributes to the damage, the regulation depends on whether the third party is responsible for the damage according to tort law or not. There has to be a legal basis for liability and the requirements of causation mentioned above in no 27 must be met. If the third party is liable, the question is governed by the general rule of multiple tortfeasors, on which see skl. §5-3 and the presentation of this rule above no 24 ff.

30 If the third party is *not* liable because the requirements of liability and causation are not met, the question will indirectly be solved by the rules of causation, more specifically the principle of equivalence. It has for a long time been held that each cause, regardless of dimension, is a cause of *all of the damage*, provided that the cause is necessary and not entirely immaterial to the damaging effect.[43] Since every necessary cause of damage will be responsible for all of the damage, the producer will be liable for all of the damage regardless of the fact that there is a third party involved that has also contributed to the damage.

31 In principle the contribution from the aggrieved party will be regulated by the general tort law rule in skl. §5–1, which has many similarities to art 8:101 of the Principles of European Tort Law. Provided that the aggrieved party was negligent, the award will *be reduced* in proportion to the gravity of fault, the nature of the respective causal contributions of the parties, the availability of insurance, and other circumstances. The broad set of factors relevant for consideration leaves the judge ample room for discretion.

VI. DEFENCES AND EXCLUSIONS

32 When drafting the Norwegian Product Liability Act, the legislator clearly presupposed that the risk should be allocated to the producer, not the victim. The provision in §2–1 (2) reads that the general consideration of the level of the product security should be fixed to the point in time when the product is put into circulation. It is still presupposed that the liability comprises development risks. The Ministry of Justice held in the preparatory works that the producer was closer to shoulder the risk of unknown risks that developed later than the consumer.[44] Moreover, it was mentioned that the Ministry of Justice could not see any arguments that in principle made it undesirable to let the product liability cover development risks. It was also mentioned that letting the consumer bear any loss stemming from development risks would contradict the considerations of risk allocations that were common and traditional to Norwegian tort law and consumer law.[45] Even though there have been no cases where liability for development risk has been assigned to the producer, such a solution would be the most consistent with the Norwegian basis of liability. A case on general strict liability from 2003 also speaks in favour of moving in this direction. In Rt. 2003, 1546 some employees sued their employer for the personal injuries caused by exposure at their workplace to a certain substance, which eventually caused lung disease. At the time of the exposure it was unknown to all that the exposure could have this effect. Still the employer was found liable according to the general, uncodified rule of strict liability mentioned in no 01 ff. The

---

43 In fact, these general requisites of causation were clearly formulated in the case on defective contraceptive pills mentioned above, Rt. 1992, 64.

44 *Rognlien* (fn 4) 201.

45 See Ot. prp. no 48 (1987–88) 40–41.

Supreme Court made in this respect some statements relevant to the question of development risks. It was held, amongst other arguments, that the employer would be closer to shoulder unknown risks than the victim. Legal theorists also hold, albeit on other grounds than in that case, that placing the development risk on the producer is the right interpretation of §2–1 PLA.[46] Hagstrøm and Stenvik also point out that product liability may only in extreme cases be limited by arguments of adequacy.[47]

33 The development risk defence may not be applied to design defects or any kind of defect, according to the stance presented above.

34 Compliance with administrative regulations will in general constitute an argument against liability; however it will not in principle be in any way a decisive argument. This is the general stance on the relationship between tort and regulatory law in Norway.[48] One should at this point note that there are a lot of acts and regulations on product control within Norwegian law.[49] These acts and corresponding administrative regulations will give guidance when deciding whether the producer has met the standards of §2–1 PLA in concrete cases. In spite of this, the producer may be liable despite having complied with the provisions or regulations. Hence it may be emphasised that the primary responsibility for avoiding damage lies with the producer.[50]

There is a special provision in §2–2 (c) PLA that the producer will be exonerated if the defect is caused by the fact that the product must comply with a regulation imposed by the public authorities. The exception clause is of minor practical importance, because it is extremely rare for the regulations to be the cause of the defect.[51] One example would, however, be if public authorities were to decide that a special kind of substance should be used in a certain kind of food production, but that substance later turns out to be damaging to health.[52]

35 According to Norwegian tort law principles, it is not possible to avoid a general liability clause by contractual exclusion. Such clauses will be deemed to be void according to the general clause on void contracts in the Act on Contracts (*Avtaleloven*, avtl.) §36.[53] Limitation clauses can easily be declared

---

46 See *M Strandberg*, in: Karnov Norsk Lovkommentar/Gyldendal Rettsdata, comments to Produktansvarsloven note 49 (2); *Rognlien* (fn 4) 200–201; and *V Hagstrøm/A Stenvik*, Erstatningsrett (2015) 312–331.

47 *V Hagstrøm/A Stenvik* (fn 46) 313.

48 See *B Askeland* (fn 19) 205–218.

49 See for example *Lov om produktkontroll* 11 June 1976 no 79, cf also *Rognlien* (fn 4) 51–54.

50 *Rognlien* (fn 4) 52.

51 See *Strandberg* (fn 41) note 55.

52 The example is mentioned in *Oftebro/Kielland* (fn 10) 73.

53 See *Lov om slutninger av avtaler* 31 May 1918 §36.

void pursuant to avtl. §36. This is a natural consequence of mandatory consumer protection regulation.

VII. REMEDIES

36 On the basis of the Product Liability Act the aggrieved party may only pursue claims for economic loss stemming from the defect. Compensation for non-pecuniary loss may, however, be claimed on the basis of the general clause on personal injury in skl. §3–5, provided that the defective product has caused personal injury and that the producer has shown gross negligence. The gross negligence must, however, be assigned to a legal person, either an individual producer or the board of directors of a company, according to the so-called 'organ theory'.[54] This means that for practical purposes it must be proven that the management of a company has shown gross negligence in the manufacturing or marketing of a product.

37 As for restoration in kind, this possibility has historically in general been at the claimant's disposal, but it is however rarely an option nowadays. Restoration in kind may only occur where a product has damaged another thing, which in turn must be replaced by the tortfeasor.

38 Non-compensatory damages are not available at all under the Product Liability Act regime. There is no tradition of such compensation within Norwegian law or Scandinavian law in general.[55]

39 The Product Liability Act does not allow the aggrieved party to request an injunction. However, the public authorities may have a legal basis for injunctions in other acts; see especially the Act on Control of Products (*Produktkontroll-loven*), and the further explanation of these issues in no 45 ff below.

VIII. PROCEDURAL AND EVIDENTIAL ISSUES

40 The burden of proof rests on the claimant, who must prove that the facts of the case on which he bases his claim did occur. The general rule on evidence within civil procedure applies.[56]

---

[54] See an elaboration of this subject in *B Askeland*, Erstatningsrettslig identifikasjon (2002) 280–294 and in *V Hagstrøm/A Stenvik* (fn 46) 249–253.

[55] See *B Askeland*, Punitive damages in Scandinavia, in: H Koziol/V Wilcox (eds), Punitive Damages in Europe (2009).

[56] *Tvisteloven* 17 June 2005 no 90 §3–21 first section.

41 This means that the claimant must convince the judges that it is more probable than not that the alleged facts of the case did occur. The facts to be proven are the existence of a defect as defined in §2-1 PLA, the damage, and a causal link between the defect and the damage. Cases on product liability in Norway sometimes revolve around the question of whether it is sufficiently proven that there is a causal link between the defect and the damage. This is often difficult to prove with sufficient certainty.[57]

42 The Product Liability Act has a special provision in §2-2 which grants the producer an opportunity to exonerate himself by proving that the product was not put into circulation by him at the time of the damage.

43 The limitation period for claims is three years from the time when the claimant ought to have discovered the damage, the identity of the tortfeasor and the causal link between the defect and the damage (see the general Act on Limitation, fel. §§9 cf 3). These general rules are supplemented by a specific twenty-year long-stop provision that specifies that the long-stop period commences on the day the product left the control of the producer. The general rules apply regarding the process of interruption of the limitation period. Hence, the limitation period is interrupted if the tortfeasor accepts that he is responsible and obligated to pay or when a lawsuit is filed against the tortfeasor (see fel. §15).

44 Attorney's fees are relatively high and may deter people from pursuing cases regarding minor losses. Since 2008 there has been the possibility of class actions within Norwegian law, but the instrument has, however, hardly ever been applied.

IX. ALTERNATIVE REGULATIONS AND REMEDIES

A. GENERAL OVERVIEW

45 Other rules of liability may within certain limits apply contemporaneously with the Product Liability Act. In this respect there has been a debate in Norway on whether the general and traditional uncodified rule of strict liability for dangerous things may apply alongside the Product Liability Act. The disagreement between theorists on this point stems from a slight contradiction between the Norwegian Act and the practice of the European Court of Justice. In §1-1 (2) PLA it is stated that the Act does not preclude the validity of other legal bases for claims on product liability. If one interprets this provision in light of the traditional Norwegian tort law rules, this means that

57 See *Oftebro/Kielland* (fn 10) 65–66.

the uncodified strict liability also applies in the area of the PLA. The ECJ has however, in several cases, stated that the Product Liability Directive is to be interpreted as a full harmonisation directive. Some scholars hold that this has no consequences for the strict liability rule.[58] Other scholars hold, on the other hand, that the ECJ cases mean that there is no room for traditional, uncodified strict liability on the area regulated by the Act. The supporting argument is that the uncodified, strict liability regime would be *stricter* towards the defendant than the PLA, and allowing for such a legal basis of liability would contradict the full harmonisation effect of the Directive.[59] For my part, I agree with the latter opinion. The other view would mean that we have a whole different liability regime in Norway and it would directly undermine the idea of full harmonisation in this area.

46 Article 13 of the Directive and the corresponding ECJ case law only forbid liability regimes that are stricter towards the defendant than the Directive. Hence, other liability regimes can in theory apply, such as the Norwegian *Bilansvarsloven* (Act on Motor Vehicle Insurance).[60] This will, however, have no practical importance.

47 If the Product Liability Act is not applicable, the victim may sue the alleged producer on the basis of *Håndverkertjenesteloven* (an act on the quality of services).

B. DUTY TO RECALL

48 §6a *Lov om kontroll med produkter og forbrukertjenester* provides a specific legal basis for recalling defective products. The provision delegates to the government the competence to recall products whenever safety is considered to be threatened.

C. PUBLIC LAW MEASURES

49 By far the most important source of remedies for victims of personal injury is the social security system. This system guarantees for example that some 60% of lost income will be compensated. A remedy worth mentioning is the administrative organ, the *Forbrukerombud*, a public entity that helps

58 See *A Kjønstad*, Det nyeste rettskildematerialet om objektivt ansvar, LoR 2004, 579–506.
59 *A Stenvik*, Erstatningsrettens internasjonalisering, TfE 2005, 33–61, 43–44; *H Gismarvik Høvik*, Produktansvar i et EØS-rettslig perspektiv, TfE 2007, 22–49, 40.
60 *Lov om ansvar for skade som motorvogner gjer* 3 February 1961.

consumers whenever their rights *qua* consumers are violated or threatened. The *Forbrukerombud* often provides in legal advices and also informs the press if there are any newsworthy situations within a certain branch of business or if specific business actors have conducted their business in an unacceptable manner. A consumer may receive monetary compensation by bargaining with the producer or seller with the support of the *Forbrukerombud*.

X. ASSESSMENT OF DOMESTIC LAW

50 The special Product Liability Act is not often much applied in practice. The reasons for this is probably first and foremost that there are relatively few defective products on the market as a result of strict and effective control mechanisms, and secondly because the possible awards in such cases are too small to make it worthwhile for the victim to pursue his case.

51 There are in my opinion no significant negative effects of the regulation seen from the perspective of the aggrieved party. The almost strict liability on the part of the producer and seller makes it relatively easy to establish that a product is dangerous whenever this really is the case. The acts and regulations of product control seem to work together with the Product Liability Act very well, meaning that the consumer is well protected.

52 For producers and sellers a possible negative effect of the regime may be that they can easily become liable once a dangerous product is put into circulation. This fact may motivate producers and sellers to avoid risks, and thus has a preventive or deterrent effect. In order to prevent risks or damage, producers and sellers may have to set up costly manufacturing processes and quality-control mechanisms. This may be perceived negatively by producers and sellers, from a strictly economic perspective because it reduces profit.

53 The definition of a 'thing' or 'product' in the Norwegian Act is not sufficient to cover all the new technologies discussed in the introduction. The fact that the Norwegian preparatory works quite crudely stated that the Act should only apply to 'material' things, hence leaving out 'immaterial things', seems to me to be entirely inadequate as a guideline for categorising new technologies. This distinction will leave modern phenomena such as data software, or cloud computing or self-configuring systems, for that matter, outside the scope of the Act, even though the legislator has not really considered whether this is the right solution taking policy into account. It seems to me that the drafters of the Act have not paid sufficient attention to the fact that an immaterial idea, principle or mechanism may have damaging effects in the real world. It is somewhat

coincidental whether such an idea or principle has a physical representation through some kind of material device, such as a floppy disk or a pen drive, for that matter, or is downloaded entirely virtually from the Internet. The state of technology was different at the time the PLA was enacted; hence the legislator did not have any incentive to discuss these kinds of problems. Today, where everyday life in Europe is highly influenced by the virtual world of devices and means of communication, it really should not play a decisive part whether or not an advanced technology has a material representation in the real world.

PRODUCT LIABILITY IN POLAND

Ewa Bagińska

I. SOURCES OF LAW AND THEIR EVOLUTION

A. THE SCOPE OF THE LAW IMPLEMENTING THE PRODUCT LIABILITY DIRECTIVE

01 Polish product liability law is based on Directive 374/85/EEC. The Directive was implemented by the Act of 2 March 2000 on the protection of certain consumer rights, on product liability and the amendment of the Civil Code, which entered into force on 1 July 2000.[1] The Act revised the Civil Code in respect of unfair contract terms and product liability.

02 No other system of compensation for losses caused by defective products or services is in place.[2]

03 The product liability regime was introduced into the Civil Code as a new title VI *prim* (articles 449^1–449^{11} *kodeks cywilny* (Civil Code, CC)) in the Book on Obligations, which follows Title VI on Torts and precedes Title VII on Performance of obligations and effects of their non-performance. In spite of this ostensible separation from tortious liability, most of the common rules concerning civil liability (arts 361–363 CC), as well as the provisions governing torts, such as those on compensation of personal injuries, are applicable to product liability claims.

04 It should be stressed that distinguishing product liability claims from tort claims is fallacious. A product liability claim is definitely a tort claim under Polish law. This is the dominant position in the legal writings and the sole position to be found in case law.[3] Title VI^1 (*prim*) of the Civil Code, which implemented the Directive, was opted for due to the fact that it was technically more convenient to create an additional chapter in the Code than to insert several new provisions in the existing section (Title VI). Nevertheless, a minority

---

1 Dziennik Ustaw (Official Journal, DzU), 2002, no 22 item 271. The Act implemented four EC Directives: Directive 85/577, Directive 97/7, Directive 93/13 and Directive 85/374/.

2 The strict liability for GMO products, prescribed by a separate legal act, should be regarded as special rules. Article 57 of Act of 22 June 2001 on Genetically Modified Organisms (DzU 2001, no 76, item 811, with amendments).

3 See *E Baginska*, Nowe unormowanie odpowiedzialności cywilnej za produkt (2000) 9 Przegląd Sądowy; *Z Banaszczyk*, in: M Safjan, in: K Pietrzykowski (ed), Kodeks cywilny. Komentarz (4th edn 2005), cmt to art 449^1 no 3; *W Czachórski*, Zobowiązania, in: M Kaliński, Szkoda na mieniu i jej naprawienie (2008) 46; *E Łętowska*, Ochrona niektórych praw konsumentów. Komentarz (2001) 113, 121; *F Mohmand*, Odpowiedzialność za produkt w prawie polskim na tle porównawczym (2008); *M Nesterowicz*, Odpowiedzialność za produkt (1993) 4 Kwartalnik Prawa Prywatnego 485; *M Jagielska*, in: A Olejniczak (ed), System prawa prywatnego, vol. 6, Prawo zobowiązań – część ogólna (2nd edn 2014). A bit unclear, but inclining towards the delictual nature of product liability *W Dubis*, in: E Gniewek/ P Machnikowski (ed), Kodeks cywilny. Komentarz (6th edn 2014) 905, no 3.

view, represented by the authors of a major textbook on the law of obligations[4] and other distinguished writers,[5] states that product liability is a risk-based regime situated in between contractual and delictual liability, and should be distinguished from the 'regular' tort liability by the following features:

- separate rules on prescription of claims;
- different regulation of joint and several liability;
- special prohibition of exclusions or limitations to the liability (art 449^9 CC); and
- a separate rule on the concurrence of liabilities.

05 The above minority position has been convincingly criticised by its opponents, who have emphasised not only the genesis of product liability in foreign legal systems, which had determined the development of a producer's tort, but also the basic elements of the cause of action, the characteristic features of liability, the incompleteness of the rules on the redress of personal injuries, and finally also the Polish traditional approach to product liability claims prior to the implementation of the Directive (see *infra* no 06 ff).[6] Further, the Product Liability Directive also does not cover all aspects of liability cases. Consequently, the provisions which implement the Directive do not cover issues such as causation and the assessment of damages (especially of non-pecuniary damages), which are governed by general rules. Moreover, the burden of proof of demonstrating liability falls on the plaintiff pursuant to art 6 CC. It is thus clear that the incorporation of the product liability rules as Title VI^1 of the Civil Code aimed at coherence and completeness of the regulation.[7]

B. PRIOR REGIME – TORTIOUS LIABILITY FOR DEFECTIVE PRODUCTS UNDER THE CIVIL CODE

06 Before the implementation of the Directive, producer's liability was based on fault. No other special liability regime, or even a single provision, with regard to product liability was in place. Products involving new technologies have so far not caught the attention of the Polish legislator.

---

4 See *Z Radwański/A Olejniczak*, Zobowiązania- część ogólna (11th edn 2014). Professor Radwański was the President of the Commission on Codification of Civil Law when the implementation of the Directive was on the agenda.

5 See *J Rajski*, Odpowiedzialnosc za produkt niebezpieczny w świetle nowych przepisów kodeksu cywilnego (2001) 100 Przegląd Prawa Handlowego 23; *Z Strus*, Odpowiedzialność za szkodę wyrządzoną przez produkt niebezpieczny (2001) 1 Palestra 25; *M Kępiński*, O zakresie odpowiedzialności za produkt, in: Rozprawy prawnicze. Księga pamiątkowa Profesora Maksymiliana Pazdana (2005) 1037.

6 In particular by *Mohmand* (fn 3) 118–121 and *Jagielska* (fn 3) 965–967.

7 See *Baginska* (fn 3) and *Nesterowicz* (fn 3) 485.

07 In common with other legal systems, the Polish product liability regime started its evolution from cases based on contract law. As contract law with its privity limitations and restrictions on recoverable damage did not offer acceptable solutions to the challenges posed by this new legal problem, the judiciary and scholars turned their attention to tort law; hence at present product liability law is firmly grounded within tortious liability.[8] In the 1960s, tortious product liability developed based on the general tortious liability clause in the Civil Code (art 415). Courts applied this provision to the liability of producers and/or sellers who marketed defective cars, food products, exploding television sets, etc. In addition to the producer's liability, the fault liability of an importer of goods was established by the Supreme Court (SN) in a decision of 26 March 1984.[9]

08 The liability based on art 415 CC is still applicable to product liability cases nowadays under the concurrence of liabilities principle, which is stipulated in art 449^1 CC (see *infra* no 79 ff). The elements of fault liability for products are:

(i) defect in the product (which resulted from defendants' fault);
(ii) damage caused to victim; and
(iii) causal link.

09 Thus, in theory at least, in addition to furnishing proof of a defect, damage and causal link, a victim would need to demonstrate fault on the part of the defendant.

10 The historical evolution of product liability law in Poland shares certain characteristic paths with other legal systems. Early judgments involving defective cars introduced the idea of sellers being liable in tort to injured buyers.[10] The Supreme Court found that selling a motor vehicle with technical defects capable of causing an accident was not only a breach of contract but also a breach of the duty not to put human life and health in danger.[11] Initially, the courts very much emphasised the need for existence of subjectively wrong conduct as a source of defect. With time, the focus of courts started shifting away from defendants' conduct to the very existence of a defect, and the concept of fault became much more objective, dependent on expectations of safety rather than focused on defendant's conduct. Taking into account the fact that defendants in such cases were companies with complex production processes and organisational

8 For a detailed explanation of this evolution, as well as a much more detailed description of Polish product liability law see *M Tulibacka,* Product Liability Law in Transition: A Central European Perspective (2009).

9 Orzecznictwo Sadów Polskich i Komisji Arbitrazowych (Decisions of the Polish Courts and Arbitration Panels, OSPiKA), 1982, no 7/8.

10 II CR 96/62, OSNCP 6/1964, item 95 and SN II CR 540/63, OSN 1965, item 32.

11 SN 28.06.1972, II CR 218/72, OSN 1972, item 228.

structures, courts used the *res ipsa loquitur* tool to impute the existence of fault when the victim showed that the product had caused an accident or damage in the course of a normal use. Further, in cases where an accident occurred and yet it was impossible to determine what exactly the cause of it was, the courts also implied the existence of a defect.[12] Later cases, such as the ones involving 'exploding television sets'[13] and defective food products,[14] illustrate how courts dealt with this issue. In the 'pin in the cake' case, the court first of all assumed that the pin must have been inside the cake (it could have been on the plate on which it was served, but this possibility was excluded). No cake should contain a pin, and thus the cake in this case was defective and the producer was held liable.

11 As regards fault, product liability adds its own characteristic features to the debate. Essentially, the defect and its exact nature and source become the integral part of the considerations of fault in product liability cases. Reasonability, predictability, avoidability, discoverability and risk–benefit analysis, all play a part in the determination of the manner in which the defendant (manufacturer, importer or retailer of a defective product) should have behaved. The objective element – unlawfulness – is linked to duties: those explicitly established by law, or those contained in general clauses such as the principles of community life. The existence of a defect in a product which caused damage is linked to a breach of 'objective standards; not fulfilling certain safety requirements and standards of conduct'.[15] Establishing unlawfulness involves complex factual and legal issues concerning the product itself: its construction and design, attached instructions and warnings, and protective equipment attached to it. Over time, unlawfulness became the main, if not the only, element which was in fact considered.

12 The above approach is still taken in newer cases, where claims are decided on the ground of art 415 CC. In the 'airbag case', an airbag inflated in a stationary car, seriously injuring a little girl sitting inside.[16] The reason for the inflation of the airbag was never found, although the manufacturer suspected it had something to do with a strong electromagnetic field in close proximity to the vehicle. The defendants (Ford Distribution – the Polish importer; and the dealer) were held liable for the girl's injuries. First and foremost, the court pointed out that the main function of the airbag was to ensure safety, and it was entirely unpredictable

---

12 See *E Bagińska/M Tulibacka*, Tort Law Poland, in: International Encyclopaedia of Laws (2014) 105–107.

13 SN 04.12.1981, IV CR 433/81, commented by *C Żuławska*, OSPiKA 2/1983, item 55.

14 SN 06.08.1981, I CR 219/81, OSPiKA 7–8/1982.

15 See *M Nesterowicz*, Odpowiedzialnosc za szkody wyrządzone wprowadzeniem do obrotu rzeczy niebezpiecznych z wadami (1979) 11 Palestra 16.

16 Judgment of the Court of Appeals in Rzeszow of 21.02.2002, I ACa 378/01, OSP 3/2004, item 39, commented by *E Bagińska*.

and unnatural for it to inflate while the car was parked. However, the defendants' liability was based on their failure to pass on the information which they held (failure to warn). Apparently, Ford Motor Co advised its dealers and service stations of the possibility of an inflation of the airbags in certain conditions, but the consumers were not warned of this possibility. While the result of this case should be applauded, and the court did manage to achieve the outcome which would also be likely to follow under the strict liability regime of the Product Liability Directive, the reasoning of the judgment could be questioned.[17] Another example is an 'exploding soda bottle' case,[18] where the Supreme Court held that the liability of the producer is established under art 415 CC when organisational fault is demonstrated by *prima facie* evidence. Such evidence permits the court to find the existence of fault which consists in deficiencies in the operation of a legal person (the technological process, storage and quality controls) that are implicated by the type of defectiveness of the product.

13 In the light of the above characteristics of the traditional basis of liability of the producer, the new European rules meant, at least on the face of it, a clear improvement of the position of the victim. Unfortunately, the number and the result of the cases brought to Polish courts in the past 15 years have not demonstrated the widely expected improvement of the position of the victim.

II. BASIC ELEMENTS OF LIABILITY

A. PRODUCT

14 According to art 4491 §1 CC: 'Whoever in the course of his economic activity (producer) produces a dangerous product is liable for damage caused by the product to anyone.'

15 Product liability, following the Directive, is strict: all the claimant must prove is that a defective product caused him or her damage. The elements of liability are: manufacturing and putting a defective (unsafe) product into circulation, damage, and causation. The producer shall not be liable for the damage if he or she has not put the product into circulation (art 449^3 §3 CC). Hence, the burden of proof of this negative condition of liability is on the producer.[19]

---

17 See *Bagińska/Tulibacka* (fn 13) 105–107.

18 SN 08.11.2006, III CSK 174/06.

19 See the Court of Appeal in Szczecin of 29.05.2014, I ACa 377/13, reversed by the Supreme Court, judgment of 02.10.2015, II CSK 816/14, unpublished.

16 A product is defined in art 449[1] §2 CC as a movable thing, even it has connected with another thing (movable or immovable), an animal or electricity. The notion of a thing should be understood widely, hence including used products or even waste. Forms of energy other than electricity are excluded from the category of product,[20] while unsafe pharmaceuticals are subject to the regime of product liability.[21] Poland has used the original option of including primary agricultural products and game into the category of 'product' (art 15).

17 The doctrinal views are almost[22] in agreement as regards the application of product liability regime to blood and bodily fluids.[23] The latter are things *extra commercium*, similarly to body parts and other components of the human body.[24] As blood, blood products and parts of a human body are not made by a typical producer, the first problem is the identification of the person liable. It is argued that the imposition of strict liability on blood banks or other banks (such as sperm banks) or transplant centres would impede progress in the medical science.[25] However, it is rightly suggested that the French and British legislative and jurisprudential developments should be seen as a certain yardstick of protection.[26] Beside the arguments stemming from the pharmaceutical law,[27] important policy arguments support the above interpretation, as it enhances the protection of victims to whom contaminated blood was transfused (in particular, the cases of the HIV, hepatitis B and hepatitis C viruses). Consequently, under Polish law blood and parts of a human body, once separated from the body, can also be regarded as *sui generis* things that are covered by the product liability rules.[28] The second question pertains to the moment when such products are put into circulation. It appears that the moment when the producer loses control over the product must be replaced by the moment when a bag of blood or a similar product is used during a medical service performed on the patient.

18 Equally disputable is the status of intellectual property products. Such products are not technically movables (tangible objects) in the meaning of

---

20 See *Jagielska* (fn 3) 976.

21 Act of 6 September 2001, Pharmaceutical Law, consolidated text DzU 2008, no 45, item 271.

22 Cf *B Gnela*, Odpowiedzialność za szkodę wyrządzoną przez produkt niebezpieczny (2000) 288 ff.

23 Act of 22 August 1997 on Public Service Related to Blood, consolidated text DzU 2014, item 332.

24 See the Act of 1 July 2005, Law on Collection, Depositing and Transplanting of Cells, Tissues and Organs, DzU no 169, item 1411.

25 See *Jagielska*, Odpowiedzialność za produkt (1999) 132–133. However, the author seems to suggest that the French and British legislative and jurisprudential developments are certain yardstick to be considered.

26 See *Jagielska* (fn 3) 976.

27 Act of 6 September 2001, Pharmaceutical Law, DzU 2008, 45, item 271 – see art 2 as regards the definition of a blood-related product, substance and medicinal product.

28 See *Mohmand* (fn 3) 195–197.

art 449[1] §2 CC and property law (art 45 CC). There is an agreement that the product liability regime should cover intellectual property products that are mass-produced, sold as durable media, or in packages such as computer software. Many of these software products include information that can be defective and hence capable of causing damage. For example, incorrect information in a cookbook or a first-aid manual can lead to the infliction of a loss when a user of the book relies on the information. Nevertheless, the dominant view in the Polish legal writings denies the information contained in the printed intellectual products the status of a product in the meaning of art 449[1] §2 CC.[29] Liability is most often admitted in the context of computer software that has been integrated into things, such as computers or aircrafts.[30] This vantage point stems from several arguments, including the existing liability of producers of component parts (where software is integrated into a machine it becomes a component of the machine), the material effects of the operation of software, and the practice of the Court of Justice with regard to the distinction between goods and services.[31] Hence, the systemic, functional and dynamic interpretation of the product liability rules supports the extension of the protection of the victims on at least some types of intellectual products.

19 So far, both courts and legal writers are silent on the applicability of product liability to digital content transmitted via the Internet. It is regarded as a service rather than the transfer of a movable.[32]

B. DEFECT

20 The Civil Code does not refer to a 'defective product', but to an 'unsafe (dangerous) product'. This very detraction from the phraseology used by the Directive has been the subject of some controversy, but its purpose was to distinguish defects in a product liability context from defects in 'mere' warranty situations (art 556 §1 CC).

21 A product is unsafe if it does not provide the level of safety which can be expected taking into account the normal uses of the product. The definition thus follows the Directive. All the circumstances present at the time of putting the product into circulation are material in determining safety, and in particular information provided to consumers and the manner in which the product is presented (art 449[1] §3). The Polish lower courts appear not to appreciate the

[29] With extensive justification based on comparative research *Mohmand* (fn 3) 212–224.
[30] See *Radwański/Olejniczak* (fn 4) and *Mohmand* (fn 3) 219.
[31] Case C-7/68, *Commission v Italy* [1968] ECR 423.
[32] Especially in the light of the Consumer Rights Directive.

element of the foreseeability of certain uses that can be expected of the consumer by the producer.[33]

22 There is also a requirement that the defect in question must have been present when the product entered the market (art 449^3 §2), although this is a defence for the manufacturer and other defendants, so it is assumed that the burden of proof falls on these defendants.

23 The courts developed a distinction between manufacturing, design and presentation (failure to warn) defects under the general fault liability regime (see *supra* nos 10–12). For example, in the judgment of 30 November 2000[34] the Court of Appeals in Bialystok,[35] holding the defendant producer liable for failure to provide adequate warnings (art 415 CC), relied on the well-approved doctrine of the liability for failure to warn.[36] The manufacturer is a professional who, being aware of foreseeable risks linked with the use of the product offered on the market, has a duty to give clear warnings. The fact that the product got a certificate from a proper State agency and fulfilled the labelling standards set out in the regulation concerning dangerous chemical substances was not a defence for the producer's negligence. Even if the plaintiff disregarded the instructions when using the product (a foam spray), the former were held to be inadequate. Moreover, the producer failed to warn the customer about a dangerous gas component and the possibility of fire if the product came into any contact with electricity. Courts have hardly continued to apply these concepts under the strict product liability.[37]

24 The lack of safety of the product is measured according to the consumer expectation test. For the concurrent fault-based liability, a proof of wrongfulness will suffice to establish liability pursuant to art 415 CC. The defect is identified with lack of safety. Hence, an unsafe product is a product which does not ensure the level of safety which one may expect taking into account the ordinary use of the products. The assessment of product safety is done on the basis of the

33 See the judgment of the Court of Appeal in Szczecin of 27.02.2014, I ACa 803/03. The case concerned the lack of safety cap on a highly toxic household product. A child, while in the supermarket with its parents, reached for the product from a lower shelf, opened the cap and consumed the toxic substance. The Court found that this was an abnormal use of the product (art 449^1 §3) and held the producer liable on the basis of fault (art 415 CC). In a silicone breast implant case, both breast implants leaked and were found partially broken in the claimant's body, and were thus entirely removed. The court did not find the implants unsafe – see the Regional Court in Wroclaw of 27.05.2013, I C 224/10.

34 I ACa 340/00, [2001] OSA 6, 33.

35 The general clause of liability (art 415 CC) was applicable to the facts at hand because the harm caused by a dangerous product occurred before the new law on producer's liability came into force (2000).

36 See *Nesterowicz* (fn 15) 11.

37 See the Court of Appeal in Szczecin of 27.02.2014, I ACa 803/03, cited above in fn 33.

circumstances existing at the time the product is put into circulation. Only used products are treated more leniently with regard to the consumer expectation test.

25 In my opinion a Polish court is not competent to change the established standard of safety for the future by means of prospective overruling.

26 A thing created by an entrepreneur from own materials based on an individualised order from a client can certainly trigger liability prescribed by art 415 CC. A case of a defective prosthesis is a good example.[38] The plaintiff sued the seller and the producer (a laboratory) for compensation for material and non-material damage, which was inflicted by the use of two defective leg prostheses. The prostheses were delivered by the seller and co-paid by the plaintiff and social benefits office. The orthopaedic devices were ordered to be specifically tailored to the plaintiff's anatomy; however both of the prostheses were delivered in such a condition that the plaintiff could not use them without enduring serious pain and suffering. The defendant seller did not meet his duties in a timely manner under the warranty regime, and moreover all the repairs to the prostheses failed to meet the expectations of the plaintiff. The Supreme Court ruled that a seller of a defective orthopaedic device commits a tort by failing to repair the device in due time and if the subsequent attempts to repair the device fail to ensure the required quality, which results in the aggravated physical effort and suffering of the disabled user. As to wrongfulness, the Court stressed that the defendant seller, acting contrary to the expectations of the disabled buyer, impaired the situation of the latter and induced her physical and mental suffering, thereby violating not only his contractual obligations but also moral principles. As Polish law recognises the concurrence of the causes of liability, the plaintiff's claim for non-pecuniary loss should be based both on tort liability for personal injury (art 445 CC) and on the breach of patient rights.[39]

27 As regards the risk-based liability, the position of a producer of individually tailored products (ie not mass-produced products) should be equated with any other producer.[40]

C. PUTTING A PRODUCT INTO CIRCULATION

28 The criterion of 'putting a product into circulation' is understood in various ways in the Polish scholarship, which reflects the different approaches present in

---

38 SN 17.12.2004, II CK 300/04, OSP 2/2006, item 20.

39 The latter basis is presently provided by art 4 of the Act on Patient Rights and Patient Ombudsman of 2008, DzU 2012, item 159.

40 Cf *Mohmand* (fn 3) 149 – inclining towards a broad understanding of 'manufacture'.

the European legal writings and the case law of the Court of Justice of the EU. The criterion that prevails in the theoretical works is the element of the control of the producer over its product. Hence, a product is put into circulation once it leaves the control of the producer, which typically occurs at the time of the first commercial transaction.[41]

29 Defectiveness can be linked to the characteristics of a given product, due to the means of putting it into circulation (eg improper storage or forwarding, faulty instructions for use, etc). This broad approach has developed in the general regime of fault-based product liability and has in practice been integrated into the new regime. The courts have broadly defined the obligations of producers and distributors (see *supra* no 11 ff).

30 The Civil Code follows the Directive rather closely; hence, no details regarding the diligence expected from the producer are specified by the Civil Code.

31 As was discussed above, the liability can be classified as strict tort liability (liability based on the principle of risk). This type of liability is introduced for the improvement of the protection of victims on the one hand, and for the provision of incentives to those who create risk of injury to others, on the other hand. Typically, the legislator who introduces such a liability prescribes exonerating facts and, in some instances, it prohibits any contractual exemptions or limitations. For example art 437 CC provides that the strict liabilities defined in arts 435 and 436 CC cannot be excluded or limited in advanced.[42] The protective aim of a risk-based liability should influence the way it is interpreted. Indeed, in other cases of strict liability, the case law demonstrates a victim-oriented approach. It is hence quite astonishing that the few reported cases involving product liability claims show the opposite trend.[43]

III. THE PERSON LIABLE FOR DAMAGE

32 Under the product liability regime (arts 449^1–449^{10} CC) the liable persons are the producer, other persons liable in the same way as a producer (quasi-producers) and importers.

33 The notion of 'producers' includes those who made the final products and those who made components or materials used in the manufacture of the final

41 For the discussion of all doctrinal concepts see *Jagielska* (fn 3) 990.
42 The same rule is expressed in art 330 of the Maritime Code.
43 See eg the Court of Appeal in Szczecin of 29.05.2014, I ACa 377/13.

products. However, the latter can avoid liability if the defect was due to the manner in which the component or material was incorporated into the final product, especially if the component was further processed by the manufacturer of the final product, or according to the final producer's instructions.[44]

34 The most common example of own-branders (or *quasi-producers*) is that of supermarkets, which place their own mark on products made by some anonymous producer. However, there is no agreement among scholars regarding situations where those supermarkets expressly indicate that products were made for them by someone else (eg 'made by x for y'). While some writers argue that their liability under the provisions of the implemented Directive is excluded,[45] the majority are in favour of stricter standards of liability which benefit consumers, and thus see the need for both the supermarket and the actual producer to bear joint and several liability, or even for the supermarket to exclusively bear liability.[46] So far there has been no response from the judiciary on this point.

35 An importer of a product is responsible 'in the same manner' as the manufacturer, but in certain situations he or she might not make use of defences available to the producer, such as the development risk defence (when the producer does not facilitate access to its documents). Therefore, his or her liability may occasionally be 'stricter' than the producer's. With regard to importers, Polish law is not entirely consistent with the Directive. The problem lies with the definition of an importer. According to art 449^5 §2 CC an importer is a person 'who puts a product of a foreign origin into the domestic circulation in the scope of his business activity'. This formula disregards art 3(2) of the Directive, which speaks of a 'person who imports into the Community a product for sale, hire, leasing or any form of distribution in the course of his business' (see *infra* no 90 ff). The Supreme Court has recently held that the victim must establish that the importer actually brought the product that had caused the damage into the EU territory (art 449^5 §2 sentence 2 CC and arts 3(2) and 7(a) of the Directive); however, he or she may benefit from *prima facie* evidence.[47]

36 As far as suppliers' liability is concerned, the Civil Code prescribes that they are obliged to inform the victim (within one month of being notified of the damage sustained) of the identity and address of the producer, quasi-producer, importer, or a person who supplied the product to them. Only when these other persons cannot be identified can the supplier be liable.

44 See *Jagielska* (fn 3) 894.
45 See *Rajski* (fn 6) 24.
46 See *Bagińska* (fn 3) 47.
47 See *infra* no 74.

37 Product liability is attached to 'whoever' in the course of his or her economic activity produces a dangerous product and puts into circulation. Hence, the law does not specify any limitation with regard to public entities. Under the Directive the liability arises regardless of the private or public status of the producer. This argument is decisive in rejecting any interpretation which would lead to the exclusion or limitation of product liability in respect of public entities who carry out commercial activities (including hybrid transactions, such as services involving the use of products). Such an interpretation includes blood banks or hospitals operated by the state or local governments.[48]

38 A commercial character of the transaction does not prevent the application of the regime, given that the damage incurred is of the nature covered by the discussed rules (ie personal injury or damage to a thing owned for personal use). Nevertheless, in the light of case law the general clause of fault liability is more favourable to the claimants who seek compensation for damage to the product itself (especially of high value) and the compensation of profits that the product could have brought.

39 The product liability provisions prescribe two instances of joint and several liability of multiple tortfeasors: arts 449^5 §1 and 449^6 CC. First and foremost, all persons involve in manufacturing or putting the product into circulation, except for the seller, are jointly and severally liable for damage. Secondly, if the third person is liable together with the producer, their liability is joint and several (art 449^6).

40 The Civil Code lays down a general rule of joint and several liability in all cases where more than one person is liable for the damage arising from a tort (art 441 §1). The basic requirements of the article are: the tortious infliction of damage, the damage for which all the persons are liable being the same, and the causal relation between the damage and the tortious event, for which each of the joint tortfeasors bears liability. Where multiple parties are responsible for the damage, it does not matter whether the actions of one party were direct or indirect or whether one party is more responsible or blameworthy than the other. As a principle, in cases where more than one person caused the damage, the degree of liability of individual persons is not to be identified or differentiated in the main lawsuit.[49]

41 Article 444 §2 and §3 CC specify the right to contribution and indemnity of the parties jointly and severally liable in tort, regardless of the basis of the

48 As regards the sphere of public authority the liability is strict and stems from an unlawful conduct – art 417 ff CC.

49 See *M Nesterowicz/E Bagińska*, Multiple Tortfeasors under Polish Law, in: WVH Rogers (ed), Unification of Tort Law: Multiple Tortfeasors (2004) 153, 156.

tortfeasor's liability (fault, strict liability or equity principle). Pursuant to art 441 §2 CC, 'if the damage resulted from acts or omissions of several persons, the person who redresses the damage may demand reimbursement from the others of the appropriate part depending on the circumstances of the case, in particular the fault of the given person and the degree to which the latter contributed to the occurrence of the damage'. By virtue of art 441 §3 CC a person who redresses the damage for which he or she is liable in spite of the absence of fault has a right of recourse against the perpetrator if the damage occurred due to the latter's fault. The right of recourse is independent from the original claim for compensation. Besides the circumstances set out in art 441 §2 CC, the scope of recourse is also determined by other factors connected to the act of commission of a tort (the motives of the tortfeasors, the actual participation in the infliction of the damage, the gains obtained). The findings of the court in the primary proceedings are not binding on the court that decides the recourse actions.[50] The right to contribution governed by art 441 §3 CC materialises when the wrongdoer's fault was the sole cause of the damage.[51] In order to determine all the liable tortfeasors, it is critical that the law imposes any (direct or vicarious) tort liability on all of them.

42 The Civil Code follows the Directive in specifying secondary liability of suppliers. The latter will be liable only if the producer or importer or a person higher in the distribution chain are unknown and the seller does not identify them within one month.

IV. THE AGGRIEVED PERSON AND DAMAGE

A. THE AGGRIEVED PERSON

43 The Civil Code does not expressly limit the scope of persons who can seek compensation under the product liability provisions. For instance, the notion of 'consumer' is not mentioned anywhere with regard to possible claimants. Product liability is a form of tort liability, hence its scope of protection covers any victim, including the consumer who bought or otherwise acquired the product, his or family members, his or her guests and passers-by. Hence, business persons injured by a defective product can also claim compensation under the product liability rules. The reference to the consumer aids in setting the standard of safety that is expected from products put on the market.

---

50 SN 30.04.1957, 3 CR 340/56, OSPiKA 4/1958, 98.

51 SN 16.10.1958, 3 CR 81/58, OSPiKA 1/1960, 6.

44 Further, scholars agree that legal persons cannot make use of product liability rules, even if they suffered damage as a result of contact with a defective product.[52] In these cases, general tortious liability rules will apply.

B. REPARABLE DAMAGE AND MONETARY LIMITS ON LIABILITY

45 There is no legal definition of damage in Polish law. Traditionally, damage is considered to be every wrong against an interest protected by law, be it property or personality interests,[53] suffered by a person against his or her will.[54] However, non-pecuniary loss is compensable in money when the law provides for such a claim. Pursuant to art 361 §2 CC, compensation includes losses that the injured person incurred (*damnum emergens*) and lost profits (*lucrum cessans*). The notion of pecuniary damage is based on the theory of difference: damage is the difference between what the victim would have had at his or her disposal (with respect to the values affected by the damage) if the event which caused the damage had not occurred, and what he or she actually has at his or her disposal as a consequence of this event.

46 The product liability rules only modify the redress for damage other than personal injury. Following the Directive, the special rules on product liability do not apply to claims that do not exceed €500. They also do not cover damage to the defective product itself and lost profits that the product could generate (art 449^7 CC). Further, as mentioned above, if property damage occurs, producer's liability only covers property which is usually used for private purposes and which was used for such purposes by the claimant (art 449^2 CC). As regards any other movables (eg business property), as well as consequential economic loss, the injured party has to bring his or her claims under the fault regime (arts 415 and 449^{10} CC).

47 Poland has not used the option of limiting the aggregate liability of the producer to an amount which may not be less 70 million ECU (art 16(1)).

48 Personal injury will be compensated based on arts 444–445 CC, regardless of whether one accepts or not the tortious nature of the liability.[55] Tort rules are

---

52 See *Jagielska* (fn 3) 975.

53 See *A Szpunar*, Ustalenie odszkodowania w prawie cywilnym (1975) 36; *A Szpunar*, Odszkodowanie za szkodę majątkową (1998) 22–24.

54 This is the dominant position, although the last part of the definition is disputable in doctrine. The case law supports the dominant view, recently in the judgment of the Supreme Court of 25.01.2007, V CSK 423/06, not published.

55 See *Radwański/Olejniczak* (fn 5) 291.

the only regime for claiming damages for non-pecuniary loss. The application of the mentioned provision is undisputed mainly due to the fact that Polish civil law admits the concurrence of claims (art 443 and art 449[10] CC).

49 As regards personal injury, there is a list of heads of damage eligible for compensation that can be drawn from arts 444–446 CC. A claim for a loss of chance has not yet been overtly approved of by Polish courts. Lost chance of healing can be compensated under the head of an annuity (eg in a case of the loss of future prospects) or in the form of compensation for non-pecuniary loss.

50 To sum up, the regular tortious liability rules will continue to apply in product liability cases as regards personal injury and damage to property not covered by the strict liability regime.

V. CAUSALITY

51 No special rules on causation have been developed for product liability. Causation is a prerequisite of liability that is governed by the common rules on civil liability – art 361 CC. In the field of liability for damage Polish law generally accepts the adequate theory of causation. Article 361 §1 CC provides that a person obliged to pay damages is liable only for the normal consequences of the action or omission from which the damage resulted. The courts first examine whether a given fact, which is presented by the plaintiff, is a *conditio sine qua non* of the alleged damage.[56] Adequate causation is principally not different from causation that exists in reality, but it links liability only with the ordinary consequences of events (or phenomena) that make up its basis. The causal link may be direct or indirect, as long as all the consequences of the causes meet the test of adequacy (normality).

52 Causation should be established between the tort and the loss or injury. Courts and legal scholars are fully in agreement that the causative event (tort) is understood as putting a dangerously defective product on the market.[57] According to Ewa Łętowska the court should use a two-pronged test: the causal link between the marketing of the product and the creation of the risk of damage, and then the causal link between the realisation of that risk and the damage inflicted by the claimant.[58]

---

56 See *A Koch*, Związek przyczynowy jako podstawa odpowiedzialności odszkodowawczej w prawie cywilnym (1975) 214 ff.

57 eg SN 04.12.1981, IV CR 433/81, commented by *C Żuławska*, in OSPiKA 2/1983, item 55, SN 12.07.2002, V CKN 1112/00, unpublished.

58 See *E Łętowska*, Prawo umów konsumenckich (2nd edn 2002) 138.

53 In some cases (such as ones involving personal injury) evidence of high probability of the causal connection between the fact and the inflicted loss will suffice. However, if the claimant fails to meet the burden of proof of causation, he or she cannot use the concept of proportional liability as it is unknown to the present rules of tort law.[59]

54 If the third person is liable together with the producer (quasi-producer, importer, or seller), their liability is joint and several (art 449^6). The provisions on multiple tortfeasors apply (see *supra* no 32 ff). Of course, the third party can be liable on the general grounds of civil liability and not in the product liability regime. This rule can lead to the exclusion of the producer's liability, which is not in conformity with the Directive – see *infra* no 96.

55 Conduct of the victim is yet another potential defence. The Directive prescribes that producer's liability should be reduced or disallowed if the damage was caused by the defect in the product as well as the fault of the injured party or a person for whom he or she is responsible (art 8(2)). The rules on product liability are silent on this issue. Scholars agree that where the damage exclusively is caused by the victim's fault, the producer would not be liable because of the lack of adequate causal link between the defect and the damage.[60] However, where the damage is caused by both the defect and the victim's fault, the producer will not be exempted from strict liability, but the extent of damages will depend on the level of contribution of the victim to the occurrence of damage pursuant to art 362 CC (contributory conduct).

VI. DEFENCES AND EXCLUSIONS

A. DEFENCES

56 The Civil Code lists five defences which can be used by producers or other persons liable (these follow the Directive, and include the development risk defence).

57 First of all, the defendant may show that he or she has not introduced the product into circulation (art 449^3 §1 CC). This provision is meant to cover situations where the product is used before the producer meant for it to enter the market, including unauthorised use in the factory or testing of the product. Further, a person who did not introduce a product into the market in the course

59 Proportional liability in its limited version existed in the code of obligations for three decades between 1933 and 1964. It was finally abolished by the Civil Code (1964).

60 See *Jagielska* (fn 3) 997.

of a business will not be liable. This rule covers cases where the product was put into circulation by the producer but outside the scope of the producer's economic activity.

58 The development risk defence, which the Directive introduces as an option, was adopted in Poland. Article 449^3 §2 provides that producers will not be liable if the unsafe features of the product might not have been foreseen, taking into consideration the state of science and knowledge at the time the product was put into circulation. There is no single published case applying this provision. Scholars agree, however, that the defence has an objective character. What the producer was expected to be able to establish depends on what this type of producer would and should be aware of considering the state of science and knowledge at the time the product was put into circulation. It is therefore not material what the particular producer in question was aware of. All persons liable for damage can make use of the development risk defence.

59 The last defence provided by the provisions implementing the Directive is available to producers who demonstrate that the unsafe qualities of the product resulted from the compliance with the provisions of law. Hence, only when a product conformed to the compulsory technical standards set by an appropriate state agency as mandatory law can the manufacturer use this as a defence against strict liability (art 449^3 §2 *in fine* CC).

60 The impact of compliance or non-compliance of conduct with regulations (administrative law, in general) on liability in tort has been considered a rather complex issue in the legal scholarship.[61] However, neither compliance with non-binding codes of conduct and other professional rules concerning products, nor compliance with binding general rules on product quality and safety (including the Act on General Product Safety)[62] satisfy the requirements of this defence, because the liability is based on risk.[63] The interpretation of this defence in the legal writings is very narrow. The mandatory regulations in question have to cover the precise quality of the product that can be linked with the damage. In other words, the producer may not escape liability by saying that the product complied with binding regulations as such. Moreover, the plaintiff may still question the level of the legal standards by trying to prove that they are outdated or do not meet the ordinary consumer expectation test, thereby basing his or her claims on fault (art 415 in conjunction with art 449^{10} CC).[64]

---

61 See *M Jagielska/G Żmij*, Tort and regulatory law in Poland, in: W Van Boom/M Lukas/C Kissling (eds), Tort law and regulatory law (2007) 223 ff.

62 Act of 12.12.2003, implementing the General Product Safety Directive, DzU 2003, no 229, item 2275, later amended.

63 See *Jagielska/Żmij* (fn 61) 224 ff.

64 See *Łętowska* (fn 58) 123.

61 It may seem at first that the list of exonerating circumstances is exhaustive and no other defences are available. However, scholars add a number of other defences that would apply in product liability cases. First of all, the damage may be due to *force majeure*. According to prominent Polish writers this would be a valid defence for producers as long as *force majeure* was the sole cause of damage (hence, lack of causation).[65] Secondly, an exclusive fault of a third person for whom the producer is not liable is another such defence, while if the third person is liable together with the producer, their liability is joint and several (art 449^6) – see *infra* no 96.

B. EXCLUSIONS

62 In the area of product liability the Polish legislator prohibited any exclusion or limitation on product liability (art 449^9 CC).

63 However, even if we permit, under the principle of freedom of contract (art 353^1 CC), the exclusion or reduction of liability between two contractual parties (hence between the buyer and the seller), such clauses would always be subject to scrutiny by the rules in the Civil Code. In particular, any exclusion or limitation of liability for personal injury would be invalid as being contrary to the principles of community life (art 58 CC). Moreover, specific provisions relating to unfair terms in consumer contracts will prevent the effectiveness of such clauses.[66] Liability for intentionally caused losses can never be excluded (art 473 §2 CC).[67]

VII. REMEDIES

64 Under Polish law an injured person may choose to have the damage cured either by restitution to his or her previous condition or by the payment of an appropriate sum of money. However, if restoration to his or her previous condition is impossible or would entail undue hardship or excessive costs to the person liable, the injured person's claim shall be limited to a monetary payment (art 363 §1 CC). This rule is fully applicable to product liability cases.

65 The forms and scope of monetary compensation for personal injuries are regulated by articles 444–448 CC. These provisions cover pecuniary and non-

---

65 See *Łętowska* (fn 3) 132 and *Bagińska* (fn 3) 58.

66 Arts 385^1–385^3 implementing the Council Directive 93/13/EEC on unfair terms in consumer contracts [1993] OJ L95/29.

67 See *Bagińska/Tulibacka* (fn 13) 138.

pecuniary damage. Compensation can take the form of a lump sum or an annuity (the latter in cases where the law permits it).

66 Polish law does not accept the concept of punitive damages, nominal damages or similar monetary sanctions.

67 Injunctions are not a typical remedy in Polish civil liability law, although there are a number of instances where a party can demand injunctive relief before a civil court. In the area of product liability the recall of the dangerous product is provided for by the Act on General Product Safety (GPS Act).[68] The recall procedure is an administrative procedure. The President of the Office for Competition and Consumer Protection orders the distributor or the seller to withdraw a dangerous product from the market and/or to withdraw the product form the consumers (art 24 of the GPS Act). The latter form of recall means that the producer has to re-purchase the product from the users at the prices they paid for it, regardless of the degree of the wear and tear. If the user has retained the receipt, he or she may approach the seller with the claim, otherwise, he or she has to go directly to the manufacturer.

VIII. PROCEDURAL AND EVIDENTIAL ISSUES

A. THE BURDEN AND STANDARD OF PROOF IN TORT LAW

68 The burden and standard of proof in civil cases is regulated in part by the Civil Code and in part by the Civil Procedure Code. Pursuant to art 6 CC, the victim carries the burden of proving causation, damage and the facts decisive for the establishment of the tort. As in other modern legal systems, the burden of proof combines the burden of production of evidence and the burden of persuasion. In general, a court may avail itself of any evidence, whether direct or indirect in order to establish causation.[69]

69 There is no codified rule as regards the standard of proof. The courts have traditionally required 'a probability bordering on certainty', which means the judge must be convinced beyond reasonable doubt ('the conviction of the judge' standard). Over the years, the standard has shifted from 'probability bordering on certainty' to 'sufficient degree of probability', thereby allowing the

---

68 Act of 12.12.2003, consolidated text DzU 2015, item 322.

69 See *E Bagińska*, Causal uncertainty and proportional liability in Poland, in: I Gilead/MD Green/BA Koch (eds) Proportional liability: Analytical and Comparative Perspectives (2013) 256–258.

courts to award compensation in more complex scenarios involving personal injuries. Nowadays, the courts typically state that the plaintiff has proved causation with a 'sufficient (sufficiently high) degree of probability'.[70] There are only subtle differences between the names given to the degree of probability.[71] What a 'sufficient degree' or a 'significant degree' of probability is depends on an individual case. In general, no numbers regarding probability of a causal contribution are reported.

70 Furthermore, the standard of proof of causation is relaxed by procedural rules. In order to facilitate the position of the victim, the courts have adopted the doctrine of *prima facie* evidence for the purpose of proving the causative connection between negligence of a doctor and a patient's injury[72] as well as in product liability cases. In addition, the doctrine of *res ipsa loquitur*, although not widely accepted in court practice, is sometimes applied in product liability cases.[73] The use of *res ipsa loquitur* can help the court attribute liability even when the source and exact nature of the defect are not clear, thus implying the existence of defect. However, the practice of lower courts has so far demonstrated that the courts have not used this opportunity too often.[74]

71 Based on art 231 of the Code of Civil Procedure (*kodeks postępowania cywilnego*, CCP), the court may recognise as established the facts that have crucial significance for the adjudication of the case if such a conclusion may be drawn from other established facts (presumption of facts). This competence has particular significance in product liability cases based on art 415 CC, where it allows for a reversal of the burden of proving causation. It should also be used in the strict product liability regime.

B. THE DISTRIBUTION OF THE BURDEN OF PROOF IN DEMONSTRATING PRODUCT LIABILITY

72 Article 4 of Directive prescribes that the injured person shall be required to prove the damage, the defect and the causal relationship between defect and damage. This article has not been transposed into the Civil Code. Hence, in product liability the burden of proof of demonstrating liability falls on the

70 SN 17.06.1969, II CR 165/69, OSPiKA 7–8/1969, item 155.
71 See *M Kaliński*, Szkoda na mieniu i jej naprawienie (2008) 400.
72 SN 02.06.2010, III CSK 245/09, unpublished.
73 SN 08.11.2006, III CSK 174/06.
74 See eg the decision by the Court of Appeal in Szczecin of 14.05.2014, I ACa 874/13. This case involved unsafe meet products made of pork which contained parasites that caused trichinelloza in more than 220 people in the locality. The producer of the meet was charged with criminal charges, but the proceedings were eventually closed for lack of firm evidence. The court held the producer liable for the claimant's personal injury.

plaintiff pursuant to art 6 CC. However, the burden of proof of particular elements is distributed in a detailed way.

73 Firstly, art 449^4 CC establishes a presumption that a defective product which has inflicted the damage had been manufactured and put into circulation within the scope of the producer's business ('economic activity').

74 In the fresh Supreme Court case, the Court for the first time dealt with the burden of proof in a product liability case involving a seller and an importer.[75] A defective mobile phone charger, made in China, caused electrocution of the user when she was using the phone when charging the battery. The plaintiff's original charger stopped working so she bought a substitute one from the defendant seller. The producer included warnings against using the phone while charging its battery. The Regional Court found that the charger was 'defective' in the sense that it was 'out of order' and did not function properly, but it was not unsafe. The Court of Appeals corrected the lower court in this respect and found that the charger had a construction defect, but the case was dismissed because the claimant failed to properly identify the person who sold the product. The court required the claimant to prove the actual transaction with the defendant seller, even though the latter pointed to the importer of the chargers such as the one the claimant bought and the latter was joined as co-defendant in this case. Clearly, the court put the burden of proof on the consumer to prove that she had bought the given product from the given seller, or that the defendant importer imported that particular charger to Poland. Before the Supreme Court, the cassation was limited to the liability of the importer. The Court interpreted both the Civil Code and arts 4 and 7 of the Directive in the same manner as did the Court of Appeals. However, it stated that the Directive makes a 'patent distinction' between the importing (bringing) of the product into the EU territory and the putting of the product into circulation in the EU (arts 3(2) and 7(a)). Such a distinction is missing from the Polish provisions and, hence, the latter must be interpreted in conformity with the Directive. In other words, the Court distinguished two elements as regard an importer: the fact of bringing the product into the EU territory and the fact of putting this product into circulation in this territory.[76] The Court held that the special rules on the distribution of burden of proof originating in the Directive do not cover the attribution of a concrete product to a concrete producer or importer. In the light of art 449^5 §2 sent 2 CC and arts 3(2) and 7(a) of the Directive, it is the victim who must identify the producer or the importer into the EU of the unsafe product that caused him or her damage. This burden flows from the general rule of art 6 CC. On the other hand, the producer or the importer may prove that they did not

[75] See SN 02.10.2015, II CSK 816/14, unpublished.

[76] Similarly the Court of Appeal in Poznan of 10.08.2011, I ACa 571/11, unpublished.

put the product in question into circulation or that they manufactured/imported the product and/or put it into circulation outside of their business activity. According to the Court, the rules should not be interpreted to permit anyone to raise their claims against any manufacturer or importer of certain line of products, and shift the burden to prove the contrary to the defendant. In order to mitigate the position of the victim, the Supreme Court indicated that the burden of proving attribution of the product to the defendant should be facilitated by presumptions of facts, and in particular by *prima facie* evidence. In particular, a court should consider whether the defendant is the only known producer of a certain kind of products on certain territory or the sole known importer.

75 Secondly, the producer is not liable where unsafe qualities of the product were *revealed* after it had been put into circulation, unless they resulted from a reason inherent in the product (art 449^3 §2 sentence 1). This is a defence which has to be proven by the producer, and once it has been proven, the burden shifts back to the claimant who can then demonstrate that the defect is due to a reason inherent in the product. In the light of art 7(b) of the Directive a court should not require the plaintiff to identify that the defect which caused the damage existed at the time the product was put into circulation. The interpretation of art 449^3 §2 sentence 1 causes some doubts. On the one hand, the prevailing opinion in the Polish legal writings[77] imposes the burden of proving the 'reason inherent in the product' on the claimant. This interpretation follows the doctrinal approach to art 559 CC[78] in its original version, which concerned the warranty liability for defective goods. On the other hand, the Supreme Court held that the burden of proof in warranty cases cannot be generalised because such cases should be decided with due consideration given to their circumstances. Consequently, the Court admitted the use of presumption in favour of the buyer that the defect was inherent in the good before the sale.[79] The negatively formulated provision of art 559 CC was revised by the Act on Consumer Rights of 30 May 2014[80] precisely because it could be interpreted as shifting the burden of proof of the reason for the defect to the buyer.[81] Therefore, I cannot agree with the prevailing doctrinal opinion, were it to be applied to product liability cases. Until a

77 See *Jagielska* (fn 3) 998.

78 'The seller shall not be liable on account of warranty for physical defects which have arisen after the peril passed to the buyer, unless the defects resulted from a reason inherent beforehand in the thing sold'.

79 See *T Bielska-Sobkowicz*, in: J Gudowski (ed), Kodeks cywilny. Komentarz. Zobowiązania III, part 1, Warszawa 2013, 839–840, see SN 26.10.2000, II CKN 305/00, unpublished and SN 27.11.2003, III CK 115/02, unpublished.

80 DzU 2014, item 827.

81 Presently, art 559 CC reads: 'The seller shall be liable on account of warranty for physical defects which existed at the moment when the peril passed to the buyer or which resulted from a reason inherent in the thing sold at that moment'.

legislative action is taken with respect to art 449^3 §2 sentence 1, the victim should be allowed to benefit from presumptions and *prima facie* evidence.

C. THE LIMITATION OF CLAIMS

76 Time limits for bringing product liability claims are a difficult issue, with regard both to the relationship of the product liability provisions of the Civil Code with the Directive and to their relationship with the general tortious liability provisions. First of all, it must be noted that limitation periods in Polish civil law are not bars to litigation, but merely defences against claims brought after the period has passed. The approach appears to have been transposed into the product liability provisions as well: thus both the three-year limitation period and what the Directive intended as the ten-year long-stop are merely such defences. This runs contrary to the express provision of the Product Liability Directive (art 11, according to which product liability claims ought to be extinguished ten years after the product was put into circulation). In other aspects the product liability provisions follow the Directive. Article 449^8 CC specifies that the opportunity to bring claims is limited to three years from when the victim learnt, or using an adequate level of care should have learnt, of the damage and the person responsible, and in any case it is limited to ten years from when the product was put into the market.

77 The second part of art 449^8 CC entails some difficulty in assessing the relationship of the product liability provisions with the general tortious liability provisions. Until 2006 the general tortious liability contained a similar approach: tort claims were to be limited to three years from when the victim learnt of the damage and the person responsible, but in any case to ten years from when the tort occurred. In 2006, the Constitutional Tribunal declared that the situation where some claims may be limited in time before the victim is even aware of the damage was unconstitutional.[82] The Code was amended following the decision,[83] and currently art 442^1 §3 CC provides that in personal injury cases the time limit for claims always expires three years after the victim learnt about the damage and the person responsible, effectively disapplying the ten-year limitation period in such cases. It is uncertain what is the correct interpretation of the consequences of the judgment of the Constitutional Tribunal with regard to the similar rule still existing within the Civil Code, but limited to product liability cases. There is no doubt that the provisions of the Civil Code concerning product liability must comply with the Product Liability Directive and thus art 449^8 CC must remain unchanged. The same approach should be taken with regard to the

---

82 Decision of the Constitutional Tribunal of 01.09.2006, SK 14/05, OTK, A-2006, no 8, item 97.

83 The Act on the amendment of the Civil Code of 16.02.2007, DzU of 2007, no 80, item 538.

very nature of limitation periods in Poland. In the context of product liability claims, they should be time-barred after ten years, not merely limited.

D. OTHER PROCEDURAL RULES

78 The Class Actions Act of 17 December 2009[84] allows for class actions to be brought by a class representative in the name of at least ten people with claims of the same kind based on the same or similar facts (the Act only applies to consumer law, product liability and tort liability claims, excluding claims for the protection of personal interests). Clearly, the aim of the new mechanism is to simplify and facilitate actions by large numbers of people seeking compensation. The first Polish class action was filed in the case of the infection of over 400 patients with hepatitis C through the administering of a drug (the class seeking approximately PLN 75 million = €18.7 million in damages). The procedure has good potential to facilitate the pursuit of liability claims against producers. However, no proof of the effectiveness of this relatively new procedural tool can be submitted yet.

IX. ALTERNATIVE REGULATIONS AND REMEDIES

A. CONCURRENCE OF BASES OF LIABILITY

79 The concurrence of actions in the area of product liability is governed by art 449^{10} CC. Accordingly, the provisions on liability for damage caused by a dangerous product do not exclude liability for damage on general rules, for damage arising from non-performance or improper performance of an obligation or liability under implied warranty for defects and quality guarantee. It should be observed that concurrence of liability *ex contractu* and liability *ex delicto* is generally permitted by art 443 CC. However, art 449^{10} has created some interpretative dilemmas.

80 I share the dominant view that art 449^{10} CC should be regarded as *lex specialis* to art 443 CC.[85] Pursuant to art 443 the fact that the act or omission from which the damage arose constituted the non-performance or the improper performance of a pre-existing obligation does not preclude a claim for damages in tort, unless the pre-existing obligation provides otherwise. There are two differences between these provisions. The first relates to the scope of concurrence. In the product liability provision, the concurrence also embraces

84 DzU 2010, no 7, item 44, in force since July 2010.
85 See the detailed discussion by *Mohmand* (fn 3) 128–135.

the choice between product liability (specific tort regime) and the liability based on general rules; it also distinguishes two types of contractual liability: the general one (non-performance or improper performance of an obligation) and the specific (the seller's) one (warranty for defects and quality guarantee). Under the general rule, on the other hand, the choice is between any tort liability and any contractual liability. The second distinction is that the Civil Code permits contractual parties to circumvent the choice of liability in relations between them (art 443 applies 'unless the contract between the parties stipulates otherwise'), while that circumvention is not possible in respect of the regimes mentioned in art 449^{10} CC. Despite these two differences, it is rightly argued that as regards the fundamental issues art 449^{10} CC should be interpreted in the same manner as art 443 CC. This approach is justified by the fact that both provisions prescribe the concurrence of bases for liability and that art 443 CC is constructed according to long-established case law and jurisprudence.

81 A minority view in the legal scholarship holds that the concurrence is limited: other bases and rules of liability (in tort and in contract) may be applied in the circumstances where the rules of product liability are not applicable.[86] Consequently, the product liability regime takes precedence over other bases of liability. This opinion, which was not well substantiated, was criticised persuasively by Fatima Mohmand, who took into consideration that both rules are rules of the same nature. Hence, the long-established and undisputed interpretation of art 443 CC should also be applied to art 449^{10} CC.

82 Consequently, other bases and rules of liability may be applied contemporaneously with rules of product liability. Instead of product liability the injured party may choose to base its action on either:

(i) general rules on tort law;
(ii) general rules on liability for breach of contract;
(iii) rules stipulating liability in warranty; or
(iv) rules stipulating liability in quality guarantee.

83 Those are the only available general bases of liability for defective products in Polish law. Hence, the law is in compliance with the Directive (art 13).

84 All alternative bases for the claims are equal.[87] Hence, this is an optional approach to concurrence of claims (or – according to some authors – an accumulation of claims).

---

86 See *Strus* (fn 6) 25, similarly *Gnela* (fn 23) 282 ff.
87 See *Mohmand* (fn 3) 132; *Jagielska* (fn 3) 1011; *Gnela* (fn 23) 282–283; *Łętowska* (fn 58) 110.

85 The fundamental questions of the application of the concurrence of liability regimes have already been solved under art 443 CC. First, there may be no concurrence with respect to a third party who remains outside of the contractual bond, because the third party may only be liable in tort. Secondly, the plaintiff may bring different claims based on different legal bases, but the court must apply the whole set of rules of a given regime of liability to the claim based on this regime (burden of proof of fault, prescription, scope of damage).[88] One may not create a mixed contractual-tortious regime for a single claim.[89] Typically, depending on the situation, one of the causes may be more favourable to the injured person. However, a court is only bound by the factual basis of the claim, and not by the legal basis indicated by the plaintiff. It is disputable whether the claimant's choice can be changed. Assuming that it can, until the claims sought under one regime are finally decided, the plaintiff may not pursue the other claims. Notwithstanding this, the court should take into consideration *ex officio* the possibility of application of the tort regime to the claim for non-pecuniary loss.

B. ALTERNATIVE REMEDIES

86 The general duty not to cause damage to anyone (*neminem laedere rule*) requires that all necessary action be taken in order to avoid damage to persons or things. Failure to do so can be wrongful, depending on the circumstances. Hence, the fact that it complied with regulations does not imply that a given conduct was not wrongful. The Supreme Court has consistently imposed liability for personal injuries arising out of conduct that complied with licences, public certificates, and product safety rules.[90]

87 Also under administrative law a manufacturer must exercise due diligence and undertake actions appropriate to the nature of the products put on the market. He or she must collect information on the risks posed by the product and undertake preventive action, including, if necessary, a recall of a defective product from the market or recall from the consumers. Hence, the duty of recall under art 10 §4 of the GPS Act is not enforced by a civil court, but by the supervisory body (the Office for Competition and Consumer Protection).

---

88 See *W Wagner*, in: D Lasok (ed), Obligations in Polish law, vol II (1974) 10–11; *W Czachórski*, Odpowiedzialnosc kontraktowa i jej stosunek do odpowiedzialności deliktowej według k.c. (1964) 10 Nowe prawo 949.

89 See *A Ohanowicz*, Zbieg norm w polskim prawie cywilnym (1963) 118; *M Nesterowicz*, Comment to SN 17 December 2004, II CK 300/04, OSP 2/2006, item 20, at 95.

90 SN 04.12.1981, IV CR 433/81, OSN 1983, no 3, item 55, Court of Appeals in Bialystok judgment of 30.11.2000, I ACa 340/00, Orzecznictwo Sadow Apelacyjnych [Decisions of the Courts of Appeal] 2001, no 6, item 33.

88 The consumer can also inform the bodies who are responsible for the monitoring of the market, the Consumer Ombudsmen or the Regional Quality Comptrollers, of the risks that are posed by the product or already materialised.

89 The social security insurance system, coordinated by the Office for Social Insurance (*Zakład Ubezpieczeń Społecznych*) is very comprehensive. It includes the following types of benefits:

(i) in cases of inability to work: (a) inability to work benefits and (b) work training benefits;
(ii) benefits for persons who lost a family member maintaining them: (a) family pensions; (b) additional benefits for orphans; and
(iii) funeral benefit.

X. ASSESSMENT OF DOMESTIC LAW

90 The product liability rules are rarely applied in practice. The reasons for this are not entirely clear. We may only speculate that the Polish consumers and users are not sufficiently encouraged by the strict liability regime to overcome the typical hurdles connected with civil litigation.[91] The reasons that hinder product liability litigation in Poland are the following: pretty modest availability of legal aid, the widely differing costs of legal advice, high costs of litigation, 'the loser pays' principle, the complex and lengthy procedural steps, the appointment and role of experts, judicial methodologies, the standard of proof rules (certainty or high probability), and many other aspects of the civil process. All of the above affect not only the process itself but also the outcome of the litigation. This potential for unpredictability is beneficial neither to claimants nor to defendants.

91 In many cases, the traditional basis of liability is more favourable to the victim, in particular as regards the defence of the compatibility of the product with binding technical standards, the redress of damage to the unsafe product and of the damage to property not exceeding the threshold of €500, as well as compensation for the lost gains that the product could bring.

92 Consequently, there are no apparent negative effects of the regulation. It is hard to assess the impact of the new provisions, as the number of cases is very small. It is, however, likely that the following issues will arise:

---

91 The cited case of the Court of Appeals of Białystok I ACa 340/00 was brought by a consumer organisation on behalf of the consumer.

(i) The position of most victims in the majority of dangerous product cases is similar to their position under the general tort system. There is no need for them to prove fault as long as they show that they suffered injuries or losses as a result of contact with a defective product. Most of the defences, including the development risk defence, contained by the new provisions would also have been relevant under the old system (as they would exclude fault).

(ii) The provisions implementing the Directive are clearly focused on business-to-consumer relations, while the old product liability system was wider in scope. For instance, it covered those who obtained products for professional use (although the requirements as to their knowledge of potential risks were higher). The old rules will continue to apply in cases not covered by the Directive.[92]

93 The Directive is a maximum harmonisation measure and as such it cannot be detracted from, for the benefit of consumers or otherwise, by national law.[93] The latter point is relevant in considering a few provisions in the Polish implementing legislation which differ from the Directive.

94 First, while the Directive defines an importer as anyone who imports a product into the EU in the course of his or her business (art 3(2)), the Civil Code limits the definition to those who 'put a product of a foreign origin into the domestic circulation in the scope of their business activity' (art 449^5 §2 CC). Hence, the Civil Code considers the sale in the national market (the Polish territory), while the Directive governs the import to the EU. The Polish rule would appear to be more advantageous for victims of defective products, as they would be able to sue the importer based on the Polish material law, while in other EU states the defendant needs to seek the person who first imported the product into the EU and who may well be based in another EU state. However, in light of the Supreme Court judgment of 2 October 2015 such a plain language construction of the Civil Code is in conflict with the Directive (see no 74). Hence, liability of any importer is strict and subject to the rules that originate in the Directive.[94]

95 The second difference relates to the prescription of claims. According to art 449^8 sentence 2 CC 'in any case the claim shall be subject to limitation upon ten years from putting the product into circulation.' Hence, *prima facie*

---

[92] See *Bagińska/Tulibacka* (fn 13) 112–113.

[93] Confirmed in the following ECJ decisions: Case C-52/00, 25 April 2002, *Commission of the European Communities v French Republic* [2002] ECR I-3827; Case C-402/03, 10 January 2006, *Skov AEg v Bilka Lavprisvarehusc A/S and Bilka Lavprisvarehus A/S v Jette Mikkelsen, Michael Due Nielsen* [2006] OJ C48/4; or Case C-327/05, 5 July 2007, *Commission of the European Communities v Denmark* [2007] ECR I-93.

[94] See also *Jagielska* (fn 3) 971.

the long-stop period is not a clear extinctive prescription as stipulated by art 10(2) of the Directive (the rights 'shall be extinguished upon the expiry of a period of 10 years from the date on which the producer put into circulation the actual product which caused the damage, unless the injured person has in the meantime instituted proceedings against the producer'). It can be observed that the mechanism of prescription in the Civil Code and the Directive is similar in the sense that the victim can interrupt the running of the prescription by taking a court action. This notwithstanding, the Civil Code is not in clear conformity with the Directive as it lists more causes of interruption of the running prescription period than of instituting proceedings against the producer.[95]

96 The third problem relates to the liability of the producer and a third party. Pursuant to art 449^6 CC if the third person is liable together with the producer, their liability is joint and several (art 449^6). This means that the victim can sue only the third party or both parties, claiming some compensation from both. It has been argued that the possible result of no liability on the part of the producer is incompatible with art 8(1) of the Directive, which dictates that producers' liability cannot be reduced if the damage is caused both by a defect in the product and by the action or omission of a third party.[96]

---

95 Art 123 §1 CC: 'The running of the limitations period is interrupted: (1) by any action before a court or other authority appointed to hear cases or enforce claims of a given type or before an arbitration tribunal taken directly to either assert or establish, or satisfy or secure a claim; (2) by recognition of a claim by the person against whom the claim is made; (3) by commencement of mediation.'

96 See *Jagielska* (fn 3) 996 and *Bielska-Sobkowicz* (fn 79) 847–848.

PRODUCT LIABILITY IN SPAIN

Miquel MARTÍN-CASALS and Josep SOLÉ-FELIU

I. SOURCES OF LAW AND THEIR EVOLUTION

A. LEGAL REGIMES APPLICABLE TO LIABILITY FOR DEFECTIVE PRODUCTS BEFORE THE IMPLEMENTATION OF DIRECTIVE 85/374/EEC IN SPAIN

01 Before the implementation in Spain of Directive 85/374/EEC, the problems relating to civil liability for damage caused by defective products were resolved by applying three possible sources of law: general rules of liability for breach of contract (arts 1486 ff CC and arts 1101 ff CC); general tort law rules (arts 1902 ff CC); and, from 1984 on, the provisions contained in Act 26/1984, of 19 July, the General Act for the Defence of Consumers and Users. The entry into force of the European Directive and its implementation in the 1994 Products Liability Act,[1] which in 2007 was recast in arts 128–176 of Royal Legislative Decree 1/2007 of 16 November, Approving the Consolidated Text of the General Consumer and User Protection Act and Other Complementary Laws (TRLGDCU-2007),[2] does

[1] Ley 22/1994, de 6 de julio, *de responsabilidad civil por daños causados por productos defectuosos*, BOE no 161, 07.07.1994.

[2] Ley 26/1984, de 19 de julio, *general para la defensa de los consumidores y usuarios*, BOE no 176, 24.07.1984. There is an unofficial English translation of this Act, which can be found

not preclude the application of most of these rules, the compatibility of which recognises art 13 Directive and current art 128.2 TRLGDCU, according to which actions for damage arising from the Directive 'do not affect the injured party's other rights to be compensated for damage, including pain and suffering, as a consequence of contractual liability, on the grounds of the lack of conformity of goods or services or any other cause of non-performance or defective performance of the contract, or of any non-contractual liability which may apply'. The only limitation is (as will be discussed *infra* no 09 ff) incompatibility between the rules laid down in the Directive and former arts 26–28 of Act 26/1984, establishing a special liability regime for damage caused by defective products, which was different from the regime provided for in the Directive. The ECJ recognised that these domestic provisions could not be applied after the entry into force of the European Directive in Spain (*María Victoria González Sánchez v Medicina Asturiana SA*[3] (on this issue in more detail, see *infra* no 09 ff).

1) *General Rules of Contractual Liability (Arts 1101 ff of the Civil Code) and Rules on Latent or Hidden Defects (Arts 1486 ff Civil Code)*

02 These are the rules that the courts preferentially used to deal with cases of damage caused by defective products until the 1970s. In fact, of the two sets of provisions, the courts mainly applied the general rules on contractual liability, since the limitation period for actions for latent or hidden defects was very brief – only six months (art 1490 CC), as compared to fifteen years (nowadays, the limitation period is of five years) for claims for contractual liability (art 1964 CC).[4]

03 Liability for latent or hidden defects (art 1486 ff CC) requires the existence of defects in the qualities of the thing sold, and these defects must be detrimental to its usefulness, in the sense that they made it unfit for the use for which it was intended, or decrease its utility to the extent that, if the buyer had known of them, he would not have purchased it or would have paid a lower price for it (art 1484 CC). In terms of remedies, the buyer can choose between terminating the contract (*actio redhibitoria*) or a reduction in the price (*actio quanti minoris*). If the buyer chooses termination, he cannot claim damages, unless the seller knew of the defect and did not communicate it to the buyer. If this is the case, the seller must compensate the buyer for the damage suffered (art 1486.2 CC). The application of these rules to cases of product liability was very exceptional,[5]

at the Portal of the Spanish Ministry of Justice <www.mjusticia.gob.es>, which is not very accurate and therefore has been used only as a starting point in this chapter.

3 Case C 183/00.

4 The current Ley 42/2015, de 5 de octubre, *de reforma de la Ley 1/2000, de 7 de enero, de Enjuiciamiento Civil* (BOE no 239, 06.10.2015), reduced the traditional limitation period from fifteen to five years, which is the period currently in force (Final Disposition 1st).

5 One of the few judgments applying these provisions was STS 12.02.1931 (Col. Leg. no 124).

and the tendency was rather to apply the general rules of civil liability for breach of contract.[6]

04 The liability regime for breach of contract is regulated in art 1101 ff CC. According to the prevailing legal doctrine, this is a liability regime based on the fault of the debtor, to the extent that art 1101 CC provides that subject to compensation for any damage caused are those 'persons who, in the performance of their obligations, should incur in wilful misconduct, negligence or default, and those who in any way should contravene the content of the obligation'. However, a growing number of authors argue that while art 1101 CC admits that the debtor's liability regime could be based on negligent or wilful misconduct of the debtor, the truth is that art 1101 CC does not provide that this is the only possible basis of liability, since there are cases in which the debtor is not relieved of its responsibility in spite of demonstrating that he acted with all due care.[7] In fact, several provisions in the Civil Code deal with specific cases of breach of contract attributable to the debtor where it is not necessary that he acted with fault, as is the case in the notion of 'debtor in good faith' of art 1107.1 CC; or the specific liability regimes of innkeepers and restaurateurs, in arts 1783 and 1784 CC, of the depositary, arts 1766–1767 CC, or of the borrower, arts 1744–1746 CC, etc.[8] Although several judgments have used these general provisions of arts 1101 ff CC to resolve cases of damage caused by defective products, the main obstacle they have faced has been applying them when the producer and the injured purchaser are not linked by any contractual relationship. This has sometimes resulted in somewhat forced constructions[9] and has led the courts to abandon the rules of contractual liability and take recourse to the general tort liability system (art 1902 ff CC).

2) The General Tort Liability System (Arts 1902 ff CC)

05 From the 1970s onwards, and more particularly during the 1980s and 1990s, the general rules of tort have been the main basis for product liability.[10] The basic rule of this regime is to be found in the general clause of art 1902 CC, which provides that 'the person who by action or omission causes damage to another by fault or negligence is obliged to repair the damage caused'. This provision establishes a system of fault liability, the basic conditions of which are: (i) an unlawful act or omission, (ii) fault, (iii) the occurrence of damage, and (iv)

6 Cf *M Martín-Casals/J Solé Feliu*, The Development of Product Liability in Spain, in: S Whittaker (ed), The Development of Product Liability (2010) 239–240.
7 *L Díez-Picazo*, Fundamentos del Derecho Civil Patrimonial, II. Las relaciones obligatorias (6th edn 2008) 714.
8 Instead of many see *Díez-Picazo* (fn 7) 711 ff.
9 SSTS 02.05.1961 (RJ 1961\1859); 29.12.1978 (Col. Leg. no 447).
10 See SSTS 14.10.1972 (RJ 1972\4004); 12.5.1976 (Col. Leg. no 132); 5.10.1983 (Col. Leg. no 492).

the existence of a causal link between the act or omission and damage,[11] The limitation period for tort liability claims is one year from the time the victim knew of the damage (art 1968.2 CC).

06 The Spanish Civil Code contains no express provision regarding the burden of proof of these conditions and therefore they are in principle governed by the general rules of evidence, which place the burden of proof on the claimant. However, proof of fault has undergone an evolution through case law that directly affects liability of manufacturers for defective products. From STS 10.07.1943 (RJ 1943\856), the Supreme Court in its case law presumed the existence of fault and reversed the burden of proof to the detriment of the defendant in cases of damage caused when carrying out specifically dangerous activities. Subsequently, this doctrine was extended to other areas, including liability for defective products,[12] and under the so-called concept of 'objectification of responsibility' it became in practice the rule for fault liability regardless of whether or not there was a situation of enhanced of risk. The current Supreme Court case law has limited the scope of this doctrine and confines it to cases of extraordinary risks, understood as significantly abnormal risks in relation to the average parameters.[13] However, liability for defective products is still one of the areas where the courts continue to apply the presumption of fault, with its corresponding shift of the burden of proof to the manufacturer.[14]

3) The Entry into Force in 1984 of the General Consumer and User Protection Act

07 In 1984 Act 26/1984 of July 19, the General Consumer and User Protection Act (LGDCU), entered into force. Articles 25–31 of this Act contained a regulation covering liability for damage caused by defective goods and services. According to the prevailing legal doctrine and case law, these provisions established a dual liability regime.[15] The first provision, art 26 LGDCU, was a general rule applicable to most goods and services establishing a fault liability regime with a rebuttable reversal of the burden of proof of fault for damage

---

11 In case law, among many others, see SSTS 29.12.2997 (RJ 1997\9602); 30.6.1998 (RJ 1998\5286). In legal doctrine see *JL Lacruz et al*, Elementos de Derecho Civil *II, Derecho de Obligaciones*, vol 2 (1999) 465; *F Pantaleón*, Com. Art. 1902, in: C Paz-Ares/L Díez-Picazo/ R Bercovitz/P Salvador, *Comentario del Código Civil*, T II (1991) 1971 ff.

12 SSTS 19.09.1996 (RJ 1996\6719); 24.07.2001 (RJ 2001\8421). On this evolution in the specific area of products liability see *M Ángeles Parra Lucán*, La protección del consumidor frente a los daños. Responsabilidad civil del fabricante y del prestador de servicios (2011) 70–80.

13 SSTS 19.07.2002 (RJ 2002\6245) and 09.02.2011 (RJ 2011\67622). *M Martín-Casals*, La 'Modernización' del Derecho de la responsabilidad extracontractual, en Asociación de Profesores de Derecho Civil, Cuestiones actuales en materia de Responsabilidad Civil (2011) 60–61.

14 Cf SSTS 19.09.1996 (RJ 1996\6719); 24.07.2001 (RJ 2001\8420) SAP Vizcaya 24.10.2013 (AC 2014\756).

15 SSTS 25.06.1996 (RJ 1996\4853); 05.02.2001 (RJ 2001\541); 14.07.2003 (RJ 2003\5837).

caused to 'consumers or users', so that producers, importers or suppliers of goods or services could only escape liability by showing that they had acted with due care. The second provision, art 28 LGDCU, provided for a specific strict liability regime for a particular type of goods and services, namely were those that 'by their own nature or as set out in the regulations, necessarily include the guarantee of certain levels of purity, efficacy or safety, under objective conditions of determination, and involve technical, professional or systematic quality controls, until they reach the consumer or user in the appropriate condition'. Article 28.2 LGDCU gave some examples of those goods or services, including 'foodstuffs, cleaning and hygiene products, cosmetics, medicines and pharmaceutical preparations, healthcare services, gas and electricity services, domestic appliances and lifts, means of transport, motor vehicles and children's toys and products'. Finally, the provision capped liability at 500 million pesetas (approx. €3 million) (art 28.3 LGDCU).

08 Both LGDCU liability regimes were applicable whether or not there was a contract between the parties and joint and several liability was established when damage had been caused by several actors.[16] These provisions, however, imposed a major constraint since they were applicable only when the injured party had the status of consumer or user, defined as the final recipient of the goods or services. In this way, and by contrast to the European Directive, third parties (bystanders) were excluded from its scope of protection.

4) The Spanish Transposition of Directive 85/374/EEC

09 As is known, Spain joined the European Union in 1986 as a Member State, one year after the entry into force of the Directive on defective products. This Directive was implemented into Spanish law in 1994 via the Product Liability Act 22/1994 (LRPD). One of the first consequences of the entry into force of this Act transposing the Directive was its impact on the double liability regime in the LGDCU regarding defective products. In this sense, Final Provision 1 of the LRPD stated that 'Articles 25–28 of the Act 26/1984, of July 19, General Act for the Protection of Consumers and Users shall not apply to the liability for damage caused by defective products included in Article 2 of this Act'. Consequently, from this time on, liability for damage caused by defective products was subject to the provisions transposing the European Directive (LRPD), while the scope of arts 25–28 LGDCU was limited to damage caused by services. This was acknowledged by the ECJ in its judgment of 25 April 2002, *María Victoria González Sánchez v Medicina Asturiana SA*,[17] which, thinking directly of

---

16 STS 14.07.2003 (RJ 2003\5837).

17 Before this judgment this was a disputed issue in Spanish legal doctrine. Some authors held that arts 25–28 were compatible with the Directive, since they were more favourable to the interests of consumers (among others, *R Bercovitz Rodríguez-Cano*, La adaptación del

arts 25–28 of the Spanish LGDCU, noted that 'a system of producer liability founded on the same basis as that put in place by the Directive and not limited to a given sector of production does not come within any of the systems of liability referred to in Article 13 of the Directive. That provision cannot therefore be relied on in such a case in order to justify the maintenance in force of national provisions affording greater protection than those of the Directive'.[18]

10 By contrast, the regime established by the LRDP was perfectly compatible with the general rules of liability in contract and in tort, as recognised in art 15 LRPD (now art 128.2 TRLGDCU), stating that: 'the actions recognised in this Act do not affect other rights which an injured person may have as a result of contractual or non-contractual liability of the manufacturer, importer or any other person'.

11 In essence, the LRPD implemented the strict liability provisions of the European Directive rather closely, and made use of the margin of appreciation that the Directive allowed Member States on various issues. Thus, it excluded from the scope of the Act compensation for non-pecuniary loss, as allowed by art 9(2) Directive, something that has been criticised by the Spanish doctrine. It also excluded 'agricultural raw materials and hunting products' from the definition of 'product', according to art 15(1)(a) Directive, although the subsequent entry into force of Directive 1999/34/EEC forced the Spanish legislature to alter this original decision and include such materials within the definition of 'product'.[19] Finally, as to the possibility of including or not including the so-called development risks defence (as permitted in art 15(1)(b) Directive), the Spanish legislator chose a compromise: it accepted this defence for the vast majority of products (art 6.3.e) LRPD), except for food, foodstuffs and medicines intended for human consumption. In relation to these two categories, art 6.3 LRPD stated that: 'in the case of medicines, food or food products for human consumption, subjects responsible under this Act may not invoke the cause of exoneration letter e) of paragraph 1 of this Article'. In general terms, the

---

Derecho español a la Directiva comunitaria sobre responsabilidad por los daños causados por productos defectuosos (1998) 2 Estudios sobre Consumo 89–91). Others, however, rejected this position, since they considered that when art 13 Directive refers to the possibility of making the Directive compatible with the 'rules of the law of contractual or non-contractual liability or a special liability system existing at the moment when this Directive is notified', this wording could only refer to the German Medicine Act (*Arzneimittelgesetz*) and not to the Spanish General Act for the Protection of Consumers and Users, since when the Directive was passed in 1985, Spain was not a member of the European Union (in this sense, *M Martín-Casals/J Solé Feliu*, Responsabilidad por productos en España y (des)armonización europea (2001) 4 Revista de Responsabilidad Civil y Seguros 7).

18 Case C-183/00, *María Victoria González Sánchez v Medicina Asturiana SA* [2002] ECR I-3901, para 33.

19 This amendment was carried out in the Additional Provision 12 of the Ley 14/2000, de 29 de diciembre, *de Medidas fiscales, administrativas y del orden social* (BOE no 313, 30.12.2000, 46631 ff).

Spanish transposition Act merely incorporated the same issues that were already in the text of the Directive (responsible subjects, product, defect, defences of the producer and recoverable damage), without regulating other general aspects of civil liability, such as the problems of factual causation or scope of liability for which recourse to the general rules of tort liability should be made.

12 In 2007, the Spanish Act transposing the Directive on Product Liability was recast into a text trying to group into a single regulatory body all the specific regulations concerning the protection of consumers and users, whether in contract or in tort. This is Royal Legislative Decree 1/2007 of 16 November, Approving the Consolidated Text of the General Consumer and User Protection Act and other Complementary Laws (TRLGDCU-2007), which is the transposition norm of the European Directive currently in force, specifically in arts 128–146. This option has been harshly criticised by the doctrine, since the Directive on Defective Products is not a norm dealing exclusively with the protection of consumers, as explicitly indicated the Preamble to the Directive.[20] Nevertheless, since this is a recast norm it does not aim to alter the implementation of the Directive carried out previously by the LRPD.

13 Besides these rules, there are neither special regulations of liability for certain categories of products, nor specific regulations regarding new technologies.

5) Specific Regulation for Liability for Damage Caused by Defective Service

14 Articles 147 and 148 TRLGDCU contain specific regulation on civil liability for damage caused by defective services when the victims are consumers or users. Accordingly, and by contrast to the rules on product liability, the provision does not protect anyone not who suffers damage, but only those persons who meet the condition of being a consumer or user, understood in the sense of 'natural persons acting for purposes outside their trade, business, craft or profession' (art 3.1 TRLGDCU). The definition of consumers and users also include 'legal persons and entities acting without profit on a trade or business' (art 3.2 TRLGDCU). This regulation, which is a recast of the old arts 25–28 of the 1984 LGDCU, establishes a dual system of liability: a general fault liability regime applicable to most services (art 147 TRLGDCU), and a strict liability regime for certain services that must meet higher safety standards (art 148 TRLGDCU).

15 Thus, according to art 147 TRLGDCU, 'service providers shall be responsible for damage caused to consumers and users, except where they can

---

20 *M Martín-Casals/J Solé Feliu*, ¿Refundir o legislar? Algunos problemas de la regulación de la responsabilidad por productos y Servicios defectuosos en el texto refundido LGDCU (2008) Revista de Derecho Privado 1 ff.

prove that they have complied with the demands and requirements established in regulations and with all the care and diligence required by the nature of the service'. It is a liability regime for rebuttably presumed fault where the reversal of the burden of proof rests withthe service provider. In its turn, art 148 TRLGCU establishes a strict liability regime for services 'which due to their inherent nature or because of the established regulations, they must include a guarantee of certain levels of effectiveness or safety, determined in objective conditions, and undergo technical, professional or systematic quality controls before reaching the consumer or user in the proper condition'. By way of example, the second section lists some of the provision of services which are subject to this regime, among which are 'healthcare services, repair and maintenance services for household electrical appliances, lifts and motor vehicles, property renovation and repair services, electricity and gas inspection, installation and similar services, and those relating to means of transport'. Finally, pursuant to the third section of this article, compensation awards according to the strict liability regime are subject to a cap of €3,005,060.52.

II. BASIC ELEMENTS OF LIABILITY

16 According to arts 135 and 139 TRLGDCU (cf arts 1 and 4 Directive), the manufacturer's liability for damage caused by defective products requires that the injured party proves the existence of damage, that it was caused by a defect in a product and that there is a causal link between the defect and damage. Thereafter, the producer – and any of the other persons in a similar position – can exonerate himself only if he proves any of the circumstances listed in art 140 TRLGDCU (cf art 7 Directive). Beyond these defences, the producer cannot claim any other circumstances to avoid liability except, of course, to prove that any of the basic conditions of liability are missing, ie that the product was not defective, that no damage occurred, or that there was no causal link between the defect and damage. All these issues are dealt with in more detail in the following sections.

A. THE NOTION OF PRODUCT

17 Following art 2 Directive, art 136 TRLGDCU defines product as 'any movable even though incorporated into another movable or into an immovable, as well as gas and electricity'. At first, the Spanish legislator excluded 'primary agricultural products and game' from the definition of product. However, following the transposition of Directive 1999/34/EEC, which eliminated the option originally foreseen in art 15(1)(a) Directive allowing the exclusion of such movables from the notion of product, the Spanish Act was amended and today primary agricultural products and game are considered products subject to the product liability regime.

18 Immovables are excluded from the definition of 'product' (cf art 334 CC), except those that, being originally movables, are incorporated into an immovable, which by express provision of art 2 Directive (and in Spain by art 136 TRLGDCU) continue to be a 'product' even though, according to the general rules of civil law, they become immovables by destination or incorporation (cf arts 333–335 CC). This is, for instance, the case of elevators, boilers, radiators, plumbing, faucets, toilets, sinks, pipework, cement, bricks, beams, doors, locks, etc.[21] This classification – which has its origins in the European Directive – may pose problems of coordination with the provisions of Act 38/1999 of 5 November, on building management (LOE),[22] arts 17–20 of which deal with liability for damage caused to the building by construction defects. To the extent that these construction defects may be caused by the use of a defective construction product, and that the LOE holds liable, among other building agents, the suppliers of products (including 'manufacturers, wholesalers, importers and sellers of building products' pursuant to art 15 LOE), concurrence of applicable rules take place. Although some authors consider that building legislation is preferential here,[23] we believe that, taking into account the jurisprudence of the Court of the European Communities,[24] the position of the authors who consider that the national rules implementing the EU Directive are preferential is more convincing. The fundamental argument is that, as recognised by the ECJ, the European Directive only allowed a very limited margin of appreciation at the time of its implementation and that this margin was the margin allowed in the text of the Directive, meaning that Member States could not go any further. For this reason, in deciding to submit the suppliers of products to the same general system of liability as producers, France was held by the ECJ to have incorrectly implemented the Directive. If this was the case as regards the suppliers of any movable, so must it also be when it comes to suppliers of a special category of movables like, in the Spanish case, the suppliers of movable construction materials that are incorporated into a building. The liability regime applicable to these movables, therefore, can only be that established according to the Directive.[25]

---

21 In this sense, in legal doctrine, among others, *M Martín-Casals/J Solé Feliu*, La responsabilidad civil por productos defectuosos, in: M José Reyes (ed), Derecho privado de consumo (2005) 159; *P Gutiérrez Santiago*, Daños causados por productos defectuosos (2008) 65 ff; *M Ángeles Parra Lucán* (fn 12) 90.

22 Ley 38/1999, de 5 de noviembre, *de ordenación de la edificación*, BOE no 266, 06.11.1999.

23 In this sense, for instance, *E Cordero Lobato*, in A Carrasco/E Cordero Lobato/MC González Carrasco, *Comentarios a la Ley de la Edificación* (2nd edn 2001) 322 and 332.

24 ECJ judgment of 25 April 2002, Case C-52/00 [2002] ECR I-139.

25 *Ángeles Parra Lucán* (fn 12) 92. In the same vein, *P Cillero del Cabo*, La responsabilidad civil del suministrador final por daños ocasionados por productos defectuosos (2000) 148–149; *Gutiérrez Santiago* (fn 21) 75–76.

19 Article 136 TRLGDCU considers that 'gas and electricity' are products. The inclusion of electricity was determined by the Directive, and the Spanish legislature expanded the reference to gas, but it probably would not have been necessary, since the prevailing legal doctrine was already classifying gas, electricity and energy in general as movables.[26] There are many judgments applying the TRLGDCU to damage caused by fluctuations in current[27] or by gas, both in relation to explosions of gas bottles and to gas deflagrations.[28] For the same reason, water – both bottled water and the network of piped water – is also considered a 'product' as long as it can be apprehended, appropriated or transported.[29]

20 As regards blood, blood products, plasma and other substances of human origin (for instance, organs and tissues), legal doctrine considers these to be products as long as they have undergone some kind of treatment that can be compared to manufacturing.[30] However, in the case of donations, the doctrine clarifies that the private donor (who obviously does not produce goods for economic purposes or in the course of professional activity) does not count as the manufacturer, but rather the laboratory or blood or organ bank that treats or processes the human materials for subsequent transplantation or transfusion.[31]

21 Regarding the application of TRLGDCU to intangible assets, there is no case law and the doctrine has raised the issue very occasionally. When defining 'product', the text of art 136 TRLGDCU speaks only of 'movables', without referring to its tangible or intangible (or immaterial) nature. In general, the authors that have raised the issue consider that one can speak of a product in cases in which the existence of possible defective information is attached to a material manifestation.[32] Thus, defective information contained in books and other publications (such as road maps, charts, etc) and computer software

26 Instead of many, see *D Jiménez Liébana*, Responsabilidad civil: Daños causados por productos defectuosos (1998).

27 Amongst many others, SSAP Asturias 20.11.2001 (JUR 2001\35199); Tarragona 28.02.2008 (JUR 2008\144040); A Coruña 31.01.2012 (AC 2012\639); Barcelona 24.10.2012 (AC 2012\1575).

28 SSAP Albacete 09.03.2000 (AC 2000\1145); Ávila 26.07.2001 (JUR 2001\325448); Islas Baleares 20.07.2011 (AC 2011\2095).

29 In this sense, *S Cavanillas Múgica*, El Real Decreto Legislativo 1/2007, por el que se aprueba el texto refundido de la Ley General para la Defensa de los Consumidores y Usuarios y otras leyes complementarias (2008) 1 Aranzadi Civil 23; *Gutiérrez Santiago* (fn 21) 55.

30 Instead of many, *J Carles Seuba*, Concepto de producto, in: P Salvador Coderch/F Gómez Pomar (eds), Tratado de Responsabilidad Civil del Fabricante (2008) 119–120, who points out that if the only thing that person treating the substance does is to analyse it or keep it, without adding anything during the process, in all likelihood he will not be considered a manufacturer in the sense of the Act; *Jiménez Liébana* (fn 26) 170–171.

31 Among others, *Carles Seuba* (fn 30) 120; *Martín-Casals/Solé Feliu* (fn 21) 161; *Jiménez Liébana* (fn 26) 171.

32 *Jiménez Liébana* (fn 26) 155.

(software, video games, etc) are considered products to the extent that they are contained in a material medium.[33] However, we have not been able to find any reference in the Spanish doctrine to cases where misinformation is put into circulation through the Internet (downloads of games, software, fonts, etc). The authors of this report believe that they should be considered products within the meaning of the European Directive, according to a teleological interpretation of the rule. First, it should be noted that the transmission of data and information via the internet is today one of the most common forms of marketing – or, to be more precise, putting into circulation – of this type of goods. From this point of view, it can be compared to the traditional circulation of intellectual or industrial works when made through a material medium. Second, from the point of view of the scope of protection of the rule, we must bear in mind that circulation via the Internet of these types of works, if they are defective, exposes potential victims to similar – or even greater – damage to products marketed in a traditional way. Finally, the way in which information and data are put into circulation through a network can be compared to the way in which electricity (understood as the flow of particles with electric charge) is distributed through the mains. If the Product Liability Directive explicitly qualifies electricity as a product, an interpretation by analogy may also allow the flow of information and data that are put into circulation through a network to qualify as a product.

22 Finally, the Spanish legal doctrine also qualifies live animals, which in general terms are considered to be movables, as 'products',[34] as well as waste or second-hand goods, provided they have undergone any activity aimed at transforming them, such as recovery or recycling.[35]

B. THE CONCEPT OF DEFECT

23 Art 137.1 TRLGDCU follows the text of art 6(1) Directive word for word and defines the defect of the product in terms of lack of legitimately expected safety, by saying that: 'defective product shall mean any product which does not provide the safety that it could legitimately be expected to provide, taking all circumstances into account, especially the presentation of the product, its reasonable foreseeable use and the time when it was put into circulation'. Although the Spanish Act does not distinguish between the three traditional categories of defect (manufacturing defects, design defects and information defects), there is a specific statement in the TRLGDCU that is not in the European Directive, referring exclusively to

---

33 Ibid.

34 *Carles Seuba* (fn 30) 169, who quotes SAP Burgos 29.09.2006 (JUR 2007\38879), considering that an animal is a movable. In legal doctrine see also *L-H Clavería Gosálvez*, Com. Art. 335, in: C Paz-Ares/L Díez-Picazo/R Bercovitz/P Salvador (fn 11) 931.

35 *Jiménez Liébana* (fn 26) 169.

manufacturing defects. According to art 137.2 TRLGDCU, 'products are defective in all cases in which they do not provide the safety normally provided by the other items in the same series.' According to the prevailing doctrine, this is a rule that aims to ease the burden of proof on the injured party, since the proof that an item offers a level of safety that is lower than the level offered by the other items of a series allows it to be presumed that the product is defective. However, legal doctrine makes it clear that this is not a substantive rule that establishes a different definition of defect based on a different safety standard, but a procedural rule of evidence, containing a rebuttable presumption of the defect. Thus, in spite of this rule, the defendant manufacturer can still prove that the product was not defective because, according to the first paragraph of art 127 TRLGDCU, it offered the safety that it could legitimately be expected to provide 'taking into account all the circumstances'.[36]

24 Beyond this rule intended for manufacturing defects, the Spanish Act does not contain specific rules regarding the operation of the notion of defect in certain product categories, such as second-hand products, energy products, digital programmes or intellectual works. However, in spite of the fact that the TRLGDCU, according to the Directive, follows the unitary concept of defect based on the legitimate expectation of safety, in practice the Spanish courts often identify the specific type of defect that caused damage, thus distinguishing between the three typical categories of defect. Thus, for instance, some decisions refer explicitly to the three categories of defect and try to offer a definition of each of them.[37] Others speak only of manufacturing defects,[38] or of design and

36 *J Solé Feliu*, El concepto de defecto del producto en la responsabilidad civil del fabricante (1997) 609; *M Martín-Casals/J Solé Feliu*, Aplicación de la ley de responsabilidad por productos defectuosos: la explosión de una botella y el defecto de fabricación, La Ley, no 5807, 20.06.2003, 1 ff.

37 Such as SAP Baleares 28.12.2006 (AC 2007\140327), which holds that 'manufacturing defects are those that occur in isolated units of a product due to the failure of a machine or a worker. Design or construction defects are those that are due to an error at the time of projecting the product, (and) appear in the entire manufacture of a product and, therefore, are those that can harm a greater number of victims. Finally, information defects appear when the manufacturer does not inform the public adequately of the characteristics and dangers of his products.' Also SAP Barcelona 18.04.2008 (AC 2008\1609) holds that 'legal doctrine usually distinguishes three types of defects, and although the Act 22/94 does not refer to this classification, it is implicitly included in its provisions: manufacturing defects, design defects and information defects. Manufacturing defects occur during the manufacturing process, affecting one or more units of a series, which for the rest of the units is normal. Art 3.2 refers to these defects when it says that "in any case, a product is defective if it does not provide the safety normally offered by the other units of the same series". Design defects affect the very conception of the product, so that the defect is repeated in all units of the affected series ... Finally, the third group of defects is the defects of information, which involve a deficiency in the data provided about the product. They would be included in the reference to the "presentation of the product" made by art 3.1'.

38 For instance, SSTS 25.06.1996 (RJ 1996\4853); 07.11.2008 (RJ 2009\137); SAP Madrid 30.12.2013 (AC 2014\192).

manufacturing defects,[39] or of design defects.[40] Finally, others speak of defects of information.[41] In spite of this, courts do not draw further conclusions in terms of applying different standards of safety, or establishing different liability regimes depending on the category of defect. In this sense, both legal doctrine and case law resolutely defend the view that the notion of defect under the Directive is a unitary one, and that all categories are subject to the same strict liability regime.[42]

25 As for the circumstances to be taken into account in the assessment of the defect, art 136.1 TRLGDCU explicitly refers to the presentation of the product, its reasonable foreseeable use and the time it was put into circulation. To the extent that this is a list of examples ('taking into account all the circumstances and especially…'), legal doctrine adds other circumstances to this list, such as the nature of the product (products which, due to their nature, generate risks which are inevitable, but which are legitimately expected), price and production cost, or compliance with administrative rules or technical standards on product safety.[43] However, in the latter case it should be noted that mere compliance with these standards is neither decisive nor sufficient to give rise to the consideration that the product was not defective. It can act as a signal from which to presume that there was no defect, allowing the claimant, however, to prove that, despite compliance, the product was defective.[44]

26 Unlike other national laws implementing the Directive, the Spanish Act does not define what is meant by 'the time when the product was put into circulation'. In this regard, attention should be paid to the definition given by the Court of Justice of the European Communities in *O'Byrne v Sanofy Pasteur*, of 9 February 2006,[45] according to which 'a product must be considered as having been put into circulation, within the meaning of art 11 of the Directive, when it leaves the production process operated by the producer and enters a marketing

39 For instance, STS 27.07.2005 (RJ 2005\5101).

40 As in SAP Granada 05.07.2013 (JUR 2013\329302).

41 Among many others, SSTS 09.12.2010 (RJ 2011\1408); 28.05.2012 (JUR 2012\194137) SAP Madrid 30.12.2013 (AC 2014\192).

42 In this sense, among others, *Solé Feliu* (fn 36) 564 ff; *Gutiérrez Santiago* (fn 21) 82. However, some authors, under the influence of the North American approach to product liability, hold that, in fact 'liability for design or information defects seems much closer to liability for fault' (in this sense, for instance, *P Salvador Coderch et al*, Guía InDret de jurisprudència sobre responsabilidad de producto (2004) 4 InDret 3. See also *P Salvador Coderch/S Ramos*, Defectos de producto, in: P Salvador Coderch/F Gómez Pomar (eds), Tratado de Responsabilidad Civil del Fabricante (2008) 162.

43 Among others, *Martín-Casals/Solé Feliu* (fn 21) 172; *Salvador Coderch/Ramos* (fn 42) 170 ff.

44 *Martín-Casals/Solé Feliu* (fn 21) 173, who point out that safety expectations whose infringement gives rise to the defect are not the 'legal' expectations, but the 'legitimate' ones; *Salvador Coderch/Ramos* (fn 42) 171.

45 Case C-127/2004.

process in the form in which it is offered to the public in order to be used or consumed' (paras 27 and 32). Previously, the Spanish doctrine defined putting into circulation as the moment of 'voluntary delivery of the product by the manufacturer',[46] which was made up of two elements, a subjective one consisting of voluntariness by the manufacturer, and an objective one consisting of the physical delivery to a person outside his own sphere of control.[47] It is also noted that this definition should be interpreted with some flexibility, in light of the ECJ judgment in *Henning Veedfald v Århus Amtskommune*,[48] which established that a product is also put into circulation when 'the use of the product is characterised by the fact that the person for whom it is intended must bring himself within that sphere of control (of the producer)' (para 17), as is the case when the victim is a patient who goes to a hospital where he suffers damage caused by a defective product. In this regard, it is stated that in cases where those two factors (physical delivery and voluntariness) do not exist, it is also understood that the product has been put into circulation when the potential victims flock to the sphere of control of the producer and the product exposes external third parties to risks arising from the defect, as in the case of products displayed at fairs and exhibitions, or in cases of transfer of the product for a test, etc.[49]

27 In any case, the assessment as to whether the product was defective should be made, at the latest, at the time when it was put into circulation, so that any activity after that time will be irrelevant to attribute liability to the corresponding manufacturer. Therefore, if the defect occurs during storage, transport or shipment, if the producer was in charge of these operations and consequently the product was still within his sphere of control, the producer is responsible under TRLGDCU. However, one must bear in mind that, before reaching its final destination, the product can be put into circulation by several manufacturers (the manufacturer of a component part or raw material delivers it to the final manufacturer, who in turn delivers the product to the supplier, who will respond only in exceptional circumstances, etc). All this implies that the time when the product was put into circulation for each of the possible responsible subjects is different and, at the same time, that it acts as the limit of liability of each of them. That is, if the manufacturer of raw materials or of the component part delivers it free from defects to the end manufacturer and the defect appears when the product was within the sphere of control of the latter, during his handling, storage or transportation activities, the former will not be liable, because at the time the former put the product into circulation there

46 *Solé Feliu* (fn 36) 263 ff.
47 Ibid.
48 ECJ Judgment of 10 May 2001, Case C-203/1999.
49 In this sense, *M Martín-Casals/J Solé Feliu*, La responsabilidad por productos defectuosos: un intento de armonización a través de Directivas, in: S Cámara Lapuente (ed), Derecho Privado Europeo (2003) 924.

was no defect.[50] Erroneous instructions for use, installation or operation given after the product was put into circulation, as well as other after-sales services, do not necessarily make the product defective, although they can give rise to fault liability on the part of the producer if a duty of care required him to have avoided them.

28 Finally, in Spain there are no categories of products subject to different and specific criteria of defects, or for which safety expectations are different from the objective and general standard deriving from TRLGDCU, which implements the Directive.

C. THE DUTIES OF CARE OF THE MANUFACTURER: PRODUCT LIABILITY AND PRODUCT SAFETY

29 The rules implementing the European Directive on product liability for defective products do not refer to any duties of care imposed on the manufacturer, infringement of which would lead to liability. In this regard, it must be borne in mind that TRLGDCU establishes a strict liability regime and that the conditions for liability – derived from the Directive – refer only to the defect, damage and the causal link between the two. So, according to this, a manufacturer's fault plays no role in the domestic Act transposing the Directive.

30 However, the manufacturer's duties of care may have a role within the framework of fault liability arising from art 1902 CC. In this regard, it is considered that the duties imposed on manufacturers by the rules on product safety are incorporated into the standard of conduct required of manufacturers. Accordingly, the infringement of these duties will give rise to negligence of the manufacturers and, if the other conditions are met, will lead to their liability.[51] These duties encompass those imposed by Directive 2001/95/EC on general product safety[52] and the Spanish implementation norm, the Royal Decree 1801/2003 of 26 December on general product safety.[53] Such duties include the duty to inform consumers and users of the risks that are not immediately obvious without adequate warnings and that follow the normal or foreseeable use of products. Manufacturers must also report these risks to distributors of their products. After the products have been put into circulation, manufacturers

---

50 *Solé Feliu* (fn 36) 300 ff.

51 See *J Solé Feliu*, Responsabilidad por productos defectuosos. Seguridad de productos. Producto defectuoso. Comentario a la STS 9.12.2010 (2012) 88 Cuadernos Civitas de Jurisprudencia Civil 101–104.

52 [2002] OJ L11/4.

53 Real Decreto 1801\2003, de 26 de diciembre, *sobre seguridad general de los productos*, BOE no 9, 10.01.2004.

must also take all appropriate measures to avoid risks arising from their products, including the obligation to inform consumers by posting special notices and, if necessary, even by withdrawal of products from the market or by recall of the products already supplied to consumers (art 4 Real Decree 1801\2003). This is, therefore, a regulation that incorporates into its norms the so-called duties of observation and monitoring of the product, and of product recall[54] when this is strictly necessary (as established by art 5(1) Directive 2001/95/EC).

31 However, it should be noted that, according to legal doctrine and case law, mere compliance with these legal safety duties (found in administrative law rules that have a preventive function, but which are not intended to establish liability) is not sufficient to consider that the manufacturer has acted with due care. In this regard, case law has consistently pointed out that in the area of product liability based on art 1902 CC mere compliance with regulations does not exempt the manufacturer from liability. The manufacturer must increase his diligence and take 'other measures of care and diligence required by the nature of the product' which are necessary to avoid damage.[55] In any case, when these rules on product safety are put in relation to the strict liability regime based on Directive 85/374/EEC, as noted above, mere compliance does not avoid liability if, despite respecting controls, safety and quality norms, tests and related inspections, the product is unsafe beyond what is legitimately expected and causes the sort of damage covered by the Directive.[56]

III. THE PERSON LIABLE FOR DAMAGE

A. LIABLE PERSONS ACCORDING TO THE TRLGDCU

32 The TRLGDCU holds the 'producer' liable for damage caused by defective products. The notion of 'producer' includes: (i) the manufacturer of the finished product, (ii) the manufacturer of any component part incorporated into the finished product, and (iii) the producer a raw material (art 138.1 TRLGDCU). For the purposes of the strict liability regime, other persons can be equated to the producer; these are: (iv) the apparent producer, namely the person who 'presents himself as such by putting on the product, either on the packaging or in any other element of protection or presentation, his name, trade mark or

[54] *Solé Feliu* (fn 36) 576–577.

[55] SSTS 10.06.2002 (RJ 2002\6198); 29.03.2006 (RJ 2006\1868). On this issue, see *Martín-Casals/Solé Feliu* (fn 6) 262–263; *Solé Feliu* (fn 51) 103.

[56] *M Ángeles Parra Lucán*, Responsabilidad civil por productos defectuosos, in: LF Reglero Campos (ed), Tratado de responsabilidad civil, T II (4th edn 2008) 585; *Solé Feliu* (fn 51) 93.

other distinguishing feature' (art 5 TRLGDCU), and (v) the importer of the product in the territory of the European Union. Exceptionally, (vi) the supplier of the product can also be held liable in two cases. The first coincides with the provisions of the Directive, which provides for the subsidiary liability of the supplier unless within three months (the Spanish legislature specifies the 'reasonable time' mentioned in the Directive) the supplier informs the injured person of the identity of the producer or of the person who supplied him with the product (art 138.2 TRGLDCU). In the second exception, the Spanish Act includes a case of liability of the supplier not foreseen in the Directive, where the supplier puts the product into circulation 'knowing the defect' (art 146 TRLGDCU). This second case has been criticised by the doctrine, as is discussed later on (nos 38–39).

33 When several of these subjects contribute to cause damage, art 132 TRLGDCU establishes that they are liable *in solido* to the injured person. Then the person who has paid compensation to the victim will be able to ask for contribution from the other liable subjects 'according to their participation in the causation of the injury'.

34 Although the text of art 138.1 TRLGDCU does not explicitly say so, the prevailing doctrine considers that the status of the liable producer implies that the manufacture or, where appropriate, the marketing of the defective product has been conducted within the framework of a professional activity or, at least, with economic purpose, as derived from the defence provided for under art 140.1.c) TRLGDCU.[57] It is also understood that liability falls on the individual who is in charge of the organisation and/or acting under his own responsibility, and not on the workers or auxiliaries.[58]

35 The manufacturer of a finished product is the person whose activity gives rise to a product that is ready to be put into circulation, even if he has merely assembled parts manufactured by others.[59] Therefore, if the defect is in a component part or in a raw material, the final producer will be liable together with the other producers since the defect is also transferred to the finished product.[60] As the SAP Madrid 08.11.2007 (RJ 2008\45612) concerning a defect in the wheel of a car, says, 'if the wheel was defective, the whole car should qualify as defective'. If so, all producers will be held liable *in solido*, but this will not prevent the final manufacturer from bringing a claim for contribution against

57 *Martín-Casals/Solé Feliu* (fn 21) 162; *F Cerdà Albero/J Carles Seuba Torreblanca*, Sujetos responsables, in: P Salvador Coderch/F Gómez Pomar (eds), Tratado de Responsabilidad Civil del Fabricante (2008) 222; *Jiménez Liébana* (fn 26) 260.

58 *Cerdà Albero/Carles Seuba Torreblanca* (fn 57) 222.

59 *Ángeles Parra Lucán* (fn 12) 150.

60 Ibid; *Cerdà Albero/Carles Seuba Torreblanca* (fn 57) 232.

the manufacturer of the component part or the raw material on the grounds of art 132 TRLGDCU (art 5 Directive). Nevertheless, it should be noted that the manufacturer of a defective component part may be exempted from liability if he proves that the defect is attributable to the design of the product in which the component has been fitted or to the instructions given by the manufacturer of the product (art 140.2 TRLGDCU).

36 Art 138 TRGLDCU does not refer to the case where the defective product has been manufactured under assignment or licensing of a patent. According to the text of the Spanish Act (and to the European Directive itself), it seems that the responsibility rests solely on the actual manufacturer, ie the transferee or licensed manufacturer, to whom the Directive refers. This is without prejudice to the fact that, once he has paid compensation, he can bring a claim for contribution against the transferor or the licensor of the patent.[61] However, art 78 of the Spanish Patent Act (Act 11/1986 of 2 March) provides for solidary liability between the transferor (or licensor) and transferee (or licensee) in the case of compensation arising from damage caused to third parties by defects inherent in the invention. The Spanish legal doctrine understands that this rule does not fit well within the structure of the system of liability arising from the Product Liability Directive. Accordingly, it discusses whether keeping the wording of art 78 of the Patent Act in force constitutes a breach by the Spanish State of its obligations under Directive 85/374/EEC.[62] However, the new Patent Act, passed in July 2015[63] and in force from 1 April 2017, reproduces in art 86.1 the same wording as in the aforementioned art 78 of the former Patent Act (now still in force).[64]

37 Regarding liability of the importer into the European Union, legal doctrine understands that this notion of 'importer' includes importers of finished products as well as importers of component parts and raw materials.[65] An isolated judgment has misunderstood the concept and applied the Spanish law transposing the Directive to the importer into Spain of a product that was manufactured in Italy.[66] Most decisions, however, understand well what the purpose of the Directive is. Thus, for instance, SAP Barcelona 29.11.2004 (AC

61 In this sense, *Ángeles Parra Lucán* (fn 12) 155; *Cerdà Albero/Carles Seuba Torreblanca* (fn 57) 230.

62 *Ángeles Parra Lucán* (fn 12) 156.

63 Ley 24/2015, de 24 de julio, *de patentes*, BOE no 177, 25.07.2015.

64 According to this new art 86, under the heading of 'liability to third parties': '1. The person who transfers a patent application or a patent already granted or who grants a license on them, will be solidarily liable with the transferee or licensee for damages that might arise as a result of damage caused to third parties by defects that are inherent in the invention to which the application or patent was made'.

65 *Martín-Casals/Solé Feliu* (fn 21) 163.

66 SAP Lleida 14.11.2002 (JUR 2002\20687).

2004\2017), explains that 'the concept of the importer that has to be taken into account is not the general one, that is, the national company or entrepreneur who introduces into Spain products from another country, either from the Community or not, for marketing'. On the contrary, 'the importer is the one who... imports products from a country outside the European Union, introducing them to any country thereof'[67] (in this sense, and also correctly applying the transposition of the Directive when excluding liability of the importer from an individual EU country to another.[68]

38 As regards the supplier, art 7 TRLGDCU defines him as 'an entrepreneur that supplies or distributes products in the market, irrespective of the entitlement or contract by virtue of which such distribution is carried out'. Just as in the Directive, his liability is exceptional and subsidiary and it takes place when the identity of the producer is unknown and the supplier has not identified him within three months. Spanish case law considers this period to start running from the time of 'formal request by the injured party'.[69] At first, some Spanish decisions did not properly enforce this liability regime and ordered suppliers to pay damages, even when the manufacturer of the defective product was identified.[70] However, the prevailing case law has subsequently rejected supplier's liability where the manufacturer is identified[71] and, conversely, has admitted liability where the manufacturer had not been identified or when such identification occurred after the three months period specified by law had expired.[72]

39 In addition to this case, the other case of liability of the supplier introduced by the Spanish legislator in art 146 TRLGDCU and not expressly provided for by the Directive refers to the supplier with fraud or intent. Thus, 'the supplier of a defective product shall be liable, as if he were a producer, when he has supplied a product knowing of the existence of the defect. In this case, the supplier shall be able to bring an action for recoupment against the producer'. According to the prevailing legal doctrine, if the injured party can prove that the supplier put a defective product into circulation 'knowingly', he does not actually need to bring a claim on the grounds of the TRLGDCU regime, and

---

67 In the same vein, STS 14.07.2003 (RJ 2003\5837).

68 Among others, SSAP Zaragoza 10.02.2004 (JUR 2004\92259) and Barcelona 20.12.2005 (JUR 2005\85658).

69 Thus, in SAP Barcelona 20.03.2012 (AC 2012\901), the date on which the *burofax* was sent.

70 See, for instance, SAP Badajoz 08.04.1999 (AC 1999\674) on the explosion of a butane gas cylinder with a manufacturing defect.

71 See, among many others SSAP Asturias 24.05.2001 (JUR 2001\214430); Asturias 31.07.2003 (JUR 2004\15503); Cáceres 21.06.2002 (JUR 2002\226019); Badajoz 14.07.2003 (JUR 2004\46697).

72 Such as SAP Barcelona 20.03.2012 (AC 2012\901), in which the supplier was held liable because he reported the identity of the manufacturer more than seven months after the injured party had filed the formal complaint.

may have recourse to the general rules of contractual (art 1486.2 CC) or tort (art 1902 CC) liability. These other rules provide for legal regimes that are more favourable for the victim than the regime derived from the provisions of the Directive. Among other consequences, all categories of damage, including non-pecuniary loss (the text the Spanish transposition excludes non-pecuniary loss, as discussed below) can be claimed for and compensation is not subject to the limit of the franchise for damage to property, etc.[73] Moreover, there are doubts about whether the introduction of a rule of this kind is in fact an infringement of EU Directive.[74]

B. PUBLIC AUTHORITIES AS PRODUCERS

40 In Spain, there are no judgments that have applied the national law implementing the Directive to cases of liability of public authorities. The cases in which public authorities are involved in any question relating to compensation for damage possibly caused by defective products, such as in cases of blood contaminated with hepatitis C or HIV, are usually dealt with in the administrative courts, and legal norms applied to these cases are those corresponding to the liability of public authorities, contained in Act 30/1992 of 26 November, on the legal regime of the Public Administrations and Common Administrative Procedure.[75] This is a result of the internal structure of the Spanish legal system established by two reforms that took place in 1998, regarding the Organic Law of the Judiciary (LOPJ),[76] and 1999, amending the aforementioned Act 30/1992,[77] which made clear that public authorities can be held liable solely before the administrative courts and in accordance with the provisions of Act 30/1992.

---

73 Legal doctrine is unanimous in this sense. Instead of many, see *Ángeles Parra Lucán* (fn 12) 160–161; *Cerdà Albero/Carles Seuba Torreblanca* (fn 57) 230; *Martín-Casals/Solé Feliu* (fn 21) 165.

74 In this sense, *Ángeles Parra Lucán* (fn 12) 161. Others scholars, however, consider that the rule does not infringe Community law, since when it establishes liability for intent of the supplier, this means that the Spanish legislature is not transposing the Directive in this point, ie it is abandoning the strict liability regime provided by the Directive. What it does is reposition liability under the general rules of liability for fault existing in Spanish law which, according to art 128 TRLGDCU (art 13 Directive), are compatible with the rules of the Directive. In this sense, *Martín-Casals/Solé Feliu* (fn 20) 105–106; *Cillero del Cabo* (fn 25) 241.

75 Ley 30/1992, de 26 de noviembre, *de régimen jurídico de las Administraciones Públicas y del Procedimiento Administrativo Común*, BOE no 285, 27.11.1992, amended by Ley 4/1999, de 13 de febrero, de modificación de la Ley 30/1992, de 26 de novembre, de régimen jurídico de las administraciones públicas y del procedimiento administrativo común (BOE no 12, 14.01.1999).

76 Art 9.4 of the LOPJ, in the wording given by LO 6/1998, de 13 de julio, del Poder Judicial (BOE no 167, 14.07.1998).

77 See fn 62.

41 The legal liability regime deriving from this legislation, although it imposes a strict liability for damage caused by normal and abnormal functioning of public services (arts 139 ff), is different from the one resulting from the legislation implementing the Directive 85/374/EEC. These differences are particularly evident in relation to the development risks defence. Thus, TRLGDCU, in implementing the Directive, does not accept the exemption of liability for a (private) producer of food and medicines intended for human consumption (as is the case, for example, with contaminated blood) when the state of scientific and technical knowledge at the time he put the product into circulation was not such as to enable the existence of the defect to be discovered. By contrast, when the person acting as producer is a public authority, art 141.1 of Act 30/1992 does allow him to be freed from liability. Some authors emphasise that this diversity of regimes could infringe the provisions of the EU Directive, since the ECJ has recognised that the Defective Products Directive applies to public authorities (*Heenning Veedfald v Åhrus Amtskommune*).[78] Additionally, as regards the development risks defence, they point out that art 15 Directive allowed Member States to choose whether or not to include it in their transposition, but not to do so only with regard to a particular category of potentially responsible subjects.[79]

IV. THE AGGRIEVED PERSON AND DAMAGE

A. THE AGGRIEVED PERSON

42 The persons who can claim compensation for damage caused by a defective product are 'all injured persons', as provided in art 128 TRLGDCU (cf also art 129.1 TRLGDCU). Thus, the scope of protection of TRLGDCU, following the same line that the Directive already marked out, is not limited to consumers and users of products, but also extends to any person who, even unrelated to the use or consumption of the product (bystander), suffers damage caused by a defect.[80] In this sense, the implementation of the European Directive extended the scope of protection of the rules existing until then in arts 25–29 of LGDCU-1984, whose scope was limited to protecting consumers from defective products.

---

78 Case C-203/99, *Henning Veedfald v Åhrus Amtskommune* [2001] ECR I-3569.

79 In this sense, instead of many, *Martín-Casals/Solé Feliu* (fn 49) 941; *Ángeles Parra Lucán* (fn 12) 185–187.

80 For this reason legal doctrine has criticised the fact that the current implementation of the Defective Product Directive has been included in the Consolidated Text of the General Consumer and User Protection Act, since as unanimously recognised by European legal doctrine and by the Preamble of the Directive itself, this is not a 'consumer Directive', but a Directive issued under the legislative powers dealing with the internal market, and seeks to strike a balance between the interests of consumers and manufacturers. In this sense, *Martín-Casals/Solé Feliu* (fn 20) 80 ff.

Along these lines, a decision of the Court of Appeal of Zamora[81] says that 'the application of the rules on product liability regarding defective products has a wider subjective scope than the rules relating to the protection of consumers and users … the circle of the persons protected being wider than the end consumer to which the Act 26/1984 referred, since it encompasses all persons injured by a defective product, in general, regardless of whether they have the strict condition of consumer or not'.

43 In this regard, it should be noted that the Directive defines the protected interests not on the basis of the subjective nature of the injured person (as a consumer or as an entrepreneur or professional), but from the perspective of the recoverable damage. Thus, personal injury and death are always compensated for, regardless of whether the injured person is a private individual with no further qualification, a consumer, an entrepreneur or a professional. However, in the case of damage to property, damage is compensated for only to the extent that the damaged property was 'objectively intended for private use or consumption, and has been used mainly as such by the injured party' (art 129.1 TRLGDCU).[82]

B. DAMAGE

44 Under Spanish law, the notion of damage in the area of product liability is different from the notion that can be found in other areas of civil liability. However, following the same criteria adopted by the Directive 85/374/EEC, compensation for damage in the area of product liability is subject to a number of limitations, both in substantive and in quantitative terms.

1) Personal Injury and Death: the Strange Exclusion of Moral Damage

45 First, and in line with what has been stated in the previous section on protected individuals, the Spanish Act covers death and personal injury, regardless of whether the victim is a consumer, entrepreneur, professional or third person or bystander (art 129.1 TRLGDCU). This should be understood in the sense that the pecuniary losses caused by death and bodily injury, such as general medical and health care expenses, rehabilitation, adaptation of housing and vehicle, burial costs, loss of earnings, etc, are recoverable pursuant to the transposition.[83] It also appears that compensation for psychophysical or

81 SAP Zamora 26.04.2013 (AC 2013\1129).
82 *Martín-Casals/Solé Feliu* (fn 21) 163.
83 *Gutiérrez Santiago* (fn 21) 95.

anatomic-functional harm can also be recovered.[84] However, paradoxically, the Spanish legislature has excluded compensation for moral damage from the protection of the law of product liability when, according to the Spanish general rules, all non-pecuniary losses enjoy a wide scope of protection.

46 Making use of the option established in art 9 Directive, which allowed Member States to exclude compensation for so-called 'non-material damage' in their national implementing legislation, in the first Spanish Act transposing the Directive the legislator excluded compensation for moral damage in art 10.2 LRPD and referred to the general civil law rules for its compensation.[85] According to the prevailing legal doctrine, the new recast of the Act transposing the Directive, now contained in the TRLGDCU, does not change this solution and, therefore, moral damage is still excluded from the scope of protection of the Spanish regulation transposing the Directive.[86] Nevertheless, a minority position advocated by the authors of this report considers that the fact that the current TRLGDCU separates into two different provisions the rules that establish the compatibility of strict liability under the Directive and the general civil liability rules, both in contract and in tort, on the one hand, and the rules on the scope of protection covered by the norm transposing the Directive, on the other, allows for a different interpretation in favour of the inclusion of moral damage into the scope of TRLGDCU. Thus, to the extent that the reference to the exclusion of moral damage has disappeared from the text of the current art 129.1 TRLGDCU, which delimits the scope of protection of the Act and declares that the strict liability regime for defective products 'includes personal injury, including death [*sic*]', it can be understood in the sense that it now also includes compensation for moral damage resulting both from personal injury and death.[87] This interpretation is not inconsistent with the fact that art 128.2 TRLGDCU, which states that the regime of strict liability under the Directive is compatible with the other general systems of contractual and tort liability, contains a reference to moral damage. What this provision in fact wants to make clear is that when the injured party has suffered damage caused by a defective product, he can choose to resort to strict liability for defective products under the Directive, or to other general liability regimes, either in contractual or in

---

84 *Martín-Casals/Solé Feliu* (fn 21) 187.

85 However, when the Spanish transposition Act was being drafted, an important part of legal doctrine favoured including compensation for non-pecuniary loss, since this was considered the most consistent solution with Spanish law. Instead of many, see *M Ángeles Parra Lucán*, Daños por productos y protección del consumidor (1990) 585; *Bercovitz Rodríguez-Cano* (fn 17) 111). In the end, the legislature did not adopt this proposal.

86 In this sense, *Ángeles Parra Lucán* (fn 12) 201; *F Gómez Pomar*, Ámbito de protección de la responsabilidad de producto, in: P Salvador Coderch/F Gómez Pomar (eds), Tratado de Responsabilidad Civil del Fabricante (2008) 704; *Cavanillas Múgica* (fn 29) 15 ff.

87 *Martín-Casals/Solé Feliu* (fn 20) 98–99.

tort, for compensation for all the 'damage, including moral damage', which is perfectly consistent with the logic of the Directive.[88]

47 That the exclusion of moral damage is alien to the Spanish civil liability system is evidenced by the fact that the Spanish courts always try to overcome this difficulty by awarding compensation for moral damage in cases governed by the Act transposing the Directive by using two different procedures that are not always in accordance with the wording of the articles of the domestic transposition norm. The first procedure is to simply ignore the wording of the transposition norm and compensate for all damage caused by the defective product, both damage to property and personal injury and death, including pain and suffering, without any reference to the problem. Quite often, when assessing the amount of compensation in the case of personal injury and death, courts apply as guidance the heads of losses and the corresponding amounts provided in the road traffic compensation scheme included in the Annex of the Road Traffic Liability Act. This scheme has many flaws and one of them is that it does not distinguish between pecuniary and non-pecuniary losses or, in the case of bodily harm, between psychophysical injury and strict moral damage.[89]

48 The second procedure, more in line with the TRLGDCU, can be found in those judgments where the court, being aware that the Spanish transposition norm has excluded moral damage from its scope of protection, finds fault of the manufacturer along with the defect of the product. In this way the court can conclude that all the conditions required to establish liability according to the general tort liability regime of art 1902 CC are also present, and that all those heads of loss which the TRLGDCU excludes are then covered by the tort liability regime. In this vein, for instance, there are some decisions stating that: 'since there is a defect it follows that the controls implemented by the manufacturer are not sufficient or have not worked properly, and a product has been put on the market with a serious flaw, so all the conditions that Article 1902 of the Civil Code requires to establish liability have been met'.[90]

49 As for compensation for death and personal injury, the Spanish legislature included a maximum quantitative limit of liability in the amount of

---

88 Art 128.2 TRLGDCU: 'The actions recognised in this book do not affect the injured party's other rights to be compensated for damage, including pain and suffering, as a consequence of contractual liability, on the grounds of the lack of conformity of goods or services or any other cause of non-performance or defective performance of the contract, or of any non-contractual liability which may apply.'

89 Thus, among many others, SSAP Granada 12.02.2000 (AC 2000\851); Cantabria 20.06.2005 (JUR 2005\176100) Sevilla 06.06.2006 (JUR 2006\40535); Murcia 22.09.2008 (AC 2009\826) SAP Barcelona 20.03.2012 (AC 2012\901); Madrid 29.10.2012 (AC 2012\1593).

90 SAP Ciudad Real 26.11.2001 (JUR 2002\32632); SAP Santa Cruz de Tenerife 19.04.2002 (AC 2002\898).

€63,106,270.90 (art 141.b) TRLGDCU). This is a ceiling for damage caused by identical items with the same defect, and corresponds to the option included art 16.1 Directive which allowed Member States to establish an overall limit on liability of producers, which could not be less than 70 million ECU. If one sticks to the provisions of Regulation (EC) No 1103/97 of 17 June 1997 on certain provisions relating to the introduction of the euro, it seems that, based on the rule of equivalence that 1 ECU = 1 euro, the limit should be €70 million. However, the Spanish legislature has made the conversion to euros from the maximum amount established in pesetas before the entry into force of the euro (1 euro = 166.368 pesetas), so that the limit originally set at 10,500 million pesetas has led to the current limit of €63,106,270.94, lower than the limit established in the Directive. This raises the question as to whether Spanish law contravenes Community law on this point.[91]

2) Property Damage and Damage to the Product Itself

50 As regards property damage caused by a defective product, art 129.1 TRLGDCU states that it is recoverable provided that it 'might affect property [and services, *sic*] … which are objectively intended for private use or consumption, and have been used mainly as such by the injured party'. In line with art 9(b) Directive, the Spanish legislature subjects the protection of damage to property to the condition that the property is for the private use of the injured party, and excludes from this protection property (commercial, industrial, professional or artisanal) that falls within to his professional sphere.[92] Similarly, this damage is defined on the basis of two criteria: an objective one, saying that damaged property must be 'objectively intended for private use or consumption' in the sense of non-professional use; and a subjective one, in the sense that the injured party has used it for private use or consumption, this criterion being relevant for products which, by their nature, can be used interchangeably both privately and professionally.[93]

51 In Spanish case law, some judgments – fortunately not a majority – have not taken this definition into account, and have compensated, according to the transposition norm, damage caused to property that was clearly for professional or business use. This is the case, for instance, of damage caused by an power surge to the equipment and facilities of the bar of the injured party (SAP Huesca 24.11.1998 (AC 1998\8667));[94] of damage caused to the facilities of

91 See *Ángeles Parra Lucán* (fn 12) 203.

92 Following the Explanation Memorandum of the Directive, *Jiménez Liébana* (fn 26) 385.

93 *M Martín-Casals/J Solé Feliu*, Veinte problemas en la aplicación de la Ley de responsabilidad por productos defectuosos y propuestas de solución (II) (2003) 10 Práctica Derecho de Daños. Revista de Responsabilidad Civil y Seguros 19; *Jiménez Liébana* (fn 26) 397.

94 See also SAP A Coruña 31.01.2012 (AC 2012\639).

a concessionaire of vehicles by a vehicle in fire due to a manufacturing defect (STS 30.04.2008 (RJ 2008\2686)); or of damage to the facilities and equipment in a hairdressing salon by a fire caused by a water heater manufactured by the defendant (SAP Burgos 13.02.2003 (JUR 2003\122404)). Other decisions, however, correctly apply the Directive and exclude compensation considering that damage was 'affecting property intended for professional or industrial use inherent to the activity of a supermarket developed by the purchaser, and not for his private use or consumption' (SAP Las Palmas 22.03.2001 (JUR 2001\170616), in a case in which the damaged goods were in the fridge of a supermarket).[95] Similarly, SAP Madrid 19.10.2010 (AC 2010\1804) excluded the application of the norms transposing the Directive because the damage caused by a defective product to a 'pool of a garden located on an office floor of an industrial building owned by a company engaged in direct sales of office furniture, is part of the premises of an immovable property which ... cannot be considered intended for private use and consumption'.

52 In line with art 9(1)(b) Directive, art 141.a) TRLGDCU includes a franchise regarding compensation for property damage, stating that '[a] release of 500.00 euros shall be deducted from the amount of compensation for damage to property'.[96] In any case, as recognised by the ECJ in the judgments issued on 25 April 2002[97] concerning the norms transposing the Directive in France and Greece, respectively, Member States cannot escape the incorporation of the franchise, since its inclusion, which aims to prevent the accumulation of claims of little economic value, is 'the result of a complex balancing of different interests ... directed at maintaining undistorted competition, promoting trade within the common market, protecting consumers and ensuring the proper administration of justice'.[98]

53 Initially, some authors were in favour of interpreting the franchise as a minimum limit, so that when damages were lower than the amount, the system provided by the transposition norm of the Directive could not apply. However, when the amount of the franchise was exceeded, all damages based on the

95 Along the same lines, SAP Alicante 08.01.2001 (JUR 2001\48487), also rejected compensating for any damage caused to food contained in the fridge of a supermarket since 'the fridge is installed in a supermarket business, intended for storage of products intended for sale, so this is a professional use or consumption not included in protected property by the Act 22/1994' (see also SAP Asturias 08.04.2002 (JUR 2002\164362)).

96 This provision provided originally a franchise of €390.66, but it has been recently amended by the Act Ley 15/2015, de 2 de julio, *de la jurisdicción voluntaria*, in the sense of harmonizing this former amount to €500.00, in accordance with the majority of national transposing legislation.

97 Cases C-52/00 and C-154/00.

98 *Commission v France*, paras 29–34; *Commission v Greece*, paras 22–24.

strict liability of the Directive could be claimed.[99] Nevertheless, the currently prevailing position, based on the wording of art 141.a) TRLGDCU holds that the amount of €390.66 must always be deducted from the amount of damages in all claims based on the transposition norm.[100] This effect forces the applicant wishing to obtain full compensation to bring, additionally, the other actions based on the general contractual or tort liability rules, in respect of which the established franchise does not operate.[101]

54 As is known, maintenance or possible removal of the franchise is one of the aspects that is periodically debated in the European context, as shown by successive Commission Reports on the implementation of Directive 85/374/EEC. However, the European Commission has so far decided to keep it and no reform of the Directive in this regard is in sight.[102] In any case, reception of the franchise in Spanish case law has been problematic, and there is a (totally wrong) line of case law that applies the TRLGDCU and compensates the full amount of the damage caused by products without deducting the amount of the excess. This gives rise to what one author has described as the 'amnesia' of the Spanish courts as regards the franchise provided for in art 141.a) TRLGDCU. Thus, for instance, SAP Zamora 26.04.2013 (AC 2013\1129), dealing with the fire of a defective oven and where the court compensated for damage to parts of damaged pottery as well as the costs of repair to the oven and for the replenishment of extinguishers used. The court calculated the damages to be €5,483.32, and did not deduct any amount for the franchise established by law.[103] On some occasions, however, the court is aware of the quantitative limitation, and in order to be able to compensate for the full amount takes recourse to the general rule of fault liability of art 1902 CC, considering that the manufacturer's fault has been established by proving the existence of the defect. Thus, for instance, in a decision of the Court of Appeal of Ciudad Real,[104] concerning damage caused by the timing belt of a vehicle that was defective, where, in response to the claim, the defendant on appeal argued for the need to deduct the amount corresponding to the franchise.

---

99 This was the opinion, for instance, of *Bercovitz Rodríguez-Cano* (fn 17) 113.

100 In favour of this position *Martín-Casals/Solé Feliu* (fn 21) 191; *Jiménez Liébana* (fn 26) 402; *Ángeles Parra Lucán* (fn 56) 1240; *Gutiérrez Santiago* (fn 21) 117–118.

101 As accepted, *inter alia*, by SSAP A Coruña 28.02.2007 (JUR 2007\142427) and Almeria 11.06.2007 (JUR 2007\358440).

102 Report from the Commission to the European Parliament, the Council and the European Economic and Social Committee, Fourth report on the application of Council Directive 85/374/EEC of 25 July 1985 on the approximation of the laws, regulations and administrative provisions of the Member States concerning liability for defective products amended by Directive 1999/34/EC of the European Parliament and of the Council of 10 May 1999, Brussels, 08.09.2011, COM(2011)547 final, 12 <http://eur-lex.europa.eu/LexUriServ/LexUriServ.do?uri=COM:2011:0547:FIN:EN:PDF>.

103 Similarly, among others, SSAP Córdoba 19.06.2002 (JUR 2002\212207); Valencia 17.09.2002 (AC 2002\1658).

104 SAP Ciudad Real 26.11.2001 (JUR 2002\32632).

The court accepted the argument, but ordered the defendant to pay damages in full on the grounds that, along with the conditions of liability required by the transposition norm, the defendant was also liable pursuant to art 1902 CC. According to the court, 'since there was a defect, it follows that that the controls implemented by the manufacturer were insufficient or did not function properly, and that he had brought a product with a serious defect on the market, and for this reason all conditions required by art. 1902 of the Civil Code are met'. Finally, on some other occasions courts apply only the norm transposing the Directive and compensate for property damage by deducting exactly the amount corresponding to the franchise.[105]

55 Article 142 TRLGDCU excludes from the scope of protection of the transposition norm (in the same way as art 9(b) Directive) property damage to the product itself, for which compensation must awarded 'in accordance with civil and commercial legislation'. As is known, the reason for this exclusion is in the idea that the damage to the defective product itself constitutes an interest protected by contract and compensation for it is determined by the rules governing contractual liability.[106] In the field of consumer goods, the contractual regulation is that resulting from Directive 99/44/EEC on certain aspects of the sale of consumer goods and associated guarantees, which Spain has implemented through arts 114–127 TRLGDCU. According to them, a product defect that causes a lack of conformity with the contract allows consumers to choose to exercise one of the contractual remedies available in arts 118 and 119 TRLGDCU, which are, alternatively, repair or replacement of the product and, subsidiarily, price reduction or termination of the contract.

V. CAUSATION

A. GENERAL RULES ON CAUSATION IN SPANISH LAW

56 Under Spanish law, there are no specific rules on causation in the field of product liability, which is therefore governed by the general rules in tort liability. The basic rule on causation in the field of product liability is in art 135

---

105 Cf SAP Burgos 13.02.2003 (JUR 2003\122404): as regards this aspect, the decision is correct, but not as regards compensation for property damage caused by the fire in a hair salon by a defective water heater manufactured by the defendant. The decision applies the transposing Act (LRPD) and despite deducting the franchise, pays damages for damage to the commercial property, consisting of repair costs, debris removal, payment of fire extinguishing services, as well as damage in the content, consisting of the equipment used in the practice of the professional activity of hairdressing. All these losses were clearly damage to property intended for business or entrepreneurial use, which is excluded from the protection of the Directive.

106 *Ángeles Parra Lucán* (fn 12) 207.

TRLGDCU, which merely states that 'producers shall be liable for damage caused by defects in the products that they manufacture or import'. At the same time, as regards proof of causation, art 139 TRLGDCU provides that 'the injured party seeking to obtain compensation for damage must prove the defect, damage and the causal link between them'.

57 Therefore, in terms of causation, we should refer to the general rules of causation in tort, where the current case law of the Spanish Supreme Court, following the approach taken by legal doctrine,[107] emphasises the need to distinguish between factual causation, based on the criterion of the *conditio sine qua non*, and legal causation or 'objective imputation', which tries to establish 'whether the harmful result produced is objectively attributable to the agent or not', in the sense that it can be charged to him.[108] Among the criteria of legal causation or 'objective imputation' used in Spanish courts are: adequate causation, which is usually the most common criterion;[109] the general risk to life;[110] the protective purpose of the rule;[111] and provocation and intervening causation.[112]

58 In the area of product liability, where there must be a causal link between the defect and damage, these conditions of factual and legal causation must also be met. Thus, once it has been proven that the defect was a *conditio sine qua non* of damage, it must be demonstrated that the type of damage suffered, according to the experience of a reasonable observer, is the specific manifestation of the typical risk of the type of defect that the product has (adequate causation), as recognised, *inter alia*, by SAP Barcelona 24.10.2012 (AC 2012\1575). In other cases, in particular when it comes to defects of information that do not meet the specifications required by regulations, the criterion of the protective purpose of the rule may also be relevant, if the risk resulting from the defect is precisely the risk that safety standards wanted to prevent. Here, for instance, the Spanish Supreme Court[113] held that there was no negligence in the case of a manufacturer of an insecticide that exploded when it was used negligently by the victim and caused damage. Although the court considered that the product had information defects, since it did not inform the user of all risks in accordance with the applicable regulations, damage was not due to the defect of the product,

107 *Pantaleón* (fn 11) 1981–1988.

108 SSTS 26.01.2007 (RJ 2007\1873); 17.02.2009 (RJ 2009\1494); 02.03.2009 (RJ 2009\169946).

109 SSTS 26.01.2007 (RJ 2007\1873); 16.02.2009 (RJ 2009\1491).

110 STS 25.03.2010 (RJ 2010\4347.

111 STS 21.11.2008 (RJ 2008\144.

112 STS 24.10.2003 (RJ 2003\7519); 17.02.2009 (RJ 2009\1494). On the state of affairs on this topic in Spain and on the dual analysis causation in fact/legal causation, see *LF Reglero Campos/L Medina Alcoz*, El nexo causal. La pérdida de oportunidad. Las causas de exoneración de la responsabilidad, in: *LF Reglero Campos/JM Busto Lago* (eds), Tratado de responsabilidad civil, T I (5th edn 2014) 768 ff.

113 STS 21.11.2008 (RJ 2009\144).

since 'the protective purpose of the rule referring to the warning that was missing was aimed at preventing poisoning by contact, inhalation or ingestion, but not inflammation of the substance', risks that had been correctly warned about and that ultimately materialised.

59 In the context of the law transposing the Directive 85/374/EEC the defect of the product is the central condition of liability and, therefore, the defect understood as 'lack of safety legitimately expected' will be the cornerstone upon which the analysis of causation, along with damage, will be built. Hence, the courts have emphasised that one should not mistake a defective product, which gives rise to liability, with a merely dangerous product, which, by this very fact, does not give rise to liability.[114] In the analysis of the defect, the circumstances expressly mentioned in art 147 TRLGDCU, ie the presentation of the product, its reasonably foreseeable use and the time the product was put into circulation, as previously seen, will play a key role.[115] By contrast, the conduct of the manufacturer during the production phase of the product is only relevant in the context of the fault liability regime based on the general rules of tort liability pursuant to art 1902 CC.[116]

60 No cases are known where Spanish case law has applied the doctrine of loss of chance or any other solutions implying proportional liability in the field of product liability.

B. MULTIPLE PERSONS CONTRIBUTING TO CAUSING DAMAGE

61 When several persons equated to the producer contribute to causing damage, art 132 TRLGDCU provides for solidary liability of all of them towards the injured party, notwithstanding the right available to the person who has paid compensation to ask for contribution from the others according to their corresponding degree of participation in the causation of damage.

62 However, when it is a third party who, together with a producer, contributes to cause damage, art 133 TRLGDCU provides that liability will not be reduced and the producer will be liable in full. Once he has paid compensation, he will be able to ask for contribution from the third party according to the latter's participation in the causation of damage. When the provision refers

---

114 So, for instance, STS 21.11.2008 (RJ 2009\144).

115 *Solé Feliu* (fn 36) 97 ff.

116 Among others, SAP Vizcaya 10.24.2013 (AC 2014\756) SAP Granada 25.01.2000 (AC 2000\266).

to a third party, the doctrine understands that this is a different person from the producer or any other person equated to him as regards liability. However, this does not necessarily mean that the third party is someone totally separate from the process of marketing the product, since it can be the installer[117] or the distributor (in cases where the producer is identified) if his conduct aggravated the damage.[118] By contrast, auxiliaries or employees of the producer are not third parties, since their actions are directly attributable to the principal and, therefore, to the producer as such.[119]

63 When contribution is between the producer and the injured party, art 145 TRLGDCU, following the same criteria as art 8(2) Directive, provides for the possibility of reducing or even of excluding liability of the producer according to the degree of participation of the injured party in the damage. Thus it holds that 'the liability provided for in this chapter may be reduced or excluded depending on the circumstances of the case, if the damage is caused jointly by a product defect and fault of the injured party or of any other person for whom he shall be civilly liable'. To establish the persons for whom the injured party must be liable, one must refer to art 1903 Civil Code, which provides for the grounds for liability of the principal for acts of his auxiliaries, which includes parents for acts of their children while in their custody, and of guardians and keepers for acts of minors or incapacitated persons under their authority and who live with them, as well as liability of the employer for the acts of their employees and, more generally, of the principal for the acts of their auxiliaries when they act within the scope of their functions.[120] In most cases, contributory negligence of the victim is directly connected with his improper or negligent use of the defective product, as was the case, for instance, in a decision of the Court of Appeal of Barcelona,[121] dealing with the burns suffered by the victim after using a plunger with a very high concentration of sulfuric acid. In the court's view, the product had a defect of information since, being a potentially dangerous product, the label did not warn about the risk of explosion or violent reaction with large heat release upon contact with water. Nor did it not warn about the need to use special antacid gloves, although it indicated that rubber gloves had to be used. The court considered that there was contributory negligence of the victim, which it quantified at 25%, since he had used the product without using any gloves, even ordinary rubber ones. According to the court, the injured party was an

[117] SAP Salamanca 15.03.2000 (AC 2000\1367).

[118] SAP Alicante 25.01.2006 (JUR 2007\135170). Among others, *Ángeles Parra Lucán* (fn 12) 191; *Martín-Casals/Solé Feliu* (fn 21) 186.

[119] *Ángeles Parra Lucán* (fn 12) 191.

[120] On the scope of this provision and the situations it covers, instead of many see *M Martín-Casals/J Solé Feliu*, Comentario al Art. 1903, in: *A Domínguez Luelmo* (ed), Comentarios al Código Civil (2010) 2055–2062.

[121] SAP Barcelona 30.05.2002 (AC 2002\1211).

industrialist, with experience in electrical, plumbing, gas and related installation and repair operations, who should have foreseen the possible consequences of not using the gloves.

VI. DEFENCES AND EXCLUSIONS

A. DEFENCES

1) Introduction

64 Defences are listed in art 140 TRLGDCU, along the same lines as in art 7 Directive, although with some particularities regarding the development risks defence. The burden of proof of the existence of any of these defences rests with the producer (art 140.1 TRGLDCU). This is also stated by case law.[122] Although the wording of the provision refers only to the 'producer', legal doctrine unanimously understands that it means all responsible persons who are equivalent to the producer, including the manufacturer of the finished product, the producer of the component part, the producer of a raw material, the so-called apparent manufacturer, and the importer on the territory of the European Union. In exceptional cases, where his liability is established, it also includes the provider.[123] Moreover, the doctrine also understands unanimously that the list contained in this provision is closed,[124] and this has been confirmed by the Spanish Supreme Court, which speaks of 'cases where a specific defence exists'.[125] This position is consistent with the positon also held by the Court of Justice of the European Communities in *Veedfald* and *O'Byrne v Sanofi Pasteur*, in the sense that the cases of exemption of liability referred to in art 7 Directive have an 'exhaustive' character and that, as exceptions, 'must be interpreted strictly', since they aim 'to protect the interests of the victims of damage caused by a defective product'.

2) The Defendant Producer Did Not Put the Product into Circulation

65 The first defence that enables the producer to be exonerated from liability is proof that he 'had not put the product into circulation' (art 140.1.a) TRLGDCU). The concept of putting the product into circulation has already been discussed in the section dealing with the notion of defect (*vide supra* no 26), including the need for a flexible interpretation of this notion, which should be understood not so

122 As in SAP Madrid 30.12.2013 (AC 2014\192).
123 In this sense, *Martín-Casals/Solé Feliu* (fn 49) 926; *Jiménez Liébana* (fn 26) 302.
124 *Gutiérrez Santiago* (fn 21) 156.
125 *Inter alia* in STS 19.04.2000 (RJ 2000\2979).

much as coming out of the strict sphere of control of the producer, but as the fact of exposing external third parties to the risks arising from the defect, as is the case, for instance, when a patient goes to a hospital that is the producer of the defective product and the product is used in its facilities (ECJ 10.05.2001, *Veedfald*).[126]

66 The prevailing legal doctrine considers that this defence is designed to free the producer from liability in all cases where a person other than him, without his consent, put the product into circulation. This is the case, for instance, if the product has been stolen from the producer's premises.[127] Therefore, rather than a true cause of exoneration, it is proof that one of the required conditions of liability is missing, ie that the defective product was put into circulation by the particular defendant producer.[128]

3) The Presumption that the Product was not Defective when it was Put into Circulation

67 According to art 140.1.b) TRLGDCU, the producer is not liable if he proves 'that, given the circumstances of the case, it may be presumed that the defect did not exist at the time when the product was put into circulation'. Once again, one of the basic conditions of liability – ie that the defect existed at the time the producer put the product into circulation – is missing here.[129] The proof of lack of defect at the relevant time can be provided in two ways: either by showing that the defect did not exist at the time the product was put into circulation, or by proving that the defect came into being afterwards. The latter test is more difficult for the producer, since he has to prove that something happened (the appearance of the defect) at a time the product was already outside his sphere of control and he lacked the ability to influence it. This explains why the law facilitates proof with the acceptance of a legal presumption ('that, given the circumstances of the case, it may be presumed'), which introduces a nuance to the original text of art 7(b) Directive, which did not speak in terms of presumptions, but of probabilities ('it is probable that the defect which caused damage did not exist … or that this defect came into being …'). Among the circumstances that serve as grounds to presume the absence of the defect at the time the product was put into circulation, or that it came into being afterwards, the Spanish legal doctrine mentions: the use or consumption of the product

126 *Martín-Casals/Solé Feliu* (fn 49) 924; *JA Ruiz García/E Farnós Amorós*, Causas de exoneración de la responsabilidad, in: P Salvador Coderch/F Gómez Pomar (eds), Tratado de Responsabilidad Civil del Fabricante (2008) 500.

127 *Solé Feliu* (fn 36) 328; *Jiménez Liébana* (fn 26) 303.

128 *Solé Feliu* (fn 36) 328.

129 According to *Ángeles Parra Lucán* (fn 12) 178, pursuant to the evidence rules in TRLGDCU, the victim must prove that the product is defective, but not that the defect was caused by the manufacturer.

beyond the expiry date; a long period of time between the introduction of the product and its use or consumption; evidence of misuse by the consumer; inadequate storage or transportation by persons participating in the further marketing process; etc.[130]

68 This is the most frequent cause of exoneration used by the defendants in Spanish judicial practice, and gives rise to very uneven results. An example would be SAP Santa Cruz de Tenerife 19.09.2008 (AC 20091\241), in a case dealing with the purchase of a cosmetic cream by a consumer that caused serious dermatitis. The cream had expired in 2003 and was sold to the consumer in 2005. The lawsuit was filed against the manufacturer of the product and against the seller. The judgment of the Court of Appeal exempted the manufacturer from liability by presuming that the cream was not defective at the time it was put into circulation, and based this presumption on the grounds that consumer sale took place two years after its expiration date. By contrast, the court held that the seller was liable for selling the product after its expiration date, but reduced the award on the grounds of contributory negligence of the victim, since he had suffered dermatitis before and could have known at the time of using the cream that it had expired.

69 In the same vein, a decision of the Court of Appeal of Córdoba[131] dealt with the serious injuries suffered by the claimant after ingesting the contents of a bottle of spring water in a nightclub. The lawsuit was filed against the water bottling company, as a producer, and against the owner of the club, as a supplier, on the grounds of both arts 1902 and 1903 CC and the Spanish transposition norm. The judgments of the courts of First Instance and Appeal exempted the bottling company from liability and ordered the owner of the nightclub to compensate the victim for the injuries suffered. Although the judgment of the Court of Appeal did not expressly mention the cause of exoneration of art 140.b) TRLGDCU (at the time, art 6.b) LRPD), the reason why the Court exempted the producer from liability lies in the fact that it was proven that when the bottle was served at the nightclub, it 'did not have the factory seal that all bottles have', from which the court concluded that the defect did not exist when the producer put the bottle into circulation, and that it was most likely that the bottle was filled or adulterated when it was already held by the supplier. Other judgments, however, reject the existence of this cause of exoneration, as the Court of Appeal of Cantabria did[132] in holding that that 'there is no indication that might encourage the possibility that the defect came into being after the product was

130 *Solé Feliu* (fn 36) 346 ff; *S Ramos González/A Rubí Puig*, Presunción de inexistencia del defecto cuando el producto se puso en circulación, in: P Salvador Coderch/F Gómez Pomar (eds), Tratado de Responsabilidad Civil del Fabricante (2008) 539–545.

131 SAP Córdoba 30.10.2000 (AC 2000\2097).

132 SAP Cantabria 19.06.2002 (JUR 2002\212110).

put into circulation … but by its very nature it must be presumed that it already existed before'.[133]

4) *Manufacture without an Economic Purpose and outside the Framework of a Professional or Entrepreneurial Activity*

70 According to art 140.1.c) TRLGDCU, the producer is exempted from liability if he proves 'that the product was not manufactured for sale or any other form of distribution with an economic purpose, nor was it manufactured, imported, supplied or distributed within the context of a professional or entrepreneurial activity'. This is a defence that, at least for now, has not raised any practical difficulties in Spain. In the same way as in art 7(c) Directive, the defence only operates when two factors cumulatively concur, ie manufacturing without an economic purpose, on the one hand, and manufacturing or commercialisation outside the framework of a professional or entrepreneurial activity on the other.[134]

5) *Manufacture Pursuant to Mandatory Rules*

71 Art 140.1.d) TRLGDCU exonerates the producer if it is established 'that the defect is due to the fact that the product was made in accordance with existing mandatory rules'. This is an exceptional defence, since it implies not only that the rules should be mandatory, but also that compliance with them must have been the cause of the defect.[135] This defence aims at avoiding the conflict between violating an administrative rule and being held civilly liable for having complied with it. The legislative message is that the producer must comply with the norm and, if the defective product causes damage, then he may avail himself of this defence.[136] Although the Spanish provision does not specify that these mandatory rules must be 'issued by the public authorities', as art 7(d) Directive does, the requirement that they are 'mandatory', and therefore binding, entails that they must be legally established by a public authority, with regulatory power, and in accordance with the procedure prescribed therein. In Spain, this includes both rules issued by the State, by the Autonomous Communities, and, in addition, those coming from the European Union, regardless of whether they have the rank of a formal Act or have a lower rank, which is the case of regulations.[137]

---

133 In the same sense, SAP Santa Cruz de Tenerife 19.04.2002 (AC 2002\898).

134 *Jiménez Liébana* (fn 26) 310.

135 *Ángeles Parra Lucán* (fn 12) 180.

136 *P Salvador Coderch/A Rubí Puig*, Elaboración del producto conforme a normas imperativas existentes, in: P Salvador Coderch/F Gómez Pomar (eds), Tratado de Responsabilidad Civil del Fabricante (2008) 569.

137 *Martín-Casals/Solé Feliu* (fn 21) 180.

72 By contrast, excluded from this defence are the so-called private norms or technical standards issued by national or international standardisation bodies (such as ISO, CEN, AENOR, DIN, etc), and also the standards issued by industrial associations grouping producers of a given sector. The reason for this is that they are not actual legal norms (mandatory) issued by a public regulatory authority.[138] Also left out are those norms where compliance results in exemption of liability, non-mandatory legal norms, and those legal norms establishing minimum legal or regulatory requirements beyond which producers are free to decide on possible alternative ways of manufacture. Thus, the mere compliance with positive or negative lists of ingredients, components, additives and other substances, which can be found in certain legal rules, does not constitute grounds for exemption of liability, to the extent that, above this minimum, producers have enough scope to decide on the process of production.[139] In short, for this defence to operate it is necessary for the legal mandatory norm to allow the producer no other alternative course of conduct when manufacturing the product.[140]

73 Compliance or breach of legal non-mandatory norms, as well as of norms or technical standards, which will not be relevant for the purposes of this defence, may, nevertheless, be considered as one of the 'circumstances' that have to be taken into account when assessing the existence of the defect. In any case, as legal doctrine has unanimously pointed out, it must be borne in mind that mere compliance with these norms is not decisive, nor is it sufficient to consider that the product is not defective, although it may become a piece of evidence leading to the presumption that the defect did not exist. However, this does not prevent the claimant from proving that, despite compliance with such norms, the product was defective,[141] to the extent that the norms were outdated and had already been outpaced by the state of scientific and technical knowledge or that, beyond compliance with such provisions, the defect could be avoided by the simple introduction of additional safety measures. Spanish case law in the field of fault liability agrees to these considerations by noting that mere compliance with regulations is not sufficient to prove the absence of fault of the actor, if due care required them to go further.[142] The Spanish doctrine also takes this approach in the field of the manufacturer's strict liability for defective products, where compliance or non-compliance acts as a parameter to be taken into account when assessing the existence of a defect.[143]

---

138 Instead of many, *Martín-Casals/Solé Feliu* (fn 21) 180; *Salvador Coderch/Rubí Puig* (fn 136) 579.

139 *Martín-Casals/Solé Feliu* (fn 21) 181.

140 *Salvador Coderch/Rubí Puig* (fn 136) 582.

141 *Martín-Casals/Solé Feliu* (fn 21) 173; *Salvador Coderch/Ramos* (fn 42) 171.

142 Among many others, see: SSTS 19.12.1992 (RJ 1992\10703); 03.06.1998 (RJ 1998\5411); SAP Valencia 12.07.2001 (JUR 2001\279709); SSAP Córdoba 20.02.2006 (JUR 2006\180346); 30.01.2007 (JUR 2007\176982); Pontevedra 10.06.2009 (JUR 2009\301632)).

143 Instead of many, see *Martín-Casals/Solé Feliu* (fn 21) 173.

6) *The Development Risk Defence*

74 The Spanish legislature made use of the option allowed by art 15(b) Directive and incorporated the development risk defence.[144] Thus, art 140.1.e) TRLGDCU provides that the producer is not liable if he proves 'that the state of scientific and technical knowledge at the time the product entered into circulation meant that the existence of the defect could not be perceived'. However, the Spanish legislature has not accepted this defence in full, since art 140.3 TRLGDCU excludes from the scope of this defence producers of foods, foodstuffs and medicines intended for human consumption. Thus, 'in the case of medicines, foods or foodstuffs intended for human consumption, the persons liable, in accordance with this chapter, cannot invoke paragraph 1.e) as cause of exemption'. The exclusion of producers of medicines for human consumption was justified on the grounds that this is one of areas where there are greater chances of development risks taking place. However, the exclusion is confined to medicines 'for human consumption', which means that the producer of veterinary medicines can avail himself of the defence.[145] As regards the producer of food and foodstuffs, it is contended that his exclusion from the scope of the defence was an option chosen by the legislature bearing in mind the enormous social impact of the Colza Oil case.[146]

75 Although the Medicines Act distinguishes, for several purposes, medicines with or without medical prescription, product liability rules make no distinction in this regard, so that all of them are considered to be included within the notion of medicine under the art 140.3 TRLGDCU, which holds producers liable for development risks.[147] At the same time, art 46 of Act 29/2006 of 26 July, on medicines and health care products (LM), includes in the notion of 'medicines' the 'derivatives of blood, plasma and other substances of human origin (fluids, glands, excreta, tissues and any other substance) and their corresponding derivatives, when used for therapeutic purposes'. The consequence is that in such cases, the producer will be held liable even though the state of scientific and technical knowledge at the time of entry into circulation did not make it possible to ascertain the defect. 'Producer' means the laboratory that treats and prepares the substances and, if this

---

144 On this defence, see *P Salvador Coderch/J Solé Feliu*, Brujos y Aprendices. Los riesgos de desarrollo en la responsabilidad de producto (1999).

145 *Ángeles Parra Lucán* (fn 12) 184.

146 SSTS, Crim, 23.04.1992 (RJ 1992\6783) and 06.09.1997 (RJ 1997\6366). For a more detailed explanation of the case, as well as of the two decisions issued by the Spanish Supreme Court on the case, see *Martín-Casals/Solé Feliu* (fn 6) 251–256.

147 *Solé Feliu* (fn 36) 557; *P Salvador Coderch/A Rubí Puig*, Excepción por riesgos de desarrollo, in: P Salvador Coderch/F Gómez Pomar (eds), Tratado de Responsabilidad Civil del Fabricante (2008) 641.

is not identified, the clinic or hospital that has made the transfusion (in the case of contaminated blood),[148] in their capacity as suppliers (arts 5 and 138 TRLGDCU). However, it does not include the private donor, since he neither produced it with an economic purpose, nor did he donate it as part of a professional or business activity (art 140.1.c) TRLGDCU).

76 This solution, which holds the (private) producer of a medicine liable even in the case of defects that were not possible to detect at the time when the product was put into circulation given the state of scientific and technical knowledge, is in clear contrast with the situation of public authorities, who can exonerate themselves for development risks in these cases. According to art 141.1 of the Act 30/1992 of 26 November, on the legal regime of public administrations and common administrative procedure (LRJAP),[149] public authorities may exonerate themselves for 'damage arising from facts or circumstances which could not have been foreseen or avoided according to the state of scientific and technical knowledge existing *at the time in which they occurred* [*sic*]'.

77 This rule, application of which is not confined to damage caused by defective products produced by public authorities, but extends to all areas in which public authorities act, was introduced to offer some support to the case law of the Supreme Court, which on the grounds of *force majeure*, exempted Spanish public authorities from liability for damage caused by HIV and hepatitis C as a result of blood transfusions made prior to the time it was possible to detect the existence of the viruses (established by Spanish courts around 1985 in the case of HIV, and around July 1989 in the case of hepatitis C).[150] From the entry into force of that new wording of art 141.1 LRJAP onwards, the Spanish Supreme Court has exempted public authorities from liability for contaminated blood transfusions performed before those dates, arguing that the state of scientific and technical knowledge did make it possible to detect the virus in the blood[151] and, conversely, holding them liable for transfusions made afterwards.[152] The same approach has also been applied to exonerate health public authorities in a case concerning the death of a patient who contracted Creuzfeldt-Jakob disease

148 *JC Seuba Torreblanca*, Sangre contaminada, responsabilidad civil y ayudas públicas (2002) 265.

149 Ley 30/1992, de 26 de noviembre, de régimen jurídico de las administraciones públicas y del procedimiento administrativo común, BOE no 285, 27.11.1992. The provision was introduced by an amendment carried out by Ley 4/1999, de 13 de enero, de modificación de la Ley 30/1992, de 26 de noviembre, de régimen jurídico de las administraciones públicas y del procedimiento administrativo común, BOE no 12, 14.01.1999).

150 On these references, see *Seuba Torreblanca* (fn 148) 290 ff.

151 Among many others, SSTS 3rd 02.04.2002 (RJ 2002\5072); 06.03.2003 (RJ 2003\2785); 09.07.2003 (RJ 2003\5948); 10.05.2006 (RJ 2006\5157); 17.05.2006 (RJ 2006\3811); 14.03.2007 (RJ 2007\2289)).

152 SSTS 3rd 22.04.2003 (RJ 2003\3513), 05.04.2007 (JUR 2007\135914).

following a dura implant made in 1984, where the medical literature did not warn of the risk until 1987.[153]

78 The existence of this specific regime for public authorities gives rise to a split of the rules on product liability depending on whether the producer is public or private,[154] which has led some academics to ask whether this difference in treatment between public and private producers, to the detriment of private ones, involves a possible infringement of the European Directive,[155] all the more so when the ECJ recognised that the Directive is applicable to public authorities (*Veedfald*).[156] For other scholars, this difference in treatment can at least be subject to harsh criticism, since it involves treating victims differently depending on whether the actor who treated them was private or public.[157]

B. CONTRACTUAL EXCLUSIONS OF LIABILITY FOR PRODUCT LIABILITY

79 In line with art 12 Directive, art 130 TRLGDCU also provides for the ineffectiveness of liability limitation or exclusion clauses against the injured party 'set forth in this book', ie of the regulation of product liability based on the provisions of the Directive. This is a rule that encompasses any limitation of the established legal regime, both as regards quantitative limits and as regards the exclusion of certain conditions, deadlines, burdens of proof, disclaimers, etc. In short, any contractual agreement that restricts or limits the liability of the producer is prohibited, as well as agreements that may indirectly affect the victim's right to compensation, such as the introduction of additional conditions or requirements to those provided in the TRLGDCU.[158] If the injured party also has the status of consumer, the invalidity of the clause modifying liability may also arise from the rules on unfair terms. In particular, art 10 TRLGDCU holds that the prior waiver of rights that the TRLGDCU provides for consumers is void. Article 82.4.b) TRLGDCU also considers unfair those clauses that 'limit the rights of consumers and users', including clauses providing for 'the exclusion or limitation of the entrepreneur's liability ... for damage, or for death or injuries caused to the consumer or user due to an action or omission of the entrepreneur' (art 86.2 TRGLDCU).[159]

---

153 STSJ Murcia 30.01.2009 (JUR 2009\192442).

154 *Salvador Coderch/Rubí Puig* (fn 147) 598.

155 Thus, for instance, *Martín-Casals/Solé Feliu* (fn 49) 940–941.

156 Case C-203/1999.

157 *Ángeles Parra Lucán* (fn 10).

158 In this sense, among others, *F Gómez Pomar*, Ineficacia de las clàusules de exoneración o limitación de la responsabilidad, in: P Salvador Coderch/F Gómez Pomar (eds), Tratado de Responsabilidad Civil del Fabricante (2008) 789–790; *Jiménez Liébana* (fn 26) 465.

159 *Ángeles Parra Lucán* (fn 12) 312.

80 However, the ineffectiveness of such clauses is only enforceable 'in respect of the injured party' (art 130 TRLGDCU). Therefore, legal doctrine considers that clauses of the same type, in which liable persons may agree among themselves in relation to any rights of recourse which may arise between them, should, however, be considered effective.[160] These clauses are valid and effective, within the limits established by private autonomy and, where appropriate, within the limits of the rules governing predisposed clauses in accordance with the provisions of Act 7/1998 of 13 April, on general contractual terms.[161]

81 Moreover, the Spanish legal doctrine considers that the prohibition is limited to the anticipated restrictive and limiting agreements, but not to what the parties may agree when liability has already arisen once the damage has already occurred and its full scope is known.[162]

VII. REMEDIES

82 The remedy provided by Spanish law for damage caused by a defective product is damages, both under the general rules of liability based on fault (art 1902 CC) and the strict liability rules transposing the Directive 85/374/EEC. In this sense, art 128 TRLGDCU provides that 'all injured parties are entitled to compensation under the terms established in this Book for damage or injury caused by goods or services'. Generally, the prevailing legal doctrine considers that liability has fundamentally a compensatory function. Accordingly, under Spanish law punitive damages and nominal damages are not allowed.[163]

83 Spanish law also allows compensation in kind. However, this form of compensation is not common and even less so in the area of product liability, where compensation is regularly in the form of a damages award. According to legal doctrine, reparation in kind (for instance, replacement of the damaged property by another of a similar condition) is a useful remedy for compensating for property damage, whenever it is possible and not excessively burdensome for the tortfeasor.[164] In this sense, it is said that when reparation in kind is

160 *Gutiérrez Santiago* (fn 21) 169.

161 Ley 7/1998, de 13 de abril, *sobre condiciones generales de la contratación*, BOE no 89, 14.04.1998.

162 Thus, *Gómez Pomar* (fn 124) 791 ff; *Ángeles Parra Lucán* (fn 12) 312.

163 See *M Martín Casals*, Notas sobre la indemnización del daño moral en las acciones por difamación de la LO 1/1982, in: Estudios Centenario del Código Civil (1989) 1231; Pantaleón Prieto, Com. Art. 1902, in: C Paz-Ares/L Díez-Picazo/R Bercovitz/P Salvador, Comentario del Código Civil, T II (1991) 1971 ff; *Martín-Casals* (fn 11) 23–28; *R de Ángel Yágüez*, Daños punitivos (2012) 57 ff; L Díez-Picazo, La responsabilidad civil extracontractual, T V (2011) 23–26.

164 STS 05.11.2002 (RJ 2002\5593). On this topic, see *E Vicente Domingo*, El daño, in: LF Reglero Campos (ed), Tratado de responsabilidad civil, T II (5th edn 2008)401.

very burdensome for the tortfeasor or is not possible given the sort of damage suffered, the alternative will be compensation by a pecuniary equivalent. However, when it comes to non-pecuniary losses, as in the case of bodily injury or moral harm, there is no alternative to monetary compensation.[165]

84 Other measures, such as withdrawal from the market, recall, destruction of the product, etc, are not regarded as remedies in the context of the rules on products liability, but are measures provided by administrative provisions on product safety. They are preventive norms, seeking to prevent the occurrence of the damage, not typical civil law remedies related to liability. In particular, the national norm implementing the European Directive 2001/95/EC on general product safety,[166] imposes upon producers certain duties aimed at preventing damage caused by unsafe products and, among them, the duty to inform consumers and users of the risks that are not immediately obvious without adequate warnings and which are the result of the normal or foreseeable use of the products. They should also report these risks to the distributors of their products. Once the products have been put into circulation, manufacturers must take all appropriate measures to avoid risks arising from their products, including the obligation to inform consumers by posting specific notices and, if necessary, even by withdrawing products from the market or recalling them from consumer (art 4 Royal Decree 1801\2003 of 26 December, on general product safety).[167]

VIII. PROCEDURAL AND EVIDENTIAL ISSUES

A. EVIDENTIARY STANDARDS OF PROOF IN SPAIN

85 Legal scholarship requires the proof to achieve the condition of certainty.[168] Even if the facts are established according to a judicial presumption (‘*presunción judicial*’, admitted by art 386 Civil Procedural Act, LEC),[169] courts declare that the judge must attain a ‘subjective certainty’, with the balance of probabilities test (ie ‘more probable than not’) used in other legal systems not being sufficient.[170] Thus, for instance, regarding causation, the Spanish Supreme Court has declared that ‘there is no place, in the sphere of the causal relationship, for mere deductions, guesswork or probabilities, but evidential certainty is required’.[171]

165 Ibid 401.
166 [2002] OJ L11/4.
167 Real Decreto 1801\2003, de 26 de diciembre, sobre seguridad general de los productos, BOE no 9, 10.01.2004.
168 As, for instance, *F Rivero*, in: JL Lacruz Berdejo et al, Elementos de Derecho Civil II, Derecho de Obligaciones, vol 2 (2005) 465; *E Roca Trías*, Derecho de daños (4th edn 2003) 159.
169 Ley 1/2000, de 7 de enero, *de Enjuiciamiento Civil*, BOE no 7, 08.01.2000.
170 See *L Yerga*, La prueba de la responsabilidad civil médico-sanitaria (2004) 404 ff.
171 SSTS 08.02.2000 (RJ 2000\1235) 16.01.2002 (RJ 2002\8).

Spanish legal doctrine contends that the standard of 'certainty' is equivalent to high probability levels, based on what corresponds to 'the regular or normal course of events (*id quod plerumque accidit*)'. In this sense, Spanish doctrine compares the Spanish standard with standards existing in other countries and points out that the Spanish standard is different from the standard that can be currently found 'in the common law', according to which 'the consideration that a fact is more likely than not is sufficient'.[172] In the area of causation, for example, some Spanish authors have recently noted that the necessary probability to establish the required 'certainty', for comparison purposes, could be placed between 80% and 100%.[173]

B. TOOLS MAKING THE PROCESS OF DEMONSTRATION EASIER IN THE FIELD OF PRODUCTS LIABILITY: BURDEN OF PROOF AND PRESUMPTIONS

86 As already seen in the context of the norms implementing the Directive, the burden of proof of the defect, damage and the causation link between these two conditions, in accordance with art 139 TRLGDCU, falls upon the injured claimant. By contrast, the burden of proof of the occurrence of any of the grounds for exemption falls on the producer, as provided in art 140.1 TRLGDCU. With reference to the defect, one must bear in mind, additionally, the rule already discussed in the section dealing with the notion of defect (*vide supra* no 23), which provides that the defect can be presumed when it is proven that the product does not 'provide the safety normally provided by other units in the same series'. This rule does not derive from the Directive and is specific to the Spanish implementation. As already stated, it aims to facilitate the proof of manufacturing defects, which are those in which it is possible to compare the actual allegedly defective unit with other units of the same series. According to the prevailing legal doctrine, the presumption is rebuttable and, therefore, the producer may furnish proof that, despite not offering the safety offered by other units of the same series, the product was not defective because the product offered the safety legitimately expected given the other circumstances of the case.[174]

87 In the context of fault liability pursuant to art 1902 CC, the burden of proof of damage, the defect, fault of the manufacturer and the causal link between

---

172 *CI Asúa González*, Pérdida de Oportunidad en la Responsabilidad Sanitaria (2008) 28 and *Yerga* (fn 170) 404.

173 *Asúa González* (fn 172) 28; *L Medina Alcoz*, La teoría de la pérdida de oportunidad. Estudio doctrina y jurisprudencial del Derecho de daños público y privado (2007) 305; *Yerga* (fn 170) 405.

174 *Martín-Casals/Solé Feliu* (fn 21) 174; *L Yerga*, in: P Salvador Coderch/F Gómez Pomar (eds), Tratado de Responsabilidad Civil del Fabricante (2008) 433.

these conditions lies, in principle, on the claimant in accordance with the general rules of evidence provided for in art 317 LEC. However, as already seen, court practice on product liability for defective products has evolved to consolidate a rebuttable presumption of fault of the manufacturer, once the defect of the product has been proven (*vide supra* no 1).[175]

C. LIMITATION PERIODS

88 When the claim is brought according to the transposition norms, the limitation period of the action follows the provisions of art 10 Directive and, accordingly, art 143.1 TRLGDCU establishes that it 'must be brought within three years, from the date on which the injured party suffered damage, whether due to the product defect or to the damage that this defect caused, provided that the person responsible for such damage is known'. The tortfeasor who has paid compensation will be able to bring a claim for contribution against the other liable tortfeasors 'within one year from the date on which he paid compensation'. For rules concerning the interruption of prescription, art 143.2 TRLGDCU refers to the general rules established in the Spanish Civil Code. In addition to this limitation period, art 144 TRLGDCU introduces into Spanish law the ten-year-period statute of repose, which bars the claim after ten years from the date on which the product was put into circulation. In the wording of this provision, 'the recognised rights of the injured party, described in this chapter, shall expire after a period of ten years counting from the date on which the specific product that caused damage was put into circulation, unless the relevant judicial proceedings are initiated within this period'.

89 When the action is based on the general rules of tort of arts 1902 ff CC, the limitation period is one year from the date the injured party knew of the damage, as provided in art 1968.2 CC. The Spanish Civil Code does not provide for statutes of repose or long-stop limitation periods. Regarding the interruption of the limitation period, the relevant rules are in arts 1973–1975 CC, which do not include suspension of the limitation period. These rules also apply to the interruption of the three-year limitation period established in TRLGDCU, according to the reference made in art 143.2 TRLGDCU. Pursuant to art 1973 CC, prescription is interrupted (i) by the exercise of the claim in court, something which is interpreted with great flexibility, so that any act involving a court summons made to the debtor has interruptive effects, including presenting an application for legal aid or the request for court-appointed counsel; (ii) by a claim on the debt made by the creditor out-of-court, which case law also

[175] See, for instance, SAP Granada 25.01.2000 (AC 2000\266). On this evolution, see *Martín-Casals/Solé Feliu* (fn 6) 246–248; *Yerga* (fn 174) 427.

construes very broadly, admitting the interruptive effect of a request made by a public notary, the exchange of letters, a letter with acknowledgment of receipt, a fax or *burofax*;[176] and (iii) acknowledgment of the debt by the debtor. As for solidary obligations, art 1974 CC provides that the interruption of prescription by one of the solidary co-creditors or co-debtors equally affects all co-debtors or co-creditors.

D. OTHER IMPORTANT PROCEDURAL RULES AFFECTING THE POSSIBILITY OF PURSUING CLAIMS

90 When the transposition norm was passed, it took some time until victims started to bring their claims for product liability according to these new rules. This was due not so much to the characteristics of Spanish procedural law, but rather to the fact that it was easier for claimants to invoke the general liability regime of art 1902 CC, which, as explained, in practice regularly implied a rebuttable presumption of the manufacturer's fault and did not suffer the limitations of the transposition norms, in terms of recoverable damage (such as franchise, exclusion of non-pecuniary losses and property damage to things of professional or entrepreneurial use, etc). Moreover, after the entry into force of the Act transposing the Directive in 1994, for some years the courts continued to apply the strict liability regime provided in art 28 LGDCU for certain categories of products, which was more favourable to the interests of consumers than the new liability regime based on the Directive. This was the situation until cases dealing with products put into circulation after the entry into force of the Act transposing the Directive started reaching the courts, after which time it was no longer possible to apply the rules contained in arts LGDCU 25–28.[177] Even after that time, the situation in the practice of the courts was confusing, until the ECJ, in the judgment in *María Victoria González Sánchez v Medicina Asturiana SA*,[178] definitively clarified that the rules of the Directive – which is not a minimum harmonisation directive – were not compatible with any other internal general system of product liability. Accordingly, the parties could not invoke the provisions of the LGDCU to resolve issues of liability for damage caused by defective products any longer, even in spite of the fact that they were more favourable to their interests.

---

176 Referring to case law, see *A Domínguez Luelmo*, Com. Art. 1973, in: A Domínguez Luelmo (ed), Comentarios al Código Civil (2010) 2140.

177 This Act (the former LRPD 1994), contained a Single Transitional provision according to which 'the present Act shall not apply to liability for damage caused by products put into circulation before its entry into force. In this case liability shall be governed by the provisions in force at the time'. Among these provisions were arts 25–28 LGDCU.

178 Case C-183/00.

91 As regards the possibility of bringing class action claims in Spanish law, art 15.1 LEC allows that possibility, but subject to certain conditions. First, this possibility is only accepted when the injured parties qualify as 'consumers or users' (cf arts 6.1.7 and 15.1 LEC). In this case the claim may be brought, either by consumers associations or by groups of consumers constituted to protect their rights and interests, or by a 'group of affected persons' provided that 'the group includes the majority of those affected' and that 'the individuals who compose the group are determined or can be easily determined' (art 6.1.7 LEC).[179] If the number or identity of the affected consumers and users is unknown or is difficult to determine, then only the consumers/users associations that, according to the Act, are representative (cf art 11 LEC) will have standing.[180] These groups, in addition to obtaining injunctions against conduct that is harmful to consumers and users, may also, according to these provisions of the LEC, bring claims to obtain compensation for damage caused by a defective product. However, the Spanish legislation does not entitle third parties or bystanders to bring collective actions.[181]

92 In Spanish court practice, there have been few class actions for product liability. Prior to the reform of the LEC-2000, which introduced the above-mentioned provisions admitting class actions, Spanish Supreme Court passed judgment in the criminal proceedings regarding the well-known case of contaminated rapeseed oil (the Colza Oil case),[182] which caused serious personal injury and death to hundreds of victims. The judgment also dealt with civil liability resulting from the criminal offences that had been committed. In this case, an association of consumers and users, OCU (Organisation of Consumers and Users), had participated in the criminal proceedings, representing a large number of victims. The Supreme Court upheld the appeal brought by the OCU and ordered compensation of the victims identified in the process, ie not only of those who had been represented in the process by OCU, but also of those, even though they were not directly represented in the proceedings and had not brought an individual claim, whose identity as victims affected by rapeseed oil was known in the proceedings. As noted by legal doctrine, the decision of the Spanish Supreme Court can only be justified by the 'radical uniqueness of the case',[183] ie the extreme seriousness of the case, on account both of the severity of

---

179 On this topic, see *JJ Marín López*, Las acciones de clase en el Derecho español (2003) 2 InDret 1–13.

180 Ibid 1–13; *LF Reglero Campos* (actualizado por Fernando Peña López), Conceptos generales y elementos de delimitación, in: LF Reglero Campos (ed), Tratado de responsabilidad civil, T I (5th edn 2014) 243–255.

181 *Marín López* (fn 179) 4, who considers that a strict application of this legislative requirement would force the judge to investigate in each case whether all class members are consumers or users in the legal sense of the term, which is a very expensive task.

182 STS 2nd 26.09.1997 (RJ 1997\6366).

183 In the words of *Marín López* (fn 179) 4.

the injuries suffered by the victims and the large number of victims, and of the social significance of the case.

93 More recently, a class action has been presented in the proceedings dealing with injuries caused by thalidomide. So far, the case has given rise to two judgments. In the first one, the Court of First Instance[184] partially upheld the claim and ordered the defendant to pay compensation to the victims. However, in the second judgment, on appeal, the first was overturned by the Court of Appeal of Madrid.[185]

94 The lawsuit was filed in 2012 by the Association of Victims of Thalidomide in Spain (AVITE) against Grünenthal Pharma, SA, in order to claim compensation for 'late damage' caused by the drug. AVITE acted on behalf of its members, who were the children of pregnant women who consumed the drug and families of the victims who had already died. At the stage of preliminary hearing, the defendant had objected, among other aspects, to the lack of standing *ad processum* of the claimant, since no specific affected consumers had been identified. This defect was remedied by AVITE by providing a list of the members who made up the group of persons affected by the claim. With this, the Court of First Instance held that the deficiency 'had been remedied with the complete identification of those who are considered to be affected'.[186] The judgment upheld the claim in part, and qualified as victims affected by thalidomide 'the members of AVITE included in the list contained in the Court Order of 6 November 2012 who receive or may receive in the future financial aid established by the Royal Decree 1006/2010 and prove this condition …, except those persons who are receiving aid from the Contergan Foundation'. At the same time, the court ordered the defendant 'to compensate each of them with the amount of €20,000 for each percentage point of disability which had been recognised by Spanish public authorities'.

95 The fundamental question in the judgments of First Instance and of the Court of Appeal was whether the osteoarthritis, lifelong pain or scoliosis that victims could eventually suffer throughout their lives, as a result of the

---

184 Decision of the Court of First Instance no 90 of Madrid of 19.11.2013.

185 Decision of the Court of Appeal of Madrid (Section 14) of 13.10.2014. For a comment on the judgment of First Instance, see *P Salvador Coderch/C Gómez Ligüerre/A Rubí Puig/S Ramos González/A Terra Ibáñez*, Daños tardíos Avite c. Grünenthal. Comentario a la SJPI nº 90 Madrid, 19.11.2013, sobre los daños causados por la talidomida (2014) 1 InDret 1–30 <www.indret.com/es/index.php>. For a comment on the Judgment of the Court of Appeal of Madrid Audiencia Provincial de Madrid, see *S Ramos González*, Nota a la sentencia de la Audiencia Provincial (Sección 14ª), Madrid, 13.10.2014 (MP: Sagrario Arroyo García), sobre los daños asociados a la talidomida, Revista CESCO, 10 noviembre 2014, 1–14 <http://blog.uclm.es/cesco/>.

186 Judgment of the Court of First Instance no 90 of Madrid 19.11.2013, FD 4).

malformations (consecutive injuries) and the emergence of new or further injuries, which have only recently been known, such as impairment of nerve, muscle and vascular systems ('late damage', according to the Heidelberg Report of 21 December 2012), could be considered 'continuing damage' or not. If this was the case, as argued by the claimant and admitted in the decision of the First Instance, the *dies a quo* for calculating the limitation period of one year for claims on tort (art 1968.2 CC) could be postponed until the time when the final scope of the injuries was known. Since this was not yet known, the action would have not been prescribed. This is what the first instance judgment holds, considering that injuries caused by thalidomide 'evolve continuously ... and unpredictably'[187] and they are neither 'fully and absolutely determined nor consolidated'.[188] Therefore, the knowledge of the actual scope of the injuries was not available and, therefore, the limitation period would have not run out. Nevertheless, it holds that the damages should be limited to compensating for injuries actually incurred at the time of the filing of the claim and that compensation could not cover the mere risk of future injury.

96 Against this position, the judgment of the Court of Appeal understands that the theory of continuing damage is only applicable when it is not possible to split, divide or separate the different sets of damage over time. Since according to the Court of Appeal this division was possible in the case, the issue is confined to establishing at what point the injured victim could bring a claim. The Court considers that those affected by thalidomide were able to bring their claims, in respect of malformations that became apparent at the time of birth, 'on reaching adulthood'. This includes injuries that could be determined directly at the moment of birth, as well as those 'sequels that could be already determined at the time of birth, for it is then when their disabling scope can be established' (SSTS 22.07.2008 and 12.03.2007, quoting many others), and which are permanent malformations (STS 02.04.2014, appeal 608/2012) following the pregnant mother's ingestion of thalidomide during the critical period. This is the first period when the determination of the first series of damage resulting from the use of thalidomide can undergo fractioning', ie it can be separated from the different sets of damage arising later, in a new and differentiated phase.

97 As to worsening or emergence of other injuries, ie the finding of new sequels not determined at the time of birth, this 'would involve a new phase or another fact differentiated from the previous one'. In these cases, which are 'cases other than the cases above (such as sequels in internal organs or other

[187] Legal Ground 6th of the Court of Appeal Decision.
[188] Legal Ground 3rd of the First Instance Decision.

organs), since they cannot be determined from the time of birth, as regards this first stage or phase, the limitation period will start running, not at the time of diagnosis, but at the time when the scope of the disablement they have caused is established". This would be the time when victims could know their scope and their causal relationship to the harmful event. In this regard and in relation to the so-called late damage, the judgment of the Court of Appeal considered that the *dies a quo* had not yet arrived and, therefore, that the action to pursue the claim for compensation had not yet been started/initiated. First, it considered that the claimant had not proved causation, neither generic nor specific, between the consumption of thalidomide and this type of new damage. In this regard, the Court of Appeal held that the so-called Heidelberg Report – which is the grounds of the first instance judgment – is merely a statistical report based on interviews which should be complemented by subsequent systematic scientific research. Moreover, secondly, the Court of Appeal considered that the association bringing the claim had not provided any evidence of the existence of this new damage (late damage) in the members it represented. According to the Court, victims may always claim compensation for late damage, within new future proceedings, under the assumption that this new damage can be duly proven.[189]

IX. OTHER REMEDIES AVAILABLE TO AGGRIEVED AND POTENTIALLY AGGRIEVED VICTIMS UNDER OTHER AREAS OF LAW (SOCIAL INSURANCE, ADMINISTRATIVE LAW, CRIMINAL LAW, ETC)

98 From the point of view of administrative law, the producers' or distributors' breach of the rules on product safety or of administrative rules laying down requirements, conditions or health standards relating to consumers' health and safety can lead to the imposition of administrative sanctions, as results from arts 49–52 TRLGDCU. Article 51 TRLGDCU provides a scale of possible sanctions, depending on whether they are considered slight (fines up to €3,005.06), serious (fines from €3,005.06 to €15,025.30) or very serious (fines from €10,025.31 to €601,012.10). In the latter case, moreover, the administration 'may agree to the temporary closure of the premises, facilities or services for a period of five years' (art 51.2 TRLGDCU). Ultimately, as accessory penalties, art 52 TRLGDCU also provides for the possibility that public authorities order

[189] A different matter is whether Grünenthal Pharma, SA should be held liable for fault for damage that was unforeseeable at the time thalidomide was put into circulation (*Ramos González* (fn 185) 4).

the 'seizure of adulterated, damaged, forged or fraudulent goods … that may involve risks to the consumer and user', and that they 'advertise the sanctions … and the names or corporate name of the responsible natural or legal persons'. It must be borne in mind that most of these measures do not constitute a remedy for the party who has suffered damage caused by a defective product, but rather are sanctions impose upon those who have breached administrative provisions, with a clearly punitive function.

99 Criminal law also provides for various sorts of offences related to damage caused by defective products, regulation of which is set out in the Penal Code (CP). Leaving aside the general categories of homicide (arts 138 ff CP), injury (arts 147 ff CP) or the offence of damage against property (arts 263 ff CP), arts 359 ff CP deal with a series of crimes 'against public health', some of which may be applicable to cases of damage caused by defective products. Most penalties which the Penal Code provides for the latter category of offences give rise to imprisonment or disqualification from the profession or trade, for lengths of time that depend on the severity of the crime.

100 Finally, in exceptional circumstances, the Spanish Social Security system has granted financial assistance aimed at protecting certain groups of victims who have suffered damage caused by certain product categories. This has occurred, exceptionally, in cases of great social relevance and with a really significant number of potential victims. Basically, benefits were granted in Spain in two specific cases, the first one dealing with personal injury and death suffered in the Colza Oil case, and the second one with blood transfusions contaminated with HIV and hepatitis C.

101 In the first case,[190] with more than 30,000 victims, including those who died and victims suffering a wide variety of personal injuries, the State passed a series of regulations establishing social allowances and benefits in order to protect the victims a few months after the outbreak.[191] These rules provided for social measures of different types, including allowances, social benefits, healthcare benefits and educational benefits, which aimed to take care of the large and various number of victims. Most of these benefits were placed under the control of the Management Office for Allowances and Social Benefits for the

[190] SSTS 2nd 23.04.1992 (RJ 1992\6783) and 26.09.1997 (RJ 1997\6366).

[191] Basically, Real Decreto 2448/1982, de 19 de octubre (RCL 1981\2553) BOE no 257, 27.10.1981 (p 25164); rect. BOE no 258, 28.10.1981 (p 25248); Fourth Additional Provision of Ley 44/1981, de 26 de diciembre, *de los Presupuestos Generales del Estado para 1982*; Real Decreto 1276/1982, de 28 de junio (RCL 1982\1579) BOE no 146, 19.06.1982 (p 16766); Orden del Ministerio de Trabajo, Sanidad y Seguridad Social, de 7 septiembre 1981 (RCL 1981, 2116 and 2248); Resolución de la Secretaría del Estado para la Seguridad Social de 12 de septiembre de 1981 (RCL 1981, 2169).

Toxic Syndrome (OGPESST) specifically set up for this purpose. Among other aspects, the allowances were granted for permanent and temporary disability, retirement, domestic assistance, social reinstatement, death and expenses associated with it (from one to three million pesetas, ie approx from €6,000 to €18,000); for widowhood and orphanage and in favour of some relatives of the deceased; for reimbursement of pharmaceutical expenses and allowances for breastfeeding children, nurseries, school expenses and children's holiday camps; for a family complementary allowance (which, because of its amount, was usually the most important); and for a discount in worker's fees, allowances for prostheses, etc. In global terms, from 1981 to the end of 2001 the Spanish State paid around 104,098.148 million pesetas (approx. €625.64 million) as social allowances and benefits resulting from the Colza Oil case.[192]

102 In the case of infections with HIV and hepatitis C resulting from blood transfusion or treatment with blood products which were carried out within the framework of public medical health care, compensation funds have been established. Thus, for instance in Royal Decree 9/1993 of 28 May on benefits in favour of persons affected by HIV as a consequence of actions within the framework of the public health care system.[193] With regard to hepatitis C, the Spanish Government passed Act 14/2002 of 5 June, establishing social benefits in favour of persons with haemophilia and other congenital diseases related to blood who developed hepatitis C as a result of receiving medical treatment with blood products within the public health care system.[194]

---

192 According to *Jiménez Aparicio*, La ejecución de la sentencia de la colza I, Indret.com, Working Paper no 112, 2003, who refers to data given by the Annual Statistic Report of the INSS (Instituto Nacional de la Seguridad Social) and to the OGPESST (Oficina de Gestión de las Prestaciones Económicas y Sociales del Síndrome Tóxico).

193 Real Decreto-ley 9/1993, de 28 de mayo, por el que se conceden ayudas a los afectados por el Virus de Inmunodeficiencia Humana (VIH) como consecuencia de actuaciones realizadas en el sistema sanitario público, BOE no 130, 01.06.1993.

194 Ley 14/2002, de 5 de junio, por la que se establecen ayudas sociales a las personas con hemofilia u otras coagulopatías congénitas que hayan desarrollado la hepatitis C como consecuencia de haber recibido tratamiento con concentrados de factores de coagulación en el ámbito del sistema sanitario público, y otras normas tributarias, BOE no 135, 06.06.2000. This Act was developed by Royal Decree 377/2003 of 28 March (BOE no 76, 29.03.2003 (correction of mistakes BOE no 99, 25.04.2003)). For a more detailed explanation of this fund, see *M Martín-Casals/J Solé*, Medical Liability in Spain, in: BA Koch (ed), Medical Liability in Europe. A Comparison of Selected Jurisdictions (2011) nos 74–81, pp 497 ff.

PRODUCT LIABILITY IN SWITZERLAND

Bénédict WINIGER

I. SOURCES OF LAW AND THEIR EVOLUTION

01 In 1993 the Swiss Federal Assembly adopted a Product Liability Act (LRFP).[1] This Act was in line with the European Directiv e of 1985.[2] After the modification of the Directive in 1999,[3] and in order to also submit

1 *Loi fédérale sur la responsabilité du fait des produits du 18 juin 1993* (LRFP) (RS 221.112.944 <www.admin.ch/opc/fr/classified-compilation/19930205/index.html>), entry into force 1 January 1994.

2 Directive 85/374/EEC, 25 July 1985 <http://eur-lex.europa.eu/legal-content/EN/ALL/?uri=CELEX:31985L0374>.

3 Directive 1999/34/EC, 10 May 1999.

untransformed products of the soil, animal farming, fishing and hunting to the regime of the LRFP, the Swiss legislation was adjusted in 2009.[4] As a result, it is now consistent with the Directive and most of the norms are identical or very close to the formulation of the Directive.

02 Prior to the LRFP, there was no *lex specialis* on product liability. Cases of product liability were submitted to the general tort law provisions of the Swiss Code of Obligations (SCO, art 41 lit f). The first Federal Court case in product liability matters seems to go back to 1923.[5] Product liability had been anticipated by the Federal Court in two key decisions, where the producer (or provider) was held liable for damage, even if he had not committed any fault.[6]

II. BASIC ELEMENTS OF LIABILITY

03 Liability according to the LRFP is based on the following requirements: (i) damage to the victim by a product, and (ii) a causal link between the product and the damaging event. The first condition tacitly includes unlawfulness, which is contained in the fact that damage has been inflicted. In a certain sense one could speak about unlawfulness of result (*Erfolgsunrecht*), which is a form of unlawfulness accepted by the Federal Court under the general tort law provision of the SCO (art 41). Like in the Directive, fault is not required.[7] Consequently, the LRFP does not mention any particular duty of care, etc. However, a hidden form of fault can be found in art 5 al 1 lit e LRFP, which enumerates the exceptions to liability. As the producer can argue that the defect of the product could not be detected by the state of science at the time the product was put into circulation, *a contrario* it is admitted that the producer of a defective product had neglected the state of science.

---

4 Abrogation of art 3 al 2 LRFP by art 20 al 2 of the Federal Act on the Security of Products (*Loi fédérale sur la sécurité des produits du 12 juin 2009* (LSPro) (RS 930.11 <www.admin.ch/opc/fr/classified-compilation/20081129/index.html>)).

5 For a short historical overview see *W Fellmann/G von Bühren-von Moos*, Grundriss der Produktehaftpflicht (1993) 24 ff; for the evolution of the idea of product liability see *P Wessner*, La responsabilité du fait des produits, un droit venu d'ailleurs!, in: C Chappuis et al (eds), Colloque en l'honneur du Professeur Gilles Petitpierre. Le législateur et le droit privé (2006) 11 ff; *C Weniger*, La responsabilité du fait des produits pour les dommages causés à un tiers au sein de la Communauté européenne. Etude comparée (1994) 21 ff with extensive bibliography.

6 ATF 110 II 456 and ATF, *i.S.G v M. & S. SA*, 14.04.1985 (unpublished, but see JdT 134 [1986] I 571 ff); *P Widmer*, Produktehaftung, in Recht 1986 Heft 2, 50–57.

7 ECJ, 10 May 2001, Case C-203/99, *Henning Veedfald v Arhus Amtskommune*, para 17 <http://curia.europa.eu/juris/showPdf.jsf?text=&docid=46357&pageIndex=0&doclang=fr&mode=lst&dir=&occ=first&part=1&cid=177817>.

A. DEFINITION OF THE PRODUCT

04 Article 3 al 1 LRFP defines the concept of 'product' as follows:

(i) All movable goods (*chose mobilière, bewegliche Sache*); these movables may be manufactured or industrially produced (cars, glasses, machines, etc), or simply extracted from the nature (coal, water, metals, etc).[8] Like the Directive, art 3 LFRP specifies that movables integrated into other movables or non-movables are products. Consequently, for example, a motor integrated into a ship is considered a product. This is also true for a movable integrated into an immovable. It is worthwhile to note this, because it forms an exception to the generally accepted principle *superficies solo cedit*, according to which the movable integrated into a non-movable adopts the juridical status of the non-movable.

(ii) Electricity is also a product despite the fact that, in principle, a movable is a material object with spatial extension.[9] Natural forces which can be harnessed are also classified as movables (art 713 Swiss Civil Code (SCC)). As such they have also to be considered as products if they have been harnessed (and put into circulation) by a producer (water power, gas, heat). However, if the exploitation of a natural force is based on an independent and durable right, such as a concession fixed in a land charge register, the natural force is submitted to rules of immovable rights.[10] It is irrelevant whether the product is new or not, bought directly from the dealer or second hand. Liability is excluded only by the rules on prescription and forfeiture (arts 9 (prescription) and 10 (*péremption*) LRFP; see *infra*).[11]

05 Since art 3 al 2 LRFP was erased in 2009 (see no 04 *supra*), untransformed goods of the soil, animal farming, fishing and hunting are considered products. This is an important point, as raw agricultural goods play an essential role and are sold in significant quantities.

06 Furthermore, body parts are movables and as such they should be considered as products.[12] This is in particular true for bred or hunted animals and their body parts once they are put into circulation. As for human body parts, such as organs for transplant or blood for transfusion, they also have to

---

8 *F Werro/S Chaulmontet*, Produktehaftpflicht, in: E Kramer (ed), Schweizerisches Privatrecht X. Konsumentenschutz im Privatrecht (2008) 422; *Fellmann/von Bühren-von Moos* (fn 5) 63 ff, also discussing products created using genetic engeneering, 65 n 143.

9 *A Heberlein/P Breitschmid/EM Belser/S Bienz*, in: P Breitschmid/A Rumo-Jungo, Handkommentar zum Schweizer Privatrecht. Sachenrecht (2nd edn 2012) art 713, 332.

10 *Heberlein/Breitschmid/Belser/Bienz* (fn 9) art 713, 333 f.

11 *Fellmann/von Bühren-von Moos* (fn 5) 66 n 146 f.

12 *S Marchand*, Droit de la consommation (2012) 111.

be considered as products. However, it is not the donor, but rather the organ or blood bank, that should be considered the producer.[13] According to the jurisprudence, prostheses implanted into a body are also products.[14]

07 It is a matter of dispute whether intellectual property can be considered a product. As explained (no 04 *supra*), art 3 LRFP defines products to be movables and electricity, a definition which without a doubt does not encompass intellectual property.[15] The question then is whether or not the definition in art 3 LRFP should be extended. There are many different points of view. Certain authors reject any possibility of extension, whether it concerns the content of books or computer software.[16] The main argument is that the LRFP only provides protection against damage emanating from material objects (and electricity). Another opinion distinguishes between damage stemming from an intellectual error, for example if an author makes a mistake in his manuscript, and damage occurring during the production of the work, for example if the editor mixes up figures in a scientific text.[17] A third opinion considers that intellectual content such as the content of books or software is a product and falls under the LRFP.[18]

08 When preparing the LRFP in 1992, the Swiss legislator did not apparently discuss the notion of movables,[19] nor in the revision of 2009.[20] Consequently it has to be assumed that the legislator adopted the traditional concept of movables. One could even say that at the latest in 2009 the legislator was aware of the controversy about intellectual property and software in the LRFP. As the law was not adjusted, this has to be interpreted as a clear expression of the legislator's decision not to submit these two 'products' to the LRFP, but to the general dispositions of the Swiss Code of Obligations (SCO). In principle it is not for jurisprudence or the doctrine to correct this, even though it may evidently lead to absurd results. It is for example difficult to understand why damage caused by a computer (hardware) should fall under the LRFP, but not damage resulting from a defective computer programme (software).

---

13 *Werro/Chaulmontet* (fn 8) 422.

14 See the Swiss Federal Court's decision ATF 137 III 226.

15 This is also true in Swiss penal law (*M Dupuis et al* (eds), Code pénal. Petit commentaire (2012) 739 marg no 12. For an alternative proposition to the LRFP and permitting intellectual 'products' to be taken into account, see *P Widmer*, Responsabilité du fait des poduits et responsabilité du fait de l'organisation, in: Mélanges en l'honneur de Jacques-Michel Grossen (1992) 349 ff, 354.

16 *H Honsell*, Schweizerisches Haftpflichtrecht (1995) §21, 133 ff, 134; *C Huguenin*, Obligationenrecht. Allgemeiner und Besonderer Teil (2nd edn 2014) 616 n 2110.

17 *W Fellmann*, Bundesgesetz über die Produktehaftpflicht (Produktehaftpflicht, PrHG), art 3 n 9, in: H Honsell et al (eds), Basler Kommentar. Obligationenrecht I (2011) 3036.

18 *Werro/Chaulmontet* (fn 8) 424 f.

19 *Message du 27 mai 1992 sur l'adaptation du droit fédéral au droit de l'EEE, Feuille fédérale* (FF) 1992 V 413 ff, 419; *Message du 24 février 1993 sur le programme consécutif au rejet de l'Accord EEE*, FF 1993 I 833 f.

20 *Message du 25 juin 2008 concernant la loi sur la sécurité des produits*, FF 2008 6780 f.

09 As far as we can see, the question of intellectual content and software has never been submitted to the Federal Court. However the court could have opened a path to get out of the dilemma. The court admits that the producer has to give sufficient instructions and warnings on the use of a product; otherwise the producer is liable under the LRFP.[21] As instructions and warnings are doubtless non-material, the Federal Court does in fact allow liability for intellectual content. This break with the principle that movables have to be material could be a first step in henceforth including other more extensive intellectual content, such as the content of books or computer programmes. It would indeed be difficult to distinguish for example between an instruction manual on how to assemble pre-fabricated furniture and an instruction manual on how to produce a chemical substance.

B. DEFECTIVENESS

10 'Defectiveness' is defined in art 4 LRFP. A product is defective if it does not offer the security 'someone' can legitimately expect. In each of the three versions (French, German, Italian) the law uses the indefinite term 'someone' ('*on*', '*man*', '*che ci si può*'), which does not indicate what person's expectations are meant.[22] According to the jurisprudence, the law refers to the average person: 'The security expected in a specific case is appreciated in an objective way, according to the average consumer's expectations'.[23] The average person is someone who is not particularly skilled, specialised or experienced, or especially untalented, obtuse or awkward.

11 However, art 4 LRFP also mentions that all circumstances have to be taken into account. This should allow the judge to adopt a low average standard, for example if the person is vulnerable because of his or her age or disability, etc.[24] Such an interpretation is supported by art 3 of the Federal Product Security Act (LSPro),[25] which states that only products representing no or solely minimal risks can be commercialised, taking into account the fact that the user or third person can be vulnerable (children, handicapped or aged persons; art 3 al 3 lit d). The doctrine emphasises that a product which infringes the conditions of the

---

21 ATF 133 III 81, 84 c 3.1; concerning the instruction see also *E Büyüksagis*, La notion de défaut dans la responsabilité du fait des produits (2005) 295 ff.

22 For the question of defect see *Büyüksagis* (fn 21).

23 ATF 137 III 226, 232 c 3.2.

24 *Marchand* (fn 12) 116. For particularly vulnerable persons, *Büyüksagis* (fn 21) 346 ff proposes a so-called 'test of an alternative reasonable concept'.

25 For the relationship between LRFP and LSPro see *T Bühler*, La législation sur les risques des produits, in: B Carron et al (eds), Droits de la consommation et de la distribution: Les nouveaux défis (2013) 8 passim.

LSPro, and which thus should have been recalled from the market, also violates *ipso facto* the LRFP.[26]

12 Doctrine and jurisprudence generally distinguish three categories of defects, stemming from: fabrication, construction and instruction.[27] (i) Defects stemming from *fabrication* concern generally well-conceived products where something however goes wrong during fabrication. This can affect the whole production or only some rare single elements (*Ausreisser*). Such a case occurred in the widely discussed slot ceiling case (*Schachtrahmen-Fall*),[28] where one of a series of pieces caused an accident while being manipulated by an employee of the consumer. (ii) Defects stemming from *construction* originate in an unsafe design, which makes the product dangerous even if it is used normally. This may be the case with a chair built from materials that are too fragile and that thus breaks under the weight of the user.[29] (iii) Defects can also result from insufficient or false *instruction* accompanying the product, and thus for example misleading the consumer in how it should be used. The producer has to call the consumer's attention to dangers when using the product and to indicate how to avoid damage.[30] According to some of the doctrine, the instruction can be less detailed if the product is destined for use by a professional and if the producer can exclude the possibility that it might fall into the hands of a layman.[31]

13 Jurisprudence and the doctrine underline that the distinction between these three categories is not based on the law and does not bind the judge. It can however be useful for better case analysis,[32] even if the distinction between the three categories is not clear-cut and sometimes even worrying.[33]

14 It has been debated whether inefficient products can be considered defective. As art 4 LRFP defines a product as defective if it does not offer the expected security, it has been argued that, for example an inefficient fire extinguisher does not compromise one's security. Formally, art 4 LRFP refers only to the security of the product, but not to its fitness for use. Indeed unfitness for use would rather fall under the (seller's) guarantee of absence of defects. According to the Federal Supreme Court and the doctrine, unfitness for use can at the same time be a defect because the expectations created by the producer can dissuade the user from acquiring a more efficient product. Consequently, an inefficient

26 *Marchand* (fn 12) 116.
27 ATF 133 III 81, 85 c 3.2.
28 ATF 110 II 456.
29 Arrêt du Tribunal fédéral du 14 mai 1985, C.564/1984.
30 ATF 133 III 81, 84 c 3.1.
31 *Fellmann/von Bühren-von Moos* (fn 5) 92 n 244, 96, 261.
32 ATF 133 III 81, 85 c 3.2.
33 *Marchand* (fn 12) 117.

product can fall under the LRFP.[34] This point of view is shared by the European jurisprudence.[35]

15 It has also been debated whether the fact that there is a newer and safer product on the market would *ipso facto* mean that an older and less safe product should be considered defective. In the message accompanying the law, the legislator clearly answered in the negative.[36]

16 Certain products are per se dangerous, such as alcohol, tobacco, drugs (narcotics) or foods with a high sugar content. However this does not mean that they have to be considered defective in the sense of the LRFP if their dangerousness is generally known and accepted by the consumer.[37] The same is true for medicines insofar as their dangerousness is known. If it is not and if a medicine considered safe does in fact cause damage, the LRFP is applicable, except if art 5 LRFP removes liability.

17 As to electricity, which is a product according to art 3 al 1 lit b LRFP (see no 04 (ii) *supra*), it has been discussed whether a defective electricity supply has to be considered a defective product. In the case of voltage fluctuations, the answer seems to be in the affirmative and any resulting damage has to be remedied under the LRFP. There is a dissent in the doctrine concerning the interruption of electricity supply. One opinion considers that interruptions of electricity supply have to be assimilated to variations of supply and that both should fall under the LRFP.[38] The opposite opinion holds that such assimilation would provoke an inopportune extension of the notion of defect.[39] The first opinion is correct that voltage fluctuations and interruption of supply should be treated in the same manner, because otherwise an electricity provider could be tempted, in the event of fluctuations, to simply cut the electricity supply in order to escape the severe liability regime of the LRFP. More generally, this opinion might be influenced by the fact that ricochet damage (a specific form of indirect damage) is generally not accepted by the Federal Supreme Court and that damage resulting from interrupted electricity supply will only be compensated if it is accompanied by material damage. This jurisprudence could be bypassed,

---

34 ATF 139 II 534, 540; 64 II 254.

35 CJEU (Ord), 11 April 2001, Case C-476/00 P (R), *Commission v Schuck GmbH* [2001] ECR I-2995.

36 '*Un produit ne peut toutefois être considéré comme défectueux par le seul fait qu'un produit plus perfectionné et plus sûr a été mis sur le marché ultérieurement*': *Message du 25 juin 2008 concernant la loi sur la sécurité des produits*, FF 2008 6780.

37 See notably *Fellmann/von Bühren-von Moos* (fn 5) 78 n 195.

38 *Werro/Chaulmontet* (fn 8) 423; probably also *Fellmann/von Bühren-von Moos* (fn 5) 67 n 152 ff.

39 *Marchand* (fn 12) 116. For a distinction between interruption and variation already *T Jäggi*, Das Bundesgesetz über die Produktehaftpflicht, in AJP 12/93 1421.

however, by assimilating the interruption of electricity supply to fluctuations in voltage.

18 However, besides the fact that the notion of defect would be overstretched, this assimilation solution has a logical problem: a non-existent product cannot be defective. If the aim of obtaining reparation for all damage resulting from the interruption of electricity supply is reasonable, the fundamental and more general question is probably what price in terms of doctrinal incoherence scholars are ready to pay in their efforts to impose their solutions on the Supreme Court.

C. PUTTING A PRODUCT INTO CIRCULATION

19 Art 5 al 1 lit a LRFP says that the producer is not liable for products he had not put into circulation. The notion of 'putting into circulation' has been defined above all by the European Court of Justice as where the product 'leaves the production process operated by the producer and enters a marketing process in the form in which it is offered to the public in order to be used or consumed. Generally, it is not important in that regard that the product is sold directly by the producer to the user or to the consumer or that sale is carried out as part of a distribution process involving one or more operators, such as that envisaged in article 3(3) of the Directive'.[40] As the LRFP is a copy of the Directive, with the legislator's intent being to harmonise Swiss and European law, it is likely that the Swiss judge would adopt the European view.[41]

20 The European Court of Justice considers that the product has been put into circulation – and thus the producer is liable – even if the consumer uses it within the sphere of the producer, for example if a patient is treated with a medicine in a hospital closely linked to another hospital, whose pharmacy produced the medicine.[42] Again, it is likely that the Swiss judge would adopt the same view.

---

40 ECJ 9 February 2006, Case C-127/04, *Declan O'Byrne v Sanofi Pasteur SA*, para 27/28 <http://curia.europa.eu/juris/showPdf.jsf;jsessionid=9ea7d0f130de026f77bfea8e4eee8830d1a570b63424.e34KaxiLc3eQc40LaxqMbN4OaNuOe0?text=&docid=55647&pageIndex=0&doclang=en&mode=lst&dir=&occ=first&part=1&cid=91173>. As to close relationships between the producer and the entity in charge of marketing, the court indicates general principles to be applied by the national judge (paras 30 and 31).

41 The Federal Court considers that EU law has no immediate and constraining force on Swiss law, but that European law is an aid in interpretation (*Auslegungshilfe*) for Swiss law. In case of doubt, Swiss law has to be interpreted in conformity with European law, ATF 129 III 335, 350 c 6.

42 ECJ, 10 May 2001, Case C-203/99, *Henning Veedfald v Arhus Amtskommune*, para 17 <http://curia.europa.eu/juris/showPdf.jsf?text=&docid=46357&pageIndex=0&doclang=fr&mode=lst&dir=&occ=first&part=1&cid=177817>. See also *F Werro*, Le droit suisse de la responsabilité du fait des produits face au droit européen, in: F Werro et al (eds), Le droit privé suisse face au droit communautaire européen (2004) 65 ff.

D. MODEL OF LIABILITY

21 In Swiss law one can distinguish different forms of liability. The general tort law provision of art 41 SCO requires (besides the existence of damage, the damaging act/conduct, and a causal link between the two) unlawfulness (*illicéité, Widerrechtlichkeit, danno illecitamente cagionato*) and a form of fault (intention, negligence or imprudence). On the other hand, there are numerous non-fault provisions. An example of non-fault liability in the tort law rules of the SCO would be liability for buildings (*bâtiments et autres ouvrages, Werkeigentümer, opera*) in art 58 SCO. Outside the SCO, numerous special acts contain non-fault (also called purely causal) liability. The Hunting Act for example says that 'the one who practices hunting is liable for the damage he causes'.[43] Acts regulating particularly dangerous activities, such as the Nuclear Power Act[44] and the Aviation Act,[45] use the same model. In between fault and non-fault liability, there are those norms that require fault, but use a reversed burden of proof. A classic example is employer's liability in art 55 SCO, where the fault of the employer is presumed, but where the employer can prove his diligence *in eligendo, instruendo* and *custodiendo.*

22 In this picture, product liability is evidently on the side of non-fault liability. We would however hesitate to call it a risk-based liability. Despite the fact that this terminology is currently used in the doctrine and in projects of revision,[46] it is not (yet) firmly established in the legislation. There is also another reason not to consider product liability to be risk-based. According to the Widmer/Wessner project,[47] activities are risky only if they cause frequent or serious damage. These requirements are not fulfilled in the Product Liability Act, as the victim can sue for damages even if the damage is seldom or minor. Besides this, product liability is not linked to an activity but to a product.

III. THE PERSON LIABLE FOR DAMAGE

23 Art 1 LRFP indicates that the liability rests with the producer and art 2 defines who is considered to be a producer: (i) the person who has produced the finished product, raw material or a component part of the product; (ii) the

43 *Loi sur la chasse et la protection des mammifères et oiseaux sauvages du 20 juin 1986* (LChP) (RS 922.0 <www.admin.ch/opc/fr/classified-compilation/19860156/index.html>), art 15.

44 *Loi fédérale sur la responsabilité civile en matière nucléaire du 18 mars 1983* (LRCN) (RS 732.44 <www.admin.ch/opc/fr/classified-compilation/19830065/index.html>), art 3 ff.

45 *Loi fédérale sur l'aviation du 21 décembre 1948* (LA) (RS 748.0 <www.admin.ch/opc/fr/classified-compilation/19480335/>), art 64 ff.

46 Révision et unification du droit de la responsabilité civile. Avant-projet de la loi fédérale par Pierre Widmer et Pierre Wessner (2000) art 50; *C Huguenin/RM Hilty* (eds), Code des Obligations suisse 2020, art 60.

47 *Widmer/Wessner* (fn 46) art 50.

person pretending to be the producer by indicating his name, trade mark or distinctive sign; or (iii) the professional importer or supplier, except if he informs the victim of the identity of the producer.

24 If there is more than one producer, they are liable *in solido* (art 7 LRFP). All of them are individually liable towards the victim for the entirety of the damage. Parties can be released from their solidary liability under the conditions of art 5 LRFP (no 37 *infra*).[48]

IV. THE AGGRIEVED PERSON AND DAMAGE

A. THE AGGRIEVED PERSON

25 The text of the LRFP does not specify the party authorised to claim damages. Potentially every victim could do so.[49] An indirect definition of the claimant results from art 1 LRFP, according to which the producer has to remedy damage: (i) in the event of the death of or physical harm to a person, in which case the heirs or the aggrieved person him/herself would be the claimants; or (ii) in the event of damage to or destruction of things, if the thing is usually and principally used for private purposes, in which case the owner of the damaged thing would certainly be entitled to file a claim, except if he principally uses it for professional purposes (thus a merchant whose *private* computer was damaged by a product could file a claim if he used the computer exceptionally for his professional duties, but he could not do so if the same occurred to his *work* computer).

26 Given that the LRFP provides damages for harm to persons and things, in practice the claimant will generally be a natural person. However it is not excluded, that a company could file a claim, for example a housing cooperative or co-proprietors of an apartment building whose goods have been damaged by a product.[50]

B. DAMAGE

27 Damage is defined in art 1 LRFP and protects persons and things: '[t]he producer is liable for damage if a defective product has: (a) caused death of a person or provoked her physical harm; (b) damaged or destroyed a thing of a kind

48 *Marchand* (fn 12) 110.
49 For the whole see also *Weniger* (fn 5) 32 ff.
50 *Marchand* (fn 12) 110.

commonly destined to private use or consummation and which had principally been used by the victim for private purpose'.[51] According to jurisprudence and doctrine, the most important provision is art 1 al 1 lit a LRFP, which is applicable in any case of personal injury and independently of whether the damage occurred during professional or extra-professional activities.

28 To the contrary, material damage is reparable only if the damaged thing (but not the product) is destined for private use. If a construction worker's personal watch is damages by a defective machine, he can claim damages under the LRFP, but he cannot if the helmet that is part of his work uniform is damaged. The distinction between private and professional use is rightly criticised by some scholars.[52]

29 Article 1 al 2 LRFP states that damage caused to the product itself does not have to be repaired. In this case, the owner of the product can base his claim on the sale contract. Thus, if a machine explodes and causes damage to the owner's goods, he can file an action based on the Product Liability Act for the damage to the goods and another claim based on the contract for the damage caused to the machine.

30 The European Court of Justice has decided that damage to persons has to be remedied in its entirety.[53] If this rule were followed by Swiss courts, it would mean notably that loss of earnings, medical expenses, and *tort moral*, eg for psychological harm, had to be remedied. However, non-material and non-physical damage cannot be remedied under the LRFP. Nevertheless, an action could be filed under the general tort law provisions of the SCO. As loss of a chance is rejected in Swiss law, it would not be remediable.[54] The possibility of applying the general tort law provisions is expressly mentioned in art 11 LRFP.

31 For material damage art 6 LRFP fixes a lower limit of Frs 900 (€750). Below this amount, the victim has to bear the damage him/herself.

V. CAUSALITY

32 The preliminary requirements for liability under the LRFP are: (i) that the defendant is the producer; (ii) that the damage has been caused by his

---

51 Art 1 LRFP; ATF 4A_16/2011 c 2.3; *Marchand* (fn 12) 107.

52 *Marchand* (fn 12) 107 f.

53 ECJ, 10 May 2001, Case C-203/99, *Henning Veedfald v Arhus Amtskommune*, para 27 <http://curia.europa.eu/juris/showPdf.jsf?text=&docid=46357&pageIndex=0&doclang=fr&mode=lst&dir=&occ=first&part=1&cid=177817>.

54 ATF 133 III 462.

product; (iii) that the producer had put the product into circulation; and (iv) that exceptions under art 5 LRFP apply, notably that the defect existed at the time the product was put into circulation and that the state of knowledge did not allow the defect to be discovered at that time.

33 The LRFP does not specify the conditions for causality. Art 1 LRFP states only that '[t]he producer is liable for damage, if a product *caused* …'. In the absence of greater precision, the general rules of causation, such as natural and adequate causality, are applicable. Firstly, the judge has to use the test of the *conditio sine qua non* and ask whether the damage would have occurred had the producer not behaved in the way he did. If the answer to the question is in the negative, natural causality is established. Secondly, the judge has to ask whether the link between the producer's attitude and the damage is not too stretched. The criterion for adequate causation used by the Federal Court is whether the damage was foreseeable according to the general experience of life and the ordinary course of things.[55] Typically this question is raised in art 5 al 1 lit e: if the state of knowledge at the time the product was put into circulation did not permit the damage to be predicted, the judge does not find adequate causation.

34 Like art 5 of the Directive, art 7 LRFP provides for solidary liability for several persons liable for the same damage. But unlike the Directive (art 8(1)), the LRFP does not regulate the question of concurrent causes between the defective product and a third party's intervention. However, certain authors rightly suppose that the Swiss judge would accept this rule, given the legislator's strong desire for compatibility with EU law.[56]

35 Contributory fault of the victim (art 8(2) Directive) does not appear in the LRFP. However, the judge does have to take the contributory fault of the victim into account on the basis of art 44 al 1 SCO, and reduce or even refuse damages depending on the gravity of the victim's fault.

36 On the subject of partial causation, where several sources might have contributed to the damage, the LRFP has nothing to day. The SCO does however permit the judge to take into account proportional liability.[57]

---

55 *'Le cours ordinaire des choses et l'expérience générale de la vie'*, among others ATF 85 II 350, 354 c 1.

56 *Marchand* (fn 12) 112.

57 *P Widmer/B Winiger*, Causal uncertainty and proportional liability in Switzerland, in: I Gilead/MD Green/BA Koch (eds), Proportional liability: Analytical and comparative perspectives (2013) 323–342.

VI. DEFENCES AND EXCLUSIONS

37 The defences are enumerated in art 5 LRFP. The producer can prove that: (i) he did not put the product into circulation; (ii) the defect did not exist when the product was put into circulation; (iii) the product was not destined for sale or distribution with economic purposes or was not distributed professionally; (iv) the default was due to the product's conformity with public law rules; or (v) the state of science and knowledge at the time the product was put into circulation did not allow the defect to be discovered. As in the Directive, the enumeration of situations is limitative.[58]

38 If the producer has not put the product into circulation, he is not liable under the LRFP. However, this does not mean that he is not liable at all. The facts can fall under the general tort law rules of the SCO (arts 41 ff), notably if the damaging object was dangerous (*Gefahrensatz*). The liability can also be contractual, for example if an employee of the producer is a victim of the product, which has not yet been put into circulation (art 328 SCO).[59] As to the definition of putting into circulation, see *supra* no 03 ff.

39 The producer can prove that the defect did not exist at the time the product was put into circulation (art 5 al 1 lit b). The Federal Court understands this as a legal presumption that the defect already existed when the product was put into circulation.[60] The doctrine underlines that art 5 al 1 lit b LRFP presupposes a precise definition of the time the product was put into circulation. Authors cite the definition given by the European Court of Justice, according to which a product is put into circulation 'when it leaves the production process … and enters a marketing process',[61] and conclude correctly that if the distributor damages an intact product (for example through careless handling) in such a way that it later causes damage, the producer will not be liable towards the victim.[62] On the other hand, the producer will still be liable if the defect develops because of the inherent properties of the product, for example if a medicine deteriorates prematurely.

---

58 ECJ, 10 May 2001, Case C-203/99, *Henning Veedfald v Arhus Amtskommune,* para 17 <http://curia.europa.eu/juris/showPdf.jsf?text=&docid=46357&pageIndex=0&doclang=fr&mode=lst&dir=&occ=first&part=1&cid=177817>.

59 *Marchand* (fn 12) 121 f.

60 ATF 133 III 81, 85 c 3.1.

61 ECJ, 9 February 2006, Case C-127/04, *Declan O'Byrne v Sanofi Pasteur SA*, para 14 ff <http://curia.europa.eu/juris/showPdf.jsf;jsessionid=9ea7d0f130de026f77bfea8e4eee8830d1a570b63424.e34KaxiLc3eQc40LaxqMbN4OaNuOe0?text=&docid=55647&pageIndex=0&doclang=en&mode=lst&dir=&occ=first&part=1&cid=91173>.

62 *Marchand* (fn 12) 122 ff.

40 If the product has not been produced for an economic or professional purpose, the producer is not liable (art 5 al 1 lit c LRFP). The European Court of Justice has given a relatively narrow meaning to this norm. It says correctly that the question is not whether the victim has paid the producer for the product, but whether the producer had an economic purpose. If the purpose of a producer of medicines is not charitable, he is liable, even if it was not the victim but a public health insurer that paid for the medicine.[63]

41 The producer can prove that the defect of his product is due to its conformity with imperative public law rules (art 5 al 1 lit d LRFP). In principle the producer can only invoke imperative legal prescriptions. He is not freed from liability if he has respected optional rules.[64] However, sometimes there might be a tension between art 4 al 1 LRFP (the expected security of the product) and art 5 al 1 lit e LRFP, if the producer has followed non-compulsory rules which are generally accepted and followed notably by professionals. Such rules (construction rules for architects, etc) are frequently referred to by the judge to find whether someone is liable. It is indeed difficult to understand that they are used as a reference by the courts, but that they have to be disregarded in product liability.

42 According to art 5 al 1 lit e LRFP the producer is not liable for defects that it was not possible to detect considering the state of science and knowledge. These so-called 'development risks' are based on the idea of foreseeability. Whether a risk was foreseeable or not is decided on an objective standard based on the generally acknowledged state of science. According to the Federal Court, the judge has to refer to the state of knowledge and science at the time the product was put into circulation. The knowledge had to be accessible to and considered as serious by the scientific community. Isolated opinions are of no importance, except if the product is particularly dangerous to the population and environment.[65]

43 As to the origins of the defect, the jurisprudence distinguishes between defects stemming from fabrication, construction and instruction (see no 12 *supra*), but considers that this is not an exhaustive or binding categorisation. It is reasonable to think that a producer would be liable for defects due to other circumstances occurring within his sphere, such as bad or over-long storage or pre-term alteration of the product.

---

63 ECJ, 10 May 2001, Case C-203/99, *Henning Veedfald v Arhus Amtskommune*, para 21 <http://curia.europa.eu/juris/showPdf.jsf?text=&docid=46357&pageIndex=0&doclang=fr&mode=lst&dir=&occ=first&part=1&cid=177817>.

64 *Marchand* (fn 12) 124; *Werro/Chaulmontet* (fn 8) 444.

65 ATF 137 III 226, 233 c 4.1; see in this context also ATF 139 II 534, 537 c 2 concerning the Product Security Act (LSPro).

44 The LRFP was modified in 2004 and the legislator introduced art 5 al 1*bis*, which formulates an exception to the exclusions of producer's liability in art 5 al 1 LRFP, for animal organs, tissues, cells, as well as standard transplants of them, when destined for transplant to humans. The message regarding the modification argues for the exception because of the numerous known and unknown risks inherent to xenotransplantation (transplantation from animals to humans).[66] In practice it means that persons undergoing xenotransplantation have to bear a substantial risk and therefore the development risk defence should not apply.

45 Contractual limitation or exclusion of the liability is not admitted if it weakens the victim's position (art 8 LRFP).

VII. REMEDIES

46 As we have seen, art 1 al 1 LRFP says that the producer is liable under certain conditions. It does not specify the mode of reparation; nor do the tort law provisions of the SCO. For the SCO it is generally admitted that all modes of reparation are possible. However the reparation in money (lump sum or pension) is clearly the most current form. The same rules should be admitted for the LRFP.

47 Swiss tort law is conceived to remedy damage. If the damage has diminished the victim's patrimony, the author has to compensate this diminution (theory of difference). In the case of *tort moral* the victim is entitled to monetary compensation in order to redress the imbalance caused by the tort; other modes of reparation, such as the publication of a judgment in newspapers, etc, are possible if they are more appropriate. Punitive and exemplary damages are excluded. If the tortfeasor was advantaged by the damaging event, the skimming off of profits is possible. Based on art 28a al 3 of the Swiss Civil Code (SCC) the judges use sometimes the norms of agency of necessity (*gestion d'affaire sans mandat, Geschäftsführung ohne Auftrag*) to transfer the tortfeasor's benefits to the victim.[67]

48 The LRFP does not regulate questions of injunctions or withdrawal of products. However, there are other means of doing this, depending on the case. The endangerment of property or of persons could be prevented by norms

---

66 *Message concernant la Loi fédérale sur la transplantation du 12 septembre 2001,* FF 2002 19, 182.

67 ATF 133 III 153.

in the SCC (in particular arts 641 ff and 28a SCC); for products requiring authorisations from the public authorities, administrative means could be used.

VIII. PROCEDURAL ISSUES

49 Unlike the Directive, art 4 of which requires the victim to prove the damage, the defect and the causal relationship between the two, the LRFP does not assign the burden of proof. In the absence of a specific norm, the Swiss judge applies art 8 SCC, according to which a party that alleges a fact has to prove it.

50 The victim has to prove the existence of the damage, the defect and the causal link between them.[68] Furthermore, he has to prove that he made normal use of the product. In this respect, the Federal Court has given some important clarifications based on art 4 LRFP: 'The victim does not have to prove the cause of the defect, but solely that the product did not offer the security an average consumer could expect in the given circumstances'.[69] In other words, the victim has to prove that he made use of the product and had reasonable expectations concerning the security offered by the product. Concerning the link between the proof of the damage and the defectiveness of the product, the Federal Court specifies: 'The damage does not prove the product's defect. Nevertheless if the injured person establishes that the product played a role in the occurrence of the damage, he will demonstrate an important clue of the defect's existence'.[70] In principle, the victim should preserve the physical evidence; however, in the case from which the preceding quote is taken, because the guests had cleaned up the kitchen after the accident and disposed the exploded cafetière, the judges admitted that the victim had proven the defect by providing a convincing description of the circumstances in which the damage had occurred.

51 The judge evaluates the proof according to his personal conviction. He admits proof if he is convinced of the truth of an allegation. If the victim cannot bring an entire proof or if it would be unreasonable to require the victim to prove the allegation *stricto sensu*, the judge can alleviate the burden and content himself with indirect proof and convincing indications (*Beweisnot*).[71]

52 The LRFP gives two different limitation periods. In art 9 LRFP the relative limitation period is three years. As in art 10 of the Directive, it starts to run

---

68 For the whole see also *Weniger* (fn 5) 66 ff.
69 ATF 133 III 81, 87 c 4.1.
70 ATF 133 III 81 c 3.3.
71 ATF 133 III 81 c 4.2.2; see also *Widmer/Winiger* (fn 57) 323–342, 328.

when the victim was or should have been aware of the damage, the defect and the identity of the producer.

53 The absolute limitation period in art 10 LRFP is ten years and starts to run at the time the product was put into circulation. According to the European Court of Justice, national legislation cannot allow the victim to appeal to join a producer to an already pending claim if this appeal comes after the expiry of the ten-year period. It is likely that the Swiss judge would adopt this rule.[72]

54 However, in the opinion of the European Court of Human Rights, limitation periods (*in casu* ten years) are too short if it is not possible for the victim to become aware of the damage within this period. This is notably the case for asbestos cases, where the illness may manifest itself more than thirty years after exposure to the damaging substance.[73] This recent decision might influence the future development of limitation periods in Switzerland and their current revision in the SCO.[74]

IX. ALTERNATIVE LIABILITY REGIMES AND REMEDIES

55 As a general principle Swiss law admits that different actions (in tort and/or contract) can be filed simultaneously.

A. REMEDIES IN CONTRACT

56 As a principle, the contractual remedies are possible only if there is a contract between the parties. Consequently, the buyer cannot act contractually against the producer, unless the contract between the producer and distributor explicitly stipulates.[75]

---

72 ECJ (Grand Chamber), 2 December 2009, Case C-358/08, *Aventis Pasteur SA v OB*, para 49 <http://curia.europa.eu/juris/document/document.jsf?docid=76602&doclang=EN>.

73 '*79. Partant, au vu des circonstances exceptionnelles de la présente espèce, la Cour estime que l'application des délais de péremption ou de prescription ait limité l'accès à un tribunal à un point tel que le droit des requérantes s'en soit trouvé atteint dans sa substance même, et qu'elle ait ainsi emporté violation de l'article 6 §1 de la Convention (voir, mutatis mutandis, Stagno, précité, §33, avec les références qui y sont citées).*' ECtHR, 14 March 2014, *Howald Moor et autres c Suisse*, 52067/10 and 41072/11, para 18 <http://caova.ch/wp-content/uploads/2014/03/affaire-howald-moor-et-autres-c-suisse.pdf>.

74 See notably the federal government's *Message relatif à la modification du code des obligations (Droit de la prescription)*, 29 November 2013 <www.admin.ch/opc/fr/federal-gazette/2014/221.pdf>.

75 *Marchand* (fn 12) 101 f.

57 Article 197 ff SCO provide for recourse against the seller. The seller is liable to the buyer for product defects. The seller is for his part able to bring an action in contract against the producer. This solution is clearly not very favourable to the buyer, who has no recourse in contract against the producer.

58 Article 197 ff also provide for recourse against the producer. The buyer can bring an action in contract against the producer in two situations: (i) where in a contract *sui generis* the producer unilaterally allows the buyer to bring an action, and the buyer accepts this contract tacitly;[76] or (ii) where the producer and the seller agree in their contract that a third party (the buyer) can act directly against the producer in the event of a product defect.[77]

B. REMEDIES IN TORT

59 The victim can bring an action in tort, based on arts 41 ff SCO, against the tortfeasor. The Supreme Court applies the theory of the *Gefahrensatz* (*responsabilité pour état de fait dangereux*), saying that it is unlawful to create a situation of danger and to neglect (ie fault) the necessary measures to prevent damage.[78] The producer should have known the danger and have taken the appropriate security measures. Article 41 SCO is applicable to design defects, while art 55 SCO (employer's liability for his employees) applies to production and presentation defects, given that in the latter cases the defect occurs because of the employees. However, if the employer proves that he was diligent (*cura in eligendo*, *instruendo* and *custodiendo*; diligence in the organisation of the enterprise), he will not be liable to the victim.[79]

C. OTHER POSSIBILITIES

60 If an action based on the liability for defective products is not possible, the victim can use the ordinary means such as described *supra* no 56 ff. There is no specific regime for defective services.

61 As far as we can see, there are no specific rules on the obligation to recall defective products. Consequently these cases should be handled according to the general tort rules.

---

[76] ATF 134 III 218 c 3.6; *Marchand* (fn 12) 102.

[77] *Marchand* (fn 12) 102.

[78] ATF 116 Ia 162 c 2; 95 II 93 c 2; 124 III 297 c 5b; 123 III 306 c 4.

[79] ATF 110 II 456 c 3a.

62 Different situations should be distinguished:

(i) The producer is aware of the danger his product poses, notably because damage has already occurred in the past. If new damage occurs, the *Gefahrensatz* could be applied (see *supra* no 59). The damage would be considered unlawful and the failure to recall the products would be considered a fault, provided that the recall would have been possible and the costs not absolutely prohibitive.

(ii) The producer is not aware of the danger his product poses, but could and should have known of it. In the event of damage, solution (i) would probably be applicable.

(iii) The producer is not aware of the danger his product poses and could not and should not have known of it. In the event of damage he would not be liable if he had not been at fault.

(iv) The most interesting case is where a product is dangerous but no damage has yet occurred. The question is then whether the mere fact that the producer has not recalled the product would make the producer liable. In other words, the question would be whether the mere fact of exposing someone to a danger would lead to liability. This is an old question which already appeared in Roman law.[80] Then the answer was negative. In Swiss law there is at least one case where danger was considered to be damage.[81] Furthermore, the exposure to very serious danger can fall under art 129 Swiss Penal Code.

63 The insurer is linked contractually (the social insurer is linked by law) to the insured victim. He has to cover damage according to the terms of contract and statutes (art 51 al 2 SCO). Normally he will pay the medical and other costs and is subrogated to the victim's rights towards the tortfeasor.[82] As to penal law, see *supra* no 62.

X. ASSESSMENT OF DOMESTIC LEGISLATION

64 In practice, the LRFP has produced very few court decisions. In 2006, 13 years after the entry into force of the law, Pierre Wessner wrote that the LRFP was still '*lettre morte*'.[83] In the meantime, the Federal Court has decided a number of cases inferior to the number of fingers on (a butcher's) hand. In contrast, the legal literature on product liability is abundant, reaching its peak

80 Digest 9.2.27.10 (*Ulpianus*).

81 ATF 98 V 166.

82 See art 72 Insurance Act (*Loi fédérale sur le contrat d'assurance du 2 avril 1908* (LCA) (RS 221.229.1 <www.admin.ch/opc/fr/classified-compilation/19080008/>)).

83 *Wessner* (fn 5) 17, with references to the situation in Europe (*ibid* fn 32).

around 1993, when the LRFP was adopted. Even in 1993 the literature was '*kaum mehr zu durchschauen*'.[84] Since then the topic has considerably developed and has become almost impenetrable. Inevitably, repetitions are predominant and well-grounded new points of view rather scarce.[85] As to new technologies, unfortunately there is no clear solution notably concerning computer programmes and the like. The source of the problem stems from the wording of art 3 LRFP, in which a product is defined as a 'mobile object' (*chose mobilière*). For the discussion of this point see *supra* no 03 ff.

84 *P Gauch*, Die Produktehaftpflichtrechtlinie der EG. Ein Überblick, in: P Tercier et al (eds), Aspects du droit européen. Beiträge zum europäischen Recht (1993) 162.

85 For a recent bibliography see *Marchand* (fn 12) 329 ff.

PRODUCT LIABILITY IN CANADA

Marie-Eve ARBOUR

01 Canada is a constitutional federation whose Head of State is Queen Elizabeth II. Despite the Conquest of New France by the English (1759–1760), crystallised by the Treaty of Paris in 1763, French-derived private law was reintroduced in the Province of Quebec, for strategic reasons, on the occasion of the Quebec Act (1774). This compromise – public law remained anchored in the common law tradition – was reiterated on the occasion of Canada's foundational Constitutional Act (1867), by virtue of which ten provinces retain competence over private law matters and property,[1] including the legal basis for liability or procedural requirements (such as time limits, class actions and the like). From a constitutional standpoint, this situation is fragmented, as the field is indeed of a provincial nature, albeit increasingly shaped by federal and provincial legislation. Despite judicial deference to the *stare decisis* principle and obvious receptiveness to persuasive authority, Canada's constitutional aesthetics, as mentioned, explain the various discrepancies between the nine common law provinces themselves. The blending of the civil law and the common law traditions, too, adds to the complexity of the Canadian legal framework: in Quebec, the coexistence of both legal traditions is particularly visible in the field of personal injury damages and product liability, whereby the circulation of French, English, American and EU models influenced Quebec's Civil Code (CCQ)[2] and Code of Civil Procedure,[3] among other pieces of legislation.

02 Both Canadian common law (which resisted the strict liability American tsunami) and Quebec's civil law (which never embraced the categories of *culpa levis*, *culpa levissima* and *culpa lata* originating in Roman law) can be said to be *sui generis*[4] when compared to their historical contexts. This characteristic has, over the years, been marked by a phenomenon of osmosis between the civilist tradition and the influence of North American common law. In addition, some provinces' personal injury framework – such as that of Saskatchewan or

1 Art 92(13) of the Constitutional Act 1867.

2 The Province of Quebec characterises itself by being the only civil law jurisdiction in all Canada; following the French tradition, it promulgated its first Civil Code in 1866 (the Civil Code of Lower-Canada), which was reformed in 1994 (current Civil Code of Quebec, CCQ).

3 A new Code of Civil Procedure will shortly be adopted. References in this chapter are made to the current version.

4 For the sake of clarity, Canadian common law will hereby refer to the law of the Anglophone provinces, whereas Quebec's law indicates the civil law tradition. This means that the present chapter is inherently of a comparative nature, providing an overview of both legal traditions evolving within the same Federation.

Quebec – have also been shaped by socialist political influences that supported, after the 1970s, the creation of a Swedish-style no-fault compensation scheme for automobiles. Along with widely adopted workers' compensation statutes, these statutory regimes have led to the cross-fertilisation of private law and administrative law in awarding damages, further eroding, specifically in Quebec, the centrality of its Civil Code. Moreover, a general safety obligation has been enacted by the federal legislator;[5] it is expected to have a great impact on the interpretation of the all consumer laws, laws of sale and tort/delictual liability in all ten provinces.

03 In the end, thus, the dichotomy between civil law and common law explains noticeable variations in legal protections in Canada. Case law, indeed, often transcends legislative variations; much like shared values sometimes explain the frequent circulation of the same policy reasons and rationales within courtrooms. This consensus surrounding the socio-economic functions pursued by product liability, for example, probably explains the true 'Anglo-Canadian attitude' to causation, non-pecuniary damages, punitive damages and access to justice. Quite often, too, Quebec embraces solutions that are designed by the common law, though reaching them through the exegesis of legal categories that come from the Roman-inspired law of obligations. Different traditions, hence, do not preclude similar results.

I. SOURCES OF LAW AND THEIR EVOLUTION

04 To begin with, in product liability there is a great divide between Quebec and the rest of Canada. Indeed, no 'product liability' as such, in its American or EU forms, exists in negligence-based Canadian common law:[6] '[i]f this law is bad law, then it is up to the Legislature or the Supreme Court of Canada to change it. Until that happens, I am bound to apply it'. The statement reflects obvious judicial reluctance to create, beyond *Donoghue v Stevenson*, any new legal category. As a result, the legal foundation for compensation remains negligence-based. Consequently, speaking of product liability in Anglo-Canadian law only refers to the source of the damage (a product), which still depends on constitutive elements of the law of negligence, or the law of sale (merchantability, fitness for purpose warranty).[7]

---

5 Canada Consumer Product Safety Act, SC 2010, c 21.

6 The matter is rather entitled 'Dangerous Chattels' in *GHL Fridman*, Law of Torts in Canada (2nd edn 2002) 519 ff.

7 The sales law is often contained in special legislation: see eg Consumer Product Warranty and Liability Act, SNB 1978, c C-18.1.

05 By comparison, Quebec's legal system provides for three grounds for 'true' product liability anchored in contract, extra-contractual liability (fault, latent defects and French-derived 'act of a thing'), as well as consumer law (latent defect, durability and fitness for purpose).[8] In other words, the 'strictness' of the law of compensation distinguishes Quebec's legal system from the rest of Canada, as it sets forth contractual presumptions of knowledge and defectiveness that do not have their equivalent in the negligence-based common law world (arts 1726 ff CCQ). Although the 1994 Civil Code of Quebec does not significantly depart from case law interpretations, it introduced new provisions regarding apportionment of liability (arts 1478–1481 CCQ), and incorporated the development risk defence (art 1473, al 2 CCQ). Following in the footsteps of Directive 1985/374/EEC on product liability, the CCQ seemingly provides for the extra-contractual liability of manufacturers towards third parties as they are 'bound to make reparation for injury caused to a third person by reason of a safety defect in the thing, even if it is incorporated with or placed in an immovable for the service or operation of the immovable' (art 1468 CCQ).

06 Beyond the Quebec/Anglo-Canadian dichotomy, provincial special legislation has established a few strict compensation schemes for some risky activities and products, such as automobiles, blood products or vaccines. Both legal systems seem to have significantly departed from their historical foundations, as Quebec's 1866 Civil Code and common law courts have adapted negligence and fault-based liability to local intellectual features and socio-economic influences. At the federal level, moreover, other special statutes have significantly shaped the legal landscape, bringing about homogeneity in personal injury. Recent examples are the adoption of the recast Nuclear Liability and Compensation Act[9] or the development of state liability.[10]

07 The result is a *sui generis* approach to the law of compensation, forged by federalism, socio-economic political choices, legal transplants, persuasive authority, international law and judicial creativity. The present chapter seeks to highlight these features.

II. BASIC ELEMENTS OF LIABILITY

08 The evolution of product liability law transversally affects the law of contracts, delict, and consumer law. Historically, these sources of law have evolved at a different pace, contributing, as mentioned, to an eclectic legal

8 Consumer Protection Act, RSQ P-40.1 (Consumer Protection Act).
9 SC 2015, c 4, s 120.
10 See the Crown Liability and Proceedings Act, RSC 1985, c C-50 <http://canlii.ca/t/52dgh>.

landscape. For the sake of clarity, however, the distinction between contract (A) and civil liability (B) shall be maintained.

A. LIABILITY IN CONTRACT

09 While liability in contract is widely used in the Province of Quebec following the French tradition (1), it is less popular in the common law provinces where negligence is still paramount in compensating victims for damages sustained by product defects, though the guarantees pass along the distribution chain to market intermediaries and retail sellers (2).

1) Quebec's Civil Law

10 In Quebec, the impossibility of choosing[11] between the most favourable regimes has fostered doctrinal developments surrounding the basis of liability, although case law favours a much more practical approach that tends to merge contract and delict law whenever information and safety obligations are involved. In practice, the distinction between the contractual and the delictual action lies in the following differences: (i) generally, the debtor must be in default;[12] (ii) solidarity among many debtors may not be presumed;[13] (iii) in contractual matters, the debtor is liable only for damages that were foreseen of foreseeable at the time the obligation was contracted;[14] and lastly (iv) the presumptions which apply to the delictual regime should not apply to the contract, though there is nowadays a great deal of confusion about this issue.[15] However, this prohibition appears quite theoretical since the plaintiff may argue for a contractual or a delictual basis in *a subsidiary* fashion.[16] Time limits are homogeneous; since 1994 the Civil Code has harmonised the two regimes.[17]

11 Art 1458, al 2 CCQ provides that 'neither [party] may … avoid the rules governing contractual liability by opting for rules that would be more favourable to them.'

12 See art 1594 ff CCQ.

13 See art 1525 and 1526 CCQ.

14 See art 1613 CCQ, though case law, in practice, does not seem to make much of a distinction between the two regimes. Non-pecuniary losses, for example, are most of the time compensated.

15 That is, art 1469 ff CCQ, related to the act or fault of another or the act of a thing. On this issue, see *J-L Baudouin/P Deslauriers*, La responsabilité civile (8th edn 2014) 48 ff and *N Vézina*, Les articles 1459 à 1469 C.c.Q. et la responsabilité civile contractuelle: plaidoyer en faveur d'une thèse dite 'restrictive' (1996) 75 R du B can 604 ff.

16 See eg *Syndicat du garage Cours Le Royer v Société immobilière du Cours Le Royer* [1994] RJQ 2987 (CS).

17 Art 2935 CCQ provides that 'an action to enforce a personal right or movable real right is prescribed by three years, if the prescriptive period is not otherwise established'.

11 The contractual legal framework in Quebec is primarily contained in the law of obligations. The word 'contract' evokes the wide, Napoleonic definition: it is deprived of any formalism, being loosely defined as 'an agreement of wills by which one or several persons obligate themselves to one or several other persons to perform a prestation'.[18] Straightforwardly enough, it is simply the 'meeting of two wills'. Article 1458, al 1 CCQ is the cornerstone of contractual liability. It reads: 'Every person has a duty to honour his contractual undertakings'. Moreover, art 1458, al 2 CCQ provides that 'where he fails in his duty, he is liable for any *bodily, moral or material injury* he causes to the other contracting party and is liable to reparation for the injury' (emphasis added).[19] Following the French tradition, the contractual action often makes the elements of proof easier in light of the intensity of the obligations (*moyen, résultat, obligation*). Article 1458 CCQ is complemented by art 1434 CCQ, which states that '[a] contract validly formed binds the parties who have entered into it not *only as to what they have expressed in it but also as to what is incident to it according to its nature* and *in conformity with usage, equity or law*' (emphasis added). This interesting principle has the effect of 'inflating' the obligations agreed upon by the parties, introducing the possibility of interpreting the contract in light of evolving policy considerations. In this context, case law 'forced' information duties (*obligation d'information*) and safety obligations (*obligation de sécurité*) into contracts, two factors that have been highly relevant in addressing liability arising from the sale or distribution of a defective product.

12 Within this general framework, special provisions related to the law of sale might apply to damages caused by defective products. Indeed, the CCQ provides for a quality warranty (a); which also has an *alter ego* in the Consumer Act (b).

a) The Quality Warranty and the CCQ

13 The quality warranty (*garantie de qualité*) – also known as latent defects – is to some extent an extension of the French *vices cachés* found in the 1866 Civil Code, by virtue of which the seller must guarantee that product sold is free from defects.[20] Similarly, art 1726 CCQ prescribes that '[t]he seller is bound to warrant the buyer that the property and its accessories are, at the time of the sale, free of latent defects *which render it unfit for the use for which it was intended* or *which so diminish its usefulness that the buyer would not have bought it or paid so high*

[18] Art 1378, al 2 CCQ.

[19] See also art 1728 CCQ, as well as art 1613 CCQ, which limit compensation to ascertainable damages: 'In contractual matters, the debtor is liable only for damages that were foreseen or foreseeable at the time the obligation was contracted, where the failure to perform the obligation does not proceed form intentional or gross fault on his part; even then, the damages include only what is an immediate and direct consequence of the non-performance'.

[20] See generally *J Edwards*, La garantie de qualité du vendeur en droit québécois (1998).

a price if he had been aware of them' (emphasis added). This provision must be read in conjunction with another principle that stems from a Supreme Court decision in which it took the view that the seller's warranty is an accessory to the property and therefore is transmitted with the product regardless successive sales. Interestingly enough, subsequent buyers shall invoke the contractual warranty against manufacturers and – unlike the European Product Liability Directive – distributors, even though they did not enter into a contract with them.[21] This solution has now been codified in art 1442 CCQ and it is also reiterated, albeit uselessly, in the specific section on sales – *les contrats nommés*.[22] The policy reasons underlying these provisions have recently been clearly stated by the Supreme Court: '[t]he development of Quebec's law of obligations has been marked by efforts *to strike a proper balance between, on the one hand, the individual's freedom of contract and, on the other, adherence by contracting parties to the principle of good faith* in their mutual relations' (emphasis added).

14 The usefulness of this legal framework lies in *the presumption of knowledge of the defect* provided for by art 1728 CCQ. It quite confusingly states: 'If the seller was aware or *could not have been unaware of the latent defect*, he is bound not only to restore the price, but to pay all damages suffered by the buyer' (emphasis added).[23] One might wonder whom exactly 'could not have been unaware of the latent defect'. The answer lies the following art 1729 CCQ, which provides for a presumption of knowledge by *professional sellers* in these terms: 'A defect is presumed to have existed at the time of a sale by a professional seller *if the property malfunctions or deteriorates prematurely in comparison with identical items of property or items of the same type*; such a presumption is not made, however, where the defect is due to improper use of the property by the buyer' (emphasis added). In line with contemporary informational asymmetry theories, professional sellers may free themselves from liability by proving their ignorance, as the presumption of knowledge is rebuttable.[24]

---

21 *Motors Products of Canada Ltd v Kravitz* [1979] 1 RCS 790. Translated into common law terms, it amounts to the removal of privity, which is provided for by art 1440 CCQ.

22 It reads: 'The rights of the parties to a contract pass to their successors by particular title if they are accessory to property which passes to them or are directly related to it'. Art 1730 CCQ states: 'The manufacturer, any person who distributes the property under his name or as his own, and any supplier of the property, in particular the wholesaler and the importer, are also bound to warrant the buyer in the same manner as the seller'.

23 See eg *Lemyre v Techni-Gestass ltée* [2000–2002] JE (CS), where a colour printer that required such a complex technical knowledge to operate it that was held not to be suitable to a normal context of utilisation was considered contrary to this definition.

24 Although this is quite a heavy burden as '[t]he manufacturer may rebut the presumption only by showing that it did not know about the defect *and that its lack of knowledge was justified*, that is, that it could not have discovered the defect even if it had taken every precaution that the buyer would be entitled to expect a reasonable seller to take in the same circumstances' (*ABB Inc v Domtar Inc* [2007] 3 SCR 461, para 69, emphasis by the Court).

15 In line with the US Second Tort Restatement, three types of defects are acknowledged: (i) material defects (which relates to a specific good); (ii) functional defects (design defects); and (iii) conventional defects (disclosure and information defects). Whereas the two first will be assessed in light of the normal use criterion, the third is evaluated in light of the factual, contractual content by which the parties are bound.[25] These defects may overlap, as happened in famous *Domtar* case. In the wake of French law, the characteristics attached to these categories of defects are the following cumulative ones: (i) it must be latent; (ii) it must be sufficiently serious; (iii) it must have existed at the time of the sale; and (iv) it must be unknown to the buyer when he/she entered the contract.

16 To this day, many uncertainties remain in the field of contractual warranties. For example, whether the development risk defence is relevant to the field of contracts remains to be seen. This situation is even more confusing when one observes that the warranties established in the CCQ and the one created by the Consumer Protection Act (CPA) often overlap.

b) The Consumer Protection Act[26]

17 The Consumer Protection Act has completely reconfigured private law in Quebec. Its application is conditional on the core notions of 'consumer'[27] and 'merchant'.[28] The Consumer Protection Act does regulate many kind of special contracts. Focusing on general principles, we shall underline that, like the CCQ (art 1442 CCQ), art 53 CPA allows consumers to file a claim against all the economic operators involved along the commercial chain. It reads:

> 'A consumer who has entered into a contract with a merchant *is entitled to exercise directly against the merchant or the manufacturer a recourse based on a latent defect in the goods forming the object of the contract,* unless the consumer could have discovered the defect by an ordinary examination.
>
> The same rule applies where there is a *lack of instructions* necessary for the protection of the user against a risk or danger of which he would otherwise be unaware.

---

25 *ABB Inc v Domtar Inc* [2007] 3 SCR 461, para 48.

26 See generally *N L'Heureux*, Droit de la consommation (5th edn 2000).

27 'Consumer' is defined at art 1(e): it 'means a natural person, except a merchant who obtains goods or services for the purposes of his business'.

28 Professionals are not defined by the Consumer Act. Nonetheless, interpretation parameters can be found at art 1384 Civil Code: 'A consumer contract is a contract whose field of allocation is delimited by legislation respecting consumer protection whereby one of the parties, being a natural person, the consumer, acquires, leases borrows or obtain in any other manner, for personal, family or domestic purposes, property or services from the other party, *who offers such property and services as part of an enterprise which he carries on*'. Article 2 of the Consumer Act states: 'This act applies to every contract for goods or services entered into between a consumer and a merchant in the course of his business'.

The merchant or the manufacturer shall not plead that he was unaware of the defect or lack of instructions.

The rights of action against the manufacturer may be exercised *by any consumer who is a subsequent purchaser of the goods*' (emphasis added).

18 Quite similar to the quality warranty in the CCQ, this action may be useful in order to seek compensation from defective goods. Though extremely favourable to plaintiffs, lawyers have been quite timid – for unknown reasons – in pleading it before the courts. However, this situation is slowly changing, as it is now evoked in conjunction with class actions. Further compensation is provided for by art 272 (including punitive damages):

> 'If the merchant or the manufacturer fails to fulfil an obligation imposed on him by this Act, ... the consumer may demand, as the case may be, subject to the other recourses provided by this Act, ... (c) that his obligations be reduced; (d) that the contract be rescinded; (e) that the contract be set aside; or (f) that the contract be annulled, without prejudice *to his claim in damages*, in all cases. *He may also claim punitive damages*' (emphasis added).

19 For example, the provision was helpful in the context of tobacco litigation, in which these legal bases are increasingly evoked together. The twin cases of *Létourneau v JTI-MacDonald Corp* and *Blais v JTI-MacDonald Corp*[29] offers the best example of this overlapping phenomenon, as the basis for action was anchored in all three bases: the extra-contractual warranty contained in the CCQ, the CPA version of the latent defects warranty, and Quebec's Charter of Rights and Freedoms.

2) Common Law in the Other Provinces

20 Regarding contractual warranties, Canadian common law is at the crossroads of tradition and contemporary legislation. Indeed, while such contractual cause of action is historically rooted in the common law, it has been greatly reconfigured by legislative initiatives. Apart from traditional common law contractual warranties stemming from the landmark case of *GH Myers and Co v Brent Cross Service Co*,[30] most provincial legislators do provide for statutory warranties, quite similar to those contained in the US Uniform Commercial Code

---

29 2015 QCCS 2382 (CanLII).

30 [1934] 1 KB 46: 'That depends upon the terms of the contract, and *I think that the true view is that a person contracting to do work and supply materials warrants that the materials which he uses will be of good quality and reasonably fit for the purpose for which he is using them*, unless the circumstances of the contract are such as to exclude any such warranty' (du Parcq J, 55) and *Young & Marten Ltd v McManus Childs Ltd* [1969] 1 AC 454 (HL), which are still part of Canadian law: see eg *G Ford Homes Ltd v Draft Masonry (York) Co* (1983) 43 OR (2d) 401 (CA).

(UCC). Unlike French or Quebec law, however, the *caveat emptor* paradigm is still central to Canadian common law. As expressed in *Tony's Broadloom & Floor Covering Ltd v NMC Canada Inc* (1995)[31] and in order to benefit from the fitness for intended use warranty, a buyer may prove that a latent defect affects one of the essential characteristics of the good. However, and unlike Quebec law, no presumption of knowledge alleviates the plaintiff's burden to prove that the defect 'was known to the seller or that the seller showed reckless disregard for what he or she should have known'.[32] Honest belief in the good's fitness for purpose is hence generally sufficient for the seller to properly abide by its contractual obligations.[33]

21 Various attitudes to contract law can be observed which thus leads to great variations in the legal protection offered. Examples include the Sale of Goods Act of Ontario, which reads:[34]

> '15. Subject to this Act and any statute in that behalf, *there is no implied warranty or condition as to the quality or fitness for any particular purpose of goods supplied under a contract of sale*, except as follows:
> 1. Where the buyer, expressly or by implication, *makes known to the seller the particular purpose for which the goods are required so as to show that the buyer relies on the seller's skill or judgment,* and the goods are of a description that it is in the course of the seller's business to supply (whether the seller is the manufacturer or not), *there is an implied condition that the goods will be reasonably fit for such purpose*, but in the case of a contract for the sale of a specified article under its patent or other trade name there is no implied condition as to its fitness for any particular purpose.
> 2. Where goods are bought by description from a seller who deals in goods of that description (whether the seller is the manufacturer or not), *there is an implied condition that the goods will be of merchantable quality,* but if the buyer has examined the goods, there is no implied condition as regards defects that such examination ought to have revealed.
> 3. *An implied warranty or condition as to quality or fitness for a particular purpose may be annexed by the usage of trade.*
> 4. An express warranty or condition does not negative a warranty or condition implied by this Act unless inconsistent therewith. R.S.O. 1990, c. S.1, s. 15' (emphasis added).

---

31 1995 CanLII 7153 (ON SC), 22 OR (3d) 244 (Gen Div), aff'd (1996) 1996 CanLII 680 (ON CA), 31 OR (3d) 481 (CA). See also *Jenkins v Foley* (2002) 215 Nfld & PEIR 257, 2002 NFCA 46 (CanLII), 2002 NFCA 46.

32 *Domtar*, at para 80 (*obiter dictum*).

33 However, if the seller could have, indeed, obtained relevant information about the essential characteristic of a product, honest belief in the good's fitness for purpose will be insufficient: see eg *Parlby Construction Ltd v Stewart Equipment Co* [1972] 1 WWR 503 (BCSC) 507–510.

34 Ont RSO 1990, Ch S.1 <www.e-laws.gov.on.ca/DBLaws/Statutes/English/90s01_e.htm#P203_11436>. As far as we know, these laws are extremely similar in all of the ten common law provinces by reason of the circulation of the model proposed by the Uniform Law Conference' Sale of Goods Act (1981) <www.ulcc.ca/en/us/index.cfm?sec=1&sub=1s2&print=1>.

22 Other provisions complete this framework, in such a way that it is not limited to the recovery of pecuniary losses:

> '51. (1) Where there is a breach of warranty by the seller, or where the buyer elects, or is compelled, to treat a breach of a condition on the part of the seller as a breach of warranty, the buyer is not by reason only of such breach of warranty entitled to reject the goods, but may, (a) set up against the seller the breach of warranty in diminution or extinction of the price; or (b) *maintain an action against the seller for damages for the breach of warranty.*
>
> (2) *The measure of damages for breach of warranty is the estimated loss directly and naturally resulting in the ordinary course of events from the breach of warranty'* (emphasis added).

23 Like Quebec's model, the right of action sometimes does away with privity and passes along the commercialisation chain,[35] although no real presumptions facilitate the proof of the actual defect itself. These warranties indeed add implied obligations to the parties, and may very well apply to defective products. However, one important obstacle is linked to the sale/service dichotomy,[36] which may bar a plaintiff from alleging a latent defect if the product was incidental to the performance of a service contract.

24 In the medical field, for example, the famous case of *ter Neuzen v Korn*[37] is a good example of the irrelevance of contractual warranties whenever the good was provided in occasion of a service. The Supreme Court held in 1992 that neither the Sale of Goods Act nor the warranty of fitness and merchantability at common law could ever apply to infected semen, since the jury came to the conclusion that the contract between the parties primarily sought the provision of services. In particular, the Court held that '[t]he jury correctly concluded that the contract to perform the [artificial insemination] procedure on the appellant was primarily a contract for medical services and not a sale of semen. *To hold otherwise would be to distort the true nature of the whole agreement between the parties'* (emphasis added).[38] The same logic was followed in a more recent case involving hip replacements, where a class action was certified, although a breach

---

35 On the convergence of torts and contracts, see also *Winnipeg Condominium Corporation No 36 v Bird Construction Co*, 1995 CanLII 146 (SCC) <www.canlii.ca/ca/cas/scc/1995/1995scc2.html>: '[I see] no adequate policy considerations exist to negate a contractor's duty in tort to subsequent purchasers of a building to take reasonable care in constructing the building, and to ensure that the building does not contain defects that pose foreseeable and substantial danger to the health and safety of the occupants' (LaForest J, para LIV.I).

36 See *Gee v White Spot Ltd* (1986) 7 BCLR (2d) 235 (SC).

37 *ter Neuzen v Korn* [1995] 3 SCR 654 <www.lexum.umontreal.ca/csc-scc/en/pub/1995/vol3/html/1995scr3_0674.html>.

38 Ibid para 71. Nonetheless, it rather came to the conclusion that a doctor had been professionally negligent in not knowing at the time of the events that HIV could have been transmitted by artificial insemination.

of the Nova Scotia Sale of Goods Act was not considered to be legally sound enough to raise a common issue.[39]

25 By contrast, the common law warranties stemming from *GH Myers and Co v Brent Cross Service Co* do not impose such a condition. They simply warrant that the parties meet the standards of a reasonably competent person in the performance of the contract: the purchaser has a remedy against the business seller, even absent negligence. However, in the medical field, they sometimes pose some other difficulties which were highlighted in the *ter Neuzen* case. Among them is the fact that the doctor cannot trace the product – blood, in this case – back to the original donor. In this particular field, Anglo-Canadian law mimics the American case law, which bars the application of these warranties to products such as human by-products.[40]

B. TORT/DELICT

1) *The Province of Quebec*

26 Extra-contractual liability in Quebec is shaped by the general provision on fault in article 1457 CCQ, which is ever hardly relevant in cases involving defective products. Indeed, the special regime created for bystanders is much more advantageous for plaintiffs, since it creates presumptions which facilitate or even reverse the burden of proof. Indeed, and as in French law, some presumptions were created in order to facilitate compensation, such as liability for the owner of an immoveable,[41] an animal[42] or a thing.[43] In practice, most product liability cases gather together these grounds for liability. The general provision of article 1457 CCQ reads:

> 'Every person has a duty to *abide by the rules of conduct which lie upon him, according to the circumstances, usage or law, so as not to cause injury to another.*

---

39 *Wright Medical Technology Canada v Taylor*, 2015 NSCA 68 (CanLII).

40 See *Perlmutter v Beth David Hospital*, 123 N.E.2d 792 (N.Y. 1954): 'If, however, the court were to stamp as a sale the supplying of blood – or the furnishing of other medical aid – it would mean that the hospital, *no matter how careful, no matter that the disease-producing potential in the blood could not possibly be discovered, would be held responsible, virtually as an insurer,* if anything were to happen to the patient as a result of "bad" blood…' (Fuld J, 595, emphasis added, cited in *ter Neuzen*).

41 Article 1467 CCQ reads: 'The owner of an immovable, without prejudice to his liability as custodian, is liable to reparation for injury caused by its ruin, even partial, where this has resulted from lack of repair or from a defect of construction'.

42 Article 1466 CCQ reads: 'The owner of an animal is liable to reparation for injury it has caused, whether the animal was under his custody or that of a third person, or had strayed or escaped. A person making use of the animal is, together with the owner, also liable during that time'.

43 Art 1465 CCQ.

> Where he is endowed with reason and fails in this duty, he is responsible for any injury he causes to another person by such fault and is liable to reparation for the injury, *whether it be bodily, moral or material in nature.*
>
> He is also liable, in certain cases, to reparation for injury caused to another by the act or fault of another person or by *the act of things in his custody*' (emphasis added).

27 Though not very useful in product liability matters, it is always evoked by default: it acts as a safety net for plaintiffs, as product liability law has developed on the margins of this general provision. Indeed, the new safety obligation that one owes third parties – extra-contractual, therefore – is increasingly relevant, as it moves towards a true strict liability regime.

28 Indeed, arts 1468 and 1469 CCQ provide for a new, special liability regime for third parties, ie bystanders. Article 1468 provides that: 'The manufacturer of a movable property is liable to reparation for injury caused to *a third person by reason of a safety defect in the thing*, even if it is incorporated with or placed in an immovable for the service or operation of the immovable. The same rule *applies to a person who distributes the thing* under his name or as his own and to any supplier of the thing, whether a wholesaler or a retailer and whether or not he imported the thing'. Although the expression 'movable property' has not, to this day, been interpreted by case law, the expression is believed, according to Baudouin, to cover non-material goods, such as electricity, gas and medical products.[44]

29 Article 1469 CCQ creates a threefold American/EU-inspired definition of defectiveness in these words: 'A thing has a safety defect where, having regard to all the circumstances, *it does not afford the safety which a person is entitled to expect*, particularly by reason of a defect in the design or manufacture of the thing, poor preservation or presentation of the thing, or the lack of sufficient indications as to the risks and dangers it involves as to safety precautions'. Much like Directive 1985/374/EEC, it includes manufacturing,[45] design and warning defects,[46] and is based on public expectations; unlike Directive 1985/374/EEC, it *does* extend the action to intermediary operators such as distributors (like the *Kravitz*-derived contractual action).

---

44 *J-L Baudouin/P Deslauriers/B Moore*, La responsabilité civile (2014) 393–394.

45 See eg *Ladouceur v Brasserie Labatt ltée*, AZ-99036382, BE 99BE-779 (CQ), the 'exploding bottle' case which applies the *res ipsa loquitur* maxim; or see the falling elevator in *London Lancashire Guarantie & Accident Co of Canada v FX Drolet* (1944) RCS 82.

46 See eg *Compagnie d'assurances Wellington v Canadian Adhesives Ltd* [1997] RRA 635 (CQ); *Mulco Inc v La Garantie, Cie d'assurance de l'Amérique du Nord* [1990] RRA 68 (CA); *Corriveau v Unicoop* [1994] RRA 915 (CS); *Therrien v Laptrise* [2001] RJQ 202, REJB 2000-21582 (CS); *Létourneau v Imperial Tobacco Ltée* [1998] RJQ 1660, REJB 98-07025 (CQ).

30 Though *a priori* a wide, modern regime, it is as today barely applied by courts, probably by reason of the predominance of the latent defect action (see *supra*); this assumption needs to be understood in light of the *non cumul* principle, which bars a contractual party from discarding the contract. Nonetheless, some courts do tend to merge the two actions by applying the safety obligation to the contractual sphere. This result can probably be explained by a gradual merging of art 1434 CCQ with art 1468 CCQ. Such an interpretation certainly seems odd (not to say incoherent), not only considering that other causes of exoneration such as *force majeure* do exist for contractual parties, but also because it introduces a new global safety obligation within the contractual sphere. Nonetheless, such a marriage has not been discarded by the Superior Court in the ambit of a pending medical device mass tort that will probably be heard in the coming months,[47] nor by the Court of Appeal in when considering a contractual action in the context of lease of machinery.[48]

31 This safety obligation is completed by some exoneration causes (among which the disturbing development risk defence) provided for by art 1473 CCQ, which states:

> 'The manufacturer, distributor or supplier of a movable property is not liable to reparation for injury caused by a safety defect in the property *if he proves that the victim knew or could have known of the defect, or could have foreseen the injury.*
>
> Nor is he liable to reparation if he proves that, according *to the state of knowledge at the time that he manufactured, distributed or supplied the property,* the existence of the defect could not have been known, and *that he was not neglectful of his duty to provide information when he became aware of the defect*' (emphasis added).

32 Many uncertainties remain regarding the application of this defence, since it is not yet clear whether it could apply to the contractual action, or whether

---

47 *Thibault v St Jude Medical Inc* (CS, 03.09.2004), SOQUIJ AZ-50268041, JE 2004-1924 (class action certified).

48 See generally *N Vézina*, L'exonération fondée sur l'état des connaissances scientifiques et techniques, dite du risque de développement, regard sur un élément perturbateur dans le droit québécois de la responsabilité du fait des produits, in: *P-C Lafond* (ed), Mélanges Claude Masse (2003) 459–461, and *Accessoires d'auto Vipa inc v Therrien* (CA), SOQUIJ AZ-50189437, JE 2003-1653, [2003] RJQ 2390, where the disposition was applied to a contract of lease, where the plaintiff was injured by wood machinery: '*En ce qui concerne le défaut de sécurité, il est exact que le législateur a mis en place un régime extracontractuel de responsabilité qui fait en sorte que, même en l'absence de contrat, une victime peut s'adresser au fabricant, au distributeur ou au fournisseur du bien meuble qui lui cause un préjudice. L'interdiction de cumul que prescrit l'article 1458 C.c.Q. ne fait cependant pas en sorte que le fabricant, le distributeur ou le fournisseur qui contracte avec la victime peut se voir automatiquement exonéré de toute responsabilité s'il y a absence d'une prise en charge expresse de l'obligation de sécurité dans le contrat*' (para 33). On this very topic: see *P-G Jobin*, Le louage (2nd edn 1996) 407 or *D-C Lamontagne/B Larochelle*, Droit spécialisé des contrats: Les principaux contrats, vol 1 (2000) 331. See *contra*: *Desrosiers v Centre hippique de la Mauricie Inc* [2004] RRA 755 (CA).

liability among the distributor and/or supplier is joint and several.[49] The EU experience will probably help in the interpretation of this provision.

33 Products are defined by the CCQ as mere 'property and its accessories' (art 1726, al 1 CCQ). There are no further restrictions as to the nature of the good itself, which could encompass a wide range of material and/or immaterial goods. In Saskatchewan, by contrast, 'consumer products' are defined as 'tangible personal property, new or used, of a kind that is commonly used for personal, family or household purposes'.[50]

34 The notion of a 'defect' is defined in the following terms: '[t]he seller is not bound, however, to warrant against any latent defect *known to the buyer or any apparent defect*; an apparent defect is a defect that *can be perceived by a prudent and diligent buyer without the need to resort to an expert*' (art 1726, CCQ, emphasis added). Case law has addressed the notion especially in the context of moveable property.

2) Common Law and the Other Provinces

35 As mentioned, Canadian common law is not known for having a particularly stringent strict product liability regime. Indeed, judges have shown reluctance towards the idea of creating a *sui generis* action based on defect; they have rather expressed their desire to leave this task to legislators. Negligence hence remains central in product liability cases and rest upon three constitutive elements: (i) the existence of a duty towards the victim (to warn or to care); (ii) proof of a breach of the standard of care; (iii) causing the injury; and (iv) causality among them.[51] Following the landmark case of *Donoghue v Stevenson*,[52] the duty to warn has significantly expanded in Canadian tort law,[53] probably granting it the status of a real product liability regime based on the reduction of information asymmetries.

36 Conceptually, Anglo-Canadian law understands 'proximity' between plaintiffs and defendants in light of the test inspired by landmark English case of *Anns v Merton London Borough Council*.[54] Decided in the context of breast

---

49 *J-L Baudouin/AM Linden*, Tort Law in Canada (2013) 76. The authors rightly point out that the situation is particularly relevant whenever the commercialisation chain reveals an element of extraneity.

50 Consumer Product Warranty and Liability Act, SNB 1978, c C-18.1, at art 1(1).

51 *L Klar*, Downsizing Torts, in: *NJ Mullany/AM Linden* (eds), Torts Tomorrow: A Tribute to John Fleming (1998) 305, 307.

52 [1932] AC 562 (HL). See also *Mustapha v Culligan of Canada Ltd*, 2008 SCC 27 (CanLII) para 3.

53 See specifically *Lambert v Lastoplex Chemicals Co*, 1971 CanLII 27 (SCC), [1972] SCR 569, 574.

54 [1978] AC 728 (HL), as applied in *Cooper v Hobart*, 2001 SCC 79 (CanLII), and *R v Imperial Tobacco Canada Ltd*, 2011 SCC 42 (CanLII)).

implant litigation, *Hollis v Dow Corning Corp*[55] expresses the underlying Canadian rationale: '[t]he duty to warn *serves to correct the knowledge imbalance between manufacturers and consumers by alerting consumers to any dangers* and allowing them to make informed decisions concerning the safe use of the product' (emphasis added).[56] On this occasion, the Supreme Court stated that a manufacturer has a duty to warn consumers of dangers which are inherent in the product's use, about he knows or ought to know. The Court further mentioned that this duty is a dynamic one, since it requires manufacturers to warn consumers not only at the time of sale, but also afterwards if dangers are discovered after the product has been put into circulation.[57] The Court moreover added that the duty is proportional to the risks posed by the product. It stated: '*Given the intimate relationship between medical products and the consumer's body, and the resulting risk created to the consumer, there will almost always be a heavy onus on manufacturers of medical products to provide clear, complete and current information* concerning the dangers inherent in the ordinary use of their product' (emphasis added).[58] The intensity of the duty is particularly strong in light of medical products and others of the like that can be 'ingested, consumed or otherwise placed in the body'.[59] A link between the duty to warn and the informed consent doctrine is thus visible: '[a] high standard for disclosure protects public health by promoting the right to bodily integrity, increasing consumer choice and facilitating a more meaningful doctor–patient relationship'.[60]

37 In some special circumstances, however, manufacturers' liability may be annulled whenever the complex information had to be filtered and/or

---

55 *Hollis v Dow Corning Corp*, 1995 CanLII 55 (SCC) <www.canlii.ca/ca/cas/scc/1995/1995scc107.html>: 'The rationale for the manufacturer's duty to warn can be traced to the "neighbour principle", which lies at the heart of the law of negligence, and was set down in its classic form by Lord Atkin in *Donoghue v. Stevenson*, [1932] A.C. 562 (H.L.). When manufacturers place products into the flow of commerce, they create a relationship of reliance with consumers, who have far less knowledge than the manufacturers concerning the dangers inherent in the use of the products, and are therefore put at risk if the product is not safe. The duty to warn serves to correct the knowledge imbalance between manufacturers and consumers by alerting consumers to any dangers and allowing them to make informed decisions concerning the safe use of the product' (LaForest J, para 21). See also *Lambert v Lastoplex Chemicals Co* [1972] SCR 569: '*Manufacturers owe a duty to consumers of their products to see that there are no defects in manufacture which are likely to give rise to injury in the ordinary course of use.* Their duty does not, however, end if the product, although suitable for the purpose for which it is manufactured and marketed, is at the same time dangerous to use; and if they are aware of its dangerous character they cannot, without more, pass the risk of injury to the consumer' (Laskin J, 574, emphasis added), and *Buchan v Ortho Pharmaceutical (Canada) Ltd* (1986) 54 OR (2d) 92.

56 *Hollis v Dow Corning Corp*, 1995 CanLII 55 (SCC) para 21 (emphasis added).

57 See *Rivtow Marine Ltd v Washington Iron Works*, 1973 CanLII 6 (SCC), [1974] SCR 1189, 1200.

58 *Hollis v Dow Corning Corp*, 1995 CanLII 55 (SCC) para 23 (LaForest J, emphasis added).

59 Ibid para 23.

60 Ibid para 26.

interpreted by a 'competent intermediary'.[61] While the *Hollis* court held that it is an exception to the general principle of complete risk disclosure to the consumer, it also stated that it was applicable to the breast implants manufactured by the respondent. In reality, the issue was rooted in the information flow between the physician and the manufacturer, which the Court found insufficient since the latter had not disclosed the device's risk of rupture in normal, regular conditions. Therefore, Dow Corporation was held liable for the damages sustained by Ms Hollis on the ground that the former did not discharge its duty to Ms Hollis *by properly warning the learned intermediate* concerning the risk of post-surgical implant rupture.

38 In another important case, *Buchan v Ortho Pharmaceutical (Canada) Ltd*,[62] the rationale had been applied by the Ontario Court of Appeal in the context of birth control pills. As a matter of fact, a duty to warn the physician of the risk of suffering a stroke caused by a contraceptive pill was acknowledged, and Ortho Pharmaceutical – just like Dow Corporation – was held liable for the damage sustained by the plaintiff.[63]

> 'In July 1971, the plaintiff was a 23-year-old, non-smoking, married woman in excellent health. She had been on a birth control program for many years. ... In January 1967, a gynecologist started her on long-lasting birth control injections of an experimental drug, Depo-Provera. She took these injections every three months until August 1970 when she was advised that the experimental program had been

---

61 This legal transplant has an American matrix: see *Sterling Drug, Inc v Cornish*, 370 F.2d 82 (8th Cir. 1966), and *Reyes v Wyeth Laboratories*, 498 F.2d 1264 (5th Cir. 1974, *cert.* denied 419 U.S. 1096 (1974)): 'As a medical expert, the prescribing physician can take into account the propensities of the drug, as well as the susceptibilities of his patient. His is the task of weighing the benefits of any medication against its potential dangers. The choice he makes is an informed one, an individualized medical judgment bottomed on a knowledge of both patient and palliative. Pharmaceutical companies then, who must warn ultimate purchasers of dangers inherent in patent drugs sold over the counter, in selling prescription drugs are required to warn only the prescribing physician, who acts as a "learned intermediary" between manufacturer and consumer' (Reyes J, para 1276).

62 (1986) 25 DLR (4th) 658 (Ont CA). See also *Lambert v Lastoplex Chemicals Co Ltd* [1972] SCR 569, where the Supreme Court held: 'Where manufactured products are put on the market for ultimate purchase and use by the general public and carry danger (in this case, by reason of high inflammability), although put to the use for which they are intended, the manufacturer, knowing of their hazardous nature, *has a duty to specify the attendant dangers, which it must be taken to appreciate in a detail not known to the ordinary consumer or user.* A general warning, as for example, that the product is inflammable, *will not suffice where the likelihood of fire may be increased according to the surroundings in which it may reasonably be expected that the product will be used.* The required explicitness of the warning will, of course, vary with the danger likely to be encountered in the ordinary use of the product' (574–575, emphasis added).

63 Contrast with *Walker Estate v York Finch General Hospital* [2001] 1 SCR 647, 2001 SCC 23 (CanLII) <www.canlii.ca/ca/cas/scc/2001/2001scc23.html> in the context of contaminated blood.

> discontinued. On June 30, 1971, she visited a doctor to obtain a prescription for birth control pills. He prescribed Ortho-Novum 1/50. In September, 1971, after having taken this pill for slightly less than six weeks, she suffered a stroke or cerebrovascular accident. This has left her permanently disabled; she has some brain damage and her left arm and left leg are substantially paralyzed.'[64]

The appeal raises the question of determining whether the relation between the defendant's contraceptive pill and the plaintiff's injury is one of cause and effect in accordance with medical or scientific notions of physical sequence (failure to warn). In this far-reaching decision, the Court presumed that the learned intermediary doctrine could find application in this case. It held that the risks of stroke should have been disclosed to Ms Buchan's physician, in order for her to properly consent to undergo a contraceptive treatment:

> 'Ortho's failure to give physicians a warning commensurate with its actual knowledge of the dangers inherent in its products combined with the efforts of its sales representatives to minimize those dangers and counteract reports of adverse side-effects *plainly influenced the doctor's opinion as to the drug's safety and the need to inform patients of the risks.* It is therefore not unreasonable to conclude, ... that the doctor's failure to disclose the risk of stroke (or, for that matter, any thromboembolic risk) to the plaintiff *was contributed to by the inadequacy of Ortho's warnings, devoid as they were of any reference to stroke, and the promotional tactics of its pharmaceutical salesmen*' (emphasis added).[65]

Indeed, it appeared that the disclosure of risk was somewhat different in the United States and in Canada; Ortho therefore breached its duty to warn Canadian consumers.

39 Apart from this duty to warn, however, Anglo-Canadian product liability emerges from the general duty of care which configures the mega-tort of negligence. A recent example was offered in the context of a youngster becoming a paraplegic after trialling a snowboard made available by the defendant.[66] Reversing the trial judge, the Nova Scotia Court of Appeal held that no duty of care existed towards the plaintiff. The same was concluded when another teenager hurt himself playing hockey. He alleged that the helmet producer (Bauer) and/or the Canadian Standard Association (CSA) were negligent in designing the product or warning him of risks; however, the British Columbia Court of Appeal found that none of these legal bases were enough to constitute a cause of action.

---

64 *Buchan v Ortho Pharmaceutical (Canada) Ltd* (1986), 25 DLR (4th) 658 (Ont CA) paras 5 and 6.

65 Ibid para 64.

66 *Burton Canada Company v Coady*, 2013 NSCA 95 (CanLII). See also *Halsbury's Laws of Canada* (First Edition) – Torts (2012) 385, para HTO-104.

40 It is not substantive law which confers a stricter character to liability, but rather procedural and proof elements. For example, courts do apply quite often the *res ipsa loquitur* maxim, in cases such as explosion, fires, falling objects, etc. Indeed, the application of the maxim sometimes amounts to creating a form of strict liability since it enables the plaintiff to shift the *factual* burden of proof to the defendant. For this reason, is was abandoned by the Supreme Court, which argued: 'the law would be better served if the maxim was treated as expired and no longer used as a separate component in negligence actions. After all, it was nothing more than an attempt to deal with circumstantial evidence'.[67] The way it is applied in Canada greatly differs from the way it is applied by English judges: to this day, the Canadian position has not evolved towards a reversal of the *legal* burden of proof.[68]

41 In Canadian common law, product liability is anything but anchored in defectiveness. Therefore, case law revolves almost entirely around the information paradigm and remains rooted in negligence. In the *Andersen v St Jude Medical Inc* case,[69] the safety of heart valves coated with Silzone® was the object of a negligence-based class action, when patients suffered thromboembolic complications. The device had been authorised for distribution and sale in Canada in 1997.[70] The valves were used until 2000, when a voluntary recall was issued by the defendants. Indeed, a post-market clinical trial (AVERT)[71] had shown 'a small, but statistically significant increase in explants due to a medical complication known as paravalvular leak PVL)'.[72] When the study abruptly ended, 36,000 devices had already been sold.

42 The victims alleged that the alleged damages had been caused by the negligence of the defendants in properly designing the device. More precisely, they argued that although defendant (St Jude) complied with the FDA's Draft

67 *Fontaine v British Columbia (Official Administrator)* [1998] 1 SCR 424, para 27.

68 See *GHL Fridman*, The Law of Torts (2nd edn 2002) 405 ff.

69 *Andersen v St Jude Medical, Inc*, 2012 ONSC 3660 (Lax J). The present comment synthetises thoughts already expressed in *M-E Arbour*, Portrait of Risk Development as A Young Defence (2014) 59 Revue de droit de McGill 1.

70 It was approved by the FDA only in March 1998.

71 For completeness: 'AVERT was a randomized control trial (RCT) sponsored and funded by St. Jude and is an acronym for Artificial Valve Endocarditis Reduction Trial. Its purpose was to study whether Silzone was clinically effective in reducing prosthetic valve endocarditis, but its protocol included the collection of data on adverse events that are complications of valve surgery. The protocol specified that the study would take four years to complete' (*Andersen v St Jude Medical, Inc*, 2012 ONSC 3660, para 26).

72 *Andersen v St Jude Medical, Inc*, 2012 ONSC 3660, para 1. For details: 'Silzone is a proprietary term for a coating comprising layers of titanium, palladium and an outer layer of metallic silver. This was applied to the polyester (Dacron®) sewing cuff that surgeons use to attach a prosthetic heart valve to heart tissue' (2, para 2).

Heart Valve Guidance, the ISO 5840[73] and ISO 10993[74] standards,[75] more testing should have been carried on following the pre-clinical (*in vitro*) and animal trials.[76] Anticipating dismissal of the case, the Court held that 'the plaintiffs *did not establish that the defendants failed to exercise a reasonable degree of care in the pre-market design and testing or in the post-market surveillance of Silzone-coated products* that would be expected of a reasonable and prudent prosthetic heart valve manufacturer in similar circumstances' (emphasis added).[77]

43 Unsurprisingly, St Jude sought regulatory approval of the device despite partial ignorance of its clinical effectiveness,[78] which cautious labelling reflected. In the eyes of the defendants, as a result, the plaintiffs were properly informed of the risks associated with the implant. The plaintiffs, conversely, contested the risk/utility assessment[79] carried out by St Jude.[80] For greater clarity, they disagreed on '(i) *the degree of certainty the defendants were required to have about the benefits* of Silzone before distributing the product, (ii) *the reasonableness of the product development process* including the testing undertaken and the manner in which the testing results were interpreted and, (iii) *the role and impact of industry and regulatory standards* and practices and regulatory approval' (emphasis added). In their opinion, the device did not offer any greater benefits than its more traditional version (marketed by the same defendant). In narrowing down the issue, the Court rather held that the test does not require 'assessing whether the benefits of the Silzone valve outweighed the benefits of the conventional valve relative to their risks. Rather, it was required to consider

---

73 International Standard Organisation, ISO 5840, Cardiovascular Implants, Cardiac Valve Prostheses <www.iso.org/iso/iso_catalogue/catalogue_tc/catalogue_detail.htm?csnumber=34164>. The abstract states: '[ISO 5840] outlines an approach for qualifying the design and manufacture of a heart valve substitute through risk management. The selection of appropriate qualification tests and methods are derived from the risk assessment. The tests may include those to assess the physical, chemical, biological and mechanical properties of heart valve substitutes and of their materials and components [and] those for pre-clinical *in vivo* evaluation and clinical evaluation of the finished heart valve substitute'.

74 International Standard Organisation, ISO 10993, Biological Evaluation of Medical Devices Package, which set standards in order to assess the biocompatibility of a medical device at the preclinical stage.

75 Candidly enough, the Ontario court states that 'the plaintiffs led no evidence at trial of Canada-specific industry standards and they acknowledge that the FDA's Guidance document and ISO standards are relevant in determining whether St. Jude met industry standards': *Andersen v St Jude Medical, Inc*, 2012 ONSC 3660, para 103.

76 Ibid para 68.

77 Ibid.

78 Ibid para 94.

79 Which 'requires a balancing or weighing of foreseeable risk against the foreseeable utility of the product based on information available to the manufacturer at the time of distribution of the product and without the benefit of hindsight': ibid para 61. The Court relied on *Rentway Canada Ltd v Laidlaw Transport Ltd*, 1989 CarswellOnt 23, paras 43–46, aff'd [1994] OJ No 50 (CA); *Ragoonanan v Imperial Tobacco Canada Ltd* [2000] OJ No 4597, paras 103–104 (SCJ).

80 *Andersen v St Jude Medical, Inc*, 2012 ONSC 3660, para 60.

whether the potential benefits associated with the addition of Silzone outweighed the potential risks of Silzone' (emphasis added).[81]

44 Methodologically speaking, the Court confines the analysis to the device itself, rejecting the 'safer alternative' paradigm of US origin. Viewed through this lens, the coated valve constituted distinctive risks, and different benefits, too, as 'PVE was a known risk with the conventional valve that the Silzone valve had the potential to address.' Accordingly, 'the conventional valve *did not meet the same need as the Silzone valve* because it did not address the risk of [prosthetic valve endocarditis]'.[82]

45 Besides negligence, the doctrine of *Rylands v Fletcher*[83] is applied where relevant. It has been used for damages to land, but only rarely to persons. In addition, stricter liability for damages caused by fire also exists in common law – rooted in English law of 1774 – although the provinces are slowly replacing it with special legislation.[84] The provinces have applied the English doctrine to a varied extent.

III. THE PERSON LIABLE FOR DAMAGE

46 Compared to EU product liability law, persons liable for damage are defined broadly. It appears correct to state that both Quebec law and Canadian common law favour a quite protective approach to consumers, as warranties generally pass along the distribution chain to the last seller.

47 A general principle of the law of obligations states that '[t]he rights of the parties to a contract pass to their successors by particular title if the rights are accessory to the property which passes to them or are closely related to it' (art 1442 CCQ).[85] In contract law, art 1730 CCQ applies this provision to the law of sale, stating that '[t]he manufacturer, any person who distributes the property under his name or as his own, and any supplier of the property, in particular the wholesaler and the importer, *are also bound to warrant the buyer in the same manner as the seller*' (emphasis added).[86] Hence, the spectrum of defendants is as wide as the product's routes into the market, in practice meaning that defendants will be chosen on the basis of which are solvent. The question whether liability of

81 Ibid para 95 (emphasis added).
82 Ibid para 96.
83 (1866) LR 1 Ex 265, aff'd (1968) LR 3 HL 330. On this topic, see *Fridman* (fn 68) especially 217 ff.
84 See eg the Ontario Accidental Fires Act, RSO 1990, c A-4. See *Fridman* (fn 68) 246 ff.
85 Before the adoption of the 1994 Civil Code, the solution was outlined in *General Motors v Kravitz*, 1979 CanLII 22 (CSC), [1979] 1 RCS 790.
86 Emphasis added.

market intermediaries is joint and several remains unclear however,[87] although the Court of Appeal has recently suggested that it be joint and several among professional sellers, and merely *in solidum* if the following sellers are non-professionals.[88]

48 As to Quebec's CPA, its application is rooted in the definition of 'consumer': a 'natural person, except a merchant who obtains goods or services for the purposes of his business'.[89] Moreover. and like the CCQ, the CPA defines a manufacturer as 'a person in the business of assembling, producing or processing goods, and, in particular, (i) *a person who represents himself to the public as the manufacturer of goods*; (ii) where the manufacturer has no establishment in Canada, *a person who imports or distributes goods manufactured outside Canada* or a person who allows his trademark to be used on goods' (emphasis added).[90] Rights of action are extended to most economic operators, and may be exercised 'by any consumer who is a subsequent purchaser of the goods' (art 53 CCQ). The same logic applies to the other warranties, such as fitness for purpose and durability (art 54 CCQ).

IV. THE AGGRIEVED PERSON AND DAMAGE

A. THE AGGRIEVED PERSON

49 There is common ground between the common law and Quebec's law regarding the law of damages and the scope of victims that are entitled to compensation. The notion of 'victim' suffices to establish a right of action in the eyes of the CCQ. However, the more 'remote' the victim, the less able he/she may be to prove the three conditions for to compensable damages (ie they must be direct, certain and legitimate. Heirs, of course, may also continue the action on behalf of victims.[91] In class actions, the status of the claimants within a particular class must be determined in every single case. To sum up, product liability law does not create any specific rules as to the required interest to sue nor the practical outcome of the judgment. Sure enough, the legal categories underlying both legal traditions greatly differ, but in the end – and especially

---

87 See *Baudouin/Linden* (fn 49) 76. The authors rightly point that the matter is particularly important in the context whereby the case reveals an extraneous element.

88 *Claude Joyal Inc v CNH Canada Ltd*, 2014 QCCA 588 (CanLII) paras 49–50. This solution is in line with idea that the defendants be bound in solidarity whenever similar faults cause the damage, or whether they respond for another's behaviour, in which case *in solidum* is preferable: see eg the malpractice case *Roy v Mout*, 2015 QCCA 692 (CanLII) <http://canlii.ca/t/ghbtd>.

89 Art 1(e).

90 Emphasis added.

91 Art 1525, al 3 CCQ.

regarding product liability cases – solutions are similar in both the common law and the civil law traditions.

B. DAMAGE AND COMPENSATION

1) *Civil Law*

50 In the absence of many rules related to the law of damages, the challenge for aggrieved persons remains that of proving the damage. In fact, art 1611 CCQ laconically provides that 'the damages due to the creditor compensate for the amount of the loss he has sustained and the profit of which he has been deprived'. Moreover, '[f]uture injury which is certain and assessable is taken into account in awarding damages'.[92] Unlike the common law, just about any kind of damage may be compensated, in line with the civilist *restitutio in integrum* principle (although contract law limits it to foreseeable damage by the co-contractor).[93] Compensable damages must be direct, certain and legitimate, as art 1607 CCQ provides that '[t]he creditor is entitled to damages for *bodily, moral or material injury* – those legal categories were adopted in 1994 – which is an immediate and direct consequence of the debtor's default'. Predictability enough, *directness* refers to the link that exists between the basis for liability and the alleged harm. Accordingly, the condition is somewhat intertwined with the different conceptions of causality and the material facts presented (see *infra* no 55 ff). As to the *certainty* condition, it is related to the possibility of linking the alleged damage to the wrong inflicted.

51 By way of a general principle, monetary awards are the most frequent tool for compensation. However, and in some circumstances, injunctions or other specific performance will be ordered by the court to prevent further or aggravation of damages. Specifically in the field of product liability, for example, some creative solutions have been devised by courts.

2) *Common Law*

52 The principle is expressed differently in common law, although the results are quite similar: '[d]amages are a monetary payment awarded for the invasion of a right at common law.'[94] Like in civil law, full compensation is the rule, as

92 Art 1611, al 2 CCQ.
93 Art 1613 CCQ states: 'In contractual matters, the debtor is liable only for damages that were foreseen or foreseeable at the time the obligation was contracted, where the failure to perform the obligation does not proceed from intentional or gross fault on his part; even then, the damages include only what is an immediate and direct consequence of the non-performance'.
94 *Canson Enterprises Ltd v Boughton & Co* [1991] 3 SCR.534, para 39, *per* LaForest J.

'a plaintiff should receive full and fair compensation, calculated *to place him or her in the same position as he or she would have been in had the tort not been committed*, insofar as this can be achieved by a monetary award. This principle suggests that in calculating damages under the pecuniary heads, the measure of the damages should be the plaintiff's actual loss' (emphasis added).[95] Accordingly, a breach of contract may give rise to the losses (expectation damages). Compensatory damages is an overarching legal category that covers both pecuniary damages and non-pecuniary damages, which include damages for pain, suffering, disfigurement, loss of enjoyment of life, damage to sexual function and loss of amenities.[96]

53 Two important limitations exist in Canadian law as to compensation law: the common law restriction of the compensation of pure economic losses, and the cap on non-pecuniary damages that was imposed by the Supreme Court (see *infra* no 70 ff).

54 Following English law,[97] in Canadian common law pure economic losses – diminution of financial worth incurred without any physical injury to the plaintiff or his or her property[98] – are not recoverable, in order to avoid creating, in tort, a 'non-contractual guaranty of fitness'. Indeed, no cause of action is to be found in negligence or in contract law. The policy reasons for this solution were made clear in 2000 by the Supreme Court.[99] Over time, though, the rule was modified whenever the conditions set out in *Canadian National Railway Co v Norsk Pacific Steamship Co*[100] are met, namely in the event of: (i) misrepresentation, (ii) negligence of public authorities, (iii) negligent performance of a service, (iv) supply of shoddy goods or structures,[101] or (v) 'relational economic losses'. As the fourth situation is particularly relevant for our purposes, the rule can be distilled down to the following assertion:

---

95 *Ratych v Bloomer* [1990] 1 SCR 940, para 71, *per* McLachlin J (emphasis added).

96 *Quebec (Public Curator) v Syndicat national des employés de l'hôpital St-Ferdinand*, 1996 CanLII 172 (SCC), [1996] 3 SCR 211, para 63.

97 *Cattle v Stockton Waterworks Co* (1874) LR 10 QB 453.

98 *Arora v Whirlpool Canada LP*, 2012 ONSC 4642 (CanLII) para 208; see also *AG (Ont) v Fatehi*, 1984 CanLII 85 (SCC), [1984] 2 SCR 536, 542, and *Rivtow Marine Ltd v Washington Iron Works*, 1973 CanLII 6 (SCC).

99 *Martel Building Ltd v Canada*, 2000 SCC 60 (CanLII), where the Supreme Court stated: 'economic interests are viewed as less compelling of protection than bodily security or proprietary interests; … an unbridled recognition of economic loss raises the spectre of indeterminate liability; … economic losses often arise in a commercial context, where they are often an inherent business risk best guarded against by the party on whom they fall through such means as insurance; … allowing the recovery of economic loss through tort has been seen to encourage a multiplicity of inappropriate lawsuits' (para 37).

100 1992 CanLII 105 (SCC), [1992] 1 SCR 1021.

101 See eg *Winnipeg Condominium Corporation No 36 v Bird Construction Co*, 1995 CanLII 146 (SCC), [1995] 1 SCR 85.

'[p]rovided that the defective product poses a substantial danger, the manufacturer is liable for the pure economic loss of the costs of repair'.[102] In the later case of *Zidaric v Toshiba of Canada Ltd*, for example, the Ontario Court held that the purchase of a defective laptop which allegedly caused data loss does not disclose any cause of action against the manufacturer. The Court rather held that '[a] tort is a civil wrong independent of contract. A contractual relationship can be coincidental with a relationship giving rise to a duty of care and potential liability in tort. … The claimed loss is really a result of the alleged failure of the seller to fulfil its contractual promise. *Thus, the plaintiff's claim properly sounds entirely in contract and not in tort*' (emphasis added).[103] The civil law tradition does not set *a priori* limits on such damages, as long as they are direct and certain.

V. CAUSALITY

55 All over Canada, causality has been characterised by the practical approach advocated for by courts. Given this commonality, it seems difficult to determine whether there is or is not a dichotomy between the civilist approach (section A) and the common law one (section B). Certainly, both traditions have witnessed significant judicial developments.

A. COMMON LAW

1) Causal Link

56 In Canadian common law, causality is anchored into the 'but for' test, even in the context of multi-cause injuries.[104] In the Supreme Court's words '*[t]he plaintiff bears the burden of showing that "but for" the negligent act or omission of each defendant, the injury would not have occurred.* Having done this, contributory negligence may be apportioned, as permitted by statute' (emphasis

[102] *Arora v Whirlpool Canada LP*, 2012 ONSC 4642 (CanLII) para 323. See also *Ducharme v Solarium de Paris Inc* [2008] OJ No 1558 (Div Ct); *Poulin v Ford Motor Co of Canada* [2006] OJ No 4625 (SCJ); *Mariani v Lemstra*, 2004 CanLII 50592 (ON CA); *M. Hasegawa & Co v Pepsi Bottling Group (Canada), Co* [2002] BCJ No 1125 (CA); *Brett-Young Seeds Ltd v Assié Industries Ltd*, 2002 MBCA 74 (CanLII); *Zidaric v Toshiba of Canada Ltd* [2000] OJ No 4590 (SCJ); *TransCanada Pipelines Ltd v Solar Turbines Inc* [1998] OJ No 3594.

[103] Emphasis added.

[104] See among others *Walker Estate v York Finch General Hospital* [2001] 1 SCR 647 (SCC), *Clements v Clements* [2012] 2 SCR 181, para 8, and *G Demeyere*, The 'Material Contribution' Test: An Immaterial Contribution to Tort Law: A Comment on Briglio v. Faulkner (2000) 34 UBC L Rev 317–334.

added).[105] In the seminal case of *Snell v Farrell*, the Supreme Court acknowledged that the 'but for' test establishes the required 'substantial connection' between the harm and the alleged negligence.[106] Causation is understood differently whether the violation is related to the duty of care or the duty to warn.

57 In the context of a failure to warn, high-tech products such as medicines and/or medical devices will raise the causation question as to whether the victim would still have undergone the treatment had she been properly warned of the risks.[107] The seminal oral contraceptive case of *Buchan v Ortho Pharmaceutical (Canada) Ltd*[108] offers a further example. The plaintiff was only 23 years old when she suffered a stroke linked to the birth control pill. The central question addressing causation is relatively simple: had she had known the risks, would she still have taken the pill? Relying mainly on the testimony of the victim (hence relying on a subjective test), the court did not experience particular problems in finding a causal connexion between the alleged failure to warn and the damage suffered. Compensation was further granted.

58 In the context of the duty to care, conversely, the test was neglected in the landmark case of *Walker Estate v York Finch General Hospital*, in which the plaintiff had contracted HIV from contaminated blood products supplied by the Canadian Red Cross Society (CRCS). The blood had been donated when quite little was known about HIV: screening was carried out with pamphlets designed to weed out risky donors (only in May 1985 did scientists developed the ELISA test that screened for the presence of HIV in blood products). These pamphlets were different from those used by the American Red Cross Society. Canadian trial courts eventually held that the CRCS had indeed been negligent in failing to update the pamphlet in light of the most recent scientific knowledge in order to meet the proper standard of care. Specifically, the causation issue was raised as the defendant proved that the infected donor continued to donate blood well

105 *Resurfice Corp v Hanke* [2007] 1 SCR 333, para 21 (emphasis added), quashing *Hanke v Resurfice Corp*, 2005 ABCA 383 (CanLII) <http://canlii.ca/t/1lxd4> on the grounds that material contribution was not to be used in this case.

106 *Snell v Farrell* [1990] 2 SCR 311, 1990 CanLII 70 (SCC) <http://canlii.ca/t/1fstw>, 327, *per* Sopinka J. The case explicitly rejects the approach set forth by English case *McGhee v National Coal Board* [1973] 1 WLR 1 (HL): 'Adoption of either of the proposed alternatives *would have the effect of compensating plaintiffs where a substantial connection between the injury and the defendant's conduct is absent.* Reversing the burden of proof may be justified where two defendants negligently fire in the direction of the plaintiff and then by their tortious conduct destroy the means of proof at his disposal' (emphasis added).

107 Here, product liability shifts away from medical practice cases, whereby an objective test based on reasonableness is preferred. The underlying rationale is synthetised in *Hollis v Dow Corning Corp*, 1995 CanLII 55 (SCC) para 46.

108 1984 CanLII 1938 (ON SC) <http://canlii.ca/t/g1dv3> (appeal dismissed at *Buchan v Ortho Pharmaceutical (Canada) Ltd*, 1986 CanLII 114 (ON CA)).

after the pamphlets were modified: therefore, the CRCS was not the cause of the damage.

59 The Canadian Supreme Court reversed the decision and suggested that the standard of care should have been considered in light of the American pamphlet. In this specific case, the standard of care established causation, as 'more likely than not'[109] adequate screening would have prevented contamination. The Supreme Court then introduced a variation of the causation test, stating that: 'the proper test for causation in negligent donor screening cases is whether the defendant's negligence materially contributed to the plaintiff's harm. Even using the strict but-for test, which is not required in these types of cases, causation is proved on the facts'.[110] Nevertheless, the 'but for' test reveals itself to be useless when multiple causes bring about the harm. Successive case law later evoked, *obiter dictum*, the 'material contribution test' (as opposed to *de minimis*) in such a way as to induce confusion in the already confusing Canadian legal landscape. Two conceptual 'beasts' are rooted in the causation debate.[111] As Justice LeBel – dissenting on other grounds – rightly pointed out: '[t]he material contribution test does not require a factual inquiry into what likely happened, *but imposes liability as a matter of policy*'. In fact, the approaches probably translate to two different perspectives on tort law anchored, respectively, in corrective justice (through regular factual causation) and fairness (legal causation).[112]

60 Probably conscious of this unwanted outcome, the Supreme Court handed down a judgment designed to shed light on the delicate question of causation. To a certain degree holding on to the English 'but for' heritage, it held in *Clements* that '[t]he "but for" causation test must be applied *in a robust common sense fashion*. There is no need for scientific evidence of the precise contribution the defendant's negligence made to the injury'.[113] Exceptionally, hence, a judicial inference surrounding the material contribution to a risk of injury may establish causation whenever the 'but for' test reveals itself to be inadequate in balancing the probabilities.[114] Such is the case when scientific uncertainty shields proper proof of causality,[115] or when multiple negligent acts obscure the factual chain.[116] In such a case, material contribution could be used: *obiter dictum*, the Supreme

109 *Walker Estate v York Finch General Hospital* [2001] 1 SCR 647 (SCC) para 96 (citing the Court of Appeal).

110 Ibid para 97.

111 *Clements v Clements* [2012] 2 SCR 181, para 14 (emphasis added).

112 As the Court added: '[t]he material contribution to risk exception to "but for" causation is not a test for proving factual causation, but a basis for finding "legal" causation where fairness and justice demand deviation from the "but for" test' (para 45, citing the Court of Appeal).

113 *Clements v Clements* [2012] 2 SCR 181, para 9 (emphasis added).

114 *Athey v Leonati*, 1996 CanLII 183 (SCC), [1996] 3 SCR 458, para 15 (Major J).

115 *Resurfice Corp v Hanke* [2007] 1 SCR 333, para 25.

116 *Clements v Clements* [2012] 2 SCR 181, para 13 (emphasis added).

Court suggested this whenever the 'but for' test is unworkable due to 'factors that are outside of the plaintiff's control'[117] and 'the defendant breached a duty of care owed to the plaintiff, thereby exposing the plaintiff to an unreasonable risk of injury;.[118] Currently, however, it seems that no 'special circumstances' have ever invited courts to use the *McGhee*-like[119] material contribution approach.[120] A product liability case – *Resurfice Corp v Hanke*[121] – illustrates the centrality of the 'but for' test, in the context of the operator of an ice-resurfacing machine being injured when hot water overflowed into the gasoline tank, releasing vaporised gasoline which, further ignited, caused an explosion and fire. The victim sought compensation from both the manufacturer and the distributor of the machine, alleging that the gasoline and water tanks were placed too close together on the machine, thus easily causing confusion.

61 In addition, on at least one occasion, a reversal of the burden of proof was proposed. This was the case in *Cook v Lewis,*[122] in which a man was shot by either one of his two fellow hunters. The evidence never revealed whoever shot the bullet. The 'but-for' test was set aside, as both defendants were found jointly and severally liable.

62 To sum up, Canadian common law appears ill-equipped to deal with more complex litigation (eg mass toxic tort litigation with multiple plaintiffs), for which neither of the above-mentioned approaches are suitable. Nonetheless, the court left the door open to new considerations in establishing causation, if, for instance, 'it is established statistically that the defendant's acts induced an injury on some members of the group, but it is impossible to know which ones'.[123] One may therefore conclude that if the 'but for' test remains the rule, courts may exceptionally favour judicial creativity whenever tort law calls for greater fairness. Reversal of the burden of proof and the material contribution test are significant indications of such willingness.

2) Multiple Causation

63 In Anglo-Canadian law, the status of the multiple tortious causes hypothesis[124] is unclear. In the seminal cases of *Athey v Leonati*[125] and *G (ED) v*

117 *Resurfice Corp v Hanke* [2007] 1 SCR 333, para 25.
118 Ibid.
119 *McGhee v National Coal Board* [1973] 1 WLR 1 (HL).
120 *Clements v Clements* [2012] 2 SCR 181, para 28.
121 [2007] 1 SCR 333, 2007 SCC 7 (CanLII) <http://canlii.ca/t/1qfl8>.
122 1951 CanLII 26 (SCC), [1951] SCR 830.
123 *Clements v Clements* [2012] 2 SCR 181, para 44.
124 Note that there is no apportionment possible among tortious and non-tortious causes.
125 [1996] 3 SCR 458.

Hammer,[126] the Supreme Court held that tortfeasors liable for separate tortious incidents will be jointly and severally liable for all of the damages, and apportionment is merely an application of the provincial Negligence Acts.[127] The courts take the following steps in assessing multiple causation: (i) identify the plaintiff's injury in order to determine whether it is 'divisible' or 'indivisible'; (ii) evaluate contributory negligence on the part of the victim; and (iii) undertake apportionment analysis in light of whether the torts are concurrent (eg committed simultaneously at a single point in time to produce the same injury to the plaintiff) or not (eg the injury is caused by separate tortious acts that are independent of one another).

B. QUEBEC'S LAW

64 Despite historical roots in French law, causation in Quebec's law embraces a pragmatic approach that underlies great judicial deference: 'Quebec's courts have approached the problem of causation from a strictly practical point of view and have steadfastly refused to involve themselves in doctrinal controversies and abstract discussion on the subject'.[128]

65 As no indication whatsoever is contained in the CCQ, causation has generated significant doctrine[129] and case law. One may even consider that causation is merely reducible to the law of 'serious, precise and concordant'[130] judicial presumptions; that is, inferences drawn from a known fact to an

---

126 2003 SCC 52.

127 See eg RSO 1990, c N.1, s 1: 'Where damages have been caused or contributed to by the fault or neglect of two or more persons, the court shall determine the degree in which each of such persons is at fault or negligent, and, where two or more persons are found at fault or negligent, they are jointly and severally liable to the person suffering loss or damage for such fault or negligence, but as between themselves, in the absence of any contract express or implied, each is liable to make contribution and indemnify each other in the degree in which they are respectively found to be at fault or negligent'.

128 *Baudouin/Linden* (fn 49) 85. Recovery as between tortfeasors follows the following rule: A tortfeasor may recover contribution or indemnity from any other tortfeasor who is, or would if sued have been, liable in respect of the damage to any person suffering damage as a result of a tort by settling with the person suffering such damage, and thereafter commencing or continuing action against such other tortfeasor, in which event the tortfeasor settling the damage shall satisfy the court that the amount of the settlement was reasonable, and in the event that the court finds the amount of the settlement was excessive it may fix the amount at which the claim should have been settled (RSO 1990, c N.1, s 2).

129 See *L Khoury*, Uncertain Causation in Medical Liability (2005) 88–89; *R Brown*, The Possibility of 'Inference Causation': In-ferring Cause-in-Fact and the Nature of Legal Fact-Finding (2010) 55 RD McGill 1; *RP Kouri*, From Presumptions of Fact to Presumptions of Causation: Reflections on the Perils of Judge-made Rules in Quebec Medical Malpractice Law (2001) 32 RDUS 213; *L Khoury*, Le juge canadien, anglais et australien devant l'incertitude causale en matière de responsabilité médicale (2014) 59 RD McGill 989.

130 Art 2849 CCQ.

unknown fact (art 2847 CCQ). As case law reveals, this pragmatic method is quite hermetic to any civilist-derived theoretical construction that could structure causation around the *causa causans, causa proxima*, etc dialectic.

66 Rather, a recent malpractice case[131] has confirmed the centrality of the presumptions in assessing causation while acknowledging that negative inferences may place an extra burden upon the plaintiff's shoulders whenever the exact cause of the damage remains uncertain. In this case, the plaintiff died of lung cancer diagnosed at an advanced stage. The question was thus the following: had he been diagnosed when the available X-rays should have invited further tests, could he have survived? In the face of contradictory evidence as to how advanced the cancer was when the medical negligence occurred, the Court held that '[t]he respondents failed to provide a concrete answer to the *prima facie* statistical proof by showing that Mr. Émond was among the 22% of persons for whom a fortuitous discovery of cancer is at a later, inoperable stage'[132] and, furthermore, 'the judge *should have found the unanswered statistical proof advanced by the appellants allowed causation to be inferred, to the disadvantage of the respondents*, given the absence of concrete evidence to the contrary' (emphasis added).[133]

67 Defendants will generally try to prove an interruption of causation due to a *novus actus interveniens*, be it the fault of a third party, fault of the victim, or the occurrence of an act of God. In the first two situations, apportionment of liability may arise, as art 1478 CCQ provides that '[w]here an injury has been caused by several persons, liability is shared between them in proportion to the seriousness of the fault of each'. Moreover, art 1480 CCQ provides that '[w]here several persons have *jointly participated in a wrongful act* which has resulted in injury *or have committed separate faults* each of which may have caused the injury, and where it is impossible to determine, in either case, which of them actually caused the injury, they are solidarily bound to make reparation thereof' (emphasis added).

VI. DEFENCES AND EXCLUSIONS

68 In common law Canada, defences in product liability actions generally revolve around the following: (i) the absence of causation; (ii) contributory fault by the plaintiff; and (iii) the 'learned intermediary' doctrine stemming from the *Hollis* case.

---

131 *St-Germain v Benhaim*, 2014 QCCA 2207 (CanLII).
132 Ibid para 144.
133 Ibid para 145 (emphasis added).

69 The most interesting – and novel – defence is to be found in Quebec, where the CCQ provides that '[t]he manufacturer, distributor or supplier of a movable property is not liable to reparation for injury caused by a safety defect in the property ... if he proves that, according to the state of knowledge at the time that he manufactured, distributed or supplied the property, *the existence of the defect could not have been known* ... and *that he was not neglectful of his duty to provide information when he became aware of the defect*' (emphasis added).[134] This 'technological advances defence' hence puts development risks on victims' shoulders. The provision has not been interpreted yet by courts. Moreover, the said defence has not been included in art 53 CPA. Conversely, it rather reads: '[t]he merchant or the manufacturer shall not plead that he was unaware of the defect or lack of instructions.'[135]

VII. REMEDIES

A. GENERAL OVERVIEW

70 The method of calculation of damages is not provided for by the CCQ itself. It is through judicial developments that the courts have come to develop a scheme for the harmonisation of this development. The first push came from the Supreme Court, which had expressed serious frustration on the methods (or the absence of such a method) used by the judiciary to award non-pecuniary damages. The awarding of non-pecuniary losses in Canada is limited by a cap which was imposed by the Supreme Court in 1978.[136] This cap has sometimes been exceeded, but generally speaking it is respected by judges and juries, as indexed every year. It amounts today to around C$300,000. Somewhat in response to the invitation of the Supreme Court, two jurists greatly contributed to the development of the law of damages in the Quebec. The first one, a scholar, published a book entitled *L'évaluation du préjudice corporel*,[137] and the second, Justice LeTarte, having handed down judgments in a few important cases in 1984, gave a further push towards the definition of a more predictable framework for victims.

71 Following the French tradition, the fault-based general clause in the CCQ provides that '[t]he creditor is entitled to damages for bodily, moral or

[134] Art 1473 CCQ. See *M-E Arbour*, Portrait of Risk Development as A Young Defence (2014) 59 McGill Law Journal 1.

[135] Art 53, al 2 CPA. See *M-E Arbour*, Garantie de qualité: droit de la consommation, in: Contrats nommés I (2011).

[136] See *Andrews v Grand & Toy Alberta Ltd* [1978] 2 SCR 229; *Arnold v Teno* [1978] 2 SCR 287; *Arnold v Teno* [1978] 2 SCR 287; *Thornton v Board of School Trustees of School District No 57 (Prince George)* [1978] 2 SCR 267, as well as *Lindal v Lindal* [1981] 2 SCR 629.

[137] *D Gardner*, L'évaluation du préjudice corporel (3nd edn 2009).

material injury which is an immediate and direct consequence of the debtor's default'.[138] Article 1611 further provided that '[t]he damages due to the creditor compensate for the amount of the loss he has sustained and the profit of which he has been deprived. Future injury which is certain and able to be assessed is taken into account in awarding damages'. In assessing damages, indeed, courts have sometimes borrowed from the common law. The Supreme Court did so, for example, when it imposed a cap in moral damages (section VII.B). Moreover and for its part, the legislator adopted punitive damages in particular cases, including situations where personality rights were infringed (section VII.C).

B. CAPS IN NON-PECUNIARY DAMAGES AND THE EVALUATION OF DAMAGES

72 A victim can get compensation for the following damages: loss of amenities, pain and suffering, and medical treatment (apart from treatments provided for by the state, ie most of them). Non-pecuniary damages are considered a head of damages, although they do not truly pursue any compensatory function.[139] The calculation of damages is however quite a confusing exercise in Quebec. In this regard, courts have tried to shift away from the French *calcul au point* method in light of which a certain amount of money is awarded for every percentage of disability determined mostly by experts. Indeed, most of Quebec's scholars argue that the calculation of the percentage of impairment is nothing but a methodological expedient useful in order to assess damages. Such a percentage – called *déficit anatomo-physiologique* (DAP) – is rather a purely scientific exercise, a tool (among other factors) that sets limit on the discretion of the judiciary. It is a transversal, objective variable that needs to be put in relation with the subjective feelings and characteristics of every single victim. In this regard, the problem is twofold.

73 Firstly, there is no unanimity as to what schedule (*barème*) should be used to reach the percentage. No-fault schemes charts of invalidity contained in regulations and guidelines?[140] The American Medical Association's charts? In fact, case law shows that although judges sometimes reject expert assessments that are based on the no-fault systems' *barèmes*, they nonetheless sometimes take into account the American Medical Association's chart in order to calculate an

138 Art 1607 CCQ.

139 The Supreme Court once stated, in *Lindal v Lindal* [1981] 2 SCR 629, that: 'non-pecuniary loss are not really "compensatory". The purpose of making the award *is to substitute other amenities for those that have been lost, not to compensate for the loss of something with a money value.* Since the primary function of the law of damages is compensation, it is reasonable that awards for non-pecuniary loss, which do not fulfil this function, *should be moderate*' (emphasis added).

140 Guides to the Evaluation of Permanent Impairment – Workers' compensations charts.

average percentage of invalidity. Considering the significant disparities which exist in light of the different policy reasons which might underlie the existence of such charts, the first problem consists in the unpredictability of the method used. As to personal injury damages, the calculation is usually done by referral to the American Medical Association's Guides to the Evaluation of Permanent Impairment.[141] Nonetheless, some courts have held that the calculation of the DAP in light of the American Medical Association standards is not sufficient to properly compensate the victim.[142] They therefore rely on other principles.

74 Secondly (and when a percentage of disability has been determined) judges either apply it in such way as to reintroduce the French method that has been banned (inducing too much objectiveness in the assessment), or use it as a mere variable in the awarding of damages which leads to further unpredictable results (inducing too much subjectiveness in the assessment).

75 In the field of non-pecuniary damages, nonetheless, losses in Canada – including in Quebec[143] – are limited by a cap that was imposed by the Supreme Court in 1978.[144] This cap, which is indexed every year, has sometimes been exceeded, but generally speaking it is respected by judges and juries. It amounts today to *circa* C$400,000. This cap has had a profound influence on Quebec's civil law, as some authors were reluctant to erode the general, civilist principle provided for by art 1607 CCQ, which states that compensation must be full, in other words *in integrum*. However, the cap is only applicable to the head of damages that refers to *bodily injuries*; this category has been interpreted narrowly by courts, who qualify, for example, non-pecuniary damages stemming from defamation[145] or copyright infringements[146] as property interests that are

141 See *Fortin v Liberté TM Inc*, 2007 QCCS 4826 (CanLII, CS) or *Saint-Maurice v Montréal (Ville)*, 2005 CanLII 9507 (QC CS).

142 In a case where the victim fell off a roof, the Court held observed that the calculation in light of the DAP procedure (in this case, 38%) would amount, considering the $315,000 cap, to $119,700. The Court nonetheless considered that this method is not appropriate since it undermines the impact of the accident on the victim's life. The Court therefore relied on the equation that had been proposed by the defendant, who had argued that the 26% DAP of the victim should justify a lump sum of $140,000. By applying this reasoning to the 38% DAP, the Court awarded $204,615.38 for non-pecuniary damages: see *Fortin v Liberté TM Inc*, 2007 QCCS 4826 (CanLII, CS). To this sum, the court added $45,000 for pain and suffering.

143 See *J-L Baudouin/P Deslauriers*, La responsabilité civile, vol I (7th edn 2007) 481–84; *D Gardner*, Le préjudice corporel (3rd edn 2009) 376–77.

144 See *Andrews v Grand & Toy Alberta Ltd* [1978] 2 SCR 229; *Arnold v Teno* [1978] 2 SCR 287; *Arnold v Teno* [1978] 2 SCR 287; *Thornton v Board of School Trustees of School District No 57 (Prince George)* [1978] 2 SCR 267, as well as *Lindal v Lindal* [1981] 2 SCR 629.

145 *Hill v Church of Scientology of Toronto*, 1995 CanLII 59 (SCC), [1995] 2 SCR 1130, para 168; see also *Snyder v Montreal Gazette Ltd*, 1988 CanLII 66 (SCC), [1988] 1 SCR 494.

146 See eg *Cinar Corporation v Robinson* [2013] 3 SCR 1168 <http://canlii.ca/t/g2fgx>. The Court added: 'It is more appropriate to characterize R's psychological suffering as a non-pecuniary damage stemming from *material* injury'.

not targeted by the cap. A strange result is that a violation of property interests often translates into greater damages for victims than, say, defective products or medical malpractice.

C. PUNITIVE DAMAGES AND NOMINAL DAMAGES

76 Punitive damages do exist in Canadian law – even in Quebec's civil law – although they usually do not reach the same level as those awarded in the United States.[147] In the common law, punitive damages were better defined in Canadian law by *Vorvis v Insurance Corp of British Columbia*[148] and *Whiten v Pilot Insurance Co*,[149] and are reserved 'for situations where the defendant *has done more than inflict injury on others by his negligence or intentional acts*. He must have acted maliciously, or with such recklessness as to indicate an indifference to the safety of others, or have engaged in some other type of behaviour which is regarded as so socially reprehensible as to justify the awarding of punitive damages'.[150] In the *Whiten* case, the Supreme Court set out the Ten Commandments in the awarding of punitive damages: (i) punitive damages are not reducible to categories; they rise out of circumstances that invite to a punishment; (ii) they intend to punish, deter and denunciate the wrongdoer; (iii) they are chiefly relevant in criminal law, and may superpose themselves to other forms of prior penalty; (iv) 'time-honoured pejorative' epithets to described the wrongdoer's conduct provide little guidance to the judge/jury; (v) rationality suggests that the lowest award suitable to fulfil one of the goals pursued on by punitive damages be imposed; (vi) the award may be, in some cases, sufficient enough not to grant him a 'licence fee' to earn greater profit; (vii) no 'formulaic approach' is suitable in awarding damages; (viii) proportionality, though, is the rule; (ix) juries must be properly addressed concerning the function of punitive damages; and (x) appellate courts shall intervene if the award is not within the boundaries of rationality.

77 Quebec also adopted punitive damages on occasion of the adoption of the 1994 Civil Code and other statutory legislation. Although the Civil Code provides for a definition, they can only be awarded in those circumstances that

---

147 On this issue, see however *Whiten v Pilot Insurance Co* [2002] 1 SCR 595, 2002 SCC 18 (CanLII) <www.canlii.org/ca/cas/scc/2002/reflex/2002scc18.html>, where high punitive damages were awarded to the plaintiff of a bad faith insurance company.

148 [1989] 1 SCR 1085, 1098–1099, where damages were awarded in the context of the unjust dismissal of the claimant.

149 2002 SCC 18 (CanLII). See also *Hill v Church of Scientology of Toronto*, 1995 CanLII 59 (SCC), [1995] 2 SCR 1130 (SCC).

150 *Legault v Tiapis*, 2015 BCSC 517 (CanLII) para 37.

are explicitly provided for 'by the legislator',[151] that is, in an express manner. Bad faith, for example, is not sufficient to justify the awarding of punitive damages to victims. The 'bridging' provision (art 1621 CCQ) rather leads to the Charter of Rights and Freedom or the CPA.

78 Finally, the category of nominal damages is found in the Canadian common law tradition, but not Quebec's civil law one. To the best of our knowledge, it has never been relevant in the product liability field.

VIII. PROCEDURAL AND EVIDENTIAL ISSUES

A. TIME LIMITS

79 In all provinces, the evidentiary standard for liability is the balance of probability. In Quebec, the CCQ provides that 'evidence is sufficient if it renders the existence of a fact more probable than its non-existence, unless the law requires more convincing proof' (art 2804). According to art 2925, '[a]n action to enforce a personal right or movable real right is prescribed by three years, if the prescriptive period is not otherwise determined'. Similarly in common law, time limitations are prescribed by statutes and resemble Quebec's legal landscape.

B. CLASS ACTIONS

80 Procedural requirements linked to class action certification are currently the main concerns in product liability cases all over Canada and beyond the civil law/common law dichotomy. Indeed, most provinces have adopted special laws surrounding certification requirements;[152] they resemble art 1003 of Quebec's

---

151 Tree Protection Act, RSQ c P-37; Transportation Services by Taxi, An Act respecting, RSQ c S-6.01, s 83 and 127; Charter of Human Rights and Freedoms, RSQ c C-12, s 49 al 2; Petroleum Products Act, RSQ c P-29.1, s 67 al 2; Régie du logement, An Act respecting the, RSQ c R-8.1, s 54.10; Securities Act, RSQ c V-1.1, s 269.2; Prearranged Funeral Services and Sepultures, An Act respecting, RSQ c A-23.001, s 56; Collective Agreement Decrees, An Act respecting, RSQ c D-2, s 31; Labour Relations, Vocational Training and Workforce Management in the Construction Industry, An Act respecting, RSQ c R-20, s 107 and 122(3); Civil Code of Quebec, s 1899, 1902 and 1968 (in terms of lease); Access to Documents Held by Public Bodies and the Protection of Personal Information, An Act respecting, RSQ c A-2.1, s 167, Forest Act, RSQ c. F-4.1, s 172.3; Labour Standards, An Act respecting, RSQ c N-1.1, s 123.15; Charter of the French Language, RSQ c C-11, s 46 al 6.

152 See eg *McSherry v Zimmer GmbH*, 2014 ONSC 5527 (CanLII) <http://canlii.ca/t/gdpvd>; recently in Manitoba, *Walls v Bayer Inc*, 2005 ACWSJ 11741 (CA), where the court certified class action proceedings in product liability action claiming damages for injuries caused by cholesterol-lowering drug Baycol, in light of the Class Proceedings Act, CCSM, c C130 of 1 January 2003. See other laws such as Class Proceedings Act, RSBC 1996, c 50 (British

Code of Civil Procedure, which provides that '[t]he court authorizes the bringing of the class action and ascribes the status of representative to the member it designates if of opinion that: (a) the recourses of the members raise identical, similar or related questions of law or fact; (b) the facts alleged seem to justify the conclusions sought; (c) the composition of the group makes the application of article 59 or 67 difficult or impracticable; and (d) the member to whom the court intends to ascribe the status of representative is in a position to represent the members adequately'.

81 In 2013 the Supreme Court also provided valuable insights into the underlying conditions for class actions.[153] Pharmaceutical law shows that the main difficulty lies in establishing general causation with 'some basis in fact'[154] in order to show the court the homogeneity between the class members. In order to do so, proper methodology based on clinical trials protocols must be used in order to aggregate potential victims around the common issues[155] that form the basis of the envisioned class action. Not doing so will lead to the denial of the certification motion.

82 An example of this was provided by the 2015 case *Charlton v Abbott Laboratories, Ltd*,[156] in which the British Columbia Court of Appeal set aside an order certifying a class action against Abbott Laboratories and Apotex Inc, the manufacturers of the weight-loss drug sibutramine. More specifically, it held that no evidence supported the hypothesis that the molecule increases certain risks

-Columbia), or Class Proceedings Act, SO 1992, c 6 (Ontario), see *Serhan (Estate) v Johnson & Johnson*, 2004 CanLII 1533 (ON SC) certification for class action for a product to be used by diabetics to monitor their blood glucose levels, Quebec Code of Civil Procedure, RSQ, c C-25, Book IX (on 3 September 2004, the Superior Court of Quebec authorised a class action against St Jude Medical Inc and St Jude Medical Canada Inc, manufacturers of a mechanical heart valve: see *Thibault v St Jude Medical Canada Inc*, 2004 IIJCan 21608 (QC CS); see also *Conseil québécois sur le tabac et la santé c JTI-MacDonald Corp*, 2005 IIJCan 4070 (QC CS) certification for personal injury caused by tobacco products), Class Actions Act, SS 2001, c C-12.01 (Sask.), Class Actions Act, SNL 2001, c C-18.1 (Newfoundland). On this very topic, see also Supreme Court cases *Western Canadian Shopping Centres Inc. v Dutton* [2001] 2 SCR 534, 2001 SCC 46; *Hollick v Toronto (City)* [2001] 3 SCR 158, 2001 SCC 68; and *Rumley v British Columbia* [2001] 3 SCR 184, 2001 SCC 69. See however *Hoffman v Monsanto Canada Inc*, 2005 Sask DJ 2378, 2005 Sask DJ LEXIS 121, 2005 SKQB 225, [2005] Sask D 770.12.00.00-01 (QB) (application for certification dismissed in an GMO field contamination litigation) or *Caputo v Imperial Tobacco Ltd*, 2004 CanLII 24753 (ON SC) (application for certification dismissed in tobacco litigation). See generally *P-C Lafond*, Le recours collectif comme voie d'accès à la justice pour les consommateurs (1996).

153 *AIC Limited v Fischer*, 2013 SCC 69 (CanLII) [2013] 3 SCR 949; *Sun-Rype Products Ltd v Archer Daniels Midland Company*, 2013 SCC 58 (CanLII), [2013] 3 SCR 545; and *Pro-Sys Consultants Ltd v Microsoft Corporation*, 2013 SCC 57 (CanLII), [2013] 3 SCR 477.

154 *Hollick v Toronto (City)*, 2001 CSC 68 (CanLII).

155 As to the aesthetic and substance of the common issues, see *Singer v Schering-Plough Canada Inc*, 2010 ONSC 42 (CanLII).

156 2015 BCCA 26 (CanLII) <http://canlii.ca/t/gg1cg>.

for all class members, in such a way as to establish general causation. The drug had been approved by Health Canada in 2000, but was voluntarily withdrawn from the market in 2010 after a post-market clinical trial (the Sibutramine Cardiovascular Outcome Trial, or SCOUT Study) had suggested a correlation between an increased risk of serious cardiovascular events and the use of sibutramine *by patients with pre-existing heart problems.*

83 Plaintiffs alleged that sibutramine causes or contributes to an increased risk of adverse cardiovascular events, increased blood pressure and heart rate, and arrhythmia. On behalf of all persons in Canada who used or purchased sibutramine and their family members, they asserted, among other things, causes of action anchored in negligence and failure to warn. In order to succeed, the plaintiffs had to demonstrate that they met the commonality and preferability requirements in the British Columbia Class Proceeding Act.[157]

84 The Court of Appeal held that where a plaintiff seeks to address questions of causation, the plaintiff must provide evidence of a methodology for proving causation on a class-wide basis. Relying on the guidelines provided for by the Supreme Court in 2013, it noted that the Court certified the case on behalf of two groups: (i) those who have suffered and actual injury, and (ii) those who were prescribed a drug that should not have been marketed at all.

85 In analysing the general causation question, the Court of Appeal noted an important discrepancy between the findings of the clinical trial and the common issues raised by the case as certified.[158] More specifically, it noted that the former all relied on the overarching assumption that sibutramine caused or contributed to cardiovascular events. Conversely, the post-market study had only demonstrated that the drug increased the risk of cardiovascular events *for patients with a history of cardiovascular disease* (and for whom sibutramine was contraindicated anyway). Scientifically speaking, nevertheless, no study documented the increase of a general risk *for all patients*; hence, no workable

---

157 Class Proceedings Act, RSBC 1996, c 50 <http://canlii.ca/t/kv3p> (art 4).

158 The common issues are the following: '1) Does sibutramine cause or contribute to heart attacks, strokes, and arrhythmia?; 2) Did the defendants breach a duty of care owed to the class in the testing, marketing, selling or distributing of sibutramine?; 3) Did the defendants knowingly, recklessly, or negligently breach a duty to warn the class of the risks of harm from the use of sibutramine?; 4) Did the defendants engage in conduct that constituted deceptive acts or practices contrary to the *Business Practices and Consumer Protection Act,* S.B.C. 2004, c. 2, or equivalent legislation in other provinces?; 5) Did the defendants' marketing and sale of sibutramine breach s. 52 of the *Competition Act,* R.S.C. 1985, c. C-34?; 6) If any of questions 1 to 5 are answered in the affirmative, does the defendants' conduct warrant an award of punitive damages?; 7) If any of questions 1 to 5 are answered in the affirmative, should the defendants be ordered to disgorge the revenues they received from the sale of sibutramine?' (Abbott J, para 57).

methodology was provided by the plaintiffs as a way to prove general causation. Therefore, the appeal was allowed. Certification had been sought in Quebec as well, with no success[159]

86 Another pharmaceutical class action, *Stanway v. Wyeth Canada Inc*,[160] had a different outcome. In this case, the plaintiffs had shown evidence of a general correlation between estrogen-progestin therapy and breast cancer, supported by a large clinical study. Many other certifications concerning innovation products have been allowed in the pharmaceutical field,[161] but no judgment on the merits has ever been made; all the cases ended with settlements.

87 The reliability of the methodology used is not the same at the certification stage and at actual trial. The British Columbia Court of Appeal mentioned that in order to prove the 'some basis in facts' requirement, '[t]he threshold is not an onerous one, and is not to be confused with the requirement of proof on a balance of probabilities applied at trial'.[162]

IX. ALTERNATIVE REGULATIONS AND REMEDIES

A. STATE LIABILITY

88 Extracontractual liability of the Crown stemming from the Crown Liability and Proceedings Act[163] is an ever increasing legal basis for liability based on fault.[164] Although the results are far from conclusive, new grounds for 'bad regulation liability' have recently emerged within the area of tort law. Most specifically in the context of GMOs and pharmaceutical law, plaintiffs have

159 *MacMillan v Abbott Laboratories*, 2012 QCCS 1684 (CanLII)).

160 2012 BCCA 260 (CanLII).

161 Those include the Vioxx saga: see *Sigouin v Merck & Co Inc*, 2006 QCCS 5325 (CanLII) <http://canlii.ca/t/1qt9q>; Pondéral/Redux: *Hotte v Servier Canada Inc*, 2002 CanLII 33243 (QC CS), [2002] RJQ 230 (CS) (settled in 2005, see <www.ponderal-reduxsettlement.ca/quebec/index.htm>); Zyprexa: *Dallaire v Eli Lilly Canada Inc*, 2006 QCCS 4233 (CanLII); *Brito v Pfizer Canada Inc*, 2008 QCCS 2231 (CanLII); *Goodridge v Pfizer Canada Inc*, 2010 ONSC 1095 (CanLII).

162 *Miller v Merck Frosst Canada Ltd*, 2015 BCCA 353 (CanLII) para 21.

163 RSC 1985, c C-50 (CLPA). Art 3 provides that: 'The Crown is liable for the damages for which, if it were a person, it would be liable (*a*) in the Province of Quebec, in respect of (i) the damage caused by the fault of a servant of the Crown, or (ii) the damage resulting from the act of a thing in the custody of or owned by the Crown or by the fault of the Crown as custodian or owner; and (*b*) in any other province, in respect of (i) a tort committed by a servant of the Crown, or (ii) a breach of duty attaching to the ownership, occupation, possession or control of property'. In Quebec, art 1376 subordinates the state to the general principles of liability.

164 See in Quebec art 1376 CCQ: 'The rules set forth in this Book apply to the State and its bodies, and to all other legal persons established in the public interest, subject to any other rules of law which may be applicable to them'.

alleged that regulation was at the source of the damage they sustained. Relying upon the American-rooted political/operational dichotomy,[165] courts, however, have been reluctant to acknowledge the existence of a duty of care towards the population in general, as 'the Crown owes a duty to the public at large but no private law duty to the manufacturers, distributors or retailers of regulated products'.[166] Nonetheless, bad regulation liability seems increasingly popular, especially in Anglo-Canadian provinces, perhaps in light of the difficulties experienced in proving negligence. A preliminary observation must be made regarding the general principles applicable to vicarious state liability. To begin with, the field is historically rooted in the common law, and followed English law. It slowly developed its own rules, based on the Supreme Court decision in *Cooper v Hobart*[167] where, in the context of financial services regulation, the famous test set out by the House of Lords in *Anns v Merton London Borough Council*[168] was adopted. Currently, the test is as follows: (i) whether the harm that occurred was *the reasonably foreseeable consequence of the defendant's act*, and (ii) whether there are reasons, notwithstanding the proximity between the parties, that tort liability should not be recognised. The proximity analysis involved at the first stage of the *Anns* test focuses on factors arising from the relationship between the plaintiff and the defendant. These factors include questions of policy, in the broad sense of the word. If foreseeability and proximity are established at the first stage, a *prima facie* duty of care arises. At the second stage of the *Anns* test, the question still remains whether there are residual policy considerations outside the relationship of the parties that may negate the imposition of the duty of care.[169]

89 There are three interesting cases addressing regulators' liability. In the first one, *Attis v Canada (Health),*[170] the Ontario Court of Appeal upheld the dismissal of a proposed class proceeding with respect to alleged negligence in relation to the government's regulation of breast implants. Applying the *Anns/Cooper* analytical framework, the judge could not find any cause of action in the absence of a private law duty of care. When defining Health Canada's margin of discretion, courts observed that the legal framework for regulators set forth by art 4 of the Department of Health Act 'provides that the Minister's

---

165 See *Canadian Food Inspection Agency v Professional Institute of the Public Service of Canada* [2010] 3 SCR 657, whereby the Court specifies that the dichotomy is relevant in Quebec's law as well: 'The fact that the federal Crown is subject to Quebec's rules of extracontractual civil liability … does not preclude it from invoking its immunity. For example, it remains open to the federal Crown to argue that a particular decision was made by its agents acting in a policy rather than an operational capacity, which would not normally attract liability' (para 27).

166 *Swarath v Canada*, 2014 FC 75 (CanLII) para 23.

167 2001 SCC 79 (CanLII).

168 [1978] AC 728.

169 *Cooper v Hobart*, 2001 SCC 79 (CanLII) para 30.

170 2008 ONCA 660 (CanLII).

obligations are to the people of Canada for the promotion of their health and the prevention of risk generally. Thus, under the statute, *the Minister's duty is to the people of Canada as a whole, not to individual residents*' (emphasis added).[171]

90 In the second case, *Los Angeles Salad Company Inc v Canadian Food Inspection Agency*,[172] the plaintiffs alleged that employees of the Crown engaged in food inspection, who found carrots to be infected with bacteria, had been negligent. All targeted lots were recalled and destroyed. The conclusion that there had been contamination was subsequently determined to be mistaken. The importer sued the state. The Court of Appeal held, as did the motion judge, that the Canadian Food Inspection Agency did not owe economic operators any duty of care, as 'the clear purpose of the relevant legislative scheme is to protect the health of Canadians by preventing the sale of contaminated food in Canada. To recognise a private duty of care to food sellers would conflict with that purpose. *It would put food inspectors in the untenable position of having to balance the paramount interests of the public with private interests of food sellers and would thereby have a chilling effect on the proper performance of their duties*. Thus, the statutory scheme excludes the possibility of sufficient factual proximity to make it just and reasonable to impose a *prima facie* duty of care in the circumstances of this case' (emphasis added).[173]

91 In the *Swarath* case, a motion to strike out was upheld when the plaintiffs, who had since 2005 held a license issued by Health Canada to sell 'Libidus', described as a natural health product intended to address symptoms of erectile dysfunction, were further notified by Health Canada to stop the sale of the product in Canada and recall it, under the Natural Health Products Regulations.[174] The decision had been based on the fact that the 'natural product' actually contained undisclosed acetildenafil, a substance regulated by the Food and Drug legislation. Against this backdrop, the plaintiffs sought compensation for the damages they suffered, alleging Health Canada's 'gross negligence, arbitrariness, bad faith and malice on the part of Health Canada employees, and a conspiracy between the defendants and the pharmaceutical industry to suppress the distribution of Libidus'.[175] The Court followed the line

171 Ibid para 54. The Statute grants the Minister of Health powers, duties and functions for the administration of the Acts, and such orders and regulations of the Government of Canada assigned to her department for, among other things, the promotion and preservation of the well-being of the people of Canada, protection against risks to health and the spreading of diseases, and investigation and research into public health.

172 2013 BCCA 34 (CanLII).

173 Ibid para 25.

174 SOR/2003-196.

175 *Swarath v Canada*, 2014 FC 75 (CanLII) para 5.

traced by the *Attis* and *Salad* cases, and concluded that '[t]he clear purpose of the relevant legislative and regulatory scheme in this matter is to protect the health of Canadians by preventing the sale of contaminated natural health products in Canada. *To recognize a private duty of care to the importers and distributors of those products would conflict with that purpose.* I am unable to agree with the argument of the plaintiffs that the duty to promote and preserve the health of the people of Canada encompasses a duty to the distributors of products such as Libidus' (emphasis added).[176] The motion to strike out was further allowed.

B. PRODUCT SAFETY LAW

92 The federal legal landscape has recently enhanced the merging of public law and private law, as a new Canada Consumer Product Safety Act (CCPSA)[177] entered into force in 2011. This statute is intended to increase product safety through the creation – like in the European Directives 1992/59/EEC and 2001/95/EC on product safety – of a longitudinal safety obligation on economic operators, and to increase the discretionary powers of the public administration (Health Canada). Except in Quebec, where it already existed, this new federal effort is likely to reshape anew the law of product liability. More specifically, the Act seeks 'to protect the public by addressing or preventing dangers to human health or safety that are posed by consumer products in Canada, including those that circulate within Canada and those that are imported'.[178] To this end, it provides that '[n]o manufacturer or importer shall manufacture, import, advertise or sell a consumer product that (a) is a danger to human health or safety; is the subject of a recall order … because the product is a danger to human health or safety'.[179] The notion of a 'danger to human health or safety' is defined by the same Act as:

> 'any unreasonable hazard – *existing or potential* – that is posed by a consumer product during or as a result of its normal or foreseeable use and that may reasonably be expected to cause the death of an individual exposed to it or have an adverse effect on that individual's health – including an injury – whether or not the death or adverse effect occurs immediately after the exposure to the hazard, and includes any exposure to a consumer product that may reasonably be expected to have a chronic adverse effect on human health'.[180]

---

176 Ibid para 28 (emphasis added).
177 SC 2010, c 21.
178 Art 3 CCPSA.
179 Art 7 CCPSA.
180 Art 2 CCPSA.

93 The CCPSA has significantly increased Health Canada's powers. For example, it may compel products to be recalled,[181] require the industry to conduct tests in order to assess compliance,[182] inspect premises, and require manufacturers or importers to provide or obtain safety information – including studies or tests – that indicate whether a consumer product meets the requirements of the CCPSA. In light of these important changes, it is likely that liability law will also constitute an important legal basis for compensation. In this regard, and despite the rejection of the above-mentioned cases (*Attis*, *Salad* and *Swarath*), this recast of the legal landscape will require adjustments to be made to coordinate tort law and product safety law.

C. COMPENSATION SCHEMES: BLOOD PRODUCTS

94 Some compensation schemes do apply to special products. Among them are the various provincial laws on automobile compensation, injuries sustained at work (workers' compensation schemes), and a federal nuclear damages law.[183] For our purposes, the most relevant is undoubtedly the quite recent strict liability scheme set out by the Act Respecting Héma-Québec and the Biovigilance Committee[184] and the Regulation respecting the conditions for compensation to victims of a Héma-Québec product,[185] by virtue of which '[t]he Minister must compensate [calculated using the automobile no-fault scheme],[186] regardless of liability, a victim[187] of *bodily injury* caused[188] by a defect in or contamination, by known or unknown pathogens, of a Héma-Québec product'.[189] The statutes specify that a bodily injury 'means any physical or mental injury suffered by a victim, including death but excepting any adverse effects determined by regulation'.[190]

181 Art 31 CCPSA. To this day, only one mandatory recall has been issued; it concerns small magnets that could have been ingested by children, harming them.

182 Art 12 CCPSA.

183 Nuclear Liability Act, RS 1985, c N-28.

184 CQLR c H-1.1 <http://canlii.ca/t/523bv>. According to art 3, '[t]he mission of Héma-Québec is to provide the health and social services institutions in Québec and the population with a sufficient supply of blood, blood products and blood components'.

185 CQLR c H-1.1, r 1 <http://canlii.ca/t/522d7>.

186 CQLR c H-1.1, art 54.3.

187 The definition of a 'victim' is provided in art 54.1: '"victim" means a person who received a Héma-Québec product, a person who contracted a disease from a person who received a Héma-Québec product, or a child conceived and born alive and viable of either of such persons or, if death occurs, the person who is entitled to a death benefit'.

188 A scientific attitude to causation seems to be privileged.

189 CQLR c H-1.1, art 54.2 (emphasis added). Such a product is defined as 'any product distributed by Héma-Québec, except (1) when such a product is used for research or clinical trials, unless the Minister decides otherwise; or (2) when such a product is made from a human biological product determined by the Government and the Government has decided to exclude it from the compensation plan for victims' (art 54.1).

190 CQLR c H-1.1, art 54.1.

D. STANDARDISATION BODIES

95 A new and noteworthy liability trend of holding the certification created by standardisation bodies (Canadian Standards Association (CSA), the equivalent of DIN) liable for alleged negligence in drafting or updating standards. This line of argument has been arisen in the context of hockey injuries sustained despite wearing a helmet, for which plaintiffs have held both manufacturer and the CSA liable. In this context, the British Columbia Court of Appeal recently passed judgment in a case where it was suggested that the helmet the plaintiff wore should have been designed to protect him against translational applications of force;[191] to begin with, the CSA 'should have developed and adopted a more rigorous certification standard for hockey helmets'. In the presence of an adequate warning,[192] however, the Court concluded that the risks were actually known to the buyer.[193] The argument related to the violation of the duty of care also did not succeed. To the contrary, the Court highlighted three policy reasons excluding liability of 'public service' entities. It held:[194]

> '[1] the reality of finding a duty of care would be that any *injured hockey player, or injured consumer, could make a claim against CSA.* ... [2] extending the risk of liability to CSA *might impact on its ability to carry on and jeopardize the valuable public service it provides.* ... [T]he threat of legal action creates the very real risk that CSA could not continue to operate, which would result in harm not only to wearers of hockey helmets, but to manufacturers, and ultimately, consumers of goods that now benefit from the establishment and certification of minimum standards. [3] the suggestion that representatives of manufacturers who participate in the Technical Committees that *establish standards might "maintain the bar at an artificially low level"* casts unfounded doubt on CSA's process for establishing standards. That process, in the case of hockey helmets, involves volunteers representing not only manufacturers, but representatives of hockey associations and leagues, consumers, academics, medical professionals, business and government, who reach decisions by consensus' (emphasis added).

For these reasons, the case was dismissed.

---

191 *More v Bauer Nike Hockey Inc*, 2011 BCCA 419 (CanLII) <http://canlii.ca/t/fnl40>.

192 Ibid para 99: 'Ice hockey is a collision sport which is dangerous. These helmets afford no protection from neck, spinal or certain types of brain injuries including those that may be caused by rotational forces. Severe head, brain or spinal injuries including paralysis or death may occur despite using this helmet'.

193 The trial court also concluded that causation was absent: 'The plaintiffs focus solely on the small CSA label on the helmet that simply says "Certified Hockey Helmet". They ignore the larger label also on the helmet that states severe head and brain injuries may occur despite wearing the helmet. Considering the effect of the smaller CSA sticker without taking the larger sticker into account is misleading'. Ibid para 16.

194 Ibid para 60 (emphasis added).

96 Finally, we may underline that the Supreme Court has recently handed down a judgment in a case of great interest for the tobacco industry, in which it confirmed the constitutionality of a British Columbia law (Tobacco Damages and Health Care Costs Recovery Act),[195] which authorises a claim by the government against tobacco manufacturers for the recovery of health care expenditures incurred by the former in treating individuals exposed to these products.[196]

X. ASSESSMENT OF DOMESTIC LAW

97 In light of the above, it can be observed that there is a great disparity between Canadian common law and Quebec's civil law. Despite commonalities in the evaluation of causation (where both the common law and civil law experience the same problems) or of the reasonable person's behaviour, both traditions understand product liability differently, as Quebec's law proposes probably one of the most victim-friendly legal landscapes. If it were not for the insertion of the quite unpopular development risk defence, the defect-based regime would appear to be particularly advantageous when coupled with the class action procedure. Over the years, there has been an increasing number of mass torts introduced in Canada, which probably testifies to the great potential of product liability as a regulation instrument. Sure enough, its flexibility allows it to encompass new products, be they material or immaterial. In the case of new products, defectiveness will be assessed by learned experts; the underlying basis for liability, however, will remain unchanged.

195 SBC 2000, c 30.

196 *British Columbia v Imperial Tobacco Canada Ltd*, 142 ACWS (3d) 425 (Supreme Court).

PRODUCT LIABILITY IN ISRAEL

Israel GILEAD

I. SOURCES OF LAW AND THEIR EVOLUTION

01 Since the enactment of the Defective Product (Liability) Law, 1980 (DPLL), one can distinguish between two sets of legal rules governing product liability in Israel. The provisions of the DPLL compose one set of rules. These rules apply to the liability of a *producer* for *bodily injury caused* by a *defective product*, as defined by the DPLL. The other set of rules, hereinafter referred to as the 'general liability arrangements' (GLA), is composed of all *tort liability* arrangements besides the DPLL, and of other *contractual* liability arrangements (including the law of sales), that apply to harm caused by products. The major *tort* liability arrangements of the GLA, embodied in the Civil Wrong Ordinance (CWO), are the tort of *negligence* and, to a lesser extent, the tort of *breach of statutory duty* (BSD).[1] GLA rules may apply to all kinds of harms (including bodily injury) caused by all kinds of defective products. Consequently, the two sets of liability rules, the DPLL and the GLA, may overlap in cases of defective product causing *bodily injury*. The aggrieved party, the plaintiff, may sue the harm-inflicting party, the defendant, in both venues of liability.[2] When the DPLL does not apply because the harm caused is not bodily injury or because another requirement of

---

1 Israeli law, although originating in the English common law, is *statutory* law. The major torts and the general principles of tort law are embodied in the CWO (Civil Wrong Ordinance).

2 The DPLL provides in sec 10 that it does not derogate from any rights under the CWO or any other law. This provision is in line with the general rule that allows concurrence of different causes of action – the plaintiff can sue for on different grounds for the same harm or occurrence.

the DPLL is not met, the plaintiff may resort to the variety of claims available under the GLA venue.[3]

02 The major difference between the liability regime in the DPLL on the one hand, and the tort of negligence as the major cause of action in tort under GLA on the other hand, is that under the former liability is, at least partially,[4] *strict* liability, while under the latter it is basically *fault-based*. Given this difference one would expect most claims for bodily injury caused by products to be made under the DPLL because strict liability is supposedly wider in scope and easier to establish than fault-based liability in negligence. In reality, however, the following factors made the DPLL less attractive than one might expect: the complexity of the 'defectiveness' concept;[5] caps in the DPLL on awards for loss of earning and for non-pecuniary harms;[6] and shorter limitation periods.[7]

03 Where the DPLL does apply, its specific provisions take precedence over the general rules of tort law.[8] In the absence of a specific provision in the DPLL the general rules of tort law, embodied in the CWO,[9] would apply, being adjust to the product liability context.[10]

04 The DPLL was inspired by early drafts (before 1980) of the European attempts to harmonise product liability in Europe.[11]

05 Notably, the proposed Israeli Civil Code includes revisions of the DPLL. These revisions, presented in the proposed Civil Code Bill of 2011, were introduced by the Tort Committee of the Codification Committee in the early 2000s (drafted by the author of this report). These revisions were inspired mainly by developments in US product liability law.

II. BASIC ELEMENTS OF LIABILITY – DPLL

06 Under the DPLL the elements of liability are: (i) bodily injury, (ii) caused to the plaintiff by a product, (iii) the product is defective, (iv) the defendant

---

3 Given the concurrence of causes of action (fn 2), however, when only the GLA applies and not the DPLL the plaintiff can still sue for the same harm by relying concurrently on a variety of causes of action such as negligence, BSD, breach of contract etc.

4 See nos 13–15 and 18–21 below.

5 See no 18–21 below.

6 See no 33 below.

7 See nos 57–58 below.

8 DPLL, sec 8.

9 See fn 1.

10 DPLL, sec 8.

11 See, eg, the first draft of the later 1985 Directive published in [1976] OJ C241/19.

is the producer of the product, and (v) the defect can be attributed to the producer.

A. BODILY INJURY

07 'Bodily injury' is defined as 'death, illness, and mental, brain or body injury or disability'.[12] It is not quite clear where the severity of mental anguish and emotional distress renders it 'bodily injury', which is governed by the DPLL, as opposed to 'pure mental and emotional harm', which is not governed by DPLL and remedy, if any, has to be sought in the GLA.[13]

B. CAUSATION

08 While under the GLA the causal link that has to be established is usually the link between the defendant's tortious conduct (or breach of contract) and the plaintiff's harm, under the DPLL the required causal link is between the product's defect and the plaintiff's harm. As to the other link in the causal chain – the one between the defendant's conduct and the defect that caused the harm – this link, the attribution of the defect to the defendant, is governed by special provisions discussed below in the context of the defences.[14] As to the causal link between the defect and the plaintiff's harm, the DPLL provides no special rules in this regard, which means that the general rules of causation in tort law apply to liability under the DPLL.[15] These general rules[16] distinguish between factual causation and legal causation. Both kinds of causation have to be established.

C. PRODUCT

09 The DPLL does not define 'product' but provides that the term 'includes component of a product, the packing of a product, a product attached to immovable property, and a building'.[17] The DPLL does not apply to farm animals, poultry and fish, and other unprocessed agricultural produce.[18] For

12 DPLL, sec 1.

13 A first instance court ruled, eg, that a person who felt disgust when viewing foreign object in a can of smashed tomatoes is entitled to compensation under the DPLL of €100 – CivC 1805/07 (Ramla) *yitzkan v Zanlakol* (27.12.2007).

14 See nos 44–45 below.

15 DPLL, sec 8.

16 See nos 36–41 below.

17 DPLL, sec 1.

18 DPLL, sec 9(a).

this purpose, cleaning, sorting, de-greening, packing, storage and refrigeration are not considered 'processing'.[19]

10 It appears that the term 'product' in the DPLL refers to *physical* objects so that intellectual property is apparently excluded. Such exclusion may also be justified on the ground that intellectual property is governed by special laws, and because it can hardly cause *bodily injury*. As to digital content, it may well be considered a part of a physical product or of its components, if integrated into them, but is probably not considered as a product per se. It is unclear whether electricity and other forms of intangible energies are included in the definition of 'product'.[20]

11 The definition of 'product' in the DPLL explicitly includes movables attached to *land*, such as playground installations. In such cases the defendant would be the producer of the attached movable. Where a movable is attached to a *building*, it would be considered either as *part* of the building which is the final product, or as a *component* of the building. In the latter case both the builder and the producer of the once movable component would be the defendants.[21] Where a product is provided to a consumer as part of a *service* contract rather than as a part of a *sale* contract, the producer of the product may still be sued under the DPLL or the GLA. As to 'tailored' products which are produced according to specifications of customers, as long as these products are produced for commercial purposes the producer may be held liable under the DPLL and the GLA.

12 A proposed revision in the draft Civil Code of the definition of 'product' in the DPLL narrows the meaning of 'product' by stating, unlike the DPLL, that a product is a 'movable', namely a tangible object. Yet the definition of 'product' also explicitly extends it to a 'building'. Moreover, it adds two items to the DPLL list of what is considered a 'product': *raw materials* and *electricity and other forms of energy* which are marketed to consumers while in their premises.[22]

D. DEFECTIVENESS

13 The DPLL provides that a product is defective (i) when it is likely to cause personal injury owing to a defect therein, or (ii) when, in the circumstances of the

---

19 DPLL, sec 9(b).

20 Regarding the doubts whether DPLL applies to the production of electricity see CivC 3061/98 (Be'er va) *Naor v Amar*, para 28 (Nevo, 20.09.2001) (Nevo is a major legal data base provider).

21 For the joint liability of the producer of the final product and the producer of a defective component of the final product see fn 28.

22 Proposed Civil Code, sec 400.

case, warnings or instructions for handling and use are called for, for reasons of safety, and they have not been provided or are inadequate to the danger involved.[23]

There are two other provisions that bear on the meaning of defectiveness. One provision stresses that 'it shall be immaterial whether or not there was fault on the part of the manufacturer'.[24] The other provision is the *state-of-the-art* defence, which provides that it shall be a defence 'that in the state of scientific and technological development at the time the product left [the producer's] control, he could not have known that with regard to its design it did not meet reasonable safety standards'.[25]

14 Given the distinction between the three kinds of defects – in design, in manufacture (construction) and in providing instructions and warnings – it is not easy to figure out how the DPLL defines each kind of defect. Unfortunately, there is no clarifying case law which copes with this question. Analysis of the above statutory definition of 'defect', together with the two other relevant provisions (no fault required and the *state-of-the-art* defence) leads to the following conclusions.[26] The state-of-the-art defence implies that a product is defective in *design* where it fails to conform with the reasonable safety level. The no-fault provision implies that a product is defective in *manufacture* (construction) under the DPLL wherever it poses a risk of bodily injury. This definition seems to be too broad: does *any* risk of bodily injury render a product defective in manufacture?[27] Finally, a product is defective in *failure to provide adequate instructions and warnings* where the danger that it creates calls for such instructions and warnings. The exact nature of this kind of defect also remains unclear: when are warnings and directions called for? What makes them adequate?

15 All in all, the present definition of 'defect' in the DPLL, which applies to all products, is vague and unsatisfactory.[28]

---

23 DPLL, sec 3(a).

24 DPLL, sec 2.

25 DPLL, sec 4(2).

26 For discussion of 'defectiveness' in the DPLL see *I Gilead*, Strict Product Liability (1990) 8 Bar Illan L Rev 179 (in Hebrew).

27 A narrower interpretation of this provision builds on the word 'likely' in the definition. Arguably, as the definition of defect refers to the 'likelihood' that the product may cause bodily injury, it can be read as requiring *reasonable foreseeability* that the product may cause such injury. The problem, however, with this interpretation is that the reasonable foreseeability requirement is usually identified with negligence – fault-based liability – and therefore such interpretation cannot be reconciled with the statutory statement that liability is strict and not fault-based. If 'likelihood' does not mean reasonable foreseeability but other kind of foreseeability, then it unclear to which kind of foreseeability the definition allegedly refers to: foreseeability by whom and at which point in time?

28 On the 'unhelpfulness' of the Israeli (and the European) definitions of defects see *G Priest*, The Modern Irony of Civil Law: A Memoir of Strict Products Liability in the United States (1989) 9 Tel-Aviv Stud L 93, 119.

16 Given the deficiencies of the definition in the DPLL, the proposed Civil Code substantially revises the definition of 'defectiveness' in accordance with the above comments, and distinguishes between the three kinds of defects. It provides that: a product is defective in *manufacture* where the specific product differs from the planned product (prototype) in ways that generate unreasonable safety risk,[29] and that a product is defective in *design* where the design of the product, its shaping or its intended use generate unreasonable safety risk.[30] As to a defect in *instructions and warnings* the proposed Civil Code basically adheres to the present definition: such defect exists in the absence of adequate instructions and warning given the safety risk generated by the product.[31] However, the proposed revision extends the *state-of-the-art defence* and applies it not just to *design* defects, as does the DPLL, but also to *defects in instructions and warnings*.

17 It is important, after the presentation of the existing and the proposed definitions of the three kinds of 'defectiveness', to provide an overview of the liability regimes involved and their development.

18 The original purpose of the DPLL, as declared in the introduction to the 1978 bill, was to create a comprehensive regime of *strict* product liability for bodily injuries, as an addition to *fault-based* liability. But what exactly is the meaning of this change? After all, strict liability may take various forms that differ from each other and there is no general standard of strict liability.[32] The answer, in principle, is that while negligence concentrates on the unreasonableness of the defendant's *conduct*, on the defendant's *carelessness*, as a pre-condition to liability, strict product liability focuses instead on the *defectiveness* of the product as the pre-condition. This difference is clearly stated in the DPLL, which provides, as mentioned,[33] that 'it shall be immaterial whether or not there was fault on the part of the producer'.[34]

19 The essence of the difference between fault-based liability (carelessness) and strict liability (defectiveness) lies in the time dimension of the assessment. When assessing whether the producer was careless, only the information available to a reasonable producer *at the time of the relevant conduct* can be taken into account. In contrast, when assessing whether the product is defective, *post-*

29 Proposed Civil Code, sec 403(a)(1).

30 Ibid, sec 403(a)(2).

31 Ibid, sec 403(a)(3).

32 Strict liability for defective products, for example, differs from strict liability for road accidents or for workplace accidents. The only common feature of strict liability regimes is that liability is imposed for the *outcome* of the defendant's conduct rather than for the *nature* of the defendant's conduct.

33 See no 13 above.

34 DPLL, sec 2.

conduct information can be taken into account, such as unforeseeable risks of a product that materialised *ex post*, new technologies and materials that increase safety, new information about the manner and intensity in which products are used, and so on. Strict liability allows what fault-based liability prohibits – *the wisdom of hindsight.*

20 So the shift from carelessness to defectiveness broadens the basis of product liability whenever defectiveness can be recognised *despite* the absence of carelessness because of the different time dimensions of the assessments. Liability is strict when is imposed also on a producer that was *not* careless. Since there are three kinds of carelessness and defectiveness – in design, manufacture and warnings and instruction – the shift from fault-based liability (carelessness) to strict liability (defectiveness) should be examined with regard to each.

21 The DPLL, as mentioned, declares its intention to impose a regime of comprehensive strict liability, but actually it has done so only with regard to *manufacturing* defects and *inadequate instructions and warnings* defects. As to *design* defects, the *state-of-the-art* defence has actually undermined most of the intended shift to strict liability because it allows the defendant producer to escape liability if the defendant establishes that the defendant was not *careless* in design when the product left the defendant's control.[35] The addition of the state-of-the-art defence, which was absent from the 1978 Bill, was therefore a retreat from strict liability back to fault-based liability.[36] The proposed Civil Code, by applying the state-of-the-art defence not just to design defects but also to defects of inadequate instructions and warnings, makes another major retreat form strict liability (defectiveness) to fault-based liability (carelessness).[37]

E. PRODUCER

22 Under the DPLL the person liable for the bodily injury caused by a defective product is its 'producer'. The term 'producer' is defined by the DPLL

---

[35] The state-of-the-art defence has actually undermined *most* of the intended shift to strict liability in design defect, and not *all* of it, because under it the reasonableness of the defendant's design is assessed not at the time of the *design*, as it should under fault-based liability, but rather at the time in which the producer lost control over the product.

[36] Indeed, under the state-of-the-art defence it is the defendant who has to establish that he or she was not careless rather than the plaintiff having to establish the defendant's carelessness. Yet, despite this shift in the burden of proof from the plaintiff to the defendant, the liability regime is still fault-based. To impose liability the court has to determine that the defendant was careless.

[37] Despite the shift in the burden of proof (fn 36).

and that definition is discussed below.[38] In its core the term 'producer' refers to 'a person who is engaged, for commercial purposes, in the manufacture or assembly of products.'[39] The proposed Civil Code leaves this definition unchanged.

F. ATTRIBUTING THE DEFECT TO THE PRODUCER

23 A finding that the defect in the product which caused the plaintiff's harm can be attributed to the defendant producer is actually, as noted,[40] a requirement of *causation* as it links the plaintiff's harm not just with the defect but also with the defendant's conduct. Under the DPLL it is actually a *negative* requirement in the sense that the burden lies on the defendant to establish, through specified defences, that the defect or the risk should be attributed not the producer but rather to another factor. These defences, discussed below,[41] deny liability if the product becomes defective after it left the producer's control, or if the defective product left the producer's control against his or her will and despite reasonable measures to avoid such loss of control. Notably, the relevant point in time in these defences is the *loss of control* rather than the *putting the product into circulation*. Indeed, the producer may sometimes preserve control over a product *after* its circulation or lose control *before* its circulation.

G. ELEMENTS OF LIABILITY – THE GLA VENUE

24 Liability under various causes of action of the GLA[42] may be imposed for any harm caused by a product if the conditions of the relevant cause of action are met. To establish negligence, for example, the plaintiff has to establish that the defendant's negligent conduct caused the plaintiff's harm, thereby breaching the defendant's duty not to harm the plaintiff.[43] To establish BSD, the plaintiff has to establish that his or her harm was caused by a breach of a statutory duty aimed to protect him or her against such harm,[44] and to establish a contractual claim the plaintiff has to establish that his or her harm was caused by a breach of contract by the defendant.

---

[38] See nos 25–30 below.
[39] DPLL, sec 1.
[40] See no 08 above.
[41] See nos 44–45 below.
[42] See no 1 above.
[43] CWO (fn 1), secs 35–36.
[44] CWO, sec 63.

III. THE PERSON LIABLE FOR DAMAGE

A. UNDER THE DPLL

25 Under the DPLL the person liable for the bodily harm caused by a defective product is its 'producer'. The term 'producer' is defined by the DPLL as 'a person who is engaged, for commercial purposes, in the manufacture or assembly of products.'[45] It also includes a person who represents him- or herself as a producer, an importer for commercial purposes, and a supplier of a product whose local producer, or importer, is not identifiable.[46] The proposed Civil Code leaves this definition unchanged.

26 As stated in the above definition, a person is considered 'a producer' only if the production of products is made for *commercial purposes*. The meaning and the scope of this limiting requirement have not been discussed by case law. That the producer is a public authority or owned or run by a public authority would not shield the public authority from liability if production is for commercial purposes.

27 Since under the statutory definition of 'product' the term also includes a *component* of the final product and it *packing*, it is evident that the manufacturer of a component or of a package is also liable under the DPLL as a 'producer' for a defect in the component or in the package that caused bodily harm.

28 When a producer of a component of a product or of its package is liable for injury caused by it, is the producer of the *final product* liable as well? The DPLL distinguishes in this regard between component and package. When the injury is caused by a defective *component*, the producer of the final product is liable with the producer of the component. No such provision of shared liability exists with regard to a defective package.[47]

29 When multiple defendants are liable to the plaintiff for the same harm, their liability, according to the general law of tort, would be *joint and several*, each responsible vis-à-vis the plaintiff for the whole harm. Their respective shares *inter se* are determined mainly by their comparative fault and their comparative causal contribution to the plaintiff's harm. When liability is strict, so that the comparative fault criterion is inapplicable, the relative shares would be determined by considerations of fairness and deterrence.[48] These rules apply

---

45 DPLL, sec 1.

46 Yet the supplier would be exempted from liability if it provides to the injured person details regarding the identity and address of the manufacture, the importer or of the previous supplier – DPLL, sec 2(c).

47 DPLL, sec 2(b).

48 CWO, sec 84.

to multiple liabilities under the DPLL. When, for example, the producers of a defective component and of the final product are both liable to the plaintiff,[49] their liability vis-à-vis the plaintiff would be joint and several with mutual rights of contribution from each other.

B. UNDER THE GLA

1) Negligence

30 Where a product causes harm to the plaintiff (bodily injury, damage to property or stand-alone economic or emotional harm), *any* person whose negligent conduct caused this harm (the defendant) may be held liable to the plaintiff in negligence if such negligent conduct breached the defendant's duty to the plaintiff. That person may be the producer of the final product or of a defective component or of the package or distributor, wholesaler, and another person who is or was in possession of the product.

2) Other Causes of Actions

31 The other *GLA* causes of action are: the tort of BSD where the defendant breached a statutory duty which intended to protect the plaintiff from a risk of a product that actually materialised; any other tort committed by the defendant with regard to the damage caused to the plaintiff by the product; contractual liability to the extent that the plaintiff's product-related harm was caused by a breach of the defendant's contract with the plaintiff. All claims under GLA may concur, and any such claim may concur with a DPLL claim in cases of bodily injury.

IV. THE AGGRIEVED PERSON AND DAMAGE

A. UNDER THE DPLL

32 Under the DPLL any person who suffered bodily injury caused by a defect in a product produced for commercial purposes may sue 'the producer' as defined.[50] 'Bodily injury', as noted, is 'death, illness, and mental, brain or body injury or disability', and it is yet unclear when the severity of mental anguish and emotional distress renders it 'bodily injury', which is governed by the DPLL.[51]

---

49 See nos 28–29 above.
50 See no 22 above.
51 See no 7 above.

33 The DPLL sets limits on the defendant's liability to the plaintiff, limits that do not apply to 'usual' tort claims. The limits are not only *per person* (as opposed to limits per *product* or per *event*) but also per *heads of damages*. One limit is a ceiling on the award for *lost earnings*. The maximum award cannot exceed the triple of the national wage average which is equivalent to about €2,000 per month.[52] For example, a person who earned €5,000 per month and due the bodily injury caused by the defect lost 25% of his or her earning capacity is entitled to an award for lost income of €500 (2,000 × 25%) rather than an award of €1,250 (5,000 × 25%). Another limit on the personal award for lost earnings is *tax deduction*. Unlike the general rule, which does not allow deduction of tax from tort awards for lost earnings, the DPLL allows such deduction up to 25% of the capped income (€2,000). Another limit in the form of a cap is imposed on awards for non-pecuniary loss (pain and suffering, loss of life expectancy). Such personal award may not exceed the ceiling, which is equivalent to about €50,000.

34 Notably, these personal limits on liability are hardly effective because, as mentioned, causes of action under the DPLL on the one hand and GLA on the other hand concur.[53] A plaintiff who is subject to these limits is incentivised, therefore, to sue in negligence or BSD or in breach of contract in order to circumvent these limits (and the shorter limitation period)[54] that do not exist in the GLA venue. This tendency to avoid the limits in the DPLL on lost earnings and non-pecuniary loss by resorting to the unlimited alternatives of GLA, mainly negligence, is one explanation for the scarcity of DPLL claims.[55] The case is quite different with regard to similar personal limits on compensation under no-fault liability regime governing, since 1976, bodily injury caused by *road accidents*.[56] As this no-fault liability regime is the *only venue* for claims for bodily injury caused by vehicles,[57] the statutory limits on lost income and non-pecuniary loss are very effective and very often applied.

B. UNDER THE GLA

35 Under the GLA there are no special product liability related limits either on the identity of the aggrieved person or on the kind of compensable harms. There are, however, limits on the scope of defendants that can be sued, plaintiffs that can sue, and harms that may be compensated for, in accordance with the general rules that govern each GLA cause of action. Under negligence law, for example,

52 DPLL, sec 5(a).
53 See no 1 above.
54 See nos 57–58 below.
55 See nos 71–72 below.
56 Road Accident Victim Compensation Law 1975, sec 4.
57 Ibid, sec 8(a).

the aggrieved person may sue not only for property damage and damage to the product itself, but also for pure economic loss and stand-alone emotional loss, as well as for consequential losses, but that depends on whether the case falls into the domain of the general rules of negligence law that allow for such liability.

V. CAUSALITY

A. CAUSALITY: DPLL AND GLA

36 The difference between fault-based liability under the GLA and strict liability under the DPLL bears on the ingredients of the causality requirement. Under the GLA the causal link that has to be established in tort is usually the link between the defendant's *tortious conduct* and the plaintiff's harm.[58] It has to be established, for example, that the defendant's negligent conduct, or the defendant's breach of statutory duty, caused the plaintiff's harm. Under the DPLL, the causal chain is divided.[59] It has to be established, firstly, that *the defect in the product caused the plaintiff's harm*, and, secondly, that the *defect in the product can be attributed in terms of causation to the defendant*. The latter causal requirement that links the plaintiff's harm not just with the defect but also with the defendant's conduct, is regulated by defences that shift to the defendant the burden to establish that the defect should not be causally attributed to the defendant.[60]

37 As to the causal link under the GLA between the defendant's *conduct* and the plaintiff's harm, and the causal link under DPLL between the *defect* in the product and the plaintiff's harm, there are no special rules of causation which relate to product liability. In both venues factual causation and legal causation of the plaintiff's harm have to be established.

38 It is worth reiterating that the causal link under DPLL is to the plaintiff's *bodily injury*, while the causal link under GLA is to *any recoverable harm* of the plaintiff.

B. FACTUAL CAUSATION

39 The major rule of factual causation (cause-in-fact) is the *but-for* test. According to this test it should be established that the plaintiff's harm would not

---

58 And if the claim is contractual it should be established that the breach of the contract caused the plaintiff's harm.

59 See no 8 above.

60 See nos 44–45 above.

have occurred but for the defendant's tortious conduct (under the GLA) or but for the defect in the product (under DPLL). The defendant's tortious conduct, or the defect in the product, respectively, must be a necessary link in the chain of causation that leads to the plaintiff's harm.

40 Usually it is the plaintiff who has to establish that factual causation is more probable than not (at least 51%), or, if the burden of proof is shifted to the defendant, it has to be established that factual causation is as probable as not (50%). Between the years 2005–2010 the Supreme Court allowed proportional liability, namely liability adjusted to the probability of factual causation where such probability is below 51%,[61] but since 2010 such proportional liability is restricted to medical malpractice cases of *lost chances of healing*. Whether such proportional liability would be allowed in cases of defective drugs or medical products is an open question.

41 Where the tortious conduct of another, a third person, is also a but-for cause of the plaintiff's harm, usually the defendant and the third party would be held liable to the plaintiff jointly and severally. Where the plaintiff's negligent conduct, which amounts to contributory negligence,[62] is also a but-for cause of the plaintiff's harm, the award to the plaintif would be reduced in accordance with his or her relative fault (under GLA) or in accordance with considerations of justice and deterrence (under DPLL).[63] Where the harm caused by the defendant is later 'overtaken' (swallowed) by harm inflicted by another liable person, the defendant, who ceases to be a but-for cause of the plaintiff's harm, would be exempted from liability under present law[64] but not under the proposed Civil Code.[65]

C. LEGAL CAUSATION

42 As to the required *legal* causal link ('proximate cause' or' remoteness') between the defendant's tortious conduct and the plaintiff's harm (under GLA), or between the product's defect and the plaintiff's harm (under the DPLL), the governing rule is now the *tortious risk test*. According to this test, the plaintiff has to establish that the plaintiff's harm materialised from a risk that contributed, respectively, to the tortious nature of the defendant's conduct, or to the defectiveness of the product. If, for example, the product is defective because of the foreseeable risk X, and the risk that actually materialised was not risk X

---

61 Or below 50% is the burden of proof is shifted to the defendant.

62 See nos 47 and 52 below.

63 See no 29 above.

64 *Hananshvili v Rotem Ins Co* (1991) 45(ii) Piskey Din (PD) 529.

65 Proposed Civil Code, sec 365(b).

but rather unforeseeable risk Y, the court will rule that the defect was not the *legal* cause of the plaintiff's harm, although it was a factual cause.[66]

VI. DEFENCES AND EXCLUSIONS

A. UNDER THE DPLL

1) *The State-of-the-Art (Development Risk) Defence*

43 The DPLL provides that it shall be a defence 'that in the state of scientific and technological development at the time the product left [the producer's] control, he could not have known that with regard to its design it did not meet reasonable safety standards'.[67] As already mentioned in the contexts of 'defectiveness'[68] and the nature of liability regimes,[69] this defence, which applies to *design* defects, has actually undermined most of the intended shift to strict liability for design defects because it allows the defendant producer to escape liability by establishing that the defendant was not careless in design when the product left his or her control. It is a retreat from strict liability for design defects back to fault-based liability – from *defectiveness* to *carelessness*. The proposed Civil Code extends this defence by applying it also to *inadequate warnings and instructions* defect.[70]

2) *Defect Created after the Product Left the Defendant's Control*

44 To establish causality under the DPLL it should be established not only that the defect in the product caused the plaintiff's harm but also that the defect can be attributed to the producer (the defendant).[71] The DPLL in this regard sets up two contrasting assumptions. The first assumption is that a defect in the product should be attributed to its producer unless the defendant can establish, as a defence, '[t]hat the defect arose after the product left the producer's control'.[72] The second assumption, embodied in the defense, which 'offsets' the first assumption, is that if 'the producer proves that the particular product underwent reasonable safety checks before leaving his control, the defect will be presumed to have arisen subsequently'. The second, offsetting, presumption, however, has

---

66 CivAp 4394/09 *Landerman v Sagiv* (30.12.2010).
67 DPLL, sec 4(a)(2).
68 See nos 13–14 above.
69 See nos 17–21 above.
70 See no 16 above.
71 See nos 8 and 36 above.
72 DPLL, sec 4(a)(1). The defence would apply, for example, if it is established that the defect in a food product was caused by the conditions in which it was transported by the distributor.

been construed narrowly. It was held that this presumption arises only where the *particular* product was checked. *Sample* tests, even if technologically and economically reasonable, would not suffice to rebut the first presumption – that the defect should be attributed to the defendant.[73]

The term 'control' in the defence is not defined. It can be interpreted as physical possession of the product but also as ability to control the defectiveness of the product while in the possession of others.[74] As mentioned, the meaning of 'losing control' differs from the meaning of 'putting a product into circulation' – a producer may sometimes preserve control over a product after its circulation or lose control before its circulation.[75]

3) *Product Left the Producer's Control against his or her Will*

45 Another defence of a causal nature denies liability if it is established 'that the manufacturer had not intended the product to leave his control and that he took reasonable steps to prevent this and to warn relevant sections of the public of the risk involved'.[76] The burden to prove the absence of carelessness in preventing theft or loss of a defective product lies on the defendant. The defence is causal in the sense that if established the law attributes the *risk* of the defect not to the defendant but rather to the person or event leading to the forced loss of control.

4) *Assumption of Risk*

46 The defence of assumption of risk (*volenti non fit injuria*) is a general defence in tort law[77] that was incorporated into the DPLL and adapted to its context. It provides that the producer would not be held liable if he or she establishes 'that the injured person knew about the defect and the ensuing risk and willingly exposed himself to that risk'.[78] To the extent that this specific defence would be interpreted like the corresponding general tort defence, it would very rarely, if at all, absolve a producer (the defendant) from liability. The reason for the limited scope of the general tort defence is that, in order to apply, all the following conditions must be met: the injured person (the plaintiff) was subjectively fully aware of the risk and its implications; the exposure to the risk was an autonomous decision not taken under pressure, including that of

---

73 CivAp 166/88 *Fenitzya Ltd v Amar* 45(ii) PD 457, 465 (1991). The producer of the final product (drink bottle) and the producer of a component (the bottle) were held both liable for harm caused by the bottle's explosion. For application of the *Fenitzya* rule in a case of a broken honey jar see *Sigal v Yad Mordechay* (31.05.2004).

74 See, eg, *Isralift (services) 1973 v Hindly* (1995) 49(i) PD 45.

75 See no 23 above.

76 DPLL, sec 4(a)(3).

77 CWO, sec 5.

78 DPLL, sec 4(a)(4).

economic distress or moral obligation; the plaintiff exposed himself or herself willingly not just to the *physical* risk of injury but also to the *legal* risk, namely, he or she actually waived his or her right to sue the defendant for the defendant's tortious conduct.[79]

5) Contributory Negligence

47 Another general defence that was incorporated into the DPLL and adapted to its context is the contributory (comparative) negligence defence.[80] Unlike the corresponding general defence, which reduces the award of damages in accordance with the relative fault of the parties, the specific defence in the DPLL allows such reduction only where the injured party (the plaintiff) was *grossly* negligent.[81] *Simple* contributory negligence on the plaintiff's part would not trigger the DPLL defence. In deciding how much to deduct, courts should consider the plaintiff's degree of negligence.

6) Children under the Age of 12

48 The special defences of assumption of risk and contributory negligence are inapplicable with regard to children under the age of 12.[82]

7) Compliance with Standards

49 No explicit special defence is provided for a defect that is due to product compliance with *mandatory* regulations issued by public authorities. As to compliance with other standards, such as industry or voluntary standards, such compliance (or non-compliance) may serve as a relevant consideration, although not a conclusive one, when deciding whether a product was safety in design, namely, whether it met reasonable safety standards.[83]

8) Contractual Exclusions

50 As the DPLL applies only to *bodily injury*, it does not allow, in accordance with the general law of contracts, contractual exclusion of tort liability for bodily injury. Such exclusion conflicts with 'public policy'. It therefore provides that 'a stipulation limiting the manufacturer's liability under this law is void'.[84] The last

---

79 The application of the defense in the product liability context was denied in the Supreme Court's decision in CivAp 6230/14 *Aslan Marketing v Polistres* (16.11.2014).

80 CWO, sec 68.

81 DPLL, sec 4(b).

82 DPLL, sec 4(c).

83 See no 13 above.

84 DPLL, sec 7.

part of this provision, however, protects the right of the manufacturer to obtain indemnity from another who did not come into possession of the product for personal, family or household purposes.

B. UNDER THE GLA

51 In claims made under the GLA, usually claims for negligence or for breach of statutory duty (BSD), the applicable defences are the general defences of tort law.[85] The following is a comparison of the specific defences of the DPLL[86] with the general defences of tort law which apply to negligence and BSD claims.

52 The *state-of-the-art* (development risk) defence is irrelevant to negligence and BSD claims because its aim is to re-establish fault-based liability for a design defect, while liability in negligence and BSD is basically fault-based at the outset.[87]

The causal defences in the DPLL, namely that *the defect was created after the product left the defendant's control*,[88] or that the *product left the producer's control against his or her will*,[89] although not recognised as statutory defences, may well deny liability, on causal grounds, if established. *Assumption of risk* and *contributory negligence* are general, statutory defences that apply to all torts. The latter defence, as mentioned, can be triggered by simple negligence and does not require *gross* negligence as does the corresponding defence in the DPLL.[90] The assumption of risk defence cannot be raised against a child under the age of 12,[91] and the contributory negligence defence is also restricted when raised against such child.[92] *Contractual exclusions* may be effective with regard to harm to property, pure economic loss or stand-alone emotional loss.[93]

VII. REMEDIES

53 The general law of tort remedies applies to DPLL and GLA claims for harms caused by defective products. The available remedies are of three kinds. The major remedy is *compensatory damages* which are governed by the *restitutio in*

85 Or contractual defences if the claim is contractual.
86 See nos 43–50 above.
87 Although BSD may accommodate strict liability, this is hardly ever the case.
88 See no 44 above.
89 See no 45 above.
90 See no 47 above.
91 CWO, sec 5(c).
92 CWO, sec 64(3).
93 But not with regard to bodily injury – see no 50 above.

integrum principle – their aim is to restore the plaintiff to the position in which he or she would have been but for the harm caused by the defendant's tortious conduct. The second kind of remedy is non-compensatory damages – punitive or nominal. *Punitive damages* are awarded only in those rare cases in which the defendant inflicts harm maliciously or intentionally. There is no record of such award in product liability cases. *Nominal damages* are hardly ever awarded. The third kind of remedy is the *injunction,* which may be either prohibitory (prohibiting tortious conduct) or mandatory (ordering the defendant to perform an act).[94] The injunction, which is basically a discretionary remedy, may order the defendant to withdraw defective products from the market. As to *restoration in kind*, no record was found regarding such order.

VIII. PROCEDURAL AND EVIDENTIAL ISSUES

A. BURDEN OF PROOF

1) *General Overview*

54 Usually the burden of proof lies on the person who makes a claim: the plaintiff has to establish the elements of the defendant's alleged liability while the defendant has to establish the elements of an alleged defence. The standard of proof is *preponderance of evidence*, namely the claim made by the party has to be found more probable than not (probability above 50%). Where probabilities regarding a disputed claim are even (50:50), the court decides against the party who bears the burden of proof. The burden of proof may be shifted from the party who makes the claim to the other party by statutory or judicial presumptions.

2) *Under the DPLL*

55 Under the DPLL the burden to prove that a product is *defective* lies upon the plaintiff. If the circumstances of the case, however, indicate that it is more probable than not that the product was defective, the burden to deny defectiveness is shifted to the defendant.[95] The burden to prove that the defect caused the plaintiff's bodily injury lies upon the plaintiff. In contrast, the burden regarding the causal link between the defect and the defendant lies upon the defendant – it is the defendant who has to establish that the defect or the risk of the defect should not be attributed to him or her but rather to another causal factor.[96]

---

94 CWO, secs 71 and 76.

95 DPLL, sec 3(b). For such shift of the burden of proof see CivAp 6230/14 *Aslan Marketing v Polistres* (16.11.2014).

96 See nos 08 and 36 above.

3) *Under the GLA*

56 In claims based on negligence, BSD or breach of contract, the burden to establish the elements of liability for each cause of action lies upon the plaintiff. In a claim in negligence, however, the major cause of action under the GLA, the burden of proof as to whether the defendant was negligent in the production of the product or otherwise may be shifted from the plaintiff to the defendant by the evidentiary statutory rule of *res ipsa loquiter* (the matter speaks for itself).[97] To shift the burden the plaintiff has to establish that: (i) relevant facts regarding the defendant's conduct cannot be ascertained; (ii) the harming product was under the defendant's full control; and (iii) in such kind of cases it is more probable than not that the harm was caused by the defendant's negligent conduct.[98] Another evidentiary (judicial) rule, that may shift the burden of proof in tort cases from the plaintiff to the defendant with regard to the tortious nature of the defendant's conduct and/or the causal link between this conduct and the plaintiff's harm, is the *evidential harm* rule. Where the plaintiff establishes that the defendant's fault negatively affected the plaintiff's evidential ability to prove a relevant factual claim, the burden is shifted to the defendant with regard to this factual claim.

B. TIME LIMITS

57 The general law of limitation of civil actions prescribes a limitation period of *seven* years which starts to run from the day the cause of action accrued.[99] The running of the limitation period may be suspended or interrupted, or the period may be extended, where the plaintiff establishes the statutory cause required for such suspension, interruption or extension. The most important rule in this regard is the *discovery rule* which suspends the running of the limitation period until the relevant facts regarding the alleged cause of action become reasonably discoverable.[100]

58 The general law of limitation apply to the GLA venue, namely product liability claims based on negligence, BSD, other torts and breach of contract. Special provisions apply to the special product liability regime under the DPLL.

---

97 CWO, sec 41.

98 It is still unclear whether the provision in sec 38 of the CWO regarding dangerous things applies to product defect and to what extent. Under this provision if the damage is caused by a *dangerous thing* controlled by the defendant the burden is shifted to the defendant to establish that the plaintiff's harm was not caused by the defendant's negligent conduct.

99 Limitation Law 1958. Some provisions regarding limitation in tort law, which the proposed Civil Code abolishes, are embodied in the sec 89 of the CWO.

100 Limitation Law 1958, sec 8.

The DPLL provides a *shorter* limitation period of *three* years (rather than seven) and further provides that no claim under this law shall be filed after *ten* years have elapsed since the product left the producer's control.[101] Otherwise the other general rules of limitation law, such as rules of suspension, interruption, apply to the DPLL. The difference in the limitation periods between the DPLL (three years) and GLA (seven years) channels claims to GLA claims where DPLL claims are time-barred.[102]

C. SPECIAL PROCEDURAL ARRANGEMENTS

59 Other than the rules discussed above, no special procedural rules apply to product liability claims made under the DPLL or the GLA. Notably, the law governing *representative actions* does not apply to product liability claims either under the DPLL or under the GLA, but it does apply to claims under the Consumer Protection Act, 1981, which are based on misrepresentation and failure to disclose information about products. Recently some attempts were made to file representative claims for harms caused by undisclosed product defects under the Consumer Protection Law.[103]

IX. ALTERNATIVE REGULATIONS AND REMEDIES

60 Product liability law in Israel, as explained at the outset of this chapter,[104] is composed of two sets of rules – two venues of liability. One venue is the special liability regime under the DPLL which applies only to cases of bodily injury. The other venue is the various causes of actions under the GLA, mainly negligence, BSD and breach of contract, which provide alternatives to the DPLL in cases of bodily injury and causes of action for all other harms caused by defective products.

61 As to alternative *remedies*, there are collateral sources of harm repair to which the plaintiff may apply with regard to product related harms. The major collateral sources of bodily injury repair are the Social Security Institution, health maintenance organisations, other statutory benefits providers, pension

---

101 DPLL, sec 6.

102 See eg CivC 7375/01 (Petach Tikva) *Shtivi v Tadiran batteries* (09.12.2003) – the plaintiff suffered a burn as a result of leakage of electrolyte fluid from a battery.

103 Over the last five years, applications to approve representative claims for violating the Consumer Protection Law were made with regard to allegedly defective food, drugs, silicon breast implants, medical eye bandage and baby carriers. Such claims are either pending, or withdrawn from or compromised.

104 See, eg, CivAp 10890/01 (Haifa) *Wytzner v Hasan* (12.08.2001).

funds and private insurance. Product-related harms other than bodily injury may be repaired by private insurance. The effect of such collateral sources of repair on the entitlements of plaintiffs, the liabilities of defendants, and the entitlements of the providers of these collateral benefits vis-à-vis defendants (eg reimbursement), are diversified and complex. Anyway, no special rules apply to product liability claims in this regard.

X. ASSESSMENT OF DOMESTIC LAW

A. NUMBER OF PRODUCT LIABILITY CLAIMS

62 Thirty-five years after the enactment of the DPLL the overall number of adjudicated cases that can be classified as 'product liability cases', either under the DPLL or the GLA, is small – a few dozens. Moreover, the overwhelming majority of these cases were adjudicated in trial courts, which means that court decisions are not binding. As to the binding authority, the Supreme Court, there are actually only two major guiding decisions in this regard, one dealing with the DPLL[105] and the other with negligence liability.[106] Otherwise there are basically only incidental references of the Justices to product liability law.[107] The following reasons may account for the scarcity of product liability adjudication.

63 To start with, a major potential source of product liability litigation – car accidents – is regulated either by no-fault liability arrangement for *bodily injury* which excludes all other sources of tort liability for defects in cars, or by insurance arrangements that render product liability claims for *property damage* unnecessary.

64 Secondly, quite often the 'suspected' product is integrated into a broader activity and it is easier for the harmed person to sue the actor rather than the producer. Prominent examples are harms suffered in the course of medical treatment or at the workplace. It is often easier for the harmed person to sue the physician or the employer rather than to sue the producer of the medical equipment or of the industrial machine.[108] The same applies to products which

---

[105] *Fenitzya v Amar* (fn 73) – bodily injury caused by exploding bottle case.

[106] CivAp 532/89 *Kibutz Nir David v Shukrun* (1992) 46 Piskey Din 221 – bodily injury caused by a defective lawnmower.

[107] See eg CivAp 7895/08 *Klina engineering v Yasin* (31.08.2011) paras 30–33.

[108] Although the sued actor can in principle sue the producer of the suspected product for contribution through third-party proceedings, the incentives to do so may be weak either because the actor is insured, or because such claim is complex and expensive. Moreover, an actor sued for bodily injury who seeks contribution from the producer of the suspected cannot rely on the DPLL because his or her loss is economic and not bodily injury – see CivC 1147/90 (Tel Aviv) *Adamov v Polaris Radiator Producers (1982)*, para 43 (Nevo, 17.12.1996).

are supplied in the course of and as part of a provision of a service. The tendency is to sue the service provider rather than the producer, especially where it is difficult to establish what was the actual cause of the harm – the defect in the product or the way it was handled or installed.[109]

65 Thirdly, it may be very complex and expensive to establish that a product is defective or was produced in a negligent manner. To establish a *design* defect the plaintiff has to provide evidence indicating that an alternative design would have been safer without substantially derogating from the usefulness of the product (cost-benefit analysis). To establish a *manufacturing* defect the plaintiff has to show that something was wrong with the quality control over the production process. These issues may involve complex questions requiring expert opinions.

66 Fourthly, Israel is a small country, and many products that may cause harm are *imported* products. It is often most complex and expensive to sue a producer abroad, and it is not always clear whether Israeli law applies to producers abroad.[110] Although the DPLL allows claims against *importers* of products, such claims may also be complex and not always fruitful (insolvent importers).

67 Finally, as to contractual claims, on the one hand such claims may often be unavailable in the absence of privity between the harmed person and the producer. On the other hand the law of sales may frequently provide a more attractive alternative than product liability law.

B. 'LABOUR DIVISION' BETWEEN THE TWO VENUES OF PRODUCT LIABILITY LAW

68 As the stricter liability regime under DPLL is limited to bodily injuries, product liability claims for other kind of harms are channelled to the GLA venue in general and to the tort of negligence in particular. But even claims for bodily injury are often based not just on the DPLL,[111] but also on negligence law.[112] Moreover, liability in these bifurcated claims is sometimes imposed in negligence, leaving aside the DPLL alternative claim.

---

109 See eg CivC 1233/00 *Taman v Amos* (01.07.2003) – allegedly leaking hot water boiler causing property harm to apartment (claim dismissed).

110 The difficulties of applying Israel's product liability on producers abroad is discussed in CivAp 1471/02 (Tel Aviv) *Metallurgique de Gerzat SA v Vilenski*, para 3 (16.02.2013).

111 See eg CivC 3037/03 (Ako) *Gentos v Willy Food Int* (25.07.2004) – stomach aches caused by contaminated can of tuna fish.

112 CivC 198940/02 (Tel Aviv) *Givaaty v David Shoes* (02.06.2005) the plaintiff fell and was injured due to defective shoe hill; CivC 88137/99 (Tel Aviv) *Oz v Pacific Car Importers* (Nevo), 29.03.2004 – plaintiff injured by defective industrial fan.

69 The reasons behind this adherence to negligence law may be diverse. Caps in the DPLL on awards for lost earnings and non-pecuniary loss obviously render this venue less attractive.[113] Ability to circumvent the shorter limitation periods under the DPLL is another explanation.[114] A different kind of explanation is that the parties and the courts feel more comfortable in the traditional domain of negligence law than in the relatively new territory of strict product liability. It should also be borne in mind that liability for *design* defects under the DPLL is actually fault-based and not strict, and therefore not really wider than liability for design defects under negligence law.[115] The complexity of the notion of 'defectiveness'[116] sometimes makes it easier to establish the defendant's negligent conduct than to establish the product defectiveness. The powerful assumptions of negligence law, which shift the burden to the defendant to prove that the injury was not caused by the defendant's negligent conduct,[117] provide another explanation for the viability of negligence law where 'competing' with the DPLL.

C. NEW TECHNOLOGIES

70 Can current product liability law cope with the challenges posed by new technologies? To answer this question one should distinguish between the different venues of liability – the GLA on the one hand and the DPLL or the other hand – and their different liability regimes.

71 Obviously, the major causes of actions of the GLA venue – negligence, BSD and breach of contract – are inherently adaptable to new technologies. Negligence law requires reasonable conduct in the design of a product and in its construction and marketing. The concretisation of this general requirement takes place on a case-by-case basis and can therefore be adapted to technological developments. The statutory duties that which generate tort liability through the tort of BSD can also be adjusted to new technologies, although the process of adapting legislation is much slower. Contractual obligations are also adaptable to changes.

72 A change that may be needed in the GLA venue, mostly in negligence, is to ease the burden of proof that in principle lies upon the plaintiff. New technologies are very complex, and it may be impossible or prohibitively expensive for the plaintiff to prove that his or her harm was indeed caused by the

---

113 See no 33 above.
114 See nos 57–58 above.
115 See no 21 above.
116 See nos 13–14 and 17–21 above.
117 See no 56 above.

defendant's product-related negligence. Although present law already embraces powerful presumptions, favourable to plaintiffs, that shift the burden of proof to the defendant,[118] it may be advisable to extend the scope and the effectiveness of these presumptions in order to cope with the challenge of liability for new technologies.

73 As the major difference between GLA and the DPLL is that the latter imposes strict liability for bodily injury caused by manufacturing defects and by lack of adequate warnings and instructions, the question is whether this regime of strict liability suits new technologies. The answer depends on the aims of this law. Is the major aim of product liability law to increase safety through the deterring effect of liability? To secure compensation for harms? To do justice? To promote efficiency? The declared aim of the DPLL, expressed in the introduction to the 1978 Bill, was to strike the right balance between the need to repair bodily injuries (compensation) on the one hand, and concerns that too heavy liability may hamper desirable production (over-deterrence) on the other hand. In retrospect, a regime of strict liability restricted to *manufacturing* defects seems to strike the right balance between the goals.[119] As with negligence law[120] it may be required, however, to extend the scope and the effectiveness of the presumptions that shift to the producers the burden to deny the existence of a manufacturing defect.

74 Finally, some statutory revisions may be required to extend the scope of the term 'product' to include new technologies which are not tangible or not part or component of a tangible product.[121] For example, 'product' may be defined as including the *electronic operating systems* of the product whether inside or outside the product (cloud).

118 See no 56 above.
119 For the proposed revision of the PDLL – applying fault-based liability where the defect is the absence of adequate warnings and instructions see no 21 above.
120 See no 75 above.
121 See nos 09–12 above.

PRODUCT LIABILITY IN SOUTH AFRICA

Johann Neethling

I. SOURCES OF LAW AND THEIR EVOLUTION

01 A distinction should be made, firstly between contractual and delictual product liability, and secondly, within these two areas, between common law and statutory product liability.[1]

---

1 See as to delictual liability *M Loubser/E Reid*, Product Liability in South Africa (2012) 38 f, 56 f; *J Neethling/JM Potgieter*, Neethling-Potgieter-Visser Law of Delict (7th edn 2015) 335 f, 399–400; *M Loubser/R Midgley* (eds), The Law of Delict in South Africa (2nd edn 2012) 247 f; *PQR Boberg*, The Law of Delict: Vol I Aquilian Liability (1984) 193 f; *JC van der Walt/JR Midgley*, Principles of Delict (3rd edn 2005) 103–104. See as to contractual liability *Loubser/Reid* 23 f.

A. DELICTUAL LIABILITY

02 Under the common law, product liability *ex delicto* is clear. The courts deal with product liability under the Aquilian action.[2] Its ordinary requirements must thus be satisfied. Accordingly, all the elements of a delict, that is conduct, wrongfulness, fault, causation and damage, must be present for delictual liability to ensue.[3] As the law on product liability is still in its infancy, much can be learned from comparative law in developing this field,[4] an approach that can be discerned in case law.[5] Be that as it may, the common law on product liability was independently developed by the courts. In light of the difficulty to prove fault on the part of the manufacturer, as well as for various other reasons, it was advocated that product liability should be strict, that is, fault should not be required for liability.[6] The willingness of the Supreme Court of Appeal to investigate this matter[7] was tested in *Wagener and Cuttings v Pharmacare Ltd*.[8] After thorough consideration, the court was not prepared to recognise strict product liability in principle and thus to become involved 'in the function of trying to "legislate" judicially in this complex field'.[9] The plaintiff's remedy was therefore limited to

---

2 See eg *Freddy Hirsch Group (Pty) Ltd v Chickenland (Pty) Ltd* 2011 4 SA 276 (SCA); *Wagener and Cuttings v Pharmacare Ltd* 2003 4 SA 285 (SCA) 300; *Ciba-Geigy (Pty) Ltd v Lushof Farms (Pty) Ltd* 2002 2 SA 447 (SCA) 470–471; *Bayer South Africa (Pty) Ltd v Viljoen* 1990 2 SA 647 (A); *A Gibb and Son (Pty) Ltd v Taylor and Mitchell Timber Supply Co (Pty) Ltd* 1975 2 SA 457 (W); cf also *Combrinck Chiropraktiese Kliniek (Edms) Bpk v Datsun Motor Vehicle Distributors (Pty) Ltd* 1972 4 SA 185 (T); *Lennon Ltd v BSA Company* 1914 AD 1; *Cooper and Nephews v Visser* 1920 AD 111. In *Herschel v Mrupe* 1954 3 SA 464 (A) 486–487 the court stated: 'By putting into circulation potentially harmful things in that manner the manufacturer is not merely exercising a legal right but is encroaching upon the rights of others not to be exposed, when going about their lawful occasions and when accepting the implied general invitation to acquire and use such commodities, to danger without warning and without their having a reasonable opportunity to become aware of such danger before use. In other words, it is an encroachment upon the rights of others to set hidden snares for them in the exercise of their own rights.' See also *J Neethling/JM Potgieter*, The continued importance of common law product liability *ex delicto* [2014] Journal of Contemporary Roman-Dutch Law (THRHR) 502 f; *MM Botha/EP Joubert*, Does the Consumer Protection Act 68 of 2008 provide for strict product liability? A comparative analysis [2012] THRHR 308-311.

3 See *Neethling/Potgieter* (fn 1) 4, 335–336; *Freddy Hirsch Group (Pty) Ltd v Chickenland (Pty) Ltd* 2011 4 SA 276 (SCA) 293; *Loubser/Reid* (fn 1) 39–40.

4 See eg *FJ de Jager*, Die deliktuele aanspreeklikheid van die vervaardiger teenoor die verbruiker vir skade veroorsaak deur middel van 'n defekte produk (1977); *CJ Hartzenberg*, Die opkoms can die risikobeginsel op die gebied van deliktuele vervaardigersaanspreeklikheid (1979); *JC van der Walt*, Die deliktuele aanspreeklikheid van die vervaardiger vir skade berokken deur middel van sy defekte produkt, [1972] THRHR 224 f; *Botha/Joubert* (fn 2) 314 f.

5 See *A Gibb and Son (Pty) Ltd v Taylor and Mitchell Timber Supply Co (Pty) Ltd* 1975 2 SA 457 (W) 461–464.

6 See *Loubser/Reid* (fn 1) 3–5; *Neethling/Potgieter* (fn 1) 339; *DJ McQuoid-Mason*, Consumer Law in South Africa (1997) 108–110; *Botha/Joubert* (fn 2) 310–312; cf *Ciba-Geigy (Pty) Ltd v Lushof Farms (Pty) Ltd* 2002 2 SA 447 (SCA) 471.

7 Cf *Ciba-Geigy (Pty) Ltd v Lushof Farms (Pty) Ltd* 2002 2 SA 447 (SCA) 471.

8 2003 4 SA 285 (SCA).

9 At 299; see also *Loubser/Reid* (fn 1) 3.

the Aquilian action, which according to the court adequately protects the person against defective products, with the possibility of gradual development of the approach to the *res ipsa loquitur* maxim and a reversal of the onus of proof. If strict liability had to be introduced, it was a task of the legislature.[10]

03 The legislature did intervene and introduce strict liability for damage caused by a defective product in section 61(1) of the Consumer Protection Act 68 of 2008 (CPA).[11] The CPA[12] provides that the producer (manufacturer) as well as the importer, distributor or retailer of goods are liable for harm caused to consumers by unsafe or defective goods, irrespective of the presence or absence of negligence; strict liability therefore applies. In this way South Africa was brought in line with many jurisdictions, including members of the European Union and the USA,[13] and in this respect the legislature most certainly draws inspiration from foreign practices. However, the common law also remains in force in terms of section 2(10) of the CPA. This applies especially to cases where the Act is not applicable, for example where a defective product causes pure economic loss.[14]

04 There are no separate regimes for separate categories of product, liable entities or injured parties, nor any special liability regimes with regard to new technologies in South African law.

B. CONTRACTUAL LIABILITY

05 Common law liability *ex contractu* for defective products is based on two grounds: an express or implied warranty by the supplier that the product is free from defects, or on a misrepresentation to that effect.[15] Contractual liability applies only to the purchaser of a defective product and does not

---

10 *Wagener and Cuttings v Pharmacare Ltd* 2003 4 SA 285 (SCA) 295–296, 300; cf *Freddy Hirsch Group (Pty) Ltd v Chickenland (Pty) Ltd* 2011 4 SA 276 (SCA) 293; see also *Neethling/Potgieter* (fn 1) 339.

11 See *Loubser/Reid* (fn 1) 56 f; *Neethling/Potgieter* (fn 1) 399–400; *Botha/Joubert* (fn 2); *C Gowar*, Product Liability: A changing playing field?, 2011 Obiter 521 f; see in general on sec 61 of the CPA, *M Loubser/E Reid*, Section 61, in: T Naudé/S Eiselen (eds), Commentary on the Consumer Protection Act (2014) [1 f].

12 Sec 61(1).

13 *B Koch/H Koziol*, Comparative conclusions, in: B Koch/H Koziol (eds), Unification of Tort Law: Strict Liability (2002) 402 declare: 'All jurisdictions but South Africa have some strict liability rule for damage caused by defective products, most of them implementing European Directive no 85/374 (which has not led to entirely identical solutions, however).'

14 Cf *Neethling/Potgieter* [2014] THRHR 507–508 on sec 61(5) of the Act; see also *Neethling/Potgieter* (fn 1) 399 fn 182; see however *Loubser/Reid* (fn 1) 93).

15 See *Loubser/Reid* (fn 1) 23–30; *Van der Walt* [1972] THRHR 225–227; *Botha/Joubert* (fn 2) 307–308.

extend to non-contracting persons. Liability for breach of an express warranty is strict. The supplier (manufacturer or retailer) is liable even if it has taken all reasonable steps to detect or prevent the defect or even if it was or became impossible to comply with the warranty. The normal remedies for breach of contract are at the disposal of the purchaser for breach of warranty.[16] Implied warranties, which are *ex lege* part of a contract, and relevant for present purposes are firstly that the product is fit for the purpose for which it is sold and of reasonable merchantable quality,[17] and secondly the warranty against latent defects in a product at the time of sale (so-called Aedilitian remedies). The latter allows purchasers to claim a price reduction or cancellation of the contract, but consequential loss may only be claimed in special instances, that is, where the seller is aware of the defect or where he is a manufacturer or dealer who publicly professes to have the skill and expert knowledge in relation to the kind of product sold. Fault on the part of the seller is not required for liability.[18] As regards a misrepresentation by the seller that the product is defect free, the Aedilitian remedies are also available if the purchaser was induced to conclude the sale by the seller's even innocent pre-contractual false material statement relating to the quality of the product sold.[19] On the other hand, a pre-contractual negligent misrepresentation that a product is defect free can give rise to a delictual claim for damages.[20]

06 The common law implied warranty that a product is fit for the purpose for which it is sold and of reasonable merchantable quality has been augmented by section 56 read with section 55 of the CPA, which also makes provision for an implied warranty of quality by the producer, importer, distributor or retailer of goods, *inter alia* that the goods are reasonably suitable for the purposes for which they are generally intended, are of good quality and free of any defects, and will be useable and durable for a reasonable period of time, having regard to normal use. It is irrelevant whether a defect was latent or patent or could have been detected by a consumer before taking delivery. The consumer's remedies in terms of section 56 are to return the defective goods to the supplier, and claim repair or replacement of the goods, or a refund of the purchase price.[21]

---

16 See *Loubser/Reid* (fn 1) 25.

17 See *Loubser/Reid* (fn 1) 25–26.

18 See *Van der Walt* [1972] THRHR 226–227; *Loubser/Reid* (fn 1) 27–29; *Loubser/Midgley* (fn 1) 248; *Kroonstad Westelike Boere-Ko-opreatiewe Vereninging Bpk v Botha* 1964 3 SA 561 (A).

19 See *Loubser/Reid* (fn 1) 29–30; *Phame (Pty) Ltd v Paizes* 1973 3 SA 397 (A) 407, 417.

20 See *Bayer South Africa (Pty) Ltd v Frost* 1991 4 SA 559 (A) 268, 270; see also *ABSA Bank Ltd v Fouche* 2003 1 SA 176 (SCA) 180, 185; *OK Bazaars (1929) Ltd v Standard Bank of South Africa Ltd* 2002 3 SA 688 (SCA) 695; *Neethling/Potgieter* (fn 1) 322–323; *Loubser/Midgley* (fn 1) 191; *Loubser/Reid* (fn 1) 30.

21 See *Loubser/Reid* (fn 1) 31–32.

II. BASIC ELEMENTS OF LIABILITY

A. OVERVIEW

07 Under common law all the elements of a delict, that is, conduct, wrongfulness, fault (negligence), causation and damage, must be present for delictual liability to ensue. Conduct is voluntary human behaviour and the producer's act consists of the human control, supervision and organising of the complex process of industrial production.[22] Wrongfulness is determined with reference to the *boni mores* or legal convictions of the community. In *Ciba-Geigy (Pty) Ltd v Lushof Farms (Pty) Ltd*[23] the court stated that '[i]t is actually self-evident that, according to the legal convictions of the community, a manufacturer acts incorrectly and therefor wrongfully if he makes a product commercially available which in the course of its designated use, and due to a defect, causes damage to the consumer thereof'. As a general rule, a product is considered to be defective if it is unreasonably dangerous;[24] and a product is unreasonably dangerous if, in the circumstances, it does not meet the expectations of the reasonable consumer with regard to its safety.[25] Seen in this light, products that are inevitably dangerous according to their form (such as a knife, blade or saw) or content (such as cigarettes or alcohol), cannot be regarded as defective. However, even shortcomings in the design of a product (such as a motor car ashtray, designed with a sharp edge, that injures a passenger's eye during an emergency stop) or insufficient warnings or information on products may be regarded as defects.[26] Van der Merwe and De Jager[27] observe:

> 'The criterion of reasonableness coupled with the community's concept of what behaviour is reasonable in given circumstances is flexible enough to take into account such factors as the type of product, the nature of the manufacturer's business enterprise, the customs and practices prevailing in a particular trade or industry, the amount of knowledge and expertise of potential purchasers and users of the product, abnormal use, and the specific stage in the production process during which a defect originated. The last-mentioned factor may influence the duties of a manufacturer in different ways. At the stage of planning or design the manufacturer must take into account the most recent knowledge available in its field. When the product is actually manufactured the

---

22 See *Van der Walt* [1972] THRHR 239; *Neethling/Potgieter* (fn 1) 356 fn 351.

23 2002 2 SA 447 (SCA) 470 (translation); cf *Freddy Hirsch Group (Pty) Ltd v Chickenland (Pty) Ltd* 2011 4 SA 276 (SCA) 294–295; see also *Loubser/Midgley* (fn 1) 248–249; *Loubser/Reid* (fn 1) 40 f.

24 *Loubser/Midgley* (fn 1) 249; *Neethling/Potgieter* (fn 1) 337; cf *Loubser/Reid* (fn 1) 44–45.

25 Cf *Van der Walt* [1972] THRHR 242; *Loubser/Midgley* (fn 1) 249.

26 Ibid; *Ciba-Geigy (Pty) Ltd v Lushof Farms (Pty) Ltd* 2002 2 SA 447 (SCA).

27 *SWJ van der Merwe/FJ de Jager*, Products liability: a recent unreported case [1980] South African Law Journal 86–87; see also *Loubser/Midgley* (fn 1) 249; *Neethling/Potgieter* [2014] THRHR 337; *Loubser/Reid* (fn 1) 45; *Freddy Hirsch Group (Pty) Ltd v Chickenland (Pty) Ltd* 2011 4 SA 276 (SCA) 296–297.

manufacturer has a duty to inspect and to control; when it is released on the market he has the duty to provide potential users with directions for use and to warn them adequately against dangers inherent in the product. Should a defect be detected after a product has been released, the general duty to act reasonably in order to prevent damage could well be concretized in a duty to withdraw the product from the market.'

08 Negligence on the part of the manufacturer must be tested against the care that the reasonable person would have exercised in the particular circumstances.[28] Here one is concerned with the reasonable foreseeability and preventability of damage.[29] Since it is normally very difficult for the prejudiced consumer to prove negligence on the part of the producer, his onus should be alleviated by a specific application of the doctrine of *res ipsa loquitur*.[30] It is

28 See eg *Wagener and Cuttings v Pharmacare Ltd* 2003 4 SA 285 (SCA) 291, 300 (*Wagener and Cuttings v Pharmacare Ltd* [2002] 1 All SA 66 (C) 68) which concerned a contaminated batch of local anaesthetic that caused harm to a number of patients but liability was excluded for lack of fault. In *Ciba-Geigy (Pty) Ltd v Lushof Farms (Pty) Ltd* 2002 2 SA 447 (SCA) the defendant company (C) was the manufacturer of a herbicide. According to C, the herbicide was suitable for eradicating weeds in pear orchards. The plaintiff bought the herbicide from a dealer, used it according to C's directions in his pear orchards and suffered damage in respect of his pear crop. He instituted action against C on the basis that the latter's defective product caused the damage. The court did not find it difficult to judge C's conduct as wrongful (470). In respect of negligence, the court found (473–474) that the fact that the damage to the pear trees was probably attributable to use of the herbicide, in conjunction with C's failure to include a warning that the herbicide was dangerous to pear trees in the instructions for use, was indicative of *prima facie* negligence on C's part. C then had an *onus* of rebuttal to convince the court that it had acted like a reasonable manufacturer in its position by performing the necessary tests to determine whether the product was safe for pear trees. C failed to do this, and hence was found to have been negligent. In *Freddy Hirsch Group (Pty) Ltd v Chickenland (Pty) Ltd* 2010 1 SA 8 (GSJ) 27 the court considered the defendant's failure to test the products involved to be negligence of such a nature that it was unacceptable.

29 *Boberg* (fn 1) 194; see also *Loubser/Reid* (fn 1) 46–50; *Neethling/Potgieter* (fn 1) 337–338. In *A Gibb and Son (Pty) Ltd v Taylor and Mitchell Timber Supply Co (Pty) Ltd* 1975 2 SA 457 (W) 464–465 a building contractor (the plaintiff) ordered scaffolding from a dealer (the defendant). On account of a defective scaffold plank an employee of the subcontractor sustained serious injuries. The plaintiff paid damages to the employee. He (the plaintiff) alleged that the defendant was 90% contributorily negligent to the employee's damage and accordingly claimed a contribution *ex delicto* from the defendant. The court came to the conclusion that a dealer may, in fact, be delictually liable for defects in the product which cause damage. *In casu* the question of whether there was liability on the part of the dealer must be answered by deciding whether the dealer had a duty to take reasonable care in detecting defects (reasonable foreseeability and preventability of damage). Such a duty to inspect does not, according to the court, arise in the case where a reasonable dealer in the position of the defendant, expects a search for defects by the client and the inspection will, in all probability, bring a defect to light. In the present case there was no duty to inspect simply because a reasonable timber merchant would have expected a building contractor to inspect scaffolding for possible defects before using it. Consequently, damage was not reasonably foreseeable.

30 See *Neethling/Potgieter* (fn 4) 338–339; cf also *Wagener and Cuttings v Pharmacare Ltd* 2003 4 SA 285 (SCA) 295–296, 300; *Combrinck Chiropraktiese Kliniek (Edms) Bpk v Datsun Motor Vehicle Distributors (Pty) Ltd* 1972 4 SA 185 (T) 190; *Bayer South Africa (Pty) Ltd v Viljoen* 1990 2 SA 647 (A) 661–662. This phrase normally refers to a situation where the facts of the

submitted that the *res ipsa loquitur* inference of negligence should at least be made where a consumer proves that he was prejudiced by a defective product and that the product was in that state when the manufacturer abandoned his control over it.[31] Finally, the plaintiff must prove a causal (factual and legal) link between the defect and the loss sustained.[32]

09 As far as statutory product liability is concerned, the CPA[33] provides that the producer, importer, distributor or retailer of goods is liable for harm caused by unsafe or defective goods, irrespective of the presence or absence of negligence; strict liability therefore applies. These conditions of liability will be discussed later.

B. CONCEPT OF PRODUCT

10 Under common law no definition of a product could be found. In terms of the CPA,[34] products or goods are defined very widely as anything marketed for human consumption; any other tangible object,[35] including any medium on which anything

matter are such as to give rise to an inference of negligent conduct and finds application where the only known facts, relating to negligence, consist of the occurrence itself (see *Boberg* (fn 1) 377–378; *Neethling/Potgieter* (fn 1) 161–162; *Sardi v Standard & General Insurance Co Ltd* 1977 3 SA 776 (A) 778).

31 See *Neethling/Potgieter* (fn 4) 339.

32 This will be discussed below nos 27–28. In *Freddy Hirsch Group (Pty) Ltd v Chickenland (Pty) Ltd* 2011 4 SA 276 (SCA) the respondent (B) was the primary operating entity in a fast-food franchise group (Nando's). As part of its operation, it supplied marinades, sauces and dressings to its partners. It sourced spices for those products from the appellant (A) who supplied B with spice packs containing cayenne pepper contaminated with a statutorily banned colourant which was unfit for human consumption. A instituted a claim against B for payment for the spice packs but B pleaded that it was excused from paying the amount claimed because it had four counterclaims against A that in total exceeded the amount of A's claim. B had unknowingly used the contaminated spice packs in the manufacture of certain of its own products and once the contamination was discovered, B and the purchasers of the affected products had had to recall and destroy them. B's counterclaims were for the losses allegedly flowing from the recall and destruction. For purposes of product liability the claim for damage suffered by C and various other business entities (purchasers of the contaminated products from B) as a result of A's alleged negligence because it had failed to detect the prohibited colourants when there was an obligation upon it to do so, is relevant. The court found that A acted wrongfully by breaching its legal duty to prevent defective products from reaching the market and causing harm (*in casu* pure economic loss) to consumers. A also acted negligently by its failure to test the products involved. As to causation, the court held that factual causation was hardly an issue because, but for A's conduct, the loss involved would not have been suffered. Legal causation was also present as the loss claimed was not too remote being reasonably foreseeable and a direct consequence of A's conduct. The claim therefore succeeded.

33 Sec 61(1).

34 Sec 1.

35 Since pharmaceutical products are tangible objects and may be marketed for human consumption, they qualify as goods (see *Loubser/ Reid* (fn 1) 90–92; cf *Wagener and Cuttings v Pharmacare Ltd* 2003 4 SA 285 (SCA)).

is or may be written or encoded; any literature, music, photograph, motion picture, game, information, data, software, code or other intangible product written or encoded on any medium; a legal interest in land or any other immovable property;[36] and gas, water and electricity.[37] There is as yet no jurisprudence on this topic. The generality of 'tangible object' in the definition would according to Loubser, Reid and Midgley qualify blood and blood products as goods,[38] and it seems that the same can be said about other body fluids and parts.[39] The definition also covers so-called informational products, which include any literature, music, photograph, motion picture, game, information, data, software or code. These goods may range from software packages (mass-produced or specifically for use in for example aeroplanes or heart-lung machines), to computer games, architectural or engineering plans in electronic format, books (such as a cookery book with incorrect information about poisonous substances) and professional advisory services (for example by a medical practitioner).[40] According to Loubser and Reid,[41] component parts of a complex product in themselves also qualify as goods. Movable property attached to immovable property in such a manner that it loses its independent existence will accordingly still be regarded as goods.

11 There can be no doubt that the thing created by the entrepreneur from his own materials based on an individualised order from a client falls in terms of the CPA within the definition of goods as a tangible object. Since a supplier of services associated with goods is regarded as a supplier of those goods for the purpose of section 61(1) of the CPA,[42] it is of no significance whether the contract between the entrepreneur and the client is classified as a contract of sale or a contract of service.

C. CONCEPT OF DEFECT

12 The CPA[43] provides that the producer, importer, distributor or retailer of goods is liable for any harm caused as a consequence of supplying unsafe goods, a product failure, defect or hazard in goods or inadequate instructions or warnings provided to the consumer pertaining to any hazard arising from

---

36 Other than an interest that falls within the definition of service, such as the renting of premises, the provision of accommodation facilities, the granting of occupancy rights and rights of access to premises (see *Loubser/Reid* (fn 1) 84).

37 See further *J Neethling*, Strikte aanspreeklikheid vir defekte produkte [2011] Journal of South African Law (TSAR) 813; *Loubser/Midgley* (fn 1) 252; *Loubser/Reid* (fn 1) 81 f.

38 *Loubser/Midgley* (fn 1) 253; *Loubser/Reid* (fn 1) 88–90.

39 See *Loubser/Reid* (fn 1) 88.

40 *Loubser/Midgley* (fn1) 253; *Loubser/Reid* (fn 1) 82–83, 88.

41 (Fn 1) 85–86, 124; see sec 53(1) of the CPA.

42 Sec 61(2) of the Act; see *Loubser/Reid* (fn 1) 87–88,126–127.

43 Sec 61(1), read with sec 53(1) of the Act.

or associated with the use of goods. Unsafe goods, a product failure, defect or hazard in goods or inadequate instructions or warnings are defined as follows.[44] 'Defect' means any material imperfection in the manufacture of the goods or components, or in performance of the services, that renders the goods or results of the service less acceptable than persons generally would be reasonably entitled to expect in the circumstances; or any characteristic of the goods or components that renders the goods or components less useful, practicable or safe than persons generally would be reasonably entitled to expect in the circumstances. 'Failure' entails the inability of the goods to perform in the intended manner or to the intended effect. 'Hazard' denotes a characteristic that has been identified as, or declared to be, a hazard in terms of any other law; or presents a significant risk of personal injury to any person, or damage to property, when the goods are utilised. 'Unsafe' means that, due to a characteristic, failure, defect or hazard, particular goods present an extreme risk of personal injury or property damage to the consumer or to other persons.

13 It is clear that all these definitions overlap and can lead to confusion. Loubser and Midgley[45] describe it as 'a puzzling interplay of definitions' – it is for example difficult to distinguish between a significant risk and an extreme risk.[46] The yardstick used by the legislator to determine the defectiveness of goods, is the reasonable expectations of consumers.[47] The objection raised by writers against this test that it is too vague to provide much guidance to the courts[48] is not acceptable.[49] There is as yet no case law on the topic. The Act does not specifically mention design defects. The previous principles will therefore also be applied to determine whether a design is defective.[50]

---

44 Sec 53(1) of the Act; see *Loubser/Midgley* (fn 1) 253–255; *Loubser/Reid* (fn 1) 57–80; *Loubser/Reid* (fn 11) [3–10]; *Neethling* [2011] TSAR 813–814.

45 *Loubser/Midgley* (fn 1) 254.

46 Clarity could perhaps have been gained if the legislator accepted as premise, as has been submitted with regard to common law product liability, that goods are defective if they are unreasonably dangerous (see above no 07).

47 *Loubser/Reid* (fn 1) 67, 68 conclude that the assessment of defectiveness is similar to that which is required by the courts in assessing the concepts of wrongfulness and defectiveness in common law (see above no 07).

48 See *Loubser/Midgley* (fn 1) 254; *Loubser/Reid* (fn 1) 63–65.

49 In other areas of South African law (such as misleading the public as to a rival's own performance or passing off as forms of unlawful competition: see *J Neethling*, Van Heerden-Neethling Unlawful Competition (2008) 154–155, 182–185) the courts apply the yardstick of the perception of the 'ordinary or average customer' with great success, and there seems to be no reason why this can also not be done with regard to the 'reasonable expectations of consumers'. The test should naturally be objective and not simply be based on the subjective opinions of consumers, although a public consumer opinion survey may play a role (cf *Van Heerden-Neethling Unlawful Competition* (fn 49) 186–187). See also *Neethling* [2011] TSAR 814.

50 Cf *Loubser/Reid* (fn 1) 68–70.

14 As to inadequate instructions or warnings provided to the consumer pertaining to any hazard arising from or associated with the use of goods, this will be present where inadequate instructions present a significant risk of personal injury to any person, or damage to property, when the goods are utilised.[51] Section 58 of the CPA elaborates on the warning concerning the fact and nature of the risks involved: a person who packages any hazardous or unsafe goods for supply to consumers must display on or within that packaging a notice providing the consumer with adequate instructions for the safe handling and use of those goods. The notice must meet the requirements of section 22 of the CPA in terms of which it must be in plain and understandable language for an ordinary consumer of the class of persons for whom the notice is intended, with average literacy skills and minimal experience as a consumer of the relevant goods or services. The producer, importer, distributor or retailer of goods will be liable even where they were not involved in the packaging operation.[52]

15 No indication could be found that defects in the context of used objects, energy, products performing their function owing to digital content (programmes) or intellectual content (for example the content of a book), or any other particular kind of product (such as medical products) are treated differently from other defects with regard to defectiveness, consumer expectations, etc. The same applies to manufacturing, design and presentation defects.

16 There is no significance in South African law attached to the criterion of 'putting a product into circulation'. Analogous descriptions used in the CPA are the making available of goods to consumers in the ordinary course of business. As has been indicated,[53] a product can be defective for reasons not related to its characteristics, such as where inadequate instructions or warnings were provided to the consumer pertaining to any hazard arising from or associated with the use of goods.

III. PERSON LIABLE FOR DAMAGE

17 The persons sued at common law for damage caused by defective products are mainly manufacturers and dealers.[54] In terms of section 61(1) of the CPA the producer, importer, distributor or retailer of goods are liable for harm caused to consumers by defective goods, that is all persons who have been involved in the production and distribution of defective products. The producer, with respect to any particular goods, means a person who grows, nurtures, harvests,

51 See *Loubser/Midgley* (fn 1) 255; *Loubser/Reid* (fn 1) 76–79.
52 *Loubser/Reid* (fn 1) 77.
53 See above no 14.
54 See above nos 05, 07–08.

mines, generates, refines, creates, manufactures or otherwise produces the goods within South Africa, or causes any of those things to be done, with the intention of making them available for supply in the ordinary course of business; or by applying a personal or business name, trade mark, trade description or other visual representation on or in relation to the goods, has created or established a reasonable expectation that the person is a producer.[55] Not only the manufacturer of completed goods, but also the maker of component parts, assembled products and reconditioned products, will qualify as the producer. The definition of producer also extends to non-manufactured goods, such as agricultural products and mining extracts (minerals, gas).[56] Where a person markets the products of other manufacturers under its own brand name, as often happens in the case of retailers (such as Spar and Checkers), according to Loubser and Reid it is reasonable that that person should be liable for its own-brand products since the consumer can then readily identify the responsible producer.

18 The importer of goods is defined as a person who brings those goods, or causes them to be brought, from outside into South Africa with the intention of making them available for supply in the ordinary course of business.[57] This means that an importer of goods for private and not business purposes will not be strictly liable for damage caused by a defective imported product.[58]

19 The distributor of goods means a person who, in the ordinary course of business, is supplied with those goods by a producer, importer or another distributor, and in turn supplies those goods to either another distributor or to a retailer. The latter is a person who, in the ordinary course of business, then supplies those goods to a consumer. The supplier means a person who markets goods or services, and supply in relation to goods includes sell, rent, exchange and hire in the ordinary course of business for consideration. In relation to services, supply means to sell the services, or to perform or cause them to be performed or provided, or to grant access to any premises, event, activity or facility in the ordinary course of business for consideration.[59] In terms of section 61(2) of the CPA a supplier of services who, in conjunction with the performance of those services, applies, supplies, installs or provides access to any goods is regarded as a supplier of those goods to the consumer, and will therefore be strictly liable if the goods are defective.[60] It is clear that only supplying of goods and services in the ordinary course of business is relevant for the purposes of the CPA – the provision

---

55 See sec 1 of the CPA, see also *Loubser/Midgley* (fn 1) 256; *Loubser/Reid* (fn 1) 122; *Loubser/Reid* (fn 11) [2]; *Neethling* [2011] TSAR 812.

56 See *Loubser/Reid* (fn 1) 122–124.

57 See sec 1 of the CPA.

58 See *Loubser/Reid* (fn 1) 125.

59 See *Loubser/Midgley* (fn 1) 256; *Loubser/Reid* (fn 1) 125–127; *Neethling* [2011] TSAR 812–813.

60 *Loubser/Reid* (fn 1) 126–127.

of goods or services outside the business sphere (for example the private sale of a second-hand car) is therefore excluded from the application of the Act.[61]

20 Public entities also bear liability for damage caused by defective products (for example, hospitals operated by the state or local government). Section 5(8) of the CPA provides that the Act is applicable irrespective of whether the supplier is an organ of state, an entity owned or directed by an organ of state, a person contracted or licensed by an organ of state to offer or supply any goods or services, or a public–private partnership.

21 Where more than one person is liable, their liability is joint and several in terms of section 61(3) of the CPA. They are therefore considered to be joint wrongdoers.[62] A court has the authority to apportion liability among persons who are jointly and severally liable.[63] The basis of this apportionment is however unclear. According to the Apportionment of Damages Act 34 of 1956, section 2 the apportionment of damages among joint wrongdoers – or for a right of recourse or recovery between them – takes place on the basis of their relative degrees of fault in a manner that is just and equitable.[64] However, since one is dealing with strict liability under the CPA, the degrees of fault of the joint wrongdoers cannot be utilised for this purpose. Loubser and Reid[65] therefore propose that comparative causation, that is, the extent to which each joint wrongdoer causally contributed to the consumer's damage – rather than comparative fault – should, in a manner that is just and equitable, constitute the basis for apportionment between joint wrongdoers under the Act. In instances of vicarious liability,[66] where an employee or agent of a person is liable in terms of the CPA for anything done or omitted in the course of that person's employment or activities on behalf of their principal, the employer or principal is jointly and severally liable with the employee or agent.

IV. THE AGGRIEVED PERSON AND DAMAGE

22 The CPA[67] provides that the manufacturer, importer, distributor or retailer of goods is liable for harm caused by unsafe or defective goods. The

---

61 *Loubser/Reid* (fn 1) 126.

62 See *Neethling* [2011] TSAR 815; *Loubser/Reid* (fn 11) [19–20]; *Loubser/Reid* (fn 1) 117.

63 See sec 6(6) of the CPA; *Loubser/Reid* (fn 1) 101, 121, 146–147.

64 See *Neethling/Potgieter* (fn 1) 279–281.

65 *Loubser/Reid* (fn 1) 146–147; cf *General Accident Versekeringsmaatskappy SA Bpk v Uijs* 1993 4 SA 228 (A) 235; *Neethling/Potgieter* (fn 1) 172. Dogmatically it has been persuasively argued that the degree of probability of a party causing damage should replace the degree of fault as criterion for apportioning damages (see *P Botha*, Die Verdeling van die Skadedragingslas by Onregmatige Daad (1993) 299–301, 399).

66 See sec 113 of the Act.

67 Sec 61(1).

aggrieved person is usually the consumer. The consumer is a person to whom particular goods or services are marketed in the ordinary course of the supplier's business; or a person who has entered into a transaction with a supplier in the ordinary course of the supplier's business, unless the transaction is exempt from the application of the Act; or, if the context so requires or permits, a user of those particular goods or a recipient or beneficiary of those particular services, irrespective of whether that user, recipient or beneficiary was a party to a transaction concerning the supply of those particular goods or services; or a franchisee in terms of a franchise agreement.[68] Since there is no requirement that the aggrieved person should be a consumer or user of the goods, a third party harmed as a result of a defective product may also claim.[69]

23 Certain persons are excluded from the application of the CPA. For example, the Act does not apply to a transaction in terms of which goods or services are promoted or supplied to the state; or in terms of which the consumer is a juristic person whose asset value or annual turnover, at the time of the transaction, equals or exceeds the threshold value determined by the minister (at present, R2 million).[70] However, and this is important, section 5(5) provides that if goods are supplied to a person in terms of a transaction that is exempt from the application of the Act, those goods, and the importer or producer, distributor and retailer of those goods, shall nevertheless be subject to the strict liability created by section 61 of the Act.[71]

24 As far as the concept of damage is concerned, section 61(5) of the CPA provides that harm for which a person may be held liable includes the death of, or injury to, a natural person; an illness of a natural person; the loss of, or physical damage to, property, irrespective of whether it is movable or immovable; and

---

68 See sec 1 of the CPA; *Neethling* [2011] TSAR 813.

69 See *Loubser/Reid* (fn 1) 93–94.

70 In terms of sec 5(2)(a) and (b) of the CPA.

71 See *Loubser/Reid* (fn 1) 128. Although strict liability applies in these cases – a state of affairs that was unfortunately overlooked by *Neethling/Potgieter* [2014] THRHR 508 (see also *Neethling/Potgieter* (fn 1) 399 n 182) – the common law on product liability is also relevant here (see eg *Freddy Hirsch Group (Pty) Ltd v Chickenland (Pty) Ltd* 2011 4 SA 276 (SCA), discussed above fn 32). In light of this the following *dictum* of Nugent JA in *AB Ventures Ltd v Siemens Ltd* 2011 4 SA 614 (SCA) 620, where he appears to limit the boundaries of common law product liability in respect of juristic persons, should be approached with circumspection: 'The considerations of policy that underlie cases of products liability have no bearing upon a case of the present kind [where the defendant delivered, installed and commissioned certain drives at a construction site]. We are not concerned in this case with anonymous consumers of mass-produced goods. We are concerned with a major construction project involving a multiplicity of contractors and sub-contractors whose co-operation was defined through a web of interrelated contractual rights and obligations. That bears no resemblance to the distant and impersonal relationship that characterises the distribution of bottles of ginger beer and motor vehicles'.

economic loss that results from harm to a natural person or property.[72] In terms of this provision, harm caused by a defective product only relates to damage to the natural person or to property, as well as to economic loss resulting from such damage – it accordingly does not include pure economic loss. An important implication of the fact that pure economic loss is not actionable under the CPA is that the common law on product liability for such loss will then apply.[73] However, Loubser and Reid[74] argue that the CPA is indeed applicable to pure economic loss. According to them, section 61(1) imposes strict liability in respect of 'any harm', which seems to imply that, although this definition 'includes' specific forms of harm, it does not exclude other forms of harm that may be caused by defective goods, specifically pure economic loss. They conclude that this may not have been the intention of the drafters of section 61, but it seems to be implied by the wording of the section. But this argument does not hold water. Section 61(1), read with subsection (5), makes it perfectly clear that only consequential economic loss and not pure economic loss is actionable. Section 61(1) explicitly provides for strict liability 'for any harm, as described in subsection (5)'. The wording thus limits 'any' harm only to harm as specified in section 61(5), leaving no room for pure economic loss. The unfortunate use of the word 'includes' should not override the clear intention of the legislature.

25 Since the CPA does not provide for any principles to determine harm and the assessment of damages in the above instances, it seems that the ordinary delictual principles will have to assist the court.[75] A court has the authority to assess whether any harm has been proved and adequately mitigated, and to determine the extent and monetary value of the damages, including economic loss.[76] As to death, the wording is wide enough to include consumers, users and third persons who died as a result of a defective product. The dependants of any of these persons will be able to claim for loss of support and the heirs and immediate family for funeral expenses.[77] As to personal injury, again the wording is wide enough to include consumers, users and third persons whose injuries were caused by a defective product.[78] They may claim damages for pain and suffering, emotional shock

---

72 See *Loubser/Midgley* (fn 1) 256; *Loubser/Reid* (fn 1) 93–99; *Loubser/Reid* (fn 11) [53 f]; *Neethling* [2011] TSAR 813.

73 As was the case in *Freddy Hirsch Group (Pty) Ltd v Chickenland (Pty) Ltd* 2011 4 SA 276 (SCA), discussed above fn 32.

74 *Loubser/Reid* (fn 1) 93.

75 See *Loubser/Reid* (fn 1) 94.

76 See sec 6(6) of the CPA. Here too the court will probably apply general delictual principles. See in general on the assessment of both patrimonial and non-patrimonial damages *ex delicto*, *Neethling/Potgieter* (fn 1) 246–248, 260–265.

77 See *Loubser/Reid* (fn 1) 94–95; see in general on these delictual claims *Neethling/Potgieter* (fn 1) 290–291, 292 f.

78 See *Loubser/Reid* (fn 1) 95–96. The kind of injuries that can be sustained is evident from instances arising in other legal systems: A pregnant woman takes a tranquilliser called Thalidomide – this causes nerve injury and she gives birth to a deformed baby; a woman

(psychological injury/lesion), disfigurement, loss of amenities of life and loss of life expectancy, as well as for consequential economic loss (such as medical expenses, loss of income and loss of earning capacity).[79] As to illness, although this kind of harm can exist independently of injury (such as cancer that developed as a result of the mining of asbestos), illness and injury clearly overlap in many instances. In general the claims for damages (also for consequential economic loss) will be the same as those for injuries.[80] Loss of or damage to movable or immovable property as a result of a defect occurs frequently, for example the destruction of a car as a result of a defective fuel system, or where a defective herbicide was used in pear orchards and caused damage in respect of the pear crop, or where a structural defect in a building causes damage to the owner's property as well as to adjacent premises. The consumer, user or a third person may claim damages for the damage to the property and for consequential loss.[81]

26 As far as could be ascertained, there are no monetary limits on liability.

V. CAUSATION

27 For strict liability the CPA requires that the defect in a product must wholly or partly have caused the harm,[82] but since the Act does not define causation, the common law principles as to factual and legal causation, which are applicable to common law product liability,[83] will in all probability also be utilised in this regard.[84] The *conditio sine qua non* or 'but for' approach is generally used to determine factual causation.[85] In its simplest formulation,

enjoys a ginger ale in a café – she suffers shock and contracts gastro-enteritis as a result of the remains of a decomposed snail poured from the dregs of the bottle; a person buys a new Corvair motor-car – he is seriously injured when a defective wheel breaks off while he is turning a corner, and the motor car overturns; a woman buys pre-packaged medicinal salt from the chemist – fine splinters of glass in the salt cause internal injuries; and a woman uses a well-known hair remedy which causes serious physical lesions (see *Neethling/Potgieter* (fn 1) 335).

79 See *Loubser/Reid* (fn 1) 95–96; see in general on these delictual claims *Neethling/Potgieter* (fn 1) 230, 253–255.

80 See *Loubser/Reid* (fn 1) 97.

81 Ibid 97–100.

82 See sec 61(1).

83 See *Freddy Hirsch Group (Pty) Ltd v Chickenland (Pty) Ltd* 2011 4 SA 276 (SCA) 297–298.

84 See *Loubser/Reid* (fn 1) 102 f; *Loubser/Reid* (fn 11) [11-16]; *Neethling* [2011] TSAR 814.

85 In *International Shipping Co (Pty) Ltd v Bentley* 1990 1 SA 680 (A) 700 the court formulated it as follows with regard to positive conduct: 'The enquiry is generally conducted by applying the so-called "but-for" test, which is designed to determine whether a postulated cause can be identified as a *causa sine qua non* of the loss in question. In order to apply this test one must make a hypothetical enquiry as to what probably would have happened but for the wrongful conduct of the defendant … If it would in any event have ensued, then the wrongful conduct was not a cause of the plaintiff's loss; *aliter*, if it would not so have ensued. If the wrongful

factual causation exits when one fact arises out of or flows from another.[86] In *Lee v Minister of Correctional Services*[87] it was emphasised that the application of *conditio sine qua non* is not inflexible since causation cannot always be answered by strict adherence to logic but that common sense sometimes has to prevail. In the final analysis the question is whether it is more likely or probable than not that the defendant caused the harm.[88] Where, apart from the defect, another factor or factors have caused the harm – which may have resulted partly from other persons or from the forces of nature – the consumer must prove that the defect in the product was a material, but not the exclusive, cause of the harm which is presumed to be indivisible. The onus is then on the defendant to rebut the presumption by proving that the harm is in fact divisible and that he did not cause all of it but only a specific part.[89] Be that as it may, the onus to prove a causal link between a defect and the harm suffered may in some cases prove to be an obstacle for the plaintiff[90] where he has to collect technical data about the product and the accident together with evidence of the conduct of the individuals concerned.[91] To alleviate the plaintiff's plight, Loubser and Reid[92] submit that, at least with regard to manufacturing defects, a dual inference should be drawn where a product failed to perform as intended and harm occurred: first, the existence of a defect; and second, a causal link between the defect and the harm. The onus is then on the defendant to overturn the inferences. A defence that may be raised in this regard is that the defect did not exist in the goods at the time when the defendant supplied them.[93] As far as inadequate instructions or warnings are concerned, in *Ciba-Geigy (Pty)*

act is shown in this way not to be a *causa sine qua non* of the loss suffered, then no legal liability can arise.' See also *Neethling/Potgieter* (fn 1) 186–187; *Van der Walt/Midgley* (fn 1) 198–199; but see *Neethling/Potgieter* (fn 1) 187 f for criticism of this approach. See further on the application of *conditio sine qua non* in cases of omissions *Boberg* (fn 1) 384; *Neethling/Potgieter* (fn 1) 191–193; *Van der Walt/Midgley* (fn 1) 198–199.

86 See *Lee v Minister of Correctional Services* 2013 2 SA 144 (CC) 161; *Neethling/Potgieter* (fn 1) 195–197.

87 2013 2 SA 144 (CC) 162.

88 See *Minister of Finance v Gore* 2007 1 SA 111 (SCA) 125; see also *Minister of Safety and Security v Van Duivenboden* 2002 6 SA 431 (SCA) 449; *Neethling/Potgieter* (fn 1) 191–192.

89 See *Loubser/Reid* (fn 1) 108–109; cf *Boberg* (fn 1) 405–406; *Kakemas Bestuursraad v Louw* 1960 2 SA 202 (A) 222; *Humphrys NO v Barnes* 2004 2 SA 577 (C) 581–582. However, in *Wright v Medi-Clinic Ltd* 2007 4 SA 327 (C) 370 the court had difficulty with the notion of a presumption of indivisibility in cases where the basic question is whether the damage is divisible or not.

90 Unlike eg in *Freddy Hirsch Group (Pty) Ltd v Chickenland (Pty) Ltd* 2011 4 SA 276 (SCA) 297 (above fn 32) where factual causation was hardly in issue; see also *Loubser/Reid* (fn 1) 110.

91 See *Loubser/Midgley* (fn 1) 251; see also *Loubser/Reid* (fn 1) 113 f where they discuss the problematic cases of defects giving rise to non-traumatic injury, and proportional liability for defective generic drugs.

92 *Loubser/Reid* (fn 1) 111–112.

93 See sec 61(4) discussed below no 32.

Ltd v Lushof Farms (Pty) Ltd[94] the court found that the damage to the pear trees was probably attributable to use of the herbicide, in conjunction with the defendant's failure to include a warning that the herbicide was dangerous to pear trees in its instructions for use. In general the consumer must prove that an adequate warning could have been provided, that it is more probable than not that the warning would have been observed, and that complying with the warning would have prevented the harm.[95]

28 Legal causation deals with the question of limitation of liability, that is, for which harmful consequences actually caused by the wrongdoer's conduct he should be held liable for; the wrongdoer will not be liable for harm which is 'too remote'.[96] The flexible basic test is whether there is a close enough relationship between the wrongdoer's conduct and its consequence for such consequence to be imputed to the wrongdoer in view of policy considerations based on reasonableness, fairness and justice.[97] The existing criteria for legal causation (such as direct consequences and reasonable foreseeability)[98] may play a subsidiary role in determining legal causation.[99] In *Freddy Hirsch Group (Pty) Ltd v Chickenland (Pty) Ltd*[100] it was reiterated that a court should be flexible in its approach to legal causation and that on the facts of the case (concerning loss caused by a defective product), on either the direct consequences or the foreseeability test the conclusion that one arrives at is the same. Applying the former, it was clear that the loss followed directly from the defendant's wrongful and negligent conduct. Applying the latter, it was reasonably foreseeable that because the defect concerned was a proscribed substance, its presence would (not just could) have as its consequence the loss suffered. These principles can also be applied to determine legal causation under the CPA.[101]

29 South African law does not recognise proportional liability. In the so-called DES and asbestos cases liability will be denied where a consumer cannot on a preponderance of probability prove which of the companies producing the goods

94 2002 2 SA 447 (SCA), discussed above fn 28.

95 See *Loubser/Reid* (fn 1) 112.

96 See *Neethling/Potgieter* (fn 1) 197 f.

97 See eg *S v Mokgethi* 1990 1 SA 32 (A) 40–41; *International Shipping Co (Pty) Ltd v Bentley* 1990 1 SA 680 (A) 700–701; *Smit v Abrahams* 1994 4 SA 1 (A) 18; *Standard Chartered Bank of Canada v Nedperm Bank Ltd* 1994 4 SA 747 (A) 765; *Neethling/Potgieter* (fn 1) 200–203.

98 See *Neethling/Potgieter* (fn 1) 205 f, 214 f; *Loubser/Reid* (fn 1) 104–107.

99 See however *Fourway Haulage SA (Pty) Ltd v SA National Roads Agency Ltd* 2009 2 SA 150 (SCA) 165 for a more restrictive interpretation of the flexible test; see also *Freddy Hirsch Group (Pty) Ltd v Chickenland (Pty) Ltd* 2011 4 SA 276 (SCA) 297–298; *Cape Empowerment Trust Limited v Fisher Hoffman Sithole* 2013 5 SA 183 (SCA) 198; see however *Neethling/Potgieter* (fn 1) 203.

100 2011 4 SA 276 (SCA) 297–298 (discussed above fn 32).

101 See *Loubser/Reid* (fn 1) 110.

caused the consumer's harmful disease.[102] If such proof succeeds with regard to more than one producer, they will be treated as joint wrongdoers which are jointly and severally liable.[103]

30 In the case of multiple tortious causes liability will be apportioned between the producer and the third party as joint wrongdoers on the grounds of fairness, reasonableness and justice. Where it is not possible to determine the specific partial contribution of each wrongdoer to the whole harm or a specific part of the harm, South African courts will hold each wrongdoer equally liable.[104] With regard to multiple non-tortious causes of harm it would also not be fair to hold the producer liable for the whole damage if it is known that only part of it was caused by him. The court should do the best it can to arrive at a just result.[105] Where, in the case of multiple tortfeasors, the aggrieved contributed to the harm, two approaches are discernable in South African law.[106] The one is that plaintiff's contributory negligence and each joint wrongdoer's negligence had to be determined separately for the purpose of apportionment.[107] The other is that the plaintiff's negligence had to be measured against the negligence of the joint wrongdoers viewed as a unity.[108] The plaintiff's contributory negligence will however only be taken into account in respect of common law product liability.[109] Since section 1(1)(a) of the Apportionment of Damages Act 34 of 1956 applies only to damage caused partly by the fault of the plaintiff and partly by that of the defendant,[110] the Act cannot apply where liability does not depend on the defendant's negligence. Thus the Act does not apply in the case of strict liability or liability without fault,[111] as is the position with regard to product liability under the CPA. In terms of section 61(1) of the Act the producer, importer, distributor or retailer of goods are liable for harm caused by defective goods irrespective of the presence or absence of negligence.

---

102 *J Neethling*, Causal uncertainty and proportional liability in South Africa, in I Gilead/MD Green/BA Koch (eds) Proportional Liability: Analytical and Comparative Perspectives (2013) 285–286.

103 See *ibid*; see also *Loubser/Reid* (fn 1) 116–118; above no 21.

104 *Minister of Safety and Security v Rudman* 2005 2 SA 16 (SCA) 43–45; *Wright v Medi-Clinic Ltd* 2007 4 SA 327 (C); see *Neethling* (fn 102) 289–290 for a discussion of these cases; see also above no 21.

105 See *Neethling* (fn 102) 290–291; cf *Wright v Medi-Clinic Ltd* 2007 4 SA 327 (C) 372.

106 See *Neethling/Potgieter* (fn 1) 175–176; *Neethling* (fn 102) 291–292.

107 *Santam Insurance Co Ltd v Vorster* 1973 4 SA 764 (A).

108 *Harrington NO v Transnet (Ltd)* 2007 2 SA 228 (C).

109 Cf *A Gibb and Son (Pty) Ltd v Taylor and Mitchell Timber Supply Co (Pty) Ltd* 1975 2 SA 457 (W) 464–465, discussed above fn 29.

110 See *Neethling/Potgieter* (fn 1) 168 f.

111 See *J Neethling*, Contributory negligence under South African law, in: U Magnus/M Martín-Casals (eds), Unification of Tort Law: Contributory Negligence (2004) 167; see also *Loubser/Reid* (fn 1) 145–146; below no 35.

VI. DEFENCES AND EXCLUSIONS

31 According to section 61(4) the following four defences are available to a particular person against strict liability in terms of section 61.[112]

First, that the unsafe product characteristic, failure, defect or hazard that results in harm is wholly attributable to compliance with a public regulation. Public regulations are directed at promoting safety and producers are obliged to comply with them. Consequently, if producers or suppliers comply with the regulations, they should not be strictly liable. But compliance with voluntary standards is not a defence in terms of the Act and will not release said persons.[113]

32 Second, that the alleged unsafe product characteristic, failure, defect or hazard did not exist in the goods at the time it was supplied by the defendant to another person alleged to be liable; or was wholly attributable to compliance by that person with instructions provided by the person who supplied the goods to that person, in which case the defence just mentioned does not apply. The purpose of the first defence is to enable the defendant to avoid liability where a defect was absent at the time of supply of the goods and therefore arose only after he relinquished control of them. So if a product became defective as a result of for example mishandling or unauthorised changes after it was supplied to another person, the supplier will not be liable.[114] The second defence deals with compliance with the instructions provided by the supplier about for example the handling or use of the goods. If this was done, the supplier may not rely on the first defence that the defect did not exist at the time the goods were supplied.[115]

33 Third, that it is unreasonable to expect the distributor or retailer to have discovered the unsafe product characteristic, failure, defect or hazard, having regard to that person's role in marketing the goods to consumers. Loubser, Reid and Midgley[116] are critical of the defence. According to them it offers distributors and retailers a means of escaping strict liability in all situations where they can establish that their conduct was reasonable and therefore blameless, which is something akin to readmitting fault-based liability through the back door. On the other hand, since the defence is not available to the producer or importer against whom the victim of a defective product may still succeed with a strict liability claim for damages, is seems reasonable and fair to allow distributors and retailers to escape liability.[117] Examples of

112 See *Loubser/Midgley* (fn 1) 256–258; *Loubser/Reid* (fn 1) 130–145; *Loubser/Reid* (fn 11) [21 f]; *Neethling/Potgieter* (fn 1) 400; *Neethling* [2011] TSAR 814–815.

113 See *Loubser/Midgley* (fn 1) 256; *Loubser/Reid* (fn 1) 131.

114 See *Loubser/Midgley* (fn 1) 257; *Loubser/Reid* (fn 1) 131–132.

115 See *Loubser/Midgley* (fn 1) 257; *Loubser/Reid* (fn 1) 133.

116 See *Loubser/Midgley* (fn 1) 257; *Loubser/Reid* (fn 1) 132; see also *Botha/Joubert* (fn 2) 316–318.

117 Cf *Loubser/Reid* (fn 1) 137.

where it will be difficult, if not sometimes impossible to discover a defect, are in goods packaged by the producer, latent defects, design defects in a packaged product or inadequate instructions accompanying goods.[118] This also applies to development risks (state of the art in scientific and technical knowledge) which may only become apparent after a product has been used.[119] Van der Walt[120] states that 'in determining what qualifies as defective, the state of human science and technology and the need for experimentation must not be lost sight of. Many human products are inevitably dangerous at a certain stage, for instance new drugs with unknown side-effects'. According to Loubser and Reid,[121] the defence should not succeed if there was knowledge of the dangerous characteristic and this was reasonably accessible to the distributor and retailer.

34 Fourth, that a claim for damages for death, injury, illness, loss of or damage to property or resultant economic loss caused by a defective product was brought more than three years after the death or injury of a person, or more than three years after the earliest time at which a person had knowledge of the material facts about an illness or the loss of or damage to property; or more than three years after the latest date on which a person suffered any resultant economic loss. Since established terminology of the Prescription Act 68 of 1969 is not used, it is uncertain whether this Act is also applicable to prescription under the CPA. However, the Prescription Act would probably be applicable for matters which the CPA does not cover, such as the interruption or suspension of prescription.[122]

35 Contributory fault on the part of the victim of a defective product may be raised by the defendant against a claim based on common law product liability. This applies to contributory negligence as well as contributory intent or voluntary assumption of risk. The first will lead to a reduction of the plaintiff's damages while the latter will be a complete defence.[123] Contributory fault may for example be constituted by the abnormal use of a product or where the consumer knowingly and deliberately exposes himself to a dangerous defect. As indicated,[124] under the strict liability regime of the CPA, the contributory fault of the plaintiff is irrelevant. However, as has been submitted with regard to joint wrongdoers, comparative causation, that is, the extent to which each party causally contributed to the consumer's damage – rather than comparative fault – may offer a solution. Although not included in the CPA, a case can be made

---

118 See *Loubser/Midgley* (fn 1) 257; *Loubser/Reid* (fn 1) 132.

119 See *Loubser/Midgley* (fn 1) 257; *Loubser/Reid* (fn 1) 133–134.

120 [1972] THRHR 242 (translation).

121 *Loubser/Reid* (fn 1) 134.

122 See *Loubser/Reid* (fn 1) 138 f for an in-depth discussion of this topic; see also *Loubser/Midgley* (fn 1) 257–258; *Neethling/Potgieter* (fn 1) 278.

123 See *Neethling/Potgieter* (fn1) 168 f, 177 f.

124 Above no 21.

out that voluntary assumption of risk should constitute a complete defence even though strict liability is applicable. It seems unjust and unreasonable to hold a producer, importer, distributor or retailer liable where the plaintiff voluntarily assumed the risk of being injured by a defective product.

36 Consent to (the risk of) harm or *volenti non fit iniura* will be a defence against a common law product liability claim.[125] The requirements for a valid consent to the risk of harm are the following: consent must be given voluntarily by a person capable of volition who has subjectively consented with full knowledge, comprehension and understanding of the nature and extent of the risk of possible harm; and the consent must be permitted by the legal order (not be *contra bonos mores*). Consent to bodily injury or the risk thereof is normally regarded as being *contra bonos mores* but exceptions are participation in lawful sport or undergoing to medical treatment.[126] So where a consumer has consented to treatment with defective medicine which caused a severe illness, the consent will be *contra bonos mores* and therefore not valid. However, the producer may still rely on voluntary assumption of risk and thus escape liability. According to Loubser and Reid[127] there is no reason in principle why this defence may not be raised against a claim under the CPA. What has been said with regard to common law product liability will then also be applicable under the Act.

37 The producer or seller of goods may free himself from liability for any defect in the goods – contractual as well as delictual – through an exclusionary (exemption) clause.[128] Liability for damage caused by intentional conduct, such as fraud, may, however, not be excluded. Under common law a seller may contract out of liability for negligence, even gross negligence.[129] But the CPA prohibits exemption of liability for gross negligence vis-à-vis consumers.[130] The precise restriction on the seller's liability will depend on the interpretation of the clause concerned.[131] A contract will not be enforceable if it is against public policy.[132] A so-called '*voetstoots*' clause (a clause stating that goods, such as

125 See on this defence *Neethling/Potgieter* (fn 1) 108 f.

126 *Hattingh v Roux NO* 2011 5 SA 135 (WCC) 14; see also *Plumridge v Road Accident Fund* 2012-05-08 case no 2656/2009 (EC) [43–44]; *Neethling/Potgieter* (fn 1) 111–114; *Loubser/Reid* (fn 1) 148–151.

127 *Loubser/Reid* (fn 1) 147.

128 See in this regard *Loubser/Reid* (fn 1) 32–35; cf *Van der Walt/Midgley* (fn 1) 62; *Neethling/Potgieter* (fn 1) 277–278; *Loubser/Midgley* (fn 1) 200–205.

129 *Government of the Republic of South Africa v Fibre Spinners & Weavers (Pty) Ltd* 1978 2 SA 794 (A) 807.

130 Sec 51(1)(c)(i); see *Loubser/Reid* (fn 1) 33.

131 See *Neethling/Potgieter* (fn 4) 277 fn 101; cf *Van der Walt/Midgley* (fn 1) 62.

132 In *Freddy Hirsch Group (Pty) Ltd v Chickenland (Pty) Ltd* 2011 4 SA 276 (SCA) 285–287 the court held that the exclusion clause that purported to exclude all statutory and common law terms, warranties or representations as to the quality or fitness of foodstuff, was contrary to public policy and unenforceable. See also *Loubser/Reid* (fn 1) 34–35.

second-hand cars, are sold 'as it is' or 'with all its defects') will exempt the seller from liability for latent defects except where he knows about the defect and did not reveal it to the purchaser.[133] The CPA also prevents the contractual exclusion of the various consumer rights protected by the Act. Proper notice must be given to consumers of any other proposed exemption from liability, and the courts are given extensive powers to correct 'prohibited conduct, unfairness, injustice or unconscionability'.[134]

VII. REMEDIES

38 Under the common law the ordinary delictual and contractual remedies are at the disposal of the prejudiced consumer. Delictual remedies are aimed at monetary compensation.[135] Similarly, compensation for harm caused by a defective product under section 61 of the CPA will be monetary.[136] Section 56 of the CPA provides for restoration in kind: within six months after the delivery of any goods to a consumer, the consumer may return the goods to the supplier without penalty and at the supplier's risk and expense if the goods fail to satisfy the prescribed requirements and standards. The supplier must then, at the direction of the consumer, either repair or replace the failed, unsafe or defective goods, or refund to the consumer the price paid by the consumer for the goods. If a supplier repairs any particular goods or any component of any such goods, and within three months after that repair the failure, defect or unsafe feature has not been remedied, or a further failure, defect or unsafe feature is discovered, the supplier must replace the goods or refund to the consumer the price paid by the consumer for the goods. Punitive or exemplary damages may not be claimed either under the common law[137] or in terms of the CPA. Injunctions (interdicts) are in principle available at common law for a threatening infringement of the consumer's rights.[138] The CPA[139] also makes provision for interim relief *inter*

---

133 See *Loubser/Reid* (fn 1) 28, 33.

134 See secs 51 and 52 of the Act; *Loubser/Reid* (fn 1) 37.

135 See *Neethling/Potgieter* (fn 1) 267–268.

136 But see sec 115(2) in terms of which a person may not institute a claim in a civil court for the assessment of the amount or award of damages if that person has consented to an award of damages in a consent order.

137 See eg *Argus Printing and Publishing Co Ltd v Esselen's Estate* 1994 2 SA 1 (A) 29–30; *Dikoko v Mokhatla* 2006 6 SA 235 (CC) 263; *Mogale v Seima* 2008 5 SA 637 (SCA) 641–642; *Seymour v Minister of Safety and Security* 2006 5 SA 495 (W) 500; *Fose v Minister of Safety and Security* 1997 3 SA 786 (CC) 823–828. However, according to Roman-Dutch law and some (particularly earlier) case law the *actio iniuriarum* may in certain cases be used to claim punitive damages from the wrongdoer. See for a full discussion *J Neethling*, Punitive damages in South Africa, in: H Koziol/V Wilcox (eds), Punitive Damages: Common Law and Civil Law Perspectives (2009) 122 f.

138 See *Neethling/Potgieter* (fn 1) 269–270.

139 Sec 114 of the Act.

alia where it is reasonably necessary to prevent serious, irreparable damage to the applicant.

VIII. PROCEDURAL AND EVIDENTIAL ISSUES

39 The standard of proof for both delict[140] and breach of contract at common law is that the plaintiff must prove the relevant cause of action on a preponderance or balance of probability. But the onus of proof may differ in respect of contractual and delictual claims. In delictual actions the onus is on the plaintiff to prove negligence on the side of the defendant.[141] As indicated,[142] this onus should be alleviated by a specific application of the doctrine of *res ipsa loquitur.* On the other hand, where a claim is instituted against a person for breach of contract where fault is required, the onus is on the defendant to show that he was not negligent.[143] In any proceedings under the CPA,[144] the standard of proof is on a balance of probability.[145]

40 Section 38 of the Constitution of 1996 lays the foundation for class and group actions in South Africa. Section 38 provides that anyone listed in this section has the right to approach a competent court, alleging that a right in the Bill of Rights has been infringed or threatened, and the court may grant appropriate relief, including a declaration of rights.[146] The persons who may approach a court are *inter alia* anyone acting as a member of, or in the interest of, a group or class of persons. Although class actions are a relatively new field in South African law, it provides the basis for mass product liability claims and defective product recalls, since many of the consumer rights that may be harmed by defective products are rights in the Bill of Rights. Be that as it may, in *Children's Resource Centre Trust v Pioneer Food (Pty) Ltd*[147] the court broadened the basis for class actions by holding that they may also be instituted for common law claims (and not just Bill of Rights claims). The court also detailed the procedure that should exist for the administration of class actions in South Africa.[148]

140 See *Neethling* (fn 102) 283 fn 1.
141 See *Neethling/Potgieter* (fn 1) 160–162; *Loubser/Midgley* (fn 1) 136–138.
142 Above no 08.
143 See *Loubser/Midgley* (fn 1) 190.
144 In terms of sec 117 of the Act.
145 As to prescription of claims, see above no 34.
146 The Companies Act 71 of 2008, sec 157 now also makes provision for a class action and will introduce this procedure into commercial activity, also as regards consumers.
147 2013 2 SA 213 (SCA).
148 They are the following: a person seeking to institute a class action must obtain certification of that class from a court; the class must be defined with sufficient precision that a particular individual's membership may be objectively determined by examining his or her situation in light of the class definition; the cause of action that is used as the basis upon which the class action is to be instituted must be a triable issue; the issues of fact or law or both must be

IX. ALTERNATIVE REGULATIONS AND REMEDIES

41 As is clear from the exposition above, other bases and rules of liability in tort and contract law may be applied contemporaneously with rules of product liability in the CPA in such a manner that the aggrieved may choose the basis for pursuing claims. Where the rules of common law or statutory product liability are not applicable, the ordinary principles of tort and contract law may be applied where they are relevant in the circumstances. There is no specific liability regime for defective services apart from related provisions in the CPA and ordinary principles of tort and contract law. Services are not considered to be goods under the strict liability regime, but a supplier of services associated with goods is nevertheless regarded as a supplier of those goods for the purpose of section 61(1) of the CPA.[149] An interest that falls within the definition of service also does not qualify as an interest in immovable property which is included in the definition of goods.[150]

42 The CPA[151] makes provision for the safety monitoring and recall of defective goods by the National Consumer Commission established in terms of the Act. The Commission must promote the development, adoption and application of industry-wide codes of practice providing for effective and efficient systems to receive notice of consumer complaints or reports of product failures, defects or hazards; the return of any goods because of a failure, defect or hazard; personal injury, illness or damage to property caused wholly or partially as a result of a product failure, defect or hazard; and other indication of failure, defect or hazard in any particular goods or in any component of them, or injury or damage resulting from the use of those goods. The Commission must then conduct investigations into the nature, causes, extent and degree of the risk to the public; notify consumers of the nature, causes, extent and degree of the risk pertaining to those goods; and if the goods are unsafe, recall those goods for repair, replacement or refund. It has been submitted that under the common law, should a defect be detected after a product has been released, the general duty to act reasonably in order to prevent damage could well be concretised in a duty to withdraw the product from the market.[152]

43 Apart from criminal sanctions provided for in the CPA for certain transgressions of the Act, and the delictual and contractual remedies referred to

---

common to all members of the class; and the representative of the class must have no conflict of interest with the class or members of the class.

149 Sec 61(2) of the Act; see *Loubser/Reid* (fn 1) 87–88, 126–127.

150 See above no 11.

151 Sec 60.

152 See *Van der Merwe/De Jager* [1980] South African Law Journal 86–87.

above, there does not seem to be other important remedies available to aggrieved and potentially aggrieved victims regulated under other areas of law.

X. ASSESSMENT OF DOMESTIC LAW

44 As is clear from the above, there are common law and statutory special product liability law applied in practice. Difficulties in its practical application are *inter alia* that it is sometimes very difficult for the consumer to prove causation, and also that the product was defective, given the puzzling interplay of definitions in this regard.[153] There are as yet no court cases on statutory strict product liability. It seems that the wide and general definition of a thing or product (goods)[154] will be sufficient to cover all the new technologies discussed in the introduction.

153 See *Loubser/Reid* (fn 1) 57 f, 102 f.
154 See *Loubser/Reid* (fn 1) 81 f.

PRODUCT LIABILITY IN UNITED STATES OF AMERICA*

Michael D Green and Jonathan Cardi

* Portions of this report are drawn from a report prepared for the initial meeting of the World Tort Law Society. *B Feldthusen et al*, North American Submission on Products Liability (forthcoming 2016).

I. INTRODUCTION

01 In the US, the substantive rules of product liability are primarily determined by state courts and legislatures. Because the US has a common law system, state courts have played an especially important role in the area of product liability and tort more generally. While strict product liability was developed exclusively by state courts, once it became established, some state legislatures enacted statutes to govern product liability cases. The more comprehensive ones tended to adopt the law that had developed through the common law and place it into statutory form.[1] In some cases, those statutes modified one or more aspects of product liability law that the courts had developed.[2] In addition, the US has had several rounds of 'tort reform', in which state legislatures have restricted tort law, and some of those reforms were targeted specifically at product liability claims or, because of their breadth, encompassed product claims as well as other tort claims.[3]

02 It is true that federal law sets some important limits on state product liability law in certain areas subject to federal regulation. For example, because, under the US Constitution, federal law pre-empts conflicting state law, manufacturers of generic drugs, medical devices, and automobiles who have satisfied federal-law regulations with respect to safe product design, or warnings of product risks, are sometimes immune from liability under state tort law.[4] In addition, the US Supreme Court has identified federal

1 See, eg, Ark. Code Ann. §4-86-102 (employing language for strict product liability regime largely drawn from §402A).

2 eg, N.J. Stat. Ann. §2A:58C-3 (limiting liability when there is no 'practically and technically feasible alternative design that would have prevented the harm without substantially impairing the reasonably anticipated or intended function of the product').

3 This includes caps on non-economic damage awards, modification of joint and several liability, various limitations on punitive damage awards, and regulation of attorney contingent fees. See *J Sanders/C Joyce*, 'Off to the Races': The 1980s Tort Crisis and the Law Reform Process (1990) 27 Hous L Rev 207.

4 See, eg, *Pliva, Inc v Mensing*, __ U.S. __, 131 S. Ct. 2567 (2011) (plaintiff's state-law product liability claim, alleging that a generic drug was defective for inadequately warning of its side-effects, is pre-empted by federal statute and by Food and Drug Administration regulations specifying how generic drug manufacturers may and may not alter their drugs' labels); *Geier v American Honda Motor Co*, 529 U.S. 861 (2000) (plaintiff's state-law product liability claim, alleging that defendant's car model was defectively designed for not having air bags, is pre-empted by federal Department of Transportation regulations allowing manufacturers to experiment with different passive safety devices rather than mandating the installation of air bags).

constitutional limits on when, how, and in what amounts punitive damages may be awarded.[5] Still, state law is the primary source of law governing liability for product-related injuries.

03 It would be a significant overstatement to say that, in substance, the US has 51 different versions of product liability law: there is a good deal of uniformity across the product liability law of each state and the District of Columbia. But there are also important differences, and thus it is often inaccurate to speak and write as if there were a single US product liability law. In what follows, we will aim to address the product liability issues confronted in this volume by reference to legal rules that have gained broad acceptance across the different US jurisdictions, and we will also try to note areas in which the law varies significantly among jurisdictions.

04 Finally, it is critically important when confronting tort law in the United States to understand that juries are employed in civil cases. The existence of civil juries has a large impact on procedural law that determines the allocation of authority between judge and jury and on the substantive law in subtle but important ways.[6]

II. THE DEVELOPMENT OF STRICT PRODUCT LIABILITY

05 Prior to 1963, a lawsuit brought in a US court seeking compensation for physical harm or property damage caused by a product would typically include claims for *negligence* and/or *breach of warranty*. Negligence, of course, is a tort and is broadly applicable to claims for personal injury and property damage. Thus, product-caused harms are within the large negligence umbrella.[7]

---

5 See, eg, *Philip Morris USA v Williams*, 549 U.S. 346 (2007) (Fourteenth Amendment's Due Process Clause prohibits juries from awarding punitive damages as punishment for harms inflicted by the defendant on non-parties); *BMW of North America, Inc v Gore*, 517 U.S. 559 (1996) (Due Process Clause sets guidelines for the maximum amount of punitive damages that can be awarded against a tortfeasor).

6 See *MD Green*, The Impact of the Civil Jury on American Tort Law (2011) 38 Pepp L Rev 337.

7 Prior to 1916, product liability suits were quite restricted by the doctrine of privity of contract, which required that a claim arising out of the performance of a contract only be pursued by one in privity of contract with the defendant. The iconic case of *MacPherson v Buick Motor Co*, 111 N.E. 1050 (N.Y. 1916) began the process that resulted in abrogation of privity limitations in tort claims. This permitted those injured by products to sue manufacturers with whom the victim had had no contractual dealings. Some privity limitations still exist for breach of warranty claims. *See* Uniform Commercial Code §2–318.

06 Breach of warranty claims belong to the law of contracts, although certain warranty claims – particularly for 'implied' warranty – have tort-like features. For example, parties' efforts to disclaim warranties were sometimes deemed void by courts. Since the 1950s when the Uniform Commercial Code (UCC) was promulgated and widely adopted throughout the United States, breach of warranty claims for 'goods'[8] have been governed by the UCC. Although largely addressed to commercial transactions in which breached warranties result primarily in economic harm, the UCC is applicable to personal injury and property damage claims. As with negligence, product-related personal injury is a relatively modest subset of all warranty claims.

07 In the decades leading up to the 1960s, prominent judges and scholars had argued that negligence and warranty law were inadequate and that suits seeking compensation for physical harm or for tangible property damage caused by products should be governed by 'strict' tort liability. Collectively, these jurists and scholars invoked multiple justifications for the move to strict liability.[9] They can be roughly categorised and described as follows:

07a *Doctrinal/Pragmatic.* Courts applying negligence law had already ruled that manufacturers owe a duty to take reasonable care that their products not cause foreseeable injuries to consumers and bystanders, regardless of whether there existed a contractual relationship between victim and manufacturer. However, they also at times applied negligence doctrine in a restrictive manner that arguably placed excessive responsibility on consumers. For example, judges would sometimes preclude juries from deeming a manufacturer careless for failing to adopt a feasible safety feature because the product's dangers were, in the judge's opinion, sufficiently obvious that product users alone should bear responsibility to guard against those dangers.[10]

Some courts had also ruled that products carry with them an implied warranty that they are safe for ordinary use. Where present, such a warranty created a form of strict liability because the warranty amounts to an unconditional promise of safety, rather than a promise to take ordinary care

---

8 'Goods' are defined in §2-105(1) of the UCC: '"Goods" means all things (including specially manufactured goods) which are movable at the time of identification to the contract for sale other than the money in which the price is to be paid, investment securities (Article 8) and things in action. "Goods" also includes the unborn young of animals and growing crops and other identified things attached to realty as described in the section on goods to be severed from realty' (section 2-107).

9 Many of the justifications offered for strict product liability are discussed in the famous concurring opinion of Justice Roger Traynor in *Escola v Coca-Cola Bottling Co of Fresno*, 150 P.2d 436 (Cal. 1944).

10 See *GT Schwartz*, Foreword: Understanding Products Liability (1979) 67 Cal L Rev 435, 455 (arguing that more robust applications of negligence law might have dampened the call for adoption of strict product liability).

to ensure safety. At the same time, liability for breach of warranty was limited in various ways. For example, courts often required that there be contractual privity between the plaintiff and the defendant in order for a warranty claim to be viable.

The imposition of strict tort liability was seen by many supporters as a reasonable extension of these precedents, particularly given that: (i) negligence law in general contains rules that sometimes ease the plaintiff's burden of proving manufacturer fault (see the discussion of *res ipsa loquitur* below); and (ii) in practice, jurors' broad discretion to make determinations of fault probably allowed some negligence plaintiffs to prevail on minimal showings of fault.

07b *Evidentiary/Process-Based.* Some supporters of strict product liability argued that negligence law placed an inappropriate evidentiary burden on plaintiffs injured by products. Particularly for mass-produced products, it can be difficult for a plaintiff to find evidence of what exactly went wrong in the production of the particular product that injured the plaintiff. Negligence law contains the doctrine of *res ipsa loquitur,* which permits a jury to find carelessness even in the absence of evidence as to how exactly the defendant was careless, and some courts permitted negligence plaintiffs to take advantage of *res ipsa* when suing for injuries caused by defective products. However, *res ipsa* is only available under certain conditions: the accident must be the kind of accident that tends not to happen without carelessness on the part of someone, and the instrumentality of harm must (at least according to some authorities) have been in the 'exclusive' control of the defendant. In some product-related cases, these preconditions for the application of *res ipsa* were not satisfied, requiring plaintiffs to produce evidence establishing exactly what had gone wrong in the defendant's production processes. A move to strict liability, proponents argued, would spare plaintiffs from having to meet this potentially difficult burden and thus would prevent careless manufacturers from avoiding liability just because of the plaintiff's inability to prove carelessness.

07c *Policy-Based.* Courts and commentators have identified various benefits or values that might be realised by moving from negligence and warranty to strict product liability. Among these are: a *right/duty* rationale, a *deterrence* rationale, and a *compensatory or loss-shifting* rationale. We briefly describe each in turn.

Right/Duty. Some maintain that strict product liability is consistent with a broad principle of consumer protection, according to which consumers are entitled to look to manufacturers to ensure that products are safe for everyday use. Likewise, manufacturers are said to be under duties to provide such products. More so than negligence and warranty, a strict liability regime arguably better ensures that consumers' rights are vindicated and manufacturers' duties are heeded.

Deterrence. The threat of tort liability can incentivise firms and individuals to change their behaviour. If one assumes that negligence law's 'ordinary care' standard requires manufacturers to adopt any safety measure that costs less than the harm expected to result from not taking the precaution – and if one further assumes that manufacturers are rational actors with perfect information – there is no difference between the deterrence signal sent by negligence and strict liability. (Under a strict liability rule, a manufacturer will not take precautions beyond ordinary care because the cheaper solution is to pay expected losses.) In practice, however, there are reasons why strict liability might consistently generate more deterrence than negligence. For example, insofar as negligence law's placement of the burden of proving carelessness on the plaintiff produces 'false negatives,' a rule of strict liability may be preferable from a deterrence perspective.[11] With a lessened ability to fend off claims for product-related injuries, manufacturers should invest more in safety, other things being equal.

Compensation. When a product causes an injury, the victim must at first bear all of the economic and non-economic costs that attend the injury. However, tort liability can enable the victim to shift some or all of those costs to the manufacturer. And strict liability, relative to negligence, shifts more costs. Moreover, when the claim is against large or well-insured manufacturers, liability not only shifts costs, it can spread them. If the manufacturer can simply increase the price of its products to reflect those costs then, in effect, it has acted like the victim's insurer, with all customers of the manufacturer bearing a tiny fraction of the victim's loss in the form of slightly higher prices.

08 It is doubtful that any one of the foregoing justifications was universally or even widely regarded as the single most important or compelling. Nor is it clear that all proponents of strict product liability had in mind precisely the same concept of 'strict liability' – though all agreed that it involved an expansion of liability relative to the then-existing negligence and warranty schemes. It is probably most accurate to say that different proponents highlighted different justifications for different iterations of strict liability, but that there was nonetheless an 'overlapping consensus' that common-law rules ought to be changed to make it easier for some victims of product-related injuries to hold product manufacturers and sellers liable.

09 The product liability scheme described in the next section is applicable to the liability of all commercial sellers of products. There are definitional issues with regard to what constitutes a 'product', as explained below with regard to blood and other blood products[12] and other intangible goods such as electricity.[13]

11 See, eg, *M Geistfeld*, Principles of Products Liability (2006) 23–24.
12 See *infra* text accompanying fn 34–38.
13 See *infra* text accompanying fn 27–28.

In addition, there are categorisation issues with regard to sales–service hybrids.[14] However, once a court concludes that a product is involved, the strict liability scheme described below is applicable to all such products. In addition, product sellers are subject to liability for negligence, but this basis for liability does not require that a product be sold or even that a product was involved. There is no special liability regime applicable to new or especially dangerous products. The general tort duty of reasonable care applies when an actor creates a risk of harm to others, and risks to others can be created in a variety of ways, including in the manufacture and distribution of products and services.

10 As strict product liability has matured in the US, there has been a recognition that other elements of a tort claim: factual cause, scope of liability, and affirmative defences based on a plaintiff's conduct (contributory negligence and assumption of risk) are governed by general tort principles. That was not the case in the early days after adoption of strict product liability when courts worked assiduously to distinguish this new basis of liability from negligence.[15] Today, courts largely employ the general standard for factual causation (either but-for or substantial factor)[16] applicable to other tort claims, scope of liability (foreseeability of the type of harm or harm within the risk) and plaintiff faulty conduct (comparative responsibility to apportion liability between a strictly liable product seller and plaintiff).[17]

III. BASIC ELEMENTS OF LIABILITY

A. SECTION 402A OF THE SECOND RESTATEMENT

11 A highly influential early formulation of the doctrine of strict product liability was contained in the Second Restatement of Torts, a work published by the American Law Institute that aims to provide, as much as possible, consensus principles of tort law from across the different states. This provision –

---

14 Restatement (Third) of Torts §20(c) (1998).

15 eg, *Barker v Lull Eng'g Co*, 573 P.2d 443, 456 (Cal. 1978) ('explaining the rejection of "unreasonably dangerous" formulation for strict liability contained in the section 402A of the Second Restatement because the Restatement test had 'burdened the injured plaintiff with proof of an element which rings of negligence'); *In re Agent Orange Prod Liab Litig*, 534 F. Supp. 1046, 1054 (E.D.N.Y. 1982) ('the policies giving rise to strict product liability reflect considerations different from those involving a negligence approach to liability'); *Horn v Gen Motors Corp*, 551 P.2d 398, 403 (Cal. 1976) ('ordinary contributory negligence is not a defense to an action for damages based on strict liability in tort').

16 Restatement (Third) of Torts §15 (1998) (providing that causal standard in product liability is 'determined by the prevailing rules and principles governing causation in tort').

17 Ibid §17 (providing that apportionment of liability between plaintiff and seller is 'governed by generally applicable rules apportioning responsibility').

section 402A,[18] which was published in 1965 – stated that a commercial seller is subject to liability for physical harm caused by a product that, at the time of sale, was '*in a defective condition unreasonably dangerous to the consumer or to his property*.'[19]

12 Section 402A further stated that this liability attaches even if the seller exercised 'all possible care' to render the product safe, and even if the consumer injured by the product had not bought it directly from the seller.[20] Finally, commentary to this provision stated that a defect renders a product 'unreasonably dangerous' only when, because of the defect, the product is 'dangerous to an extent beyond that which would be contemplated by the ordinary consumer who purchases it, with the ordinary knowledge common to the community of its characteristics.'[21] By linking the idea of a defective product to consumer expectations rather than lack of care on the part of the seller, while at the same time eliminating the requirement of contractual privity, section 402A brought together elements of negligence and warranty law to create a new form of tort liability. How drastically this form of liability departed from negligence is discussed below, as is the definition of defect under the more recently adopted Third Restatement of Torts, which the American Law Institute regards as superseding the Second, although a number of state courts continue to employ standards for strict liability from the Second Restatement.

13 Section 402A limited recovery to 'physical harm',[22] which was understood to mean personal injury and damage to tangible property. The Third Restatement is more explicit, subjecting the seller of a defective product to liability for 'harm to persons or property caused by the defect'.[23] Thus, strict product liability does not extend to economic loss; US courts have instead left warranty law to determine how economic loss should be allocated between manufacturer and

---

18 Restatement (Second) of Torts §402A (1965) ('Special Liability of Seller of Product for Physical Harm to User or Consumer') reads as follows:

'(1) One who sells any product in a defective condition unreasonably dangerous to the user or consumer or to his property is subject to liability for physical harm thereby caused to the ultimate user or consumer, or to his property, if
  a) the seller is engaged in the business of selling such a product, and
  b) it is expected to and does reach the user or consumer without substantial change in the condition in which it is sold.

(2) The rule stated in Subsection (1) applies although
  a) the seller has exercised all possible care in the preparation and sale of his product, and the user or consumer has not bought the product from or entered into any contractual relation with the seller.'

19 Ibid (emphasis added).

20 Ibid.

21 Ibid cmt i.

22 Restatement (Second) of Torts §402A (1965).

23 Restatement (Third) of Torts: Products Liability §§1 and 21 (1998).

consumer.[24] Notwithstanding substantial consensus on this matter, a few courts have recognised a 'sudden and calamitous' exception to the bar on economic loss claims.[25] Thus, if an accident of the sort that tort law ordinarily would address, such as the crash of a helicopter, occurs but the only harm is to the helicopter itself and the purchaser's finances, these courts would permit a product liability claim. This exception might be thought of as invoking 'looks like a tort, must be a tort' reasoning.

B. THE DEFINITION OF 'PRODUCT'

14 'Product' as used in section 402A went undefined. It was generally understood to include personal property, and although a few courts have applied it to real property, most have not.[26] Electricity, by contrast, as something that is 'manufactured' and distributed in the stream of commerce has been treated as subject to strict product liability, especially when it causes harm due to power surges.[27] Similarly, the provision of water has been held to subject the supplier to strict product liability, in one case because the water was contaminated with flammable gas.[28] 'Fixtures', tangible products that are permanently attached to real property such as hot water heaters, windows and furnaces, have been widely accepted as products subject to product liability law.[29]

15 Product liability doctrine has always extended beyond the case of the mass-produced product. It is limited to injuries caused by products made or sold by *commercial sellers* – sellers who are in the business of making and/or selling the product in question. However, it is not restricted to industrial manufacturers. A local artisan who is in the business of selling crafts can be held strictly liable if one of her products is defective and causes injury.

16 Extension of the concept of 'product' to software or digital content first requires appreciation that economic loss caused by defective software would not be subject to product liability for the independent reason explained above limiting product liability to personal injury and property damage. Currently no

---

24 See *East River Steamship Corp v Transmerica Delaval Inc*, 476 U.S. 858 (1986).

25 See *Lloyd v Gen Motors Corp*, 916 A.2d 257 (Md. 2007); *DA Fischer et al.*, Products Liability: Cases and Materials (5th edn 2014) 652.

26 See, eg, *Martens v MCL Constr Corp*, 807 N.E.2d 480, 493 (Ill. App. Ct. 2004) ('Based on policy considerations supporting the strict liability doctrine, courts have consistently held that buildings and indivisible component parts of the building structure itself, such as bricks, supporting beams and railings, are not deemed products for the purpose of strict liability in tort.'). But see *Schipper v Levitt & Sons, Inc*, 207 A.2d 314 (N.J. 1965).

27 See, eg, *Pierce v Pac. Gas & Elec Co*, 212 Cal. Rptr. 283 (Ct. App. 1985).

28 *Moody v City of Galveston*, 524 S.W.2d 583, 589 (Tex. Civ. App. 1975).

29 See *DG Owen*, Products Liability Law (3rd edn 2015) 1104.

case law addresses whether software manufacturers or sellers are subject to strict product liability or negligence liability for software that does cause physical harm.[30] Commentators, however, generally favour the imposition of product liability on sellers of defective software[31] and have identified several hypothetical scenarios in which defective software could cause physical injury.[32]

17 With regard to digital content, the robust role of the First Amendment to the US Constitution, which bars goverment action 'abridging the freedom of speech', must be appreciated. When the product involves communication, whether in a book, newspaper, electronic image, movie, or other form, including transmissions on the internet, courts are reluctant to declare the message defective and impose liability, even if such liability might not violate the strictures of the First Amendment. Thus, in an early and influential case, *Winter v GP Putnam's Sons*,[33] a book about mushrooms allegedly misidentified poisonous mushrooms as safe for eating. Victims of mushroom poisoning sued the publisher and seller in a product liability suit. The court of appeals affirmed dismissal of the case explaining the 'high priority on the unfettered exchange of ideas,' reflected in US society and law. Courts have also rejected claims against video game manufacturers and other visual entertainment products, ruling that they are not 'products' for the purposes of product liability.[34]

18 Blood and other human tissue is not treated as a product for purposes of product liability.[35] Since the first cases arose, state legislatures have enacted provisions that limit the liability of blood providers to instances in which they have failed to exercise reasonable care.[36] Today, 49 states have enacted 'blood shield laws,' which are statutes immunising blood providers from strict liability or breach of warranty actions for injuries caused by contaminated blood products.[37] These laws were intended to respond to the unavailability, at the

---

30 See *Owen* (fn 29) 1045 ('the case law so far is limited to commercial contexts involving claims for economic loss without physical harm'). Owen notes that in the commercial arena, mass produced software has been held to be a 'good' subject to the warranty provisions in the UCC. Ibid.

31 See, eg, *EG Durney*, Comment, The Warranty of Merchantability and Computer Software Contracts: A Square Peg Won't Fit in a Round Hole (1984) 59 Wash L Rev 511; *BL Horovitz*, Note, Computer Software as a Good Under the Uniform Commercial Code: Taking a Byte Out of the Intangibility Myth (1985) 65 BU L Rev 129; *DJ Hanson*, Note, Easing Plaintiffs' Burden of Proving Negligence for Computer Malfunction (1983) 69 Iowa L Rev 241.

32 See *TG Wolpert*, Product Liability and Software Implicated in Personal Injury (1993) 60 Def Couns J 519.

33 938 F.2d 1033 (9th Cir. 1991).

34 *Owen* (fn 29) 1113.

35 Restatement (Third) of Torts: Products Liability §19(c) (1998).

36 Ibid §19 cmt c.

37 New Jersey is the only state that has not adopted a shield law, but its case law protects blood providers from strict liability; the same is true for the District of Columbia. See *RD Eckert*, The AIDS Blood-Transfusion Cases: A Legal and Economic Analysis of Liability (1992) 29

time of their adoption, of tests to screen blood donations for hepatitis C or HIV. They limit liability for hospitals, blood banks, and in some cases pharmaceutical companies by requiring proof of negligence or wilful misconduct to establish liability.[38]

19 In the face of the blood shield statutes, most courts have held blood providers to a professional standard of care rather than ordinary negligence.[39] Under ordinary negligence principles, a party is held to an objective standard of reasonable care that is left to the jury to determine. Professionals, by contrast, are held to the standard actually employed by reasonable professionals, requiring expert testimony about customarily employed care.

20 Influenced by section 402A of the Second Restatement, state courts and legislatures in the United States overwhelmingly embraced the idea of strict product liability, which they understood as liability based on *product defectiveness* rather than manufacturer fault.[40] Henceforth, and still today, a person alleging physical harm caused by a product was required to prove only that she was injured by a product that was in a defective condition at the time it left the control of the manufacturer or seller and that her injury resulted from a foreseeable use of the product. (We leave aside here any discussion of affirmative defences, such as comparative fault.)

C. THE CONCEPT OF 'DEFECT'

21 It is important to emphasise that strict product liability law was first adopted in the 1960s and 1970s with certain kinds of cases in mind. These tended to involve defects that could be identified in a relatively straightforward and commonsensical manner: for example, glass bottles of carbonated beverages

San Diego L Rev 203, 205–06 n 8 (noting that forty-nine states adopted shield laws, and citing cases). Litigation in New Jersey and the District of Columbia has been limited because, early on, courts provided immunity from strict liability. See *Brody v Overlook Hospital*, 332 A.2d 596 (N.J. 1972); *Fisher v Sibley Memorial Hospital*, 403 A.2d 1130 (D.C. Ct. App. 1979).

38 Most states enacted shield laws in the 1960s and 1970s; by 1972, for example, there were already forty-one states with this type of law on the books. See *MA Franklin*, Tort Liability for Hepatitis: An Analysis and a Proposal (1972) 24 Stan L Rev 439, 474 and n 203 (noting that only nine states had not yet adopted a shield law by 1972 and citing statutes).

39 See, eg, *Zaccone v Am. Red Cross*, 872 F. Supp. 457, 460 (N.D. Ohio 1994) ('[Red Cross] cannot be negligent if it met the generally recognised and accepted practices of blood bank professionals'); *Osborn v Irwin Memorial Blood Bank*, 5 Cal. Rptr. 2d 101, 121 (Ct. App. 1992) (requiring blood bank 'to exercise with respect to blood testing and donor screening that reasonable degree of skill, knowledge, and care ordinarily possessed and exercised by other blood banks under similar circumstances').

40 Forty-six of the 51 jurisdictions in the United States have adopted some form of strict product liability. See *Owen* (fn 29) 270–271 and n 196.

that exploded during normal use[41] or cars with steering mechanisms that caused the car to veer violently off the road.[42] A key point of contention today among judges and scholars is the degree to which genuinely strict product liability has been applied, or should be applied, to less glaring dangers – for example, to products that might have been made less hazardous by designing with an additional safety feature.

22 As strict liability was developing and becoming widely adopted, claims were made that went beyond exploding bottles and cars that made uncommanded turns. Some of these claims were that the product should have been made safer than it was by adding additional safety features or modifying the design in a way that eliminates or reduces the risk posed by the product. Claims were also made that products should have been accompanied with instructions for safe use or warnings about latent dangers posed by the product. During this time, the concept of defect developed to recognise three different types of defect: (i) manufacturing defects; (ii) design defects; and (iii) informational inadequacies. That tripartite understanding of defect is widespread in US jurisdictions today.[43]

23 There is broad consensus on the idea of a 'manufacturing defect'. It consists of a single unit or item (for example, one particular car) that departs from the manufacturer's own specifications for that product line in a way that renders the particular item or unit more dangerous than it would be if it conformed to the manufacturer's specifications. Strict liability, in the sense that a failure to exercise reasonable care by the manufacturer is not required, is widely accepted.[44]

24 Design defects, by contrast, have historically been defined in terms of one of two tests: (i) the consumer expectations test and (ii) the risk-utility test. The first stems from the Second Restatement, which provided, based on the contractual roots of section 402A, a consumer expectations standard as explained above.[45] Under this test, a product is deemed defective if it contains a danger that an ordinary consumer would not expect to find in such a product, and the question of what an ordinary consumer would expect is largely for the jury.

25 The second standard was developed after the adoption of section 402A, largely in response to the aggressiveness of a plaintiffs' bar that pushed the

---

41 See, eg, *Escola v Coca-Cola Bottling Co of Fresno*, 150 P.2d 436 (Cal. 1944).

42 See, eg, *Vandermark v Ford Motor Co*, 391 P.2d 168 (Cal. 1964).

43 The Third Restatement distinguishes among these three different types of defects and provides different standards for determining whether a defect exists for each of the three. Restatement (Third) of Torts: Products Liability §2 (1998).

44 See Restatement (Third) of Torts: Products Liability §2(a) & cmt c (1998).

45 See *supra* text accompanying notes 19–21.

boundaries of strict liability by bringing claims that raised the question of how much safety must be built into a product.[46] Durable products can almost always be made safer by adding safety features (at additional cost) or by reducing risk (often by trading off utility). Thus automobiles could be made almost completely safe by turning them into tanks that travel at only four miles per hour and that consume vastly more fuel than automobiles. While no plaintiff's lawyer argued that cars must take the form of tanks to be non-defective, many suits asserted theories of defect that raised the difficult question of how much safety tort law should mandate. Courts and commentators became concerned about the indeterminacy of the consumer expectations test for these kinds of cases and the concomitant unconstrained discretion it afforded juries.[47] In addition, some courts[48] became dissatisfied with the consumer expectations standard because of the way it treated open and obvious dangers – no matter how much risk was created by an obvious danger and how minimal the costs to correct it, the product would not violate consumer expectations and therefore was not defective.

26 Thus, courts developed a risk-utility test that, after some early misconceptions,[49] employs cost-benefit methodology to compare the additional safety that an alternative safer design would provide with the costs of employing such a design. Those costs might implicate economic, functionality, aesthetic or other issues that, as with safety in the personal injury realm, cannot be quantified. But such cost-benefit methodology provides a framework for addressing questions about design defects of these sorts. This risk-utility test also generally requires expert testimony about the existence and availability of safer alternative designs and the relevant trade-offs that exist. In the product liability provisions of the Third Restatement of Torts, published in 1998, the risk-utility test was adopted as the sole standard for determining whether a design defect exists.[50]

---

46 See *supra* section III.A of Discussion Questions.

47 See *Soule v General Motors Corp*, 882 P.2d 298 (Cal. 1994) (limiting the availability of consumer expectations for design defects to instances when the design violates 'consumers' reasonable minimum assumptions' about safety); *MJ Davis*, Design Defect Liability: In Search of a Standard of Responsibility (1993) 39 Wayne L Rev 1217, 1236–37 (explaining dissatisfaction with the consumer expectations test for design defect claims).

48 See, eg, *Camacho v Honda Motor Co.*, Ltd., 741 P.2d 1240 (Colo. 1987); see also Restatement (Third) of Torts: Products Liability §2 cmt g (1998) (conformance with consumer expectations is not a basis for exonerating a design).

49 Many courts relied on a list of factors from an early canonical article. See *JW Wade*, On the Nature of Strict Tort Liability for Products (1973) 44 Miss LJ 825. Wade's factors were not appropriate for the type of cost-benefit analysis described above. See *MD Green*, The Schizophrenia of Risk-Benefit Analysis in Design Defect Litigation (1995) 48 Vand L Rev 609.

50 Some jurisdictions, including California, employ both a risk-utility and consumer expectations test either of which can be the basis for finding a design defective. In California, at least, the consumer expectations standard is limited to cases in which the product's failure

27 We should observe that the risk-utility test draws on the famous *Carroll Towing*[51] algebraic formulation for negligence: B < P x L.[52] Although juries are not routinely instructed in these algebraic terms, the factors contained in the Hand formula play an important and often determinative role in jury determinations of negligence in some cases[53] and in appellate review, such as it exists, of these jury determinations. Thus, today, in many, but by no means all, US jurisdictions, design defects are determined by a negligence standard or something closely akin to a negligence standard.

28 The role of warnings in a jurisdiction employing a risk-utility standard is quite different from the role described above with regard to consumer expectations. Even dangers that are open and obvious, or of which the consumer is subjectively aware, may render a product defective if the design's risks outweigh its utility. Thus, the existence of even an adequate warning does not of itself preclude a finding that the product was defectively designed. However, the obviousness of the risk and the consumer's actual awareness of it can be considered factors within a risk-utility analysis of the product's design.[54]

29 Before leaving strict liability theories–more accurately theories based on product defect–one other basis for liability deserves mention. Section 3 of the Products Liability Restatement explains that the existence of a defect can be inferred in some cases from the circumstances of the accident.[55] It is closely

justifies an inference that it is defective, equivalent to section 3 cases in the Third Restatement of Torts, which we explain below in text accompanying note 55. See *Soule v General Motors Corp*, 882 P.2d 298 (Cal. 1994).

51 *United States v Carroll Towing Co*, 159 F.2d 169 (2d Cir. 1947).

52 Where 'P' is the foreseeable probability of an accident occurring, 'L' represents the magnitude of any such loss, and 'B' is the burden of preventing such accidents from occurring. (The concept of the expected value of an accident, reflected in the product of P and L, simplifies the reality that many different accidents with different probabilities and magnitudes might be implicated, requiring something more akin to determining the area under a curve representing a function expressing those various possibilities.)

53 The Hand formula factors are generally not helpful when personal inadvertent careless conduct is the basis for a claim of negligence.

54 The Third Restatement explains: 'Warnings are not … a substitute for the provision of a reasonably safe design … [O]bviousness of risk does not necessarily obviate a duty to provide a safer design.' Restatement (Third) of Torts: Products Liability §2 cmt l (1998).

55 The text of section 3 provides:
'It may be inferred that the harm sustained by the plaintiff was caused by a product defect existing at the time of sale or distribution, without proof of a specific defect, when the incident that harmed the plaintiff:
(a) was of a kind that ordinarily occurs as a result of product defect; and
(b) was not, in the particular case, solely the result of causes other than product defect existing at the time of sale or distribution.'
Restatement (Third) of Torts: Products Liability §3 (1998).

related to the classic negligence doctrine of *res ipsa loquitur*, which recognises that circumstantial evidence may support an inference of carelessness even though the specific careless acts of the defendant are not known. Thus, if a brand-new car being driven home by its new owner suddenly veers to the left on its own, section 3 might be invoked to permit a jury to find it was defective.[56] Such a finding most likely would be the result of a manufacturing defect but is not limited to such.

D. COMMERCIAL SALE OR DISTRIBUTION OF A PRODUCT

30 The paradigm for invocations of strict product liability is the sale of a new chattel.[57] That sale must be made by one who is in the business of selling products to others, although it need not be the sole or even primary business of the seller. Casual sales by consumer owners of products, such as the sale of a used car, thus, are excluded from the reach of strict liability.

31 A number of different mechanisms for putting products into the hands of consumers or exposing consumers to the risks of products have expanded the reach of strict products beyond 'selling' to 'distributing' a product.[58] Thus, distribution includes renting,[59] bailing, or providing a product in the course of promoting a sale.[60]

E. SPECIAL PRODUCTS

32 Pharmaceuticals and medical devices have been singled out for special treatment. The special consideration applicable to these products is with regard to design defects and to a lesser extent warnings; the standards for defectiveness based on manufacturing defects remains the same as for other products.[61]

---

56 At least one commentator claims that these were the types of defects that strict product liability was intended to address and explains why no attention was paid to the different types of defects in section 402A. See *MD Green*, The Unappreciated Congruity of the Second and Third Restatements on Design Defects (2009) 74 Brook L Rev 807. But see *GL Priest*, Strict Products Liability: The Original Intent (1989) 10 Cardozo L Rev 2301 (claiming that section 402A was intended to address only manufacturing defects).

57 *Owen* (fn 29) §16.1, at 995.

58 Thus, the Third Restatement imposes liability on those who 'sell or distribute' a product. Restatement (Third) of Torts: Products Liability §1 (1998).

59 The seminal case is *Cintrone v Hertz Truck Leasing & Rental Serv*, 212 A.2d 769 (N.J. 1965).

60 Restatement (Third) of Torts: Products Liability §20(b) (1998); see also *Owen* (fn 29) §16.2, at 1003–1004.

61 Restatement (Third) of Torts: Products Liability §6(b)(1) (1998).

33 The beginning of special treatment for drugs was an inscrutable provision in the Second Restatement known as 'Comment k'.[62] Comment k provided:

> '*k. Unavoidably unsafe products.* There are some products which, in the present state of human knowledge, are quite incapable of being made safe for their intended and ordinary use. These are especially common in the field of drugs. An outstanding example is the vaccine for the Pasteur treatment of rabies, which not uncommonly leads to very serious and damaging consequences when it is injected. Since the disease itself invariably leads to a dreadful death, both the marketing and the use of the vaccine are fully justified, notwithstanding the unavoidable high degree of risk which they involve. Such a product, properly prepared, and accompanied by proper directions and warning, is not defective, nor is it unreasonably dangerous. The same is true of many other drugs, vaccines, and the like, many of which for this very reason cannot legally be sold except to physicians, or under the prescription of a physician. It is also true in particular of many new or experimental drugs as to which, because of lack of time and opportunity for sufficient medical experience, there can be no assurance of safety, or perhaps even of purity of ingredients, but such experience as there is justifies the marketing and use of the drug notwithstanding a medically recognizable risk. The seller of such products, again with the qualification that they are properly prepared and marketed, and proper warning is given, where the situation calls for it, is not to be held to strict liability for unfortunate consequences attending their use, merely because he has undertaken to supply the public with an apparently useful and desirable product, attended with a known but apparently reasonable risk.'[63]

34 Many US courts adopted the basic premise of Comment k that drugs and similar products were special and should not be subject to the same rules with regard to design defectiveness as other products. Note that Comment k specifically invokes the requirement that such products are 'properly prepared' and 'proper warning is given' and, thus, courts held that drugs could be defective for inadequate warnings or if adulterated.

35 With regard to drug design, two schools of thought developed. Some courts found Comment k to be an absolute barrier to drug design claims.[64] By contrast, others insisted that whether a drug is 'unavoidably unsafe' and therefore within the Comment k mantle of protection should be determined on a case-by-case

---

62 One commentator has observed that: 'Whether and how pharmaceuticals should be treated differently from other types of products has consumed more time and effort, and resulted in the gnashing of more teeth, than any other particularized issue in all of products liability law.' *Owen* (fn 29) §18.1, at 1100.

63 Restatement (Second) of Torts §402A cmt k (1965).

64 See, eg, *Brown v Superior Court*, 751 P.2d 470 (Cal. 1988); *Stone v Smith, Kline & French Labs*, 447 So. 2d 1301, 1303 (Ala. 1984) ('As has been noted, Comment k provides for drugs and vaccines an exception to the strict liability defined in Section 402A').

basis, which seemed to contemplate the court (rather than the jury) making an assessment of the benefits of the drug compared to its adverse effects.[65]

36 Although a variety of grounds have been proffered for special treatment of pharmaceuticals,[66] the best reason in our view is that drugs cannot, for the most part, be designed differently.[67] Drugs are biologically active chemicals that provide therapeutic benefits but also come with adverse effects.[68] Unlike durable goods, there is not a way to add a safety guard or otherwise eliminate the adverse effects attached to that specific chemical compound.

37 As a result, a risk–benefit test for determining defectiveness cannot be employed with drugs, unlike durable goods, because of the lack of an alternative design. To be sure, the courts that adopt a case-by-case approach seem to contemplate that the court will do a comparison of the drug's overall benefits with its overall risks, sometimes labelled 'categorical liability'. Such a meta-balancing of risks and benefits to determine defectiveness is rarely employed for other products. The Third Restatement adopted a very limited basis for finding

---

65 See, eg, *Toner v Lederle Labs, a Div of Am Cyanamid Co*, 732 P.2d 297, 303–08 (Idaho 1987); *White v Wyeth Labs, Inc*, 533 N.E.2d 748, 753–54 (Ohio 1988).

66 Those reasons are:
'(1) Drugs are highly regulated by the Federal Food, Drug, and Cosmetic Act. (2) Drugs have high social utility. Or, to put the point in economic terms, drugs provide substantial consumer surplus; most of us would pay more for drugs than we are charged because drugs have a value to most consumers well in excess of their price. (3) Learned intermediaries, physicians, assist their patients in determining which drugs will be appropriate for those individual patients. (4) Drugs that are harmful for some patients may be beneficial for others.
In addition, drugs are different from other durable goods but not from other toxic agents in that they frequently involve risks that cannot be identified through reasonable research and testing. Only after the extensive premarketing approval testing required by the Food and Drug Administration for drugs and upon distribution to the general public do those risks emerge, often after many years of use by the public.'
MD Green, Prescription Drugs, Alternative Designs, and the Restatement (Third): Preliminary Reflections (1999) 30 Seton Hall L Rev 207, 211.

67 There are exceptions. Combination drugs can be designed differently by removing or adding an additional chemical compound. Inert ingredients used to preserve or deliver the drug to patients can be replaced with other ingredients. The most notable example of this is the Sulfanilamide fiasco, in which the active ingredient, sulfanilamide, the first of the sulfa drugs, was suspended in diethylene glycol solvent (essentially antifreeze) to deliver the active ingredient. See *P Temin*, Taking Your Medicine: Drug Regulation in the United States (1980) 42. More than 100 people died as a result of using the drug. See *C Ballentine*, Taste of Raspberries, Taste of Death: The 1937 Sulfanilimide Incident <www.fda.gov/aboutfda/whatwedo/history/productregulation/sulfanilamidedisaster/default.htm>.

68 Some of those adverse effects can be eliminated or reduced with proper warnings. Thus, a drug that might put a heavy burden on the liver should be so identified so that those with reduced liver function can avoid taking the drug.

a drug defectively designed.[69] Thus, for drugs, 'the liability game is with the warnings candle, not with design'.[70]

38 Without much consideration or explanation, prescription medical devices were also subject to the same limited design defect standard as was adopted for drugs. Since 1976, medical devices, like drugs, have been subject to extensive regulation, including that pre-marketing approval be obtained from the federal regulatory agency, the Food and Drug Administration. And, like drugs, some medical devices have great social utility. However, unlike drugs, most medical devices are durable goods that can be designed in a different fashion. An MRI that, because of the design of its electrical system, shocks one in a thousand patients can be redesigned so that it does not do so. Perhaps the best that can be said for the Third Restatement's collapsing medical devices into the same special design standard applicable to drugs is that some medical devices are implants. Implants, unlike MRI machines, can only be assessed for effectiveness and safety in the same fashion as drugs: employing clinical trials to determine the device's safety and efficacy. Redesigning the product in a courtroom through expert witnesses would, given these circumstances, be an arguably inappropriate exercise.

F. STANDARD OF LIABILITY

39 Product liability brings together several different theories of liability. Breach of warranty, a contractual, strict-liability, standard is one. The most important of the three warranties in product liability is the implied warranty of merchantability, which requires that a product be 'fit for the ordinary purposes for which goods are used'[71] and be 'adequately contained, packaged, and labeled as the agreement may require.'[72] While these standards were developed for use in commercial transactions between suppliers and purchasers, they have been widely adapted and used in product liability cases as one basis for liability.

40 The second theory in use is negligence. Claims based on negligent design, warning, and manufacturing preceded the adoption of strict product liability in 1965 and were unleashed with the decision in *MacPherson v Buick Motor Co*,[73]

---

69 A prescription drug or medical device is not reasonably safe due to defective design if the foreseeable risks of harm posed by the drug or medical device are sufficiently great in relation to its foreseeable therapeutic benefits that reasonable healthcare providers, knowing of such foreseeable risks and therapeutic benefits, would not prescribe the drug or medical device for any class of patients. Restatement (Third) of Torts: Products Liability §6(c) (1998).

70 *Owen* (fn 29) §18.1, at 1101 (quoting *Green* (fn 66) 209).

71 UCC §2-316(c).

72 Ibid §2-316(e).

73 111 N.E. 1050 (N.Y. 1916).

which began the demise of the requirement of privity of contract for tort suits in which the defendant's performance or conduct was pursuant to a contractual arrangement.[74]

41 The third theory is 'strict product liability'. This theory, which does not require a showing of fault, reflects a melding of the strict liability of contract/warranty and negligence law in its protection of the person and private property. The 'strict' in strict product liability has been softened in the years since this theory was first adopted. While it does not require a showing that defendant engaged in an unreasonable act or conduct that threatened harm to others, courts have coalesced around a requirement that before liability may be imposed on a product manufacturer, there must be a showing that the risk that made the product defective was foreseeable, a central element for fault-based (negligence) liability.[75] To be sure, there remain several pockets of true 'strict' liability in modern products theory. Manufacturers are liable for manufacturing defects regardless of the degree of care taken in the manufacturing and quality assurances processes.[76] Similarly, retailers and others 'downstream' in the chain of distribution who had no role in the product's defectiveness, but who sold the product in that defective state are liable without regard to their lack of fault.[77] Finally, when a product fails to perform in such a way that a defect may be inferred – a car that enters into an uncommanded left turn and goes off the road – the manufacturer is strictly liable and foreseeable risk would not be an issue whether the defect that caused the deficient performance was of design or manufacturing origin.[78]

IV. THE PERSON LIABLE FOR DAMAGE

A. COMMERCIAL SELLERS AND DISTRIBUTORS

42 To be liable on a product liability theory, the defendant must be a seller or distributor[79] of a defective product. In addition, the seller or distributor must be in the business of selling or distributing products. Such sellers need not be exclusively in the business of selling the product alleged to be defective, so

---

74 While MacPherson was a product of the common law tradition and written so that it appeared only to extend those exceptions, in fact it turned out to be the genesis for the abandonment of privity in tort in United States courts over the next several decades. MacPherson, although an application of negligence law, was a critical first step in the development of product liability in the US.

75 See *Owen* (fn 29) §10.4, at 672–81.

76 See Restatement (Third) of Torts: Products Liability §2(a) & cmt c (1998).

77 Ibid §2 cmt o.

78 Ibid §3.

79 See *supra* text accompanying notes 58–60; see also *Sukljian v Charles Ross & Son Co, Inc*, 503 N.E.2d 1358 (N.Y. 1986).

long as such sales are part of the course of business for the seller. Thus, sales of refreshments by a movie theatre would qualify as business sales. Casual sellers, however, are not subject to product liability theories, although they may be liable based on pure negligence concepts.[80] Thus, a movie theatre that sells a surplus projector would not be covered by strict product liability.

43 We are not aware of and have been unable to locate any cases involving government entities that were sued on a product liability theory. While there may be such a case or even a few such cases, there are good reasons to think such a situation would be quite rare. First, governments rarely manufacture or sell products. Second, most hospitals in the US are not owned by governmental entities. In addition, although hospitals often 'sell' products in connection with providing medical services, most courts hold that hospitals are not the seller of products that are provided to patients in the course of providing medical care.[81] Finally, statutes that authorise suit against the federal government and many individual states do not permit suits based on strict liability, although negligence claims are permitted.[82]

B. APPORTIONMENT AMONG MULTIPLE DEFENDANTS

44 When multiple defendants are held liable for the same harm to an injured plaintiff, apportionment rules are employed to determine how much of the liability will be borne by each such defendant. Defendants may include several that are within the chain of distribution of the defective product as well as defendants who have contributed to causing the harm independently of the product. Thus, a careless driver who causes an accident that, because of a defective airbag, results in the death of a passenger is subject to liability for negligence along with the manufacturer (and retailer and perhaps the airbag manufacturer) of the automobile.

---

80 Thus, an individual selling a car that she had owned who knows that the car has brakes that could give out at any time would be subject to liability to the purchaser based on acting unreasonably in failing to inform the purchaser of the significant risk posed by the automobile. See Restatement (Third) of Torts: Products Liability §8 cmt c (1998) ('Noncommercial and casual used-product sellers may be liability under the general principles of negligence. But such sellers are outside the scope of this [Products Liability] Restatement' (citation omitted)); cf *Gebo v Black Clawson Co*, 703 N.E.2d 1234, 1238 (N.Y. 1998) (acknowledging possibility of negligence liability for a casual seller but concluding that defendant had acted reasonably under the circumstances).

81 See Restatement (Third) of Torts: Products Liability §20 cmt d (1998).

82 See *MD Green/WJ Cardi*, The Liability of Public Authorities in the United States, in: K Oliphant (ed), The Liability of Public Authorities in Comparative Perspective (forthcoming 2016).

45 We begin by addressing the basis of apportionment between the manufacturer (we address the implications of other product sellers below) and the negligent driver. First, we assume for purposes of this illustration that the manufacturer is responsible for the defect in the airbag. Because each defendant has acted tortiously, comparative responsibility would be employed to determine the share of plaintiff's harm that each of the driver and the manufacturer would be responsible to pay.[83]

46 This apportionment would likely occur in the underlying suit by the injured victim against the driver and manufacturer and would require the fact finder to assign comparative percentages of responsibility to each of the defendants (and to the plaintiff's decedent as well if contributorily negligent). Even if the decedent's estate only sued the driver, procedural rules would permit the driver to join the car manufacturer in the suit. Alternatively, the driver could wait to see if she was held liable and, if so, bring a recourse action against the car manufacturer.

47 Universal joint and several liability has largely been replaced in the US with a variety of alternative schemes. Some states limit joint and several liability to defendants whose comparative responsibility is above a specified threshold, often 50%. Other states limit joint and several liability to pecuniary damages and employ several liability for non-pecuniary damages. Some states reallocate the share of an insolvent or partially insolvent defendant to the remaining parties in proportion to their comparative share of responsibility. Some states use pure several liability. In any case, when all defendants are solvent, the joint and several or several liability scheme is not of great importance. Joint and several liability matters when one or more responsible defendants is financially unable to pay its share.[84]

48 All parties in the chain of distribution are subject to full liability to the injured victim. This is often described as joint and several liability, but that is not quite accurate. Liability in this instance is vicarious rather than joint and several. The significance of the distinction is that even if a jurisdiction has modified its rules on joint and several liability, vicarious liability makes each party liable for the entirety of the harm. Hence, the risk of insolvency remains with vicariously liable parties.

---

83 See Restatement (Third) of Torts: Apportionment of Liability §23 (2000).

84 See Restatement (Third) of Torts: Apportionment of Liability §A18 cmt a (2000) (explaining the two consequences of joint and several liability: the risk of insolvency is placed on other liable defendants and the burden of suing other potentially liable parties is placed on defendants).

49 Apportionment among parties within the chain of distribution in a product liability claim requires determining which of those parties was responsible for the defect. Most often this is the manufacturer, but it can be others. A retailer who misassembles the parts of a bicycle resulting in the handlebars flying off while the owner is riding it would be responsible for the defect in the bicycle. Similarly, the manufacturer of the airbag, a component part, may be responsible for the defect. Notwithstanding responsibility for the defect, all who sell a defective product are subject to liability for harm caused by the defect. However, those who are held liable for simply selling a defective product are being held vicariously liable: they are liable not for anything they did but for their status as seller of the product. Thus, in this instance, those 'innocent' parties would be entitled to indemnity from the party responsible for the defect.[85]

50 Finally, it may be that some within the distribution chain, while not responsible for the defect, have acted tortiously in connection with the defect. Thus, it may be that although the airbag was defective, the car manufacturer's failure to test it was, under the circumstances, negligent. In that event, the basis for apportionment between the airbag manufacturer and the car manufacturer would be contribution rather than indemnity and the fact finder would assign comparative shares of responsibility to each of the manufacturers.

V. THE AGGRIEVED PERSON AND DAMAGE

A. WHO MAY PURSUE A CLAIM?

51 Since *MacPherson v Buick Motor Co*[86] rid tort claims of privity limitations, any person suffering personal injury or injury to property (other than the product itself) may sue entities in the manufacturing/distribution chain in tort, subject to the limitations of causality and scope of liability. Privity remains a significant barrier to warranty claims in many states, however. First, with regard to vertical privity, most states limit the right to sue for breach of warranty to those with a direct buyer–seller relationship. Thus, the purchaser of a defective

85 '(a) When two or more persons are or may be liable for the same harm and one of them discharges the liability of another in whole or in part by settlement or discharge of judgment, the person discharging the liability is entitled to recover indemnity in the amount paid to the plaintiff, plus reasonable legal expenses, if:
(1) the indemnitor has agreed by contract to indemnify the indemnitee, or
(2) the indemnitee
...
(ii) was not liable except as a seller of a product supplied to the indemnitee by the indemnitor and the indemnitee was not independently culpable.'
Ibid §22.

86 111 N.E. 1050 (N.Y. 1916).

chair from a retail store is typically barred from suing the ultimate manufacturer for breach of warranty.[87] A minority of states would allow such a suit.[88] Liability in cases involving horizontal privity – that is, claims brought by someone other than the purchaser – are even more mixed. The Uniform Commercial Code reflects the diversity of approaches among jurisdictions by providing three alternatives, pursuant to which suit may be brought by: (i) 'any natural person who is in the family or household of his buyer or who is a guest in his home', (ii) 'any natural person who may reasonably be expected to use, consume or be affected by the goods', or (iii) 'any person who may reasonably be expected to use, consume or be affected by the goods,' except that it extends to property damage as well as personal injury.[89]

52 When strict product liability developed in the early 1960s, there was initially some confusion about how to treat bystanders. Strict product liability doctrinally was an amalgam of contract (warranty) and tort law,[90] and from the former perspective privity of contract continued to impose considerable limitations on who could recover. A caveat to section 402A of the Second Restatement of Torts explicitly left unresolved whether a bystander could assert a claim based on strict liability.[91] An influential early case, drawing on the tort strand of strict product liability, extended strict liability to bystanders:

> 'If anything, bystanders should be entitled to greater protection than the consumer or user where injury to bystanders from the defect is reasonably foreseeable. Consumers and users, at least, have the opportunity to inspect for defects and to limit their purchases to articles manufactured by reputable manufacturers and sold by reputable retailers, whereas the bystander ordinarily has no such opportunities. In short, the bystander is in greater need of protection from defective products which are dangerous, and if any distinction should be made between bystanders and users, it should be made, contrary to the position of defendants, to extend greater liability in favor of the bystanders.'[92]

53 This reasoning has captured the day with regard to who can assert a strict product liability claim, and today bystanders are as able to assert strict product liability claims as purchasers and consumers.[93] Indeed, from a tort perspective, bystanders are more sympathetic victims than purchasers as they did not select the product purchased and thus were involuntarily exposed to it and garnered none of the benefits of consuming the product.

---

87 See, eg, *Compex International Co, Ltd v Taylor*, 209 S.W.3d 462 (Ky. 2006).

88 See *JJ White/RS Summers*, Uniform Commercial Code (5th edn 2006) §11–3, at 744–745 n 8.

89 UCC §2–318.

90 See *supra* text accompanying notes 19–21.

91 Restatement (Second) of Torts §402A caveat (1) (1965).

92 *Elmore v American Motors Corp*, 451 P.2d 84, 89 (Cal. 1969).

93 See *Owen* (fn 29) §5.3, at 261–262.

B. DAMAGE

54 The concept of harm generally is not different in the product liability context from other torts, although there exist a few differences among the types of harm compensable under negligence, strict liability, and breach of warranty theories. Most significantly, the economic loss rule remains a barrier to collecting purely economic damages pursuant to claims for negligence and strict liability,[94] whereas there is no per se bar to economic loss in warranty claims. Warranty claims are subject to the general limitation on consequential damages – that the potential for such harm must have been contemplated by the parties at the time of contracting.[95] This limitation sometimes results in the exclusion of consequential economic harms, but it does not serve as bright line exclusion.

55 Similarly, a plaintiff may not collect damages in tort for harm to the product itself, although such damages are squarely within the purview of warranty protection. By contrast, most courts apply generally applicable rules to purely emotional distress damages regardless of the type of claim. Specifically, such pure emotional distress is recoverable in negligence, strict product liability, and warranty under the same labyrinthine restrictions applicable in other kinds of negligence cases[96] – although not all courts are in agreement as to this approach.[97] Finally, with proof of malice, a plaintiff might collect punitive damages via tort; punitive damages are not, however, recoverable for breach of warranty.

56 Finally, as part of the tort reform movement in the US, business lobbyists and many state legislatures have targeted product liability lawsuits in an effort to curb what they view as excessive recoveries. Thus, a number of states have, by statute, imposed damages caps in product liability lawsuits, applicable either to damages generally or noneconomic or punitive damages in particular.[98]

---

94 A plaintiff may sue for purely economic losses that result from the tort of misrepresentation, however.

95 See, eg, *Hadley v Baxendale* (1854) 156 Eng. Rep. 145.

96 See, eg, *Walker v Clark Equipment Co*, 320 N.W.2d 561 (Iowa 1982) (applying negligence standards for emotional distress to strict liability claim); *Sease v Taylor's Pets, Inc*, 700 P.2d 1054 (Or. 1985) (extending rules to strict liability and warranty claims).

97 Compare *Kately v Wilkinson*, 148 Cal. App. 3d 576 (Ct. App. 1983) (allowing recovery more liberally for emotional distress to strict liability than would be the case in negligence) with *Pasquale v Speed Products Eng'g*, 654 N.E.2d 1365 (1995) (requiring proof of physical harm in a bystander case, an element not required when the suit is brought in negligence).

98 See, eg, MCLA §600.2946a(1) (imposing cap of $280,000 on noneconomic damages in product liability actions); *State ex rel. Ohio Acad of Trial Lawyers v Sheward*, 715 N.E.2d 1062, 1073 n 6 (Ohio 1999) (describing Ohio statutory damages caps in products cases).

VI. CAUSALITY

A. FACTUAL CAUSATION

57 Although some courts tend to collapse factual causation and scope of liability,[99] we address them separately here. Factual causation is a largely empirical inquiry that, framed by legal standards, inquires into what happened. Legal standards frame the inquiry by mandating that the tortious conduct of the defendant be the relevant matter to determine whether it was responsible for certain legally cognizable harm suffered by the plaintiff. In product liability, the relevant tortious conduct is selling or distributing a defective product, so the causal inquiry becomes whether the defect in defendant's product caused plaintiff's personal injury or property damage.

58 Two tests for factual causation are in use in the US. One employs the *sine qua non* (or but-for) standard that inquires whether the plaintiff's harm would have occurred in the absence of the defendant's tortious conduct.[100] This standard for factual cause has to be supplemented when the plaintiff's harm is over-determined by two or more multiple sufficient causes.[101]

59 The other standard for causation in use in the US inquires whether the defendant's tortious conduct is a 'substantial factor' in the plaintiff's harm. Originally developed to address the over-determined outcome situation, it nevertheless is in widespread use in the United States in ordinary cases in which over-determination is not in issue.[102] Sometimes court employing it recognise that, at least as set forth in the first and Second Torts Restatements,[103] a requirement of the substantial factor test is that the harm would not have

99 We use the term 'scope of liability,' rather than 'legal cause' or 'proximate cause' because it better expresses the function that it performs in a tort case. We note that both the Principles of European Tort Law and the Third Restatement of Torts employ 'scope of liability.'

100 See Restatement (Third) of Torts: Liability for Physical and Emotional Harm §26 (2010).

101 Ibid §27.

102 See, eg, *Am. Fed'n of Teachers-Oregon, AFT, AFL-CIO v Oregon Taxpayers United PAC*, 189 P.3d 9, 17 (Or. 2008) ('"Factual causation" exists when a defendant's conduct "was a substantial factor in producing [the] plaintiff's injury"'). For a perceptive analysis of the choice between substantial factor and sine qua non for factual causation, see *June v Union Carbide Corp*, 577 F.3d 1234 (10th Cir. 2009).

103 The first two Torts Restatements adopted the substantial factor test for factual causation but caused significant confusion by employing 'legal causation' as an umbrella term to include both factual causation and scope of liability. See Restatement (Second) of Torts §431 (1965).

occurred without the defendant's tortious conduct[104] (ie *sine qua non*), other courts fail to appreciate or articulate this aspect.[105]

B. SCOPE OF LIABILITY

60 There are multiple tests employed for scope of liability in the US: some courts use a foreseeability test,[106] some distinguish between direct and remote causes, others use a harm-within-the-risk test.[107] In addition, intervening acts may 'cut the chain of causation', in the vernacular of some courts, meaning that plaintiff's harm is outside the defendant's scope of liability.

61 When strict product liability first was adopted, a number of auxiliary doctrines developed that appeared to be distinctive from the standard tort rules for factual causation and scope of liability. 'Misuse' was employed in a variety of ways; among them was that a plaintiff or third party acted in a sufficiently unforeseeable or culpable way so as to release the defendant from liability. 'Substantial change', a term employed in section 402A, was also employed when a product was altered in a sufficiently egregious matter that the courts felt the defendant should not be held responsible. Nevertheless, most of the time, courts used familiar standards and language for determining the scope of product liability defendant's harm.

62 In 1998, the Third Restatement provided necessary clarification, explaining: 'Whether a product defect caused harm to persons or property is determined by the prevailing rules and principles governing causation in tort.'[108] Although the language refers only to 'causation', its context reveals that it is about both factual causation and scope of liability.

---

104 Ibid §432(1) ('the actor's negligent conduct is not a substantial factor in bringing about harm to another if the harm would have been sustained even if the actor had not been negligent').

105 See *Hoeffer v Rockwell Automation, Inc*, 2006 WL 185479 (Cal. Ct. App. 2006) (stating that 'substantial factor' is not a stringent test for causation and that exposure to defendant's asbestos products could constitute a substantial factor so long as the contribution to causing plaintiff's disease was 'more than negligible or theoretical').

106 In the early days of strict liability, the foreseeability standard for scope of liability required adaptation because courts often held that knowledge of the risk, ie, foreseeability, was not required. See, eg, *Collins v Navistar, Inc*, 155 Cal. Rptr. 3d 137, 156 (Ct. App. 2013).

107 See *JA Page*, Proximate Cause (2003).

108 See Restatement (Third) of Torts: Products Liability §15 (1998). The Reporters' Note to Comment a to section 15 elaborates: 'The basic rules governing causation in product liability litigation are the same as those governing tort law generally. It is unnecessary, therefore, to draft a set of causation standards limited in application to product liability; the prevailing rules and principles of causation may be applied in products litigation. Defect-related increases in harm are sufficiently unique to the product liability field to warrant separate, special treatment. See §16(c). Otherwise, the general rules governing causation in tort law should suffice.'

C. PROPORTIONAL LIABILITY

63 Two forms of proportional liability have been recognised in the US, although not unanimously. The first is loss of chance and the second is market share. Loss of chance in the US has been largely limited to the medical context and not employed in product liability,[109] so we do not elaborate here.

64 Market share liability, however, emerged from a product liability case and, so far as we are aware, has only been employed in the product liability arena. It emerged from litigation over the drug DES, a synthetic oestrogen used to prevent miscarriages:

> '[I]n the middle part of the 20th century to prevent miscarriage, DES, because it was not patented, was manufactured by hundreds of pharmaceutical companies. DES caused disease in the offspring of the mothers who took the drug, typically 20 years after exposure, and at a time when evidence of which manufacturer produced the DES the mother had consumed was, quite often, unavailable.'[110]

65 Beginning in 1980, led by the California Supreme Court,[111] several courts recognised a new market-share liability that enabled a DES victim to recover without identifying the manufacturer that had supplied the DES that her mother took. Of the approximately 18 courts that have addressed the issue, about half have accepted the doctrine while the other half have rejected it.[112] Details of the doctrine in the courts' adopting vary with regard to the definition of the market,[113] whether liability is joint and several,[114] whether a defendant can exculpate itself by showing it did not produce the DES for plaintiff's mother,[115] and whether defendants are proportionally responsible for manufacturers that no longer exist or were not joined in the case.[116]

66 While market share was a much-hyped development when it first emerged, it has played a considerably subdued role because it is limited to products that are equivalent in the risks that they pose. Thus, many asbestos plaintiffs who could not identify the manufacturers to whose asbestos products the victims had been

---

109 See *DB Dobbs et al*, The Law of Torts (2nd edn 2011) §197, at 669–678; Restatement (Third) of Torts: Liability for Physical and Emotional Harm §26 cmt n (2010).

110 Restatement (Third) of Torts: Liability for Physical and Emotional Harm §28 cmt p (2010).

111 *Sindell v Abbott Labs*, 607 P.2d 924 (Cal. 1980).

112 Restatement (Third) of Torts: Liability for Physical and Emotional Harm §28 rptrs. note to cmt p (2010).

113 Compare *Hymowitz v Eli Lilly & Co*, 539 N.E.2d 1069, 1077–1078 (N.Y. 1989) (adopting a national market share) with *Conley v Boyle Drug Co*, 570 So. 2d 275 (Fla. 1990) (market share should be 'as narrowly defined as the evidence in a given case allows').

114 See ibid 1078.

115 See ibid.

116 See *Brown v Superior Court*, 751 P.2d 470 (Cal. 1988).

exposed sought unsuccessfully to use the market-share theory to bridge their evidentiary gap. Because asbestos products pose different risks, those efforts have been largely turned away. Only a very small number of cases have extended market share to products other than DES.[117]

D. APPORTIONMENT AMONG MULTIPLE CAUSES

67 Multiple actors or events may contribute to a plaintiff's harm and, when that is the case, apportionment of liability may be required. The first instance in which apportionment may be required is when different actors, whether acting tortiously or not, cause different harms to a victim. Thus, if a negligent driver collides with another car, causing the occupant a broken arm, while a defective airbag fails to inflate, resulting in the occupant crashing into the windshield and suffering head gashes, the first basis for apportionment between the car manufacturer and the negligent driver is causation. The driver is the only tortious cause of plaintiff's broken arm; both the driver and the manufacturer are a cause of the head gashes. In such a situation, the court must isolate the harms for which each of the two can be held liable because of the central tort principle that parties are not held liable for harms that they do not cause.[118] In this hypothetical, apportionment based on causation is straightforward; in other cases, the available evidence may not so readily permit causal apportionment.[119]

68 When multiple tortfeasors are each a cause of the same harm, as with the head gashes in the foregoing hypothetical, liability is apportioned between them, as explained above no 44 ff. That would be equally true if the victim contributed to her own injuries, as would be the case if a driver of an automobile negligently gets into an accident that results in the same injuries described above.[120]

69 In rare cases, the particularly egregious or unforeseeable subsequent tortious acts of another may result in a court concluding that the later tortious act is a superseding cause that prevents the plaintiff's harm from being within the first tortfeasor's scope of liability. Thus, for example, if a defect in an automobile results in it breaking down on a remote road and a sexual predator is thereby enabled to assault the female driver, the automobile manufacturer would likely not be held liable for the assault on scope of liability grounds.

---

117 See *MA Franklin et al*, Tort Law and Alternatives (9th edn 2011) 382–383.

118 See Restatement (Third) of Torts: Apportionment of Liability §26 (2000).

119 This is particularly true in 'crashworthiness' cases and in toxic harm cases in which plaintiff is exposed to multiple defendants' toxic agent. See Restatement (Third) of Torts: Products Liability §16 (1998) (crashworthiness cases); *MD Green*, A Future for Asbestos Apportionment? (2006) 12 Conn Ins LJ 315 (toxic substances).

120 See Restatement (Third) of Torts: Products Liability §17 (1998).

70 Ordinarily, that there was a non-tortious event or conduct that was a cause of the harm would not change the apportionment analysis set forth above. Thus, if the driver of the car was distracted by a busker (acting non-negligently) on the sidewalk and thereby drove into a tree, the conduct of the busker would not be relevant to any apportionment between the automobile manufacturer and the plaintiff.[121]

VII. DEFENCES AND EXCLUSIONS

71 In American product liability, there are six general types of defences, arising from both common law and statute: (i) contributory or comparative fault and assumption of risk, (ii) unforeseeable misuse, alteration and modification, (iii) disclaimers and contractual limitations on liability, (iv) statutory defences, (v) compliance with statute and pre-emption, and (vi) state of the art.[122]

(i) Comparative fault (or, in a few jurisdictions, contributory negligence) exists as a defence in product liability suits in the same manner as other torts. Historically, contributory negligence was not a defence to a strict liability claim,[123] but with the advent of comparative fault most jurisdictions permit a plaintiff's faulty behaviour to reduce her recovery.[124] In negligence and strict liability suits, assumption of risk is generally regarded as a part of the comparative fault calculus, except that in some cases, the assumption of risk analysis may appear as a means by which the court holds that the product was not defective or that the plaintiff's conduct serves as a superseding cause, thus negating proximate cause.

(ii) A plaintiff's unforeseeable misuse of a product might be treated as evidence of three things: (a) that the product was not defective, (b) that the harm that occurred was not within the scope of liability of the defendant, or (c) that the plaintiff is liable for his or her own comparative fault.[125] In some jurisdictions, courts discuss misuse as if it were its own freestanding defence; in others, the discussion is folded into the context of the doctrines listed here.

---

121 Some exceptions to this principle exist in toxic torts where at least one court permitted a reduction in the liability of an asbestos manufacturer for plaintiff's lung cancer based on the plaintiff's smoking without consideration of whether the smoking constituted contributorily negligent conduct. See *Dafler v Raymark Industries, Inc*, 611 A.2d 136 (N.J. Super. Ct. App. Div. 1992). But see *Champagne v Raybestos-Manhattan, Inc*, 562 A.2d 1100, 1118 (Conn. 1989) (permitting apportionment based on plaintiff's negligence in smoking).

122 See *Dobbs* (fn 109) §470–475 (2nd edn 2011).

123 See Restatement (Third) of Torts: Products Liability §17 cmt a (1998).

124 Ibid §17(b).

125 *Dobbs* (fn 109 122) §471.

(iii) A discussion of disclaimers and contractual limitations on liability appears separately below.
(iv) Statutory defences to actions for product liability vary from separate statutes of limitations or statutes of repose,[126] to damages caps, to substantive matters such as the state of the art. A complete collection of such statutes is impracticable here, as there is such a broad array of approaches across the states.
(v) The effect of compliance with regulation is discussed separately below. Federal pre-emption, as explained earlier,[127] is a defence or limitation to state common-law tort suits in a number of important areas of product liability – namely tobacco, generic prescription drugs, medical devices, certain consumer products, auto safety, aviation, hazardous substances, vaccines, trains, and insecticides, fungicides, and rodenticides.[128] Pre-emption can either be expressly provided in the federal statute or implied; it can be narrow or comprehensive; and it is an area of the law too complex to describe in detail in this report.
(vi) The 'state of the art' issue is sometimes described by courts to constitute a defence to a product liability suit.[129] However, 'state of the art' is used to mean several quite different things.[130] Sometimes it is used to mean whether the product's risk was foreseeable at the time of manufacture.[131] Alternatively, it is treated merely as one piece of the inquiry into existence of a defect. In design defect cases, for example, a defendant might argue that the design of its product comported with the 'state of the art', meaning that the available or predominant technology at the time of manufacture is relevant to a risk/utility analysis defect – relevant to the feasibility of an alternative design.[132] Sometimes 'state of the art' is used to mean the highest safety technology that has been developed. Similarly, in the context of a negligence claim, if a defendant could not reasonably have known of a potential alternative design, then the defendant cannot be negligent for failing to adopt it.

---

126 See *infra* no 88 ff.

127 See *supra* text accompanying notes 4–5.

128 See generally *Fischer* (fn 25) 617–637 (5th edn 2014).

129 eg Ariz. Rev. Stat. §12–683 (1); Mo. Ann. Stat. §537.764 (defining state of the art to mean the 'dangerous nature of the product was not known and could not reasonably be discovered at the time the product was placed into the stream of commerce' and providing that it is a complete defence to a failure to warn claim).

130 See *Owen* (fn 29) §10.4, at 659 ('Due in part to the diffuse nature of state-of-the-art concept, which embraces such diverse aspects of manufacturer responsibility as the foreseeability of risk, the feasibility of implementing a safer design, and the proper scope of "strict" liability, courts and legislatures have yet to agree on a definition of the term').

131 See *infra* text accompanying notes 166–167.

132 See, eg, *Boatland of Houston v Bailey*, 609 S.W.2d 743 (Tex. 1980).

72 In some states, this issue is mediated by the common law; in others, statutes set the standard.[133] Virtually every jurisdiction holds that defendants are not liable for 'unknowable risks' or for designs that were not technologically knowable or feasible at the time of manufacture.[134] On the other hand, most jurisdictions do not adopt an industry's prevailing customary standards as sufficient for a state of the art defence.[135] The majority approach is to define state of the art as 'the level of scientific, technological, and safety knowledge existing and reasonably feasible at the time of design.'[136]

73 The state-of-the-art defence is not only relevant to design defect cases. In some jurisdictions, it is also applied to both warning defect claims and manufacturing defect claims. In warning cases, the state-of-the-art defence addresses the knowability or foreseeability of product risk that would enable a warning to consumers of the danger.[137] In this context, the issue is different, focusing on the foreseeability of the risk, rather than the feasibility of an alternative design. Courts are split on whether the state of the art defence should be relevant to manufacturing defect claims.[138]

---

133 See, eg, Ariz. Rev. Stat. §12–683 (state of the art); N.C. Gen. Stat. §99B-1.1, 99B-4 & 99B-6 (no strict liability; state-of-the-art defence for prescription drugs; requirement of feasible alternative design); N.J. Stat. Ann. §2A:58C-3 (manufacturer not liable if there was no feasible alternative design); Ohio Rev. Code Ann. §2307.75(A)(invoking risk-benefit test for design defect cases).

134 *Dobbs* (fn 115) §471.

135 See, eg, Ark. Code Ann. §16–116–104 ('consideration' may be given to industry practice); Colo. Rev. Stat. §13–21–403 (1) (a) (imposing rebuttable presumption that product is non-defective if product conformed to the state of the art 'as distinguished from industry standards'); Kan. Stat. Ann. §60–3307 (a) (evidence of industry's improvements inadmissible); La. Rev. Stat. §9:2800.59 (no liability for manufacturer if at the time the product left his control he did not know and could not have known 'in light of then-existing reasonably available scientific and technical knowledge' of the danger); N.H. Stat. Ann. §507:8-g (an affirmative defence if risks were not discoverable using 'prevailing research and scientific techniques'); Tenn. Code Ann. §29–28–105 (scientific knowledge available to the manufacturer at the time 'is applicable', but consideration is also given to industry custom and standards).

136 *Potter v Chicago Pneumatic Tool Co*, 694 A.2d 1319, 1346 (Conn. 1997).

137 See fn 129.

138 Compare *Reed v Tiffin Motor Homes, Inc*, 697 F.2d 1192, 1196 (4th Cir. 1982) (S.C. law) ('In manufacturing defect cases courts have excluded evidence of the state of the art because the plaintiff need only show the product does not conform to the manufacturer's specifications to prove it is defective') (citing case applying Md. law), *Sturm, Ruger & Co, Inc v Day*, 594 P.2d 38, 44 (Alaska 1979) ('state-of-the-art evidence could have no bearing on the issue of whether a product had a manufacturing defect, i.e., that it deviated from the manufacturer's intended result'); *Cunningham v MacNeal Memorial Hospital*, 266 N.E.2d 897, 902 (Ill. 1970) ('To allow a defense to strict liability on the ground that there is no way, either practical or theoretical, for a defendant to ascertain the existence of impurities in his product would be to emasculate the doctrine and in a very real sense would signal a return to a negligence theory'), with *Indianapolis Athletic Club, Inc v Alco Standard Corp*, 709 N.E.2d 1070 (Ind. Ct. App. 1999) (statutory state-of-the-art defence covered manufacturing defects as well as defects in warning and design); *McGuire v Davidson Mfg Corp*, 258 F. Supp. 2d 945 (N.D. Iowa 2003), aff'd, 398 F.3d 1005 (8th Cir. 2005) (jury properly could find that ladder which

A. COMPLIANCE WITH REGULATION AS A DEFENCE TO PRODUCT LIABILITY

74 Compliance with voluntary standards has a similar effect as compliance with an industry standard;[139] compliance is relevant and may be persuasive in proving reasonableness, or knowledge of defectiveness; however, 'compliance with a statute is not in itself a defence to a negligence action.'[140] In a few jurisdictions, however, courts have attempted to provide protection for 'manufacturers whose products might be found defective although in compliance with federal statutes.'[141] Some provide that compliance is admissible as evidence to show that the product was not defective (or even negligently made).[142] Others provide that where compliance is proven, the product is 'rebuttably "presumed" non-defective'.[143] Still others provide that punitive damages are not available where certain safety standards are met.[144]

B. CONTRACTUAL EXCLUSION OF LIABILITY

75 Product manufacturers and distributors may limit implied warranties of merchantability, subject to limits imposed by the Uniform Commercial Code and a federal statute known as the Magnuson-Moss Act.[145] The Magnuson-Moss Act standardises certain aspects of warranty law and sets out standards of clarity and honesty.

---

broke did not contain a manufacturing defect, because it conformed to the state of the art, but that defendant was negligent in manufacturing the ladder with manufacturing defects; Iowa's state-of-the-art statutory defence explicitly applies to manufacturing as well as design and warning defects).

139 'The rule is the same with respect to a defendant's compliance with industry customs or standards. See *Jablonski v Ford Motor Co*, 955 N.E.2d 1138 (Ill. 2011) (manufacturer's compliance with industry standards in the design of the vehicle's fuel tank was probative but not determinative of the manufacturer's negligence in designing the fuel tank as it did, and thus the defectiveness of the design in a products case brought on a negligence theory); *Howard v Omni Hotels Management Corp*, 136 Cal. Rptr. 3d 739 (Cal App. 2012) (manufacturer's compliance with industry standards was not necessarily determinative, but in this case tended to prove that the manufacturer met the applicable duty of care with respect to the design of a bathtub). *Dobbs* (fn 109) §474.

140 *Dobbs* (fn 109) §474.

141 Ibid.

142 Ark. Code Ann. §16-116-105; Rev. Code Wash. §7.72.050 (1) (but providing a complete defence where the defendant was in compliance with 'a specific mandatory government contract specification').

143 Colo. Rev. Stat. Ann. §13-21-403 (1) (b); Kan. Stat. Ann. 60-3304; Tenn. Code Ann. §29-28-104; see also *Wright v Ford Motor Co.*, 508 F.3d 263 (5th Cir. 2007) (applying Tex. Civ. Prac. & Rem. Code §82.008).

144 Or. Rev. Stats. §30.927 (as to regulated prescription drugs).

145 15 USCA §2301 et seq.; see *Dobbs* (fn 109) §472.

76 Under the UCC, the disclaimer of warranties is acceptable if made by clear and conspicuous language.[146] The UCC also allows the seller of goods to 'limit remedies for breach of warranty in stand-alone economic harm cases, but a limitation as to damages for personal injury is prima facie unconscionable and unenforceable.'[147]

77 In the torts context, the Restatement (Third) of Torts: Products Liability provides that an exculpatory provision may not bar or reduce otherwise valid products claim 'for harm to persons'.[148] However, disclaimers or exculpatory provisions should not be confused with warnings. A valid warning obviously precludes a defective warning claim, and it may play a role in courts' assessment of the adequacy of the design of a product.[149] Specifically, if a court applies the consumer expectations test for defect (a minority) under section 402A, an effective warning typically defeats a design defect claim. Even pursuant to a risk-utility test, the plaintiff's awareness of the defect plays a role in the determination of the risk posed by the design of a product.[150]

VIII. REMEDIES

78 In a warranty-based product liability claim, a plaintiff may collect compensatory damages for harm to the product itself, personal injury and harm to the plaintiff's other property, and, if foreseeable to the parties at the time of contracting, purely emotional or economic harm. If the product is unique or otherwise difficult to replace, plaintiff may also seek replacement of the product with one that is non-defective – an *in personam* court order that is a form of specific performance.[151] Neither nominal nor punitive damages are available for breach of warranty.[152]

79 In tort-based product liability actions, monetary compensation is far and away the most common form of remedy. As with negligence, nominal damages are not permissible.[153] A plaintiff may recover punitive damages under the right set of facts, however. Punitive damages are available where the plaintiff has suffered actual damages and can prove that the defendant acted with 'malice',

---

146 UCC §2–316(2).
147 *Dobbs* (fn 109) §472.
148 Restatement (Third) of Torts: Products Liability §18 (1998).
149 'Although disclaimers will not absolve the defendant of liability for a defective product, adequate warnings may make some products reasonably safe.' *Dobbs* (fn 109) §472.
150 See Restatement (Third) of Torts: Products Liability §2 cmt f (1998).
151 UCC §2–716(1).
152 *Owen* (fn 29) §5.3, 268.
153 eg *Bic Pen Corp. v Carter*, 251 S.W.3d 500, 510 (Tex. 2007).

typically defined as actual knowledge of the defect and conscious or deliberate disregard of foreseeable harm likely resulting from the defect.[154] Punitive damages are most common in cases where a defective product has already caused harm to others prior to the plaintiff's injury, a fact of which the defendant was aware.

80 Plaintiffs also sometimes request specific relief in products cases – for example, an injunction ordering the defendant to stop manufacturing defective products, or mandating the use of a particular alternative design or quality control process, or compelling a recall or retrofit of a line of defective products.[155] Although there is no general doctrinal bar to obtaining such relief, it is the rare case in which such relief is granted. The reason is that in order to obtain injunctive relief, a plaintiff must prove that legal remedies would be inadequate.[156] In most product liability cases, the plaintiff has already been harmed, and damages are typically deemed adequate to compensate that harm. It is the unusual case in which the plaintiff anticipates future harm to herself/himself from a product necessitating an injunction; nor does a plaintiff have standing to sue on behalf of other potential future victims.[157] Courts sometimes depart from this general approach, however, particularly in cases of continuing relationships between the buyer and manufacturer.[158]

81 By contrast, regulatory agencies are frequently vested with the power to require specific actions of manufacturers and distributors of defective products. For example, the Food, Drug, and Cosmetic Act of 1938[159] gives the Food and Drug Administration two tools for the removal of defective products from the marketplace: seizure and injunction.[160]

---

[154] eg *Owens-Illinois, Inc. v Zenobia*, 601 A.2d 633, 653–54 (Md. 1992).

[155] See, eg, *Lucia v Teledyne Continental Motors*, 173 F. Supp. 2d 1253 (S.D. Ala. 2001) (describing suit by owner of general aviation aircraft against manufacturer of aviation parts seeking injunction to force manufacturer to conduct particular quality control checks to correct defects in parts). With regard to claims involving failure to recall or retrofit defective products, most courts dismiss such claims on duty grounds, without even addressing the remedies question. See *Owen* (fn 29) §10.8, 706–07.

[156] *eBay Inc v MercExchange, LLC*, 547 U.S. 388, 391 (2006).

[157] eg *Silverstein v Procter & Gamble Manuf Co*, 2008 WL 4889677 (S.D. Ga. 2008) ('[T]he rule requiring injunction-seeking plaintiffs to demonstrate an ongoing injury makes it difficult for consumers to obtain injunctions against manufacturers of defective products. The result of the rule, in most applications, is that once a plaintiff learns about a product's defect, he has lost his standing to enjoin the manufacturer from producing it').

[158] *Owen* (fn 29) §10.8, 706 (citing examples in the context of recall/retrofit cases).

[159] 21 USC §§301–92 (1970).

[160] Ibid §§332, 334.

IX. PROCEDURAL AND EVIDENTIAL ISSUES

A. THE BURDEN AND STANDARD OF PROOF AND PRESUMPTIONS

82 The plaintiff bears the burden of proof on the prima facie elements of a product liability claim. Those elements, based on the Third Restatement of Torts: Products Liability, include: (i) defendant sold or distributed a product defective at the time of sale or distribution; (ii) defendant is engaged in the business of selling or distributing products; (iii) the defect in the product was a factual cause of personal injury or property damage to the plaintiff; and (iv) plaintiff's harm is within the scope of defendant's liability.[161] Additional *prima facie* elements would depend on the specific type of defect alleged by plaintiff. Thus, in a design defect case, plaintiff would have to prove the existence of a reasonable alternative design that, in light of the foreseeable risks posed by the product, rendered the product not reasonably safe because of the failure to adopt the alternative design.[162]

83 There are numerous affirmative defences where the burden of proof would be on the defendant. A few of the most prominent ones include: (i) comparative responsibility by the plaintiff; (ii) in a few jurisdictions, assumption of risk; (iii) statutes of limitations; and (iv) statutes of repose. The significance of characterising an element as an affirmative defence is that the defendant bears the burden of proving it.

84 The standard of proof in US civil cases is a preponderance of the evidence, which is understood to mean that the proposition is more likely than not. For a very few matters, the burden of proof is sometimes ratcheted up to clear and convincing evidence, a standard intermediate between the preponderance standard and the criminal standard of beyond a reasonable doubt. Thus, a number of jurisdictions require that the culpability required for punitive damages be demonstrated by clear and convincing evidence.[163]

---

161 Additional elements would be required based on the specific type of defect that the plaintiff attempted to prove. Courts relying on the Second Restatement would require additionally that: (i) the defective product was unreasonably dangerous; and (ii) the product was expected to and did reach the consumer in without substantial change. See, eg, *Whitted v Gen Motors Corp*, 58 F.3d 1200, 1205 (7th Cir. 1995).

162 See Restatement (Third) of Torts: Products Liability §2(b) (1998).

163 See, eg, *Jonathan Woodner Co. v Breeden*, 665 A.2d 929, 932 (D.C. 1995), opinion amended on denial of reh'g, 681 A.2d 1097 (D.C. 1996); *Darcars Motors of Silver Spring, Inc v Borzym*, 841 A.2d 828, 837 (Md. 2004).

85 Two areas in which some jurisdictions employ presumptions in product liability cases are with regard to proof that an inadequate warning caused a plaintiff's harm and with regard to the foreseeability of risk posed by a product.

86 Proof that an adequate warning would have resulted in the plaintiff avoiding harm almost always requires proof that the plaintiff would have read and heeded an adequate warning. Because such proof would be self-serving, possibly speculative, *post hoc* testimony by an injured victim, some courts have adopted what is known as a 'heeding presumption.'[164] This heeding presumption shifts the burden of proof[165] on causation to the defendant. Although this presumption commands a slight majority of jurisdiction,[166] the Products Liability Restatement did not adopt it.[167]

87 Another area in which some courts employ what is effectively a presumption is with regard to the foreseeability of the harm. Since courts in the mid-1980s retreated from imposing liability for unknowable risks, foreseeability of risk is an issue in product liability cases. While in negligence this is an element of demonstrating negligent conduct, some courts have instead shifted the burden of proof to defendants by adopting a 'state-of-the-art'[168] affirmative defence that permits a defendant to avoid liability by proving that the risk that rendered the product defective was not something that could have been determined at the time of manufacture.[169] For the vast majority of durable goods, foreseeability of risk exists and is undisputed. Thus, making this a defence is sensible for the reason that it avoids the necessity of proof in many cases where it is not reasonably in dispute. Where shifting the burden of proof makes a significant difference is in the toxic substances area where, because of the long latency period before the existence of disease manifests, knowledge of risk may not develop for many years after the product is first marketed, as was the case with DES and asbestos.

---

164 *Owen* (fn 29) §11.4, 741–46.

165 More specifically, this presumption shifts the burden of producing sufficient evidence on the matter to the defendant. If the defendant succeeds in providing sufficient evidence that would enable the fact finder to determine that an adequate warning would not have prevented plaintiff's harm, then the burden of persuading the jury on this matter would remain with the plaintiff.

166 *Owen* (fn 29) §11.4, 743.

167 See *Delaney v Deere & Co*, 999 P.2d 930, 937–38 (Kan. 2000) (no heeding presumption adopted by the Restatement (Third) of Torts: Products Liability).

168 We should caution that 'state of the art' is used for a variety of meanings in US product liability decisions. See *Owen* (fn 29) §10.4, 659 ('Due in part to the diffuse nature of state-of-the-art concept, which embraces such diverse aspects of manufacturer responsibility as the foreseeability of risk, the feasibility of implementing a safer design, and the proper scope of "strict" liability, courts and legislatures have yet to agree on a definition of the term'). We employ it here for only one of those meanings.

169 See, eg, Mo. Ann. Stat. §537.764 (state of the art 'means that the dangerous nature of the product was not known and could not reasonably be discovered at the time the product was placed into the stream of commerce').

B. STATUTES OF LIMITATIONS AND OF REPOSE

88 Statutes of limitations in the US are creatures of state legislation and there is considerable variance in their provisions, including the length of time within which the plaintiff must begin suit to avoid the bar imposed by the statute of limitations. As well, states have different periods for different kinds of claims. Thus, for torts involving personal injury, several states employ a one-year period, while a few have a six-year period. More typically, the period provided is two or three years.[170] Generally, both negligence and strict product liability tort claims (warranty claims are different and addressed below) are subject to the statute of limitations generally applicable to tort actions for personal injury or property damage.[171] For death cases, separate statutes of limitation are prescribed.

89 In a number of states that have enacted product liability legislation, statutes of limitations specific to product liability claims are provided.[172]

90 Claims ordinarily accrue – ie start the statute of limitations clock running – upon the occurrence of the last event required for a valid claim. In product liability actions that event is harm to the plaintiff or the plaintiff's property. In most jurisdictions, the act that must occur within the prescribed period is filing of the complaint with the court clerk.[173]

91 There are several reasons that can toll the running of the statute of limitations clock, including, in some jurisdictions, the minority or incapacity of the injured victim. The most important tolling doctrine in product liability is the discovery rule. Discovery rules toll the statute of limitations until the victim knows or reasonably should have known of certain matters. Those matters vary across states, some requiring only that the plaintiff be aware of the existence of the injury. Others require not only knowledge of the injury but also that the defendant (or the defendant's product) caused the injury. And in the most protective versions, victims must also know that tortious conduct was responsible for the harm.[174] In toxic tort cases, in which insidious and progressive disease of unknown causes and sources often exist, discovery rules are critical to the plaintiff's ability to timely file a complaint.

---

170 *Owen* (fn 29) §14.6, 915.

171 See *SR Shapiro*, Products Liability: What Statute of Limitations Governs Actions Based on Strict Liability in Tort, 91 A.L.R.3d 455, at §3.

172 See, eg, Ark. Rev. Stat. §16–116–104 ('All product liability actions shall be commenced within three (3) years after the date on which the death, injury, or damage occurs').

173 Some jurisdictions require that the complaint and summons ('process') be served on the defendant before the prescribed period expires.

174 *Fischer et al.* (fn 25) 775–776; *Owen*, (fn 29) §14.6, 921–922.

92 For warranty claims, the statute of limitations reflects the commercial background in which the UCC was drafted and provides that a claim for breach of warranty accrues upon 'tender of delivery',[175] which in most cases is the time when the product is sold. The period specified is four years, which means that the statute expires four years after sale. Thus, for a plaintiff injured by a product more than four years old, ordinarily no warranty claim is available based on the UCC.

93 Statutes of repose are different from statutes of limitations in that they begin to run upon sale of the product rather than upon injury to the plaintiff.[176] Thus, like the warranty statute of limitations in the UCC, statutes of repose can bar a claim before a plaintiff is harmed and can sue.[177] Enacted in the 1960s through 1980s and typically employing a period between six and twelve years, these statutes of repose moderated the lengthy time before suit that could occur in the toxic substances arena (with latency periods running several decades before disease manifestation) and for durable goods with long useful lives, such as industrial machinery that may remain in use in excess of 25 or even fifty years. In a number of states, courts have declared these statutes of repose to be unconstitutional as infringing on 'open court' or equal protection provisions in the state constitution.[178]

C. ACCESS TO JUSTICE ISSUES

94 The 'American Rule' provides that the parties bear their own attorney's fees. Although some exceptions exist, none is applicable to product liability claims. While this rule might be a significant impediment to injured victims being able to recover for their injuries, the sanctioning of contingent fees largely ameliorates this concern. Contingent fees enable victims who could not afford to pay for legal services to obtain those services and insurance (from the contingent fee lawyer) for the risk that the case will be unsuccessful. Often contingent fee lawyers will also bear the substantial cost of litigating a product liability case, which will be reimbursed from the recovery if the suit is successful and, often, be borne by the lawyer if the case is unsuccessful.

---

175 UCC §2-725(1). Section 725(2) extends accrual when the seller has explicitly extended the warranty to future performance.

176 See, eg, N.C. Gen. Stat. §1-50(6) ('No action for the recovery of damages for personal injury, death, or damage to property based on or arising out of any alleged defect or any failure in relation to a product shall be brought more than six (6) years after the date of initial sale').

177 See generally *MM Martin*, A Statute of Repose for Product Liability Claims (1982) 50 Fordham L Rev 745.

178 *Fischer et al* (fn 25) 781-782 (citing such cases as well as cases finding statutes of repose constitutional).

95 The contingent fee does not solve all access to justice issues. Because of the high cost of litigation – and product liability cases are among the most expensive tort cases to litigate because of the frequent need for multiple expert witnesses and extensive discovery – plaintiffs who suffer minimal or even modest injuries may not be able to find a lawyer willing to take her case even if the case is meritorious. The requirement that plaintiff prove the existence of a reasonable alternative design in design defect claims along with reform limiting the admissibility of expert witnesses unless their testimony is found reliable by the court has ratcheted up the costs of prosecuting a product liability claim and consequently the number of plaintiffs whose injuries are not severe enough to support a product liability case.

96 After experimenting with class actions when similarly situated plaintiffs suffer personal injury in the latter part of the 20th century, US courts have decided that class actions are inappropriate procedural devices for product liability claims.[179] There is one aggregation device that is widely employed for mass product liability cases that permits consolidated discovery and other pre-trial proceedings for related cases thereby saving time and duplication that would otherwise be required if each case proceeded individually. This mechanism permits transfer of all cases to a single judge for pre-trial proceedings exists at the federal level and is known as the Multi-district Litigation Act.[180] Many states have similar provisions for related cases filed in state courts, although these are limited to cases filed within that state.[181]

X. ALTERNATIVE REGULATIONS AND REMEDIES

97 The three different theories that may be employed by a product liability plaintiff are set forth above no 39 ff. For non-products, including services, the negligence regime would be the primary, if not exclusive, basis for recovery, as neither strict product liability nor UCC warranty claims[182] would be available.

98 No duty to recall is imposed by product liability law. Regulatory agencies, such as the National Highway Transportation Safety Administration (NHTSA)

---

179 *RL Marcus et al*, Complex Litigation (5th edn 2010) 331–349; *BG Stier*, Resolving the Class Action Crisis: Mass Tort Litigation As Network (2005) Utah L Rev 863, 865 ('But, as courts have increasingly held, multiple-incident, personal-injury class actions are not appropriate for class treatment because they involve numerous individualized issues that require unmanageable individualized adjudication'); see generally *RH Klonoff*, The Decline of Class Actions (2013) 90 Wash UL Rev 729.

180 28 USC §1407. For a history of the Act and Panel that administers it, see *RL Marcus*, Cure-All for an Age of Dispersed Litigation? Toward a Maximalist Use of the Multidistrict Panel's Transfer Power (2008) 82 Tulane L Rev 2245.

181 See, eg, Cal. Rules of Court 1500 et seq.

182 The UCC provisions on warranty are limited to 'transactions in goods'. UCC §2–102.

have the authority to order recalls of automobiles if they have safety-related defects or do not meet federal safety standards.[183] Frequently, NHTSA will work with automobile manufacturers to arrange for a voluntary recall.

99 While tort law does not impose a duty to recall, manufacturers do have a post-sale duty to warn when they discover information about dangers in the product that was not reasonably known at the time of sale. This post-sale duty is limited to 'substantial risks' and imposes an obligation (i) to notify those who are reasonably ignorant of the risk and can be identified, (ii) when a warning can be effectively communicated and acted upon, and (iii) the existing risk is sufficiently great to justify the warning.[184]

100 Alternative sources of remedies for victims outside the tort system are quite limited. While a variety of regulatory agencies, including the National Highway Traffic and Safety Administration (automobiles), the Federal Aviation (Agency (aircraft), the Consumer Protection and Safety Administration (consumer products), the Food and Drug Administration (food, drugs, vaccines and medical devices), and other agencies regulate the safety of many products, they do not provide compensation for those injured by regulated products.

101 While the US has a handful of targeted compensation schemes, the only one that deals specifically with products is the Childhood Vaccine Injury Act of 1986, which was adopted because of concerns that tort liability was affecting the availability of childhood vaccines from their manufacturers.[185] Designed to provide compensation for those injured by childhood vaccines while furnishing protection to vaccine manufacturers, the Act provides for compensation for vaccine victims without a showing of fault. However, claimants must demonstrate causation unless their injury is on a scheduled list of recognised harms (a list that has shrunk over time), and many claims founder on an inability to demonstrate that element. Unsuccessful claimants may pursue tort claims, but must demonstrate causation as well as negligence by the manufacturer or defectiveness of the vaccine.[186]

102 Social insurance does provide modest compensation for those who suffer disability.[187] However, substantial replacement of lost earnings due to disability

---

183 Other federal agencies have the authority to order recalls of a variety of products. See *A Bernstein*, Voluntary Recalls (2013) U Chi Legal F 359, 407 n 6.

184 See Restatement (Third) of Torts: Products Liability §10 (1998).

185 See *N Freeman Engstrom*, A Dose of Reality for Specialized Courts: Lessons from the VICP (2015) 163 U Pa L Rev 1631 ff.

186 See *RL Rabin*, The Renaissance of Accident Law Plans Revisited (2005) 64 Md L Rev 699, 707–708.

187 See <www.ssa.gov/disability/>.

requires private insurance, which is among the least prevalent forms of loss insurance with only about 25% of the US population covered by a short-term disability policy and 10% by a long-term disability policy, usually provided by or purchased through an employer.[188]

103 Criminal prosecutions of companies arising from their product manufacturing activities are extremely rare in the US[189] Restitution for victims of such criminal acts as an aspect of sentencing would be even rarer still and depend on the specific restitution statute in the state where the manufacturer was convicted.[190]

104 Among the many mass torts in the United States, including cigarettes, asbestos, the Dalkon Shield IUD, and a variety of drugs going back to the 1960s, there has been but a single handful of criminal prosecutions and those that resulted in convictions were often for misdemeanours.[191]

XI. ASSESSMENT OF DOMESTIC LAW

105 In practice, plaintiffs sue those responsible for defective products not only pursuant to general negligence, misrepresentation, and warranty law, but under the product-specific doctrine of strict product liability. There is widespread disagreement among academics regarding which body of law serves the area best.[192] Moreover, the confluence of these available actions creates what is arguably unnecessary complexity, and courts and lawyers often seem to find it difficult to keep the various areas of law distinct. Add to

---

188 See I The American Law Institute, Reporters' Study, Enterprise Liability for Personal Injury (1991) 157–158.

189 In the 2013 fiscal year, only 172 business organisations (or other organisations) were successfully prosecuted. And, of course, those prosecutions cover the full panoply of corporate misconduct that exists, including financial fraud, antitrust, and environmental crime. US Sentencing Comm'n, Overview of Federal Criminal Cases Fiscal Year 2013, at 3 (2013) <www.google.com/url?sa=t&rct=j&q=&esrc=s&source=web&cd=1&ved=0CB8QFjAA&url=http%3A%2F%2Fwww.ussc.gov%2Fsites%2Fdefault%2Ffiles%2Fpdf%2Fresearch-and-publications%2Fresearch-publications%2F2014%2FFY13_Overview_Federal_Criminal_Cases.pdf&ei=dBoTVZbtLcO0ggSe3YLwDw&usg=AFQjCNEm22t8Tsyaov5Ue7u7WLThSswB6Q&sig2=KUFGZNcGqAHF-_rMZj7bLg&bvm=bv.89217033,d.eXY>.

190 See generally *CE Lollar*, What Is Criminal Restitution? (2014) 100 Iowa L Rev 93; *LM Lavenue*, The Corporation as a Criminal Defendant and Restitution as a Criminal Remedy: Application of the Victim and Witness Protection Act by the Federal Sentencing Guidelines for Organizations (1993) 18 J Corp L 441.

191 See *MD Green/WJ Cardi*, Basic Questions of Tort Law from the Perspective of the USA, in: H Koziol (ed), Basic Questions of Tort Law from a Comparative Perspective (2015) 444 ff.

192 See, eg, *R Posner*, Strict Liability: A Comment (1973) 2 J Legal Studies 205; *S Shavell*, Strict Liability Versus Negligence (1980) 9 J Legal Studies 1; *AM Polinsky/S Shavell*, The Uneasy Case for Product Liability (2010) 123 Harv L Rev 1437.

this various layers of statutory and regulatory requirements and the scientific aspects of many cases, and product liability law has become one of the most complicated areas of tort law.

106 One emerging area of difficulty is in the application of product liability law to new conceptions of products. Courts have, for some years, faced this issue in the context of human and animal biological products, such as blood and transplant tissues. In this context, courts have generally held that such chattels – although bought and sold on the market – are not 'products' but are rather treated as services for purposes of product liability law.[193] Courts are less clear about, for example, whether computer software is a 'product' for purposes of product liability.[194] Similar issues are likely to be faced by plaintiffs suing for injuries caused by the results of 3D printing – ie whether the digital designs on which the printouts are based are themselves products. 3D printing entails other problems for product liability law as well – for instance, whether digital designers or the hobbyists who print the designers are 'commercial sellers' and whether alterations in designs by hobbyists are sufficient to 'materially alter' the products, thereby relieving the original designer of liability.[195]

107 Although it will be interesting to see how courts resolve such questions, there is not much thought that new technologies will require dramatic change in product liability law. Rather, innovations seem more likely to require new applications – sometimes, as with human biological products, infused with significant policy considerations – of longstanding doctrine.

---

193 *Owen* (fn 29) §16.9, 1047.

194 *Winter v GP Putnam's Sons*, 938 F.2d 1033, 1036 (9th Cir. 1991) (suggesting in dictum that computer software might be considered a product).

195 See generally *N Freeman Engstrom*, 3-D Printing and Product Liability: Identifying the Obstacles (2013) 162 U Pa L Rev Online 35.

PART III

ECONOMIC ANALYSIS OF PRODUCT LIABILITY

Michael Faure

I. INTRODUCTION

01 It is logical in a project which focuses on the effectiveness of the Product Liability Directive, especially with a view on potential damage that could be caused by new technologies, to also pay attention to the economic approach to product liability. The European Group on Tort Law has a long tradition of incorporating economic analysis in its earlier work,[1] and hence it is also useful to incorporate the economic approach into the debate on a potential reform of product liability. This is all the more the case since even in the early law and economics literature that emerged in the 1970s the economic analysis of product liability was already well developed.[2] Moreover, several authors in the US have paid extensive attention to product liability as it was held that this was a mechanism that could potentially lead to high liability costs and thus to 'crushing liability' for industry.[3] There is, moreover, not only the 'old' law and economics approach to product liability, which emerged in the 1970s and 1980s; indeed, a lot of the more recent law and economics literature has also addressed product liability in an empirical manner, addressing *inter alia* the question of to what extent product liability regimes have been able to contribute to safer products and adequate compensation of victims.[4]

02 This contribution will provide the traditional economic analysis of product liability law and also apply those insights to the liability regime as it has been incorporated into the Directive. However, an interesting aspect of the economic

---

1 See eg for the economic analysis of fault *M Faure*, Fault. Economic Analysis, in: P Widmer (ed), Unification of Tort Law: Fault (2005) 311–330; for strict liability, *M Faure*, Strict Liability. Economic Analysis, in: BA Koch/H Koziol (eds), Strict Liability (2002) 361–394 and for contributory negligence *M Faure*, Economic Analysis of Contributory Negligence, in: U Magnus/M Martin-Casals (eds), Unification of Tort Law: Contributory Negligence (2004) 233–256.

2 I am referring *inter alia* to *J Buchanan*, In defence of *caveat* emptor (1970) 38 University of Chicago Law Review 64–73; *R McKean*, Products liability: trends and implications (1970) 38 University of Chicago Law Review 3–63; and *R McKean*, Products liability: implications of some changing property rights (1970) Quarterly Journal of Economics 611–626.

3 See *MJ Trebilcock*, The social-insurance deterrence dilemma of modern North American tort law: a Canadian perspective on the liability insurance crisis (1987) 24 San Diego Law Review 929–1002.

4 See *MA Geistfeld*, Products liability, in: M Faure (ed), Tort law and economics (2009) 287–340.

approach is that it has equally generated criticism with respect to the question whether a European approach to product liability is warranted at all. This is done in the so-called economics of federalism and is also worth a brief discussion.

03 The project description rightly asks for attention to be paid to specific problems related to causation in the specific case where multiple parties are involved in a product accident or where there is uncertainty concerning the producer. Moreover, specific problems may occur with new technologies whereby the question arises as to what extent product liability standards and legislation can and should be rapidly adapted to technological developments, still providing sufficient incentives for prevention to operators. Hence, this question of changing technological knowledge, more particularly related to new products and developments (known in the product liability literature as 'development risk') should also be discussed.

04 The goal of this chapter is not to provide an in-depth analysis of the wide economic literature on product liability, but rather to show how some economic insights can provide complementary arguments to the legal debate and to indicate how this economic literature can equally contribute to agenda-setting for academic research in this area.

05 This contribution is structured as follows: after this introduction we will first discuss product liability within the framework of the economics of federalism (II); then we move to the simple case where parties have a contractual relationship, and the victim is a consumer of the product and informed about the risks related to the product (III). Next we move on to the more realistic situation where either the consumer has no information about the risks related to the product, or third parties also suffer losses (IV). These basic insights concerning the economics of product liability law lead to a brief discussion of the economic effects of the Product Liability Directive (V). Then we turn to the problem of multi-party causation and more particularly the question how one should deal with causal uncertainty in that respect (VI). A few more recent developments in the literature will be discussed (VII) and specific attention will be paid to the problem of development risks (VIII). With respect to the central question of whether the Directive is able to ensure sufficient safety for individuals and adequate compensation for victims, it will be recalled that (as is often stressed in the economic literature as well) (product) liability can only play a modest role as far as both prevention and compensation are concerned; other instruments may equally (and in some cases more effectively) contribute to safe products and adequate compensation of victims (IX). Section X concludes.

II. PRODUCT LIABILITY AND THE ECONOMICS OF FEDERALISM

A. COMPETITION BETWEEN LEGAL ORDERS

06 The question whether product liability regulation should be issued at national (Member State) level or rather at a central (EU) level has equally been addressed in the economic literature. The starting point for the analysis is usually Tiebout's theory about the optimal provision of local public goods.[5]

07 Tiebout argued that when people with the same preferences cluster together in communities, competition between local authorities will, under certain restrictive conditions, lead to allocative efficiency. If, for example, in one community there are citizens who greatly prefer sporting facilities and in another the majority of citizens prefer opera, the first community will probably construct sporting facilities, whereas the second may build an opera house. If someone living in the second community preferred sporting facilities to the opera house, he could then move to the first community, which provides services more to his tastes. The idea is that well-informed citizens will move to the community that provides the local services that best suit their personal preferences. Through this so-called 'voting with the feet', competition between local authorities will lead citizens to cluster together according to their preferences.[6] In practice, it is clear that different communities do indeed offer a variety of different services. The idea is that the citizen can have an effect on this provision of local public goods either by influencing the decision-making (vote) or by moving (exit).

08 This basic idea applies not only to community services, but also, for example, to fiscal decisions[7] and environmental choices.[8] In addition, this idea of citizens moving to the community that provides services which best correspond to their preferences can also be applied with respect to legal rules. Thus, it has been argued that competition between legislators will lead to legal systems competing with each other to provide legislation that corresponds

---

5 *C Tiebout*, A pure theory of local expenditures (1956) Journal of Political Economy 416. For a discussion see *S Rose-Ackerman*, Rethinking the progressive agenda: the reform of the American regulatory state (1992) 169 ff.

6 Compare *DC Mueller*, Federalism and the European Union: A Constitutional Perspective (1997) 90 Public Choice 255–280.

7 See, eg, *R Inman/D Rubinfeld*, The EMU and Fiscal Policy in the New European Community: An Issue for Economic Federalism (1994) International Review of Law and Economics 147; *G Kirchgässner/W Pommerehne*, Tax Harmonisation and Tax Competition in the European Community: Lessons from Switzerland (paper presented at the Cost Meeting in Luzern, November 1993); and *W Oates*, Fiscal Federalism (1972).

8 So *W Oates/R Schwab*, Economic Competition among Jurisdiction: Efficiency Enhancing or Distortion Inducing? (1988) 35 Journal of Public Economics 333–354.

best to the preferences of citizens. The various lawmakers in the nation states will create a competitive market for the supply of law.[9] The idea therefore is that in an optimal world citizens will cluster together in states that provide legal rules that correspond to their preferences. Well-informed citizens who are dissatisfied with the legislation provided could move (voting with their feet) to the community that provides legislation that corresponds best to their preferences. This idea, assuming that different legal systems offer different legal rules to satisfy the demands of the citizens, thus explains the variety and differences between legal systems.[10] Moreover, it also shows that differences between the various legal rules of different countries should not necessarily be judged negatively, as is often the case in Europe today.

09 In economic literature, the Tiebout model is used to argue that, from an economic point of view, decentralisation should be the starting point, since competition between legislators will lead to allocative efficiency. Van den Bergh also uses his theory to provide criteria for centralisation/decentralisation within the European Union. Taking Tiebout as a starting point and assuming that competition between decentralised legislators will lead to an optimal provision of legal rules, the crucial question is: why centralise? Van den Bergh criticises that part of the current discussion in the European legal literature which seems to focus on the question of why there should be decentralisation (referred to by Van den Bergh as 'top down federalisation'). According to economic theory, that is the wrong question. Starting from Tiebout's model, there is reason to believe in what Van den Bergh calls 'bottom up federalisation', assuming that in principle the local level is optimal, since the local level has the best information on local problems and on the preferences of citizens. Decision-making should be moved to a higher level only when there is a good reason.[11] Economic theory has indeed suggested that there may be a variety of reasons why the local level is not best suited to take decisions and that there are occasions when central decision-making can lead to more efficient results.

---

9 *A Ogus*, Competition between National Legal Systems: A Contribution to Economic Analysis to Comparative Law (1999) International and Comparative Law Quarterly 405–418, and see *A Ogus*, The Contribution of Economic Analysis of Law to Legal Transplant, in: J Smits (ed), The Contribution of Mixed Legal Systems to European Law (2001) 27–37.

10 *R Van den Bergh*, Subsidiarity as an Economic Demarcation Principle and the Emergence of European Private Law (1998) 5 Maastricht Journal of European and Comparative Law 134 and *R Van den Bergh*, Towards an institutional legal framework for regulatory competition in Europe (2000) 53 Kyklos 437–439.

11 A major American supporter of this 'presumption in favour of decentralisation' is Revesz. See, eg, *R Revesz*, Environmental Regulation in Federal Systems, in: H Somsen (ed), Yearbook of European Environmental Law (2000) 1–35 and *R Revesz*, Federalism and Environmental Regulation: An Overview, in: R Revesz/P Sands/R Stewart (eds), Environmental Law: The Economy and Sustainable Development (2000) 37–79.

10 I will now apply these criteria for centralisation and relate them to the harmonisation of product liability in Europe.[12]

B. CROSS-BORDER CHARACTER OF THE EXTERNALITY

11 The Tiebout argument in favour of competition between local communities obviously works only if the problem to be regulated is indeed merely local. Once it has been established that the problem to be regulated has a cross-border character, there may be arguments to be made in favour of centralisation. First, there is an economy of scale argument for shifting powers to a higher legal order that has competence to deal with the externality over a larger territory. This corresponds with the basic insight that if the problem to be regulated crosses the borders of competence of the regulatory authority, the decision-making power should be shifted to a higher regulatory level, preferably to an authority which has jurisdiction over a territory large enough to deal with the problem adequately.[13] 'Economic theory provides a straightforward but unrealistic answer to regional problems: draw "optimal" jurisdictional boundaries'.[14] This 'economics of scale' argument is thus related to the argument that transaction costs will be lower if regulation is made at the higher level.[15] There is, however, another argument in favour of centralisation which relates to the fact that in cases of cross-border externalities states would have no incentive to impose stringent regulations upon their own citizens if the consequences of harmful actions were only felt outside their own territories. Cross-border externalities thus may create inefficiencies in the absence of central regulation.[16]

12 The question arises as to how this 'cross-border externality' argument relates to a tort area like product liability. One can certainly argue that the product liability area is different from traditional tort as far as the potential for affecting international trade is concerned. The chance that a 'normal' tort might have an interstate effect is, with a few exceptions (like the cross-border pollution case) relatively small, whereas, given mass production, products nowadays are seldom meant just for the domestic market. Indeed, as Schwartz

---

12 See also *M Faure*, Product Liability and Product Safety in Europe: Harmonisation or Differentiation? (2000) 53 Kyklos 467–508.

13 Compare: *Ogus* (fn 9) 414 and *C Kimber*, A Comparison of Environmental Federalism in the United States and The European Union (1995) 54 Maryland Law Review 1; *D Esty*, Revitalizing Environmental Federalism (1996) 95 Michigan Law Review 625; and *Rose-Ackerman* (fn 5) 164–165.

14 So *S Rose-Ackerman*, Controlling Environmental Pollution: The Limits of Public Law in Germany and the United States (1995) 38.

15 It is thus related to the 'transaction cost' argument, to be discussed below.

16 See, for the 'interstate externalities' and 'economies of scale' justifications for centralisation, *Revesz* (fn 11) 67.

argued in the American context, the imperatives of mass production require a manufacturer to sell the same product throughout the federal nation, so that the need for uniformity in state product liability law seems huge.[17] For the same reason Ackerman argues that product liability is in principle a good candidate for federal law.[18] These arguments, however, mainly amount to the point that uniformity in product liability law would 'come in handy' in the American context;[19] they do not explain why the mere fact that products cross national borders would constitute the risk that states would be able to shift external costs to others.

13 Indeed, the starting point for the analysis remains that different communities in the Member States may have different preferences concerning both the level of product safety and product liability law. The fact that these differing preferences lead to differing legal solutions should in principle, as was discussed above, be considered a benefit instead of a problem.[20] A problem arises only if, say, a producer in the Netherlands were to produce products which comply with the Dutch (supposedly low) product liability and product safety standards and export them to, say, Belgium and France, where (again supposedly) the required level of product safety is much higher. In this hypothesis a 'cross-border externality' problem would only arise if the consumers in Belgium and France had no possibility of filing a lawsuit against the Dutch manufacturer. This problem is, however, not very realistic, since the victims would in this case be the French and Belgian citizens who would presumably have a higher product liability standard, which could then be applied to the Dutch manufacturer. In other words, manufacturers of defective products are generally liable to pay damages for harm suffered in export markets.[21]

14 Of course, the fact that in the example given the manufacturer is located in the Netherlands and the products marketed in Belgium and France and the harm is suffered equally in those countries may lead to a few practical problems for victims, but these do not necessarily immediately justify central regulation, with the corresponding loss of differentiated regulation according to preferences. First of all, choice-of-law regimes may be used to guaranteeing, for example, that the French and the Belgians can have their (supposedly higher-standard) product safety and product liability law applied. This, however, is criticised by Schwartz who points out the fact that in this example the court

17 *GT Schwartz*, Considering the Proper Federal Role in American Tort Law (1996) Arizona Law Review 924.

18 *RM Ackerman*, Tort Law and Federalism: Whatever Happened to Devolution? (1996) 14 Yale Law & Policy Review 451.

19 And might therefore fit into the transaction cost argument, to be discussed below no 29 ff.

20 *Van den Bergh* (fn 10) 133–134.

21 Ibid 141.

in, say, France will apply high-standard French law to the Dutch manufacturer. The effect therefore is that the Dutch manufacturer will be confronted with the higher-standard French law. From this Schwartz implies that a regime of state product liability law is inconvenient as a means of expressing state values. In the view of Schwartz, France would express its sovereignty by subordinating the sovereignty of the Netherlands through the application of French law.[22] Still, it can hardly be seen how this argument can justify central regulation. The effect of the choice-of-law regime is precisely that the Dutch manufacturer will not be able to externalise harm by shifting this only to export markets. Of course this presumes that a system is in place which allows the Belgian and French victims to sue the Dutch manufacturer. But this is, in the European context, in fact provided for through the European Regulation on jurisdiction and execution of judgments. Of course one should be aware that even with this Regulation it might still remain difficult for victims to recover losses in another state.[23] This practical problem, however, cannot be remedied by harmonisation. It is indeed not differences in legal rules that cause difficulties in the cross-border enforcement of claims, but different rules of civil procedure in the Member States.

15 In sum, the mere fact that different states have different preferences with respect to product liability and product safety and that therefore different regimes exist can as such hardly be considered an argument for centralisation as long as states are not capable of externalising harm to victims in third countries. A problem might in that respect only exist if the rules of the import country do not allow a full internalisation because the injurer may escape the payment of damages. Van den Bergh gives the example of a situation where a state would not allow recovery in tort in cases of causal uncertainty, meaning that the manufacturer could not be held liable unless the victim could prove 'beyond reasonable doubt' that the particular manufacturer caused his loss. A problem could, according to Van den Bergh, also arise if a legal system were to not allow the recovery of non-pecuniary losses.[24] In those cases there would be loopholes in the national product liability law of the importing state which would indeed allow exporting manufacturers to externalise harm. This, however, assumes that, for example, the decision not to compensate non-pecuniary losses would lead to the inefficient use of resources and would not be a reflection of national values and the preferences of the citizens.

---

22 *Schwartz* (fn 17) 931–932 and 937–941.

23 See *R Kirstein/AR Neunzig*, Internationale Zuständigkeit von Gerichten und die Anerkennung ausländischer Urteile, in: K-E Schenk/D Schmidtchen/ME Streit/V Vanberg (eds), Jahrbuch für neue politische Ökonomie, Globalisierung und Rechtsordnung (1999) 345–368.

24 *Van den Bergh* (fn 10) 142.

C. THE RACE FOR THE BOTTOM

16 There may be an economic argument for centralisation, in that there is a risk that a 'race for the bottom' might emerge between countries to attract foreign investments. As a result of this, prisoner's dilemmas could arise, whereby countries would fail to enact or enforce effective legislation. Centralisation can be advanced as a remedy for these prisoner's dilemmas. This race-for-the-bottom argument could in theory play a role in the case of product safety as well.[25] It would mean that local governments would compete with lenient environmental legislation to attract industry.[26]

17 The race-for-the-bottom argument could in theory play a role in the case of product safety as well.[27] It would mean that local governments would compete with lenient product-safety regulation to attract industry.[28] The result would be an overall reduction of product safety below efficient levels. This should correspond with the traditional result of game theory that prisoner's dilemmas create inefficiencies.

18 The basic idea behind this argument, when applied to product liability, would be that product liability law may impose costs on industry. If governments fear these costs greatly and would prefer to favour national industry, they could do so by lowering product standards. If lowering product standards were a way to attract industry, distortions could occur which would justify centralised decision-making.

19 There are, however, some weaknesses in the application of this argument to the area of product liability. First of all, product liability and product safety law may effectively create costs for manufacturing but, as will be explained in the economic analysis,[29] these costs can often be passed on to the purchasers of the product.[30] Second, as far as the liability of a producer in the sense of the Product Liability Directive (being the manufacturer) is concerned, it is also difficult for states to take part in a race to the bottom for the simple reason that the harm

---

25 For a detailed discussion of this argument, see *D Esty/D Geradin*, Environmental Protection and International Competitiveness. A Conceptual Framework (1998) 32 Journal of World Trade 16–19.

26 Compare *Rose-Ackerman* (fn 5) 166–170.

27 For a discussion, see *Van den Bergh* (fn 10) 136–139.

28 Compare *Rose-Ackerman* (fn 5) 166–170.

29 For an economic analysis of product liability, see *P Burrows*, Products Liability and the Control of Product Risk in the European Community (1994) Oxford Review of Economic Policy 68–83 and *F Silva/A Cavaliere*, The Economic Impact of Product Liability: Lessons from the US and the EU experience, in: G Galli/J Pelkmans (eds), Regulatory Reform and Competitiveness in Europe, vol I, Horizontal Issues (2000) 292–323.

30 *Van den Bergh* (fn 10) 137–139. See also below no 41 ff.

may well occur in another state. Imagine, again, that France would like to attract industry with a lenient product liability regime. In doing so it can hardly attract manufacturing industries that largely depend upon an export market. Their exposure to product liability will indeed depend upon the legislation applicable in the state where the harm will occur. It is therefore, especially as far as the liability of manufacturers is concerned, unlikely that states would engage in a race to the bottom to attract industry.[31]

20 This shows that the theoretical basis for a race-to-the-bottom risk in cases of product liability is relatively weak.[32] This argument would only justify centralisation if it could be proven that without centralisation a risk of destructive competition would indeed emerge.[33] There is no proof of such destructive competition leading to lower product safety standards and this risk is, moreover, not very realistic.[34] Indeed, it is doubtful whether the law of tort, and more particularly product liability, plays a significant role in attracting or repulsing businesses to or from a given state. Other elements, such as labour conditions, the amount of direct government regulation and taxes, may be far more important than the level of product liability in the location decisions of businesses.[35] Moreover, if product liability were to have any effect as far as a race for the bottom is concerned, it is even more likely that states would wish to protect victims rather than corporate interests. Consumer advocates may call this a 'race for the top', although a system whereby foreign manufacturers are penalised by overprotective product liability law may well be considered inefficient and in that (reverse) sense a race towards the bottom.[36]

D. INTERNAL MARKET

21 This race-for-the-bottom argument, that competition among jurisdictions for economic activity will be 'destructive', corresponds – to some extent – to the European legal argument that the creation of harmonised conditions of competition is necessary to avoid trade distortions. This argument was traditionally used to harmonise legislation of the Member States in a variety of areas. Simply stated, the argument is that complying with legislation imposes

---

31 See *Ackerman* (fn 18) 458, and *Van den Bergh* (fn 10) 139.

32 *R Van den Bergh* (fn 10) 136–137.

33 In the words of Rose-Ackerman: 'If state and local laws seem designed to protect local business rather than reflect genuine differences in tastes across jurisdiction, the federal government should take a hard look to determine the possible interference with interstate commerce (*Rose-Ackerman* (fn 5) 173).

34 *M Faure*, Aktuelle Regulierungspraxis bei Heilwesenschäden in Europa mit Ausblick auf die EG-Rechtsharmonisierung (1998) 46–47.

35 *Ackerman* (fn 18) 459.

36 Ibid 458 and *Schwartz* (fn 17) 932.

costs on industry. If legislation is different, these costs would therefore differ as well and the conditions of competition within the common market would not be equal. The argument apparently assumes that total equality of conditions of competition is necessary for the functioning of the common market.

22 There are, however, some problems with this traditional European argument which in fact claims that any difference in legislation between the Member States might endanger the conditions of competition and therefore justifies harmonisation of legal rules.[37] From an economic point of view, the mere fact that conditions of competition differ does not necessarily create a risk of a race to the bottom. There can be differences in marketing conditions for a variety of reasons, and if the conditions of competition were indeed totally equal, as the argument assumes, there would also be no trade.

23 Let us now have a brief look at the contents of the Product Liability Directive of 1985 to analyse whether this directive is capable of creating legal certainty and achieving full harmonisation, which are necessary to realise the proclaimed 'harmonisation of marketing conditions'.

24 The European Product Liability Directive had two goals:[38] first, it aimed at creating equal marketing conditions to 'avoid distortions of competition', and second, it wished to achieve a high level of consumer protection. Both goals can, within the focus of this chapter, be rephrased in economic terms. The question whether the Product Liability Directive actually leads to harmonisation is obviously useful in judging the desirability of European action in the first place. If the Directive had been able to create full harmonisation of product liability, it might have saved transaction costs (an aspect which will be discussed in the next subsection) to such an extent that they might have outweighed the advantages of differing product liability laws.

25 The question which therefore should be asked is whether the justification given in the considerations preceding the Directive, which was that the existing divergences in law before the Product Liability Directive may have distorted competition and affected the movement of goods within the common market, is actually correct. It is undoubtedly true to argue that before 1985 there were different product liability regimes in the Member States, but the question arises whether these differences were so important that they 'may [have] distort[ed] competition and affect[ed] the movement of goods within the common market',

---

37 See also *J Spier/OA Haazen*, The European Group on Tort Law ('Tilburg Group') and the European Principles of Tort Law (1999) Zeitschrift für Europäisches Privatrecht 478.

38 See on the goals of the Directive also *AJO van Wassenaer van Catwijck*, Products liability in Europe (1986) The American Journal of Comparative Law 793–794.

as the Product Liability Directive argues. A Dutch author, Van Wassenaer van Catwijck indicated that although the product liability regimes did indeed differ, insurance premiums to cover the product liability risk were not substantially different. If that is true, the differences in market conditions where probably not as large as the Commission holds. Obviously more important is the question of whether the Directive in the 1985 version could reach the harmonisation goal at all. It is in fact very unlikely that this is the case.[39]

26 Indeed, according to article 13 all the different, already existing, product liability laws remain in effect, which means differences that already exist will remain unchanged. In addition, at many points the Directive itself refers to national legislation, for example, with respect to the rights of contribution or recourse (articles 5 and 8(1)), with respect to non-material damage (article 9), the suspension or interruption of the limitation period (article 10(2)) and with respect to nuclear accidents (article 14). It should also be mentioned that in three cases the Directive expressly allows the Member States to derogate from the provisions of the Directive – namely liability for primary agricultural products, liability for development risks and the introduction of a financial limit on liability. Moreover, the Directive cannot of course create any harmonisation for all the product accidents to which it does not apply, because of limitations in the definitions of 'product', 'producer' and 'damage'. Many notions in the Directive are also unclear and can give rise to interpretation problems.[40] Interpretational problems are all the more likely in practice since even the language differences of the various translations of the Directive can lead to different interpretations of the same provision.[41] It has already been mentioned that the Product Liability Directive gave several options to the Member States, including (originally) primary agricultural products, the liability for development risks and the possibility of introducing a financial limit on liability. This has obviously also caused differences, as we just indicated. These differences are shown in annex 1 to the Green Paper on Liability for Defective Products.[42]

---

39 Almost all authors agree on that point. See *H Duintjer Tebbens*, De Europese Richtlijn Produktaansprakelijkheid (1986) Nederlands Juristenblad 373–374; *P Storm*, Een gebrekkig produkt (1985) Maandblad voor Ondernemingsrecht 245; *AJO van Wassenaer van Catwijck*, Produktaansprakelijkheid, in: Serie Praktijkhandleidingen (1986) 81; and *M Martin Casals/ J Solé Feliu*, Responsabilidad por productas en España y (des)armonizacion Europea (2001) 4 Revista de responsabilidad civil y seguros 1–17.

40 Consider the defect notion in article 6, which might have different interpretations.

41 See for instance the different meaning of the 'lower threshold' of article 9 in the French and the Dutch version. Another example is that in the English text producer liability is called a 'liability without fault', whereas in the Dutch version it is just 'liability'. For other examples see *M Faure/W Vanbuggenhout*, Produktaansprakelijkheid. De Europese richtlijn: harmonisatie en consumentenbescherming (1987–1988) Rechtskundig Weekblad 1–14 and 33–49.

42 Green Paper on Liability for Defective Products, COM(1999)396 final.

27 Since it is clear that the Product Liability Directive cannot approximate to the Member States legislation, it has been suggested that this could be an argument for giving the (then) EC competence in this matter.[43] For all these reasons, some authors qualify the Directive itself as a defective product.[44]

28 From this it follows that the Product Liability Directive still relies highly on national law and can for that reason never lead to a 'levelling of the playing field' or a 'harmonisation of marketing conditions'. The European Product Liability Directive therefore nicely shows that the harmonisation of the conditions of competition argument is not a useful basis for European action towards centralisation.

E. REDUCTION OF TRANSACTION COSTS

29 There may, however, be one final economic argument in favour of harmonisation, based on the reduction of transaction costs.[45] This argument is often advanced by European legal scholars pleading for harmonisation of private law in Europe, and is based on the belief that differences in legal systems are very complex and only serve law firms.[46] This argument cannot be examined in detail here.[47] It is obviously too simple to state that a harmonised legal system is always more efficient than differentiated legal rules because of the transaction cost savings inherent in harmonised rules.[48] This argument neglects the fact that there are substantial benefits stemming from differentiation whereby legislation can be adapted to the preferences of individuals.[49] Moreover, given the differences between the legal systems (and legal cultures) in Europe, the costs of harmonisation may be huge – if not prohibitive – as well.[50] The crucial question therefore is whether the possible transaction cost savings

---

43 Article 100 of the EEC Treaty indeed gave legislative competence to the community in order to harmonise the different legislations of the Member States. It was, however, heavily debated whether this article 100 was an appropriate basis on which to ground the legislative power of the EC with respect to product liability (see *L Krämer*, EEC Consumer Law, in: Droit et Consommation (1986) 274–275).

44 This is the title of the article by *Storm* (fn 39) 241–246.

45 A somewhat related but different argument relates to economies and diseconomies of scale in administration, see *Rose-Ackerman* (fn 5) 165–166.

46 This is one of the arguments made by the Danish scholar Lando in favour of harmonised private law. *O Lando*, Die Regeln des Europäischen Vertragsrecht, in: P-C Müller-Graff (ed), Gemeinsames Privatrecht in der Europäischen Gemeinschaft (1993) 473–474.

47 It is further developed and criticised by *Van den Bergh* (fn 10) 129–152.

48 Compare *Rose-Ackerman* (fn 5) 172, who argues that uniform federal regulation may reduce search costs and tends to produce a more stable and predictable jurisprudence.

49 See, for the environmental case, *R Mendelsohn*, Regulatory Heterogeneous Emissions (1986) Journal of Environmental Economics and Management 301.

50 That point has especially been made by *P Legrand*, The impossibility of legal transplants (1997) Maastricht Journal of European and Comparative law 111.

of harmonisation outweigh the benefits of differentiated legal rules. There is little empirical evidence to support the statement that transaction cost savings could justify European harmonisation of all kinds of legal rules. Moreover, the transaction cost savings are likely to be relatively small.[51]

30 The question, however, arises as to whether these transaction cost savings as a result of harmonised rules can also be expected for product liability. One could argue that a manufacturer who markets his products across the whole of Europe would, in the absence of harmonisation, need specialised legal counsel in every state and that their insurance underwriters would have to calculate the liability exposure separately in accordance with each state's product liability law.[52] This argument, however, neglects the fact that there is a benefit in differentiated liability rules that reflect varying preferences. Moreover, the cost of harmonisation in the field of private law (which is so rooted in legal culture) may be huge and the alleged transaction cost savings may be less than expected. Indeed, even in the case of a harmonised legal rule, manufacturers would still need local counsels to bring their case to court. Accordingly, economies of scale under a harmonised rule would probably be insignificant.[53] Here again 'the proof of the pudding is in the eating', so that the question arises as to whether the European Product Liability Directive has been able to create the legal certainty required, reducing transaction costs for manufacturers.[54]

31 Above we looked more closely at the Product Liability Directive and argued that, given its dependence on national law, it can never lead to a harmonisation of marketing conditions. The Product Liability Directive in fact adds an additional layer of complexity to the labyrinth of conflicting standards of liability. It can therefore never lead to uniformity or a lowering of transaction costs.[55]

F. POLICY ANALYSIS

32 The result of applying economic criteria to the question of whether tort law should be harmonised is that there would only be arguments in favour of centralised European rule making (i) if inefficiencies were fostered by national product liability law so that damage could be externalised to other

51 Thus *Van den Bergh* (fn 10) 146–148.

52 *Ackerman* (fn 18) 453.

53 Thus *Ackerman* (fn 18) 453 n 135.

54 Van den Bergh rightly points out lots of interpretation problems in the European Product Liability Directive, which backs up the conclusion that the transaction cost savings may be small, simply because a full harmonisation of the rules of private law is apparently difficult to achieve (*Van den Bergh* (fn 10) 146–147).

55 See *Ackerman* (fn 18) 454.

countries or (ii) if it could be established that states would attract industry by their lenient standards. The latter is, however, unlikely since states would, on the contrary, be more likely to enact legislation to protect victims of product-related accidents within their own jurisdiction with high tort standards. However, there may be transaction cost savings if European intervention were able to create legal certainty and achieve full harmonisation. Other arguments, such as the need to create a 'level playing field' or 'the harmonisation of marketing conditions' cannot, at least from an economic perspective, justify centralisation.

33 A closer look at the European Product Liability Directive has shown that the case for European harmonisation is weak. Comparing the Directive to the criteria for centralisation we can conclude as follows:

(i) The Product Liability Directive is not able to correct for the risk of interstate externalities caused by product damage, if such a risk already exists.
(ii) There is no empirical evidence of a risk that states could attract manufacturers with lenient product liability legislation (the Directive would only apply to manufacturers). On the contrary, there might be a risk of a race to the top, protecting national victims of product-related accidents.
(iii) The Product Liability Directive, given its high reliance on national law, can never lead to a 'levelling of the playing field' or a 'harmonisation of marketing conditions'.
(iv) The Product Liability Directive, which in fact, adds an additional layer of complexity to the labyrinth of conflicting standards of liability, does not lead to uniformity or a lowering of transaction costs.[56]

34 A question which obviously cannot be avoided when inefficiencies are found is whether this can be explained on the basis of public choice theory. Indeed, one notices that many of the harmonisation efforts do not fit into the economic theory of centralisation and would hence, at least from an economic perspective, not be considered as promoting social welfare. If a certain legislative action cannot be said to promote public interest, public choice scholars would ask the question whether the legislation favours special interest groups.[57] Of course, one can generally hold that the lack of transparency at the European level is a highly useful cover for lobbying activities.

56 Compare *Ackerman* (fn 18) 454.

57 For a discussion of harmonisation efforts in Europe from a public choice perspective, see *Van den Bergh* (fn 10) 148–151 and *Van den Bergh* (fn 10) 448–451, and see the recent paper of *R Revesz*, Federalism and Environmental Regulation: a public choice analysis (2001) Harvard Law Review 553–641.

35 Some have argued that comparative lawyers themselves can be considered a lobby group. Harmonisation efforts will undoubtedly serve their interests since harmonisation requires knowledge of the various legal systems that need to be harmonised. A call for harmonisation does undoubtedly create a demand for comparative lawyers and may hence serve their interests.[58]

36 One should obviously also mention the interests of the European bureaucracy itself. Until 1985 Europe had done relatively little as far as the harmonisation of private law was concerned (because differing legal cultures hampered it). Maybe a European Product Liability Directive, although it did not fulfil the economic criteria for centralisation, might have served the interests of the Brussels bureaucracy to show that Europe could bring about a piece of legislation in an area which is considered important by many lawyers, touches upon manufacturers' interests and is moreover very sensitive to public opinion. Hence, the fact that the Commission wanted a European Product Liability Directive may to some extent also simply have been due to the prestige that this Directive, as one of the first in the area of private law, would give the European Commission.

37 Several aspects of the European Product Liability Directive can undoubtedly be considered to be the result of lobbying. Interest group considerations might explain why a Product Liability Directive came into being in the first place. Since it cannot achieve a 'harmonisation of marketing conditions', the Directive might have been promoted for a reason other than the formally stated goal. One important reason might have been the fear of producers in Europe that a product liability crisis similar to that seen in the US would develop. One motive for the Directive was to avoid some Member States going too far in their wish to protect 'consumers'. The Directive aims at a balanced approach, or so it is stressed many times in the Green Paper of Liability for Defective Products.[59] For that reason, manufacturers have been 'protected' with some defences, thresholds, relatively short statutes of limitations and the option to impose a financial cap on liability. Since the Directive is clearly mandatory for the areas it covers (meaning that Member States are not allowed to go further in protecting victims in the areas which the Directive covers), the Directive could at least avoid some Member States imposing overbearing product liability regimes. But the Directive may also be considered 'defective' in reaching that goal since precisely those areas which could have led to an increase in liability exposure, such as non-pecuniary losses, are not dealt with by the Directive.

[58] So *Ogus* (fn 9) 405, and *Ogus* (fn 9) 28–32, as well as *Van den Bergh* (fn 10) 449.

[59] Green Paper on Liability for Defective Products, COM(1999)396 final, 18–20.

38 Public choice explanations might also have influenced specific features of the Directive. This is obviously the case for the exclusion of primary agricultural products from the scope of the Directive in its original form. Some authors held that indeed the increased protection of strict liability was only necessary against the increasing risks of modern industrial production. Strict liability for agricultural products would unnecessarily increase the insurance burden.[60] This explanation, however, is not convincing. Even if agricultural products were produced industrially, they were still excluded from the scope of the Directive. This means that a consumer was not able to claim damages against a breeder of veal who had used artificial hormones or against a grain producer who had used dangerous pesticides.[61] It is not at all clear why strict liability does not apply in those cases. The real reason for the exclusion of primary agricultural products was the fact that European farmers engaged in successful lobbying and convinced the politicians that the Directive's strict liability should not be applicable to them.[62]

39 There was increasing criticism of the exclusion of primary agricultural products after the BSE crisis. One effect of the exclusion of primary agricultural producers from liability under the Directive was obviously that the liability would in fact be passed on to the industrial processor or producer. If, for example, baby food was derived from veal which had been treated with hormones, this would not lay a strict liability on the farmer, but on the producer of the finished product.[63] Of course, the cattle breeder might have been liable under a fault rule, according to his national tort law.[64] For these reasons the Product Liability Directive was amended by Directive 1999/34/EC of 10 May 1999 to include defective agricultural products.

40 Another example may be seen in the proposal made during the discussion preceding the EC Product Liability Directive to set up a compensation fund as an alternative to product liability. This, however, stood no chance in the face of lobbying by the insurance industry, which feared losing business.[65] Therefore, Van den Bergh argues, the European Product Liability Directive is to a large extent to be considered the result of rent seeking by industry instead of an instrument to increase economic welfare.[66]

---

60 *Duintjer Tebbens* (fn 39) 370.
61 *N Reich*, Product Safety and Product Liability (1986) Journal of Consumer Policy 143.
62 Ibid 143.
63 Ibid.
64 [1999] OJ L141.
65 See *M van Empel/H Ritsema*, Aansprakelijkheid voor producten (1987) 53.
66 *Van den Bergh* (fn 10) 151.

III. ECONOMIC THEORY OF PRODUCT LIABILITY: COASE THEOREM

A. OPTIMAL ALLOCATION

41 In the economics literature attention has mostly been paid to the question of how the law can give incentives to producers to induce them on the one hand to take efficient care of the products they manufacture and on the other hand to produce an efficient number of products. Indeed, if too many products were to be put on the market, the risk of a product accident might also increase. The relevant question would then be whether the law should set rules to induce parties to reach these efficient care and production levels. If it were found that a legal intervention was necessary, the next question that would arise would be whether these efficient levels could best be reached through a fault rule or through a strict liability rule.

42 The starting point is the Coase theorem.[67] The first publications on economic analysis of product liability applied the Coase theorem on product liability.[68] They showed that in a zero-transaction costs setting, the choice of the liability rule will have no effect on the care taken by the producer, nor on the quantity of products put on the market. The well-informed consumer will always base his purchase decision on the full price of the product, being the cost price plus the expected accident costs.[69] As long as the conditions for the Coase theorem are met, both an efficient output and efficient care will follow, irrespective of the legal rule applied (no liability, negligence or strict liability).

43 The application of the Coase theorem to product liability can be illustrated by a well-known example presented by Polinsky[70] concerning the question whether a producer of beer should sell beer in bottles or in cans. Bottles have a lower production price than cans, but do create a higher expected damage. It can be illustrated in the following table:

Choice	Cost price	$p \times D$	Full price
Bottle	40	10	50
Can	43	2	45

67 *RH Coase*, The problem of social cost (1960) Journal of Law and Economics 1–44.

68 *McKean* (fn 2) 3–63; *McKean* (fn 2) 611–626; *Buchanan* (fn 2) 64–73; and especially *W Oi*, The economics of product safety (1973) Bell Journal of Economics 3–28.

69 For simple examples see *S Shavell*, An economic analysis of accident law (1987) 78–80 and *M Polinsky*, An introduction to law and economics (1983) 95–97.

70 *Polinsky* (fn 69) 95–97.

44 The table clearly illustrates both the efficient care and efficient production level: optimal care in this case is producing the beer in cans. The marginal cost of a can is 3, but this leads to a marginal reduction of the expected damage of 8. The lowest full price is 45 (production price + expected damage), which will equally lead to an efficient production level. The consumer will only have a demand for beer when his expected utility is higher than 45. Under the conditions of the Coase theorem the output will be efficient irrespective of the liability rule. If the producer is not held liable (under a *caveat emptor* rule) the production price is 40 when beer is sold in bottles and 43 when beer is sold in cans. Well-informed consumers will, however, add the expected damage to the production price and only take into account the full price in their purchase decision. As a consequence, the rational consumer will chose to buy the beer in cans at the lowest full price of 45. As a result efficient levels of both care and production are reached. The result is not different under a producer liability rule (*caveat venditor*). Also in that situation will the producer chose to sell the beer in cans. It will reduce his total price. Since the market price reflects the full price of the product, it will again generate an efficient output. Consumers will only purchase the beer in cans if it generates a utility higher than 45.

45 It is also important that under these conditions the choice of the legal rule also has no distributional consequences.[71] Indeed, in a Coasean setting choosing a strict liability rule for example to 'protect' the consumer seems meaningless, since the expected accident costs will then still be passed on to the consumer through the price system. Therefore, in these circumstances, a legal intervention does not seem very useful. On the contrary, if consumer groups are not homogeneous, but the expected accident costs differ for every consumer,[72] the introduction of a strict liability rule might have adverse effects, since safer products might disappear from the market.[73] The reason for this is that the producer does not know which consumers have high expected accident costs. He will therefore set the quality (care) standard at the level of an average consumer and safer products will disappear from the market.[74] These problems caused by a heterogeneous consumer group have often been advanced as an argument against strict liability.

---

71 *K Hamada*, Liability rules and income distribution in product liability (1976) American Economic Review 228–234.

72 A common example is that the potential loss caused by the burning of one's hand through a defective toaster will be much higher for a high quality piano-player than for the average economist.

73 This point has been made by *Oi* (fn 68) 5 and has been developed by *M Adams*, Produkthaftung: Wohltat oder Plage – Eine Ökonomische Analyse (1987) Betriebsberater, Beilage 20 zu Heft 31/1987, 5–10.

74 The reason is of course asymmetrical information (see *G Akerlof*, The market for lemons: quality uncertainty and the market mechanism (1970) Quarterly Journal of Economics 488).

B. CRITICISM

46 The papers using the Coase theorem to analyse product liability were subjected to criticism; it was held that the theorem does not help since the conditions will almost never be fulfilled in a product liability setting. One argument often heard in this respect is that the consumer has no information on the risk of accidents.[75] Although consumers can indeed be poorly informed with respect to some risks,[76] this is certainly not true for all risks. The consumer might be well aware of the risks of for example a lawn-mower. In addition, it should be mentioned that information can often be provided through legislative measures. If these were successful, the conditions for the Coase theorem could again be met. Only if a consumer underestimates the accident risk and the information deficiency cannot be cured through regulation or otherwise would a liability rule induce the producer to expend enough care on the safety of his products. If consumers remain uninformed, no liability will certainly not lead to an efficient result since producers will have no incentive to invest in safety equipment if this benefit (reduction of expected accident costs) is not recognised by the consumer.

47 That problems arise in the event of a lack of information can also easily be illustrated using the simple Polinsky example concerning the sale of beer presented above. The result of a lack of information is that the expected damage (p x D) is no longer added by the consumer. Hence, in the hypothetical situation of a no liability, rule the consumer will simply buy the cheapest product, which in the example is beer produced in a bottle at 40. Hence, both an inefficient care level (production in a bottle rather than in a can) and an efficient production level (consumer already purchasing bottles at 40) result. If a fault rule were put in place the producer would be held liable if he produces beer in bottles rather than in cans. In order to avoid having to pay the expected damages, producers will have an incentive to produce in cans and put beer on the market, produced in cans at the price of 43. Hence, a fault (or negligence) regime does lead to an efficient care level (production in cans rather than in bottles) but still too a high production level (consumers purchase at the price of 43 rather than at the full price of 45). This can only be avoided under a strict liability rule. In that case the manufacturer will not only produce the beer in cans, but will equally add the expected damage of 2 to the production price of 43 and put the beer on the market at the price of 45. Hence, only under strict liability does an efficient level

75 This was especially stressed by Goldberg in a critique on the work by Oi: *V Goldberg*, The economics of product safety and imperfect information (1974) Bell Journal of Economics 683–688. For a reaction see *W Oi*, The economics of product safety: a rejoinder (1974) Bell Journal of Economics 689–695.

76 For example the carcinogenic effects of asbestos.

of both care and production follow. In that sense strict liability constitutes an alternative to a lack of consumer information.

48 There is one more interesting criticism of those early papers, formulated by Israel Gilead. He argues that these early papers, applying the Coase theorem to product liability, assume that consumers and producers can freely negotiate in a competitive market without any transaction costs, whereas this in fact is not the case.[77] Gilead argues that in the classic Coase theorem the potential victim and the potential injurer can directly negotiate. This is, on the contrary, not the case in the product market as there are built-in transaction costs that prevent an application of the Coase theorem to product safety. Only liability rules can therefore guarantee efficient allocations.[78] This thus constitutes yet another powerful reason why the Coase theorem may in practice only have limited relevance in product liability cases.

IV. PRODUCT LIABILITY AND THIRD PARTIES

A. BASIC MODEL

49 As was just shown, the analysis using the Coase theorem undoubtedly has its limits since it is based on the strong assumption of information on the product risks. In the event of information asymmetry, more particularly in case of poorly informed consumers, some intervention by the legal system is necessary. It is generally held that a fault rule can induce the producer in such case to take efficient care, but only a strict liability rule will also lead to an optimal output of products. In this respect strict liability is considered to be a good remedy for underestimation of the risk by consumers.[79]

50 The latter conclusion is also true when harm is caused to third parties, for example bystanders, who have no connection at all with the producer. A Coasean solution is of course excluded under these circumstances since the transaction costs will be prohibitive. There is also no 'contact' between a producer and third parties through the price mechanism.[80] Again, a fault rule would induce the producer to take efficient care, but consumers would purchase

---

77 *I Gilead*, 'Coase theorem', competitive market and products liability law (1985) 20 Israel Law Review 39–48.

78 Ibid 42.

79 See *Adams* (fn 73) 12; *Polinsky* (fn 69) 99; *S Shavell*, Strict liability versus negligence (1980) Journal of Legal Studies 4.

80 See *Hamada* (fn 71) 230 and *CG Veljanovski*, The economic theory of tort liability – toward a corrective justice approach, in: P Burrows/C Veljanovski (eds), The economic approach to law (1981) 31.

too many products. Therefore, the market price would be too low, since it would not reflect the expected accident costs and, given this demand, too large an output of products will follow.[81] This inefficiency can again only be remedied by the introduction of a strict liability rule. Since under such a rule the market price will reflect the expected accident costs, both efficient care will be taken by the producer and an efficient quantity of products will be produced.[82] Again the example of Polinsky concerning the production of beer in cans or in bottles illustrates that with damage caused to third parties the same problems arise as in the case of a lack of consumer information. Only strict liability is able to reach an efficient care level (production of beer in cans rather than in bottles) and an efficient output level (consumers only purchasing beer when their utility is higher than 45).

51 It has been shown that the economic theory does not jump to hasty general conclusions with respect to the desirability of a fault or a strict liability rule. Such answer depends on whether the victim is a consumer or a third party, and if it is a consumer a further distinction is made depending on whether or not the consumer underestimates the risk of a product accident. However, if consumers do underestimate the risk or if the harm is caused to third parties, the literature clearly points at the advantages of strict liability from an efficiency viewpoint. These advantages are mainly to do with the full *internalisation* of the harm through the strict liability rule.

B. REFINEMENTS

52 It has so far been assumed that the behaviour of the victim had no influence on the accident risk, that both producers and consumers were risk-neutral and that the market was perfectly competitive. When these assumptions are relaxed the advantage of strict liability, expressed earlier, does not prevail any longer.

53 It has been stressed that in a bilateral accident situation, where the victim also influences the accident risk, liability rules should also give victims an incentive to take appropriate care and not to engage too often in dangerous activities. If the victim has a significant influence on the accident risk, most authors hold that a fault rule will be preferred to a strict liability rule, even if the latter is combined with a contributory negligence defence.[83] One of the reasons given is the unwillingness of courts to consider the contributory negligence of victims, which might easily affect their incentives. In addition, only a fault

81 See *Polinsky* (fn 69) 103; *Shavell* (fn 69) 49–50.
82 *Shavell* (fn 79) 3.
83 *Shavell* (fn 69) 58.

rule will lead to an efficient activity level by the victim. It is therefore held that if the victim has a significant influence on the accident risk and it is thus more important to control his activity level than it is to control the injurer's, a fault rule will be preferred.[84]

54 It has also been pointed out by Polinsky and Rogerson that a strict liability rule might be problematic if the producer has market power and consumers underestimate the risks of a product accident.[85] When producers have market power, market prices will be relatively high, which will lead to too low a demand for the product. This process is amplified in the case of strict liability. Then the market price will still be higher than the full price of the product (cost price + expected accident costs). Under a fault rule the market price will be lower since the expected accident costs are not added into it. The basic idea of Polinsky and Rogerson is that when consumers underestimate the risks and producers have market power, a fault rule might be preferable. The reason is that under a fault rule the market price will be lower and since the consumers underestimate the risk they will not take the expected accident costs into account in their buying decision. Thus demand will increase. Therefore, they argue that with a fault rule one can make use of consumers' underestimation of the accident risk in order to fight the natural tendency of the monopolist to limit output. So the surprising conclusion is that when the producer has market power he should almost be 'rewarded' for it by introducing a fault rule. Thus it is possible to ensure that the monopolist does not reduce output and puts an inefficiently limited number of products on the market.[86]

C. INFLUENCE OF RISK AND INSURANCE

55 Finally it should also be mentioned that risk neutrality of all the market participants has so far been assumed. If one introduces risk, one could examine whether producers or consumers are risk averse and allocate the liability accordingly, given the insurance function of a strict liability rule for victims.[87] This is, however, not very useful, since it is often difficult for the regulator to examine the attitude of either victims or producers to risk. It seems easy to assume that consumers would always be averse to product-related risks.

---

84 *Shavell* (fn 79) 7, 20; *Shavell* (fn 69) 48–51. This will often be dependent upon the nature of the activity and the potential harm.

85 *M Polinsky/W Rogerson*, Products liability, consumer misperceptions and market power (1983) Bell Journal of Economics 581–589.

86 Similar points have been made by *Hamada* (fn 71) 233 and by *D Epple/A Raviv*, Product safety, liability rules, market structure and imperfect information (1978) American Economic Review 86.

87 For an analysis along these lines see *S Shavell*, On liability and insurance (1982) Journal of Economics 120–132.

However, producers might also be averse to particular risks. Producers might for example be averse to the risks of serial damage. Therefore it is hard to draw conclusions on the desirability of a certain liability rule merely on the basis of attitude to risk.

56 In addition, one would only have to rely upon the insurance function of some liability rules for risks for which no commercial insurance coverage can be found on the market. In practice both producers and consumers can insure the product risk. In this respect there is, however, an important difference between various types of insurance which follow from different liability rules. Under a strict liability rule producers will always have to pay compensation. If they are risk averse, they will purchase third party insurance. Victims will always be compensated through the strict liability rule so, irrespective of their attitude towards risk, they would have no demand for insurance. Under a fault rule, rational producers will have an incentive to take due care to avoid liability. Since producers will not be found liable, consumers will not be compensated through liability rules and risk-averse consumers might purchase first party insurance.[88]

57 There is, however, an important difference between both insurance schemes when it comes to the question whether the adverse selection problem can be cured. Under first party insurance the victim him- or herself knows if he or she poses a high or a low risk and what type of insurance coverage he or she needs. Given the different preferences for different types of insurance coverage a narrowing into small risks pools by the insurer is possible and the adverse selection problem can be avoided. This is not the case in third party insurance schemes. Due to asymmetrical information on the size of the risk between the insurer and the insureds, the premium will be set at an average level.[89] For the low-risk members of the group this premium will be relatively too high, which will lead the good risks to leave the risk pool. According to Priest this leads to a process whereby the best risks will always be leaving the pool, which leads to an overall unravelling of the risk pool. Priest argues that the insurance crisis in the US has been caused by this incurable adverse selection problem.[90] He argues however that these problems are much more serious in third party insurance than in a first party insurance scheme and that the development towards the increasing use of third party insurance schemes has caused the insurance crisis in the US. If this were true one would of course have another strong argument against strict liability, since only under this rule will risk-averse producers take out third party liability insurance.

88 See *Polinsky* (fn 69) 100–101.

89 See the basic article by *Akerlof* (fn 74).

90 *G Priest*, The current insurance crisis and modern tort law (1987) Yale Law Journal 1521–1590. The point had also been made by *R Epstein*, Product liability as an insurance market (1985) Journal of Legal Studies 650–652.

58 In sum, the economic theory advances in its basic model strong arguments in favour of a strict liability rule when consumers underestimate the risk of a product accident or when the harm is caused to third parties. However, if the victim has a substantial influence on the risk of an accident, or if the producer has market power and the consumers underestimate the accident risk or if one takes into account the influence of insurance, strong arguments could be advanced in favour of a fault rule as well.

V. ECONOMIC EFFECTS OF THE PRODUCT LIABILITY DIRECTIVE[91]

A. GENERAL VERSUS DIFFERENTIATED RULES

59 Apparently the drafters of the Directive judged that the best way to realise the 'protection of the consumer', of which they spoke so much, was to implement a generalised strict liability rule for harm caused by a product defect. The first point that is striking when one compares this rule to the economic theory of product liability discussed above is that the Directive advances one single rule to solve all product accidents, whereas the economic theory is much more balanced and detailed. Depending upon whether or not the victim is a consumer, whether or not the latter has information on the product risk, what the influence of insurance is, etc, economic theory would only hold that a strict liability rule is efficient in some cases, but certainly not in all.

60 On the policy level it is, based on all the relevant criteria, almost impossible to advise the legislator to use one single rule for all product accidents. It can even be questioned whether the legislator would have to define such a rule. An obvious alternative would be to let the judge decide what type of liability rule should govern the product accident. Thus case law could take into account all the relevant criteria and the application of the strict liability rule could be limited to certain product accidents. The Directive, which introduces one strict liability rule for all product accidents, disregards all the various factual situations which make different liability rules efficient. Thus, by using one single rule, inefficiencies will unavoidably be created, since the strict liability rule will also be applied where this would be inefficient taking into account the above-mentioned criteria. It is also doubtful whether the savings in administrative

91 In the scope of this chapter only a few brief remarks concerning the economic effects of the Directive can be made. For a more thorough analysis see *J Finsinger/J Simon*, An economic assessment of the EC Product Liability Directive and the product liability law of the Federal Republic of Germany, in: M Faure/R Van den Bergh (eds), Essays in law and economics. Corporations, accident prevention and compensation for losses (1989) 185–214.

costs by using one legal rule outweigh the inefficiencies. The costs of applying the economic criteria for strict liability should not be that high either. Especially if the criteria can easily be recognised (eg whether the victim was a consumer or a third party), an individualised product liability system where strict liability will only be applied in some cases could be used by the judge at relatively low costs.

61 One of the criteria was also applied for a long time in legal practice. Indeed, in most legal systems product accidents where the victim has a contractual relationship with the producer were treated differently from those where the victim is a complete stranger to the producer.[92] One of the reasons for introducing the generalised strict liability in the Directive was that this different treatment was considered 'unjust'. However, this distinction is quite sound from an economic point of view. As was mentioned above, if the victim has a contractual relationship with the producer, a Coasean solution is in principle possible if the consumer is well informed of the accident risk. Such solution is of course always excluded if the victim is a third party because of the prohibitive transaction costs. So there is a good economic reason for treating both situations differently.

B. STRICT LIABILITY FOR DEFECTS

62 Of course the Directive does not introduce a general strict liability rule for all damage caused by a product. The producer will only be liable when the damage was caused by a defect in the product. This looks more like fault liability, since a product is often defective because the producer did not take sufficient care. However, the liability is indeed strict since the producer will always incur liability when harm was caused by a defect in his product even if he can prove that he took due care. The producer only escapes liability when the harm was not caused by a defect of the product. Given the broad notion of defect in the Directive, a product is almost already considered defective by the mere fact of having caused the harm.[93] Therefore, there is, from an economic point of view, not a substantial difference between strict liability for all damage caused by a product and strict liability for damage caused by a defect in the product as introduced in the Directive.[94]

---

92 This is especially the case for Member States where product liability for damage caused to consumers was based on a contract rather than on tort such as for example in Belgium or France.

93 One could argue that as soon as a product causes serious injuries it does not provide the safety which a person is entitled to expect and is therefore defective according to article 6 of the Directive.

94 For an economic analysis of liability for defective products see *Shavell* (fn 69) 58–60. For an analysis of the defect notion in the Directive see *Finsinger/Simon* (fn 91) 200–207.

63 A further differentiation could be made between different types of defects. The US economic literature in particular (as well as the legal literature) distinguishes between *inter alia* manufacturing defects, design defects and warning defects.[95] The European Product Liability Directive seems to adopt a so-called consumer expectations test by considering a product defective when it frustrates the safety expectations of the ordinary consumer.[96]

C. INSURANCE CRISIS?

64 An important question is of course whether Europe could expect to follow the American product liability explosion and the above-mentioned insurance crisis. The question is important since the Directive introduced a general strict liability rule for product defects, which leads to an increasing use of third party liability insurance, which in turn caused the insurance crisis in the US, according to Priest. There are of course differences in the legal systems of Europe and the US which are relevant for the development of accident law. In the US the amounts of damages awarded are often much higher than in Europe for several reasons, not only because of the use of punitive damages[97] but also because in general tort judgments are often given for much higher amounts. One explanation for the latter fact might be that damage awards in the US are often fixed by juries.[98]

65 There are also structural differences between both legal systems which explain why more liability suits are brought in the US and why plaintiffs are often that successful. One is that attorneys in the US are often paid on a contingency fee or a no-win-no-fee basis.[99] Another reason is that in Europe (unlike in the US) victims are often generously compensated by the welfare state, thus reducing their need to call on liability law; moreover, access to justice in Europe is still costly, which may equally reduce the likelihood of product liability suits in Europe.[100]

---

95 For further details see *Geistfeld* (fn 4) 310–315.

96 *Geistfeld* (fn 4) 309.

97 In most European legal systems punitive damages are excluded. It is held that a tortfeasor should compensate for the total damages, nothing less, but also certainly nothing more than the actual damage.

98 According to *Krämer* (fn 43) 291–292 and *T Bourgoignie*, Responsabilité du fait des produits: arguments connus pour un nouveau débat (1986) I Revue Européenne de Droit de la Consommation 20–21.

99 This so-called *pacta de quota litis* is prohibited in most European countries either by a code of civil procedure or by legal ethics or by both.

100 So *A Cavaliere,* The economic impact of product liability and product safety regulations in the European Union (2001) Quaderni dell dipartimento di economía pubblica e territoriali, Working Paper No 4, 11–15.

66 Will the insurance crisis also follow in Europe? Based on the above-mentioned differences from the US one could at least say that fewer liability suits will be brought in Europe and that the amount of liability will in general be lower. However, Priest warned that it is not the jury system alone and the high amount of damages which caused the insurance crisis in the US. The main reason is that tort law in the US was no longer seen as a system of liability rules but as a system of compensation that should provide insurance for victims.[101] Indeed, some authors argue that now the doctrine of product liability has finally grown up and that Europe will go through a similar evolution as the US went through in the past.[102] If this will be true, we might have expected a similar product liability explosion in Europe. Most authors do, however, believe that given the differences with the situation in the US, the Directive would not lead to an insurance crisis.[103] This might be all the more true since the strict liability of the Directive in fact has only a limited scope of application and is for example not applicable to professional damage, non-material damage and damage caused to the product itself. Moreover, the Directive is now thirty years old and the various reports on the functioning of the Directive do indicate that the national laws implementing the Directive are only seldom used and that, moreover, the application of the Directive has so far not led to insurability problems of any importance.

D. INEFFICIENCIES AND REDISTRIBUTION?

67 It was mentioned above that the general strict liability rule for all activities, which is used in the Directive, might create inefficiencies since it will also be applied in cases where a fault rule would be preferable from an efficiency viewpoint. It should, however, not be forgotten that the purpose of the Directive was the harmonisation of product liability law in Europe. If this were to succeed it could create benefits that could easily outweigh the aforementioned disadvantages of the generalised strict liability rule. Indeed, if a single product liability rule were to be created in all Member States, this could contribute to the creation of equal marketing conditions and thus to the realisation of the internal market. This could bring substantial savings[104] which could easily outweigh the inefficiency of the use of one single rule. This, however, will not be the case in practice since the Directive can never bring about the harmonisation of product liability law in Europe. So the inefficiencies remain without any compensating benefit for the realisation of the internal market.[105]

---

101 *Priest* (fn 90) 1582–1590.

102 *Van Wassenaer van Catwijck* (fn 39) 114.

103 *Bourgoignie* (fn 98) 18–19; *Krämer* (fn 43) 292.

104 Cf *R Van den Bergh*, Competition law and law of unfair competition in Europe after 1992, unpublished manuscript.

105 See in that respect the criticism on the 'internal market' justification for the harmonisation of product liability law at EU level, above no 06 ff.

68 One could go one step further and argue that the Directive not only creates several inefficiencies, but that it is also problematic from a distributive point of view. Many lawyers favour the introduction of strict liability since it would protect the consumer. It is even argued that strict liability would be necessary 'to restore the broken balance between producers and consumers'. The Coase theorem teaches that from a distributive point of view there also will be no difference between a fault rule and a strict liability rule. Fully informed consumers will only take into account the full price of the product (cost price + expected accident costs) and will base their purchase decision upon this full price. Even if the legislator would like to protect the consumer by introducing a strict liability rule, the producer will still add the expected accident costs to the cost price. The consumer will again pay the full price since the expected accident costs are passed on to him, which is reflected in a higher market price. Since producers and consumers are bound together through the price mechanism, every shift of liability to the producer will be passed on to the consumer. In this setting a legal intervention to redistribute wealth to the consumer by introducing a strict liability rule therefore seems useless.[106]

69 When consumer groups are heterogeneous, the introduction of strict liability will even have adverse distributional effects. Indeed, the most important part of damages is lost income. The expected damages are therefore of course higher for high-income consumers than for low-income consumers. The producer will, however, take into account an average expected damage and will add this to his cost price to get one single market price for all consumers. The effect is that when low-income consumers still buy the product, they 'pay' for the expected damages of the high-income consumers. Therefore strict liability in a product liability setting creates a redistribution from poor to rich consumers.[107] For the same reason Priest argued that the product liability explosion in the US especially hurts low-income groups.[108]

70 This effect will be made even worse if the strict liability rule not only applies to harm suffered by consumers, but is extended to damages caused to third parties, such as the Directive does. In that case the market price will again be higher since the producer will also have to pay for damage caused to third parties. The increased expected damages will again be passed on to the consumer who pays a higher market price for the damage a product he bought can cause to third parties. The consumer has no possibility of passing on this increased price and therefore he, in fact, pays for the protection of third parties.

---

106 See *Hamada* (fn 71) 228–234.

107 See *Adams* (fn 73) 6–7.

108 *Priest* (fn 90) 1521–1590.

71 So the expansion of strict liability to damage caused to third parties redistributes wealth from consumers to third parties. Consumers will indeed have to pay for the protection of third parties. This again increases the adverse redistributive effect that poor consumers will pay higher prices for the expected damages of third parties. Since lost income is an important part of the damage, again high-income groups do indeed benefit from the redistribution.

72 This shows that the generalised strict liability introduced by the Directive may not only create inefficiencies, but is also based on wrong ideas concerning the protection of consumers.

VI. MULTI-PARTY CAUSATION

73 A specific problem that can arise within the context of product liability is that multiple producers may have brought a specific product on the market.[109] Problems in that respect especially arise when it is not clear who manufactured the particular product that caused the damage to the victim. It may well be that many producers brought a similar product onto the market and hence causal uncertainty arises as to the particular producer that caused the damage to the victim. The question arises as to how the law should deal with this problem of causal uncertainty. The DES case provides an example of causal uncertainty.

74 The case dealt with a product referred to as DES, which has been given to pregnant women. As a result of mothers taking DES, their daughters suffered birth defects and personal injury. The causal link between the use of DES by the mother and the daughter's symptoms was not disputed. It was also known that certain manufacturers had brought DES onto the market. However, uncertainty existed with respect to which manufacturer had sold a specific product to a particular mother. Several 'DES daughters' in a variety of countries sued some of the producers that had brought DES onto the market at the time, although they could not prove from which manufacturer their mother had bought the drug. This gave rise, *inter alia* in the Netherlands, to a debate about whether a proportionate liability rule should be applied to apportion the burden of liability between the manufacturers. Market-share liability would be an example of such a proportionality rule. The Dutch Supreme Court, however, applied a so-called 'alternative causation' rule, meaning that the DES daughters are allowed to claim full compensation from any of the manufacturers.[110] A manufacturer can still

---

109 In the questionnaire this is also addressed as a specific issue under section III.A.

110 For a discussion of alternative causation under German law, see *J Köndgen*, Multiple Causation and Joint Tortfeasors Pollution Cases according to German Law, in: JM van Dunné (ed), Transboundary Pollution and Liability, the Case of the River Rhine (1991) 99–106 and

rebut the presumption by proving that he did not sell DES to the particular mother, but this will often be impossible in practice.[111] Hence, this result is similar to a joint and several liability rule.[112]

75 This means that any victim can claim full compensation from any of the manufacturers. The insurer of the particular manufacturer then becomes *de facto* the insurer of the whole market. It is therefore held that this tendency towards joint and several liability endangers the insurability of domestic tort liability.[113]

76 This case shows that the crucial question arises as to how the law should deal with this causal uncertainty in the event of multi-party causation. One option is, as the Dutch Supreme Court did in the DES case, to shift the risk of causal uncertainty entirely to the manufacturer. He is then *de facto* held liable for the entire loss and has to seek recourse against individual other producers, if they are still in the market. The insolvency risk is thus also shifted to the producer. A more fine-tuned alternative would be to adopt a proportional solution. Proportional liability in this specific context of product liability amounts to a market-share liability. As a result of market-share liability the particular producer will only be exposed to liability for the risk that he caused with his activity.[114] The result of the market-share liability is that the producer will have optimal incentives for accident prevention, so it is generally held in economic literature.[115] In summary, there is, from an economic perspective, a strong case in favour of market-share liability in the event of uncertainty over causation.

---

the interesting article of *T Bodewig*, Probleme Alternativer Kausalität bei Massenschäden (1985) Archiv für die civilistische Praxis 505–558.

111 Note, however, that the Dutch Supreme Court only considered the causation question. Formally, it still had to be decided whether bringing DES on the market was in itself wrongful. See Hoge Raad 9 October 1992 [1994] Nederlandse Jurisprudentie 535 (C.J.H.B.). See on this case, *J Spier/JH Wansink*, Joint and Several Liability of DES Manufacturers: A Dutch Tort Crisis (1993) International Insurance Law Review 176–181.

112 So *J Spier*, How to Keep Liability within Reasonable Limits?, in: J Spier (ed), The Limits of Liability: Keeping the Floodgates Shut (1996) 123–124.

113 *A Monti*, Environmental Risk: A Comparative Law and Economics Approach to Liability and Insurance (2001) European Review of Private Law 51–79, 58. And see *L Bergkamp*, The proper scope of joint and several liability (2001) Tijdschrift voor Milieuaansprakelijkheid (Environmental Liability Law Review) 154 who argues that under joint and several liability civil liability becomes unpredictable and hence uninsurable.

114 It is a solution that has more particularly been proposed by *S Shavell*, Uncertainty over causation and the determination of civil liability (1985) Journal of Law and Economics 587–609.

115 See also *inter alia J Makdisi*, Proportional liability: a comprehensive rule to apportion tort damages based on probability (1989) North Carolina Law Review 163; *G Robinson*, Probabilistic causation and compensation for tortuous risk (1985) Journal of Legal Studies 797–798; and *O Ben-Shahar*, Causation and foreseeability, in: M Faure (ed), Tort law and economics (2009) 83–108.

VII. RECENT LITERATURE

A. INTRODUCTION

77 The basic economic theory of product liability, as summarised in sections III and IV, is grounded in publications of Steven Shavell from 1980 and 1987. Theoretically those findings are still extremely valuable. However, in the past thirty years more literature has been published, fine-tuning some of the literature on product liability (B). Moreover, Shavell himself, in a provocative article with Polinsky in the Harvard Law Review, questions whether there should be any role at all for product liability law (C). Furthermore, unlike in the 1980s, the economic approach to accidents and also to product liability has become increasingly empirical. It is also interesting to briefly look at the most important findings of this empirical literature (D). Another point that changed in the analysis is that behavioural law and economics (BLE) has gained a lot of influence (E).

B. SIGNALLING, INNOVATION AND DEFECTS

78 In a literature review Geistfeld shows how the literature has evolved since the early publications of Shavell.[116] One aspect that has been examined in more depth in the literature is the relationship between the quality of products and their safety. Recall that the original signalling model as presented by Oi held that a higher price would signal higher quality. More recent literature has cast serious doubt on the ability of consumers to draw correct inferences about the product safety from the price.[117] Equally, literature has emerged on the relationship between product liability and innovation. The policy debate in the US has held that increased product liability would reduce innovation and undermine the competitiveness of domestic products in a global economy.[118] However, the literature has indicated that liability can increase investment in safety and hence lead to a higher full price of products. But in those circumstances liability could even encourage safety innovations rather than hindering them.[119] An increase in product liability would therefore also increase expenditure on research and development and hence spur

116 *Geistfeld* (fn 4) 287–340.

117 See *inter alia Burrows* (fn 29) 68–83; *P Burrows*, Consumer safety under products liability and duty to disclose (1992) 12 International Review of Law and Economics 457–478 and *A Kirmani/AR Rao*, No pain, no gain: a critical review of the literature on signaling unobservable product quality (2000) 64 Journal of Marketing 66–79.

118 *Geistfeld* (fn 4) 304.

119 See *inter alia A Endres/R Bertram*, The development of care technology under liability law (2006) 26 International Review of Law and Economics 503–518.

innovation.[120] Empirical evidence seems to confirm that firms do increase their R&D expenditures as a result of liability concerns.[121] This shows that expanding product liability should hence not necessarily hinder innovation, but can, on the contrary, stimulate it.

79 The literature has also been refined to the extent that the classic Shavell models assumed liability would arise for any damage resulting from a product. In fact strict product liability only applies to *defective* products. Geistfeld has examined the consequences of reducing product liability to defective products and has held that it reduces insurance costs substantially and still provides the right incentives for prevention by freeing producers from damage that would result from products that are not defective.[122] Various tests are employed to examine the defectiveness of a product, such as *inter alia* a consumer expectation test. The latter enables the role of contracting over product risk to be incorporated.[123] Moreover, a large literature has developed, mostly in the US, distinguishing between the various defects, such as construction/manufacturing defects, design defects and warning defects,[124] and the different incentive effects that liability for those specific defects would have.

80 Furthermore, some scholars have paid attention to the enforceability of contractual limits on product liability. Whereas these are in most legal systems held to be not enforceable,[125] some law and economics scholars have argued that it would be important to rely more on contractual limitations on seller's liability. The argument is that the limit on the seller's liability would signal information concerning the riskiness of the product to consumers.[126]

C. POLINSKY/SHAVELL

81 In 2010 the Harvard Law Review published a remarkable article by two of probably the most well-known law and economics scholars, Mitchell Polinsky and Steven Shavell.[127] Polinsky and Shavell argue in that article that from a

---

120 *AF Daughety/JF Reinganum*, Product safety: liability, R&D and signaling (1995) 85 American Economic Review 1187–1206.

121 *Geistfeld* (fn 4) 305.

122 *MA Geistfeld*, Principles of product liability (2006) 51–58.

123 *Geistfeld* (fn 4) 309.

124 For an overview see *Geistfeld* (fn 122) 85–102 and *Geistfeld* (fn 4) 310–315.

125 *Geistfeld* (fn 4) 316.

126 See more particularly *R Epstein*, Modern product liability law (1980); *R Epstein*, The unintended revolution in product liability law (1989) 10 Cardozo Law Review 2193–2222; and *P Rubin*, Tort reform by contract (1993).

127 *AM Polinsky/S Shavell*, The uneasy case for product liability (2010) 123 Harvard Law Review 1438–1492.

cost-benefit perspective the benefits of product liability are weak compared to the costs for a wider range of products. They argue for example that the role of product liability law in providing incentives for increased product safety is modest. First of all consumers would punish firms that largely sell harmless products and moreover safety regulations equally play an important role in the prevention of harm caused by products. Their main objection is specific to the American context, namely that product liability does indeed lead to price increases, but that these do not always reflect product risks. A substantial proportion of increased costs for producers is simply the result of high litigation costs. They state that 'for each dollar that an accident victim receives, two dollars of legal expenses are incurred. In all then, the tort system, and thus the product liability system, is very expensive'.[128] Moreover, they equally refer to the large amounts awarded for pain and suffering and mention the classic law and economics argument that victims would not ordinarily purchase insurance for this type of damage.[129] In sum, Polinsky and Shavell argue that the benefits of product liability law are doubtful or could at least also be achieved via other mechanisms.[130] Moreover, they especially point out the excessively high costs of the product liability system, as compared to the doubtful benefits.

82 This analysis is of course powerful and important. They therefore argue in favour of limiting or eliminating product liability in certain industries. However, one has to take into account that a significant part of their criticism fits into the particular American tort litigation context with excessively high lawyers' fees, large awards for pain and suffering and substantial amounts of the compensation being paid to the plaintiff bar rather than to the victims.[131] These problems may not have yet appeared to the same extent in Europe, but still they constitute an important warning, particularly in view of the potential tort reforms in Europe.

D. EMPIRICAL LITERATURE

83 An important difference between the economic approach of the 1980s and the approach today is that, simply because computer skills were lacking at the time, the original law and economics approach was largely theoretical. However, since computational skills, aided by computer programmes, have greatly

128 Ibid 1470. See for an overview of the administrative costs of the tort system also *BCJ van Velthoven*, Empirics of tort, in: M Faure (ed), Tort law and economics (2009) 470–471.

129 See the argument made by *SP Croley/JD Hanson*, The non-pecuniary costs of accidents: pain and suffering damages in tort law (1995) 108 Harvard Law Review 1785–1917.

130 See also below no 99 ff.

131 See on these points also above no 64 ff.

increased the possibility of regression analysis, an empirical revolution has taken place in law and economics. Some of this has also affected the area of product liability, although some of the empirical research still comes from the time when those tools were not as powerful as today, which hence also leads to particular methodological flaws.[132] Some early (and therefore less reliable) studies held that there were no clear effects of product liability litigation on accident rates, thus casting doubt on the argument that the benefits of expanded product liability would have been large.[133] But a problem with the data used is that they do not separate accidents involving defective products from accidents involving non-defective products.[134] Other studies, which relied on interviews showed that according to corporate executives product liability significantly influences manufacturers concerning product design decisions. Many companies would equally have decided not to introduce new products because of the fear of product liability.[135] There is some evidence that in particular cases liability burdens have been the reason for product withdrawals[136] but there is equally evidence that product liability cost would increase research and development intensity in this domain.[137] Van Velthoven summarises the empirical findings concerning the effects of product liability law as follows: 'In conclusion, strict liability would seem to stimulate R&D towards safer products, to drive defective products out of the market and to raise prices'. However, he adds that some research 'suggests that liability can go too far in its cover of non-economic damages'.[138] Also Polinsky and Shavell provide an interesting overview of studies which according to them show 'that product liability has had no noticeable impact on accident rates'.[139]

E. BEHAVIOURAL

84 Yet another revolution that has taken place since the 1980s in the domain of law and economics is not only that it has become much more empirical, but also that the traditional rational choice paradigm has been refined by incorporating

[132] Good overviews of the empirics of product liability are provided by *Geistfeld* (fn 4) 301–304 and of empirics of tort generally by *DM Dewees/D Duff/MJ Trebilcock*, Exploring the domain of accident law: taking the facts seriously (1996) and by *Van Velthoven* (fn 128) 453–498.

[133] See for example *GL Priest*, Products liability law and the accident rate in liability: perspectives and policy, in: RE Lietan/C Winston (eds), Liability: perspectives and policy (1988) 184–222 and *PW Huber/R Lietan*, Overview, in: PW Huber/RE Lietan (eds), The liability maze: the impact of liability law on safety and innovation (1991) 1–27.

[134] *Geistfeld* (fn 4) 302.

[135] Ibid 303.

[136] *Van Velthoven* (fn 128) 483.

[137] So *WK Viscusi/MJ Moore*, Product liability, research and development, and innovation (1993) 101 Journal of Political Economy 161–184.

[138] *Van Velthoven* (fn 128) 484.

[139] *Polinsky/Shavell* (fn 127) 1455–1459.

insights provided by cognitive psychology into the analysis. This has merged into a new domain which is now sometimes referred to as behavioural law and economics.[140] This behavioural approach has equally affected the economic analysis of tort law.[141] The behavioural approach has to some extent had an influence on the economic analysis of product liability as well. Studies have devoted attention to the way in which consumers valuate particular risks.

85 Interesting in this respect is Kahneman's theory on heuristics and biases, which points *inter alia* at so-called availability heuristic, which holds that individuals often overestimate risks that are brought to their attention. The more easily the memory of a particular accident comes to people's mind, the more likely it seems that the accident will occur. It is a mental shortcut that individuals use on the basis of which they assume that memorable events are memorable precisely because they are common or have recently occurred.[142] This could potentially lead to an overestimation of product risks by consumers.[143] However, most product risks are not very salient since product accidents remain relatively rare for most individuals. Hence, there is rather a probability that consumers would not worry about product risks and even tend to underestimate product risks and undervalue product safety.[144] The danger of an underestimation of product-related risks could also be related to the phenomenon of 'selective optimism': individuals believe that good things are more likely than average to happen to them and that bad things are more likely than average to happen to others.[145] This selective optimism may hence lead to an underestimation by consumers of the potential dangers of particular products, for example smoking.

86 The lessons from behavioural law and economics are more particularly relevant as far as the effectiveness of information remedies are concerned. Traditional economic literature has prescribed information duties as a remedy to address information asymmetry.[146] The idea is that legislation could improve consumer welfare by prohibiting fraud, the distribution of false information

---

140 See *CR Sunstein*, Behavioural analysis of law (1997) 64 University of Chicago Law Review 1175–1195 and *C Jolls/CR Sunstein/R Thaler*, A behavioural approach to law and economics (1998) 50 Stanford Law Review 1471–1550.

141 For a summary see *HB Schäfer/F Müller-Langer*, Strict liability versus negligence, in: M Faure (ed), Tort law and economics (2009) 35–36 and *JC Teitelbaum*, A unilateral accident model under ambiguity (2000) 37 Journal of Legal Studies 431–477.

142 See *Sunstein* (fn 140) 1188.

143 *A Schwarz*, Legal implications of imperfect information in consumer markets (1995) 151 Journal of Institutional and Theoretical Economics 31–48.

144 *Geistfeld* (fn 4) 292.

145 See *C Jolls*, Behavioural economic analysis of redistributive legal rules (1998) 51 Vanderbilt Law Review 1659.

146 See G Hadfield/R Howse/MJ Trebilcock, Information-based principles for rethinking consumer protection policy (1998) 21(2) Journal of Consumer Policy 131–169.

and the imposition of duties to inform.[147] However, the behavioural literature has shown that most of the heuristics and biases indicate cognitive deviations on the part of consumers and hence suggest opportunities for sellers to take advantage of consumers.[148] Empirical evidence also casts serious doubts on the effectiveness of disclosure duties. Consumers often do not read particular warnings and consumers continue (as a result of various biases, such as over-optimism) to have incorrect interpretations of the contract terms.[149] As a result, the effectiveness of information duties is undermined by consumer biases and heuristics. Consumers are hence not able to discipline the market and in that sense improve product quality. These behavioural insights hence lead to the important conclusion that (as information economics hoped and expected) merely imposing information duties (eg duties to warn about the potential dangers of a product) on manufacturers will not necessarily lead to effective risk perceptions by consumers. The policy consequence is that information duties cannot be considered an alternative for liability rules.

VIII. DEVELOPMENT RISK[150]

A. RETROSPECTIVE VERSUS DEVELOPMENT RISK LIABILITY

87 One area of law that has long struggled with the need for regulation to provide flexibility whilst guaranteeing a clear standard of foreseeability in unstable regulatory environments is the field of product liability. One of the primary aims of product liability is to incentivise the potential tortfeasor to act so as to prevent his action or inaction from causing harm to others. A great deal of research has been conducted on the negative effects of retroactive regulation in liability[151] and law and economics scholarship has clearly shown – as deterrence theory would suggest – that an *ex post* finding of liability for behaviour that was

---

147 *R Van den Bergh*, Competition law and consumer protection legislation, in: AM Hatzis (ed), Economic analysis of law: a European perspective (2003).

148 *MG Faure/HA Luth*, Behavioural economics in unfair contract terms. Cautions and considerations (2011) Journal of Consumer Policy 337–358.

149 See *inter alia F Marotta-Wurgler*, What's in a standard form contract? An empirical analysis of software license agreements (2007) 4(4) Journal of Empirical Legal Studies 677–713.

150 This section of the chapter relies and builds further on *M Faure/M Goodwin/F Weber*, The regulator's dilemma: caught between the need for flexibility & the demands of foreseeability. Reassessing the lex certa principle (2014) 24(2) Albany Law Journal of Science & Technology 283–364.

151 See, eg, *K Abraham*, Environmental liability and the limits of insurance (1988) 88 Columbia Law Review 957–959 and *J Boyd/H Kunreuther*, Retro-active liability or the public purse? (1997) 11(1) Journal of Regulatory Economics 79–90.

not considered wrongful at the time that it took place rarely serves the purposes of accident prevention.[152]

88 However, the same scholarship has also shown that in situations in which rapid technological developments lead either to the emergence of new risks or to improvements in the ability of regulatees to prevent risks at lower costs, it may be optimal for courts to impose more severe sanctions or to extend liability to behaviour that was not previously deemed wrongful. This research in the law and economics field has concluded that, in situations in which standards could be stricter for no greater cost and could further reduce the risk to human health and the environment, it would lead to suboptimal regulation if manufacturers were only to be held liable for compliance with an existing standard and could under no circumstances be held liable for risks that had not been foreseen.[153] Instead, this research asserts that a regulatee's knowledge or ability to foresee that they may be held liable *ex post* for behaviour that causes harm creates incentives for a potential tortfeasor to obtain as much information as possible about the risks associated with their behaviour.[154] The creation of such incentives is referred to in the literature as 'development risk liability', and is intended to provide the regulatee with sufficient and appropriate incentives to invest in research on the risk of their activities and into optimal technologies to prevent or minimise those risks.[155]

B. THE TECHNIQUE OF 'DEVELOPMENT RISK LIABILITY'

89 The application of development risk to a party obviously leads to a flexibility/foreseeability dilemma. On the one hand, flexibility demands that the standard-setting process in civil law is seen as a learning process whereby the standard of care is not static but changes over time.[156] It would clearly lead to regulatory disconnect and thus ineffectiveness to hold that due care standards should never

---

152 See *M Faure/P Fenn*, Retroactive liability and the insurability of long-tail risks (1999) 19 International Review of Law and Economics 487. It might of course, however, serve other purposes, such as sparing the taxpayer the cost of providing victims with compensation.

153 See, eg, *A Schwartz*, Products liability, corporate structure and bankruptcy: toxic substances and the remote-risk relationship (1985) 14 Journal of Legal Studies 689.

154 This point has been made by *S Shavell*, Liability and the incentive to obtain information about risk (1992) 21 Journal of Legal Studies 259. And see *LT Visser/HO Kerkmeester*, Kenbaarheidsvereisten en gewoonten als verweren tegen een aansprakelijkheidsaktie: een rechtseconomische benadering (1996) Tijdschrift voor Milieuaansprakelijkheid 48.

155 See *M Faure/D Grimeaud*, Financial assurance issues of environmental liability, in: M Faure (ed), Deterrence, insurability and compensation in environmental liability. Future developments in the European Union (2003) 59.

156 This argument has been powerfully stressed by *C Ott/H-B Schäfer*, Negligence as untaken precaution, limited information and efficient standard formation in the civil liability system (1997) International Review of Law and Economics 15–29.

change. There may be many reasons, for instance new technological insights, for why judges might impose a more stringent standard of care than is generally recognised as representing the legal standard at that moment. This new standard can, moreover, have an important signalling function for other manufacturers in the market who can adapt their future behaviour to the new circumstances. However, the foreseeability question, and thus one of fundamental rights, arises with regard to the individual defendant in the particular case in which a new standard of care is set. Is it acceptable to sacrifice the guarantee of legal certainty for the benefit of a more efficient standard in the future by rendering an individual operator retroactively liable for behaviour that was not considered wrongful at the time it was committed?

90 A case from the German system, in which a court applied the idea of development risks but was able to create flexibility without sacrificing foreseeability, serves as a nice example. The German *Bundesgerichtshof*, the highest German civil and criminal court,[157] in a 1980s case concerning a skiing accident that had occurred on the well-known Zugspitzeplatte, in which the victim had hit an unprotected ski lift pillar, came up with an interesting approach to standards of liability. The Court first held that the party responsible for the ski lift had violated a general duty of care owed to the skier. It grounded this judgment in the following way:

> '*Die mit einer solchen Abpolsterung verbundenen Kosten stehen nicht außer Verhältnis zu ihren aus den Schleppliften zu erzielenden Einnahmen. Zudem ist der Unternehmer in der Lage, die Aufwendungen über den Fahrpreis weiterzugeben.*' [The costs associated with the padding of the ski lifts are not disproportionate to the expected gains. In addition, the business is in the position to pass on the related expense to the users via the ticket price.]

91 However, in considering the question of whether the ski lift operator was also to blame for the accident, the Court concluded that it was not:

> '*Jedoch muß den Verkehrssicherungspflichtigen der Pflichtverstoß bei Anwendung verkehrserforderlicher Sorgfalt erkennbar gewesen sein, wobei Bewertungszweifel über die Pflichtmäßigkeit oder Pflichtwidrigkeit des schädlichen Verhaltens zu seinen Lasten gehen. Hier fällt ins Gewicht, daß Entscheidungen Deutscher Gerichte zur Sicherung von Liftstützen zum Schutze der Skiläufer bei derartigen Pistenverhältnissen im Unfallzeitpunkt, soweit ersichtlich, nicht ergangen waren. Eine solche Sicherungspflicht lag auch nicht ohne weiteres in der Tendenz der bis dahin ergangenen Rechtsprechung zur besten Sicherungspflicht.*' [However, when applying a reasonable standard of care in social life, the fact that a duty of care has been violated should be knowable to

[157] See Bundesgerichtshof, 23 October 1984 [1985] Neue Juristische Wochenschrift (NJW) 16–20 and Bundesgerichtshof, 14 March 1995 [1985] NJW 26–31.

the individual. Doubts concerning the question of whether his behaviour violated or complied with the duty of care are otherwise held against the individual who has to comply with the duty. In this respect, an important aspect is that as far as we can see, at the moment of the accident, there were no decisions of German courts concerning the padding of ski lifts to protect skiers. Such a duty of care was moreover not foreseeable based on the, until now, applicable case law concerning the best duty of care.]

92 In announcing that it would abide by existing norms – here relating to duty of care – in the case before it but that it would apply a different, stricter standard in the future, the *Bundesgerichtshof* made use of the technique of prospective overruling.[158] The advantage of this technique was that it allowed the Court to introduce a stricter standard of the duty of care – to update the regulation in this area to take account of changes in the cost to operators of padding ski lifts – while at the same time respecting the guarantee of legal certainty for the defendant before it.

93 As the German case makes clear, a distinction has to be made between the retrospective application of a new liability regime and liability for development risks. Holding actors liable for risks that are not yet known is not necessarily inefficient, especially where, if they know in advance that a strict form of liability applies, it will provide incentives to acquire information about potential new risks and on the optimal techniques for preventing that risk from occurring. Thus strict liability could well provide appropriate incentives for investment in optimal preventive techniques. This, however, does not require, or indeed perhaps justify, the retrospective application of new standards or new contexts that do not positively affect future incentives for prevention, ie where the regulatee was unaware that they would be held to a strict liability standard. Development risk liability refers exclusively to risks that could not be known by (industrial) operators at the time of the design of their practice, process or product and that appear later in the course of the process of operation or manufacture; this definition also includes technological improvements that enable risks to human health or to the environment to be reduced, ie that do not increase the risk of the product or primary process but that create the possibility of reducing risk further. In such cases, the legal rule as such does not change, but the standard of liability to which an operator is held is viewed flexibly.

94 Liability for development risks is desirable from an economic perspective where it has the possibility of positively influencing incentives for prevention

158 The decision in this case has been supported in the Dutch legal literature by *J Drion*, Stare decisis. Het gezag van precedenten (1950) and by *O Haazen*, De temporele werking van een rechterlijke uitspraak, in: HG Schermers et al (eds), De rol van de rechter in de moderne Westerse samenleving (1993) 171.

and where the development risk liability is not retroactive liability in disguise, which of course is unattractive for other reasons than merely being inefficient.[159] Development risk liability is then a valuable technique for ensuring that regulation keeps pace with technological developments. Moreover, where manufacturers are aware that they will be held to a strict liability standard, the law provides sufficient certainty both to incentivise risk minimisation and to protect individual rights. However, where a standard of strict liability has not previously been used, applying a development risks approach in determining the appropriate standard of liability falls foul of the principle of foreseeability. It is in these circumstances that the use of prospective overruling as a judicial technique for preventing an equal injustice in applying a development risk approach may be more appropriate.

C. PROSPECTIVE OVERRULING

95 Prospective overruling is a judicial technique in which a previous precedent or authority is overruled without the new ruling having retrospective effect. It thus represents a departure from the fundamental notion that judicial decisions that develop or change the law necessarily have retroactive effect. It is or has been used where a court wishes to overturn or amend bad law but is wary of the consequences of the retrospective application of their finding, whether because of the inherent unfairness that would result to an individual who had relied on the existing law in good faith or for reasons of practicality where the decision would have sweeping consequences for the operation of the judicial system.[160]

96 The application of prospective overruling should, however, be done with caution, otherwise it could *de facto* amount to a no liability rule. Moreover, if the application of a new standard would lead to a finding of no liability in the particular case at hand, it would equally remove the incentives for plaintiffs to sue in all cases where, precisely as a result of technological change, the standard has increased. That is why development risk liability should in principle provide

159 A similar – balanced – conclusion concerning the efficiency of a development risk defense is reached by *G Wagner*, Haftung und Versicherung als Elemente der Techniksteuerung (1999) Versicherungsrecht 1441–1480.

160 See *Linkletter v Walker*, 381 U.S. 618 (1965), in which the US Supreme Court decided not to apply its finding in *Mapp v Ohio* (367 U.S. 643 (1961)) – extending an earlier ruling that the fourth amendment of the Constitution prohibits unreasonable searches and seizures by government agents, thereby excluding evidence gained by violating the amendment, to the states – retrospectively to judgements that had become final before *Mapp*. For consideration of these cases, and others, see *RJ Traynor*, Quo Vadis, Prospective Overruling: A Question of Judicial Responsibility (1977) Hastings Law Journal 792–796.

incentives to innovate, whereas on the other hand prospective overruling should in principle be reserved for cases where applicable rules change in an unforeseeable manner and hence where a finding of liability would not have provided additional incentives for prevention or investments in innovation.

97 Here what we see occurring is the limitation of liability of producers and operators precisely because of a reluctance on the part of the regulator to use development risk liability for fear of applying standards retrospectively. The EU Product Liability Directive,[161] for example, explicitly excludes liability if the producer can prove that, having regard to the circumstances, it is probable that the defect did not exist at the time when the product was put into circulation. Moreover, art 7(e) of the Directive provides for the 'state-of-the-art defence', which protects the producer from liability if she can prove that the state of scientific and technical knowledge at the time the product was put into circulation was not such as to enable the existence of the defect to be discovered, ie signalling a preference for the opposite of development risks liability.[162] Article 15(1)(b) does provide an option for Member States to introduce liability for development risks; however, this option has only been used to date by Luxembourg and Finland.[163] This reluctance to apply development risks liability may lead to inefficiencies and may reduce the incentives for producers to reduce the risk of products where they are able to do so in a cost-effective manner. In such a situation, the use of prospective overruling would avert the fear of new standards being applied retrospectively, whilst at the same time allowing for standards of liability to be made stricter over time as new technology develops and allowing producers to adapt their products to minimise the risk of harm.

98 The economic impact of the development risk clause has been analysed in a study for the European Commission, and it was held that an outright removal of the development risk clause would encourage more process innovation and an increased rated of incremental innovation.[164]

---

161 Art 7(b) of the European Product Liability Directive of 25 July 1985 [1985] OJ L210/29 excludes liability of the producer if he proves 'that, having regard to the circumstances, it is probable that the defect which caused the damage did not exist at the time when the product was put into circulation by him or that this defect into being afterwards'.

162 The state-of-the-art defence has also been addressed in the American context by *J Boyd/ DE Ingberman*, Should 'relative safety' be test of product liability (1997) Journal of Legal Studies 433–473. They show that the 'customary practice test' tends to induce inadequate safety, whereas the 'technological advancement test' tends to induce excessive safety.

163 And by Spain for food on medical products, as well as by France for products derived from the human body. See the overview of the transposition in domestic law, provided in the Green Paper on the Liability for Defective Products, COM(1999)396 final, 35–36.

164 See *Fondazione Rosselli*, Analysis of the economic impact of the development risk clause as provided by Directive 85/374/EEC on liability for defective products.

IX. ALTERNATIVE INSTRUMENTS

A. INTRODUCTION

99 Product liability is, as may be clear, an area of great controversy between law and economics scholars. Even the traditional theoretical approach presented by Steven Shavell in the 1980s, where, at least from a theoretical perspective, the benefits of product liability in providing more product safety were advanced, has, thirty years later, apparently given way to a more sceptical approach, in which Polinsky and Shavell, convinced by the empirical evidence about limited positive effects of product liability and high costs, even argue in favour of limiting/abolishing product liability in particular areas. An important point to stress is that the goals of product liability law (compensation and prevention/deterrence) can be achieved potentially just as well, and probably even better, via alternative mechanisms.

B. PREVENTION

100 As far as prevention is concerned, Shavell's classic criteria certainly indicate weaknesses in the tort system in providing adequate deterrence:[165] information on optimal preventive measures can in some cases, especially when compared to smaller manufacturers, be better obtained at lower costs by a government institution; liability may suffer from a lack of a deterrent effect because of insolvency; and in some cases a liability suit may never be brought because of, for example, latency, problems of access to justice, or uncertain causation. That may hence make safety regulation through *ex ante* public standard setting the primary method to control product-related risks. However, notwithstanding the advantages of safety regulation, it would surely be a mistake to assume that product safety can be fully achieved through regulation.[166] After all, regulation may not capture all possible situations; regulation can quickly become out of date and may not change with rapidly evolving technological evolutions; regulation may also be the result of lobbying by private interest groups (industry) and thus be inefficient; and, moreover, regulation only guarantees high safety standards if full compliance through effective enforcement can be guaranteed. That will, given high costs of enforcement, not always be the case. For that reason it is important to keep in mind that, especially as far as new and quickly developing

---

165 See *S Shavell*, Liability for harm versus regulation of safety (1984) 13 Journal of Legal Studies 357–374.

166 See for economics arguments to combine liability rules and safety regulation and for the mutual interdependencies *M Faure*, Economic analysis of tort and regulatory law, in: WH van Boom/M Lukas/C Kissling (eds), Tort and regulatory law (2007) 399–416.

technologies are concerned (where legislators necessarily often fall behind), liability law can still play an important, albeit complementary, role in providing (some) deterrence. But the empirical evidence shows that the proof of positive effects on product safety of liability law is at best debateable; hence, expectations in that respect should also not be too high.

101 Obviously the fact that product liability never functions in a vacuum but is *de facto* always combined with product safety regulation raises a variety of interesting questions. One of those questions is to what extent mandatory safety regulation imposed by government affects product liability (for example the interpretation of the defect notion in the Directive).[167] Yet another question may be to what extent the fact that government regulation may equally have contributed to a defect in the product could give rise to public authority liability. These are undoubtedly important and relevant questions that, however, go beyond the scope of this chapter.

C. COMPENSATION

102 As far as compensation is concerned, the classic economic analysis of the Product Liability Directive, presented above,[168] pointed at the fact that using the liability system for compensation is problematic since a liability regime leads to third party insurance, which is more costly than the alternative of first party insurance by victims. First party insurance would be better able to deal with the well-known insurance problems of moral hazard and adverse selection and thus lead to better 'insurability' of product liability.[169] Moreover, we can also point to the criticism made by Polinsky and Shavell that the tort system is, at least in the US context, an extremely costly method of providing compensation.[170] Other empirical research has equally indicated that the tort system is discriminatory, in the sense that only a relatively small number of victims receive (large amounts of) compensation, whereas vast numbers of people do not.[171] Hence, it is clear that if compensation were the goal of the product liability regime other mechanisms like first party insurance, but eventually even no-fault compensation schemes,[172] could equally prove to be effective systems of compensation.

---

167 This is *inter alia* addressed by *Cavaliere* (fn 100).

168 Above no 59 ff.

169 So *Eptein* (fn 90) 645–669 and *Priest* (fn 90) 1521–1590.

170 *Polinsky/Shavell* (fn 127) 1469.

171 See the summary of the claiming rates by *Van Velthoven* (fn 128) 463–465.

172 See for the economic perspective on those *K Fiore*, No-fault compensation systems, in: M Faure (ed), Tort law and economics (2009) 406–432.

X. CONCLUDING REMARKS

103 Product liability has probably been one of the most studied areas in the economic analysis of law. It has been one of the domains that has been studied since the early literature that emerged in the 1970s and 1980s. The first studies considered product liability to be an interesting domain to test the Coase theorem. Given the contractual relationship between potential injurers (the manufacturer) and victims (the consumer) product liability was one of the domains where the Coase theorem could potentially be applied in action. However, a problem with that type of literature was that it was often based on unrealistic assumptions concerning consumer behaviour, more particularly full information on the part of consumers. Long before the behavioural revolution came to law and economics, scholars criticised the assumption that consumers would be aware of product risks and would on that basis be able to choose the appropriate level of safety they would desire, corresponding with the price they would pay for the product. By the 1980s new models were therefore developed, on the one hand accepting that consumers may be misinformed about product-related risks, but also addressing the situation where the victim is not a consumer and hence does not have a contractual relationship with the manufacturer. More particularly, Polinsky and Shavell showed in many studies that a strict liability rule is preferable as a mechanism providing both incentives for efficient levels of both care and output.

104 Meanwhile the theoretical insights have probably, notwithstanding a few refinements, been very much further developed in the subsequent thirty years. What did change, however, is that the new tools of empirical law and economics were also applied to the domain of product liability. That was important more particularly since the classic analysis of product liability was based on a strong belief in prevention of product-related risks via deterrence by means of liability rules. The classic idea was that exposure to product liability would provide incentives to manufacturers to invest in innovation and thus lead to safer products. The empirical insights now increasingly cast doubt on whether product liability has had any added value at all as far as increasing product safety is concerned. More particularly Polinsky and Shavell have argued in a provocative paper that the added value of product liability as far as bringing safer products to the market is concerned can be seriously doubted.

105 The economic literature with respect to product liability can undoubtedly also have its importance for the European debate on a desirable reform more particularly of the Product Liability Directive. The contribution of the law and economics approach lies probably not so much in a detailed analysis of the specific regime installed by the Directive, but rather in the economics of federalism. The advantage of that approach is that it has provided detailed criteria for centralisation. Applying those criteria to product liability casts serious doubts on whether there is an actual need of a harmonisation of product liability at EU level at all. The economic approach at least shows that the seemingly economic arguments of 'harmonisation of marketing conditions' and 'levelling the playing field' are probably not the rights justifications for a harmonisation of product liability law in Europe. Moreover, the economic approach equally shows that, given the specific features of the Directive, it is doubtful whether the Directive can reach its goal of creating a harmonised regime, thereby reducing transaction costs.

106 The economic approach to product liability also shows that it is important to structure liability rules in such a way that incentives are provided to manufacturers to innovate and develop new technologies that go beyond the current state of the art. In that respect the current Product Liability Directive may be too afraid of development risk liability. In order to protect manufacturers from unexpected or unforeseeable changes, even a regime of prospective overruling could be considered. Moreover, it was equally held that probably the most problematic aspects of a product liability regime (from a manufacturers' perspective) may be joint and several liability, which could potentially expose manufacturers to so-called 'crushing liability'. The application of a proportional liability rule – in the product liability context, market-share liability – could keep product liability within reasonable (and insurable) limits.[173] The application of such a proportional liability would, moreover, be in line with the European Principles on Tort Law, which equally advocate for a proportional liability rule in the case of causal uncertainty.[174]

107 An important insight of the more economic literature is the fact that both the compensatory and preventive functions of product liability are probably limited, as a result of which the importance of liability rules in realising both functions should not be overestimated. Given the highly selective nature of the liability regime, product liability may actually only provide compensation to a relatively small number of victims; other mechanisms like social security, workman's compensation or first party insurance may *de facto* play a more important role. The same may be true for the preventive function where regulation aiming at product safety can in practice be considered more important than the deterrent function of liability rules. That, however, does not mean that there is no role whatsoever for product liability to play. An important

---

173 For a detailed, also economic, analysis of proportional liability see *I Gilead/MD Green/BA Koch* (eds), Proportional Liability: Analytical and Comparative Perspectives (2013).

174 More particularly in art 3:103(2) of the Principles of European Tort Law.

point for further research may be how the comparative advantages of product liability (for example its flexibility and dynamic character, being more easily able to adapt to rapid changes in technology than regulation) could be combined with regulation in order to provide optimal incentives to manufacturers for innovation aiming at increasing product safety.

PART IV

CONCLUSIONS*

Piotr MACHNIKOWSKI

* I would like to express my gratitude to everyone involved in the project for inspiring discussions that had their influence on the final text of this paper, and particularly to Prof Bernhard Koch for his valuable comments. Possible mistakes may only be attributed to myself. I am deeply grateful to Ms Nina Baranowska for her generous support throughout the project and to Matthew La Fontaine for his help in preparing the results.
In this chapter, the following two-letter codes are used in citing the reports: EU (Product Liability Directive), AT (Austria); CA (Canada); CZ (Czech Republic); DK (Denmark); EW (England and Wales); FR (France); DE (Germany); IS (Israel); IT (Italy); NL (the Netherlands); NO (Norway); PL (Poland); ZA (South Africa); ES (Spain); CH (Switzerland); US (the United States of America); and EA (Economic Analysis).

I. HARMONISATION OF LAW IN THE EUROPEAN UNION

A. EUROPEAN PRODUCT LIABILITY LAW COMPARED TO OTHER NATIONAL LIABILITY REGIMES

01 This section will discuss the law of the European Union Member States, but also Norwegian law and Swiss law, because – as was demonstrated above – these two systems of law are to a large extent modelled on or inspired by EU legislation. However, it should be remembered that those states enjoy a special status – they are not parties to the EU treaties and are not obliged to implement EU directives.[1]

02 In all the legal systems examined in this volume, at the time of the entry into force of Directive 85/374/EEC there were legal grounds to claim compensation from the producer of a defective product. They were based on tort liability or contractual liability with numerous modifications and limitations.

03 Liability caused (at least theoretically) by the fault or negligence of the producer played the key role in tort liability. This type of liability was provided for in Austrian, Danish, English, French, German, Italian, Dutch, Polish and Spanish law.[2] A few countries, such as Spain,[3] Norway[4] and probably Switzerland, had also, or exclusively, introduced liability independent of fault.[5] The differences related to the extent to which an act of parliament, or more often case law, modified general principles of the tort regime. Those modifications usually involved adopting a more or less formalised principle stating that even the marketing of a dangerous product may constitute a tort. At times this principle was connected with a presumption of fault or some measures that facilitate proving the fault, eg inferring the existence of a fault from the fact of damage.[6] There were also systems in which general principles of liability had not been extensively modified, even with regard to the process of proving fault.[7] However, there were differences in the detailed conditions that triggered liability; those conditions were of key importance from the perspective of the injured party and the producer. An important difference concerned liability for

---

1 This is the cause of some differences in the Norwegian law; See NO nos 19 and 43.

2 Cf AT no 02; DK no 01; EW no 02; FR no 5 ff; DE no 01 ff; IT no 1 ff; NL no 01; PL no 06 ff; SP no 06. Likewise probably in the Czech law, see CZ no 01.

3 See ES no 07.

4 See NO no 01.

5 See CH no 02.

6 Cf AT no 02; FR no 5 ff; DE no 01 ff; IT no 1 ff; NL no 32 ff; PL no 06 ff; ES no 06.

7 See EW no 02.

employees and subcontractors – a crucial factor in respect of products produced on an industrial scale. In some countries (Austria, Germany) limitations on an undertaking's liability for its employees compromised the protection of persons injured by the product.[8] Other jurisdictions extended tort liability for a defective product to trade intermediaries,[9] but most of them limited it to the producer only. It was often connected with differences in the personal scope of contractual liability.

04 Contractual liability in individual countries protected to varying degrees persons injured by defective products and remedied, to differing extents, the possible shortcomings of the tort regime. Usually they adopted the most rudimentary model of liability, in which the debtor (seller, etc) is liable towards the creditor (buyer) for a breach of contract, including defects in the product sold. Such liability applied only to the parties of the contract, and it did not extend to injured third parties, nor did it allow for claims of compensation from the preceding members of the sales chain, the producer included.[10] The rights of the creditor usually included compensation for the damage caused by the product, including damage to the product itself.[11] The advantages of this liability are that it is usually independent from the fault, or that it applies a presumption of fault and broad liability of the debtor for persons involved in contract performance. Additionally, some legal systems developed mechanisms for extending the personal scope of contractual liability. In Austria, liability was imposed on the producer as a consequence of adopting the premise that the sales agreement between him and the product distributor included protection obligations with regard to final users of the product that authorise the latter to bring contractual claims against the producer.[12] A disadvantage of this solution was that bystanders were not protected, and that it allowed for exclusion of liability by means of a contractual provision included in a contract that the final user neither concluded nor negotiated. In France, on the other hand, the buyer could submit contractual claims not only against the seller, but also directly against previous actors in the sales chain.[13] This model seems to have the same limitations as the Austrian solution presented above. German contracts for the benefit of a third party or contracts that protect a third party, applied in other cases of contractual liability, ensure protection neither to a product user who is not a party to the agreement, nor to bystanders.[14]

---

8 See AT no 03; DE no 04.
9 See DK no 01; FR no 08.
10 Cf DE no 03; EW no 03; IT no 02; NL no 103; NO no 01; PL no 79 ff; ES no 02 ff.
11 See DK no 02.
12 See AT no 04 ff.
13 See FR no 02.
14 See DE no 03.

B. SINGLE MODEL OF TORT LIABILITY FOR PRODUCTS IN EU MEMBER STATES

05 As was explained in detail in the chapter on the Product Liability Directive, the purpose of Directive 85/374/EEC was to introduce a single model of liability for products in all EU Member States. The liability was imposed on the product producer or the entity that represents itself as the producer, producer of materials or parts, importer to the EU and, under the subsidiarity principle, on the product supplier. The liability was to be independent from the producer's fault, although he could exempt himself from liability by demonstrating that when the product was brought to market, the current state of scientific and technical knowledge was insufficient to ensure safety. The conditions of liability are as follows: defect (understood as a lack of safety that can be legitimately expected), damaged goods and interests set forth in the Directive (life, health and property intended and used for consumer purposes), and a causal link between them. Without delving into the details, one may say in a somewhat simplified manner that a producer is liable if the defect had already existed when he brought the product to market, and if he manufactured or distributed the product for commercial purposes or in the framework of his business activity; however, all those circumstances are presumed – the producer may invoke their absence as a defence. Individual countries have their own ways of classifying this liability, depending on their tort law; it may be classified as strict liability, no-fault liability or risk-based liability, but this does not affect the interpretation and application of provisions of law.[15] Liability cannot be excluded by a contractual provision.

06 The implementation of Directive 85/374/EEC in the European Union Member States encountered some difficulty (this was especially visible in France, and to some extent also in Denmark).[16] Even though the implementation was not a complete success, it seems that the shortcomings are in most cases negligible.[17] Many countries decided to apply the safest technique of directive transposition – faithfully transferring its text into national legislation.

07 When implementing the Directive, some countries modified their earlier rules of contractual or tort liability,[18] while others left them unchanged. In some

---

15 Norway is however a characteristic case. As a non-member of the EU, it defines (or explains) this liability in a way that makes strong reference to negligence. However, it has no practical importance. See NO no 18.

16 See FR no 14 ff; DE no 08.

17 eg regulations on importer liability in the Polish and Austrian law (see AT no 47; PL no 93 ff); scope of compensable damage in the law of the Czech Republic (see CZ no 20), time limits in the Polish and Czech law systems (see PL no 93 ff; CZ no 32) and the possibility to interrupt the run of the extinction period by recognition of the claim in Italy (see IT no 125). One may also have doubts as to the correctness of the upper liability limit in the German law; see DE no 08.

18 See *inter alia* DK no 03 ff; FR no 14 ff and 21 ff; NL no 07; ES no 09.

countries there are also special regimes of compensation for damage caused by some categories of products (medicines, medical devices, vaccines, products made using gene technology). However, neither do they always resemble classic tort liability, nor impose the obligation to compensate for damage on the producer.[19]

C. SCOPE OF HARMONISATION

08 Product liability is only a part of a broader problem area of liability for damage caused to another person by means other than failure to perform an obligation. This area is regulated by several rules. They answer the following questions:

(1) What kind of damage to goods or interests are subject to compensation (what is considered damage in a given system of law)?
(2) What events causing the damage justify the obligation of compensation (what occurrences are considered torts in a given system)?
(3) What kind of causal link between these events and the damage justifies the requirement of providing compensation (what idea of a causal link is adopted in a given system for the purposes of liability for damages)?
(4) Who should compensate for damage caused by a given event (which entity is held liable) and how is this obligation distributed among a multiplicity of liable entities?
(5) How should damage be remedied (what is the compensation obligation, what are the damages)?
(6) What is the liability time frame (how does the passage of time affect the existence and the duty to pay compensation)?

One should also add to these basic substantive issues procedural matters regarding the burden of proof and evidentiary standards in the given system.

09 Numerous systems of law try to provide general answers to some of those questions, applicable to the entire tort liability law or, even more generally, to liability for damage. As a result, the tort law is often regulated by detailed provisions that specify individual types of torts and indicate parties liable (item 2 and, partly, item 4) and by more general provisions that define damage (sometimes divided into material and non-material damage) and the causal link, the principles of compensating for damage (with some exceptions for specific categories of damages), relations between the injured party and numerous liable entities and among these entities, as well as time limitations on claims (items 1,

---

19 Cf DK no 27 ff; EW no 39 ff; DE nos 15 and 27; NO nos 04 and 17; PL no 02.

3, 5 and 6, together with a part of item 4) for all kinds of torts. Various systems regulate that matter using, to varying degrees, general and detailed provisions.

10 The European regulation concerning product liability regulates only some of the matters referred to above. Several aspects of this liability are regulated in the Directive; others were explicitly left to be regulated by provisions of national law, while still others were overlooked. The Directive describes the circumstances to which the obligation to compensate for damage applies (arts 1, 2 and 4), indicates the liable entities (art 3), partly regulates the kinds of damage to be remedied (art 9), partly regulates the issue of numerous causes of damage and sets time limitations on liability in the form of a statute of limitations (art 10) and long-stop period (art 11), although the statute of limitations is not regulated exhaustively.

11 The Directive did not force the Member States to harmonise their legislation with regard to all aspects of product liability covered by it.[20] However, the possibility to diverge from the basic liability model of the Directive was used only to a limited extent. The majority of Member States did not introduce a maximum liability limit.[21] Of the countries covered by this project, only France and Spain excluded the possibility for an enterprise to invoke the development risk defence with respect to some products.[22] This decision does not seem to have strongly affected the functioning of the liability regime, the situation of potentially liable parties, the insurance market, etc.

12 Most countries stick to the letter of the Directive in the legal acts that transpose it into their national legislation. However, there have been sporadic attempts at complementing or elaborating the provisions of the Directive in national legislation. This refers to the notion of putting the product into circulation – Austria, France and Italy made attempts at defining this notion.[23] Not all of these initiatives are convincing; some of them raise doubts as to their compliance with the interpretation of the Directive adopted by the CJEU.[24]

13 Divergences between the EU Member States exist in those areas in which the Directive gives, explicitly or implicitly, some flexibility to the national legislators. Some of those divergences may affect the level of protection of the injured parties, as well as the situation of producers in individual countries of the EU.

---

20 See EU no 21 ff and 30 ff.

21 See however DE no 08; ES no 49.

22 Apart from the group of investigated countries this defence is not admissible in Luxembourg and Finland.

23 See AT no 40 ff; FR no 37 ff; IT no 50.

24 See EU nos 144 and 176.

14 Several matters have been explicitly left to the discretion of the national legislator. Article 5 of the Directive provides for joint and several liability of two or more persons liable for the same damage under the provisions set forth in the Directive, while art 8(1) stipulates that the liability of the producer is not reduced if the damage was jointly caused by an act or omission of a third party. Both of these provisions leave the issue of recourse among the jointly liable entities to be regulated by national law. Furthermore, pursuant to art 13, the Directive does not limit contractual liability (ie seller's liability to the buyer) nor tort liability under the general regime based on fault or strict liability other than product liability. This approach is sufficient to protect the injured party, but it hampers the possibility of achieving the Directive's objectives, which are the removal of barriers in the flow of goods by equally distributing the burden falling on producers putting their products on markets in various countries. By means of various regulations regarding the area where contractual and tort claims meet, as well as by redistributing the burden of compensation between the producer and another person, a state may create more or less favourable conditions for manufacturing or distributing goods on its territory. This is well-illustrated by regulations in force in the Netherlands. The Dutch legislator assumed that the Directive's objective is ultimately to attribute liability to the producer of the defective product. He narrowed down the scope of application of provisions on contractual liability to reduce the area of competing claims against various entities.[25] Other countries did not introduce such limitations, which – at least theoretically – should lead to attributing greater liability to the sellers, because seeking compensation from the seller is usually the easiest solution for an injured buyer. Various ways of using recourse mechanisms among entities liable under the same or different provisions of law may also have various economic consequences. Adopting the principle that all liable parties assume the burden of compensation *per capita* will result in a different situation than a decision to establish the extent to which every one of them contributed to the damage. In addition, a different outcome will result from adopting the principle that the one among the liable parties who is at fault will assume the burden of the compensation.[26] The assumption that suppliers are vicariously liable and that they are entitled to full recourse claims against their predecessors[27] shifts the responsibility towards the producer, while a principle that gives the liable person who is not at fault a recourse claim against the person who is at fault[28] may generate the opposite result.

15 Article 9 of the Directive stipulates that its provisions relative to compensable damage 'shall be without prejudice to national provisions relating

25 See NL no 37.

26 Cf eg AT no 52; CZ no 18; DK no 46; EW no 46; FR no 47 ff; DE eg no 54; IT no 76; NL no 41; NO no 23; PL no 41; ES nos 33 and 36.

27 See DK no 32.

28 See FR no 59; PL no 41.

to non-material damage'. It is beyond any doubt that the admissibility or inadmissibility of seeking compensation for non-material damage is crucial in determining whether a given liability regime is favourable for the injured parties. This is demonstrated by an increase in the number of cases to which product liability provisions apply in Germany after the introduction of compensation for non-material damage into the regime,[29] and also by efforts of the Spanish courts to adjudicate compensation for non-material damage even without explicit legal grounds in the legislation.[30] Undoubtedly, highly diverse provisions and practice in Member States with regard to the admissibility and amount of compensation for damage affect the burden imposed on a producer distributing goods in various countries. This diversification is not inherently unsuitable – it stems from differences in wealth among societies, the amount of payments available from other sources (in particular from the public social security system), insurance coverage and numerous other factors, including the legal culture of a given country.

16 Article 10 of the Directive includes an obligation to set a limitation period for compensation claims and specifies the date when the limitation period starts to run, as well as the duration of this period. Provisions regarding suspending or interrupting this period were left to the discretion of the national lawmaker, which allows for granting the injured parties stronger or weaker protection against the lapse of the period, and restricts the harmonising effect of the Directive. This issue was not the main research area,[31] but even a cursory analysis shows differences in the level of protection afforded the injured party against the consequences of the passage of time. For example, some countries allow suspension the limitation period during negotiations,[32] or interrupting its run by summoning the debtor to compensate for damage.[33]

17 Apart from the above examples, several other matters crucial for the liability regime were implicitly left to the discretion of the national legislator. Among them is the notion of a causal link, which is required, but not specified in the Directive. Depending on additional criteria adopted in a given system to identify cases of causing damage or to limit the scope of liability (directness,[34] no intervening events,[35] foreseeability,[36] adequacy or normality of the effect[37]

---

[29] See DE no 14.

[30] See ES no 45 ff. Non-material damages are not remedied in Norway, except in cases of gross negligence, see NO no 36.

[31] This is currently being tackled in a separate project.

[32] See DE no 92.

[33] See NL no 89 ff; ES no 89.

[34] See FR no 56.

[35] See EW no 58.

[36] See CH no 33.

[37] Cf AT no 66; CZ no 24; DE no 67; IT no 21; NO no 27; PL no 51.

and other, more complex criteria), the situation of the liable entity will change according to the applicability of various laws.[38] Some countries also allow proportional liability, albeit in the majority of them such liability is excluded.[39]

18 A situation in which the injured party contributed to the damage was treated in a similar manner. Article 8(2) of the Directive stipulates that the liability of the producer may be reduced or disallowed when, having regard to all the circumstances, the damage is caused both by a defect in the product and by the fault of the injured person or any person for whom the injured person is responsible. Making the reduction or disallowance of liability contingent on the contribution of the injured person or on the fault of the injured person will inevitably be interpreted in various ways in various countries. Usually, general provisions on the injured party's contribution apply to product liability; these do not always refer to fault, and they often apply purely causal criteria and equity judgements.[40] There are probably similar differences with regard to identifying the person for whom the injured person is responsible. In addition, some jurisdictions unequivocally exclude liability in the case of voluntarily exposing oneself to the risk of damage.[41]

19 Damage and remedies constitute another area of hidden disharmony. Article 9 of the Directive stipulates that for its purposes 'damage' means damage caused by death or by personal injuries and damage to or destruction of an item of property intended for consumption. There is no doubt that every injured person is an entitled entity.[42] Individual types of compensable damage may, however, be interpreted differently in national systems of law.[43] There may also be various claims for compensation for the damage, especially with regard to personal injury.

20 With regard to the first issue – the notion of compensable loss in strict product liability – there is a broad agreement that liability covers not only direct loss in the above-listed goods, but also consequential economic loss, though at times – when they take the form of lost profits – compensation is contingent

---

38 For a more detailed study of that issue see *J Spier* (ed), Unification of Tort Law: Causation (1994).

39 See NL no 59 ff; CH no 36. For more on that see *I Gilead/MD Green/BA Koch* (eds), Proportional liability: Analytical and Comparative Perspectives (2013).

40 Cf AT no 69; DK no 47; EW no 59; FR no 60; DE no 71; IT no 94; NL nos 66 and 77; NO no 31; PL no 55; ES no 63; CH no 35. For a more detailed analysis of the problem see *U Magnus/M Martin-Casals* (eds), Unification of Tort Law: Contributory Negligence (2004).

41 See DK no 69; IT no 96; NO no 19.

42 See AT no 57.

43 As pointed out in the ruling of the CJEU 25 April 2002, C-154/00, *Commission of the European Communities v Hellenic Republic* [2002] ECR I-3879, item 23.

on meeting additional criteria.[44] Furthermore, some systems of law seem to allow for compensation of pure economic loss;[45] however, there are doubts as to whether this complies with the Directive, and it is of little importance from a practical point of view. On the other hand, non-material damage caused by death or personal injury is subject to compensation.[46] There are also differences in the approach of individual legal systems to the issue of liability for destruction of a product caused by defects in its parts.[47] Moreover, the majority of Member States do not treat loss of chance as compensable damage, although there are exceptions to this rule as well.[48]

21 As for the other matter – remedies available to the aggrieved – some of the differences are only superficial. The fact that some systems of law allow for restitution in kind, while others accept only restitution in value is of no importance. The English law is the only legal system in the EU that allows for punitive damages, but most likely it does not extend to the area of product liability.[49] On the other hand, the possibility of taking into account profits resulting from a tort while calculating the compensation (present in the Dutch and Swiss law) may have some practical implications in the domain of product liability.[50] There are also differences with regard to personal injury – with respect to both the direct claims that the injured party is entitled to, and a list of relatives of the deceased entitled to make a claim and the scope of claims they can make (including compensation for non-material damage).[51]

22 Lastly, the Directive does not harmonise differences in procedures arising from the provisions of law or court practice. The required standard of proof (credibility level of statements or the degree of conviction that a judge must reach in order to deem a fact proven) oscillates in some jurisdictions (at least theoretically) between more likely than not[52] to a higher degree of likelihood or full confidence,[53] or they are left to the judge's discretion.[54] Varying scopes of admissibility of prima facie evidence, the greater or lesser role of factual presumption in proving circumstances that are difficult to prove (a causal link or

44 See AT no 83.
45 See FR no 53 ff.
46 The Spanish law constitutes an exception, but in practice it diverges from the wording adopted in the legislation; see ES no 45 ff.
47 Cf AT no 60; DE no 60; IT no 85; NO no 24.
48 See FR no 53 ff; NL no 59.
49 See EW no 68.
50 See NL no 81; CH no 47.
51 Cf AT no 81 ff; DE no 55; EW no 68 ff; NL no 44 ff; PL no 48 ff; CH no 30.
52 See EW no 71; NO no 40.
53 See AT no 87; DE no 90; PL no 69; ES no 85.
54 See CZ no 31; FR no 71; CH no 51.

a defect), result in a situation in which the actual functioning of harmonised law in individual countries may vary.[55]

23 One may also note that differences among national regulations transposing the Directive stem from the fact that in the EU there are numerous official languages.[56] Hence, EU legislative acts are published in a large number of languages, which often leads to substantive differences among individual language versions. This can be exemplified by differences among various language versions of the content of art 9 of the Directive regarding limiting liability.[57] As a result, national legislation in some of the Member States interprets limiting liability as a franchise or deductible of the injured party, ie the amount deducted each time, regardless of the amount of loss, from the compensation,[58] while other legal systems establish a threshold that the loss must exceed in order to be compensated for in full.[59] The efficiency of the harmonisation objective may be hampered by poor coordination of language versions of the harmonising instrument itself, and the necessity for the Court of Justice of the European Union to interpret it. The more strictly legal terms there are in a piece of legislation, the greater the discrepancies among its language versions. Legal terms, as opposed to technical terms, carry a plethora of semantic subtleties unique to individual national systems of law, which are at times tied to basic institutions and notions of those systems and which are interpreted according to a tradition that often goes back several centuries.[60] This phenomenon surfaces with regard to one of the major issues – the notion of a product, which will be discussed below.

D. LIMITATIONS OF MAXIMUM HARMONISATION

24 As a side remark to the observations made above, it is worth pointing out that information presented in the preceding chapters of this book constitute interesting material for studies on the mechanism of harmonisation (in

---

55 Cf DK nos 44 and 55; EW no 71; FR no 72; IT no 114 ff; NL no 84 ff; PL no 70; ES no 86; CH no 50.

56 None of them is superior vis-à-vis the others, see CJEU ruling of 2 April 1998, C-296/95, *R v Commissioners of Customs and Excise, ex parte EMU Tabac SARL, The Man in Black Ltd, John Cunningham* [1998] ECR I-1605 and of 20 November 2003, C-152/01, *Kyocera Electronics Europe GmbH v Hauptzollamt Krefeld.*

57 See EU no 158 ff.

58 See DK no 37; ES no 52.

59 See AT no 64; CZ no 22; EW no 51; FR no 55; DE no 65; IT no 83; NL no 55; PL no 46.

60 This issue is discussed in detail in the context of the European contract law by G Ajani, 'A Better Coherence of EU Private Law' and Multilingualism: Two Opposing Principles?, in: R Schulze (ed), Common Frame of Reference and Existing EC Contract Law (2008) 33 ff. See also G Ajani/M Ebers (eds), Uniform Terminology for European Contract Law (2005).

particular maximum harmonisation) of private law by means of directives, as well as on limitations of its use and the difficulties it creates. Two aspects of Directive 85/374 make it a good subject for research on the harmonisation method. First of all, it has been in force for thirty years, and its implementation has been subject to review by the Court of Justice, which means that there is plenty of material for analysis. Second, this Directive pertains to one of the pivotal issues in the private law – liability for damage. When the European legislator introduced uniform rules of liability for a given category of events causing damage, this also entailed the creation of an obligation to incorporate them into complete and coherent tort liability systems already in existence that had been developing over decades or even centuries. The applied mechanism of harmonisation (although not necessarily the content of the harmonised rules) resembles to some extent attempts at harmonising contract law. This observation allows for a judicious transfer of conclusions drawn from the former to the latter.

25 The first important remark refers to discrepancies between the actual and declared motives and objectives of the European legislator. The development of the concept to implement a separate regulation for liability for damage caused by defective or dangerous products in Europe is undoubtedly associated with incidents entailing mass damage caused by defective pharmaceuticals and food products in Western Europe during the second half of the 20th century. Therefore, it seems justified to state that regulations included in the Directive originate from an actual need or from social expectations with regard to ensuring protection to potential injured parties.[61]

26 However, protecting potential victims of defective products was not the intention of the European Communities. At that time (in the era preceding the Maastricht Treaty), it was not even consumer protection. The legal grounds for this measure could only have been art 100 of the Rome Treaty, which allowed the Council to pass unanimously directives approximating national laws and administrative legislation of the Member States that directly affect the establishment or functioning of the single market.[62] This article (art 114 TFEU is its modified equivalent today) granted the general authority to harmonise legislation for the purpose of completing the internal market. As a result, the Directive had to be devised, and, first and foremost, justified as a means of removing obstacles to the functioning of the internal market. This brings us to the second important, but rather obvious, remark: EU legislation may be shaped not only by its actual objectives and substantive factors determining the desired direction for regulation of a given matter, but it may also be affected by the treaty provisions on which a given piece of legislation is based, ie the scope of powers to

61 See EU no 01 ff.
62 See EU no 14 ff.

regulate a given area. As a result, a collision of objectives may appear which must then be resolved in individual provisions. If one of those objectives is important as a justification of the powers to pass a given law, and the other objective is irrelevant in that matter, the collision may be resolved in favour of the first objective, even though the second objective would be supported by substantive arguments. Discrepancies in the objectives of Directive 85/374 can be seen in the initial provisions of the preamble.[63] A clash between those objectives surfaced when it was necessary to decide on the nature of the harmonisation required under the Directive. The minimal character of the Directive was supported by numerous references to consumer protection in its preamble, while one of the key arguments supporting its maximal character was the first item of the preamble, which mentioned the requirements of the internal market as the grounds for harmonisation.[64] This allows a cautious formulation of a third thesis: it is the legal grounds (the scope of powers), and not the substantive objectives of a law, that determine the applied harmonisation method.

27 The fourth observation relates to the requirement of a link between the adoption of a Directive and functioning of a common or internal market. The existence of such a link may be challenged in the case of directives that harmonise private law.[65] Whether it is actually challenged by authorised entities – the Member States – before the Court of Justice depends on the extent to which those countries approve of the content of such a directive. Weak arguments in support of the power to pass such a law make its proposer more likely to seek compromise with the Members States. This adds to the natural need to seek compromise that results from the rules of the legislative procedure. In this aspect, Directive 85/374 is unusual, because its legal basis – art 100 of the Treaty establishing the European Community in its wording from before the Single European Act – required unanimity for the Council to adopt a Directive. That provision forced the parties to go even further in search of compromise in the form of regulatory options.[66]

28 Further conclusions that can be drawn from the history of the Product Liability Directive relate to the consequences of applying the maximum harmonisation method. Here attention should be directed to the conditions of the producer's liability.[67] Specifying those conditions, together with the liability standard required by the Directive, is necessary to establish which area of social relations (and provisions that regulate it) were encompassed by its harmonising effect. Identifying the degree of a directive's interference in the national system

63 See EU no 14 ff.
64 See EU no 26 ff.
65 See EA no 21 ff and 32 ff.
66 See EU no 21 ff.
67 See EU no 133 ff.

of law is also important in the case of minimum harmonisation, but it becomes crucial with regard to maximum harmonisation. If a directive does not permit the retention of any other liability regulations (not only those less beneficial for the protected entity) in the national legal system, it is not possible to achieve the required effect without explicitly establishing the field of intervention of the directive. In the case of Directive 85/374, there are some attempts at solving this problem through the provisions of art 13, which describes the relationship between the liability regime introduced by the Directive and the liability rules already in place in the given national legal system.[68] The Directive is supposed to introduce a parallel, additional liability regime existing alongside contractual liability or fault-based liability, which supersedes only general regulations potentially already present in national legislation regarding no-fault liability for damage caused by the products. In practice, the decision on whether national product liability regulations that differ from the provisions set forth in the Directive is made following comparison of the scope of application in both liability regimes and their structure. A parallel system regulating liability for damage caused by a defective product may operate together with the system introduced by the Directive if its application is limited to specified products (ie medicinal products), or if liability is based on other liability principles than the regime introduced by the Directive, ie if it is fault-based liability or contractual liability (eg warranty for hidden defects of a product).[69] Despite the efforts of the EU legislator, it was not easy to solve some problems concerning the relations between the new, harmonised liability regime and the national laws not covered by the harmonising effect of the Directive. It was necessary to compare the scope of the Directive with the scope of the national liability regime with regard to the event that caused the damage, with regard to obligations imposed by the Directive and those imposed by national legislation, with regard to the type of interests that are protected, and finally with regard to the personal scope of the Directive and of the national laws. All those issues were accompanied by the difficulties typical of maximum harmonisation and related to the comparison of degrees of protection required by the Directive and ensured by the national legislation.

29 Another group of problems that surfaced after the adoption of Directive 85/374 and which seem to be common to all attempts at harmonising the private law (and some of them to all attempts of harmonising legislation in general),

---

68 See EU no 44 ff.

69 See CJEU rulings of 25 April 2002, C-154/00, *Commission of the European Communities v Hellenic Republic* [2002] ECR I-3879, no 18; 25 April 2002, C-52/00, *Commission of the European Communities v French Republic* [2002] ECR I-3827, no 22; 25 April 2002, C-183/00, *Maria Victoria González Sánchez v Medicina Asturiana SA* [2002] ECR I-391, nos 31–33; 10 June 2006, C-402/03, *Skov Æg v Bilka Lavprisvarehus A/S and Bilka Lavprisvarehus A/S v Jette Mikkelsen, Michael Due Nielsen* [2006] ECR I-199, no 47.

especially in cases of maximum harmonisation, relate to the possibility of attaining actual uniformity among systems of law within the scope covered by a given harmonising measure. Observations presented in no 08 ff above on the scope of harmonisation seem to corroborate the thesis that in the area of tort law (and probably in the entire law of obligations) harmonisation that is limited only to chosen areas of law or certain aspects of its functioning never fully covers even the area which it tries to regulate. Its fragmentary scope on the one hand hampers the functioning of the national law, while on the other it limits or even excludes the possibility of attaining the objective set out by the EU lawmaker, namely the removal of barriers to the flow of goods. The consequences of existing differences are naturally mitigated by the norms of the private international law, which also justifies the question whether it was appropriate to choose a substantive mechanism rather than a mechanism based on conflict of laws in order to deal with discrepancies among systems of law. In any case, attempts at harmonising core elements of national contract law always require defining the limits of interference of the European law in the national law. The provisions of art 9(2) of the Directive probably constitute a good example of setting such limits. However, it is not always possible to draw a clear line, as demonstrated by problems with defining the notion of damage in the context of art 9(1) of the Directive. Partial interference of this provision with national laws (it lists all types of interests that are protected, but fails to define damage or particular forms of damage) leads to contradictions that seem unsolvable.[70] In addition, in this case harmonisation may become a never-ending process. If one accepts the main argument supporting it – that differences among national systems of law are obstacles to the free flow of goods – while at the same time remaining unable to precisely define which of those differences constitute actual obstacles and which do not affect the functioning of the common market, it becomes impossible to set the limits of interference by EU legislation. It is only natural that the EU lawmaker would try to achieve full unification, and decisions to extend harmonisation to other areas of law are purely political.

30 Another obvious observation that can be made in the context of development of views in the matter of product liability is that the law proposed by the Commission and approved by the Council (and, currently, also by the Parliament), ie the law approved by the Member States, evolves with time. The main driver of this evolution is the Court of Justice, whose main tool consists of its interpretations of a given directive. The law in force is not necessarily identical to the law that the lawmakers had in mind. This is nothing new, and such developments can be observed in every system of law. However, they take on a different meaning in the context of laws passed by an international organisation given legislative powers by its members. They may also undermine

[70] See EU no 151 ff.

the stability of a given national legal system. Transposition of a directive that may have seemed correct in terms of its content and adopted according to the EU legislative process may turn out to be incorrect as a result of how it is interpreted by courts.[71] Those difficulties should not overshadow the fact that the Court of Justice's ability to interpret the law fosters the development of laws, allowing them to adapt smoothly to changing social conditions and to take into consideration special cases overlooked by the lawmaker. One may quote as an example the CJEU's comments on the notion of a product, putting it on the market and its defects that were included in the rulings in *Veedfald* and *Boston Scientific Medizintechnik GmbH*.[72] Such developments would also be possible on the national level and they would be probably faster and more efficient, but they would also mean giving up approximating national systems of law.

31 This brings us to the final, more general remark that can be made about the Product Liability Directive. Regulating an issue by means of a directive, which means excluding the legislative powers of a Member State with regard to the same issue, takes away from a Member State the possibility of quickly and adequately responding to changing economic circumstances, legal environment and public opinion. At times, taking these changes into consideration is possible only through strict or narrow reading of the scope of the directive's rules. For instance, Directive 85/374 defines a product as a movable property. It thus seems appropriate that compensation for damage caused by defective non-material goods (software, other digital content or information) is not regulated in this Directive, and that the Member States retain their full legislative powers in this regard. This issue will be discussed below. However, there are cases when there is no doubt that a given issue should be included in the scope of the Directive, and the manner of this regulation may be deemed inadequate in terms of social expectations or even requirements set forth in superior rules of law. An example can be found in art 11 of the Directive, which refers to the ten-year extinction period.[73] From the same perspective, it may be controversial to limit the application of product liability only to damage in excess of €500. The only justification for taking such a decision may be fear of an excessive number of small claims. The relatively small number of cases resolved on the basis of harmonised provisions in the Member States seems to put this fear to rest, and this limitation undoubtedly decreases the effectiveness of the law as a tool for consumer protection and for supporting the functioning of the common market. It is also worth pointing out that applying a single quota in all of the countries of the post-enlargement EU (where major differences exist in levels

[71] See EU nos 28 and 40.
[72] See EU no 59 ff, 83 and 160 ff.
[73] See EU no 187.

of wealth across societies) raises doubts in connection with the equal treatment principle.

E. APPLICATION OF THE EUROPEAN LAW

32 Most of the reports on national systems of law mentioned the marginal or moderate practical application of the harmonised legislation.[74] Enough time has definitely passed for the new liability regime to become solidified in the public awareness (or at least in lawyers' awareness), and the circumstances to which it applies have had enough time to occur. The reasons why the regulations described above have found little practical application lie elsewhere. Moreover, even though the number of cases resolved on the basis of strict product liability rules is generally low, there are clear differences among individual EU Member States in this area. First of all, it should be realised that we lack precise data about the number of product liability cases brought before the courts prior to the entry into force of provisions implementing the Directive and resolved under the liability regimes previously in force. The lack of data stops us from drawing valid conclusions on the influence of the EU regulation at the level of protection for injured parties.

33 It seems that there is no one single source of the relatively low practical importance of the European regulation and discrepancies among individual Member States. Informal observations and reflections, not supported by empirical research, suggest that the following factors may be the cause of low interest in product liability:

(1) relatively high level of product safety, ensured both by purely market mechanisms and by administrative oversight of the activity of producers and sellers;
(2) exclusion of the possibility to claim compensation under the European regime in the case of material damage with a value lower than €500;[75] it may be assumed that in many cases damage to consumer goods due to a defect in the product does not exceed this value;
(3) addressing the majority of personal injuries (costs of treatment and medical care, loss of livelihood) via various mechanisms of social security or public healthcare;

74 Cf AT no 97; CZ no 37; DK no 64; EW no 86; FR no 93; DE no 13; IT no 135; NL no 113; NO no 50; PL no 90; CH no 64.

75 In some countries a lower threshold was established as an effect of currency conversion when euro was introduced – see EW no 51; IT no 83; ES no 52 ff.

(4) the relative appeal of liability regimes existing prior to the entry into force of the Directive, which – although often formally fault-based – provided sufficient protection to the injured parties, especially when they allowed for a presumption of fault and/or a presumption of a causal link, or to infer the existence of fault or of a causal link from the fact of damage instead of demonstrating that a product was defective and how the given defect resulted in damage;
(5) competition between claims based on the regime introduced by the Directive and contractual claims against the seller, which are often much easier to pursue;
(6) the growing importance of services in the economy and using products to provide services, which lead to filing compensation claims for damage in the first place against the service provider;
(7) the relatively high cost of pursuing claims resulting from the obligation to prove the existence of a defect, which may require expensive expert opinions; and
(8) availability of professional legal assistance in this type of case, ie whether lawyers are willing to engage in such cases, taking into account the value of the claim, the workload and lawyers' fees (a hypothesis that should be examined further).

34 It is more difficult to find the roots of differing popularity levels enjoyed by the European product liability regime across the EU Member States. The factors listed in item 1 above do not really apply, because they are excluded by the principle of free flow of goods and the universal character of numerous provisions concerning product safety.[76] Neither does the factor mentioned in item 2 above apply, because occasional differences in regulations regarding the lower threshold of compensable damage do not match the conclusions regarding the number of cases in individual countries. Austria is a characteristic example – it probably has the highest number of cases resolved on the basis of harmonised regulations in the EU (and even more so *per capita*), while it has faithfully implemented the €500 threshold. It does not seem that popularity of first party insurance has any influence in that regard, because in this respect there are no material differences between countries such as Austria and, for instance, Switzerland, where product liability cases are rare. The most likely reasons for the aforementioned differences are the relative appeal of competing, non-harmonised liability systems, the possibility to claim compensation for loss of profit as well as for pain and suffering, and the amount of compensation awarded, taking into account the level of protection ensured by public insurance systems (in the case of workplace accidents or occupational diseases) and healthcare, as well as the possibility of recourse granted to operators of those

[76] See EU no 188 ff.

systems vis-à-vis persons responsible for damage. This matter, however, requires further and more detailed investigation.

II. DEVELOPMENT OF LAW OUTSIDE THE EU

35 As previously mentioned, regulating an area of social reality using a directive requiring maximal harmonisation blocks or at least seriously slows down the development of law applicable to that area. Directives are rarely amended and implementation of any change is a lengthy process, while the law-making activity of the Court of Justice is limited by the existing paradigm of interpretation. Furthermore, the Court itself can hardly be described as a dynamic institution. For this reason it would not be an exaggeration to state that by adopting Directive 85/374 the EU has blocked or seriously slowed down the development of that branch of law in Europe. Moreover, the Directive's normative approach reflects views on security threats and compensation for damage originating in the 1970s. Over time, the positions of lawmakers in other parts of the world may have evolved, and it is worth taking a closer look at those developments. It may be particularly instructive to examine the development of opinions of the courts, lawmakers and jurisprudence in the USA that have obviously served as inspiration for the final shape of the EU Directive.

36 All the systems of law analysed in this book that are not modelled on the EU Directive at some stage of their development had to resolve the issue of damage caused by products within the framework of general contractual and tort liability (as fault-based liability or the tort of negligence).[77] Moreover, not all of them have abandoned this model. Israel, South Africa and the USA have adopted a special tort liability regime for products, but Canada (except for Quebec) has not opted for that solution.

37 All of these special product liability regimes (the American, Israeli, South African and Quebec models) can be classified in the category of strict liability, in which the obligation to remedy the damage caused by a defective product is imposed on the producer (or other persons).[78]

38 The stringency of those regimes is mitigated in various ways. In the USA, liability of the producer (but not intermediaries) in the case of design defects and warning defects is contingent on whether the risk that made the product defective was foreseeable, which makes the regime similar to negligence.[79]

77 See CA no 04 ff; IS no 01 ff; ZA no 02 ff; US no 05 ff.
78 Cf CA no 28; IS no 06; ZA no 03; US no 41.
79 See US no 41.

This is related to the practice of assessing the product's defects (in the case of so-called design defects and warning defects) by means of the risk/utility test. It is probable that similar results are obtained by applying the state-of-the-art defence to a design defect, which requires that account be taken of the technology available at the time when carrying out the risk/utility test. This depends on how availability of technology is defined – whether it is within reach given the current state of human knowledge or whether it can be put to practical use. It is not clear whether it is possible to apply this defence (conceived as the impossibility to understand a risk that justifies a warning) to warning defect and to manufacturing defect (which would mean the lack of technical possibility to detect a defect in a product specimen).[80]

39 A similar defence is present in the legal system of Quebec, and its wording challenges the assertion that we are dealing with strict liability. The relevant provision in the Civil Code seems to cover all types of defects and results in a situation in which the manufacturer, distributor or supplier is not liable if she proves that, according to the state of knowledge at the time that she manufactured, distributed or supplied the product, the existence of the defect could not have been known, and that she was not neglectful of her duty to provide information upon becoming aware of the defect.[81] First of all, the defence refers to being unaware of the defect, and not to the defect being impossible to avoid. Second of all, this regulation extends liability to situations when a previously unknown defect appears, and the liable entity failed to inform about it.

40 Israeli law also allows the respondent to invoke the development risk defence, although only in cases of design defects.[82] South African law introduces a less stringent liability standard with regard to distributors and sellers (but not for producers or importers). They may defend themselves by stating that, considering their role in putting the product on the market, they cannot reasonably be expected to detect a defect.[83]

41 The South African legislation contains the widest range of products to which special rules of liability apply. It does not differentiate between material and non-material goods, but it treats as a product everything that may be put to use, including blood and tissue, IT products (software, data, intellectual and digital content), as well as professional consultancy and goods manufactured pursuant to the customer's order as the provision of a service.[84] Such a broad scope of product liability is unique among the systems of law examined in this

---

80 See US no 71 ff.
81 See CA no 31.
82 See IS no 43.
83 See ZA no 33.
84 See ZA no 10 ff.

book.[85] American law focuses on movable property, though it also applies strict liability to electricity, water and software. Blood and tissue are not covered by liability regulations. Nor do liability regulations apply to intellectual content (books, movies) due to protection of freedom of speech.[86] The Civil Code of Quebec defines a product as movable property, and the scope of definition probably also includes electricity and natural gas.[87] Israeli law, although ambiguous in that respect, seems to apply strict liability only to material items. In consequence, digital content is not a product by itself, but it may be a part of a product that is a material item.[88]

42 The systems of law discussed in this book take various approaches to product defects. Some of them define three types of defect: design defects, manufacturing defects and informational (warning) defects;[89] others treat defects as a general category.[90] In the legislation of Quebec, product defects are very clearly defined. In the South African and Israeli systems of law there are complex and sometimes murky definitions of defect, but the matter essentially boils down to failure to fulfil reasonable or legitimate expectations with regard to product safety.[91] The Israeli practice allows for inference of defect from the circumstances of the occurrence of damage.[92] There is a different approach to that issue in the US, and – importantly – this difference results from its evolution in recent years. The test of the average consumer's expectations, used in the Second Restatement, has been replaced by the risk/utility test or cost/utility test with regard to design defects (and to some extent to warning defects). Those tests are based on investigating the possibilities and costs of alternative product design.[93] It should be stressed that there are exceptions to this rule, but they are invoked only if the circumstances of the damage occurring (the product's performance) indicate the existence of a defect.[94] A unique trait of US law is that it takes a special approach to medicinal products and medical devices, where the likelihood of succeeding in proving a design defect is limited. It seems, however, that it usually pertains to those forms of drug 'defects' (threat of damage) that are inextricably linked to its medical effects.[95]

---

85 The South African statute is the most recent piece of legislation of all that have been discussed here, a fact one should assess in the light of what has been said (under no 31 above) about the effect that directives have on the development of law in Europe.

86 See US no 14 ff.

87 See CA no 28.

88 See IS no 10.

89 See IS no 13 ff; US no 22; CA no 29.

90 See ZA no 12 ff.

91 Cf CA no 29; IS no 13 ff; ZA no 12 ff.

92 See IS no 55.

93 See US no 26 ff.

94 See US nos 29 and 41.

95 US no 32 ff.

43 These non-EU systems of law under examination provide differing definitions of the group of entities liable for damage. The Israeli and Quebec legal systems have many similarities with the EU approach in this respect and impose liability on the producer who is an entrepreneur, on the apparent producer, importer and intermediary (Canada), or on the producer pursuing a commercial activity, the apparent producer, the producer of a defective part or package and importer pursuing commercial activity, but on the intermediary only when the importer and producer are unknown (Israel).[96] Liability is imposed on those parties when a defect existed at the time when they relinquished control over the product (the burden of proof falls on the person liable), unless they lost control over the product against their will. Joint and several liability applies if more than one person is liable, while the regulations on dividing the cost of compensation among them are quite flexible and refer to fairness and deterrence.[97] In the case of South Africa, the group of liable entities is larger because there is a broad definition of a product, and the liability regime applies not only to the producer (and producer of parts), importer, distributor and seller, but also to breeders, persons extracting minerals and service providers – as long as those people provide those goods to consumers in the framework of their commercial activity. All of them are jointly and severally liable, while the rules of recourse are not clearly defined.[98] On the other hand, in the US every seller is held liable (regardless of her position in the product distribution chain), and sale is broadly defined as any form of product distribution in the framework of some commercial activity, as well as renting or sharing a product for promotional purposes. This manner of defining liable entities has an impact on how recourse is regulated – individual participants in the distribution chain have recourse claims against the entity that is responsible for the defect in the product. In the case of persons liable for damage on various grounds it is characteristic for US law to replace joint and several liability with various forms of sharing liability proportionally to the extent of the responsibility for the defect.[99]

44 There are also substantial differences with regard to the injured party and compensable damage. In Israel, a strict liability regime applies only to personal injuries, suffered by any person, but the amount of compensation is limited by rather low thresholds.[100] The legal system of Quebec stipulates that all types of damage must be remedied (damage to property and personal injury, material and non-material damage, with a high threshold applying to the latter), but strict liability is limited only to injured bystanders (which reflects the French '*non*

96 Cf IS no 25 ff; CA nos 28 and 48.
97 See IS no 23.
98 See ZA no 16 ff.
99 See US nos 30 and 42 ff.
100 See IS no 7 and 32 ff.

cumul' principle).[101] According to South African legislation, all types of damage caused to any entity must be remedied (except for, probably, pure economic loss, which is dubious in the context of the fact that intellectual goods and services – eg consultancy – are also defined as products).[102] In the USA, a general notion of damage is applied to strict liability, except for damage to the product itself and excluding pure economic loss. However, statutory caps on damages were introduced in some states.[103] In addition, the law of the USA, Canada and Israel allows for the adjudication of punitive damages.[104]

45 It is also worth examining the admissibility, albeit controversial, in the USA of using proportional liability in the form of market-share liability in cases when it is impossible to establish who from among the many producers was liable for a given product, while all of the products of the same type pose the same risk.[105]

46 Finally, in all of the discussed systems of law, liability is limited in time. The Israeli law strongly resembles the EU Directive in that regard.[106] Legislation in the US provides for various limitation periods and statutes of repose; the latter raises doubts with regard to the right to a fair trial, which may be interesting in the context of European discussion on that matter.[107] According to reports on Canadian and South African systems of law, in those systems there are no limitation periods on filing claims that would run independently of whether damage emerged or not.[108]

III. ADEQUACY OF THE EUROPEAN PRODUCT LIABILITY REGIME FOR THREATS POSED BY NEW TECHNOLOGIES

A. KEY FEATURES OF NEW TECHNOLOGIES

47 The key feature of the new technologies described in the first chapter of this volume is the fact that they function on the basis of data stored in digital form and transmitted without any physical media. Data is understood here as both software that controls the operation of devices and information used by devices and stored in digital form, including texts, images, sounds, geodetic

101 See CA nos 28, 51 and 71.
102 See ZA no 22 ff.
103 See US no 51 ff.
104 See IS no 53; US no 79; CA no 76.
105 See US no 64 ff.
106 See IS no 58.
107 See US no 88 ff. Cf EU no 187.
108 Cf CA no 79; ZA no 34.

data, etc. First of all, collecting, processing and transmitting data is an activity in itself, and data is the subject of this activity – production and circulation. Therefore, data can be an autonomous good which is subject to trading, as well as the source of a threat to the property and interests of its users or third parties. Secondly, data become a fundamental 'component' of material objects which facilitates their functioning, and which can therefore also determine their defectiveness. Moreover, data are frequently supplied after the purchase of the device itself as part of an update service; they can therefore be supplied by another entity than the producer of the device itself. The importance of data as a non-material object is the only feature of new technologies which is, to some extent, indeed a new phenomenon, differentiating in a qualitative manner these sources of danger from defective traditional products. This is, nevertheless, not entirely the case, as a similar issue had already existed before (and was not uniformly resolved in individual countries). It concerned the possibility of finding a material product defective (eg a book) because of errors contained in its intellectual content.

48 The remaining two features of the advanced technologies discussed herein are not new, but constitute previously known phenomena occurring with increased frequency. The first, dependency on networks, is rather a feature of an economy based on new technologies than the technologies themselves. The manufacturing of products and provision of services is based nowadays to a greater extent than ever before on the interaction or combination of independent activities of two or more entities. The Internet of Things, 3D printing and dispersed sources of renewable energy are all examples of this phenomenon. The second feature of new technologies – although, truth be told, a feature of the technological progress itself – is the fact that they are associated with a large degree of imperceptibility and uncertainty. From the point of view of an average user, the way that devices or services based on new technologies work are not only unknown, but can potentially be impossible to figure out due to insufficient cognitive capacity. This is something that clearly distinguishes modern technology from its counterpart from half a century ago. While this may be an illusion, it also seems that the complexity of new technologies results in a higher risk of them malfunctioning or causing damage in the long run – a risk that can be impossible to detect with the current level of knowledge. As far as consumption goods are concerned, this phenomenon is aggravated by competition between entrepreneurs and their desire to launch new products as soon as possible in order to gain an advantage, which is, in turn, facilitated by extensive and efficient distribution networks. In the field of health care (where gene technology and nanotechnology are applied), trying to introduce new technologies as quickly as possible results from medical needs (although administrative supervision over drug safety and medical products is stricter).

B. POSSIBILITY AND PURPOSE OF APPLYING THE EUROPEAN PRODUCT LIABILITY MODEL TO NEW TECHNOLOGIES

1) *Introduction*

49 The key characteristics of new technologies presented below make several aspects of the Directive 85/374 particularly important in assessing whether legislation based on this Directive applies to those technologies. The key issue is the notion of a product in which defect has caused damage. Another important matter is how defect is defined, especially in the context of admissibility of the development risk defence. Finally, the group of liable entities and the manner in which the Directive solves the problem of multiple causes of damage, including multiple tortfeasors, can also play an important role.

2) *Notion of a Product*

50 The Directive defines products as all movables, even if incorporated into another movable or into an immovable, as well as electricity. One may express various reservations and advance interpretation proposals with regard to this definition,[109] although it is clear that such a solution is a sign of the times in which the Directive was drafted, and it reflects the state of technology at that time. Nevertheless, in the national legislation the notion of a product is usually interpreted as including only material items; it does not include non-material goods, unless they are stored on a material carrier. What qualifies as a product is, however, still a matter of dispute in many countries.[110] The issue that is not explicitly regulated in the Directive, and which is not always tackled in legal writing or by court rulings in the Member States, is whether non-material content written on a material item (first and foremost software and digital content stored on a device) may be treated as a component or raw material, which would allow their authors to be treated as producers and justify their liability (art 3(1) of the Directive).[111] It seems that the terms 'component' and 'raw material' themselves, as well as limiting the notion of product to tangible goods, argue against this reasoning. The system of law would be inconsistent if a producer of such goods was not held liable for a product after putting them on the market as a separate good, but would be held liable if the same product became a part of a tangible good manufactured by another person.

109 See EU no 53 ff.

110 Cf AT no 13 ff (which is particularly instructive, given that a broader interpretation would be justified in the context of the Austrian civil law); CZ no 10; DK no 17 ff; EW no 19; FR no 25 ff; DE no 20 ff; IT no 32 ff; NL no 11 ff; NO no 07; PL no 16 ff; ES no 17 ff (see however no 21 ff); CH no 3 ff and 7 ff.

111 See however DK no 21; EW no 19; PL no 18.

51 The Directive, especially interpreted in the context of the *Veedfald* ruling, applies the term 'product' not only to goods produced on a mass or industrial scale, but also to goods produced individually. Moreover, in some national laws the notion of a product is interpreted in a manner that also includes goods produced upon the individual order of the buyer.[112] There are some doubts as to whether such situations should not be classified as provision of services.[113] It seems, though, that the dividing criterion lies elsewhere. It is not the character of the contractual relation between the product manufacturer and the first buyer of the product, but the issue of whether the product was put into circulation in the meaning of the Directive. For this reason, if a product (a movable item) is created as the result of the performance of some service and is made available to another person, we are dealing with putting a product into circulation, and the service provider is held liable as its producer. If a service is provided with the use of a product that had been put on the market earlier or only at that time, and its defect (and not the manner in which it is used by the service provider) is the cause of the damage, the product manufacturer is held liable (usually being a different person than the service provider). If there is no link between the service and any given product – ie no product is used to perform the service and no product is made as a result of performing the service – then there are no grounds for product liability.

52 The Directive treats electricity as a product, probably due to doubts regarding its material character. In most countries there is no controversy over treating other energy carriers as products, which seems understandable given their material character.[114]

53 The Directive's provisions are silent with regard to whether blood, other bodily fluids, bodily tissues and, generally speaking, products of the human body should be treated as products.[115] In most national legislation this issue is resolved in favour of treating them as such, assuming that those goods are in some way processed or otherwise treated.[116]

3) *Defect and Development Risk Defence*

54 The Directive gives a very general definition of the notion of a defect in a product by making reference to the safety which a person is entitled to

---

112 See AT no 23; FR no 29; DE no 28; NO no 08; PL no 27.

113 See AT no 23; IT no 33; NL no 16.

114 See AT no 18; CZ no 12; DK no 19; EW no 21; DE no 25; ES no 19; CH no 04. Cf however PL no 16.

115 See EU no 65 ff.

116 See AT no 19; FR no 27; DE no 26; IT no 38; NL no 14; NO no 07; PL no 17; ES no 20; CH no 06. Slightly different EW no 22.

expect.[117] Interestingly, despite explicitly basing the notion of defectiveness on the safety expectations test, in some countries there is a tendency to examine whether those expectations are rational using the production costs criterion – which means introducing a cost/utility analysis to the notion of defect.[118] This is congruent with the development in the US in recent years,[119] and it also allows for consideration of the fact that various products serve various purposes (this applies in particular to medicinal products). It is questionable, however, whether this practice is compliant with the Directive.

55 In cases where the product itself is material, but its defectiveness (absence of expected safety) is the result of intellectual property contained in the product (incorrect information in a printed source; error in the operating system of an electronic device or in data transmitted by that device to the user) the Directive does not clearly state whether a defect giving rise to liability has occurred. Opinions are split on that matter.[120]

56 An important issue from the point of view of this project's objective is the role of developments in human knowledge, attitudes and perception of events in time when considering whether a product is defective. The Directive ties assessment of a product's defect in various ways to the moment when it is put on the market. It requires that, when assessing whether the product provides the safety which a person is entitled to expect, we take into account the time when the product was put into circulation (art 6(1)(c)), and explains that a product shall not be considered defective for the sole reason that a better product is subsequently put into circulation (art 6(2)). This justifies the conclusion that changes in social expectations with regard to safety ensured by a product may not lead to finding defective a product that was put on the market and that had until then been perceived as safe. The development risk defence (art 7(e)) plays a similar role – it allows the producer to avoid liability for a product that does not ensure safety if the producer demonstrates that the state of scientific and technical knowledge at the time when it put the product into circulation was insufficient as to enable the existence of the defect to be discovered. Both of these solutions are beneficial for the producer, because they tie liability to a decision taken at the time the product was put on the market, exclusively on the basis of available data and opinions on the adequate level of product safety. The interests of users of products that are already on the market and that do not ensure the safety required at a given time may be protected first and foremost by general tort law, if it provides (even in the general tort cause of action) for liability for failure

117 See EU no 77 ff.
118 See AT no 33 ff; EW nos 29 and 42; FR no 32; NL no 29.
119 See US no 26 ff.
120 Cf AT no 20 ff; EW no 19; FR no 36; NO no 12; PL no 19; ES no 21.

to inform users about a known defect of a product that is already in circulation or failure to recall such a product. This form of liability remains outside the harmonising effect of the Directive. The second mechanism that national courts may use – if their powers, their position in the state structure and their judicial tradition allows them to – is the introduction of new standards of users' expectations for future use by means of so-called prospective overruling.[121] However, the legality of this mechanism with regard to product liability may be challenged. It does not make the producer of a particular product specimen that caused damage liable towards the injured party, but it still goes against the Directive's assumption that the determination about the product's defectiveness is linked to the moment when it is put into circulation. Prospective redefining of justified expectations makes a given group of products (in the case of design defect, all products of a given type that are already on the market) defective from the next day on, even though until the day before they were considered safe.

4) The Entity Liable for Composite Products

57 The rules of Directive 85/374 aim to make the manufacturer of the finished product, defective material or component parts, as well as the importer to the European Economic Area liable for defects. Suppliers are liable only as an alternative, when the producer or importer cannot be identified. On the other hand, the liability of a quasi-producer is meant to protect injured persons when there are difficulties in establishing the identity of the actual producer. As a rule, those who were involved in the production of a defective product are liable under the Directive (but not necessarily those who prepared a defective design).[122] All of them are jointly and severally liable. If the concurrent cause of a damage is the behaviour of a person who is not a producer, importer or supplier in the meaning of art 3 of the Directive (nor an injured person), the issue of that person's liability is determined on the basis of national law; this however cannot exclude or limit the producer's liability (art 8(1) of the Directive). In both cases – joint liability of the persons listed in art 3 of the Directive and joint liability of these people and other entities – national laws are decisive for possible recourse claims. Decisions about this vary from place to place, as already mentioned (see no 14 above).

5) Time Limits

58 One of the most important decisions of the Directive is the decision to limit the producer's liability for a product introduced to the market to a maximum of ten years thereafter. From the very beginning there were some doubts regarding this provision, including recent doubts concerning its compliance with the

---

121 See DE no 35; NL no 25.

122 See EU no 105 ff.

European Convention on Human Rights.[123] The controversy centred primarily on products which were defective from the start, but either their defectiveness became apparent only after a longer period of time had passed, or the damage caused by them arose or showed only after some delay. It may be that when it comes to new technologies this will in practice apply foremost to drugs and medical equipment, and to other products made of materials with unverified long-term safety, as well as organs for transplantation obtained with the help of gene technology.

C. ALTERNATIVE LIABILITY REGIMES

59 It is worth noting that all EU Member States retained their liability regimes created before the implementation of the Directive, and that previously they also applied to damage caused by products.[124] These models are diverse, most often based on fault or negligence, which are understood in different (more or less objective) ways. They also differ in their approaches to using the relaxation of the burden of proof by means of factual presumption or *prima facie* evidence concerning the fault, defectiveness of the product, and the causal relationship between this defectiveness and the damage. Their common feature is the fact that they have a much wider scope than just the damage caused by products. Their application to products consisted in applying more general rules to specific facts, possibly with a small modification of the rules. Therefore one can, with a large degree of probability, state that any cases of damage caused by putting into circulation goods which do not guarantee the usual level of safety, and which are not covered by EU rules concerning product liability, can be resolved on the basis of alternative causes of action.[125] The outcome of such cases will be different in individual countries, though, as their regimes differ in the conditions of liability and the scope of damage which can be remedied. Therefore, as far as this area is concerned, the EU's planned effect, which was to lower transaction costs, and thus make it easier to transfer goods (regardless of the accuracy of the assumptions of these plans)[126] will not be achieved, and in practice the level of customer protection will differ across the Member States. These consequences

[123] See EU no 183 ff.

[124] See AT no 92; CZ no 1; DK no 13 ff; EW no 74 ff; FR no 82 ff; DE no 18 ff; IT no 127 ff; NL no 102 ff; PL no 82; ES no 05 ff.

[125] This phenomenon already exists, for example liability for fault in product monitoring can function in practice as a supplement to strict liability in cases where the latter would be excluded due to the development risk defence (see AT nos 29 and 94; NL no 109 ff). The general regime may also provide for liability for defective immovables, services, etc (see eg DE no 18 ff; DK no 22; NL no 102); justify the liability of suppliers (see, for example, FR no 83) or designers (see CH no 59).

[126] See EA no 6 ff.

are particularly evident in relation to intangible property (software and digital content), transmitted via computer networks, which makes it exempt from at least some factual restrictions to trade.

D. POSSIBLE DEVELOPMENT PATHS FOR PRODUCT LIABILITY LAW

60 Considering the consequences of the phenomena discussed in no 47 ff above, one can, at the outset, formulate a rather general question: will the scope of cases in which a defective product causes injury expand or shrink? Some new technologies (primarily cloud computing and its use in processing data and the Internet of Things) lead to changes in an economic model based on ownership of material goods and information (proprietary model) to one based on access to these goods (access model). As a result, conventional distribution of a good is replaced by a service consisting in providing access to that good. Traditionally understood liability for a marketed product does not fully suit that model. Moreover, the growing significance of data or digital content means that some cases of damage extend beyond the scope of application of the product liability regime if that regime is founded on the assumption that a product is only defined as a physical object. On the other hand, the automation of services (eg teaching) and widespread presence of advanced robots (eg in medicine), and the resultant assumption of previously human-performed functions by devices may mean that situations previously classified as defective services will be also viewed as damage caused by defective products, although even then it may be more convenient for the harmed person to seek liability of the service provider.

61 Equally general is the conclusion that administrative regulations concerning product and service safety will play an important role in the face of potential risks associated with new technologies.[127] It is worth paying attention to interactions that will develop between public and private law, especially to the way in which public law safety standards and authorisations for individual products affect legitimate expectations of consumers which determine whether a given product is seen as defective or not.

62 Turning to more specific matters, it should be stressed that the majority of the issues discussed below are policy issues which have to be resolved by a democratically elected legislator in accordance with commonly accepted social values and on the basis of expert knowledge. The role of the lawyer is merely

127 Although it may take a longer time for the public law to introduce security standards than for private law courts to apply general liability clause to a newly emerged risk.

to draw attention to the existing legal conditions for resolving these issues, and, possibly, to indicate available solutions.

63 As the Internet of Things, 3D printing and other new phenomena are based on the joint operation of many devices or on connecting elements from a number of sources in one product, the primary consequences are increased difficulties in determining the causes of a product's poor performance, in assigning the cause to a particular entity and – when someone is assigned liability – in determining the principles for recourse claims among the product's 'co-creators'. Furthermore, technically advanced products with their functioning based on external data (including statistical generalisations based on the analysis of large volumes of individual data) make it increasingly difficult to determine the cause of faulty operation. Should this justify the broader application of strict liability or the presumption of fault and causal nexus, and thus arbitrary assigning of liability to a defined entity in the interests of the aggrieved? One should also take into account that modern devices not only receive data and transmit it to the user. They also collect data from the user (including highly personal information such as health data) and transmit it to their producers, system operators and third parties. This may create threats to other goods than those protected by the Directive (life, health and property), in particular to privacy and human dignity. Does this justify expanding the scope of protection provided by product liability law to goods other than life, health and personal property?

64 The use in medicine of materials previously not applied (stem cells and organs harvested from them, the creation of DNA and its implantation into the cells of a patient) requires research to determine whether such creations are and can be products in terms of regulations governing product liability.

65 Does the fact that the long-term security of some new innovations may not be fully tested, including after their period of use has expired (safety of waste), justify extending limitation periods[128] or excluding or limiting the potential for invoking the development risk defence (eg through the necessity of taking account of *post hoc* knowledge when assessing the defectiveness of a product or through determining new standards of safety/defectiveness via prospective overruling)?

---

128 Which, for slightly different reasons, could also be justified in respect to digital content, if considered as a product; cf recital 43 of the proposed Digital Content Directive: 'Due to its nature the digital content is not subject to wear and tear while being used and it is often supplied over a period of time rather than as a one-off supply. It is, therefore, justified not to provide a period during which the supplier should be held liable for any lack of conformity which exists at the time of the supply of the digital content.'

66 Some technologies lead to democratisation of the production process – products and their constituent elements are not created by enterprises alone, but also by hobbyists (eg mobile applications, designs for 3D printing) and by people who create a good for their own use but market the excess (this may be the future of energy – diffuse production of green energy, storage of surplus, local distribution). This leads to several questions: Should energy thus created continue to be treated as a product? Can only entrepreneurs bear liability for a product? For the needs of a product liability regime, how should we treat people who occasionally make their creations available to others, such as hobbyists, prosumers, etc?

67 Some contemporary business models lead to the establishment of long-term relationships between the producer (and other entities) and the users of goods (software updates, removal of defects, etc). Should defective services provided in the framework of such relationships justify the same liability as defectiveness of the original product? What should be done in the case of changes in the entities providing such services over the course of years?

68 Only a few of these questions have clear answers so far. The development of the practice of application of the law based on Directive 85/374[129] allows one to formulate the thesis that both organs produced from stem cells and agents used in gene therapy constitute products within the meaning of European law, and that the entity which manufactured them (carried out the process through which they were acquired) is liable for their defectiveness. This status should not change.

69 Taking into account both the content of the Directive (although this can be attributed to the times in which it was drafted) and the way it is transposed and understood by the Member States, one should accept the view that intangible goods (software, digital content) as such are not products. However, the consequences of this view are hard to accept. First of all, there is no way to justify the assumption that the creation of an enterprise becomes a product, and thus the regulations concerning the producer's liability change, when that creation is put into circulation on a physical device, but not when the same occurs online, even though the creation itself is the same in both situations. Secondly, there is no convincing justification for the idea of defining ‚products' as only material objects. None of the reasons for introducing strict liability for a product – from the need for compensation of loss, to fair allocation of risks, to deterrence, to loss spreading – loses any of its strength in a situation where the loss was caused by a product which is manufactured and distributed within the framework of a

[129] Especially in light of the *Veedfald* judgment; see EU no 59 ff.

commercial enterprise, but which has no material form. Therefore, it would be justified to determine (either through legislative means or by means of a CJEU judgement) that data, ie software and digital content, may be products within the meaning of the Directive, and that making them available constitutes putting them into circulation.[130]

70 This is connected with further issues concerning material objects which use data in their operations. The prevalence of technology based on data which may originate from people other than the manufacturer of the product means that the understanding of the term 'component part' is important. Unlike in the case of a product, the Directive does not state that a component part must be a material object. Given the date of the Directive's creation, one can likely assume that the problem of software and digital content was not contemplated by its authors. Certainly, the role that software or digital content play in composite products is not different in any significant way from the role that material component parts play in traditional products. Therefore, it seems reasonable to also apply the provision on liability of the producer of component parts to creators of software and digital content, if they are defective and cause the product to be defective. Furthermore, data which are not stored on the product itself but which are made available to the product via cloud technology should also be treated in the same way.[131] However, in the current legal situation, the adoption of such a solution without a simultaneous recognition of intangible goods as products would result in legal inconsistency. A producer of software and digital content would not be liable for damage caused by putting it into circulation in any way other than on a tangible medium, but would be liable as the producer of a component part if the producer's defective component part was used to manufacture a material product. The second problem is related to the fact that software put into circulation can subsequently be changed by means of updates. There is a general problem related to this issue and a more specific one. The general problem concerns an obligation to update software which enables the functioning of a product. This is not about updates that improve the way the product functions, but about updates that are meant to prevent the product's defective functioning. There are some cases in which a product is not defective at the moment it is put into circulation, but becomes defective, not because of any changes in the product itself, but because of the development of external threats – eg hacking techniques or computer viruses which may threaten the product's functioning (for example medical equipment, cars, equipment installed in intelligent houses) and thus threaten the interests of their users and third parties. One could categorise this as an example of the development risk defence, but it would not be entirely convincing

130 See AT no 98; ES no 21; IS no 77. Cf South African law, ZA no 44.
131 Cf AT no 98; IS no 77.

because the general vulnerability of the product is already recognised at the time of putting it into circulation; it is only the particular form of threat that appears afterwards. It seems therefore more adequate to put it as a question of defectiveness. The Directive defines defectiveness as the absence of the safety which one is entitled to expect, which allows for the assumption that a product that fails to guarantee protection against newly arisen threats related to information technology throughout the entire period of its use is indeed a defective product. The liability for such defectiveness should be borne both by the producer of the complete product and the producer of the component part, that is, the software. This would also, by means of a secondary effect, create an incentive to update software. This concept is justified in particular because the desired objective in the form of product safety cannot be achieved merely by means of imposing an obligation to monitor product safety and to warn about threats, because the user does not know software codes and cannot respond to such warnings and remove the threat independently. There is no doubt that the obligation to monitor and update software involves additional costs, thereby slowing down technological development. It seems, however, that the consumer is entitled to this kind of expectation.[132] A specific issue arises when the update is distributed by a person other than the producer of the original product. In this case, it does not seem reasonable to make the producer of the complete product liable, as the producer had no influence on the formation of the product's defectiveness (aside from cases in which an update is needed to remove a defect that already existed at the moment when the product was put into circulation). Instead, consideration should be given to broadening the meaning of 'the producer of a component part' and the related liability, so that it would include an entity updating the digital content of a product previously put into circulation.[133]

71 In national reports, mention is frequently made of a problem with the limited practical possibility of obtaining compensation because of the practical difficulties and costs involved in proving that a product is defective, and with proving the causal link between the defect and the damage.[134] The rapid development of technology and the increase in its complexity will most likely only exacerbate this problem. This issue is only partially regulated in the Directive – a causal link is the condition of liability, and the burden of proof lies with the injured person (art 4), but the technique for proving the link is defined by national laws. Different procedural mechanisms which facilitate the provision of such evidence may therefore develop in the legal practice of

---

132 The interpretation of a product's defectiveness assumed by the CJEU in the *Boston Scientific Medizintechnik* judgment is a potential step in this direction; see EU no 83 ff.

133 See DE no 45.

134 Cf EW no 15; CA no 98; IS no 76; ZA no 44.

individual countries – including even a practical disregard for the burden of proof as determined in the Directive. This tendency in itself is not bad, but it leads to restrictions on the scope of harmonisation. An application of the presumption of the existence of a defect and the relevant causal link should be therefore considered in the event of damage occurring as a result of the product's use. As a rule, it is the producer who has more knowledge about the principles of the product's operation, and also the economic potential which allows the actual cause of the damage to be determined.

72 The complex nature of modern products described in the preceding passages, along with the fact that many entities take part in their production, suggest that reconsideration ought to be given to the issue of a producer's recourse claims. Leaving it as a matter to be determined by national laws which apply different criteria in deciding upon the final distribution of the burden of liability[135] means that the Directive does not lead to the creation of a uniform structure of liability. If its goal was to impose the costs of remedying the damage on the entity which contributed to the greatest extent to the creation of said damage, then this goal has not been achieved. We cannot be sure that this was the purpose of the European legislator, although it would be a goal worth considering, as the structure of recourse claims has an influence on the rules of liability fulfilling at least two of its functions – deterrence and fair allocation of risks. This is particularly evident in relation to those participants of the product manufacturing process who are not producers within the meaning of the Directive and who may be liable for damages only on different grounds, yet who have influence on the defectiveness of the product – designers and software developers (if we assume that software does not constitute a component part).[136]

73 It also ought to be reconsidered whether the decision of the European legislator about uniform treatment of all categories of products was justified.[137] Drugs are products that may deserve separate regulation, and the rapid technological progress in their design and production seems to reinforce this need.[138] Several features determine the unique nature of this type of product. First of all, its user does not make completely free decisions about the product and its use – the decision is dependent on the state of the user's health and their doctor's recommendations. If we were to consider this in the light of fair allocation of risk as a function of liability, it would support the idea of strengthening the position of the injured person by, for example, excluding the

135 See no 14 above.
136 See also FR no 47 ff.
137 See also EA no 59 ff.
138 See DK no 27 ff; FR no 94.

possibility of holding the development risk defence against her.[139] Secondly, in relation to drugs, there is a particularly high risk of damage being far removed in time from the moment the product is used, which results in the difficulty of securing evidence (particularly considering the extensive access to generic drugs from different manufacturers) and increases the practical significance of time limits on liability. This could also justify a relaxation of the limits of liability. Thirdly, however, in some respects drugs are inherently dangerous products, as, in addition to therapeutic effects, their active ingredients also cause harmful side effects, and this danger cannot be avoided (one can only provide relevant information). In this respect (but only in this respect) the risk connected to the product does not constitute a design defect. It seems, however, that the uniform concept of a defect as the absence of safety which can be legitimately expected, as adopted in the Directive, allows this feature of drugs to be taken into account when making judgements about liability in the context of drugs.

74 This is related to the following issue. Both from the point of view of the protection of human rights and in order to ensure a truly fair distribution of risk, it would be advisable to rethink the legitimacy of the limitation of liability to a ten-year term counted from the date of the product's being put into circulation. An alternative option could be to exclude the application of the term in relation to personal injury (not property damage), or possibly to combine it with a limit on the amount of compensation for pain and suffering and/or loss of profit.[140]

75 The national reports have not indicated that the availability of the development risk defence currently results in socially or economically unacceptable results in the field of liability. On the other hand, if the worry that the quick entry of untested technologies to the market will result in a greater threat to the consumer's interests due to issues related to long-term safety proves well founded, it may be necessary to exclude this defence, at least for some categories of products. The current state of the law leaves it to national legislators to decide whether this type of defence is admissible. There is no need to change, as it allows for a quick and adequate response to the threats that may arise, and is balanced enough not to slow down technological progress too much.[141]

139 See also EA no 53.
140 Cf EA no 69 ff.
141 See EA no 13 ff, but also no 78, 83 and 88 ff.

76 The issue of protection of rights in personality other than life and health should be approached with caution. The fact that some modern technologies use personal information the further use, transfer or loss of which (eg due to the lack of appropriate security measures) may result in violations of privacy or dignity can justify the assignment of liability for non-economic consequences of such an event to the producer. Such a decision would, however, require a broader examination of how this liability is currently shaped in individual Member States and how much of the problem can be resolved by application of the law on personal data protection.

77 Finally, the position of non-professional producers of products (prosumers) should be reconsidered in situations where they produce certain goods mostly for their own use, but with some quantities put into circulation. The wording of art 7(c), which mentions 'any form of distribution for economic purpose', would justify making such people liable under the Directive (for example, producers of electricity which is distributed locally). It seems, however, that this would not be reasonable. Prosumers cannot apply loss spreading, and they do not generate profit that is significant from the perspective of fair apportionment of risk, so strict liability would function for them mostly as deterrence, while the activity in question is usually regarded as socially beneficial and worth promoting.

www.ingramcontent.com/pod-product-compliance
Ingram Content Group UK Ltd.
Pitfield, Milton Keynes, MK11 3LW, UK
UKHW051844310526
6126IPUK00024B/1752

9 781780 683980